D1589873

THE GREAT WAR 1914–1918

WITHDRAWN

Wyggeston QE I

00289369

MODERN WARS IN PERSPECTIVE

General Editors: *H. M. Scott and B. W. Collins*

This ambitious new series offers wide-ranging studies of specific wars, and distinct phases of warfare, from the close of the Middle Ages to the present day. It aims to advance the current integration of military history into the academic mainstream. To that end, the books are not merely traditional campaign narratives, but examine the causes, course and consequences of major conflicts, in their full international political, social and ideological contexts.

ALREADY PUBLISHED

THE GREAT WAR
1914–1918

IAN F. W. BECKETT

Longman

An imprint of **Pearson Education**

Harlow, England · London · New York · Reading, Massachusetts · San Francisco
Toronto · Don Mills, Ontario · Sydney · Tokyo · Singapore · Hong Kong · Seoul
Taipei · Cape Town · Madrid · Mexico City · Amsterdam · Munich · Paris · Milan

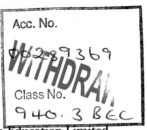

Acc. No.
0628 9369
WITHDRA
Class No.
940. 3 BEC

Pearson Education Limited
Edinburgh Gate
Harlow
Essex CM20 2JE
England

and Associated Companies throughout the world

Visit us on the World Wide Web at:
http://www.pearsoneduc.com

First published 2001

© Pearson Education Limited 2001

The right of Ian F. W. Beckett to be identified as author of
this Work has been asserted by him in accordance with
the Copyright, Designs and Patents Act 1988.

All rights reserved; no part of this publication may be reproduced, stored
in a retrieval system, or transmitted in any form or by any means, electronic,
mechanical, photocopying, recording, or otherwise without either the prior
written permission of the Publishers or a licence permitting restricted copying
in the United Kingdom issued by the Copyright Licensing Agency Ltd,
90 Tottenham Court Road, London WlP 0LP.

ISBN 0 582 32248 0

British Library Cataloguing-in-Publication Data
A catalogue record for this book is available from the British Library

Library of Congress Cataloging-in-Publication Data
Beckett, I. F. W. (Ian Frederick William)
    The Great War, 1914–1918 / Ian F. W. Beckett.
        p.   cm. — (Modern wars in perspective)
    Includes bibliographical references and index.
    ISBN 0–582–32249–9 — ISBN 0–582–32248–0 (pbk.)
    1. World War, 1914–1918.   I. Title.   II. Series.

    D521.B376 2001
    940.3—dc21   00–051508

10 9 8 7 6 5 4 3 2 1
05 04 03 02 01

Typeset by 35 in 11/13 pt Baskerville MT
Produced by Pearson Education Asia Pte Ltd
Printed in Malaysia

CONTENTS

Wyggeston QE1 College
Library

PREFACE AND ACKNOWLEDGEMENTS

In endeavouring to convey to students the significance and complexities of a conflict fought on such a vast scale as the Great War, the author can adopt two potential approaches – either chronological or thematic. Both have their advantages and disadvantages. The chronological approach requires students to make the appropriate connections, and it can become little more than a narrative heavily biased towards military and political events. The thematic approach is generally more analytical and, consequently, more rewarding, but it requires students to have some grasp of the chronology. The analytical approach is consciously chosen for this volume in the knowledge that there are a number of chronological narratives available, but all too few thematic analyses. Moreover, of the latter, none treat the war in sufficient depth or at sufficient length to reveal the wider political, diplomatic, social, economic, military and cultural contexts. It is also intended to introduce students to the enormous amount of new research, which has so greatly expanded academic knowledge of the war and taken the 'new military history' into so many new and exciting areas. Consequently, the footnotes are designed to be as comprehensive as possible. It is hoped that the true global significance of a war that shaped the twentieth century will emerge from this volume and that, at the same time, it will go some way to demythologising the popular memory of a war which is widely misunderstood.

It is that popular memory which first aroused my own interest in the war since, although my father and his generation had so recently fought in the Second World War, it was the earlier conflict that seemingly held more significance for so many of those among whom I grew up. I never knew my maternal grandfather. A regular soldier in the Royal Artillery, he arrived in France with the 85th Battery, 11th Brigade, Royal Field Artillery, attached to the Third Indian (Lahore) Division, in October 1914 and saw service at Festubert, Aubers Ridge and Loos in 1915, on the Somme in 1916, at Arras in 1917, and again on the Somme in 1918. He died as a result of his war injuries in 1938. My maternal grandmother was employed on war work, as was her sister, and I remember vividly my great uncle's account of being aboard HMS *Aboukir* when it was torpedoed in September 1914. Subsequently, he served with the Dover Patrol and in the monitor, HMS

Lord Clive, which, among other duties, bombarded German coastal batteries in support of the raids on Zeebrugge and Ostend in April 1918. There were many men in the village in which I was born – Whitchurch in Buckingham-shire – who had seen service with the Royal Bucks Hussars at Gallipoli and in Palestine or with the Bucks battalions of the Territorial Force in France and Italy. The names of families still well represented within the village appeared on the war memorial in the church.

Since turning professionally to the subject of the Great War some twenty years ago, I have benefited enormously from the expertise of many friends and colleagues. There has also been the challenge of teaching students brought up on the received 'myth' of the war as well as testing out arguments before the knowledgeable audiences at branch meetings of the Western Front Association. A series of lectures to schools delivered in Sydney and Newcastle (Australia) at the invitation of Alf Pickard and the New South Wales History Teachers Association in 1998 was also a valuable opportunity to try out various theories.

I was lucky that colleagues at the Royal Military Academy, Sandhurst, included such distinguished historians of the war as John Keegan, Richard Holmes, Keith Simpson and, later, Gary Sheffield, Stephen Badsey and Paul Harris. That 'lost company' may exist now only in memory, but fortunately its members and many other friends are frequently to be found at meetings of the British Commission for Military History and the military history seminars run at the Institute of Historical Research by Brian Bond and Michael Dockrill of the Department of War Studies at King's College, London. My thoughts on the interconnection between strategy and war aims were greatly assisted by my visiting period in the Department of Strategy at the US Naval War College, Newport, Rhode Island in 1992–93, in the company of scholars such as Douglas Porch, George Baer, David Kaiser, William Fuller and John Maurer. It is difficult to include everyone who has done so much to help me towards an understanding of the war over the years, but mention should be made of David French, John Gooch, Toby Graham, Keith Grieves, Keith Jeffery, John Lee, Chris McCarthy, Alf Peacock, Nick Perry, Bill Philpott, Peter Scott, Peter Simkins, Edward Spiers, Hew Strachan, Rod Suddaby, Tim Travers, Jay Winter and David Woodward. I have also benefited from the work of my postgraduate students, Tim Bowman, Bill Mitchinson and Denise Poynter. This is, I hope, a better book for the insights of all these. None, of course, is responsible for the failings that remain.

I am also grateful to the series editor, Bruce Collins, and successive Long-man editors, Andrew MacLennan, Hilary Shaw and Heather McCallum, and finally the project editor, Jill Birch for their great patience.

Note: Place names are rendered in the form most familiar to English readers. Where they have changed substantially, the modern name is given in parentheses.

Until February 1918, Russia used the Old Style or Julian calendar, which, at the time of the Great War, was thirteen days behind the western, New Style, or Gregorian calendar. All dates are given according to the Gregorian calendar. In the case of some particularly significant dates in 1917, however, the Julian date is given in parentheses. Bulgaria adopted the Gregorian calendar in 1916.

Ian F. W. Beckett

Publisher's acknowledgemenmts

We are grateful to the following for permission to reproduce copyright material:

Map 1 and Map 4 from *The Origins of the First World War*, Longman (Joll, J. 2000); Map 2 adapted from *The First World War*, Hutchinson (Keegan, J. 1999), used by permission of The Random House Group Ltd; Map 5 and Map 6 adapted from *Britain and the First World War*, Routledge (Allen & Unwin) (Turner 1988).

While every effort has been made to trace the owners of copyright material, in a few cases this has proved impossible and we take this opportunity to offer our apologies to any copyright holders whose rights we have unwittingly infringed.

ABBREVIATIONS

AEF   American Expeditionary Force
AEG   Allgemeine Elektrizität Gesellschaft (General Electric Company)
AFL   American Federation of Labor
AHR   *American Historical Review*
AIF   Australian Imperial Force
ANMEF   Australian Naval and Military Expeditionary Force
Anzac   Australian and New Zealand Army Corps
AOK   Armee-Oberkommando (German Army High Command)
Asdic   Anti-Submarine Detection Investigation Committee
AT&T   American Telephone and Telegraph Company
ATS   Auxiliary Territorial Service
AZS   Abteilung für Zurückstellungswesen (Exports and Exemptions Section)
BBC   British Broadcasting Corporation
BEF   British Expeditionary Force
BHR   *Business History Review*
BIHR   *Bulletin of the Institute of Historical Research*
BSP   British Socialist Party
BUF   British Union of Fascists
CEF   Canadian Expeditionary Force
CEH   *Central European History*
CGT   Confédération Générale du Travail (General Labour Confederation)
CGW   Comrades of the Great War
CHR   *Canadian Historical Review*
CID   Committee of Imperial Defence
CIGS   Chief of the Imperial General Staff
CJH   *Canadian Journal of History*
CTA   County Territorial Association
CWC   Clyde Workers Committee
DHV   Deutscher Handlungsgehilfen-Verband (German Clerks Association)

DMO	Director of Military Operations
DORA	Defence of the Realm Act
DSIR	Department of Scientific and Industrial Research
EcHR	*Economic History Review*
EEQ	*Eastern European Quarterly*
EHR	*English Historical Review*
ESR	*European Studies Review*
GHQ	General Headquarters
GMCC	*Guerres Mondiales et Conflits Contemporains*
GOC	General Officer Commanding
GQG	Grand Quartier Général (French General Headquarters)
HJ	*Historical Journal*
HJFRT	*Historical Journal of Film, Radio and Television*
HS	*Historical Studies*
HWJ	*History Workshop Journal*
IHR	*International History Review*
ILP	Independent Labour Party
INV	Irish National Volunteers
IRA	Irish Republican Army
IRB	Irish Republican Brotherhood
ISB	International Socialist Bureau
IUX	International Union of Ex-servicemen
IWMR	*Imperial War Museum Review*
JAH	*Journal of African History*
JBS	*Journal of British Studies*
JCH	*Journal of Contemporary History*
JICH	*Journal of Imperial and Commonwealth History*
JMH	*Journal of Modern History*
JMilH	*Journal of Military History*
JRUSI	*Journal of the Royal United Services Institute for Defence Studies*
JSAHR	*Journal of the Society for Army Historical Research*
JSS	*Journal of Strategic Studies*
KEA	Kriegsernährungsamt (War Food Office)
KPD	Kommunistischen Partei Deutschlands (German Communist Party)
KRA	Kriegsrohrstoffabteilung (Raw Materials Section of German War Office)
MA	*Military Affairs*
MI	Mobilitazione Industriale (Industrial Mobilisation)
MID	Munitions Invention Department
MM	*Militärgeschichtliche Mitteilungen*
MRC	Military Revolutionary Committee (Russian)

NADSS	National Association of Discharged Sailors and Soldiers
NAMPI	National Association of the Motion Picture Industry
NAWSA	National American Woman Suffrage Association
NCF	No Conscription Fellowship
NCO	Non-commissioned officer
NFDSS	National Federation of Discharged and Demobilised Sailors and Soldiers
NUX	National Union of Ex-servicemen
NWAC	National War Aims Committee
OHL	Oberste Heersleitung (German General Headquarters)
P&P	*Past and Present*
PLP	Parliamentary Labour Party
RAF	Royal Air Force
RFC	Royal Flying Corps
RIC	Royal Irish Constabulary
RIHM	*Revue Internationale d'Histoire Militaire*
RNAS	Royal Naval Air Service
RSL	Returned Services League
RSSADL	Returned Sailors' and Soldiers' Australian Democratic League
RSSILA	Returned Sailors' and Soldiers' Imperial League of Australia
RWA	Reichswirtschaftsamt (Imperial Economic Office)
SANLC	South African Native Labour Corps
SAZ	Ständige Ausschuss für Zusammenlegungen (Standing Committee on Consolidations)
SPD	Sozialdemokratische Partei Deutschlands (German Social Democratic Party)
SR	Socialist Revolutionary
SSAU	Soldiers, Sailors and Airmens' Union
SWC	Supreme War Council
TsVPK	Tsentral'nyi Voenno-Promyshlennyi Komitet (Central War Industries Committee)
TUC	Trades Union Council
UDC	Union of Democratic Control
UF	Union Fédérale (Federal Union)
Ufa	Universum-Film-Aktiengesellschaft (Universal Film Joint Stock Company)
UGAPE	Union des Grandes Associations contre la Propagande Ennemie (Union of Associations against Enemy Propaganda)
UNC	Union Nationale des Combattants (National Union of Veterans)
UNMR	Union Nationale des Mutilés et Réformés (National Union for the Disabled and Discharged)

USPD	Unabhängige Sozialdemokratische Partei Deutschlands (German Independent Social Democratic Party)
UVF	Ulster Volunteer Force
VPK	Voenno-Promyshlennya Komitet (War Industries Committee)
VTC	Volunteer Training Corps
WAAC	Women's Army Auxiliary Corps
W&S	*War and Society*
WEWNC	War Emergency Workers' National Committee
WH	*War in History*
WIB	War Industries Board
WRAAF	Women's Royal Auxiliary Air Force
WRNS	Women's Royal Naval Service
WSF	Women's Suffrage Federation
WUMBA	Waffen und Munitionsbeschaffungsamt (Weapons and Munitions Procurement Office)
YMCA	Young Men's Christian Association

For two who knew the face of battle

My maternal grandfather, Warrant Officer Class I Master
Gunner Arthur George Beer, Royal Artillery (1904–34),
and my father, Randolph Alexander Beckett, 1st Battalion,
Royal Berkshire Regiment (1939–46).

By altars old their banners fade
Beneath dear spires; their names are set
In minster aisle, in yew tree shade;
Their memories fight for England yet.

CHAPTER ONE

Another Country?

The Great War of 1914–1918 is an event which is just within living memory. There are men and women alive today who experienced it as children, and a very few still living who participated in it as young adults. While wartime events clearly shaped the twentieth century, however, it is too often forgotten that those who experienced the events continued themselves to guide the political destinies of the former belligerents sometimes up to over fifty years later.

Winston Churchill, both Cabinet minister and front-line soldier between 1914 and 1918, did not retire from office as British prime minister until 1955 and both his successors, Anthony Eden (1955–57) and Harold Macmillan (1957–63), had served in the trenches of the Western Front. Macmillan may have been the 'last Edwardian' in Downing Street, but President Charles de Gaulle, wounded and taken prisoner by the Germans at Verdun in March 1916, continued in power in France until 1969. United States president Dwight D. Eisenhower (1952–60) had been a West Point cadet and had not seen active service, but his predecessor, Harry S. Truman (1945–52) had been an artillery officer on the Western Front in 1918. The veteran politician and former president of Turkey, serving a third term as prime minister between 1961 and 1965, Mustaf Ismet Pasha (known as Inönü), had been an exceptionally young divisional commander during the war. On the political left, Nikita Khrushchev, who had played a minor role in the Russian Revolution and then fought in the Russian Civil War (1917–21), was not ousted from power in the Soviet Union until 1964. Ho Chi Minh, who had tried unsuccessfully to plead the Vietnamese nationalist cause at the Paris peace conference in 1919, led North Vietnam from 1954 until his death in 1969. A veteran of the Spartacist rising in Berlin in 1918, Walter Ulbricht remained at the helm of the German Democratic Republic

1

as first general secretary of the Communist Party from 1946 until 1971. Josip Broz, better known from his Second World War pseudonym of Tito (The Hammer), was first exposed to communism as an Austro-Hungarian conscript in a Russian prisoner of war camp. He was to be president of Yugoslavia, itself a creation of the Great War, from 1946 until his death in 1980.

Whatever the obvious consequences of the Second World War for Europe and the wider world, the political arena in which these men operated owed as much, if not more, to the twentieth century's first global 'total' conflict. It was the Great War that destroyed four empires – those of Imperial Germany, Austria-Hungary, Tsarist Russia and Ottoman Turkey. The consequences were profound, not least in the Middle East, whose politics remain conditioned by events between 1914 and 1918 and the post-war settlement effected by Britain and France. Rather similarly, the Great War had a profound impact upon Ireland, with consequences that have contributed materially to contemporary divisions. The war gravely weakened Europe's influence generally, even if the United States chose to wield its new-found power in financial rather than military or diplomatic terms. Without the Great War, communism would arguably not have triumphed in Russia, nor fascism been given its opportunity in Germany and Italy. Indeed, Churchill was not alone in choosing to regard the two world wars as a second Thirty Years' War, echoing the conflict that had consumed much of Europe from 1618 to 1648.[1]

In another sense the Great War is also still in the visual memory in that not only photographs but also early moving images on film survive. Malcolm Smith has made the important point that, prior to the expansion of cheap photography in the early years of the twentieth century, only a few adults with a wealthy background 'had any clear idea of what they looked like as children, or what their parents looked like when they were younger, and probably only the dimmest recollection of what their grandparents had looked like at all'. Thus, the Great War just falls within what Smith has called 'a more dependable popular memory'.[2] Apart from the rituals of annual remembrance and the physical evidence of war cemeteries and remains of trenches in France, Flanders and elsewhere, there are other reminders of the Great War, at least in Britain. Until recently, there were licensing laws which had endured since 1914, while British Summer Time remains a legacy of 1916. Popular linguistic usage in Britain reflects soldiers' slang, such as Blighty, conchie, Jerry and so on. There is, too, an enduring literary and artistic legacy with which many are familiar through the medium of a handful of well-known, but hardly representative, poets such as Siegfried Sassoon and Wilfred Owen. Some historians would claim that this cultural legacy, which has endured in the work of contemporary writers such as Pat Barker, represents a 'modern memory'.[3]

Certainly, the collective British popular memory embraces persistent myths. Indeed, it might be argued that the Great War was refashioned at the time of its fiftieth anniversary through popular histories of the time such as Leon Wolff's *In Flanders Fields* or Alan Clark's *The Donkeys*, and the musical play and film, *Oh! What A Lovely War*. Interestingly, when, in 1964, John Terraine, Correlli Barnett and others sought in the scripts of the landmark BBC television series *The Great War*, to counter what they regarded as the pervasive misinterpretation of the war, audience research reports showed that the visual content had reinforced the popular concept of the war's futility for a mass audience estimated at 8 million per episode.[4] As recently as 1998, tabloid headlines in the *Daily Express* demanded the removal of Field Marshal Earl Haig's statue from Whitehall on the grounds that his wasting of his men's lives rendered him no better than a war criminal. Surveying much Great War popular historiography, one is reminded of the newspaper editor's refrain in John Ford's classic western, *The Man Who Shot Liberty Valance*: 'when legend becomes fact, print the legend'.[5]

The capacity for myth-making derives largely from the fact that, despite those genuine historical echoes around us, we are now as distanced from 1914 as those who fought it were from the Great Reform Act of 1832. The past, to echo L. P. Hartley's novel of the Edwardian era, *The Go Between*, is a 'foreign country' when it stretches beyond immediate memory. In 1967, Geoffrey Barraclough wrote that, 'on a purely practical level of daily life, a person living today who was suddenly put back into the world of 1900 would find himself on familiar ground, whereas if he returned to 1870, even in industrialised Britain, the differences would be more striking than the similarities'.[6] It was in this sense, therefore, that Barraclough characterised the 1890s as the beginning of 'contemporary history'. Certainly, the Great War has become regarded as a great catalyst of change, a 'total' war fought on such a scale seemingly to demonstrate irrefutably Leon Trotsky's dictum that war is the 'locomotive of history'.

In the 1960s and 1970s, historians such as Arthur Marwick began to construct models of the inter-relationship between total war and social change, emphasising that, even where change might have been attributable to longer-term evolutionary trends, war fought on a global scale was likely to accelerate the pace of changes already taking place. In essence, therefore, Marwick's interpretation of the Great War was as an event marking a discontinuity with the past.[7] The issues of change and continuity are central to much historical debate, therefore it is not altogether surprising that this should be reflected in much of the continuing debate on the Great War, the thrust of recent contributions being to emphasise continuity rather than change.[8]

Industrialisation and the state

Any attempt to measure the impact of the Great War on Europe and the wider world must perforce begin with an examination of the nature of the world of 1914. Certainly, as indicated by Barraclough's observation, there had been considerable change in Europe at the end of the nineteenth century as the technological, scientific and material explosion of social effort that had been earlier known only to Britain reached the continent. In 1870, there were perhaps as many as seventy European cities with a population of over 100,000, but Paris and London alone exceeded 1 million, the majority of Europe's approximately 300 million people living on the land or in small towns.

Industrialisation and its attendant urbanisation allowed European societies to sustain growing populations through the increase in productive wealth, advances in preventative medicine and the beginnings of a global economy. This last resulted in more, better and cheaper foodstuffs becoming available from extra-European sources. By 1900, therefore, over two hundred European cities exceeded a population of 100,000, and Berlin, Moscow, St Petersburg, Vienna, Constantinople and Glasgow had all matched Paris and London as urban conurbations of over 1 million inhabitants.[9]

Europe's population had grown rapidly to some 400 million in barely thirty years. It was a population with not only a longer life expectancy than ever before, but also far more educated, since industrialisation demanded a more skilled labour force. In 1850, half of Europe's people had been illiterate, but this was to fall steadily to about 10 per cent by 1930. In part, Imperial Germany's rapid industrial rise can be explained in terms of a sophisticated state educational system, particularly in scientific and technical subjects, but Prussia had pioneered universal primary education before 1870. By 1880, the example had been emulated by Belgium, Britain, Italy, the Netherlands and Switzerland. Educational progress naturally varied, however, from state to state. It was suggested, for example, that, whereas 1 out of every 1,000 conscripts entering the German army would be illiterate, the proportion would rise to 68 out of every 1,000 in the French army, 220 in the Austro-Hungarian army, and to 330 in the Italian army.[10]

Moreover, while emphasis has been placed on the consequences of urbanisation and industrialisation, this was not experienced by European society as a whole, for it was only Britain and Imperial Germany that had a higher percentage of their labour forces engaged in industry than agriculture. Indeed, whereas 34.6 per cent of the British population and 21.0 per cent of the German was urban-based in 1913, this was true of only 14.8 per cent of the French population, 11.6 per cent of the Italian, 8.8 per cent of the Austro-Hungarian and 7.0 per cent of the Russian population.[11]

The rapid pace of change wrought by industrialisation in western Europe sharpened the contrast with most of the states of central, southern and eastern Europe. These remained in effect peasant societies, for all that the agricultural depression of the 1870s to 1890s had accelerated the movement of the rural population towards towns and, in the case of southern Europe, to the United States. In fact, some of the more rapid increases in population were measured among the predominantly peasant societies of eastern Europe, the rural population of Tsarist Russia increasing by some 25 per cent between 1877 and 1897 and by the same factor again between 1897 and 1917. The Italian population also increased by some 4 million between 1880 and 1900.[12]

Mechanisation had entered agriculture, but it was still labour intensive and life in much of Europe remained governed by the unchanging pattern of the agricultural year, and by the speed of man and of horse. Railways had spread significantly across Europe since the 1840s and even the trans-Siberian railway had been completed by 1902, but it should be borne in mind that Marconi had transmitted the first wireless message across the Atlantic only in 1901, and both aircraft and motor vehicles were still in their infancy. The Wright brothers flew for the first time in 1903, and the first mass production motor vehicle, Henry Ford's Model T, was only announced in 1909.

While there was increasing primary education, it was also the case that the majority of children in Europe did not progress to secondary education and, both in rural and urban areas, many lived in abject poverty. Charles Booth's *Life and Labour of the People of London*, published in 1902, and Seebhom Rowntree's study of York, *Poverty: A Study of Town Life*, published in the same year and intended to challenge the preoccupation of earlier social researchers with London, came up with broadly similar results. Booth calculated 30.7 per cent of London's population living below what he regarded as the poverty line and Rowntree 27.84 per cent in York.[13]

As the growth of population indicated, many diseases had been arrested by the advance of science. Immunisation against typhoid was available from 1896 and against diphtheria from 1913, while the bacillus responsible for tuberculosis had been identified in 1882 and that for both tetanus and the plague by 1900. Aspirin had been introduced in 1899, vitamins discovered in 1902, and the first antibiotic, Salvarsan, brought out in 1909. Yet, as Jay Winter has pointed out, despite the advances, 200 out of every 1,000 infants still failed to survive the first year of life in areas like Birmingham, Blackburn, Salford, Sheffield and Wolverhampton. Thus, although the average life expectancy of English males in 1910–12 was now greater than before, at 51.5 years, it was about the same as that of Ecuadorian males in 1961–63 and Iraqi males in 1970–75. As Winter puts it, therefore, in large parts of working-class Britain, 'there were before 1914 conditions of poverty and ill health which today we associate with countries of the Third World'.[14]

If such conditions pertained in Britain, then it is not a feat of great imagination to envisage the conditions routinely endured by those Europeans in less advanced states. There was especially serious poverty in southern Italy, with life expectancy among Italian males rising only from an average of 35 years in 1874 to 44 years by 1905. Tsarist Russia was the most rapidly industrialising state in Europe by 1914, quadrupling its coal production between 1890 and 1914, increasing steel production tenfold since 1880 and expanding its rail mileage by one-quarter. But industrial progress existed alongside rural poverty exacerbated by the export of grain to sustain industrial expansion, harvest failures, and, in 1891–92, famine.[15]

Those who went to war in 1914 were not only more intimately acquainted than ourselves with hard labour, long hours and, at best, subsistence wages but, again to quote Winter, they 'knew untimely death more frequently and experienced bereavement perhaps with a greater degree of fatalism than we do today'.[16] In a very real sense, therefore, the peoples of Europe were conditioned by their ordinary expectations to endure the kind of ordeal that was to soon to confront them.

Such conditioning was enhanced by the growth in the power of the state. The majority of European states witnessed the gradual emergence of mass politics, representative legislatures and more responsible governments. The corollary was increasing state interference in various aspects of industrial and social life, enhanced state educational and welfare provision being but one spur to the growth in the size of state bureaucracies.[17]

Prior to 1870, only Belgium, Britain and France had any form of representative government but, in 1871, both France and Imperial Germany introduced universal male suffrage for national elections. Switzerland followed suit in 1874; Belgium, Norway and Spain in the 1890s; and Portugal, Sweden and Austria (though not Hungary) by 1914. During the same period the electorates of Britain, Italy and the Netherlands were enlarged, while even Tsarist Russia and Ottoman Turkey secured elected assemblies for the first time in 1905 and 1908, respectively. Between 1907 and 1913, Denmark, Finland and Norway all introduced measures of female suffrage, New Zealand having done so in 1893 and Australia in 1902.

In each state in which the franchise was widened, working class political organisations emerged such as the Sozialdemokratische Partei Deutschlands (SPD; German Social Democratic Party), founded in Imperial Germany in 1875, and the Independent Labour Party (ILP) in Britain in 1893.

Meanwhile, mass trade unions for the unskilled rather than narrowly based craft unions became common in Austria-Hungary, Britain, France, Germany and Spain.[18]

Yet, despite scientific progress, education, democratisation and reform, as Ferro puts it, 'The mass of . . . men were outside public affairs. They were prisoners in a universe whose mechanism was a mystery'.[19] Europe remained overwhelmingly monarchical and aristocratic, its ruling royal families closely linked by blood. King Edward VII was uncle to both Tsar Nicholas II and Kaiser Wilhelm II, while the grandchildren of Queen Victoria also ruled Greece, Spain, Romania, Sweden and a host of German states and principalities. Below the hereditary monarchies, absent only from France among the major powers, and Switzerland and (from 1910) Portugal among the lesser powers, traditional aristocratic and landed elites remained effectively in control of the main structures of government in much of Europe.[20]

It should be said that most leading politicians did not see themselves as representatives of a class interest. Moreover, most administrations had to work with more than one social group in order to carry on the business of government, reconciling conflicting interests in an increasingly complex domestic political context. Generally, however, political elites were consistently successful in cultivating sufficient consensual support to maintain and consolidate their power. This reflected not only the largely successful adaptation of the capitalist methods of the middle classes or bourgeoisie by the landed elite as in Britain, France and Austria-Hungary, but also the readiness of the middle classes themselves to accept assimilation rather than undermine that elite.[21] Indeed, in the case of Germany, it has been argued by Michael Gordon that, despite its industrial growth, social structures remained largely pre-industrial. According to Jürgen Kocka, industrial wealth conferred less social mobility than elsewhere while the *Mittelstand* (middle class), equating to a lower middle class of white-collar workers, artisans and shopkeepers, was easily mobilised by the traditional landed elite in defence of the status quo. By contrast, historians such as Geoff Eley and David Blackbourn have argued that the German bourgeoisie was as influential in the social and economic spheres as was the traditional elite. They acknowledge, however, that any social and economic power was not reflected in political influence.

It is clear, therefore, that Imperial Germany was a state in which political, economic and social life was in flux. In much of eastern and southern Europe, including Tsarist Russia and Italy, there was hardly a significant middle class at all. It should also be noted that, in many states of central and eastern Europe, differentiation of class could actually be one of nationality.[22]

The concept of class is a difficult one and there were many strata between and within various social groups, but the working class was often deferential in its attitudes to traditional elites and conservative in nature. Gerard De Groot, in pondering the response of working-class British soldiers to the trials of trench warfare has turned round the apocryphal phrase attributed to Colonel Max Hoffman, that the British army was one of 'lions led by donkeys', to the suggestion that it was actually a case of donkeys led by lions. Similarly, de Groot suggests the rejection after the war by British ex-servicemen of radical veterans' organisations in favour of the officially sponsored British Legion proves their 'sheep-like' qualities.[23]

Ideology and the nation-state

The growing incidence of industrial unrest in pre-war Europe might suggest that the industrial labour force was far from deferential and presents a ready contrast with the apparent readiness of the European working class to sacrifice itself for the state in the war itself. In 1913, France experienced over 1,000 strikes, Britain over 1,400, Germany over 2,100 and Russia over 2,400. There had been general strikes in Italy in 1904, in Spain in 1905 and in Portugal in 1912, while the revolution in Russia in 1905, in the wake of defeat in the Russo-Japanese War was the most significant revolutionary experience in Europe since the Paris Commune of 1871.[24] The emergence of mass politics, however, while seemingly offering a widening of the democratic process, was in reality a spur to a nationalism which aristocratic governments invariably found ways to manipulate to their advantage.

Thus, where the ideal of the nation-state was a reality rather than an aspiration, nationalism reinforced and buttressed the state. In new constructs such as Imperial Germany and Italy after 1871, the state assiduously cultivated the ideal of national unity, although without ever entirely overcoming the parochial nature of much of European society. Nevertheless, the expansion of education was a powerful tool in establishing national identities, with images of the Franco-Prussian War and the loss of the two provinces of Alsace and Lorraine being firmly planted in the minds of French schoolchildren, the Germans teaching of their traditional role as a bulwark against the Slavs, and so on.[25]

Conscription for military service, too, contributed to the process. Originally, universal military service had been envisaged by some as a catalyst of social and political change, in which the army would become a school of the nation and service in it a route to the franchise. By the late nineteenth century, the rhetoric of the nation in arms was not to be taken so literally in political terms, and the social and political implications of military service were to be seen in the context of the moulding of the individual by the state. To Niccola Marselli, the new Italian army after 1871 was to be the 'great crucible in which all provincial elements come to merge in Italian unity'. The French army would similarly turn peasants into Frenchmen, while the German High Command consciously attempted to effect a permanent eradication of SPD influence over its recruits through such means as political instruction classes and even retraining in agricultural skills. The imperial army of Austria-Hungary, with its loyalty firmly focused on the emperor, was a particularly important supranational institution in an empire in which less than 24 per cent of the population was German.[26]

A comparison of the maps of Europe in 1848, 1871 and 1914 forcefully illustrates the power of nationalism. Before 1850, only Greece, in 1827, and Belgium, in 1831, had joined long-established nation-states such as France, Portugal and Spain. Imperial Germany and Italy were unified after a fashion in 1871. New states were carved out of the crumbling Ottoman Empire such as Romania in 1877, Bulgaria and Serbia in 1878, and Albania in 1912. Norway also split from Sweden in 1905. European nationalism as a whole was also intimately connected with imperial expansion in the last two decades of the nineteenth century as the powers rushed to partition Africa and to divide the decaying Manchu Empire in China into exclusive spheres of influence.[27]

Belgium, Britain, Denmark, France, Germany, Italy, the Netherlands, Spain and Portugal all had overseas possessions. The United States, too, had begun to extend its influence overseas as a consequence of the Spanish–American War of 1898. By contrast, Tsarist Russia and Austria-Hungary were great continental empires, while Germany's failure to secure what many Germans regarded as an overseas empire commensurate with her European status fed imperial aspirations not only overseas but within Europe itself. This was perhaps epitomised by the first words of the imperial anthem, *Deutschland über Alles*: 'Von der Maas dis an die Memel, von der Etsch bis an den Belt' (From the Meuse to the Niemen, from the Adige to the Belt). Of these rivers, only the Niemen was within German territory and only for its last few miles.

In some respects, nationalism had still to run its course and could therefore threaten the identity of the state, principally in the form of local separatism, as in the case of Ireland within the British Empire and in parts of the multinational Austro-Hungarian Empire. Some states maintained irredentist claims to others, not least in the Balkans. Tsarist Russia was also beset by the problem of what might be termed internal nationalism, proclaiming pan-slavism abroad while practising 'russification' at home, affecting such peoples as the Finns, Latvians, Armenians, Georgians, Estonians, Ukrainians and Belorussians. In Russia in particular, but elsewhere in Europe, internal nationalism was similarly evident in the increase in anti-semitism in the 1880s and 1890s fed by crudely racial theories such as those of Joseph-Arthur Gobineau and Houston Stewart Chamberlain. The Dreyfus affair in France was one manifestation of the intensity which issues of national identity could evoke, again pointing to the capacity of European peoples for the kind of hatred which could be manipulated to sustain national war efforts. What, therefore, might be termed defensive nationalism would prove just as powerful as aggressive nationalism and imperialism in stimulating national sacrifice.

In Germany, *Ostjuden* or eastern Jews bore the brunt of the popular view that they were *Schnorrer und Verschwörer* (cadgers and conspirators). Austria-Hungary, and especially Vienna, was rife with anti-semitism although, in the case of Hungary, anti-semitic political parties did not attract much support. More serious were the periodic pogroms of Russia's 5 million Jews, confined to the 'Pale of Settlement' in Poland and other parts of western Russia. Many Jews emigrated to Britain or the United States. Another potential solution, attuned to the wider ideals of the nation-state, was the concept of a Jewish national home, as espoused by Theodor Herzl's polemic *The Jewish State*, published in 1896, and his foundation of the Zionist Congress at Basle in Switzerland in the following year.[28]

Nationalism was equally stirring among indigenous subjects of the European imperial powers. In India, a Hindu-based Indian National Congress had been formed as early as 1885 and major concessions were initiated by the British authorities in the Morley–Minto reforms of 1908. In the case of the white dominions of the British Empire, effective independence had been granted to Canada in 1867, Australia in 1901, New Zealand in 1907 and South Africa in 1910. Indeed, such was the independence of spirit evinced by the Canadian delegation at the 1911 Imperial Conference that the British government began to fear that the Canadians could not be relied upon to support Britain in any European conflict.[29]

Nationalism and imperialism enabled ruling elites to continue to exercise power through the manipulation of their popular appeal but, to the occasional uncertainties manifested in nationalism, might be added the threat which ruling elites still perceived in those political parties and interest groups attempting to exploit wider franchises and growing press freedom. Literacy, social awareness and urbanisation exposed the population to manipulation through the oral and written word by opposition, both parliamentary and extra-parliamentary, as well as by government. In this process, the evolution of a mass circulation press was of some significance. Lord Northcliffe's *Daily Mail*, launched in Britain in May 1896, for example, reached a circulation of close to 2 million by 1908. On the continent, the *Berliner Margenpost* had a circulation of half a million by 1900 and *Le Petit Parisien* some 800,000. It is a matter of debate how far the press moulded rather than followed popular opinion. One radical contemporary, J. A. Hobson, believed the press one means by which public opinion and public policy were moulded by the 'industrial and financial forces of Imperialism'. Another, Norman Angell, believed that vested interests could not create public sentiment, but merely exploit existing sentiment.[30]

In any case, as yet, the influence of political ideologies other than nationalism was weak in Europe so that there was no coherent challenge to the power of the state. Socialism, communism, anarchism and fascism all had their roots in the mid-nineteenth century. They were notably unsuccessful in political terms, however, prior to 1914. Violent anarchism had certainly had an impact in Russia, Italy and Spain. A number of prominent individuals had fallen victim to assassination (though this was not always the work of anarchists), including Tsar Alexander II in 1881, the Spanish prime minister Canovas del Castillo in 1897, Empress Elizabeth of Austria-Hungary in 1898, King Humbert I of Italy in 1900, and the chairman of the Council of Ministers in Russia, Pyotr Arcadievich Stolypin, in 1911. In Russia, revolutionary violence resulted in 9,000 casualties between 1905 and 1907 and in 17,000 over the period from 1905 to 1910. Yet, the existing European political order remained strong and development of the European labour movement had occurred primarily in the economic sense.

Outside of Scandinavia, social democratic parties had achieved relatively little, although the extension of the franchise ensured that socialist parties were rapidly growing in electoral strength. In April 1914, the socialist, René Viviani, formed a government after the French national elections, while the German SPD had become the largest party in the Reichstag by securing 34.7 per cent of the vote in the 1912 elections. However, the SPD was effectively neutralised by the electoral system pertaining in Imperial Germany's constituent states, which had narrower franchises and which held the real power.

Certainly, there was a sense of international solidarity between socialist movements in different European states but, like much else, the supposed solidarity of the Second International, the Workingmen's Association established by socialists in Paris in 1889 following the collapse of the first in 1876, was to be swept away by the appeal of patriotism in 1914. Indeed, even the powerful French anarcho-syndicalist trade union movement, the Confédération Générale du Travail (CGT; General Labour Confederation), which had an unambiguously pacifist outlook, succumbed to the appeal for national political and social unity expressed by the *Union Sacrée* (Sacred Union), much as the German trade unions succumbed to the appeal of the similar *Burgfrieden* (fortress truce). The British labour movement was largely indifferent to international affairs. Like the ILP leader Keir Hardie, the French socialist leader Jean Jaurès, had always believed that international socialism could only succeed in preventing a war through strike action in a pre-war diplomatic crisis. In the event, Jaurès indicated his general support for the French government in the July Crisis, although he was still assassinated by a nationalist on 31 July 1914.[31]

There is a natural tendency to see the appeal of militarism rather more strongly than that of internationalism in the pre-war world and, certainly, many European societies were militarised to a greater or lesser degree. In Britain, the pressure for continental-style conscription increased as Britain's political isolation became more apparent and as her position in relation to the other major powers came under threat. By 1900, Britain had already been outstripped by both Germany and the United States in terms of industrial production in areas such as coal, pig-iron and steel. Britain's claim to economic superiority rested more on financial capital, shipping and primary products than upon manufactured goods, new technology or new industries such as petrochemicals and precision engineering.

Moreover, Europe generally, despite its overall increasing industrial production and the development of new industries such as chemicals in Germany, was still losing economic ground to the United States. Thus, in 1913, energy consumption in the United States, as measured in millions of tonnes of coal equivalent, was approximately equal to that of Britain, Germany, France, Russia and Austria-Hungary together.[32]

Europe retained primacy in investment overseas, amounting to £350 million a year between 1900 and 1913. In terms of financial primacy, Britain was still the most significant of the great powers, with over 43 per cent of the world's foreign investments in 1913. Yet, British financial primacy and the Empire could not compensate for long-term decline and Britain could no longer out-build naval opponents with her former ease or realistically match continental states where numbers secured by conscription were the yardstick of military power.

In 1902, the journalist W. T. Stead, who was to be lost with the *Titanic*, published a popular polemic, *The Americanisation of the World*, predicting the future global power of the United States. With more precision, the geographer, Sir Halford Mackinder, in a lecture to the Royal Geographical Society on 25 January 1904, announced the dawning of a new era. According to Mackinder, a correlation between 'the larger geographical and the larger historical generalisations' would result in the decline of maritime power and the emergence of a Eurasian strategic pivot or 'heartland' based on size and numbers as the determinant of international development.[33]

The shock of early defeats in the South African War resulted in an increasing concern in Britain with the physical and moral condition of the nation. This fuelled such movements as the National Social Purity Crusade and the National Service League, which campaigned for conscription.

Concerns with eugenics and 'national efficiency' coincided with the social investigations of Booth and Rowntree mentioned earlier, the latter in particular equating poverty in York with diminished physical efficiency. The same essentially military concept of poverty was also adopted by A. L. Bowley when he surveyed urban poverty in Reading, Northampton, Warrington, Stanley and Bolton between 1912 and 1914. The trend towards the quasi-military organisation of British youth was continued with the creation of the Boy Scouts in 1907, while military drill was widely accepted as the most appropriate form of physical education in schools.

Beyond the schoolroom and adolescence, popular writers such as G. A. Henty and H. Rider Haggard, the popular press, popular entertainment such as the music hall and the infant cinema all did similar service in transmitting nationalist themes. As in the rest of Europe, popular culture was redolent with the assumptions of Social Darwinism as popularised by Benjamin Kidd's *Social Evolution*, published in 1893. Yet, militarism in Britain existed, to quote Michael Howard, only in 'mild solution'.[34]

While the fact that war did break out in Europe in 1914 against such a background cannot be ignored, those factors which suggest that war was not inevitable should not be readily dismissed. There was a pacifist movement in Britain as elsewhere, albeit it in fragmented state. While arguably aimed more at a German audience than a British, Norman Angell's pacifist tract *The Great Illusion*, published in 1910, was just as popular with the British reading public as G. F. Wyatt's militaristic *God's Test by War*, published in 1912. In Germany, membership of radical nationalist groups such as the Army and Navy Leagues was not extensive and the SPD had won the 1912 elections largely on a platform of opposing increased military expenditure.[35]

International co-operation and international organisations characterised banking, transportation and communication. As John Keegan has pointed out, European, if not international, tourism was also well established among the wealthier classes. If the international conferences on the limitation of war held at The Hague in 1901 and 1907 had not resulted in much tangible progress, the Olympic Games had been revived by Baron Pierre de Coubertin in 1896, although even they soon took on the guise of national rivalries rather than peaceful sporting occasions promoting international harmony.

Other sports were also taking on an international aspect. The Fédération Internationale de Football Associations (FIFA), for example, was founded in Paris in May 1904; curiously, Glasgow Celtic played Burnley before a crowd of 20,000 in an exhibition match in Budapest in May 1914.[36] Religious belief, too, remained strong in much of Europe, especially in rural areas, despite the enforced separation of Church and state in Italy after unification and in France in 1905, and the state-sponsored anti-clericalism represented by the *Kulturkampf* (cultural struggle) initiated by the German chancellor, Otto von Bismarck, in Imperial Germany in the 1870s. Indeed, religious conflict between Catholic and Protestant remained a significant and volatile factor in German politics.[37]

Europe in 1914, therefore, presents a number of contrasts between the effects of industrialisation and urbanisation on the one hand, and the persistence of an older economic system on the other. Increasing wealth existed alongside abject poverty. Similarly, the apparent emergence of mass democracy contrasted, in most cases, with the realities of continuing governance by traditional power elites. A general fatalism arising from the conditions of everyday existence, together with the ability of those elites to manipulate much of the population through the appeal of nationalism, when coupled with the growth of the power of the nation-state itself, meant that Europe and its peoples were largely conditioned in advance to sustain even a war that would be waged on an unimaginable scale.

Even given the undoubted acceptance of, or at least acquiescence in, war in 1914 by Europe's peoples, it should be remembered that, while a state could not wage war without a degree of popular support, the crucial decisions in every belligerent state in 1914 were taken by very small groups of policy-makers. If anything, these men revelled in their detachment from the influence of 'the people'. In Britain, politicians regularly professed to recognise the significance of public opinion, not least in matters of war and peace. Yet, the Foreign Secretary between 1906 and 1916, Sir Edward Grey, felt little need to cultivate press or public, later writing that many of the shortcomings of democratic government were 'due to the fact that public opinion is not necessarily a great statesman at all'.[38] What James Joll has characterised as the underlying 'unspoken assumptions' of 1914 will need to be addressed again but, in turning to the causes of the war, the irony should be borne in mind that the handful of largely patrician and self-consciously detached policy-makers whose views mattered in July and August 1914 considered themselves in no way bound by their perceptions of the prevailing public opinion they had so often manipulated.

Notes and references

1. Winston S. Churchill, *The Second World War* (London, 1948), I, p.ix; Arno J. Mayer, *The Persistence of the Old Regime* (Beckenham, 1981), p.1.

2. Malcolm Smith, 'The War and British Culture', in Stephen Constantine, Maurice Kirby and Mary Rose, eds, *The First World War in British History* (London, 1995), p.170.

3. As extreme examples, see Paul Fussell, *The Great War and Modern Memory* (Oxford, 1975); and Omar Bartov, 'Trauma and Absence: France and Germany, 1914–45', in Paul Addison and Angus Calder, eds, *Time to Kill* (London, 1997), pp.347–58.

4. Leon Wolff, *In Flanders Fields* (London, 1958); Alan Clark, *The Donkeys* (London, 1961); Alex Danchev, 'Bunking and Debunking: The Controversies of the 1960s', in Brian Bond, ed., *The First World War and British Military History* (Oxford, 1991), pp.263–88.

5. Ian Beckett, 'The Military Historian and the Popular Image of the Western Front, 1914–1918', *The Historian* 53 (1997), pp.11–14; Brian Bond, 'A Victory Worse than Defeat? British Interpretations of the First World War', Liddell Hart Centre for Military Archives Annual Lecture, King's College, 20 November 1997 (London, 1997).

6. L. P. Hartley, *The Go Between* (Harmondsworth, 1958), p.7; Geoffrey Barraclough, *An Introduction to Contemporary History* (Harmondsworth, 1967), pp.45–6.

7. Arthur Marwick, *Britain in the Century of Total War* (London, 1968); idem, *War and Social Change in the Twentieth Century* (London, 1974); Ian Beckett, 'Total War', in Colin McInnes and Gary Sheffield, eds, *Warfare in the Twentieth Century* (London, 1988), pp.1–23.

8. See, for example, Gerard De Groot, *Blighty: British Society in the Era of the Great War* (London, 1996); and Constantine, Kirby and Rose, *First World War in British History*.

9. Michael Biddiss, *The Age of the Masses* (Harmondsworth, 1977), p.30; J. M. Roberts, *Europe, 1880–1945*, 2nd edn (London, 1989), p.28; Barraclough, *Introduction to Contemporary History*, p.53; Jean-Louis Robert, 'Paris, London, Berlin on the Eve of the War', in Jay Winter and Jean-Louis Robert, eds, *Capital Cities at War: London, Paris, Berlin, 1914–19* (Cambridge, 1997), pp.25–53.

10. Biddiss, *Age of the Masses*, pp.34–5; Paul Kennedy, *The Rise and Fall of the Great Powers*, 2nd edn (New York, 1989), p.210.

11. A. Milward and B. Saul, *The Development of the Economies of Continental Europe, 1850–1914* (London, 1977), pp.19–20; Kennedy, *Rise and Fall*, pp.199–200.

12. Hans Rogger, *Russia in the Age of Modernisation and Revolution, 1881–1917* (London, 1983), pp.76–7; James Joll, *Europe since 1870: An International History*, 4th edn (Harmondsworth, 1990), p.175; Roberts, *Europe*, p.581.

13. B. Seebohm Rowntree, *Poverty: A Study of Town Life*, 2nd edn (London, 1902), pp.299–301; E. P. Hennock, 'The Measurement of Poverty: From the Metropolis to the Nation, 1880–1920', *EcHR* 2nd ser., 40 (1987), pp.208–27.

14. Barraclough, *Introduction to Contemporary History*, pp.47–8; Jay Winter, 'Army and Society: The Demographic Context', in Ian Beckett and Keith Simpson, eds, *A Nation in Arms: A Social Study of the British Army in the First World War* (Manchester, 1985), p.195.

15. Roberts, *Europe*, pp.24–6, 175, 194; Joll, *Europe since 1870*, p.31.

16. Winter, 'Army and Society', p.196.

17. Roberts, *Europe*, p.73; Marc Ferro, *The Great War 1914–1918* (London, 1973), p.3.

18. Biddiss, *Age of the Masses*, p.38; Barraclough, *Introduction to Contemporary History*, pp.127–8.

19. Ferro, *Great War*, p.4

20. David Kaiser, *Politics and War: European Conflict from Philip II to Hitler* (Cambridge, MA, 1990), pp.271–82.

21. J. V. Beckett, *The Aristocracy in England, 1660–1914* (Oxford, 1988), pp.206–37, 436–67; Robert Anderson, *France, 1870–1914* (London, 1977), p.33; C. A. Macartney, *The Habsburg Empire, 1790–1918* (London, 1969), pp.620–3; Mayer, *Persistence of Old Regime*, pp.1–23, 77–88, 135–7.

22. Michael R. Gordon, 'Domestic Conflict and the Origins of the First World War: The British and German Cases', *JMH* 46 (1974), pp.191–226; Jürgen Kocka, *Facing Total War* (Oxford, 1984), pp.78–81; David Blackbourn and Geoff Eley, *The Peculiarities of German History: Bourgeois Society and Politics in Nineteenth Century Germany* (New York, 1984), pp.1–61; Martin Clark, *Modern Italy, 1871–1892* (London, 1984), pp.28–30.

23. De Groot, *Blighty*, pp.173, 269.

24. Ferro, *Great War*, p.178; Roberts, *Europe*, p.242; Joll, *Europe since 1870*, p.74; Kennedy, *Rise and Fall*, p.237.

25. Ferro, *Great War*, pp.11–13.

26. John Gooch, *Armies in Europe* (London, 1980), p.118; E. Weber, *Peasants into Frenchmen: The Modernisation of Rural France, 1870–1914* (Stanford, CA, 1976); V. G. Kiernan, 'Conscription and Society in Europe before the War of 1914 to 1918', in M. R. D. Foot, ed., *War and Society* (London, 1973), pp.143–58; Raymond Pearson, *National Minorities in Eastern Europe, 1848–1945* (London, 1983), p.46.

27. For the 'new imperialism' generally see R. Hyam, *Britain's Imperial Century, 1815–1914: A Study of Empire and Expansion*, 2nd edn (Basingstoke, 1993); and A. N. Porter, *European Imperialism, 1860–1914* (Basingstoke, 1994). For its impact on European politics, see Kaiser, *Politics and War*, pp.282–307.

28. Kaiser, *Politics and War*, pp.307–25; Joll, *Europe since 1870*, pp.103, 111.

29. John Gooch, *The Plans of War: The General Staff and British Military Strategy c.1900–1916* (London, 1974), pp.149–55.

30. Keith Robbins, *Politicians, Diplomacy and War in Modern British History* (London, 1994), pp.85–100, 125–47; Roberts, *Europe*, p.234.

31. Niall Ferguson, *The Pity of War* (London, 1998), pp.28–9; Joll, *Europe since 1870*, pp.49–70.

32. Roberts, *Europe*, pp.38, 214–15; Kennedy, *Rise and Fall*, pp.200–2, 209–15, 224–32.

33. Roberts, *Europe*, p.52; Kennedy, *Rise and Fall*, p.230; idem, *Strategy and Diplomacy, 1870–1945* (London, 1983), pp.41–86; Ferguson, *Pity of War*, pp.35–9; H. J. Mackinder, 'The Geographical Pivot of History', *Geographical Journal* 23 (1904), pp.421–44.

34. Hennock, 'Measurement of Poverty', pp.208–27; M. D. Blanch, 'Imperialism, nationalism and organised youth', in J. Clarke, C. Critcher and R. Johnson, eds, *Working Class Culture* (London, 1979), pp.103–20; Anne Summers, 'Militarism in Great Britain before the Great War', *HWJ* 2 (1976), pp.104–23; H. W. Koch, 'Social Darwinism as a Factor in the New Imperialism', in H. W. Koch, ed., *The Origins of the First World War: Great Power Rivalry and German War Aims*, 2nd edn (London, 1984), pp.31–42; Michael Howard, 'Empire, Race and War', *History Today* 31 (1981), pp.4–11.

35. Robbins, *Politicians, Diplomacy and War*, pp.175–88; H. Weinroth, 'Norman Angell and *The Great Illusion*: An Episode in pre-1914 Pacifism', *HJ* 17 (1974), pp.551–74; Ferguson, *Pity of War*, pp.20–6; James Joll, '1914: The Unspoken Assumptions', in H. W. Koch, ed., *The Origins of the First World War* (London, 1972), pp.307–28. Joll's essay was not included in the second edition referred to in n.34 above.

36. John Keegan, *The First World War* (London, 1998), pp.12–16; Ferro, *Great War*, pp.13–14; Bill Murray, *Football: A History of the World Game* (Aldershot, 1994), p.67.

37. Joll, *Europe since 1870*, pp.43–7.

38. Viscount Grey of Fallodon, *Fallodon Papers* (London, 1926), p.3; Robbins, *Politicians, Diplomacy and War*, pp.125–47; Zara Steiner, *Britain and the Origins of the First World War* (London, 1977), pp.168–70.

CHAPTER TWO

Guns in August

There have been myriad explanations of how the assassination of the heir to the Austro-Hungarian Empire, Archduke Franz Ferdinand, at Sarajevo by the young Bosnian Serb student Gavrilo Princip, on 28 June 1914 became translated into a global conflict within 37 days.[1] In 1918, the victorious Allies had little doubt that the prime responsibility for the war lay in German actions, hence article 231 of the Treaty of Versailles, which categorically stated that 'Germany accepts the responsibility of Germany and her allies for causing all the loss and damage to the Allied governments and their nationals imposed on them by the aggression of Germany and her allies'.[2]

Germans responded in the 1920s to the *Kriegsschuldfrage* or 'war guilt' clause by an officially co-ordinated campaign to shift the blame to France and Russia through highly selective release of their diplomatic archives. Assisted by an increasing guilt on the part of the Entente and by the conclusions of the American revisionists Harry Barnes and Sidney Fay, a consensus emerged by the late 1930s that, in the words of David Lloyd George, all the great powers had 'slithered over the brink into the boiling cauldron of war'.[3]

The new revisionism was challenged by others such as Pierre Renouvin, Bernadotte Schmitt and, especially, Luigi Albertini, whose work became available in English translation in the 1950s.[4] Yet, surprisingly, the concept of equal responsibility and miscalculation even survived the German role in beginning a Second World War. What reopened the whole controversy regarding the causes of the Great War was the work of a German revisionist historian, Fritz Fischer, whose new interpretation, *Griff nach der Weltmacht* (Struggle for World Power), appeared in 1961, to be followed by *Krieg der Illusionen* (War of Illusions) in 1969.[5]

It was Fischer's contention, based on extensive archival research, that Germany did indeed bear the primary responsibility for war and that all the key decisions were those taken in Berlin. Fischer was subjected to considerable hostility by fellow German historians, who resisted the theory that there was an essential continuity in German policy from 1871 to 1945. Fischer was supported by Imanuel Geiss,[6] but others like Gerhard Ritter, Egmont Zechlin and Karl Dietrich Erdmann attacked his thesis.[7] Fischer relied on the record of crucial meetings such as that of the so-called War Council on 8 December 1912 and on documents like the September Programme issued by the German chancellor, Theobald von Bethmann-Hollweg, on 9 September 1914. Fischer's critics fastened on the diaries of Bethmann's private secretary, Kurt Riezler, edited by Erdmann, about the reliability of which considerable doubts soon arose.[8]

Fischer's interpretation of the relationship of German foreign policy to domestic politics was also taken up in a wider context of a spirited debate on the rival claims of the *Primat der Innenpolitik* (primacy of domestic policy) over the *Primat der Aussenpolitik* (primacy of foreign policy) in Hans-Ulrich Wehler's *Das Deutsche Kaiserreich* (The German Empire), which postulated a beleaguered elite determined to preserve its privileges at all costs.[9]

While historians have cast the net much more widely in recent years in examining the inter-relationship of various themes in the approach of war, the parameters of the debate remain as established by Fischer.[10] In terms of the build-up to war, the debate over the German role is still in essence between those who believe German policy was dictated by domestic political considerations, and those who believe policy was determined largely by external events. Some German historians have also returned to the theme of the overall responsibility of other powers, such as Britain, for not being able or willing to accommodate German ambitions within the international system.[11] In terms of the July Crisis of 1914, it is primarily a debate about whether Germany blundered, whether Germany gambled, or whether Germany deliberately provoked a general war.[12]

Alliances and the European state system

The centrality of the German role clearly needs to be set in the context of the European state system. However, while acknowledging that there are both immediate and long-term causes of any war, the structures in themselves were not the cause of the international breakdown but the given conditions in which decisions were made. Indeed, policy-makers made every decision with deliberation, often after debate and sometimes in the face of opposing ideas, and could have as well prevented as precipitated general war.[13]

There had been undoubted stability in the system between 1815 and 1848 through the alliance of conservative powers in the Concert of Europe. This was clearly followed by a period of instability from 1848 until 1871, not least through the emergence of nationalism as a potent political force. Stability was then restored in 1871, in essence through the reconstruction of a conservative alliance by Bismarck.[14] The alliance system itself has frequently been seen as crucial to the events of 1914, through the polarisation after 1894 of a new Franco-Russian alliance and the existing Triple Alliance between Austria-Hungary, Germany and Italy. Romania was also attached to the Triple Alliance by secret protocol. Having considered agreements with Germany in both 1898 and 1901, Britain then reached less formal agreements with France in April 1904 and Russia in August 1907.[15]

Stability within such a system rested on an approximate balance of power, in which it was important that those powers most interested in the status quo were the stronger. It so happened that those powers who should have been most interested in the status quo, Germany and Austria-Hungary, believed themselves increasingly undermined. German policy-makers tended to dwell increasingly on the insecurity of Germany's geographical position in Europe, on her inferiority to Britain in colonies and seapower, to Russia in population, to the United States in terms of the scope for future material growth, and on the danger that the years in which she could still use her power were numbered.

In turn, Germany's own material primacy in Europe was a powerful stimulus towards contracting alliances among the other powers, which served only to increase German suspicions of encirclement. Indeed, it was aggressive German policy which converted Britain's essentially colonial agreements with France and Russia into something rather more concrete, arousing particular fears among military and foreign affairs specialists in Britain.[16]

Austria-Hungary, on the other hand, was equally challenged. Having lost influence in central Europe to Germany after the Austro-Prussian War of 1866, and having lost Venetia and Lombardy to Italy in 1871, Austria-Hungary's only opportunity to preserve the notion of great power status lay in the Balkans. Here, however, the empire was confronted by the emergence from the Ottoman Empire of new states with nationalist and irredentist claims on her own imperial possessions. In particular, pan-Slavism was becomingly increasingly linked to the continued existence and ambition of Serbia, which not only rivalled the Habsburgs for the allegiance of the Slavs within the Austro-Hungarian Empire, but also had a natural recourse to Tsarist Russia for diplomatic support.

As James Joll has remarked, the alliance system may have conditioned expectations about likely partners in the event of war and, therefore, in some measure conditioned the likely form the war would take.[17] Yet, it has to be noted that the rival alliance systems were by no means as solid as they might have appeared for, as John Keiger has remarked, 'Fluctuations, agreements and *ententes* across the alliances were commonplace'.[18] Italy's commitment to the Triple Alliance, in the words of the Austro-Hungarian Chief of Staff, Franz, Baron Conrad von Hötzendorf (usually referred to simply as Conrad), was 'a pointless farce'.[19]

Similarly, Franco-Russian commitment was by no means a certainty.[20] Thus, George Kennan's view that the Franco-Russian alliance made war unavoidable is an exaggeration.[21] Similarly, British ministers, albeit for internal political reasons within the Liberal Cabinet after 1905, maintained a convenient fiction that there was no moral obligation to either France or Russia.[22] It should also be noted that it was the effective breakdown of the older stability within the system that encouraged smaller states in the Balkans to exert their independence of the great powers.

Imperial Germany and *Weltpolitik*

Fearing the balance of power was increasingly threatened, German and Austro-Hungarian policy-makers reacted accordingly, and very differently from Bismarck. That raises the question of what kind of state Germany was within the international system that was breaking down after 1890. Paradoxically, as already seen, it was a state in which the Reichstag was elected by universal male suffrage but had only limited powers to approve legislation and the budget. Thus, as Germany's economic progress was not matched by any social and political progress, it immediately created internal tensions.[23]

As suggested in the first chapter, there is something of a debate on the nature of the challenge posed to the traditional elite in Germany. Certainly, the avowedly Marxist SPD was thought to pose a significant threat to those who continued to exercise power.[24] In response, nationalism was strongly articulated in Germany, although the definition varied from group to group. Indeed, what was to become known as *Weltpolitik* (world politics) – in essence a more aggressive foreign policy expressed through the construction of a new modern fleet – was adopted in 1897 by the chancellor, Prince Bernhard von Bülow, primarily as a response to the internal threat from socialism and democracy.[25] Through forging a degree of unity between different groups, *Weltpolitik* reconstructed the alliance of 'steel and rye' first forged by Bismarck in the late 1870s between the agrarian power elite and heavy industry, the alliance in effect empowering the upper middle class who dominated industry.[26]

Maintaining the alliance was not to be that easy. Despite his ready access to the Kaiser, Bülow lost office in 1909 when attempting to impose inheritance tax and death duties to help continue the expansion of the armed forces.[27] His successor, Bethmann-Hollweg, tried to rebuild the alliance, especially that of Conservatives and National Liberals. Bethmann, however, was increasingly unable to satisfy the volatile radical right, as represented by the Pan-German League, whose enthusiastic support for radical nationalism far outstripped the intentions of those within the government who had sponsored its creation.

Weltpolitik was increasingly failing in other ways. The army, whose role would be crucial should the elite be threatened by social revolution, had not been noticeably successful in converting the working class from its allegiance to the SPD.[28] Moreover, *Weltpolitik* failed to undermine the political support of the SPD among the working class. Not perhaps surprisingly, the extreme political right grew increasingly hostile to the whole concept of parliamentarianism and spoke of a possible coup against the SPD in the wake of the 1912 election.[29] Indeed, politics was at such an impasse between 1912 and 1914 that many Germans began to see war as a possible catalyst for stabilisation at home as well as abroad before time ran out.

War as a way of stabilising Germany's position abroad raises the point that, while *Weltpolitik* was intimately linked with domestic policy, there were those for whom overseas expansion was an end in itself. What precisely was meant by the idea of a 'place in the sun' was never clearly defined. Some saw it being achieved by economic imperialism, some by accommodation with Britain, some by war against Britain. Indeed, in many ways, *Weltpolitik* was Anglophobic: only Britain was challenged by the construction of a fleet.[30] Bülow, however, envisaged no immediate conflict with Britain. More often than not, what was later to be articulated as the *Mittelafrika* (Central Africa) policy tended to see the Belgian Congo or the Portuguese African colonies as the prize.

Mittelafrika had lost some of its appeal by 1912 and was largely supplanted by the *Mitteleuropa* (Central Europe) policy, much favoured by industrialists such as Walther Rathenau, chairman of Allgemeine Elektrizität Gesellschaft (AEG; General Electric Company), who wished to escape Germany's dependence upon 'the charity of the world market' in terms of raw materials, foodstuffs and safe markets.[31] *Mitteleuropa* was in essence the concept of a customs union protected by high tariffs to include Austria-Hungary, the Balkans and Ottoman Turkey, linked to the idea of a Berlin-to-Baghdad railway.[32]

Expectations of German expansion were clearly being raised, and Germany was no more immune than any other state to the lure of Social Darwinism.[33] Indeed, it could be argued that the theories of seapower adopted by the State Secretary of the Reich Navy Office, Admiral Alfred von Tirpitz, from those of the American naval theorist Alfred Mahan, were little more than naval Social Darwinism. In fact, Tirpitz was cautious in believing that expansion could not succeed until the fleet was sufficiently strong to deter Britain, and consistently opposed risking war. By contrast, Bethmann believed British neutrality could be bought by slowing naval construction. At the same time, increased army expenditure would enable Germany, in the words of David Kaiser, 'to extort or conquer a colonial empire on the battlefields of Europe'.[34]

Imperialism, capitalism and militarism

Imperialism in itself has been another explanation advanced for the war, despite the fact that the great imperial rivals of the mid- to late nineteenth century were those that allied themselves through settlement of colonial disputes between 1904 and 1907, namely Britain, France and Russia.[35]

It can be argued that the imperial rivalry that mattered was that between Britain and Germany. Certainly, the construction of a modern German fleet to rival that of Britain and the fates of the Portuguese and Ottoman Empires became irritants in Anglo-German relations.[36] Nevertheless, imperialism in the accepted sense of overseas colonies did not play any real role in the outbreak of war in 1914 although, again, imperial rivalries helped to inform decisions that were made.[37] If, however, imperial expansion is interpreted in terms of German ambitions for expansion in Europe as epitomised by the concept of *Mitteleuropa* then clearly it did play a significant role.

Imperialism was often explained as a product of capitalism, and capitalism itself was advanced as a cause of the war by Marxists led by Lenin, whose celebrated pamphlet *Imperialism – The Highest Stage of Capitalism* appeared in 1916. In turn, capitalism has been connected with militarism and the arms race, since it was held by Sir Edward Grey, amongst others, that the activities of arms merchants had made war inevitable.[38] The Marxist argument was that war was inherent in capitalism and inevitably resulted from imperial rivalries caused, in turn, by the need for capitalists to maintain profits by expanding markets. As Sir Harry Hinsley has pointed out, it is not entirely surprising that the war was fought by capitalist societies since all European societies in 1914 were such. Therefore, it was not necessarily because they were capitalist societies that there was a war.[39]

There was an element of economic hostility between the powers since, with the exception of Britain, whose Unionist government had fallen apart on the issue in 1905, most maintained protective tariffs.[40] Obviously, too, there were trading rivalries which, in the case of Germany, did contribute to insecurity. Yet, between 1905 and 1914 Russo-German trade was immensely important, with Russia sending 44 per cent of her exports to Germany and receiving 47 per cent of her imports from Germany. Moreover, despite the deteriorating political relationships in Europe, German banks continued to co-operate with French banks in business dealings with Ottoman Turkey, and with British banks in dealings with Portuguese Africa and China right to the end of the July crisis.[41]

It could also be argued that the existence of an international economy was a factor in negating more parochial nationalism. Business hardly welcomed war, as the considerable economic uncertainty in July and August 1914 indicated. Austrian state bonds fell by 5–10 per cent between 27 June and 27 July, interest rates increased from 4 to 8 per cent at the end of July, and payments of gold for paper currency were suspended on 5 August. Similarly, German and Russian state bonds fell by approximately the same amount as Austrian during July. British government bonds fell by between 5 and 7 per cent in the last week of July, interest rates rose from 3 to 10 per cent between 29 July and 1 August, and there was a run on the banks. The stock exchanges in Berlin, Paris and London all closed, the latter not having done so in any crisis during the nineteenth century.[42]

Similarly, there is little real evidence of the existence of what might be termed a military–industrial complex in Europe in that the arms manufacturers had neither power nor inclination to influence foreign policy. In so far as they did try to influence governments, armaments firms were primarily interested in introducing changes likely to disadvantage their domestic competitors.[43] Consequently, the armaments race itself was in many respects a reaction to events, particularly the Bosnian Crisis of 1908–09 and the two Balkan Wars of 1912–13. While traditionally seen in terms of the naval race between Britain and Germany, what is actually more significant is the race for preparedness for war on land. That should be judged not in terms of the purchase of weapons, for the large-scale technical developments had been absorbed by the 1890s at the latest, but in terms of improvements in the speed of mobilisation resulting from measures such as double tracking and increased investment in signalling on railways, and raising the proportion of manpower under arms.[44]

The most rapid augmentation resulted from the Balkan Wars, with Russian military improvements the trigger to the shift in German armaments expenditure from the navy to the army, since the new strategic railway lines into Poland and the military reorganisation of the Russian army would substantially decrease Russian mobilisation times by 1917–18.[45]

The faster mobilisation times that could be achieved by 1914 certainly enabled the politicians to run greater risks. They also persuaded each alliance system that they could be victorious, especially if it were perceived that windows of military opportunity were fast closing.[46] However, as David Stevenson has written in an echo of Trotsky, armaments were 'the wheels and pistons of the locomotive of history, not the steam'. Indeed, the general increase in armaments between 1909 and 1913 was not of the same magnitude as that in Europe in either the 1930s or the 1950s.[47]

Connected to the question of armaments and militarism is the notion of war by timetable, as popularised by A. J. P. Taylor, whose contention was that German mobilisation was decisive 'because of the academic ingenuity with which Schlieffen, now in his grave, had attempted to solve the problem of a two-front war'.[48] But it cannot be said that the war plans of the great powers of themselves caused the war. Certainly, those of Germany and, to a much lesser extent, Britain, were sufficiently rigid to deny their governments room for manoeuvre once war had been decided upon. In particular, Germany's Schlieffen Plan required her to invade France irrespective of whether the quarrel was, as in 1914, primarily with Russia. Moreover, the practical constraints of the military plans were such that Germany must secure the Belgian fortress of Liège within 72 hours if the 42 day timetable for the defeat of France was to be adhered to. In this sense, indeed, once German mobilisation began on 30 July, German policy came under military control.[49]

Certainly, the German army viewed war as inevitable and, preferably, wanted it sooner rather than later. Indeed, the need for a preventative war to avoid Germany's having to fight France and Russia simultaneously was an act of faith for such influential soldiers as Friedrich von Bernhardi, head of the historical section of the General Staff from 1898 to 1907, and the inspector of fortresses from 1899 to 1901, Colmar von der Goltz.

More is said of the Schlieffen Plan in the next chapter but, for the Chief of German General Staff between 1891 and 1906, Alfred, Count von Schlieffen, the strategic problem facing Germany required an appropriate military solution regardless of political considerations. While some military aspects of Schlieffen's scheme were adjusted by his successor, the younger Helmuth von Moltke, the subordination of political considerations to military exigencies remained unaltered. Moltke, too, subscribed to the belief that time was running out for Germany in view of the improvements in Russian military capability. Moreover, the growing Russian threat coincided with constraints on Germany's own capabilities, which suggested to the military and political leadership that Germany could not match French and Russian defence spending in the long term, necessitating a pre-emptive strike.[50]

One manifestation was the celebrated War Council on 8 December 1912. Attended by the Kaiser, Tirpitz, Moltke and other military and naval officers, the council centred on the inevitability of conflict, although both Moltke and Tirpitz appear to have counselled delay. Interpretations of the significance of the War Council vary.[51] The army, however, was clearly reluctant to postpone conflict for much longer and the conventional wisdom that Germany must soon fight continued to be expressed by Moltke and others on frequent occasions down to July 1914.[52]

There is a danger in viewing the German leadership as monolithic in its intentions. Certainly, the army represented an entirely different hierarchy from that represented by the politicians. Similar views to those of the army, however, were held within the parallel hierarchy represented by Bethmann and his advisers within the Foreign Ministry, principally the Secretary of State, Gottlieb von Jagow, the Under-secretary of State, Arthur Zimmermann, and the head of the political department, Wilhelm von Stumm. Reference to 1917 as a crucial year is commonplace among the German political and military leadership.[53] Bethmann himself may have been a relatively late convert to war,[54] but, while he was clearly reluctant to see Germany at war with Britain, this does not appear to have been the case with respect to war against France and Russia.

Vienna and the domestic imperative

Assumptions on the part of policy-makers have led historians to focus upon the background against which the key decisions were made and the possibility that foreign policy decisions were taken for domestic reasons.[55] Since the adoption of *Weltpolitik* did not actually halt the political advance of the SPD, therefore, war could be regarded as a further possible means of establishing social stability in Germany.

Similarly, Austro-Hungarian action against Serbia would deal with the potent threat posed to the empire by pan-Slavism. It has been argued that Russia had fought the disastrous war against Japan as an ultimately unsuccessful 'short victorious war' to stave off internal revolution. Russian foreign policy thereafter reflected calculations of its results in relation to the domestic situation, not least during the Bosnian Crisis of 1908, although the consensus to avoid war at all costs broke down after Stolypin's assassination.[56]

Britain, too, had an escalating internal problem in the Irish Home Rule crisis, which culminated, during and after the Curragh incident of March

1914, in the open disaffection of much of the army's officer cadre, effectively paralysing the government in the face of the possibility of civil war in
Ireland. Yet, despite what has sometimes been described as the Edwardian
crisis within British society, it remained stable: as Zara Steiner has written,
it 'was not a society on the eve of dissolution'.[57] In the British case, therefore,
foreign policy was not determined by considerations of domestic politics, but
by perceived dangers both to the Empire and to the balance of power in
Europe.[58]

The clearest pressure for war to solve internal difficulties was in Austria-
Hungary. Vienna was confronted by the aspirations of a more militaristic
Serbian dynasty, which had taken power in Belgrade by a coup in 1903. The
aim was for a greater Serbia embracing Montenegro, parts of Macedonia
and, ultimately, the southern Slav provinces of the empire, Bosnia and
Hercegovina. Dalmatia, Croatia and Slovenia also appeared to be in the
sights of the Serb leadership. Vienna had mobilised its forces against Serbia
both during the annexation of Bosnia and during the Balkan Wars. Conrad
and influential young members of the Foreign Ministry like Count Forgách,
Baron von Musulin, Count Hoyos and Baron von Franckenstein – followers
of the former Foreign Minister, Count Lexa von Aehrenthal – all looked to
solve the empire's problems through a preventative war.

Aehrenthal himself, who had died in 1912, had sought expansion without war but, as argued by Fritz Fellner, his young disciples lacked his diplomatic finesse. Aehrenthal's successor, Leopold, Count Berchtold, was greatly
influenced by this group and, in any case, shared their determination
to exploit Archduke Franz Ferdinand's assassination. Indeed, the Austro-
Hungarian ambassador to Belgrade was instructed as early as 7 July 1914
that war must be forced on Serbia, and it is apparent that Berchtold continued to fear that Berlin might accept a diplomatic solution to the crisis.[59]

Franz Ferdinand had led those advocating a peaceful solution to the
empire's relationship with Serbia.[60] His reported ideas, however, of recon-
structing the empire by giving the Slavs the same autonomy as enjoyed by
the Hungarians since 1867 was precisely what made him a target for the
Serbian secret society known as the Black Hand. In reality, Franz Ferdinand
seems to have intended to reassert German dominance within the empire
as a whole. The Black Hand's leader was Serbia's chief of the military
secret service, Colonel Dragutin Dimitrijevic (nicknamed 'Apis' or the Bull),
but the Serb government of Nikola Pasic was not involved in the Sarajevo
assassination and even Dimitrijevic tried to prevent it at the last moment.[61]
Theoretically, the Black Hand was also distanced from the deed since the
assassins were members of the Mlada Bosnia (Young Bosnia) movement
and Austrian subjects. Clearly, however, Conrad and Berchtold were determined to exploit the assassination from the beginning.

No one mourned Franz Ferdinand, for all that mattered was to act decisively to preserve the empire and Austria-Hungary's status as a great power. As Samuel Williamson has put it, the Austro-Hungarian leadership 'consciously risked a general war to fight a local war'. It did so in order 'to save itself', without contemplating how war would actually achieve such an objective.[62] Only the Hungarian prime minister, Count Tisza, hesitated, but he was sympathetic towards Germany. He accepted war once assured of German support and of Romanian neutrality, and that Serbia itself would not be annexed after its intended defeat.[63]

German support, without which Vienna would not act, was secured as early as 5 July. Count Hoyos went to Potsdam with a letter from Emperor Franz Joseph to the Kaiser and received an unequivocal statement of support, known henceforth as the 'blank cheque'.[64] It has been suggested on occasions that Hoyos exaggerated the degree of support, but other documents make it clear that the German military and political leadership was fully committed to backing Vienna and well knew the likely outcome. Indeed, Zimmerman told Hoyos that there was 'a probability of 90 per cent to a European war' if Austria-Hungary took action against Serbia.[65]

Agreed upon at a meeting on 14 July and finalised on 19 July, the Austro-Hungarian ultimatum, which was drafted by Musulin, was presented to the Serb government on 23 July. As will be seen, part of the delay was owing to the movements of the French president, and there also appears to have been concern to ensure bringing in most of the harvest. Delay was also urged by Conrad, who after such frequent demands for preventative action in the past, had had to admit that delay was necessary to complete mobilisation. The ultimatum was always intended to be unacceptable in its demands for the suppression of the Black Hand and of anti-Austrian propaganda, the dismissal of Serbian officers implicated in anti-Austrian activities, the arrest of named suspects, tightening of border controls and the participation of Austrian representatives in an official enquiry to be carried out by the Serbs.

In fact, the Serbs accepted the ultimatum on 25 July with the exception of allowing Austrian officials on Serbian soil, but this was still sufficient for Vienna to go to war.[66] The draft declaration of war was put before Franz Joseph on 27 July, Berchtold having argued that a compromise might be found 'unless a clear situation is created by a declaration of war'.[67]

From 'Third Balkan War' to world war

Austro-Hungarian determination to 'settle accounts' and seek a 'final and fundamental reckoning' with Serbia, as Conrad and Berchtold separately termed it, goes far to explain the outbreak of a 'Third Balkan War' in July 1914.[68] It cannot explain the conversion of that localised conflict into a world war. That leads back to the calculations made in Berlin and whether the German leadership miscalculated, gambled or deliberately provoked war, although, in a sense, there has also been a related question as to whether Germany fought merely a preventative war or a war of conquest.

The idea that Germany miscalculated the reaction from other powers rests largely on the assumption that the continued existence of Austria-Hungary was of vital national interest to Germany, and that it was absolutely necessary to support Vienna on the assumption that Britain and France would restrain Russia from supporting Serbia. Germany was not obliged to issue the 'blank cheque' under the terms of its alliance with Austria-Hungary since this was couched in purely defensive terms. Therefore, it is argued that it did so through fears that the possible collapse of the Habsburg empire would tip the wider balance of power against Germany. In reality, the German leadership does not appear to have been motivated at any point by real concern for Vienna's interests and Serbia was regarded as a quite minor issue.[69]

As it happened, Austria-Hungary did not declare war on Russia until 6 August, while Britain and France did not reciprocate until 12 August. In any case, backing Vienna clearly involved considerable risks of escalation. Moreover, in order to mobilise for military operations against France, Germany needed to take a decision for war at least two weeks before opening its campaign against France, Belgium and Luxemburg.[70] A second element of miscalculation on the part of Bethmann was the attitude of Britain, but, as suggested below, this made little difference.

By contrast, there is the contention that the German leadership took a calculated risk.[71] According to this interpretation, the expectation was that the threat of war would force Russia to break with Britain and France, the intention being to ensure a limited and successful war by Austria-Hungary against Serbia. Much rests on the interpretation of the diaries of Chancellor Bethmann's private secretary, Riezler. These suggest that Bethmann did not believe Russia would assist Serbia if Vienna acted sufficiently quickly, and because the Serbs were implicated in the murder of a member of the Austrian royal family. But, while Bethmann and the Kaiser had doubts from time to time, it seems that there was no real belief that Russia would stay out of a war.[72]

The suspect nature of the Riezler diaries recalls the arguments of German historians in the 1920s that Britain and France had not done enough to prevent the war but, as the German ambassador in London, Prince Karl Max Lichnowsky later expressed it, peace would have been maintained only 'on the condition that Russia would give her blessing to the annihilation of Serbia'.[73] If Germany was engaged on a 'leap in the dark' – the phrase used by Riezler – then its leadership was certainly prepared to accept war as an outcome of any risk taken, in the belief that it was a risk well worth taking.

The third interpretation is that Germany deliberately provoked war. As already indicated, much testimony exists as to the willingness of both the military and political leadership to contemplate a general war. It is argued by opponents of this interpretation that there is no direct line from the War Council in December 1912 to the July crisis and even Fischer later accepted that the War Council did not make a definite decision for war.[74] This does not alter the underlying assumptions of the German leadership, and more evidence is becoming available, as documents once thought lost reappear from eastern archives, to suggest a deliberate decision on war taken at an early stage in 1914.[75]

What is not known is precisely when the decision for war was taken. It was probably no later than when Hoyos arrived in Berlin on 5 July and, conceivably, even before the July crisis developed.[76] Indeed, Germany's only concerns as the crisis unfolded were to ensure that any mediation failed, and that the blame for war fell on others. In particular, the blame was to be pinned on Russia, since this would assist the acceptance by the SPD leadership of the need for German mobilisation.[77]

It has been argued that, even if deliberate, the war was in essence a preventative one, embarked upon in the increasing sense of Germany's coming decline. However, Germany was in no immediate danger of being attacked by the Entente powers even if her military position was one of long-term decline in terms of manpower compared with that of Russia. Thus, in view of the frequent discussion of such an option since 1912, John Rohl has commented that, in this context, 'it is then hard to distinguish between a preventative war and a war of aggression'. Equally, as Niall Ferguson has remarked, a preventative strike 'is by no means incompatible with the idea that the outcome of such a strike, if successful, would be German hegemony in Europe'.[78]

There is evidence that Germany intended from the beginning to pursue wider war aims. One such piece long known is the comprehensive and wide-ranging list of German war aims announced on 9 September 1914 and known as the September Programme. The other belligerents took months, if not years, to formulate their war aims. It has been argued that Bethmann's support for the September Programme, outlined to him by Walther Rathenau on 28 August, resulted primarily from a new realisation that Germany was now engaged in long-term economic warfare with Britain and that there was no continuity between pre-war and wartime desire for expansion.[79] The balance of evidence suggests, however, as Harmut Pogge von Strandmann has argued, that there was a general willingness to fight an expansionist war 'disguised as a defensive or preventative action'.[80]

The role of powers other than Germany and Austria-Hungary in the July Crisis needs to be considered. There was little the Serbs could do to prevent Vienna declaring war on 28 July but critics of Fischer's interpretation of German guilt argue that Russia failed to place a restraining hand on Serbia. Indeed, much has been made of Russian partial mobilisation on 29 July, followed by full mobilisation on 30 July. This then triggered the German ultimatum to Russia on 31 July and both German mobilisation and a declaration of war on 1 August.[81] In fact, the Germans had earlier picked up the signs of Russian pre-mobilisation measures.[82] Russia is seen by some as more expansionist than Austria-Hungary in the Balkans and encouraging Serbian defiance.

Russia was initially ambivalent in its support for the Serbs, who were fully independent actors in the crisis,[83] but the Russian leadership was not prepared to yield to Austro-Hungarian or German demands in the way it had done in previous Balkan crises. Russia had recovered substantially from defeat in the Russo-Japanese War to the extent that military and naval expansion was being accommodated with considerably less financial strain than was the case in Germany, and with knock-on effects for the benefit of the Russian economy as a whole albeit largely unplanned.[84]

Thus, while advising the Serbs to concede to Vienna, the Russian Council of Ministers resolved to undertake preparatory mobilisation measures. It regarded mobilisation as a diplomatic lever and warning rather than as a prelude to any offensive action. Indeed, in response to a telegram from the Kaiser, the Tsar halted partial mobilisation on 29 July. He was then convinced by the military that this left Russia in a hopeless situation since the multi-racial nature of the Tsarist empire dictated that Russian regiments did not draw their reserves from single military districts and it was all but impossible to mobilise only four districts as the Council had intended. Full mobilisation was then ordered.[85]

The French president, Raymond Poincaré, and his prime minister, René Viviani, who doubled as Foreign Minister, were actually out of France from 15 to 29 July on state visits to Russia and Scandinavia. As a result, they played little role in the crisis other than trying to ensure British support once they hurriedly returned to Paris. Indeed, the isolation of Poincaré and Viviani from events was compounded by Vienna deliberately delaying despatch of the ultimatum to Serbia until the Frenchmen had sailed from St Petersburg for Sweden on 23 July. The French ambassador in St Petersburg, Maurice Paléologue, certainly encouraged the Russian Foreign Minister,

Sergei Sazonov, to take a firm line with Germany, but contrived to add to the isolation of French policy-makers by concealing and then delaying news of Russian mobilisation.[86]

It has also been argued that the domestic controversy over the legislation to increase the term of military service to three years in 1913, and the possibility that it might be amended, led Poincaré to reassure the Russians of continued French support by giving them unconditional and uncritical backing.[87] However, Paléologue made little contribution to the decision-making process in St Petersburg and even less to that in Vienna and Berlin. Poincaré also clearly tried to avoid a provocation. In the event, the German declaration of war on 3 August alleged a wholly fictitious French air raid on Nuremberg as justification.[88]

Germany had already invaded Luxemburg on 2 August and demanded passage through Belgium, the invasion of Belgium beginning on 4 August. Belgium hardly had time to react at all, but King Albert and his prime minister had no hesitation in refusing the ultimatum, immediately appealing to the guarantors of its neutrality under the Treaty of London of 1839, principally Britain.[89] There was an expectation on the part of Grey that he could mediate successfully and, in view of the difficulties of carrying the British Cabinet on intervention, it was only the threat of resignation by Grey and the prime minister, Asquith, which brought an honouring of pre-war naval commitments to France on 2 August to safeguard the Channel while the French fleet deployed to the Mediterranean. The German ultimatum to Belgium, and not actual German invasion, then triggered the British ultimatum to Germany, which expired at 11p.m. on 4 August. It has been argued that firmer British diplomatic action would have had an additional deterrent effect in view of the hesitations of the Kaiser and Bethmann and, indeed, that the outbreak of war represented a general breakdown of deterrence since Germany failed to deter Austria-Hungary and Britain failed to deter Germany.[90]

It appears highly unlikely, however, that any firmer British declaration of support for France and Russia would have made any real difference to events. It has become an increasingly fashionable view that British entry to the war was unnecessary, even if the intervention of the British Expeditionary Force (BEF) probably did prevent a German victory. It was the case that the Foreign Office had concluded that the 1839 treaty did not require Britain to go to Belgium's assistance in all circumstances. Some British military and naval planners had themselves contemplated violating Belgian neutrality, if necessary, in order to take the war to Germany. There is also no doubt that the extent of Britain's 'moral commitment' to France since the initiation of staff talks between the British and French general staffs in 1905 had been concealed from most ministers until 1911.

Nevertheless, it was not in Britain's long-term strategic interests to allow Germany either to dominate the Low Countries and the Channel ports or to upset the balance of power in Europe. Nor is it likely that, even if Germany's immediate war aims had been limited by a need to ensure British neutrality, a victorious Germany would not have soon threatened British interests. Unpleasant though the consequences were for Britain, it was a necessary war.[91]

Once war was imminent, it is usually assumed that there was a readiness and even eagerness to accept its challenge amongst many of Europe's peoples, but the contribution of the popular mood to actual events in July 1914 was limited. While the idea of the unspoken assumptions of 1914 is primarily connected to James Joll, it was actually commonplace in the 1920s to stress the inevitability of war. Caroline Playne's *The Pre-war Mind in Britain*, published in 1928, spoke of the mood as being one of infectious mental contagion which 'swept down the mindless, expectant, half-frightened, wondering crowds, and . . . swept down progressives, earnest people, intelligent people as well'.[92] In part, this is attributed to the incipient militarism of pre-war society fuelled by nationalism, imperialism and Social Darwinism. Indeed, how else, it is reasoned, could the pre-war expectations of international solidarity have been so easily overcome?

Yet, in many cases, and especially so in the case of Britain, the public had little time in which to react to events. There was no noticeable sense of impending foreign crisis in the British press until 29 July, attention having been fixed on the continuing Irish problem. The final crisis unfolded over the Bank Holiday weekend, the news of the German ultimatum to Belgium reaching London on the morning of Bank Holiday Monday, 3 August. In Manchester at least, the opposition to intervention on the part of the *Manchester Guardian* reflected the fears of the local and influential business community as to the economic consequences of involvement.

Rather similarly, attention in France was diverted by the sensational murder trial of Madame Henriette Caillaux, second wife of the French Finance Minister, Joseph Caillaux, which began on 20 July. Indeed, *Le Temps* devoted twice as much space to the verdict as to the deepening European crisis, John Keiger suggesting that, for all practical purposes, the July crisis 'never existed for French public opinion'.[93] Jean-Jacques Becker's study of public opinion in France supplemented by P. J. Flood's study of the *département* of the Isère, centred on Grenoble in south-eastern France, suggests not all were eager to embrace war. The notion of *revanche* (revenge) for the lost provinces of Alsace-Lorraine had long since lost any wider currency beyond a minority of nationalists.[94]

The mood in Austria-Hungary was also subdued for most of the four weeks of the July Crisis, popular enthusiasm for war becoming apparent only in the first days of August, although the press had become steadily more bellicose. Even in Germany, where it is generally supposed that the war was met with particular enthusiasm, studies of towns such as Hamburg and Darmstadt have suggested that the 'August experience' was by no means uniform.[95] Indeed, it would seem that, with the exception of some sections of the population in Austria-Hungary and Serbia, most Europeans were, to quote L. L. Farrar, 'probably apathetic regarding the question of war' between the assassination of Franz Ferdinand and the issue of their own country's ultimatums.[96]

While it was important that the people accept the risk and inevitability of war or, perhaps, the illusion of what war would be like, it was not the people who made the decisions in 1914. In each case, a handful of policy-makers made decisions with due deliberation and with careful calculation. The balance of evidence suggests that, from the beginning, the German leadership was intent on war. It was not inevitable that a localised conflict should lead to a general European war, but the German leadership had no intention of keeping it localised and embarked on war with determination, confidence and belief in ultimate victory. Everyone else simply reacted to the German challenge. European policy-makers could as easily have prevented war as precipitated it. Many, however, undoubtedly shared the assumptions not only that war was inevitable, but also that it would be short and that they would win, especially as the best chance of victory lay in an immediate offensive.[97] All such assumptions were to prove tragic delusions.

Notes and references

1. Z. A. B. Zeman, 'The Balkans and the Coming of War', in R. J. W. Evans and Hartmut Pogge von Strandmann, eds, *The Coming of the First World War*, 2nd edn (Oxford, 1990), pp.19–32; Wayne S. Vucinich, 'Mlada Bosnia and the First World War', in Robert A. Kann, Béla Király and Paula Fichtner, eds, *The Habsburg Empire in World War I: Essays on the Intellectual, Military, Political and Economic Aspects of the Habsburg War Effort* (Ithaca, NY, 1977), pp.45–70.

2. James Joll, *The Origins of the First World War* (London, 1984), p.1.

3. H. E. Barnes, *The Genesis of War: An Introduction to the Problem of War Guilt* (New York, 1926); S. B. Fay, *The Origins of the World War*, 2 vols (New York, 1930); David Lloyd George, *War Memoirs* (London, 1924), I, p.52.

4. P. E. G. Renouvin, *The Immediate Origins of the War* (New York, 1927); B. E. Schmitt, *The Coming of the War, 1914*, 2 vols (New York, 1930); Luigi Albertini, *The Origins of the War of 1914*, 3 vols (London, 1952–57).

5. Fritz Fischer, *Germany's Aims in the First World War* (London, 1967); idem, *War of Illusions: German Policies from 1911 to 1914* (London, 1975); idem, *World Power or Decline* (New York, 1974); idem, *From Kaiserreich to Third Reich: Elements of Continuity in German History, 1871–1945* (London, 1979).

6. Imanuel Geiss, *July 1914: The Outbreak of the First World War, Selected Documents* (London, 1967); idem, ed., *Juli 1914: Die europäische Krise und der Ausbruch des Ersten Weltkrieg* (Munich, 1965); idem, 'The Outbreak of the First World War and German War Aims', *JCH* 1 (1966), pp.75–91; idem, *Das Deutsche Reich und die Vorgeschichte des Ersten Weltkrieges* (Munich, 1978); idem, *Das Deutsche Reich und der Erste Weltkrieg* (Munich, 1985).

7. Useful summaries of the views of Fischer's critics can be found in the articles by Zechlin, Erdmann and Karl-Heinz Janssen (on Ritter) reproduced in Koch, *Origins of First World War*, 2nd edn, pp.189–318, 343–85. Koch himself is also to be counted in the anti-Fischer camp – see his introduction in the same collection, pp.1–29.

8. Bernd Sösemann, 'Die Tagebücher Kurt Riezlers: Untersuchungen zu ihrer Echthiet und Edition', *Historische Zeitschrift* 236 (1983), pp.327–69; Fritz Fischer, *Juli 1914: Wir sind nicht hineingeschlittert. Das Staatsgeheimnis um die Riezler-Tagebücher. Eine Streitschrift* (Hamburg, 1983). On Riezler generally, see John A. Moses, *The Politics of Illusion: The Fischer Controversy in German Historiography* (London, 1975), pp.27–44.

9. Hans-Ulrich Wehler, *The German Empire, 1871–1918* (Leamington Spa, 1985). For a useful summary of the course of the debate on the nature of Imperial Germany see James Retallack, 'Wilhelmine Germany', in Gordon Martel, ed., *Modern Germany Reconsidered, 1870–1945* (London, 1992), pp.33–53.

10. The most obvious examples are the volumes in the Macmillan series on the origins of the war: Volker Berghahn, *Germany and the Approach of War in 1914* (London, 1973); John Keiger, *France and the Origins of the First World War* (London, 1983); D. C. B. Lieven, *Russia and the Origins of the First World War* (London, 1983); Samuel Williamson, *Austria-Hungary and the Origins of the First World War* (London, 1991), and Steiner, *Britain and Origins*.

11. Volker Berghahn, *Germany and the Approach of War*, 2nd edn (London, 1993), pp.1–14; Klaus Hildebrand, *Deutsche Aussenpolitik, 1871–1918* (Munich, 1989); Gregor Schöllgen, ed., *Escape into War? The Foreign Policy of Imperial Germany* (Oxford, 1990), pp.1–17, 121–33.

12. For a general survey of the historiography of the causes of the war, see J. W. Langdon, *July 1914: The Long Debate, 1918–90* (Providence, RI, 1991).

13. Sir Harry Hinsley, 'Introduction', in Keith Wilson, ed., *Decisions for War, 1914* (London, 1995), p.4.

14. F. R. Bridge, *1914: The Coming of the First World War*, 2nd edn (London, 1988), pp.5–8. See also F. R. Bridge and R. Bullen, *The Great Powers and the European State System, 1815–1914* (London, 1980).

15. Joll, *Origins*, pp.34–57; R. J. Crampton, 'The Decline of the Concert of Europe in the Balkans, 1913–14', *Slavonic and East European Review* 52 (1974), pp.393–419; R. T. B. Langhorne, *The Collapse of the Concert of Europe: International Polictics, 1890–1914* (London, 1981).

16. Keiger, *France and Origins*, pp.13–20.

17. Joll, *Origins*, p.56.

18. Keiger, *France and Origins*, p.87.

19. Joll, *Origins*, p.51; Richard Bosworth, *Italy and the Approach of the First World War* (London, 1983), pp.51–76.

20. Keiger, *France and Origins*, pp.88–9.

21. G. F. Kennan, *The Fateful Alliance: France, Russia and the Coming of the First World War* (New York, 1984).

22. Michael Brock and Eleanor Brock, eds, *H. H. Asquith: Letters to Venetia Stanley* (Oxford, 1982), p.123; John W. Coogan and Peter F. Coogan, 'The British Cabinet and the Anglo-French Staff Talks, 1905–1914: Who knew What and When did he know it?', *JBS* 24 (1985), pp.110–31; Keith M. Wilson, *The Policy of the Entente: Essays on the Determinants of British Foreign Policy, 1904–14* (Cambridge, 1985), pp.121–34.

23. Berghahn, *Germany and Approach of War*, pp.5–24; Joll, *Origins*, pp.108–18.

24. R. J. Evans, ed., *Society and Politics in Wilhelmine Germany* (London, 1978); Geoff Eley, *Reshaping the German Right: Radical Nationalism and Political Change after Bismarck* (New Haven, CT, 1980); D. Blackbourn, *Class, Religion and Local Politics in Wilhelmine Germany* (London, 1980). A useful discussion of varying interpretations of competing nationalist ideologies in Germany can be found in Niall Ferguson, 'Germany and the Origins of the First World War: New Perspectives', *HJ* 35 (1992), pp.734–42.

25. Geiss, *July 1914*, pp.21–35; David E. Kaiser, 'Germany and the Origins of the First World War', *JMH* 55 (1983), pp.442–74; idem, *Politics and War*, pp.295–300; John Rohl, *Germany without Bismarck: The Crisis of Government in the Second Reich, 1890–1900* (Berkeley, CA, 1967), pp.156–75, 212–22; Woodruff Smith, *The Ideological Origins of Nazi Imperialism* (New York, 1986), pp.41–82; On the Kaiser, see John Rohl, *Kaiser, Hof und Staat: Wilhelm II und die deutsche Politik* (Munich, 1987); Lamar Cecil, *Wilhelm II: Prince and Emperor* (Durham, NC, 1989); and T. A. Kohut, *Wilhelm II and the Germans: A Study in Leadership* (Oxford, 1991).

26. Kaiser, 'Germany and Origins of First World War', pp.447–8.

27. Katherine Anne Lerman, *The Chancellor as Courtier: Bernhard von Bülow and the Governance of Germany, 1900–1909* (Cambridge, 1990).

28. Geoff Eley, 'Conservatives and Radical Nationalists in Germany: the Production of Fascist Potentials, 1912–28', in Martin Blinkhorn, ed., *Fascists and*

Conservatives (London, 1990), pp.50–70; idem, 'The Wilhelmine Right: How it Changed', in Evans, ed., *Society and Politics*, pp.112–35; Ferguson, *Pity of War*, pp.16–17.

29. Kaiser, 'Germany and the Origins of the First World War', p.461; Berghahn, *Germany and Approach of War*, pp.145–64.

30. Paul Kennedy, *The Rise of Anglo-German Antagonism, 1860–1914*, 2nd edn (London, 1987), pp.410–31; R. T. B. Langhorne, 'The Naval Question in Anglo-German Relations, 1912–14', *HJ* 14 (1971), pp.361–87; Gregor Schöllgen, 'Germany's Foreign Policy in the Age of Imperialism: A Vicious Circle', in Gregor Schöllgen, ed., *Escape into War*, pp.121–33.

31. Kaiser, *Politics and War*, p.299; Fritz Fischer, 'World Policy, Power and German War Aims', in Koch, ed., *Origins of First World War*, 2nd edn, p.168.

32. Fritz Fischer, 'German War Aims 1914–1918 and German Policy before the War', in Barry Hunt and Adrian Preston, eds, *War Aims and Strategic Policy in the Great War, 1914–1918* (London, 1977), pp.105–23.

33. Joll, *Origins*, pp.186–8, 192–3.

34. Kaiser, 'Germany and Origins of First World War', pp.456–8, 463–4.

35. Joll, *Origins*, pp.148–70.

36. Ibid., pp.156–58; R. T. B. Langhorne, 'Anglo-German Negotiations Concerning the Future of the Portuguese Colonies, 1911–14', *HJ* 16 (1973), pp.361–87.

37. Joll, *Origins*, p.167.

38. Viscount Grey of Fallodon, *Twenty-five Years, 1892–1916*, 2 vols (London, 1925), I, p.90.

39. Hinsley, 'Introduction', in Wilson, ed., *Decisions for War*, p.6.

40. Joll, *Origins*, pp.123–47.

41. Lieven, *Russia and Origins*, p.134.

42. L. L. Farrar, 'Reluctant Warriors: Public Opinion on War during the July Crisis, 1914', *EEQ* 16 (1983), pp.431–3; Ferguson, *Pity of War*, pp.189–97; Jon Lawrence, Martin Dean and Jean-Louis Robert, 'The Outbreak of War and the Urban Economy: Paris, Berlin and London in 1914', *EcHR* 45 (1992), pp.564–93; Jon Lawrence, 'The Transition to War in 1914', in Winter and Robert, eds, *Capital Cities*, pp.135–63.

43. David Stevenson, *Armaments and the Coming of War: Europe, 1904–1914* (Oxford, 1996), pp.18–39, 62.

44. Ibid., pp.1–14.

45. Ibid., pp.246–53.

46. David G. Herrmann, *The Arming of Europe and the Making of the First World War* (Princeton, NJ, 1996), pp.227–8.

47. Stevenson, *Armaments*, p.421.

48. A. J. P. Taylor, *War by Timetable* (London, 1969), p.101; Charles S. Maier, 'Wargames: 1914–1919', *Journal of Interdisciplinary History* 18 (1988), pp.81–49.

49. F. H. Hinsley, *The Causes of the First World War* (Hull, 1964), p.12.

50. Niall Fergusson, 'Public Finance and National Security: The Domestic Origins of the First World War Revisited', *P&P* 142 (1994), pp.141–68; idem, 'Germany and Origins', pp.742–52; idem, *Pity of War*, pp.121–5, 129–42.

51. Fischer, *War of Illusions*, pp.161–9; John Rohl, *The Kaiser and His Court: Wilhelm II and the Government of Germany* (Cambridge, 1994), pp.162–89; idem, *Kaiser, Hof und Staat*, pp.175–202; idem, 'Admiral von Müller and the Approach of War, 1911–14', *HJ* 12 (1969), pp.651–73; idem, 'An der Schwelle zum Weltkrieg: Eine Dokumentation über den Kriegsrat vom 8 Dezember 1912', *MM* (1977), pp.77–134; Moses, *Politics of Illusion*, pp.73–93.

52. Rohl, 'Germany', in Wilson, ed., *Decisions for War*, pp.44–5; Wolfgang Mommsen, 'The Topos of Inevitable War in Germany in the Decade before 1914', in Volker Berghahn and Martin Kitchen, eds, *Germany in the Age of Total War* (London, 1981), pp.23–45; Berghahn, *Germany and Approach of War*, p.203; Annika Mombauer, 'A Reluctant Military Leader? Helmuth von Moltke and the July Crisis of 1914', *WH* 6, (1999), pp.417–46.

53. Rohl, 'Germany', pp.33–4, 36–7, 46; W. C. Wohlforth, 'The Perception of Power: Russia in the pre-1914 Balance', *World Politics* 39 (1987), pp.353–81.

54. Wolfgang J. Mommsen, 'Domestic Factors in German Foreign Policy before 1914', *CEH* 6 (1973), pp.3–43; Koch, 'Introduction', in Koch, ed., *Origins of First World War*, 2nd edn, pp.14–15.

55. Gordon, 'Domestic Conflict and Origins of First World War', pp.11–226; Mommsen, 'Domestic Factors in German Foreign Policy', pp.3–43; Joll, 'Unpsoken Assumptions', in Koch, ed., *Origins of First World War*, pp.307–28; Avner Offer, 'Going to War in 1914: A Matter of Honour?', *Politics and Society* 23 (1995), pp.213–41.

56. David M. McDonald, 'A Lever without a Fulcrum: Domestic Factors and Russian Foreign Policy, 1905–14', in Hugh Ragsdale, ed., *Imperial Russian Foreign Policy* (Cambridge, 1993), pp.268–314.

57. Ian F. W. Beckett, ed., *The Army and the Curragh Incident, 1914* (London, 1986), pp.1–29; Steiner, *Britain and the Origins*, p.153; David French, 'The Edwardian Crisis and the Origins of the First World War', *IHR* 4 (1982), pp.207–21.

58. Joll, *Origins*, p.7.

59. Fritz Fellner, 'Austria-Hungary', in Wilson, ed., *Decisions for War*, pp.9–25; Samuel Williamson, 'Vienna and July 1914: The Origins of the Great War

Once More', in Samuel Williamson and P. Pastor, eds, *Essays on World War I: Origins and Prisoners of War* (New York, 1983), pp.8–36.

60. R. J. W. Evans, 'The Habsburg Monarchy and the Coming of War', in Evans and Strandmann, eds, *Coming of First World War*, p.35.

61. Vladimir Dedijer, *The Road to Sarajevo* (New York, 1967), pp.118–41, 371–95; Joll, *Origins*, p.74.

62. Williamson, *Austria-Hungary and the Origins*, pp.196, 211, 215; John Leslie, 'The Antecedents of Austria-Hungary's War Aims: Policies and Policy-making in Vienna and Budapest before and during 1914', *Wiener Beiträge zur Geschichte der Neuzeit* 20 (1993), pp.307–94.

63. Evans, 'Habsburg Monarchy', in Evans and Strandmann, eds, *Coming of the First World War*, pp.38–9; József Galántai, *Hungary in the First World War* (Budapest, 1989), pp.39–48.

64. Fellner, 'Austria-Hungary', p.17; Geiss, *July 1914*, pp.76–80.

65. Fritz Fellner, 'Die Mission Hoyos', in W. Alff, ed., *Deutschlands Sonderung von Europa, 1862–1945* (Frankfurt-am-Main, 1984), p.296.

66. Mark Cornwall, 'Serbia', in Wilson, ed., *Decisions for War*, pp.55–96.

67. Fellner, 'Austria-Hungary', p.16.

68. Holger H. Herwig, *The First World War: Germany and Austria-Hungary, 1914–1918* (London, 1997), pp.10, 12.

69. Fellner, 'Austria-Hungary', p.22.

70. Ibid., p.20.

71. Apart from the contributions of Erdmann and Zechlin to Koch, ed., *Origins of the First World War*, 2nd edn, pp.343–85, see also K. H. Jarausch, 'The Illusion of Limited War: Chancellor Bethmann-Hollweg's Calculated Risk, 1914', *CEH* 2 (1969), pp.48–76; and Andreas Hillgruber, 'Riezlers Theorie des Kalkulierten Risikos und Bethmann-Hollwegs Politische Konzeptionen in der Julikrise, 1914', *Historische Zeitschrift* 202 (1966), pp.333–51.

72. Marc Trachtenberg, *History and Strategy* (Princeton, NJ, 1991), pp.47–99; H. F. Young, 'The Misunderstanding of August 1, 1914', *JMH* 48 (1976), pp.644–65; S. J. Valone, '"There Must be Some Misunderstanding": Sir Edward Grey's Diplomacy of August 1, 1914', *JBS* 27 (1988), pp.405–24.

73. John Rohl, ed., *1914, Delusion or Design: The Testimony of Two German Diplomats* (London, 1973), pp.51–2.

74. Fritz Fischer, 'Twenty-five Years Later: Looking Back at the "Fischer Controversy" and its Consequences', *CEH* 21 (1988), pp.207–23.

75. John Rohl, 'Germany', in Wilson, ed., *Decisions for War*, pp.27–54.

76. Ibid., p.40.

77. D. Groh, 'The "Unpatriotic Socialists" and the State', *JCH* 1 (1966), pp.151–77.

78. Rohl, *1914, Delusion or Design*, p.28; Ferguson, 'Germany and Origins of the First World War', p.734.

79. Egmont Zechlin, 'Cabinet versus Economic Warfare in Germany: Policy and Strategy during the Early Months of the First World War', in Koch, ed., *Origins of the First World War*, pp.237–45, 258–60.

80. Hartmut Pogge von Strandmann, 'Germany and the Coming of War', in Evans and Strandmann, eds, *Coming of First World War*, pp.106, 123.

81. L. C. F. Turner, *Origins of the First World War* (London, 1970); idem, 'The Russian Mobilisation in 1914', in Paul Kennedy, ed., *The War Plans of the Great Powers, 1880–1914* (London, 1979), pp.252–68. However, Turner also echoes Taylor in regarding the Schlieffen Plan as central to the outbreak of war: 'The Significance of the Schlieffen Plan', in Kennedy, ed., *War Plans*, pp.199–221.

82. U. Trumpener, 'War Premeditated? German Intelligence Operations in July 1914', *CEH* 9 (1976), pp.58–85.

83. Cornwall, 'Serbia', pp.79–81, 83–4.

84. Peter Gatrell, *Government, Industry and Rearmament in Russia, 1900–1914: The Last Argument of Tsarism* (Cambridge, 1994), pp.117–25, 161–3.

85. D. W. Spring, 'Russia and the Coming of War', in Evans and Strandmann, eds, *Coming of First World War*, pp.57–86; Keith Neilson, 'Russia', in Wilson, ed., *Decisions for War*, pp.97–120; Lieven, *Russia and the Origins*, pp.139–51.

86. M. B. Hayne, *The French Foreign Office and the Origins of the First World War, 1898–1914* (Oxford, 1993), pp.302–8.

87. Gerd Krumeich, *Armaments and Politics in France on the Eve of the First World War* (Leamington Spa, 1984), pp.215–30, 240–1.

88. Keiger, *France and the Origins*, pp.145–64; idem, 'France', in Wilson, ed., *Decisions for War*, pp.121–49.

89. Jean Stengers, 'Belgium', in Wilson, ed., *Decisions for War*, pp.151–74.

90. Jack S. Levy, T. J. Christensen and Marc Trachtenberg, 'Mobilisation and Inadvertence in the July Crisis', *International Studies* 16 (1991), pp.189–203; John H. Maurer, *The Outbreak of the First World War: Strategic Planning, Crisis Decison-making and Deterrence Failure* (Westport, CN, 1995), pp.29–45, 101–7; Sean M. Lynn-Jones, 'Détente and Deterrence: Anglo-German Relations, 1911–14', Marc Trachtenberg, 'The Meaning of Mobilisation in 1914' and Jack S. Levy, 'Preferences, Constraints and Choices in July 1914', all in Steven E. Miller, Sean M. Lynn-Jones and Stephen Van Evera, eds, *Military Strategy and the Origins of the First World War: An 'International Security' Reader*, 2nd edn (Princeton, NJ, 1991), pp.165–94, 195–225, 226–61.

91. Michael Brock, 'Britain enters the War', in Evans and Strandmann, eds, *Coming of First World War*, pp.145–78; Keith Wilson, 'Britain', in Wilson, ed., *Decisions for War*, pp.175–208; idem, *Policy of the Entente*, pp.135–47; idem, *Empire and Continent: Studies in British Foreign Policy from the 1880s to the First World War* (London, 1987), pp.149–68; Trevor Wilson, 'Britain's "Moral Commitment" to France in July 1914', *History* 64 (1979), pp.380–90; idem, *The Myriad Faces of War* (Cambridge, 1986), pp.22–7; Coogan and Coogan, 'British Cabinet and Anglo-French Talks', pp.110–31; Niall Ferguson, 'The Kaiser's European Union: What if Britain had stood aside in August 1914?', in Niall Ferguson, ed., *Virtual History: Alternatives and Counterfactuals* (London, 1997), pp.228–80; idem, *Pity of War*, pp.xxxix–xl, 56–81, 158–73, 443–4, 458–9.

92. L. L. Farrar, 'The Primacy of Foreign Policy: An Evaluation of the Role of Public Opinion during the July Crisis', *International Interactions* 7 (1981), pp.651–72; Caroline Playne, *The Pre-war Mind in Britain* (London, 1928), pp.329–30.

93. Zara Steiner, *The Foreign Office and Foreign Policy, 1898–1914*, 2nd edn (London and Atlantic Highlands, NJ, 1986), pp.155–6; John Keiger, 'Britain's "Union Sacrée"', in Jean-Jacques Becker and Stéphane Audoin-Rouzeau, eds, *Les sociétés européennes et la guerre de 1914–1918* (Nanterre, 1990), pp.39–52; idem, *France and the Origins*, pp.145–6.

94. Jean-Jacques Becker, *The Great War and the French People* (Leamington Spa, 1985), pp.94–102; P. J. Flood, *France, 1914–18: Public Opinion and the War Effort* (London, 1990), pp.5–12; Keiger, *France and the Origins*, pp.74–81.

95. Evans, 'Habsburg Monarchy', pp.42–3; Volker Ullrich, *Kriegsalltag: Hamburg im Ersten Weltkrieg* (Cologne, 1982); Gerd Krumeich, 'L'entré en guerre en Allemagne', in Becker and Audoin-Rouzeau, eds, *Les sociétés européennes*, pp.65–74; B. Ziemann, 'Zum Ländlichen Augusterlebnis 1914 in Deutschland', in B. Loewenstein, ed., *Geschichte und Psychologie. Annährungsversuche* (Pfaffenweiler, 1992), pp.193–203; W. Kruse, 'Die Kriegsbegeisterung im Deutschen Reich zu Beginn des Ersten Weltkrieges: Entstehungszusammenhänge, Grenzen und ideologische Strukturen', in M. van der Linden and G. Mergner, eds, *Kriegsbegeisterung und Mentale Kriegsvorbereitung: Interdisziplinäre Studien* (Berlin, 1991), pp.73–87; Christian Geinitz and Uta Hinz, 'Das Augusterlebnis in Südbaden: Ambivalente Reaktionen der deutschen Öffentlichkeit auf den Kriegsbeginn', in Gerhard Hirschfeld, Gerd Krumeich, Dieter Langewiesche and Hans-Peter Ullman, eds, *Kriegserfahrungen: Studien zur Sozial- und Mentalitätsgeschichte des Ertsen Weltkriegs* (Essen, 1997), pp.20–35; Roger Chickering, *Imperial Germany and the Great War, 1914–1918* (Cambridge, 1998), p.16.

96. Farrar, 'Reluctant Warriors', p.436.

97. Michael Howard, 'Europe on the Eve of the First World War', in Evans and Strandmann, eds, *Coming of First World War*, pp.10–12.

CHAPTER THREE

Over by Christmas

The expectations of most European soldiers and politicians alike was that the war would be over by Christmas. Hindsight would suggest an extraordinary failure to comprehend the changes in warfare so evident in the mid- and late nineteenth century. The impact of technology upon warfare had been enormous, dramatically increasing the destructive capacity of armies by providing them with weapons of enhanced range, accuracy and rate of fire. Indeed, by the 1890s, magazine rifles, quick-firing artillery and machine guns had all entered service with the major European armies. Just prior to the war, armies were also experimenting with aircraft. At sea, too, wood, sail and round shot had given way steadily to iron and steel, steam, the screw propeller and shell. Mines, submarines and torpedoes all now threatened the traditional supremacy of the capital ship.

Through systems of universal conscription, though selective in practice, states also had the ability to mobilise millions of men. Such armies could be mobilised and sustained in the field by the advances in transportation, particularly railways. Widely varying proportions of those eligible for military service, however, were called up in peacetime. Thus, the French called up 84 per cent of those eligible in 1913 compared with 53 per cent in Germany, 29 per cent in Austria-Hungary and about 20 per cent in Russia. In 1914, the peacetime strength of the Russian army was approximately 1.4 million men; followed by between 700,000 and 910,000 in France, between 761,000 and 891,000 in Germany, and between 420,000 and 478,000 in Austria-Hungary.[1]

Upon mobilisation, through the call-up of trained reserves, Austria-Hungary could field between 2.5 and 3 million men, France between 3.5 and 4 million, Russia between 4.4 and 5.5 million and Germany between 3.9 and 4.5 million men.[2] By contrast, Britain's small regular army numbered but

247,432 officers and men in August 1914, although the addition of reservists and the part-time Territorial Force brought its potential strength to
733,514.[3] The sheer numbers involved might have suggested both that
victory would prove difficult and that casualties would be horrendous.

Expectations of war

It is traditionally reasoned that the significance of the changes that had
taken place was underestimated through the innate conservatism of European military and naval officer corps and their contempt for technology.[4]
Thus, the evidence of such conflicts as the American Civil War (1861–65),
the Franco-Prussian War (1870–71), the Russo-Turkish War (1877–78), the
South African War (1899–1902) and the Russo-Japanese War (1904–05)
was wilfully ignored. Generally, indeed, it is often suggested that the most
accurate prediction of the future of warfare was not by a soldier, but by a
Polish Jewish banker and railway magnate, Jan Bloch. Originally published
in Polish in 1897, the six volumes of *The War of the Future in its Technical,
Economic and Political Aspects* was translated into Russian in 1898 and into
French and German in 1900. The last volume also appeared in English in
1899 as *Is War Impossible?* Many of Bloch's predictions were in fact no more
accurate than other contemporary futurologists but his vision of an indecis-
ive, attritional stalemate was certainly striking. But, as a pacifist polemicist,
Bloch had little chance of influencing soldiers or politicians in pre-war
Europe and he was particularly criticised in Germany.[5]

Contrary to popular belief, however, soldiers had long recognised the
problem in crossing the so-called empty battlefield in the face of modern
firepower. But they had also noted the phenomenon of the 'flight to the
front' by men under fire and they believed, mistakenly, that they could
overcome the difficulty of incoming firepower largely by closing with the
enemy more rapidly.[6] In part, this miscalculation derived from both the
American Civil War and the Russo-Turkish War being dismissed as not
sufficiently relevant to a European context in the light of the more recent
experience of the rapid victories in the German Wars of Unification. It was
also the case that, despite the apparent modernity of rifled muskets, the
American Civil War was actually fought tactically more as if it were the last
Napoleonic encounter than the first 'modern' war.[7]

Secondly, the lessons of the most recent conflicts were far more contradictory than generally supposed. In the case of the South African War, it
is usually assumed that traditional cavalry proved unsuccessful and that
mounted infantry was the key to the future of the mounted arm. In reality,

the lessons were not clear-cut, enabling British cavalry traditionalists such as Sir John French and Sir Douglas Haig to argue that the principles of offensive mounted action remained unchanged.[8]

The capacity for drawing different lessons from the same experience was even more marked during the Manchurian campaign of the Russo-Japanese War, fought by some 2 million men. In all, 83 observers from 15 armies were present on one side or the other and the Austrians, the Russians, the Germans and the British all produced official histories of the war. There was little unanimity among them.[9] Some observers believed that the predominant lesson was the way in which the Japanese infantry prevailed in mounting frontal assaults on entrenched Russian positions through their superior morale. Equally, others emphasised the poor standards of Russian musketry and the lengthy and methodical preparation by the Japanese prior to their assaults. Some of the British observers fully recognised the significance of entrenchment both in attack and defence, of indirect artillery fire, of howitzers, and of machine guns. Some even foresaw the likelihood of a future war being one of position rather than manoeuvre: in 1907 an article by Captain C. E. P. Sankey in the *Royal Engineers Journal* predicted a situation of stalemate in which 'each army will then practically become the garrison of an enormously extended fortress'.[10] However, in most cases, official doctrine fell prey to the prevailing military assumption that the greatest advantage derived from the offensive rather than the defensive. This was particularly so when the actual victor in the Russo-Japanese War had been the attacker, namely the Japanese.[11]

In Britain, the military theorist G. F. R. Henderson, a distinguished student of the American Civil War and whose collected writings were published posthumously in 1905, believed that a principal lesson of the South African War was the need for manoeuvre and envelopment in order to avoid the destructive power of modern weapons. Yet, successful manoeuvre itself also depended upon the offensive power of those same weapons. Given the seeming reluctance of some officers and men to face modern firepower on occasions in South Africa, Henderson also stressed the need for high morale and an offensive spirit. The Manchurian experience seemingly reinforced a requirement for an offensive spirit since firepower did not appear decisive and the substitute for firepower was cold steel. As Major-General E. A. Altham put it in 1914, the Russo-Japanese War had 'wiped out the mistaken inference from South African experience that bayonet fighting belongs to the past'.[12]

In fact, the 'offensive spirit' was common to all European armies. Moreover, the use of the bayonet, sabre and lance implicit within it ideally complemented traditional military ideals of honour and glory. On the one hand, some traditionalists undoubtedly did fear that these ideals would be devalued by the unwelcome intrusion of technology and professionalism into what remained a seemingly aristocratic, or at least gentlemanly, occupation. On the other hand, the widespread suspicion that ordinary soldiers might not push the attack in the face of overwhelming fire carried a Social Darwinist undercurrent. British proponents of the offensive spirit were clearly concerned with the prospects of degeneration within society and that the British public would not be prepared for the kinds of casualties suffered by both sides in Manchuria.[13]

On the continent, soldiers were even more obsessed with the possible lack of enthusiasm on the part of conscripted youths in the face of fire and over extended battlefields on which command and control might be problematical. Indeed, there was a decided reaction within the French army against new infantry regulations introduced in 1904. Drawing upon the British experience in South Africa, these abandoned the close formations prescribed in those of 1894, which had specified advancing 'elbow to elbow in mass formations, to the sound of bugles and drums'. Thus, French generals such as Joseph Joffre, who was appointed to the new post of Chief of General Staff, in July 1911, and Ferdinand Foch, the director of the École de Guerre (War School), invested the offensive with the power of renewing the spirit of the French nation itself. The author of new field service regulations for larger formations in October 1913, Colonel Louis de Grandmaison, who was to be killed in 1915, proclaimed that the army, 'returning to its traditions, recognises no law save that of the offensive'. It is perhaps symptomatic of the obsession that French infantry continued to carry colours into action until 1916.[14]

In France, the spirit of the offensive served all political purposes in offering perceived traditional values to the political right, moral rejuvenation to the political left and the revival of the army's prestige to 'colonial' soldiers like Grandmaison and Joffre, who were concerned most by the damage done the army's reputation by the Dreyfus affair. At the same time, however, it also reflected perceptions of weakness deriving from unresolved internal doctrinal confusion, from organisational defects and from material shortages. In many respects, therefore, military audacity would compensate for such weaknesses.[15]

In Germany, Schlieffen, the Chief of Staff, argued in December 1905 that the losses in Manchuria had been exaggerated: an average daily loss of between 2 and 3 per cent of those engaged was considerably less than the 40 to 50 per cent commonly experienced in battle during the Napoleonic Wars. Similarly, the Russians and Japanese had lost fewer casualties in the battle of Mukden (21 February to 10 March 1904) than the French and Germans had sustained in the single day's engagement at Mars-La-Tour (16 August 1870). Another motivation for the offensive spirit in Germany was the belief that a quick and decisive victory would avoid an apocalyptic escalation of violence damaging to the very structure of society.[16]

It might be added that soldiers and politicians were equally unprepared for the demands that modern warfare would put upon economy and society as suggested by what in Britain has been referred to as the strategy of 'business as usual'. The Chancellor of the Exchequer, David Lloyd George, announced on 4 August 1914 that the government would 'enable the traders of this country to carry on business as usual'. It was recognised that some limited intervention might be required in food supply, transport, maritime insurance and the money market, but the expectation was that this would be only for a few weeks.[17]

Little thought had been given to the need to increase production of munitions and the actual expenditure of ammunition and other war supplies had been greatly underestimated. In Britain, reserves of ammunition remained predicated on the South African experience, the lesson drawn from the Russo-Japanese War being the need to ensure fire economy rather than increase the ammunition available. Thus, each of the army's standard eighteen-pounder artillery pieces was allocated only 1,000 rounds for active service with a further 300 rounds in reserve in the UK and another 500 to be manufactured within the first six months of a war. This represented a stock in hand two and a half times greater than at the start of the South African War but, as Jonathan Bailey has remarked, each gun at battery level had only 176 rounds, which would sustain fire for just 44 minutes at what was called rate four (four rounds per minute). Six such periods would exhaust all ammunition in the field, another 75 minutes would account for the reserve in the UK and a further 60 minutes those shells intended to be manufactured within the first six months of war.[18]

In reality, the South African War had already suggested that the output of the state's own ordnance factories was inadequate, but it was assumed the private sector could supply any wartime needs.[19] Many contractors both at home and abroad simply failed to meet promised targets. Existing arms manufacturers in Britain could produce just over 47,000 rifles a year in 1914, whereas the estimated requirement by July 1915 was 1.1 million a year with British manufacture being supplemented by orders placed in Canada, the United States and Japan. Similarly, by May 1915, of 29.9 million rounds of eighteen-pounder artillery ammunition ordered since August 1914, only 1.4 million rounds had been delivered. Other calculations were equally misplaced. Winston Churchill, First Lord of the Admiralty, had confidently predicted on 1 August 1914 that naval operations would cost no more than £25 million a year. The reality was £280 million spent on the armed forces by March 1915 with total direct war costs an estimated £359 million.[20]

The French went into the war with 1,390 rounds for each of their 3,500 75 mm quick-firing guns but, in a matter of weeks, supplies had dwindled to only 695 rounds per gun. French industry had produced 10,000–12,000 shells a day initially but the requirement was now judged to be 80,000–100,000 rounds. By 1918, the French were producing 230,000 rounds a day for the 75 mm gun alone. Nor had the French army given any priority to the defence of the most industrially productive region of the north-east, the Briey basin, from which had been derived much of France's iron ore, pig-iron and coal. With the German seizure of much of north-eastern France in the first campaign, the French found themselves without 55 per cent of their coal resources, 70 per cent of their steel production, and 80 per cent of both iron ore and iron production.[21]

In Russia, where it had originally been thought that the war would last only between two and six months, stocks of munitions largely met pre-war norms. As early as 23 August 1914, however, the supply chief of the North-western Front warned that ammunition expenditure greatly exceeded expectations and the same warning came from the south-western front five days later. By September 1914, Russian headquarters, Stavka, was demanding 1.5 million shells per month or three times the pre-war estimate, a total soon amended to 3.5 million shells per month.[22] In the case of Germany, the Secretary of State for Finance declined in July 1914 to buy up additional stocks of grain in Rotterdam on the grounds that war preparation was a purely military matter.[23]

War plans

In such circumstances, it is not altogether surprising that the war plans of the major belligerents in 1914 were traditional. Indeed, Schlieffen, had been much taken by the classic encircling movement executed by Hannibal at the battle of Cannae in 216 BC. The strategic dilemma for the Germans was the potential problem of having to fight war on two fronts simultaneously, hence the perennial concern to fight a preventative war against either France or Russia. Both France and Russia had been selected for the honour at various times between 1871 and 1891 by Schlieffen's predecessors as Chief of Staff, the elder Helmuth von Moltke (1857–88) and Alfred von Waldersee (1888–91).[24]

When Schlieffen became Chief of Staff, the greater density of railways in north-west Europe, the construction of new Russian fortifications in Poland and the re-emergence of the French army from the shadow of defeat in 1870–71 brought him to the same conclusion earlier reached by both Moltke and Waldersee, namely that France must be defeated first. Nothing, however, was firmly ruled out, although Schlieffen increasingly contemplated a *Westaufmarsch* (western deployment) between 1898 and 1905. The final version of what became known as the Schlieffen Plan, contained in Schlieffen's *Denkschrift* (study) in December 1905, resembled what Basil Liddell Hart called 'a giant revolving door'.[25]

No less than seven German armies would be committed to the west and, of these, five were to advance through Belgium, Luxemburg and the Netherlands – a solution first included in Schlieffen's calculations in 1899. The remaining two armies allocated to the west would hold an expected French advance into Alsace-Lorraine. The German First and Second Armies on the extreme right of advance would swing around Paris to pin the French armies on their own frontier, ensuring the climatic and decisive *Kesselschlacht* (cauldron battle). All this would be accomplished in just 42 days and, as Schlieffen put it, the 'last grenadier on the right wing should brush the Channel with his sleeve'. Schlieffen's response to the fact that the First Army would have a considerable distance to cover in the allotted time was merely to remark that the men would have to make 'very great exertions'.[26]

The plan did not take account of the logistical problems involved in supplying such an advance on the assumption that sufficient supplies could be captured en route through the Low Countries. Nor did it take any account of French counter-moves or what the German military theorist Carl von Clausewitz had termed 'friction'. It was also the case that the divisions committed to the plan at this stage largely existed only on paper.

It is possible, however, that the *Denkschrift* may not have been written until just after Schlieffen's retirement in January 1906 and that it represented merely a statement of what might be achieved if German manpower were fully utilised. Indeed, recent doubt has been thrown on the whole concept of the *Denkschrift* as the culmination of Schlieffen's planning by Terence Zuber's interpretation of new documents emerging from former eastern archives. All previous accounts have been based upon the *Denkschrift* and the subsequent special pleading of former members of Schlieffen's staff, who criticised the younger Moltke for not adhering to the plan. It would appear, however, that the basis of German planning under both Schlieffen and Moltke remained the need to meet the anticipated French offensive into Lorraine and then to launch a counter-attack across the Meuse, to encircle the French frontier armies inside French territory and to break the frontier fortress line. This would not involve a deep penetration of French territory and a second campaign would be required to complete French defeat. It is now suggested that there is no evidence beyond the *Denkschrift* that the Germans intended to march to the west of Paris and a re-evaluation by Moltke in 1911 concluded that it was not feasible.[27]

The complete military technician, Schlieffen was not at all concerned by the political implications of invading neutral states or by the requirement to invade France should Germany's ostensible quarrel be only with Russia. In fact, his approach to operational planning was not without its critics in the German army. In defence of Schlieffen, it might be noted that he regarded what Michael Geyer has characterised as 'a professionally autonomous war' as a means of limiting the effects of conflict through swift victory.[28] Moreover, when Schlieffen had raised the issue of Belgian and Dutch neutrality with successive chancellors, no political objections had been raised.[29]

Schlieffen had been recovering from a horse riding accident at the time of the first Moroccan Crisis in 1905 and was not available to press for the early war he believed necessary. He was now 72 years old and had two years previously asked the Kaiser to think of choosing a successor. It was, therefore, as much Schlieffen's age and health that precipitated his retirement in January 1906 as the Kaiser's unwillingness at that time to contemplate an immediate war.[30] Schlieffen's successor, the younger Helmuth von Moltke, nephew of the elder Moltke, was confronted by the sheer impracticalities of the *Denkschrift* and by his own self doubts. A courtier where Schlieffen was a technocrat, Moltke had joined the General Staff only in 1905 and owed his unexpected choice as its chief entirely to the Kaiser. Much influenced by the theosophy of Rudolf Steiner, Moltke was deeply fatalistic and pessimistic. Although he concealed his doubts about German strategy from the politicians, Moltke always harboured fears that a short war might prove an illusion.[31]

Moltke pressed for the necessary increases in the size of the army but the additions made in 1912 and 1913 still fell one-third short of his requirements. Moltke also set his staff to work on the logistical problems. Consequently, any advance through the Netherlands was struck out and the extremity of the right wing's advance was confined to Brussels rather than the Channel coast. Leaving the Netherlands free also provided some insurance against the possibility of a prolonged war necessitating access to foreign markets. Moltke reduced the overall frontage of the potential German advance by approximately 250 miles, but at the price of losing the use of Dutch railway lines and increasing the early congestion at the vital Belgian railway junction of Liège, around which some 600,000 men would now be moving over a frontage of but 12 miles.

Moltke was equally concerned by the threat posed by any unexpected early Russian advance as well as by the anticipated French advance into Alsace-Lorraine. Accordingly, it is argued that he changed the ratio of the German right wing to the left wing. There is some debate as to the extent of the changes since some of the ten divisions now reallocated south of Metz were from new formations raised during the army's expansion. Moreover, as suggested by recently discovered documents, both Schlieffen and Moltke recognised the possibility of the main battle taking place in Lorraine without a need for a German counter-thrust through Belgium. It was previously generally accepted that the ratio of right wing to left wing changed from 7:1 to 3:1, a total of 55 divisions being allocated north of Metz and 23 divisions to its south, whereas the plan Moltke inherited had allocated 59 divisions north of Metz and nine to its south. In one respect, Moltke made no changes: in his acceptance of the need for war sooner rather than later.[32]

It was the sense that time was running out for Germany that led Moltke to try to enlist more concrete Austro-Hungarian support on the Eastern Front. His opposite number in Vienna, Conrad, was an equally complex personality and by no means a conventional soldier in that he, too, dabbled in philosophy. A convinced Social Darwinist and fatalist, Conrad also believed in the inevitability of war, his search for a likely enemy often bordering on fantasy since, on occasions, he contemplated war against both Japan and China. More specifically, he was concerned with the possibility that Austria-Hungary, too, might face war on different fronts simultaneously. Russia, Italy and Serbia all posed threats. Increasingly, Conrad saw a war against Serbia as the solution to Austria-Hungary's difficulties.

The elder Moltke had had no great faith in Austro-Hungarian military prowess.[33] Equally, Schlieffen had enjoyed a poor relationship with Conrad's predecessor, Beck, and there was no real contact between the two general staffs between 1896 and 1909. Moltke wished, however, to secure Conrad's co-operation since the bulk of the German army would be in the west at the start of any future war, while Conrad was also anxious to discover German intentions. As a result, Conrad and Moltke exchanged correspondence between January and March 1909. Conrad formed the impression that Germany would support Austria-Hungary in any future war and that Moltke had promised an early offensive by the German Eighth Army in the east. In turn, Moltke formed the impression that there would be Austro-Hungarian help in defending east Prussia against the Russians through an immediate Austro-Hungarian offensive.[34]

In so far as Moltke had made any promises he had effectively changed the defensive nature of the Dual Alliance of 1879 into an offensive alliance. Correspondence continued thereafter but, in the event, neither the Austro-Hungarians nor the Germans were to hold to what the other believed had been promised. The failure to achieve any degree of co-ordination between Germany and its sole ally at the start of the war would become critical.[35]

In 1914, Conrad had his army divided into three groups, just over 28 infantry divisions and 10 cavalry divisions of A-Staffel (A Echelon) opposite Galicia (southern Poland within the Austro-Hungarian Empire), 8 infantry divisions in the Minimalgruppe Balkan (Balkan Task Force) opposite Serbia and the B-Staffel (B Echelon) – the Austro-Hungarian Second Army – of one cavalry and 12 infantry divisions as a reserve. Conrad assumed he could safely attack Serbia in the expectation that Russia would not intervene and decided to commit the reserve to this front as well. In order to redirect B-Staffel to the Russian front, Conrad would need to do so no later than five days after mobilisation began, the fifth day as events unfolded being 1 August 1914.

The time needed reflected the fact that all Austro-Hungarian military trains moved at the speed of the slowest – about 10 miles per hour compared with about 20 miles per hour in the case of German military trains. Conrad knew that the Russians had mobilised on 31 July but did not choose to order the recall of B-Staffel until 6 August, presumably through his determination to crush Serbia. It was then probably the German failure to open an offensive against the Russians which compelled Conrad to act. A *post facto* excuse was offered that, for 'technical considerations', relating to the constraints of railway timetabling, B-Staffel could only be transported back to Galicia once full deployment had taken place on the Russian front. Yet, Conrad did alter the mobilisation plans in July by having A-Staffel detrain much further back from the Galician frontier than originally intended, inevitably delaying the Austro-Hungarian offensive against the Russians. Conrad chose not to inform Moltke of the delay.[36]

Compared with the German and Austro-Hungarian planning, that of France was straightforward, Plan XVII being a dash into Alsace and Lorraine by the French First, Second and Third Armies in order to ensure that France seized the military initiative. However, it was only in 1911 that the French had reconsidered an out-and-out offensive. Plans VIII and IX in 1887 and 1888 had been offensive but then Plans X to XVI between 1889 and 1909 had reverted to what might be termed a defensive-offensive strategy to soak up an opening German offensive before the French went on the offensive themselves.[37]

Believing Plan XVI inadequate, Victor Constant Michel, vice-president of the Conseil Supérieur de la Guerre (Superior War Council) – and, thereby, designated Commander-in-Chief in the event of war as the Minister sat as president – considered operations inside Belgium in 1911. However, these plans did not recommend themselves either to French soldiers or to politicians. In particular, the Belgian option would expose France if the Germans did advance from Alsace-Lorraine. Moreover, while aware of the outline of the Schlieffen Plan, French intelligence remained unconvinced of the likelihood of a German threat to Belgium.[38] As a result, Michel was promptly replaced by Joffre as the newly designated Chief of Staff.

As indicated earlier, Joffre was a convinced advocate of an early offens-ive – the *offensive à outrance* – believing this to be essential to victory in what would be a short war: in July 1914 he was to remark that every 24 hours lost in beginning mobilisation meant the loss of between 12 and 15 miles of territory. Conversion to the offensive also reflected greater confidence in the overall military balance. Initially, Joffre was prepared to countenance an offensive into Belgium, but the problem of Belgian neutrality and the likely response of the British to its violation precluded serious consideration of this option.[39] This left an offensive into the lost provinces of Alsace-Lorraine, which would have the additional role of a spoiling attack to disrupt the opening German offensive. The resulting Plan XVII, adopted in April 1913, aimed to strike first into the lost provinces, at the cost of leaving the Belgian frontier undefended but for the French Fifth Army.

At the same time, Plan XVII offered, in the words of Douglas Porch, 'the negative political advantage of not alienating the British' through a violation of Belgian neutrality.[40] Some French commanders believed that the Germans would come through Belgium, notably Pierre Ruffey (Third Army), Charles Lanrezac (Fifth Army) and Joseph-Simon Galliéni (Sixth Army). They were ignored by Joffre.[41]

The success of French plans was dependent not only upon the Ger-mans attacking from Alsace-Lorraine, but also upon Russian co-operation. The Russian army had made considerable progress since the end of the Russo-Japanese War.[42] Unfortunately, Russian military planning was bedevilled by factionalism, much as the officer corps as a whole was split between those supporting the military reforms of the War Minister, V. A. Sukhomlinov, and his opponents, principally Grand Duke Nicholas, the Tsar's uncle.

It had long been recognised that Russian Poland was vulnerable to a German offensive from east Prussia in the north and an Austro-Hungarian offensive from Galicia in the south. As a result, after the Russo-Japanese War it had been decided to abandon Poland and rely on defence in depth in the event of war. As Russian military recovery proceeded, however, this seemed increasingly incompatible with the offensive spirit. Therefore, by 1912, Sukhomlinov and General M. I. Dragomirov, one-time director of the General Staff Academy, were arguing for an offensive against east Prussia. Others, including the influential M. Alekseev, commander of the Kiev military district, argued for an offensive against Galicia, which was less risky and could have an important moral effect on Slavic peoples within the Austro-Hungarian Empire.

Such was the division of opinion that the unhappy compromise of 'Plan 19 Altered Variant A' was adopted in May 1912. This would attempt a simultaneous offensive against both east Prussia and Galicia with sixteen corps assigned against Austria-Hungary and nine against Germany. Neither would be strong enough to succeed and the east Prussian offensive was further weakened by the late consideration given in August 1914 to the possibility of an advance from Warsaw direct towards Berlin.[43]

Rather as in the case of Germany and Austria-Hungary, the military alliance of France and Russia left much to be desired. Clearly, the success of the French Plan XVII depended on an early Russian offensive, but the French had little real expectation of the Russians coming quickly to their assistance. Equally, some Russians believed the French to be pushing them into premature military action, which would benefit French rather than Russian interests. The relationship improved after 1910 and the Russians undertook in 1911 to be ready to mount an offensive within fifteen days of mobilisation. Grand Duke Nicholas certainly believed that an early offensive was also necessary to demonstrate the commitment to France.[44]

The French were no more confident of British assistance materialising and did not include the British Expeditionary Force in their line of battle. British military planning had changed dramatically, with a strategic reorientation since 1902, the concern of the Victorian army being either the defence of India against Russia or the possibility of French invasion of the United Kingdom itself.[45] Indeed, the newly established Committee of Imperial Defence (CID) considered the defence of India at fifty of its eighty meetings between 1902 and 1905 and conducted three major invasion enquiries between 1903 and 1913.[46]

Those agreements reached with France in 1904 and Russia in 1907, however, reflected not only alarm at Britain's diplomatic isolation but also a growing concern that Germany threatened the European status quo. The entente with France implied no real commitment, but in April 1905 a wargame played in the War Office suggested that, if the Germans were to invade Belgium, any British intervention must be swift if there was to be any hope of its being effective. Keeping Belgium and the Channel ports out of hostile hands was deemed of vital strategic interest to Britain.

In December 1905, while the general election campaign was being fought, an informal caucus from the CID – the so-called Whitehall Gardens subcommittee – agreed that the British should intervene in such circumstances and authorised the general staff to seek military staff talks with the French general staff. As it happened, the Director of Military Operations (DMO) at the War Office, who had presided over the wargame, Sir James Grierson, had come to the same conclusion independently and was also keen to approach the French. He joined the others in their deliberations in January 1906, contacts with the French being established through the agency of the military correspondent of *The Times*, Charles Repington, and the French military attaché in London, Colonel Huguet.[47]

A meeting of the CID itself on 6 January 1906 concluded that the Admiralty's scheme for an amphibious assault on the north German coast was impracticable and it became a matter of whether any British expeditionary force should be placed in Belgium or with the French army in the event of war. Talks, which had never been authorised, were concealed from many members of the incoming Liberal government. The resulting plans for intervention were considered by a sub-committee of the CID in October 1908. Since the Admiralty chose to boycott the proceedings because its own plans had been rejected, the CID resolved on 24 July 1909 to send four infantry divisions to France on the outbreak of war. It remained a plan only in principle until Major-General Henry Wilson became DMO in June 1910. A passionate Francophile, Wilson even left a fragment of the British mobilisation plan on the steps of the statue of France at Mars-La-Tour on one of his periodic bicycle trips to France in 1911.[48]

At a famous meeting of the CID on 23 August 1911, Wilson effectively demolished the Admiralty case for non-intervention, although Churchill and Sir John French demonstrated a concern that the British should not be too closely tied to the French army and should be free to co-operate more with the Belgians. Even under Churchill's more realistic guidance, the Admiralty still fought a sufficient rearguard action in the 1913 invasion enquiry to ensure that two of Britain's six divisions were kept back from the continent on the outbreak of war.[49]

Nevertheless, it should be noted that Britain remained an imperial and maritime power, while the actual shape of the British Expeditionary Force after the Haldane reforms of 1906–1908 was determined more by financial calculations than by those of strategy.[50] Moreover, even within the army, some like Sir John French remained attracted to what is sometimes called the Belgian option as likely to serve British strategic interests better than simple subordination to French military planning. At the War Councils held on 5 and 6 August 1914, the Belgian option manifested itself once more in a preference for a descent on Antwerp rather than a concentration at Mauberge as dictated by Wilson's plans. Failing that, a concentration at Amiens on the French coast was also suggested. In the event, both Sir John French as designated Commander-in-Chief of the British Expeditionary Force, and the newly appointed Secretary of State for War, Lord Kitchener, were persuaded by 12 August that the British Expeditionary Force should adhere to Wilson's mobilisation plans.[51] There were British politicians, too, for whom a strategy of strictly limited liability, confining British effort to imposing an economic blockade and bankrolling the French and Russians to undertake the main effort on land, was very attractive.[52]

The failure of the war plans in the west

Turning to the course of events in August 1914, both the Schlieffen Plan and Plan XVII failed. In the case of the latter, the French were thrown back from Alsace-Lorraine in a series of bloody attacks between 10 and 28 August: by the end of the month, Joffre had dismissed an army commander, 3 corps commanders and 36 divisional commanders. The reverses were due not simply to the offensive spirit but also to elementary failures on the part of French commanders and tactical ineptness on the part of their men.[53]

If the new interpretation of German intentions is accepted, then the main German thrust through Belgium was a counter-offensive which became a pursuit. Instead, however, of taking 48 hours, as hoped, to reduce the Liège forts, it took ten days. The battle by the small British Expeditionary Force, caught unexpectedly at Mons in the path of the German First Army on 23 August, and the subsequent delaying actions fought by the British as they retreated, most notably by Sir Horace Smith-Dorrien's II Corps at Le Cateau on 26 August, as well as by the French Fifth Army under the command of Lanrezac at Guise on 29 August, also imposed crucial delays on the German timetable. Moreover, the arc of German advance was always within reach of the French strategic rail network. Once he had belatedly realised the extent of the German advance under the prompting of Lanrezac, Joffre was able to begin switching formations on 15 August to confront it. Ironically, the west to east orientation of the French rail lines between Paris and the eastern frontier, which Joffre was able to exploit, had originally been constructed on the assumption of a German offensive through Alsace-Lorraine.

As Moltke always knew it would, the logistical support for the German army soon proved insufficient. Schlieffen had assumed that use could be made of Belgian, French and Dutch railways, but the Dutch had been excluded from the equation and the Belgian rail lines were extensively damaged during the German advance. The critical distance between the marching columns and Germany's own railheads stretched to an average of 70–80 miles in the case of Alexander von Kluck's First Army. By the end of the campaign, Karl von Bülow's Second Army was 105 miles from its original railheads. As they marched deeper into France, intense summer heat took its toll of the German infantry and the poor roads took similar toll of their boots as they endeavoured to keep to the timetable by covering an average of fifteen miles a day. The horsed supply columns simply could not keep pace and it was fortunate that the fields were full of crops, although the Germans were still short of bread and, especially, of fodder. Indeed, it proved necessary to feed the cavalry, artillery and transport horses largely on green corn with consequent increases in sickness and weakness exacerbated by exhaustion.[54]

The handling of the advance was itself highly nervous on the part of Moltke and Oberste Heersleitung (OHL; General Headquarters). Moltke suffered from heart trouble and in effect surrendered control to his field commanders. Poor communications exacerbated the situation and OHL steadily lost contact with its forward units. Initially located at Koblenz, OHL was 206 miles from Kluck at the extreme right of the German front. Field telegraph lines could not be laid sufficiently quickly to keep pace with the advance and field telephones had a range of only about 25 miles. Wireless transmitters were maintained principally at Metz, Strasbourg and Cologne but with a range of about 180 miles.[55] Moreover, while Kluck had two wireless transmitters, OHL had only one receiving set. Transmissions were slow to decode and the French were using the Eiffel Tower transmitter in Paris to jam the German signals, forcing OHL to send out staff officers in motor cars.

OHL moved to Luxemburg on 29 August but still could not regain control while Moltke continued to detach troops from the advance. He did so first to mask the Belgian army as it fell back into Antwerp. Then Moltke did so again on 25 August, detaching two corps in response to an urgent request from his commander in east Prussia, Maximilian Prittwitz und Gaffron. Conrad had added to the pressure earlier on 21 August by demanding an immediate German offensive in the east to draw Russian forces from Galicia. When Churchill landed British marines at Antwerp on 27 August, Moltke suffered a virtual nervous collapse.

Meanwhile, co-ordination between Kluck and Bülow was also poor and a gap of some thirty miles had opened between their armies by 27 August. In response to urgent demands to close the gap, Kluck decided to alter his line of march on the following day. In doing so, he exposed the flank of his army to the Paris garrison and the move was seen by Allied reconnaissance aircraft on 3 September. This enabled the military governor of Paris, Joseph-Simon Galliéni, commanding the French Sixth Army, to mount the beginning of the Allied counter-attack, the Battle of the Marne, on 5 September. Moltke immediately sensed danger and, on 6 September, despatched a staff lieutenant-colonel, Richard Hentsch, with full powers, to assess whether to stop Kluck's advance. On the same day, the British Expeditionary Force advanced into the gap between the two German armies and, in view of the deteriorating situation, Hentsch used his authority on 9 September to order a German retreat.

In following up the German retreat, the French Fifth Army encountered an organised trench system before Rheims on 13 September and, within a matter of days, the other Allied formations came up against other German entrenchments. Moltke, who was replaced as operational commander by Erich von Falkenhayn on 13 September, had not intended that these trenches should be more than a temporary measure to gain a respite for his army. Therefore, in search of more mobility, each side began to attempt to out-flank the other, leapfrogging to the north by turn, beginning on the Aisne and the Chemin des Dames range. This 'race to the sea' culminated in the First Battle of Ypres between 20 October and 11 November 1914, to which Falkenhayn committed five newly formed reserve corps of German Fourth Army to an offensive around Langemarck.

Almost at once, these formations were mythologised as students or other volunteers when, in reality, the composition was extremely mixed and only some 18 per cent were actually university or high school students and teachers. They supposedly advanced singing 'Deutschland, Deutschland über alles', conceivably doing so as a means of battlefield identification in a fog. The so-called *Kindermond* (slaughter of the innocents) proved an enduring myth, kept alive into the Nazi era by the participation of Hitler, who was present with the 16th (Bavarian) Reserve Infantry Regiment. Their efforts were not sufficient to break through the British Expeditionary Force, whose defence of the 'immortal salient' around Ypres was itself characterised as the 'death of the old [British regular] army'.[56] The Belgians, too, though losing Antwerp on 10 October, had been able to extract much of their army. They then flooded the area between the Yser and the sea by opening the sluices on 25 October, closing the last gap so that the front line was virtually continuous from the Alps to the Channel.

The Eastern Front

In the east, without full use of the additional reserves from B-Staffel, the offensive into Serbia by the Austro-Hungarian Fifth and Sixth Armies failed between 19 and 21 August. In the oft-quoted words of Winston Churchill, the B-Staffel left the Austro-Hungarian commander in Serbia, Oskar Potiorek, 'before it could win him a victory. It returned to Conrad in time to participate in his defeat'.[57] In Galicia, the Austro-Hungarian advance begun on 23 August resulted in mixed fortunes, the First and Fourth Armies enjoying some success but the Third Army being thrown back. Only six divisions of the Second Army arrived at the end of August since four were delayed on the Serbian front when they became involved in fighting and two were still in transit. All had arrived by 8 September but, in a general engagement against the best of the Russian armies at Lemberg between 3 and 10 September, the Austro-Hungarian front collapsed. Conrad, who blamed Austrian misfortunes on German failure of support, was forced to order a retreat to the Carpathians. Indeed, the Austro-Hungarian army had lost 300,000 men – one-third of its combat effectives – in the first three weeks of war and 750,000 men in the first six months.[58]

There were no more successes for the Austrians against the Russians, Lemberg in effect ending the Austro-Hungarian army as a significant military force. Belgrade was taken on 2 December, but a Serbian offensive forced the Austrians to abandon the city on 15 December. Potiorek was dismissed on 22 December 1914.[59]

The Russian advance into east Prussia, though only beginning on 17 August, greatly alarmed the German commander, Prittwitz, whose forces were pushed back from Gumbinnen on 20 August. Prittwitz had only 11 divisions with which to confront the 21 divisions of the Russian First and Second Armies. In face of Prittwitz's decision to abandon east Prussia and his virtual collapse, he was dismissed. Moltke sent east the partnership of Paul von Beneckendorf Hindenburg as Commander-in-Chief and Erich Ludendorff as Chief of Staff. Both men had been in disgrace for some time. Hindenburg had allowed the Kaiser to lose the annual manoeuvres on one occasion and had retired in 1911. Ludendorff had pressed too hard on Moltke's behalf for increases in the army before the war and had been sent to a provincial command in 1912, although he had then been recalled to lead the German attack on Liège.

Arriving on 23 August they found that the head of operations of the German Eighth Army, Lieutenant-Colonel Max Hoffmann, had already worked out a scheme for counter-attack. This they promptly adopted, using strategic railways to concentrate all forces against Alexander Samsonov's Second Army and simply ignoring Pavel Rennenkampf's slow-moving First Army. The situation was not assisted by the fact that the two Russian commanders were hardly on speaking terms. Moreover, the Russians, whose wireless signals were intercepted by the Germans, confused the movement of German forces to the south as a retreat. Samsonov's army had advanced without one-fifth of its infantry complement partly in order to comply with the promise to the French to advance within fifteen days and partly because Samsonov had little faith in his second-line and reserve formations. He was defeated in a spectacular double envelopment at Tannenberg between 27 and 30 August, which cost the Russians some 50,000–70,000 casualties with an additional 92,000 captured.[60]

Ludendorff originally intended to call the battle after the village of Frögenau but Hoffmann suggested the adjacent Tannenberg since this had been the site of the defeat of the Teutonic knights by Polish and Lithuanian forces in 1410. It thus suggested suitable revenge over the Slavs. It was not the first echo of medieval battle to intrude into the Great War: Franz

Ferdinand's assassination had occurred on the day of the Serbian national holiday to commemorate the defeat of the medieval Serbian kingdom by the Turks at Kosovo in 1389. An early British propaganda story suggested that the British Expeditionary Force had been assisted at Mons by the English archers of Agincourt (1415) firing heavenly arrows at the Germans (in other versions the archers were angels).

Getting hopelessly lost in forest while going forward to take command of one of his corps and blaming himself for betraying the trust placed in him by the Tsar, Samsonov committed suicide. Rennenkampf promptly retreated after meeting German troops around the Masurian lakes on 9 and 10 September. In doing so, Rennenkampf suffered the loss of 70,000 men as casualties and 30,000 taken prisoner. In turn, the Germans advanced into Poland, although this was temporarily halted by the need to assist the Austrians further south. Resumed in November, the German advance took Lodz on 6 December, but then failed to take Warsaw through the Russians entrenching themselves. The winter campaigning in November and December 1914 cost the Germans 100,000 casualties and the Russians 530,000.[61]

There had been heavy losses in the west as well, the French alone suffering 385,000 in the first six weeks and 995,000 by the end of the first five months. The Germans had suffered 750,000 casualties in the west in the same period. The pre-war British estimate of wastage rates had been approximately 40 per cent for the first six months and 65–75 per cent for the first twelve months. The actual British casualty rate in the first three months was 63 per cent.[62]

The impact of industrialisation upon warfare, not least in terms of weapons development, the growth in the size of armies, and the inability of soldiers to predict what would occur on the future battlefield all contributed to the emergence of what would be called 'total' war. Pre-war international conferences such as those at The Hague had also failed to find a universal readiness among nation-states to compromise their future freedom of manoeuvre by accepting meaningful limitations on the actual conduct of war. Following their experience of guerrilla opposition by so-called *francs tireurs* (voluntary riflemen) after the defeat of the main French armies in the Franco-Prussian War, the Germans had been particularly unwilling to accept anything curtailing the 'rights' of the invader.

This was all too obvious during the German advance into Belgium when at least 5,000 civilians were executed and over 18,000 houses destroyed, including much of Louvain (Leuven) burned to the ground between 25 and 27 August 1914. In all, over 1 million Belgians fled the country. Much the same fate befell the Polish town of Kalisch on the Silesian frontier, which was shelled into oblivion on 14 August after snipers had supposedly fired on

German troops. Moreover, the German commandant subsequently imposed a financial 'contribution' of 27,000 roubles on the townsfolk.[63]

A final factor in the transition to total war in 1914 was the greater acceptance of war and the prolongation of war as an appropriate test of nationhood and national virility. Confronting the failure in the west, Falkenhayn, who formally succeeded Moltke as German Chief of Staff on 6 November 1914, suggested to Bethmann that it was time to seek a separate peace with Russia. Such a proposal hardly accorded with the war aims Bethmann had accepted on 9 September and it was rejected.[64] The war would not be over by Christmas.

Notes and references

1. Stevenson, *Armaments and Coming of War*, pp.1–8; Kennedy, *Rise and Fall*, p.203; Herrmann, *Arming of Europe*, p.234; Gatrell, *Government, Industry and Rearmament*, p.300; Ferguson, 'Public Finance and National Security', pp.148–54; idem, 'Germany and Origins of First World War', p.734; idem, *Pity of War*, pp.91–5, 105–11.

2. Herrmann, *Arming of Europe*, p.234; Ferguson, *Pity of War*, pp.91–5.

3. Ian Beckett, 'The British Army, 1914–1918: The Illusion of Change', in John Turner, ed., *Britain and the First World War* (London, 1988), p.99; John Brophy, *The Five Years* (London, 1936), p.133.

4. John Ellis, *The Social History of the Machine Gun* (London, 1975) pp.47–56.

5. Brian Bond, *The Pursuit of Victory: From Napoleon to Saddam Hussein* (Oxford, 1996), pp.88–91; Tim Travers, 'Technology, Tactics and Morale: Jean de Bloch, the Boer War and British Military Theory, 1900–14', *JMH* 51 (1979), pp.264–86; Roger Chickering, *Imperial Germany and a World Without War: The Peace Movement and German Society, 1892–1914* (Princeton, NJ, 1975), pp.387–92, 403–5; J. W. Chambers, 'The American Debate over Modern War, 1871–1914', in Manfred Boemeke, Roger Chickering and Stig Förster, eds, *Anticipating Total War: The German and American Experiences, 1871–1914* (Cambridge, 1999), pp.241–79.

6. Paddy Griffith, *Forward into Battle* (Chichester, 1981), pp.57–72; Hew Strachan, *European Armies and the Conduct of War* (London, 1983), pp.119–21.

7. Jay Luvaas, *The Military Legacy of the Civil War: The European Inheritance*, 2nd edn (Lawrence, KS, 1988); Maureen P. O'Connor, 'The Vision of Soldiers: Britain, France, Germany and the United States Observe the Russo-Turkish War', *WH* 4 (1997), pp.264–95; Paddy Griffith, *Rally Once Again: Battle Tactics of the American Civil War* (Ramsbury, Wiltshire, 1987), pp.189–92.

8. Stephen Badsey, 'Mounted Cavalry in the Second Boer War', *Sandhurst Journal of Military Studies* 2 (1991), pp.11–28. For more critical views of the cavalry's performance in South Africa and its consequences, see Brian Bond, 'Doctrine and Training in the British Cavalry, 1870–1914', in Michael Howard, ed., *The Theory and Practice of War: Essays presented to Captain B. H. Liddell-Hart on his 70th Birthday* (London, 1965), pp.97–125; E. M. Spiers, 'The British Cavalry, 1902–1914', *JSAHR* 57 (1977), pp.71–9.

9. Gary P. Cox, 'Of Aphorisms, Lessons and Paradigms: Comparing the British and German Official Histories of the Russo-Japanese War', *JMilH* 56 (1992), pp.389–401.

10. Keith Neilson, '"That Dangerous and Difficult Enterprise": British Military Thinking and the Russo-Japanese War', *W&S* 9 (1991), pp.17–37. See also Philip Towle, 'The Russo-Japanese War and British Military Thought', *JRUSI* 116 (1971), pp.64–8; and Shelford Bidwell and Dominick Graham, *Fire-power: British Army Weapons and Theories of War, 1904–45* (London, 1982), pp.17–21, 49–58.

11. Azar Gat, *The Development of Military Thought: The Nineteenth Century* (Oxford, 1992), p.139.

12. G. F. R. Henderson, *The Science of War* (London, 1905), pp.338–64, 382–434; Tim Travers, *The Killing Ground: The British Army, the Western Front and the Emergence of Modern Warfare, 1900–1918* (London, 1987), p.153; idem, 'The Offensive and the Problem of Innovation in British Military Thought, 1870–1915', *JCH* 13 (1978), pp.531–53; Keith Simpson, 'Capper and the Offensive Spirit', *JRUSI* 118 (1973), pp.51–6.

13. Major J. E. D. Ward, 'Some Lessons of the Russo-Japanese War Applied to 1912', *United Service Magazine* 45 (1912), pp.651–7.

14. Michael Howard, 'Men against Fire: The Doctrine of the Offensive in 1914', in Peter Paret, ed., *Makers of Modern Strategy*, 2nd edn (Oxford, 1986), pp.510–26. A slightly different version of Howard's paper appears as 'Men against Fire: Expectations of War in 1914', in Miller, Lynn-Jones and Van Evera, *Military Strategy*, pp.3–19.

15. Douglas Porch, *The March to the Marne: The French Army, 1871–1914* (Cambridge, 1981), pp.213–32; idem, 'The French Army and the Spirit of the Offensive, 1900–14', in Brian Bond and Ian Roy, eds, *War and Society: A Yearbook of Military History* (London, 1975), pp.117–43; Gat, *Development of Military Thought*, pp.134–72; Jack Snyder, *The Ideology of the Offensive: Military Decision-making and the Disaster of 1914* (Ithaca, NY, 1984), pp.41–106.

16. Arden Bucholz, *Moltke, Schlieffen and Prussian War Planning* (Providence, RI, 1991), pp.212–13; L. L. Farrar, *The Short War Illusion: German Policy, Strategy and Domestic Affairs, August to December 1914* (Santa Barbara, CA, 1973); Snyder, *Ideology of the Offensive*, pp.107–56; Stephen Van Evera, 'The Cult of the

Offensive and the Origins of the First World War', in Miller, Lynn-Jones and Evera, eds, *Military Strategy*, pp.39–108.

17. David French, *British Economic and Strategic Planning, 1905–15* (London, 1982), pp.85–97; Paul Kennedy, 'Strategy versus Finance in Twentieth Century Britain', *IHR* 3 (1981), pp.44–61.

18. Jonathan Bailey, 'British Artillery in the Great War', in Paddy Grifith, ed., *British Fighting Methods in the Great War* (London, 1996), pp.2–49; French, *British Economic and Strategic Planning*, pp.41, 45–6; idem, 'The Rise and Fall of "Business as Usual"', in K. Burk, ed., *War and the State: The Transformation of British Government, 1914–18* (London, 1982), pp.7–31.

19. Clive Trebilcock, 'War and the Failure of Industrial Mobilisation, 1899 and 1914', in J. M. Winter, ed., *War and Economic Development: Essays in Memory of David Joslin* (Cambridge, 1975), pp.139–64.

20. French, *British Economic and Strategic Planning*, pp.139, 171.

21. Ferro, *Great War*, p.55; R. D. Challenor, *The French Theory of the Nation in Arms, 1866–1939* (New York, 1955), pp.92, 96–8, 132–3.

22. Gatrell, *Government, Industry and Rearmament*, pp.298–99; Lieven, *Russia and Origins*, p.113; David R. Jones, 'Imperial Russia's Forces at War', in Allan R. Millett and Williamson Murray, eds, *Military Effectiveness: The First World War* (Boston, 1988), pp.262–9; Norman Stone, *The Eastern Front, 1914–1917* (London, 1975), pp.49, 144–5.

23. Ferro, *Great War*, p.27.

24. The evolution of German military planning can be traced in Gerhard Ritter, *The Schlieffen Plan: Critique of a Myth* (London, 1958, and Westport, CN, 1979). Background on the mechanics of staff planning processes can be found in Bucholz, *Moltke, Schlieffen and Prussian War Planning*.

25. Basil H. Liddell Hart, *A History of the World War, 1914–18* (London, 1934), pp.68–9.

26. Ritter, *Schlieffen Plan*, 2nd edn, pp.145–6.

27. Holger H. Herwig, 'Strategic Uncertainties of a Nation-state: Prussia-Germany, 1871–1918', in Williamson Murray, MacGregor Knox and Alvin Bernstein, eds, *The Making of Strategy: Rulers, States, and War* (Cambridge, 1994), pp.254–60; Terence Zuber, 'The Schlieffen Plan Reconsidered', *WH* 6 (1999), pp.262–305.

28. Gerhard Ritter, *The Sword and the Sceptre* 4 vols (Miami, FL, 1969), II, pp.193–226; Gunther E. Rothenberg, 'Moltke, Schlieffen, and the Doctrine of Strategic Envelopment' and Michael Geyer, 'German Strategy in the Age of Machine Warfare, 1914–45', both in Paret, *Makers of Modern Strategy*, pp.314–15, 530–3; Bucholz, *Moltke, Schlieffen and Prussian War Planning*, pp.127–34.

29. Ibid., pp.176–7; Ritter, *Schlieffen Plan*, 2nd edn, pp.91–6.

30. Bucholz, *Moltke, Schlieffen and Prussian War Planning*, pp.207–8.

31. Bucholz, *Moltke, Schlieffen and Prussian War Planning*, pp.214–22; Correlli Barnett, *The Swordbearers: Studies in Supreme Command in the First World War* (London, 1963), pp.13–106; Stig Förster, 'Der deutsche Generalstab und die Illusion des kurzen Krieges, 1871–1914: Metakritik eines Mythos', *MM* 54 (1995), pp.61–95; idem, 'Dreams and Nightmares: German Military Leadership and the Images of Future Warfare, 1871–1914', in Boemeke, Chickering and Förster, eds, *Anticipating Total War*, pp.343–76; Jost Dülffer, 'Kriegserwartung und Kriegsbild vor 1914', in Wolfgang Michalka, ed., *Der Erste Weltkrieg: Wirkung, Wahrnehmung, Analyse* (Munich, 1994), pp.778–98; Mombauer, 'Reluctant Military Leader', pp.417–46.

32. Bucholz, *Moltke, Schlieffen and Prussian War Planning*, pp.265–7; Zuber, 'Schlieffen Plan Reconsidered', pp.262–305.

33. Dennis E. Showalter, 'The Eastern Front and German Military Planning, 1871–1914', *EEQ* 15 (1981), pp.163–80.

34. Norman Stone, 'Moltke–Conrad: Relations between the Austro-Hungarian and German General Staffs, 1909–14', *HJ* 9 (1966), pp.201–28; idem, 'Moltke and Conrad Plan their War', in Kennedy, ed., *War Plans*, pp.222–51; Graydon Tunstall, *Planning for War against Russia and Serbia: Austro-Hungarian and German Military Strategy, 1871–1914* (New York, 1993), pp.81–108.

35. Herwig, 'Strategic Uncertainties of a Nation-state', pp.258, 266; idem, 'The Dynamics of Necessity: German Military Policy during the First World War', in Millett and Murray, eds, *Military Effectiveness*, pp.87, 89; idem, 'Disjointed Allies: Coalition Warfare in Berlin and Vienna, 1914', *JMilH* 54 (1990), pp.265–80; Maurer, *Outbreak of First World War*, pp.29–45.

36. Gunther Rothenberg, *The Army of Francis Joseph* (West Lafayette, IN, 1976), pp.178–80; Norman Stone, 'Austria-Hungary', in Ernest R. May, ed., *Knowing One's Enemies: Intelligence Assessment before the Two World Wars* (Princeton, NJ, 1986), pp.53–9; idem, *Eastern Front*, pp.73–9; Maurer, *Outbreak of First World War*, pp.17–27; Tunstall, *Planning for War*, pp.189–209.

37. Samuel R. Williamson, *The Politics of Grand Strategy: Britain and France Prepare for War, 1904–1914*, 2nd edn (London and Atlantic Highlands, NJ, 1990), pp.115–30; Gat, *Development of Military Thought*, pp.129–30.

38. Jan Karl Tanenbaum, 'French Estimates of Germany's Operational War Plans', in May, ed., *Knowing One's Enemies*, pp.150–77; Allan Mitchell, *Victors and Vanquished: The German Influence on Army and Church in France after 1870* (Chapel Hill, NC, 1984), pp.53–8, 98, 113–14.

39. Gat, *Development of Military Thought*, pp.156–8; Krumeich, *Armaments and Politics*, pp.24–5; Bucholz, *Moltke, Schlieffen and Prussian War Planning*, p.310.

40. Krumeich, *Armaments and Politics*, pp.22–5; Douglas Porch, 'The French Army in the First World War', in Millett and Murray, eds, *Military Effectiveness*, p.201; Williamson, *Politics of Grand Strategy*, pp.205–26.

41. Tanenbaum, 'French Estimates of German Plans', pp.170–1.

42. Keith Neilson, 'Watching the "Steamroller": British Observers and the Russian Army before 1914', *JSS* 8 (1985), pp.199–217; Jones, 'Imperial Russia's Forces at War', pp.257–61.

43. Walter Pintner, 'Russian Military Thought: The Western Model and the Shadow of Suvorov', in Paret, ed., *Makers of Modern Strategy*, pp.370–4; William Fuller, 'The Russian Empire', in May, ed., *Knowing One's Enemies*, pp.115–17, 124–5; Stone, *Eastern Front*, p.54; idem, *Strategy and Power in Russia, 1600–1914* (New York, 1992), pp.423–38, 442–5; Snyder, *Ideology of Offensive*, pp.157–98.

44. Fuller, 'Russian Empire', p.103; Krumeich, *Armament and Politics*, pp.18, 26–30, 118–25; Douglas Porch, 'Arms and Alliances: French Grand Strategy and Policy in 1914 and 1940', in Paul Kennedy, ed., *Grand Strategies in War and Peace* (New Haven, CN, 1991), pp.129–31, 136; Lieven, *Russia and Origins*, pp.101–6.

45. Gooch, *Plans of War*, pp.278–98; J. McDermott, 'The Revolution in British Military Thinking from the Boer War to the Moroccan Crisis', *CJH* 9 (1974), pp.159–78; Williamson, *Politics of Grand Strategy*, pp.30–58; K. M. Wilson, 'To the Western Front: British War Plans and the "Military Entente" with France before the First World War', *British Journal of International Studies* 3 (1977), pp.151–68.

46. Michael Howard, *The Continental Commitment: The Dilemma of British Defence Policy in the Era of Two World Wars* (Harmondsworth, 1974), p.17; Ian Beckett, 'H. O. Arnold-Forster and the Volunteers', in Ian Beckett and John Gooch, eds, *Politicians and Defence: Studies in the Formulation of British Defence Policy, 1845–1970* (Manchester, 1981), p.48.

47. Williamson, *Politics of Grand Strategy*, pp.59–88; Nicholas D'Ombrain, *War Machinery and High Policy* (Oxford, 1973), pp.81–90.

48. Major-General Sir C. E. Callwell, *Field Marshal Sir Henry Wilson: His Life and Diaries*, 2 vols (London, 1927), I, p.105; Brian Bond, *The Victorian Army and the Staff College, 1854–1914* (London, 1972), pp.244–73.

49. Williamson, *Politics of Grand Strategy*, pp.167–204, 300–10; D'Ombrain, *War Machinery*, pp.92–105.

50. E. M. Spiers, *Haldane: An Army Reformer* (Edinburgh, 1980), pp.48–91; John Gooch, 'Mr Haldane's Army: Military Organisation and Foreign Policy in England, 1906–7', in John Gooch, ed., *The Prospect of War: Studies in British Defence Policy, 1847–1942* (London, 1981), pp.92–115; idem, 'Haldane and the "National Army"', in Beckett and Gooch, eds, *Politicians and Defence*, pp.69–86.

51. William J. Philpott, 'The Strategic Ideas of Sir John French', *JSS* 12 (1989), pp.458–78; Williamson, *Politics of Grand Strategy*, pp.364–7; Roy A. Prete, 'French Strategic Planning and the Deployment of the BEF in France in 1914', *CJH* 24 (1989), pp.42–62.

52. David French, 'Allies, Rivals and Enemies: British Strategy and War Aims during the First World War', in Turner, ed., *Britain and First World War*, pp.22–35.

53. John Keegan, *Opening Moves: August 1914* (London, 1973), pp.58, 73; Bond, *Pursuit of Victory*, p.100.

54. Martin van Creveld, *Supplying War: Logistics from Wallenstein to Patton* (Cambridge, 1977), pp.122–41; Holger, 'Dynamics of Necessity', p.93; Richard Holmes, 'The Last Hurrah: Cavalry on the Western Front, August–September 1914', in Hugh Cecil and Peter Liddle, eds, *Facing Armageddon: The First World War Experienced* (London, 1996), pp.278–94.

55. Bucholz, *Moltke, Schlieffen and Prussian War Planning*, pp.183–4, 281.

56. Colin Fox, 'The Myths of Langemarck', *IWMR* 10 (1991), pp.13–25; Karl Unruh, *Langemarck: Legende und Wirklichkeit* (Koblenz, 1986), pp.10, 61, 63, 156; Bernd Hüppauf, 'Langemarck, Verdun and the Myth of a New Man in Germany after the First World War', *W&S* 6 (1988), pp.70–103.

57. Winston S. Churchill, *The World Crisis: The Eastern Front* (London, 1931), p.132; Holger Herwig, *The First World War: Germany and Austria-Hungary, 1914–18* (London, 1997), pp.88–9; Gunther Rothenberg, 'The Austro-Hungarian Campaign against Serbia in 1914', *JMilH* 4 (1989), pp.127–46.

58. Rothenberg, *Army of Francis Joseph*, p.180; idem, 'The Habsburg Army in the First World War', in Kann, Király and Fichtner, eds, *Habsburg Empire*, pp.74–86 [also in Béla Király and N. F. Dreisziger, eds, *East Central European Society in World War 1* (Boulder, CO, 1985), pp.289–300]; Stone, *Eastern Front*, pp.80–91.

59. Herwig, *First World War*, pp.111–13; Tunstall, *Planning for War*, pp.237–59; Dimitrije Djordjevic, 'Vojvoda Putnik, the Serbian High Command and Strategy in 1914', in Király and Dreisziger, eds, *East Central European Society*, pp.569–89.

60. Dennis E. Showalter, *Tannenberg: Clash of Empires* (Hamden, CT, 1991); Richard W. Harrison, 'Alexander Samsonov and the Battle of Tannenberg', in Brian Bond, ed., *Fallen Stars: Eleven Studies of Twentieth Century Military Disasters* (London, 1991), pp.13–31; Stone, *Eastern Front*, pp.54–69.

61. Stone, *Eastern Front*, pp.96–108; Herwig, *First World War*, p.110.

62. Porch, *March to Marne*, p.213; Herwig, *First World War*, p.120; French, *Economic and Strategic Planning*, p.26.

63. John Horne and Alan Kramer, 'German "Atrocities" and Franco-German Opinion, 1914: The Evidence of German Soldiers' Diaries', *JMH* 66 (1994), pp.1–33; Mark Derez, 'The Flames of Louvain: The War Experience of an Academic Community', in Cecil and Liddle, eds, *Facing Armageddon*, pp.617–29; Imanuel Geiss, 'The Civilian Dimension of the War', ibid., p.18; Alan Kramer, '"Greueltaten": Zum Problem der deutschen Kriegsverbrechen in Belgien und Frankreich, 1914', in Gerhard Hirschfeld and Gerd Krumeich, eds, *Keiner fühlt sich hier als Mensch: Erlebnis und Wirkung des Ersten Weltkrieges* (Essen, 1993), pp.85–114; idem, 'Les "atrocités allemandes": Mythologie populaire, propagande et manipulations dans l'armée allemande', in J.-J. Becker, J. M. Winter, G. Krumeich, A. Becker and S. Audoin-Rouzeau, eds, *Guerre et Cultures, 1914–18* (Paris, 1994), pp.147–64 [also in *GMCC* 171 (1993), pp.47–68]; John Horne, 'Les Mains Coupées: "Atrocités Allemandes" et Opinion Française en 1914', ibid., pp.133–46 [also in *GMCC* 171 (1993), pp.29–46]; Gerd Krumeich, 'The Myth of Gambetta and the "People's War" in Germany and France, 1871–1914', in Stig Förster and Jörg Nagler, eds, *On the Road to Total War: The American Civil War and the German Wars of Unification, 1861–1871* (Cambridge, 1997), pp.641–56; Manfred Messerschmidt, 'The Prussian Army from Reform to War', ibid., pp.278–81; Jay Winter, *The Experience of World War I* (London, 1988), p.167; Harold B. Segel, 'Culture in Poland during World War I', in Aviel Roshwald and Richard Stites, eds, *European Culture in the Great War: The Arts, Entertainment and Propaganda, 1914–18* (Cambridge, 1999), pp.68–9.

64. Holger Afflerbach, *Falkenhayn. Politisches Denken und Handeln im Kaissereich* (Munich, 1994), pp.198–203.

CHAPTER FOUR

Widening Horizons

When the war broke out in August 1914 the Entente comprised Britain, France, Belgium, Russia and Serbia on the Allied side while Germany and Austria-Hungary comprised the Central Powers. In reality, the war automatically involved the empires of the major European powers from the beginning. Technically, Australia, Canada, New Zealand, South Africa and Newfoundland were all autonomous states but Britain declared war on behalf of the Empire as a whole.

The existence of overseas German colonies immediately widened the struggle beyond Europe and at once involved British, French and Belgian colonial contingents in the war effort. In Africa, the German colony of Togoland was overrun by the British and French as early as 26 August 1914 and the surrender of German South-west Africa was taken by South African forces on 9 July 1915. In the Pacific, New Zealand forces secured German Samoa by 30 August 1914 and the Australians accepted the surrender of German New Guinea on 13 September, occupying Nauru on 6 November 1914. Japan, who entered the war on 23 August, occupied German Micronesia, comprising the Marshalls, Carolines, Marianas, Palaus and Yap, by 21 October 1914. The German port in China, Tsingtao (Qingdao), fell to Japanese and British forces on 6 November 1914. Kamerun (Cameroon), however, did not fall to British, French and Belgian forces until March 1916.

In theory, an international agreement guaranteed the neutrality of the Belgian Congo in the event of a European war. The British, however, declined to allow Belgian neutrality in Africa, and the Belgians themselves seized the German colonies of Rwanda and Burundi by June 1916. In German East Africa, however, the able German commander, Paul von Lettow-Vorbeck, did not finally surrender until 25 November 1918. With only a handful of troops, Lettow-Vorbeck not only defied British, Indian, South African and Belgian forces, but also invaded Portuguese Mozambique and the British colony of Northern Rhodesia: it was in the latter that Lettow-Vorbeck surrendered.[1]

On 5 August 1914, too, Montenegro demonstrated its solidarity with Serbia by declaring war on Austria-Hungary. By the end of 1914, the Ottoman Empire had joined the Central Powers, as Bulgaria was to do in 1915. Other Balkan and southern European states subsequently joined the Entente, Italy coming into the war in 1915, Portugal, Albania and Romania in 1916, and Greece in 1917. In that same year, the United States joined the Entente, as did China, Liberia and Siam (Thailand), as well as several states in Latin America. More Caribbean and Latin American states joined the Entente in 1918. Thus, what initially might have been characterised as the Third Balkan War not only took on the appearance of a much wider struggle as soon as the colonial empires were taken into account, but also rapidly became an expanding global conflict. In addition, the war naturally impacted upon those states choosing to remain neutral and had implications for the global economy as a whole.

The contribution of empire

Colonial empires represented a manpower reserve and an economic resource to be employed in the interests of the metropolitan power. In the event, however, the war not only further stimulated the development of distinctive national identities in the case of Britain's white dominions, but also generally encouraged limited degrees of indigenous nationalism and economic independence.

Britain had by far the largest empire in 1914, and some 2.8 million men from the Empire fought during the war, of whom over 1.4 million were from the Indian army. The imperial effort also embraced a high percentage of the white male populations of the dominions, amounting to 19.3 per cent from New Zealand, 13.4 per cent from Canada, 13.4 per cent from Australia and 11.1 per cent from South Africa. This compares favourably with the 22.1 per cent of the British male population who served in the wartime army and, compared with Britain, Australia, New Zealand and South Africa, all had a certain military advantage in having adopted elements of compulsion prior to the war.[2]

In the case of Australia, which was in the midst of an election campaign when war broke out, the incumbent (and soon to be defeated) Liberal prime minister, Joseph Cook, and his Labor opponent, Andrew Fisher, vied to demonstrate imperial loyalty. It was Japan rather than Germany that was most feared but, legally, Australia had no choice but to follow Britain's lead. In any case, Australia's political and economic security was widely perceived as being ultimately dependent upon a British victory.[3]

There was more resistance to initial recruitment efforts in Australia than sometimes supposed: the 52,561 men enlisted by the end of 1914 represented only 6.4 per cent of those eligible, albeit that rigorous physical standards were applied to recruits for the Australian Imperial Force (AIF). A disproportionate number of the first cohort of the AIF was British-born as opposed to Australian-born. Underlying divisions within Australian society deriving from class (defined by income), religion and national origin, were to become even more pronounced during the subsequent referenda on conscription in October 1916 and December 1917. Those most likely to oppose its imposition were Labor voters, Catholics and those of Irish extraction; those most likely to support it were women, males of military age and recent migrants. On both occasions, conscription was rejected: by the narrow margin of 72,476 votes in a poll of 2.5 million in 1916, and by a larger margin of 166,588 in 1917. The controversy over the first referendum split the Labor Party and William Morris Hughes, who had succeeded Fisher as prime minister in October 1915, was compelled to create a national coalition with the Liberals in January 1917. Ironically, the secretary of the Anti-Conscription League was John Curtin, who would introduce conscription as Labor prime minister in the Second World War.

In some respects, however, opposition to the war and, later, to conscription was economic in character. It reflected the increase in unemployment and short-time working at the outbreak of war, and the subsequent fears that conscription would further denude the rural labour force. It did not, therefore, reflect anti-war feeling as such and there was a certain feeling that a just war would find its own recruits without compulsion. Indeed, Hughes and the new Nationalist Party won the general election in May 1917 and Labor was swept from office everywhere but Queensland by 1918.

In all, between 412,000 and 416,000 Australians enlisted in the Australian Imperial Force, of whom approximately 331,000 served overseas. Expecting to go direct to France via England, the initial Australian and New Zealand Army Corps (Anzac) was instead diverted to Egypt, largely through the difficulties of adequately accommodating it on Salisbury Plain, where the Canadian Expeditionary Force (CEF) had already suffered deaths from pneumonia and meningitis. Subsequently, the Anzacs – arguably the first word formed from initials to enter English usage – served at Gallipoli and in Palestine. From March 1916, however, the principal Australian presence was in France and Flanders, two Australian corps eventually being formed.[4]

New Zealand's level of mobilisation was the highest of the dominions and its manpower policy sounder than most through a system of linked battalions. Nonetheless, conscription was introduced in August 1916 and, as in Australia, it was opposed by the labour movement, Catholics and those of Irish extraction. As in Australia, a leading opponent of conscription, Peter Fraser, would (as prime minister) preside over its introduction in the Second World War. The government of William Massey, however, resolved not to impose conscription on Maoris, though over 2,000 Maoris still served with the New Zealand forces. Approximately 128,000 New Zealanders enlisted, of whom 112,000 served abroad. Initially, the New Zealanders formed part of a mixed division with Australians in the Anzac Corps. A separate division was formed in January 1916 but it nonetheless served within the Australian Corps in France.

The South Africans initially had to deal with an Afrikaner rebellion led by two Boer veterans of the South African War, Koos De la Rey and Christiaan De Wet. While the rebellion had been defeated by January 1915, it delayed the South African advance into German South-west Africa. After the fall of the German colony, South Africa made a major contribution to the campaign in German East Africa, as well as committing a brigade to France and Flanders. With the Australian Imperial Force, the South Africans remained the only all-volunteer force on the Western Front throughout the war: 136,000 South Africans enlisted, of whom 76,000 served abroad. Southern Rhodesia, which had only paramilitary police and volunteer units in 1914, raised from scratch the 1st Rhodesian Regiment with 5,716 Rhodesians serving during the war.[5]

In Canada, parliament was not even recalled until two weeks after the Conservative prime minister, Sir Robert Borden, decided to despatch the Canadian Expeditionary Force to wherever the British government wished. Borden took the principled view that Canada was fighting the war in its own right, for wider freedom and civilisation, though he did assume that such a disinterested contribution to the war deserved recognition for Canada's right to have a voice in imperial decisions. The opposition leader, Sir Wilfred Laurier, was equally committed to the war effort. Yet, just as some Afrikaners resisted fighting for the British Empire, there were also divisions in Canada.

As in the case of the Australian Imperial Force, the men of the Canadian Expeditionary Force were also unrepresentative of the population as a whole in being largely British-born. French Canadians – between one-quarter and one-third of the population – were most resistant to enlistment, feeling themselves excluded from political power and being resentful of restrictions on the French language. Yet, loyalty to France was also muted by distance and through the more secular nature of Catholic society in Quebec. It also so happened that Quebec and the eastern maritime provinces generally had a smaller proportion of single males than western provinces. Men in Quebec tended to marry at a younger age than elsewhere in Canada and, under the rules for enlistment introduced by the Canadian government, married men required the written consent of their wives in order to enlist. The rural nature of much of Quebec was also a factor in inhibiting enlistment since most recruits were derived from urban areas. Significantly, when the government finally authorised a specifically French Canadian battalion, most of its recruits were either recent immigrants or unemployed.

As casualties mounted and expanding wartime industry began to compete for manpower, so difficulties were experienced. Borden, therefore announced the introduction of conscription in May 1917. Conscription proved controversial and Borden won a bitterly contested election. Exemption was widely sought until most exemptions were cancelled in April 1918 in the wake of the German spring offensive on the Western Front. There were anti-conscription riots in Quebec that same month, where, ironically, tribunals had been especially lenient. In the event, only 46,000 conscripted Canadians reached France before the end of the war. Despite the opposition to recruitment, however, some 628,000 Canadians enlisted during the war, of whom 365,000 went overseas. A Canadian corps was formed in September 1915. Legally separate from Canada, Newfoundland raised its own war loan of C$6 million and its infantry contingent served both at Gallipoli and in France.[6]

Initially, an Indian corps was despatched to France, the first elements arriving at Marseilles on 26 September 1914 but it was not a success on the Western Front. This was largely owing to the sub-division of battalions by caste, which made replacement difficult, the smaller field strength of Indian as compared with British battalions, and the shortages of white officers. With continuing morale problems, deriving from heavy casualties and unfamiliar conditions of warfare and climate, the infantry component was withdrawn in December 1915. The extension of the war, not least the entry of Ottoman Turkey, however, opened up new theatres of direct concern to India. Indeed, the campaign against the Turks in Mesopotamia was to be directed from India.

Indian troops also served in Egypt and German East Africa, greatly increasing the manpower demands in India itself. In March 1915, the viceroy, Lord Hardinge, supported by his Commander-in-Chief, General Sir Beauchamp Duff, refused to send more troops out of India unless directly ordered to do so, in view of the depletion of the garrison and the fear that this would encourage a tribal descent from the North-west Frontier or rebellion in India itself. They were overruled by the Secretary of State for India. The manpower pressures resulted in a considerable broadening of the pre-war preference of enlisting only perceived martial classes, and the 826,855 men enlisted during the war included recruits drawn from no less than 75 new 'classes'. Indeed, the introduction of a quota system on districts from 1917 onwards contributed greatly to immediate post-war unrest as local Indian officials increasingly resorted to coercion in order to meet the quotas. Significantly, the Punjab, which was most affected by the disturbances in 1919, was forced to find over 98,000 men alone in the last six months of the war, although it has been argued that the recruitment drive increased the importance of loyal rural notables in the province.[7]

Britain also raised about 56,000 troops from Black Africa and, after some reluctance, even 15,000 from the West Indies. In addition, non-combatant labour corps were raised from the Empire, providing much needed logistical support for the British army. On the Western Front alone, by 1916 there were 193,500 native labourers serving the British army drawn from China, India, South Africa, Egypt, the West Indies, Malta, Mauritius, the Seychelles and Fiji, with similar labour corps in Mesopotamia, East Africa, Egypt, Italy and at Salonika.[8]

Just over 1 million Africans were employed by the British as labourers or carriers during the war, the prevalence of tsetse fly making the use of baggage animals impossible in German South-west Africa and, especially, German East Africa. Ironically, labour conscription actually exacerbated the spread of sleeping sickness through depleting the labour force normally available to clear the bush, where the tsetse fly flourished. Service conditions were hard and mortality, especially from dysentery, high. Over 94,000 carriers died, although a reasonably effective vaccine for dysentery was introduced in 1917. The death rates, however, varied considerably among Africans recruited from different regions and serving in different areas. Some 616 men of the South African Native Labour Corps (SANLC) were lost on the SS *Mendi*, sunk off the Isle of Wight in February 1917. About half the total of African carriers and labourers were conscripted, the earlier reliance upon voluntary effort – often in effect 'involuntary conscription' – and selective compulsion giving way to a mass levy of males aged between 18 and 30 in British East Africa in July and August 1917.[9]

In 1914 the French had approximately 122,000 indigenous troops serving in their colonial formations, conscription having been extended to the Empire in 1912. During the war, the French Empire provided some 600,000 additional troops, comprising about 6.6 per cent of the wartime army. More than half were from North Africa and one-third black, principally from Senegal and Niger. Between 66,000 and 71,000 French colonial troops died on wartime service. Indeed, following the French army mutinies in the spring of 1917, Senegalese troops suffered proportionally more casualties than French troops. Similarly, the Empire provided not only 200,000 labourers for field service, but also large numbers of workers for French factories. Between 109,000 and 122,000 Algerians had worked in French industry by 1918, together with 50,000 'Annamites' or Indo-Chinese, and even 13,000 Chinese. In all, overseas workers comprised about 7 per cent of those employed in war-related industries and 16 per cent of the munitions industry. Their high visibility, indeed, resulted in a series of race riots against immigrant workers in France in 1917, Moroccans in particular becoming targets.[10]

At the same time that the colonial empires were proving a manpower quarry, they also represented an economic resource. The British Empire's financial contributions to the war effort were considerable. In India, military expenditure, which fell entirely on the Indian taxpayer, increased from £20 million in 1914 to £140 million in 1918 and the government of India gifted £100 million to the British government as a war loan in 1916. The dominions equally paid for their own forces. Similarly, colonial production of both raw materials and manufactured goods was increased to assist the British war effort. To give but one example, nearly 3 million tons of Indian wheat were shipped to Britain or its European allies by 1917 alone.[11]

The military, political and economic impact of imperial participation was varied. In terms of casualties, the British imperial contingents together suffered over 203,000 dead, the Australian total of something between 58,000 and 63,000 exceeding that of the United States.[12] Generally, military and labour conscription was the single most important factor in terms of the impact of the war on native peoples. This was particularly so as the needs for labour brought European administrators into remote areas they had previously left alone. In some cases, indeed, pacification of the interior was completed during the war as in Portuguese Mozambique, the Barué revolt in 1917 being set off by wartime conscription.

There is some evidence that the minority of educated indigenous subjects in French Africa such as the Senegalese deputy in the National Assembly, Blaise Diagne, supported the war effort relatively willingly in the expectation of further opportunities of advancement to citizenship. This did not apply, however, to the majority of ordinary Africans, and tribal elders resisted the undermining of their authority by the concessions of future exemption from labour service frequently extended to recruits. Thus, when the French increased the rate of labour conscription in West Africa in 1916, possibly as many as 150,000 people fled into Liberia and neighbouring British colonies. There was a revolt against the French in West Volta between November 1915 and July 1916 and other unrest in Niger and French Soudan. The Portuguese simply resorted to seizing Africans for service.

In the East African Protectorate and Nyasaland, where John Chilembwe led a brief revolt against conscription, the British authorities resorted to rounding up tax defaulters, in effect holding families hostage until men surrendered themselves for labour, and threatening chiefs with removal from office unless they found sufficient recruits. Militant Kikuyu nationalists began to appreciate that European power was dependent on the co-operation of chiefs and the war undoubtedly widened the already increasing tension between chiefs and people in both East and West Africa. It also served to further antagonism between Africans and the white settler population in East Africa, which resented the loss of labour to the carrier service and the higher rates of pay afforded carriers.

War service itself, however, was not a significant factor in stimulating indigenous nationalism in East Africa. A handful of future nationalist leaders served in the small and well organised Kikuyu Mission Volunteers, raised in April 1917, but, as Geoffrey Hodges has commented, 'literacy in English and Swahili, not war experience was the passport to leadership'. Most educated Kikuyu like Jomo Kenyatta spent the war in clerical or similar administrative appointments. Moreover, it was settler pressure on land and growing settler power that created support for post-war nationalism. Similarly, only a few of those who served in the South African Native Labour Corps subsequently became political activists in South Africa, although the war further stimulated African migration towards urban areas and unionisation of the African labour force.

In Nigeria, there was also considerable resistance to military service in southern districts, where wartime revolts in Egboland appear to have resulted from increased government activity. The wide net cast by military and labour conscription also had the effect of creating amongst Africans a greater sense of a larger political entity than tribal groups. In Southern Rhodesia, on the other hand, military recruits were found relatively easily either from labour migrants or from areas which had been sources of migrant labour in the past. Similarly, Egyptians appear to have been attracted by the relatively well paid short-term contracts on offer for military labourers.[13]

Irrespective of the degree of nationalism among indigenous peoples, the 're-partition' of Africa in 1919, through the division of the former German colonies, took place without reference to indigenous peoples. Yet, the fact that Britain was engaged in a war against Ottoman Turkey, whose sultan-caliph, Mehmet V, was the recognised leader of Islam, did have considerable implications for the Muslim population in India. In August 1917, concessions to Indian nationalism were announced, with a recognition that the ultimate goal would be 'the progressive realisation of responsible government'. On the back of the 1919 disturbances, India also received a measure of autonomy under the Government of India Act of that year.[14]

Elsewhere, the war's political consequences were of more immediate significance. Ireland was to disintegrate into chaos after the war, nationalists having already staged the abortive Easter Rising in Dublin in 1916. Arguably most significant, however, was the growth of a national consciousness within the white dominions. Following the Afrikaner rebellion, Afrikaners drifted towards the National Party, which became the largest party in the South African parliament in 1920. At the same time, the experience of the Anzacs at Gallipoli assisted the cultivation of a new national myth in Australia, although this was not initially seen as being incompatible with loyalty to Empire. In reality, the Anzacs had been only a minority of the forces employed at Gallipoli, and 87 per cent of Australia's war dead were lost on battlefields elsewhere. But, bolstered by the efforts of journalists like Keith Murdoch, Ellis Ashmead-Bartlett and, especially, C. E. W. Bean, Gallipoli gave Australians an authoritative heroic tradition. The first Anzac Day (25 April) was celebrated in 1916, a year after the landings at Anzac Cove.[15]

Command over the Australian Corps became symbolic of independence of spirit, the Australian authorities also rebutting the attempts of the British High Command to extend to Australians the death penalty for disciplinary offences on the same basis as applied to British troops. Ultimately, the Australian Sir John Monash was elevated to the command of the Australian Corps in May 1918. The Canadians also insisted on acting only as an integrated corps. To the despair of British officers, the Canadian voluntary militia system had long been prone to interference on the part of Canadian politicians. The tradition was continued by the Canadian Minister of Militia and Defence, Sam Hughes, until his dismissal in October 1916. All Canadian politicians, however, intended Canadian formations to remain distinct, and an unprecedented Ministry of Overseas Military Forces of Canada was established in London. Moreover, at a time when Canadian criticism of General Headquarter's conduct of the war on the Western Front was increasing, Borden took the opportunity to insist on a Canadian being appointed to command the Canadian Corps in June 1917, the choice falling on Lieutenant-General Sir Arthur Currie. Some Canadians regarded the performance of the Canadian Corps, as at Vimy Ridge in April 1917, as playing the same role in nation-building as the Anzacs at Gallipoli, and the Canadian military contribution to the war undoubtedly strengthened Canada's status within the Empire.[16]

Increasing dominion independence was a matter recognised in part by the attendance on occasions of Borden and William Hughes at Cabinet meetings when in London. Australian and Canadian representatives also attended the Allied economic conference at Paris in June 1916. Above all, there was the establishment of an Imperial War Cabinet in December 1916, although the consultation process amounted to little in real terms and the British saw it mainly as a means by which more manpower might be obtained. There was also an Imperial War Conference in 1917, which included two Indians in the three-man Indian delegation.

Although the South African prime minister Jan Smuts joined the War Cabinet, the influence of the dominion prime ministers was limited by the time they could spend in London. Thus, though Borden characterised the consultative process as transforming Canada 'from colony to nation', Hughes felt Australia disadvantaged by his absence in 1917 and was prominent in 1918 in demanding the right of the dominions to communicate direct with the British prime minister on matters of Cabinet importance.[17]

Australia, Canada and New Zealand all insisted on separate representation at the post-war peace conference and were represented both within a British Empire Delegation and by their own delegates, as well as being recognised as separate signatories of the Treaty of Versailles. Moreover, their increasing refusal to automatically follow the lead of the British government in foreign policy, as they had in 1914, was soon to be demonstrated during the Chanak Crisis in 1922.[18]

In terms of economic developments, the colonial empires derived some general benefit from the increased wartime demands for raw materials and other products. Indian nationalists had persistently argued that industrial development had been deliberately retarded in order to retain India merely as a source of raw materials for British manufacturers. With the demands of the war, new capital was made available for industrial development, and tariffs on Indian manufactured exports such as cotton, previously maintained to protect the Lancashire cotton industry, were removed. On the other hand, war closed some traditional markets and shipping and inland transport shortages resulted in shortages in commodities such as salt, spices and oil. The result was that some prices rose to offset the rising prosperity. Consequently, there were wartime disturbances in a number of areas and export of wheat and other foodstuffs was halted in 1918, apart from supplies sent to Indian forces in Mesopotamia.[19]

In British West Africa, what had been an ailing local economy hit by pre-war drought and famine, as well as the cessation of previously profitable exports of palm kernels to Germany, was stimulated anew by the wartime demand for groundnuts and palm products. The withdrawal of many Europeans for war service also opened up new labour opportunities for Africans on the railways and in the mines.

Australia was equally dependent upon export of agricultural and mining primary products and, after an initial period of depression, the Australian economy generally benefited from the war. Britain's agreement in 1916 to purchase the entire wool clip was of considerable significance. Australia's surplus meat was also purchased by the British government in its entirety, though purchase of the wheat crop was initially rejected owing to shipping shortages. When the British government did buy up the entire wheat crop in 1917, it proved impossible to transport it and the wheat mouldered at Australian ports. Nevertheless, as E. M. Andrews has commented, British purchases of Australian primary products 'provided for Australia's commercial security'. There was also some diversification with the stimulus given to domestic production of some goods such as textiles in the absence of competition from British imports and to development of some new areas such as chemicals. The war therefore accelerated Australia's progress towards becoming a modern industrialised state.

Canada benefited from its greater proximity to the Atlantic route, exporting 70 per cent of its wheat crop in 1917 and twice as much as the United States. Although there was a degree of wartime industrial diversification, the continued demand for Canadian wheat had the long-term disadvantage of further stimulating the agricultural sector. South Africa suffered from the depression of the gold market and its economy remained largely dependent upon imported manufactured goods.[20]

Overall, the actual expansion of the British and French Empires in 1918, as a result of the acquisition of former German and Turkish territories, was to bring a new consciousness of the economic value of empire. In the French Empire, new investment was largely a result of the loss of between two-thirds and three-quarters of all existing French overseas investment when Tsarist Russia collapsed in 1917. Rather similarly, a sense of the need to exploit the resources of the Empire more systematically, and to do so within the context of a system of greater imperial protection emerged in Britain. In the process, the European economic stake in the colonial empires substantially increased, ironically diminishing the degree of autonomy enjoyed by indigenous economies during the war.[21]

The Balkans and beyond

Apart from the involvement of colonial empires, the most obvious expansion of the war was that in southern and eastern Europe. For Montenegro, the smallest of all the Allied belligerents with just 250,000 inhabitants, entry to the war was a relatively simple matter of solidarity with neighbouring Serbia. In fact, this did not necessarily serve the interests of its ruler, King Nikita, who rejected a tempting offer of Serbian territory from Austria-Hungary in return for staying neutral. In the event, while the tiny Montenegrin army could make little real contribution, Montenegro's strategic position on the Dalmatian coast not only threatened the Austro-Hungarian naval base at Cattaro, but also safeguarded the Serbian left flank. Consequently, in

January 1916, a major Austro-Hungarian offensive overran Montenegro, forcing Nikita into exile in France. A small-scale guerrilla war continued thereafter against the Austro-Hungarian occupation forces.[22]

The next entrant to the war in the Balkans after Montenegro was Ottoman Turkey, allying itself with the Central Powers. Its decision was of far more consequence in compelling the Entente to open new fronts in the east, while it also cut Russia's lifeline from the Black Sea to the Mediterranean. Primarily, Turkish entry was a result of a protracted internal political struggle within the ruling Ittihad ve Terakki Cemiyeti (Committee of Union and Progress). The Unionists, who had dominated Turkish politics since the revolution of the so-called Young Turks in 1908 and had increased their power by a military coup in 1913, had seen their ambitions for a revival of the power of the Ottoman Empire destroyed during the First Balkan War. Remaining Turkish frontiers in Europe were vulnerable to Greece and Bulgaria, while Russia appeared to retain its interest in the Straits of the Dardanelles and the Bosphorus. Between 1912 and 1914 some of the Turkish leadership favoured alliance with one of the great powers, while others wished to reach accommodation with all the powers. Still others, of whom the most prominent was the Minister of War, Mehmet Enver Pasha, wished to overthrow the whole post-Balkan Wars settlement. In the scenario projected by Enver, Russia's Turkic territories in the Caucasus and Turkestan might be won for the Ottoman Empire with the support of Germany and Austria-Hungary.

Germany had no apparent territorial ambitions in Turkey and had been more sympathetic to Turkish nationalism than the other great powers, seeing the advantage of opening markets in the Ottoman Empire for German goods. Thus, the Turks had willingly turned to Germany, reaching agreement on a German military training mission led by Otto Liman von Sanders in October 1913, though it should be noted that the gendarmerie remained under the command of a French officer and the navy under the command of a British admiral, Hugh Limpus. It was also the case that France held 62.9 per cent of Turkey's foreign debt and that Britain was the next largest overseas investor. Any approach to Turkey by the Entente, however, was hampered by Anglo-French indifference coupled with Russian ambitions, and the Turks were mindful of the possibility that their neutrality might give Russia the pretext to seize the Straits.[23]

Initially, the Turks were more concerned with an increasing confrontation with Greece over some of the Aegean islands, but they did make overtures to Germany in July 1914. This resulted in a secret treaty of alliance on 2 August, albeit one concluded with the knowledge of only a handful of Unionist leaders. The alliance was concluded on the assumption that the war would be over quickly, that both Bulgaria and Romania would join the Central Powers, and that Turkey could fight a war with Bulgarian assistance against Greece and Serbia. The Germans were anxious to bring the Turks into the war and accepted the invitation of Enver to send to the Straits two warships, the battle cruiser *Goeben* and the light cruiser *Breslau*, which had been cruising in the Mediterranean out of ready access to safe refuge. It was a clear violation of international law, which prohibited neutral powers from harbouring belligerent warships.

The arrival of the two ships on 10 August 1914 brought considerable internal debate, the difficulty being overcome by an immediate (but fictional) announcement that the two ships had been purchased by Turkey. Limpus resigned his appointment as soon as the German vessels passed the Dardanelles, being in effect replaced by the German rear-admiral Wilhelm Souchon, while the German Military Mission extended its control over the Turkish army and began preparations for campaigns against Egypt and Odessa on Russia's Black Sea coast.

In September, the Turkish leadership unilaterally abrogated the so-called Capitulations, by which foreign nationals enjoyed immunity from Turkish taxation and justice and by which changes in custom duties required the consent of the great powers. The Straits were also closed to shipping. Negotiations followed with Balkan neighbours and the Entente. Enver and Talât Bey, the Interior Minister, increased pressure on their colleagues, resolving to break the deadlock within the leadership by securing a German financial loan and then authorising the *Goeben* and *Breslau* to commence raids on Russian shipping on 29 October. Britain had already imposed an economic blockade on Turkey in early October and made preparations to declare Cyprus, held by Britain since 1878 but still nominally part of the Ottoman Empire, a Crown colony. Russia formally declared war on Turkey on 2 November, followed by Britain and France on 5 November. The formal Turkish counter declaration on 11 November 1914 invoked a *jihad* (holy war) against the infidel.

Apart from the Entente's Dardanelles expedition, Turkish entry into the war brought an unsuccessful Turkish advance towards Egypt in February 1915; the campaign waged by the government of India in Mesopotamia from November 1914 to the fall of Baghdad in March 1917; the British advance into Palestine in 1916, culminating in the fall of Jerusalem in November 1917 and of Damascus in October 1918; and British promotion of the Arab Revolt, normally dated as beginning on 7 June 1916.

The latter was arguably the most significant, since the Ottomans had ruled the Arabs for over four centuries. There had been anti-Ottoman conspiracies by Arab secret societies before the war, two of these societies, al-Fatat (The Society of the Young Arab Nation) and al-'Ahd (The Covenant) beginning to co-operate in early 1915, following the first wave of executions of Arab activists by the commander of the Turkish Fourth Army based at Damascus, Jemal Pasha. Some estimates of the numbers of Arabs executed in 1915 and 1916 are as high as 50,000, while Jemal also oppressed the Jewish population. The Entente's blockade of exports such as Lebanese silk and Palestinian citrus fruit, coupled with bad harvests, led to considerable privation: income at Islam's holy places was also cut by the effect of the blockade on pilgrimages. When the independent ruler of Najd, Ibn Sa'ud, declined to become involved in any revolt, Sharif Hussein (Husayn) of Mecca was approached by the Entente. His son, Faisal (Faysal), became the undisputed leader of the revolt following the withdrawal in November 1916 of 'Aziz 'Ali al-Misra of al-'Ahd.

At peak, there were some 40,000 Arabs under arms, mostly tribesmen from the Hijaz, but it was by no means the case that all Arabs supported the revolt. Al-Misra had purposely not taken Medina at the start of the revolt because he favoured a dual Turko-Arab federation modelled on Austria-Hungary. Nor was Hussein's pan-Arab concept of a unified Arab state shared by advocates of a greater Syria, Lebanese separatists, or Ibn Sa'ud. Egyptian nationalism was separately stimulated by the imposition of conscription for the British labour corps in 1916, Britain having announced the establishment of a protectorate over Egypt when Turkey entered the war. Such divisions did not assist the Arab cause, especially in dealings with the Entente, and caused considerable problems both during the war and long after.[24]

While Turkey sided with the Central Powers in 1914, Italy, a member of the Triple Alliance, significantly did not. Primarily this was because of Italy's continued rivalry with Austria-Hungary in the Adriatic and her irredentist claims: some 800,000 Italians lived under Habsburg control in *Italia irredenta*. Technically, Vienna's failure to notify Italy in advance of its ultimatum to Serbia, and its refusal to contemplate awarding Italy territorial compensation for its own likely gains in the Balkans under the terms of the Triple Alliance, provided an excuse for an Italian declaration of neutrality made public on 3 August 1914.

The able Italian Foreign Minister, Antonino Di San Giuliano, did not denounce the Triple Alliance as such. He did argue, however, that it was a defensive alliance and that Italy could not legally take part in a war of aggression, such as that begun by Germany and Austria-Hungary without any significant consultation with their nominal ally. The decision came as a complete surprise to the Italian Chief of Staff, Luigi Cadorna, who had succeeded to the appointment only in July 1914. As recently as 31 July 1914, Cadorna had sought authority to send the first Italian contingent to join the German army on the Rhine.

The early setbacks for Germany in the west and for Austria-Hungary in Serbia and Galicia then presented an opportunity for Italy to realise its territorial ambitions by joining the Entente, since Italian neutrality would not result in gains at the peace table. Di San Giuliano remarked in September 1914 that 'the ideal situation for us would be if Austria and France were both beaten'. Such an outcome, of course, was unattainable and it was clearly the case that Italy stood to gain more from an Entente victory. Accordingly, the Italian prime minister Antonio Salandra, the Colonial Minister Ferdinando Martini, Di San Giuliano, who died in October 1914, and his successor as Foreign Minister Sidney Sonnino, had resolved on intervention by September although they did not communicate this to the rest of the Cabinet. Their main problem was not only Italy's military weakness but also the government's parliamentary weakness.

This decision did not prevent the Italian leadership from negotiating with Germany and Austria-Hungary for territorial compensation once the Austro-Hungarians occupied Belgrade in December 1914. Vienna would not budge and, with the opening of the British bombardment of the Dardanelles in February 1915, the Italians began negotiations with the Entente, demanding Trentino, part of the Tyrol, Trieste, Dalmatia and the expansion of Italian possessions in Africa as the price for intervention. As it happened, the Italians were facing a continuing major revolt by the Senussi in Libya, which forced them to abandon much of Tripolitania in January 1915.

The Entente promised to Italy northern Dalmatia, the southern Tyrol up to the Brenner Pass, Trieste, Istria up to the Quarnero, Gorizia and Gradisca, the Curzolari islands, the Dodecanese, the Albanian port of Valona, which the Italians had seized in December 1914, possible territorial gains in Africa, a substantial British loan and the exclusion of the Vatican from any peace conference. The deal, which involved Italy receiving more Slavs and Germans than Italians, enabled the Treaty of London to be concluded on 26 April 1915. Italy undertook to enter the war within one month, although Cadorna did not discover this until 2 May. Public indifference, parliamentary opposition, the faltering of the Allied expedition at the Dardanelles, and the Russian retreat on the Eastern Front then caused some difficulties for Salandra and Sonnino. Salandra resigned on 12 May, only to be reappointed by King Victor Emmanuel III, who strongly supported entry to the war, four days later.

Earlier, pro-war agitation had been largely manufactured by those like the leader of the intellectual movement known as the futurists, Filippo Marinetti; the veteran nationalist, Gabriele D'Annunzio; and the young newspaper editor, Benito Mussolini, who had resigned from the socialist organ, *Avanti!* in October 1914 to found the pro-interventionist *Popolo d'Italia*. Now, by contrast, the nationalist demonstrations of 'Radiant May' were more spontaneous, although the influence of nationalists and other elements over government policy itself has been much exaggerated. Indeed, there was also strike action in Turin against intervention. Moreover, it was an overwhelmingly neutralist chamber which voted by 407 to 74 for a war, which appeared, in the words of John Thayer, 'a cure for every conceivable national deficiency, domestic or diplomatic'. In the process, Italian parliamentary democracy lost much of its credibility.

The Italians had signed an agreement to co-operate with Romania in September 1914 since, if both entered the war together, they could demand a higher price from the Entente. In the event, however, Sonnino's grasp of diplomacy was much less sure than that of Di San Giuliano, and the Romanians opted to remain neutral. Indeed, the Italians had managed to join the Entente at a moment when its fortunes, as evinced by the setbacks at the Dardanelles and in Galicia, were not bright. Moreover, seduced by the enduring myth that Italy was a great power, neither government nor armed forces were actually ready for war. Italy declared war only on Austria-Hungary on 24 May 1915, but there was no declaration against Turkey until October 1915, and none against Germany until August 1916. San Marino also declared war on Austria-Hungary on 3 June 1915.[25]

The Italian bargaining with both sides was not atypical of the attitude of those Balkan states as yet uncommitted. Few had been satisfied by the outcome of the Balkan Wars and the patchwork arrangement of frontiers cutting across national and religious divisions gave all irredentist claims on others. Tortuous negotiations between the Balkan states and both sides thus became commonplace, but, naturally, promises by either the Entente or the Central Powers were dependent upon entry into the war on their side. Thus, the maintenance of genuine neutrality became increasingly difficult for those in receipt of such promises, while the belligerents had to juggle promises that were often contradictory and incompatible.

In many respects, Bulgaria epitomised the self-interested approach of the Balkan states to the war. Its own strategic position contiguous to Serbia, Greece, Romania and Turkey and across the route between Turkey and Austria-Hungary made it a useful prospective partner for both sides. Indeed, the Entente was even prepared to force Serbia to make territorial concessions to the Bulgarians, although it had less to offer beyond Turkish territory, since the Entente wished to bring both Greece and Romania into the war as well. King Ferdinand of Bulgaria and his prime minister, Vasil Radoslavov, were sympathetic towards the Central Powers. Nonetheless, Bulgaria was mindful of the progress of the respective sides. Thus, the Entente failure at the Dardanelles and the success for German and Austro-Hungarian armies in 1915, together with the apparent likelihood that Romania would join the Entente, tilted the balance in favour of the Central Powers.

Accordingly, in return for the promise of all of Macedonia, the return of the Maritsa valley from Turkey, access to the Adriatic and a corridor between Bulgaria and Austria-Hungary along the Danube, Bulgaria attacked Serbia without declaration of war on 5 October 1915. As a result, Britain declared war on Bulgaria on 15 October and France on the following day. British and French forces landed at Salonika in Greece later that month to open a new front against Bulgaria. Subsequently, Italy and Russia declared war on Bulgaria on 19 October 1915. Meanwhile, the Central Powers' offensive against Serbia had resulted in the fall of Belgrade on 9 October, compelling the Serbs to retreat through Albania to the sea and to evacuate their remaining troops to Corfu.[26]

Romania, which shared with Bulgaria a strategic position on the Danube between Germany and Turkey, had equally strong ties with the Central Powers. Her decision, however, was to be different, largely as a result of an intensification in Romania's irredentist claims on the Austro-Hungarian provinces of Banat, Bukovina and Transylvania. Romanians had not actually controlled Transylvania since 1699 nor Bukovina since 1775, but some 3 million ethnic Romanians were under Vienna's control. Thus, Romania repudiated its alliance with the Central Powers and declared for neutrality in August 1914.

While King Carol of Romania favoured the Central Powers, the prime minister, Dmitri Bratianu, had few doubts that Romania should join the Entente, but felt it necessary to negotiate a formal alliance with some care so as not to provoke any immediate attack from the Central Powers or Bulgaria. Carol died in October 1914, and his successor, Ferdinand, was more sympathetic to the Entente. The negotiations were complicated during the course of 1915 by the Entente's unwillingness to meet all Bratianu's demands when the war was going well for them. Subsequently, further difficulties arose from Bratianu's equal hesitation to enter the war when the Entente was driven by military failure to concede all his demands, despite the conflict with the ambitions of both Serbia and Russia.

The success of Russia's Brusilov offensive in the summer of 1916 was an important factor in pushing the Romanians into the war. They had few illusions since, if either Russia or the equally war-weary Austria-Hungary went for a separate peace, Romania would have little opportunity to realise her territorial ambitions. Bratianu sought further assurances of direct military support from the Entente, including an Allied offensive from Salonika and the delivery of munitions. In return, he agreed to enter the war against Austria-Hungary only, Romania's declaration of war following on 27 August 1916. The Germans, who had been taken by surprise, declared war on Romania the following day. Bulgaria also attacked Romania, but without declaration of war, on 31 August.

Romanian entry had an immediate impact for both sides. Austria-Hungary found itself cut off from Romanian grain supplies while the Romanian offensive into Transylvania undermined Tisza's government in Hungary. It also forced OHL (German General Headquarters) to divert troops from Verdun and contributed to Falkenhayn's dismissal. In the event, the promised Anglo-French offensive from Salonika was not forthcoming and the Russians also failed to support the Romanian offensive into Transylvania. Ironically, Falkenhayn commanded the German and Austro-Hungarian forces that drove into Romania in September 1916, linking with German, Bulgarian and Turkish forces from the south. Despite a daring Romanian counter-attack across the Danube, Bucharest fell to the Germans on 6 December 1916.

Romanian defeat forced the Russians to lengthen their own front while ending realistic expectations of securing the Dardanelles. The loss increased war-weariness in Russia and weakened both Briand's government in France and that of Asquith in Britain. Confined to Moldavia, the Romanians attempted a new offensive in July 1917 but, by December, had all but exhausted their military resources. An armistice was concluded with the Germans in March 1918 followed by the Treaty of Bucharest, taking Romania out of the war, on 7 May 1918.[27]

Greece, too, was minded from the beginning to join the Entente or, more specifically, the Greek prime minister, Eleutherios Venizelos, was so minded, since Greek opinion was evenly divided between intervention and neutrality. The Entente, however, rejected Venizelos's comprehensive offer of alliance in August 1914 because they feared it might immediately bring Bulgaria and Ottoman Turkey into the war, and because the Russians had little intention of becoming indebted to a power which had its own claims on the Bosphorus. Venizelos saw intervention as a way of securing Greece's grandiose irredentist ambitions. The so-called *Megali* (Great) Idea envisaged uniting all territories inhabited by Greeks and establishing control of Constantinople, Greek successes in the Balkan Wars having increased the national land area by almost 70 per cent and the population by 2 million. However, King Constantine of Greece, who was married to the Kaiser's sister, and the Greek military were concerned at Greece's potential vulnerability, especially from attack by Bulgaria. Nor were they convinced that Greece could successfully hold down the large area of Asia Minor around Smyrna (Izmir), being offered by the Entente, in the face of likely Turkish hostility after the war. Thus opened the 'national schism' within Greek political life.

When Constantine declined to assist the Allied offensive against the Dardanelles, Venizelos resigned on 6 March 1915 but, following new elections, was back in office in June to resume his duel with the king. When Bulgaria began to mobilise in September for its war against Serbia, Greece was in theory obliged to assist Serbia under a treaty of May 1913. On 24 September

1915, Venizelos promptly invited the British and French to land troops at Salonika although, publicly, the Anglo-French request to do so was refused.

Venizelos had secured the king's approval of his request to the Entente for troops but Constantine changed his mind on 3 October, prompting Venizelos's resignation two days later. The British offered Cyprus as a further inducement to the Greeks but this was refused. Nonetheless, the Anglo-French landing went ahead and, by January 1916, with the Serbs in full retreat, German and Bulgarian forces confronted the Entente at Salonika. Troops from both belligerents were now on Greek soil and, indeed, when the Greeks declined to permit the Serbian army to be evacuated to Corfu, French troops simply occupied the island. A pro-Venizelist coup was mounted in Salonika in August 1916 in the name of a National Defence Movement. Venizelos himself established a provisional government on his native Crete and, in its name, declared war on both Germany and Bulgaria on 23 November 1916. The Entente powers recognised the provisional government in December 1916, imposing a blockade on mainland Greece after being repulsed in an attack upon Athens. Subsequently, they forced Constantine's abdication in favour of his second son, Alexander. Venizelos returned to Athens on 27 June 1917 and promptly declared war officially on behalf of all Greece.

Even before becoming involved in the war, Greek forces had been deployed to pursue territorial claims in Albania. Created only in 1912–13 and policed by an international peacekeeping force until August 1914, Albania was fated like Poland to be something of a battleground of other powers. Greek and Italian forces moved into Albanian territory in October 1914. Montenegrin and Serbian forces then occupied parts of Albania in June 1915, with French forces occupying the area around Korca at the end of the year as the Greeks withdrew. The fall of Serbia resulted in the replacement of Serb forces by Bulgarians, while Austro-Hungarian forces forced out the Montenegrins in January 1916, at which point Albania technically declared war on Austria-Hungary. The French gave their part of Albania a degree of autonomy in December 1916, but took over full control once more when Greece joined the Entente.[28]

The last European power whose entry into the war should be noted is Portugal. As in Greece, opinion was divided on whether to support Britain as Portugal's 'oldest ally' or to remain neutral. Neutrality in itself, however, might be regarded as assisting the Entente through making available Portuguese resources and those of other neutrals. Initially, government was in the hands of the pro-German general, Pimenta de Castro, until he was overthrown in May 1915. Britain had offered to assist the defence of Portuguese colonies in return for the ability to move forces through them. When the Portuguese responded to a British request to seize those German vessels which had been in effect interned in Portuguese ports, the Germans responded by declaring war on Portugal on 9 March 1916. On 15 July 1916 the Entente 'cordially invited' Portugal to make a further contribution to the Allied cause and a small Portuguese expeditionary force was sent to the Western Front, where it was known to British troops as 'The Pork and Beans'. Portuguese policy was greatly influenced by a wish to re-establish Portugal's international status and clearly differentiate the country's role from that of neighbouring Spain, which was periodically believed to be harbouring ambitions to intervene to restore the Portuguese monarchy.[29]

Distant waters

It remains to discuss the expansion of the war beyond the confines of Europe and its colonies. The Japanese government of Count Shigenobu Okuma entered the war almost immediately on 23 August 1914. This was not simply a result of the British asking for naval assistance to hunt down German commerce raiders in the Pacific under the terms of the Anglo-Japanese treaty but because the Japanese government was concerned with security. It envisaged a land threat from Russia to its acquisitions from the Russo-Japanese War such as the Korean peninsula and a maritime threat from the United States. While annexation of Chinese territory was not apparently intended at this early stage, the Japanese were clearly mindful of American interest in the preservation of China and the advantage to be accrued from acting within the Entente. Moreover, as the war was expected to be short, Japan needed to act quickly to acquire international advantage and seize the opportunity presented by what Kaoru Inoue, one of the influential *genro* (elders) who advised the emperor, characterised as a 'providential chance'. It was also clear that there was resentment of Germany's attitudes towards Japan, the Germans having joined with France and Russia in forcing Japan to give up some of her gains at the time of the Sino-Japanese War of 1894–95.

There was expectation on the part of Britain that Japanese action would be strictly limited to assisting in the protection of shipping from German commerce raiders. The Japanese did not wish to limit their role and, as a result, Britain in effect withdrew its request for assistance since it had not envisaged Japanese occupation of Germany's Pacific possessions. The Japanese ultimatum to Germany, sent without prior consultation with the British, demanded the withdrawal or surrender of German vessels in eastern waters and the ceding of the German mandated territory of Kiaochow in China. With no reply being received, Japan declared war, at once blockaded Tsingtao, and, using the excuse of the need to hunt down the German East Asian squadron commanded by Count Maximilian von Spee, moved to occupy German islands in Micronesia and the Pacific. Subsequently, the Japanese were to send a naval squadron to assist in patrolling the Mediterranean in 1917 and to participate in the Allied intervention against the Bolsheviks in Russia in the following year.[30]

The war had a significant impact upon Japan's economy. The level of exports such as cotton and silk to existing markets such as China and the United States not only increased dramatically but Japan also reached new markets such as Australia, India and the Dutch East Indies. Shipping shortages resulted in reduced imports into Japan and stimulated domestic production in areas such as engineering, shipbuilding, chemicals, and iron and steel. Japan had been industrialising rapidly in the pre-war period and the war further contributed to the emergence of a pattern in which Japanese trade consisted primarily of a high level of exported manufactures and imported raw materials. Japan ran up large balance of payments surpluses and emerged from the war in the short term as a net creditor.[31]

Australia feared Japanese ambitions in the Pacific and had been deeply unsettled by the Anglo-Japanese alliance. On the outbreak of war, Australia responded to British requests by despatching its navy to search for Spee's two cruisers, SMS *Scharnhorst* and SMS *Gneisenau*, and by preparing the Australian Naval and Military Expeditionary Force (ANMEF) to seize German radio stations in New Guinea, on Yap in the Palau islands and on Nauru. A contingent from New Zealand was also despatched to Samoa. The Japanese, however, seized Yap with the rest of German Micronesia in October 1914 and, while Okuma was initially prepared to give up Yap to an Australian garrison, domestic opposition in Japan caused him to retract the offer. The British Cabinet was itself divided over policy regarding the Pacific islands, but made it clear to the Australians in November 1914 that the Japanese would not be dispossessed and the matter would be left until after the war.[32]

German rule in the Pacific had been relatively relaxed, with the result that the military administrations imposed by Australia, New Zealand and Japan in 1914, and perpetuated after the war, marked a distinct change for Melanesians and Micronesians. Generally, the new administrations were far less willing to accept indigenous customs and practices and, in retrospect, there was some nostalgia for German rule. By the end of the war, Melanesians were trying to get the Japanese replaced by another power, while Nauruans and Samoans were voicing increasing dissatisfaction with dominion control. Some Samoans, indeed, wanted unification with American Samoa. Elsewhere in the Pacific, there were also signs of unrest. New Caledonia rose against French military conscription in 1917, while there had also been disturbances in the New Hebrides in 1916. There were to be disturbances in the Gilbert Islands and on Fiji in 1918, and riots by returning servicemen on the Cook Islands in March 1919.[33]

Ironically, whereas Japan had not posed a direct threat to Australia prior to 1914, the Japanese wartime advance into the Pacific made the threat a reality. The principal Japanese interest, however, remained in Asia. Whatever the initial Japanese intentions towards China, the presentation by the Japanese government of the Twenty-one Demands to China in January 1915 extended Japanese influence over a variety of trade outlets and sources of raw materials and included the renewal, for a further 99 years, of leases in Manchuria first acquired in 1905. This left the Japanese in a strong economic position.

China itself was gravely weakened as a result of its revolution in 1911, which had led to incipient civil war and 'warlordism'. It initially adopted neutrality in order to try to prevent the war spreading to China by virtue of the European presence there. The Entente had favoured pressing China into war against Germany but this had foundered on Japanese opposition. Nonetheless, the Chinese Foreign Ministry entered a contract with the French in May 1916 to supply up to 50,000 Chinese labourers for use in France. The British followed suit three months later, although the first of the 96,000 labourers raised by the British in China left for France only in January 1917.

China's weakness in the face of the Twenty-one Demands had made the Chinese all too aware of the need to secure some representation at a post-war peace conference in order to submit their dispute with the Japanese to international arbitration. Accordingly, in February 1917, when the United Sates circulated a note inviting neutrals to sever diplomatic relations with Germany as a gesture of protest against the introduction of unrestricted submarine warfare, the Chinese saw a means of securing China's own interests vis-à-vis Japan by enlisting American support. The Chinese government therefore decided to sever diplomatic links with Germany on 10 March 1917.

The entry of the United States into the war in April 1917, however, posed a particular problem since it formally allied the Americans with Japan, making it even more important to secure China a seat at the peace conference. An internal political crisis delayed the matter of Chinese entry but the success of the prime minister, General Tuan Chi-jui, in ousting the more cautious president, Li Yuan-hung, brought formal declaration of war on Germany and Austria-Hungary on 14 August 1917. Japanese sensitivities were assuaged by the Lansing–Ishii Agreement on 2 November 1917, by which the American Secretary of State, Robert Lansing, in signing an agreement with the Japanese ambassador to Washington, Kikujiro Ishii, recognised that Japan had 'special interests' in China.

Equally aware of the dangers of neutrality in the event of victory by the Entente, Siam (Thailand) had also declared war on Germany and Austria-Hungary on 22 July 1917, despatching approximately 1,300 men to France in June 1918.[34]

Like China, the United States had also initially seen its aim as preserving what President Woodrow Wilson interpreted as neutrality. On the one hand, Wilson was very much an idealist and believed in international arbitration as a means of settling international disputes. He was also concerned not to jeopardise the progress of his modest domestic social reform programme by entry into the war. At least publicly, Wilson endorsed the view held by many Americans that no vital American interests were threatened by the outbreak of war, remarking that the conflict was one 'with which we have nothing to do, whose causes cannot touch us'. On the other hand, however, Wilson had concluded that long-term American interests would not be served by a German victory.

Wilson clearly wished to ensure a degree of national unity on foreign policy issues. Yet, the United States was a polyglot society in which national loyalties were still evident among differing immigrant groups. Those of German, Irish, Jewish and Polish origin were generally pro-German, through hatred of either Britain or Russia, but many Americans favoured the Entente since there were the obvious cultural affinities with Britain, the sentimental attachment to France for its role in American independence, and admiration for Belgian resistance to German aggression. Anglo-American relations had improved considerably after the Venezuelan dispute of 1895–96. By contrast, there were exaggerated Americans fears of German ambitions in the Pacific and the Caribbean.[35]

Nevertheless, while it was recognised that Germany was the aggressor, Britain posed the most potent threat to American interests as a maritime power intent on imposing blockade on the Central Powers. The Anglo-American War of 1812–14 had centred on the issue of the rights of neutral shipping and the British role in supporting Confederate commerce raiders during the American Civil War had resulted in the long-running dispute over the 'Alabama' claims. More recently, British attempts to impose economic blockade on the Boer republics during the South African War had resulted in renewed Anglo-American tension, and a determination on all sides to review maritime law with regard to belligerent and neutral rights. In February 1909, the Declaration of London saw a measure of agreement on the definition of contraband. The British were prepared to surrender the concept of 'continuous voyage', by which even a vessel sailing between neutral ports might be stopped on the assumption that the goods being carried were intended ultimately for conveyance to the enemy. In the event, however, fears that too much was being conceded persuaded the

House of Lords to reject legislation ratifying the declaration in December 1911.[36]

The British Cabinet reversed its pre-war policy by the Order in Council of 20 August 1914 and, without formally announcing it as such, imposed an economic blockade on the Central Powers which clearly repudiated the restrictions of belligerent rights implicit in the Declaration of London. The definition of contraband was steadily extended to include materials such as foodstuffs, which had previously not been regarded as either absolute or conditional contraband, with the Royal Navy not only stopping shipping on the high seas, but also forcing vessels into port for examination. The British similarly extended the definition of continuous voyage, compelling ships headed for neutral ports to stop in Britain to obtain detail of safe passage. Shipping was also impeded by British mining of the North Sea, which was declared a military area on 3 November 1914.

Wilson did not believe neutral rights sufficiently important to justify breaking with the Entente and was ever mindful that, in 1812, the United States had been forced into a war in which it had in effect sided with tyranny in the shape of Napoleonic France. Wilson therefore declined to confront the British openly and chose instead to make remonstrations through his Anglophile ambassador in London, Walter Hines Page.[37]

There was thus a considerable element of self-delusion in Wilson's belief that he had not compromised the neutrality or the interests of the United States. The *de facto* acceptance of the blockade by the United States meant, in the words of John Coogan, that Wilson's administration 'had become a partner, and not always a silent partner, in the Allied economic campaign to strangle Germany'.[38]

The war took on a new dimension for the Americans with the declaration by the German government on 18 February 1915 that the waters around Britain were a war zone, in which enemy shipping was to be sunk on sight rather than being stopped and identified first. Indeed, the Germans warned that, since Allied merchantmen might fly neutral flags, neutral shipping should avoid the designated zone altogether. Britain responded with another Order in Council on 11 March 1915, which made all neutral trade subject to confiscation. Again, there was a contrast in Wilson's response. A protest to the German government was despatched within six days but the response to the British retaliatory action took a month. Inevitably, neutral ships were sunk although Wilson chose to act cautiously over the loss of the British steamship *Falaba* in March, in which an American life was lost. Wilson had spoken of holding the Germans to 'strict accountability' but inclined at this stage more towards the non-interventionist policy of his Secretary of State, William Jennings Bryan, who opined that Americans took passage on belligerent ships at their own risk.

Then, on 7 May 1915, the British passenger liner, *Lusitania*, was sunk by *U-20* off the Irish coast with the loss of 128 Americans among the 1,198 who died. This produced an American note to the German government which, while representing neither an ultimatum nor a threat, made it clear that an unrestricted submarine campaign was unacceptable. It was sufficiently strong to force the resignation of Bryan, who was replaced by the counsellor from the State Department, Lansing. Like Wilson's policy adviser, Edward M. House, Lansing was pro-Entente.

The German reply was highly abrasive but the strong American reaction to the sinking of the liner *Arabic* on 19 August, in which two Americans died, then brought a German declaration that passenger ships would not be attacked without warning. Not surprisingly, the Germans believed that Wilson should also take a firm line against the British blockade. Wilson did send a harsher note on blockade policy to the British government in October 1915. The British delayed their reply but took particular exception to the naive suggestion by Lansing in February 1916, which was welcomed by the Germans, that the British should agree not to arm merchant ships in return for a German promise not to sink unarmed ships without warning.[39]

With the sinking of an unarmed ferry, the *Sussex*, in the Channel in March 1916, costing four American lives, there was a strong public reaction against Germany in the United States, to which Wilson responded with a further note. In line with their generally inept propaganda machine in the United States, the Germans initially claimed that they had not torpedoed the *Sussex* but another vessel at the same time and place.[40] The affair, however, brought another German pledge of restraint on 4 May 1916. This was despite the belief of the German military leadership that American intervention in the war could not be in enough strength sufficiently quickly to offset the advantages from an intensification of the submarine war, and that United States opinion could be neutralised by German propaganda. British propaganda was rather more successful. The Bryce report in May 1915, for example, had made considerable capital out of such incidents as the German execution of the British nurse Edith Cavell in Belgium. As a well respected former British ambassador in Washington, the attachment of Bryce's name to the report brought credibility to the otherwise doubtful accounts of German atrocities.[41]

German involvement in Mexico also raised new tensions in US–German relations.[42] At the same time, however, the temperature of Anglo-American relations was similarly raised by the British suppression of the Easter Rising. In July 1916 the British also blacklisted American firms believed to be doing business with Germany.

Wilson was increasingly convinced that he could only keep America out of the war by ending it, hence his increased efforts at mediation in the winter of 1916–17, marked by the formulation of his Peace Note to all belligerents on 18 December 1916, calling for a peace without annexations and one founded on equality, self-determination, freedom of the seas, limitation of armament and a permanent international organisation. By this time, however, American investment in Entente contracts and the extension of loans to the Entente was such that the possibility of peace led to the worst fall on the New York stock market for fourteen years. It must be noted, however, that American financial investment in the Entente was secured on American or Canadian collateral and would not have been at risk even if the Entente had lost the war.[43]

On 1 February 1917, the Germans announced the revival of unrestricted submarine warfare around the British Isles and in the Mediterranean, although one American steamer per week would be permitted through the war zone if clearly identified and carrying no contraband. This immediately prompted the breaking of diplomatic relations by the United States. More American lives were lost when the British *Laconia* was torpedoed on 26 February, followed by the publication of the Zimmermann telegram of 19 January. This instructed the German ambassador to propose an alliance to the Mexican government, the Mexicans being promised the return of those territories it had lost to the United States in 1848 in the event of German victory. The British had intercepted the telegram and passed it to Page.

Four more American vessels were sunk in March and the Entente cause also received a fillip through the abdication of the Tsar on 15 March 1917, since the new Russian provisional government could be regarded as sufficiently democratic to remove any moral objections to American participation in the Entente. Wilson finally requested a declaration of war from Congress on 2 April on the grounds that the world 'must be made safe for democracy', the resolution passing the Senate by 82 votes to 6 on 4 April and the House of Representatives, by 373 to 50, two days later. Those opposed to American entry were mostly Democrats and Republicans representing the agrarian west and south, despite the implied threat of the Zimmermann telegram to their interests. Their opposition, however, was partly explained by the fact that there was a large German vote in these regions. Thus, the United States came into the war not as an ally of the Entente powers, but as an 'associated' power.[44]

The economics of belligerency and neutrality

American entry into the war posed immediate questions for Latin America. American influence was all the stronger from the fact that there had been a substantial US Marine presence on Haiti since July 1915 and in the Dominican Republic since November 1916, while a legation guard had been stationed in Nicaragua since the withdrawal of larger Marine forces in January 1913. The United States retained the ability to intervene in Panama to enforce order or sanitation in the terminal cities of the canal zone while a second military occupation of Cuba had ceased only in January 1909.

From the beginning of the war, most Latin American countries had been broadly sympathetic to the Entente. All, however, had declared neutrality. Indeed, the Latin Americans were confronted both with the raids on British shipping off the west coast of the subcontinent by von Spee's squadron, until it was destroyed by the Royal Navy off the Falkland Isles on 8 December 1914, and also the blockade imposed by the Royal Navy on non-British shipping using east coast ports. At the initiative of Argentina, commerce between Latin American countries was declared to be coastal trade even if the ships were flying belligerents' flags. In the case of Peru, coastal trade was escorted by Peruvian naval vessels, while Chile shipped some nitrate exports in its own naval vessels. Co-operation between Latin American states, however, was limited by traditional rivalries.

With American entry to the war, Panama and Cuba joined the Entente on 7 April 1917 and declared war on Germany, though not doing so against Austria-Hungary until December. Nine other states broke off diplomatic relations with Germany: Bolivia (13 April 1917), Costa Rica (21 September 1917), the Dominican Republic, Ecuador (7 November 1917), Guatemala (27 April 1917), Honduras (17 May 1917), Nicaragua (19 May 1917), Peru (6 October 1917), and Uruguay (7 October 1917). In the case of Peru, the German sinking of a Peruvian vessel, the *Lorton*, was cited by way of justification. The German recourse to unrestricted submarine warfare was also instrumental in bringing Brazil into the war on 26 October 1917. A Brazilian medical unit was despatched to France, a detachment of airforce pilots underwent training in Britain and a Brazilian naval squadron proceeded to West African waters on anti-submarine duties.

In 1918, five more Caribbean and Latin American states declared war on Germany, four of which had already broken off diplomatic relations in the previous year: Guatemala (23 April 1918), Nicaragua (8 May 1918), Costa Rica (23 May 1918), and Honduras (19 July 1918). The fifth was Haiti (12 July 1918). In a bizarre twist, the Onondago American Indian nation also declared war on Germany on 31 July 1918. In Africa, Liberia, which had been created by the United States in 1821 as a refuge for freed slaves, had also followed the American lead in declaring war on Germany on 4 August 1917.[45]

Generally, however, the impact of the war upon Latin America was economic. Just as the New York stock exchange was closed for almost four months at the start of the war, so exchanges and banks closed throughout Latin America in August 1914 and, as in Europe, workers were laid off or dismissed. The reason was that Latin American states were highly dependent upon foreign capital investment, foreign shipping and insurance, foreign imports, and access to export markets for primary products such as Argentinian wheat and maize, Brazilian coffee and rubber, Chilean nitrates, and Peruvian copper and sugar. The initial economic uncertainty with regard to export markets was compounded by the same shortage of shipping that also affected the United States, and by the virtual suspension of credit as British banks began to call in long-term loans. Britain's suspension of coal exports, on which Latin American extraction industries and transport heavily depended, also had an immediate effect.

By 1915, the export trade had begun to recover, but imports were considerably curtailed throughout the war and the lack of such vital imported commodities as coal impeded any wider import-substitution industrialisation. Coupled with increasing inflation, not least higher food prices, and falling real wages, the lack of growth in domestic consumer industry helped to fuel rising industrial militancy between 1917 and 1919.

In turn, the recognition of Latin America's economic vulnerability and the increasing economic manipulation by the Entente through control of such areas as shipping, purchasing and blacklisting of firms trading with the Central Powers, fuelled a kind of cultural nationalism. Such nationalism was given further stimulus by the way in which the United States increased its regional economic dominance at the expense of Britain and Germany during the war, both in terms of trade and finance. While Britain's share of Latin American trade declined from 29 per cent to 20 per cent, that of the United States increased from 18 per cent to 42 per cent.[46]

While the United States and Brazil had been persuaded to join the war by the German imposition of unrestricted submarine warfare, there were other states that remained neutral and were affected equally by the economic blockade of the Central Powers by the Entente. Most directly affected were Denmark, the Netherlands, Norway, Sweden and Switzerland. Denmark was self-sufficient in foodstuffs but needed to import raw materials, while Norway and the Netherlands were self-sufficient in neither foodstuffs nor raw materials. Switzerland, Denmark and the Netherlands were also vulnerable to external pressure from their geographical proximity to Germany, the sea, or both.

Generally, agreements, whether formal or on the basis of trust, were reached with the Entente whereby imported goods would not be re-exported to the Central Powers. The Netherlands, which declined a defensive alliance with Britain in August 1914, established the Nederlandsche Oversee Trustmaatschappij (NOT; Netherlands Overseas Trust Company) in

November 1914 to regulate Dutch imports. Only in the case of Denmark was there initial resistance to accepting the demands of the Entente and this resistance crumbled in January 1915, following threats by Britain to seize Danish imports. Neutrals remained free to export their own products to the Central Powers: in the case of the Netherlands, the entire export surplus amounting to at least 1 million tons of food reached Germany in 1915. Dutch banks became a conduit for American financial loans to Germany. British exports and re-exports through neutral ports were also reaching the enemy.

With the intensification of the blockade in March 1915, however, new agreements were reached with Denmark, the Netherlands and Switzerland, extending Allied control not only over neutral imports but also over exports of neutral products to the Central Powers containing more than 25 per cent imported raw materials or semi-manufactures. With Norway and, particularly, Sweden, agreements were reached on particular commodities. In the case of Norway, these included fish, copper and pyrites. Norway was broadly sympathetic to the Entente, but there was some sympathy in Sweden for the Central Powers. The Entente, however, needed Swedish iron ore, ball bearings and timber as much as the Germans and, in addition, there was a need to keep open a vital supply route to Russia once Turkey had closed the Dardanelles. As a result, the Swedes were permitted to export as much to Germany as the Entente sent to Russia through Sweden until the fall of Russia released the Entente from the necessity of accommodating Swedish sensitivities.

Where commodities were not covered by the agreements, the Entente purchased the export surplus. With the entry of the United States into the war, there was an attempt to restrict virtually all exports to the European neutrals and a further round of negotiation. In the case of the Netherlands, negotiation was not actually concluded until after the armistice although the Entente had seized much of the Dutch merchant fleet in March 1918. By this time, however, many of the neutrals were more concerned with the prospect of the spread of revolution.[47]

As epitomised by the contradictory attitudes of King Alfonso XIII, Spanish opinion was divided as to the merits of the protagonists. Spaniards recognised the economic links with both Britain and France and their liberal demo-cratic systems. They disliked, however, French anti-clericalism, the refuge Spanish anarchists had found in France in the past and, especially, the British hold on Gibraltar. Equally, there was admiration for German sci-ence and efficiency, with both clerics and the military broadly sympathetic to Germany, but there were less direct links with Germany and a lingering resentment of German policy towards Spain in the past. In many respects, however, most Spaniards adopted an attitude of what has been characterised as 'Sanchopancisme', but benefiting from the orders placed by the Entente for commodities such as iron, wolfram and lead.[48]

In global terms, the increasing economic dominance of the United States was highly significant, the process beginning while the United States was still a neutral. By 1914, the United States had liquidated much of its foreign debt and was poised to become a net international creditor. The outbreak of the war was certainly seen as an opportunity to break into new markets such as Latin America, especially as the Panama Canal opened for traffic in August 1914. The difficulty was the small size of the American merchant fleet and the way in which Britain had soon drawn in no less than 95 per cent of the world's merchant tonnage to carry its own war trade across the Atlantic. The Entente lodged effective objection to a tentative American plan to purchase German ships bottled up in American ports and, of course, the blockade of Germany imposed delay and disruption on American trade. Moreover, just as the German plans for *Mitteleuropa* threatened to exclude future American trade from Europe in the event of German victory, so the Allied economic conference at Paris in January 1916 threatened similar American exclusion through the creation of a comparable post-war trading bloc.

At the same time, however, neutrality reaped economic rewards through the increasing reliance of the Entente upon American raw materials and manufactured goods. Indeed, even the shipping shortage benefited the United States economy since it forced the Allies to eschew purchases from more distant primary producers such as Australia and Argentina. Substantial profits were made in the export boom, the United States merchant fleet growing to 40 per cent of the size of the British merchant marine by 1918.[49]

Yet more important was the increasing Entente dependence upon American credit. Initially, Britain and France used their gold reserves to purchase war needs. As these reserves were depleted, so they acquired dollar-denominated securities, which could be liquidated in the United States without further increasing their negative trade balances either through dollar exchange or as collateral for loans. By 1917, the United States had become a new international creditor: Britain owed the New York bank J. P. Morgan alone US$400 billion by June 1917, having acted as banker for its Allies largely on the strength of American loans and having guaranteed French, Russian and Italian purchases in the United States.

The process culminated in a major sterling crisis in December 1916 and the effective refusal of the American government to maintain the sterling–dollar exchange rate by advising member banks of the Federal Reserve System not to buy short-term foreign securities. Anglo-American relations were strained by the cool reception the British had accorded the president's mediation attempts and Wilson appears to have wanted to apply further diplomatic pressure for peace. It has been argued that a weaker pound would not have been seriously damaging to the British war effort and that, in any case, Britain's leverage as a major debtor made it all but impossible for the United States not to maintain sterling at a reasonable level without endangering its own financial institutions. Nonetheless, this was not how it was perceived at the time and the United States found the threat to sterling a useful bargaining counter.

At times during the early months of 1917, until American entry into the war, Britain occasionally had barely more than a week's money in hand to meet American interest payments. Even after their entry into the war, the Americans did not, as the British expected, take on the full financing of Entente purchases in the United States, although this was partly owing to the unexpectedly heavy demands being made on the United States Treasury for war funding. By July 1917, Britain had reached the point at which no more gold could be sent to the United States without destroying the whole basis of British credit. Subsequently, in February 1918, the British Treasury had to accept the subrogation of the rights of its collateral to the United States. Indeed, it was not until 1923 that the United States released US$300 million worth of British securities deposited as collateral against war loans under the subrogation agreement. Even then, Britain was forced to accept the American schedule for debt repayment. New York had passed London as the world's financial centre, although Britain's declining economic independence owed as much to the changes in the international economy generally as to American policy.[50]

Overall, the United States increased its share of world trade from 11 per cent to 15 per cent, though many trading customers were economically exhausted and required substantial American investment in order to sustain the volume of trade generated by the war. Europeans had some leverage in responding to suspension of American loans by cancelling contracts in 1919, but the fact that the United States itself was a major producer of primary products meant that it did not play the same mediatorial role in the world economy as Britain had done before 1914. Since the United States was far more important to the world economy than the world economy was to the United States, the result was that the international economic system was far less stable after 1918.[51]

In fact, the volume of international trade was only just beginning to attain its pre-war level by 1929, at which point the onset of global economic depression promptly cancelled out the recovery. Clearly, war resulted in considerable economic costs, although the exact calculation of direct and indirect costs are difficult to make. In 1919, John Maynard Keynes calculated that the material damage of the war amounted to £2.1 billion in the case of the Entente, excluding Russia. Similarly, in 1920, E. L. Bogart calculated a total direct and indirect cost of US$338 billion. This was achieved by a process which included placing a monetary value on each life lost whereby, for example, a dead British or American soldier was a far greater loss to the economy than a dead Serb or Turk. Another calculation after the war was in terms of the delay in levels of production so that, for example, it was suggested that, but for the war, the level of global food production recorded in 1929 would have been reached in 1923, that of industrial goods in 1924, and that of raw materials in 1927.

In fact, quantitative evaluations may not be especially helpful since structural changes are more significant. In this regard, it can be said that the Great War resulted in global depreciation of currency values, with significant repercussions for currency stability in the inter-war period. The gold standard, which represented a fixed exchange rate pegging currencies to the value of gold and to each other, was in effect abandoned in 1914. For all practical purposes, it was not revived so that there was no real post-war system of fixed exchange rates. There was also what has been described as a decentralisation of the global economy. Europe's share of world production fell from 43 per cent in 1913 to 34 per cent by 1923, and its share of world trade from 59 per cent to 50 per cent. Since the principal beneficiary was the United States, the shift in economic gravity remained with an existing dominant industrial power, although Europeans were also to be challenged by newly industrialising states claiming a share in the market. Another legacy of the war was a complex web of international debt whereby, for example, Allied governments owed both the United States and Britain over US$7 billion each by 1918, while Britain's share of the debt to the United States was US$3.6 billion.[52]

In terms of international political consequences, the defeat of Germany and, especially, Austria-Hungary, together with the collapse of Tsarist Russia would result in considerable changes of frontier. The redrawing of the map of Europe was also to reflect the widening of the war in the Balkans. Equally, the defeat of Turkey in the war was substantially to redraw the map of the Middle East as well. The division of the former German colonial empire was to have a wide impact, not least in the Pacific. Thus, a European conflict had rapidly grown into a global war. The escalation had resulted equally from the strategic aims of the original belligerents and from the calculation of self-interest among the smaller powers.

Notes and references

1. Wolfgang Petter, 'Der Kampf um die deutschen Kolonien', in Michalka, ed., *Ertse Weltkrieg*, pp.392–412; Eric Grove, 'The First Shots of the Great War:

The Anglo-French Conquest of Togo, 1914', *Army Quarterly and Defence Journal* 106 (1976), pp.308–23; Jean Nouzille, 'La campagne de Cameroun, 1914–16', *RIHM* 63 (1985), pp.9–20. Other general accounts include Charles Burdick, *The Japanese Siege of Tsingtao: World War I in Asia* (Hamden, CN, 1976); Edwin Hoyt, *The Fall of Tsingtao* (London, 1975); Brian Gardner, *German East* (London, 1963); Leonard Mosley, *Duel for Kilimanjaro* (London, 1963); Charles Miller, *The Battle for the Bundu: The First World War in East Africa* (London, 1974); Byron Farwell, *The Great War in Africa, 1914–18* (New York, 1987).

2. A. J. Stockwell, 'The War and the British Empire', in Turner, ed., *Britain and First World War*, p.37.

3. Michael McKernan, *The Australian People and the Great War* (Melbourne, 1980), p.15; John Robertson, *Anzac and Empire: The Tragedy and Glory of Gallipoli* (London, 1990), pp.15–17; E. M. Andrews, *The Anzac Illusion: Anglo-Australian Relations during World War I* (Cambridge, 1993), pp.6–7; Avner Offer, *The First World War: An Agrarian Interpretation*, 2nd edn (Oxford, 1991), pp.164–214; Judith Smart, '"Poor Little Belgium" and Australian Popular Support for War, 1914', *W&S* 12 (1994), pp.23–42.

4. Andrews, *Anzac Illusion*, pp.43–5; J. N. I. Dawes and L. L. Robson, *Citizen to Soldier: Australia before the Great War. Recollections of Members of the First AIF* (Melbourne, 1977), p.66; L. L. Robson, 'The Origin and Character of the First AIF, 1914–18: Some Statistical Evidence', *HS* 15 (1973), pp.737–49; Joan Beaumont, 'The Politics of a Divided Society', in Joan Beaumont, ed., *Australia's War, 1914–18* (St Leonards, 1995), pp.35–63; Bill Gammage, *The Broken Years: Australian Soldiers in the Great War*, 2nd edn (Ringwood, Victoria, 1975), pp.19–20, 283; A. D. Gilbert, 'The Conscription Referenda, 1916–17: The Impact of the Irish Crisis', *HS* 14 (1969), pp.54–72; McKernan, *Australian People and Great War*, pp.4, 11, 38, 197; idem, 'Catholics, Conscription and Archbishop Mannix', *HS* 17 (1977), pp.299–314; Bobbie Oliver, *War and Peace in Western Australia: The Social and Political Impact of the Great War, 1914–26* (Nedlands, 1995), pp.90–125; Ian Beckett, 'The Nation in Arms, 1914–1918', in Ian Beckett and Keith Simpson, eds, *A Nation in Arms: A Social Study of the British Army in the First World War* (Manchester, 1985), p.20; Robertson, *Anzac and Empire*, pp.31–2; K. S. Inglis, 'Anzac and the Australian Military Tradition', *RIHM* 72 (1990), pp.1–24 [also in John Lack, ed., *Anzac Remembered: Selected Writings of K. S. Inglis* (Melbourne, 1998), pp.120–47]; idem, 'The Anzac Tradition', in Lack, ed., *Anzac Remembered*, pp.18–42.

5. Ian McGibbon, *The Path to Gallipoli: Defending New Zealand, 1840–1915* (Wellington, 1991), pp.171–80; Paul Baker, *King and Country Call: New Zealanders, Conscription and the Great War* (Auckland, 1988); P. S. O'Connor, 'The Recruitment of Maori Soldiers, 1914–18', *Political Science* 19 (1967), pp.62–83; Bill Nasson, 'A Great Divide: Popular Response to the Great War in South Africa', *W&S* 12 (1994), pp.47–64; N. G. Garson, 'South Africa and World

War I', *JICH* 8 (1979), pp.68–85; T. R. H. Davenport, 'The South African Rebellion, 1914', *EHR* 78 (1963), pp.73–94; S. B. Spies, 'The Outbreak of the First World War and the Botha Government', *South African Historical Journal* 1 (1969), pp.47–57; Peter McLaughlin, *Ragtime Soldiers: The Rhodesian Experience in the First World War* (Bulawayo, 1980), p.140.

6. Robert C. Brown, 'Sir Robert Borden, the Great War and Anglo-Canadian Relations', in J. S. Moir, ed., *Character and Circumstance: Essays in Honour of Donald Grant Creighton* (Toronto, 1970), pp.201–24; idem, 'Sir Robert Borden and Canada's War Aims', in Barry Hunt and Adrian Preston, eds, *War Aims and Strategic Policy in the Great War* (London and Totowa, NJ, 1977), pp.55–66; Desmond Morton, 'The Military Problem of an Unmilitary People', *RIHM* 51 (1982), pp.10, 17; idem, 'The Canadian Military Experience in the First World War, 1914–18', in R. J. Q. Adams, ed., *The Great War, 1914–18: Essays on the Military, Political and Social History of the First World War* (London, 1990), pp.79–98; Robert C. Brown and Donald Loveridge, 'Unrequited Faith: Recruiting the CEF, 1914–18', *RIHM* 51 (1982), pp.53–79; R. Matthew Bray, 'Fighting as an Ally: The English-Canadian Patriotic Response to the Great War', *CHR* 61, (1980), pp.141–68; Paul Maroney, ' "The Great Adventure": The Context and Ideology of Recruiting in Ontario, 1914–17', *CHR* 27 (1996), pp.62–98; J. L. Granatstein and J. M. Hitsman, *Broken Promises: A History of Conscription in Canada* (Toronto, 1977), pp.22–104; Réal Bélanger, 'Albert Sévigny et la Participation des Canadiens Français à la Grande Guerre', *RIHM* 51 (1982), pp.80–108. On the Canadian experience generally, see Desmond Morton and J. L. Granatstein, *Marching to Armageddon: Canadians and the Great War, 1914–19* (Toronto, 1989).

7. Jeffrey Greenhut, 'The Imperial Reserve: The Indian Corps on the Western Front, 1914–1915', *JICH* 12 (1983), pp.54–73; David Omissi, *The Sepoy and the Raj: The Indian Army, 1860–1940* (London, 1994), pp.38–40, 123–5; D. C. Ellinwood, 'Ethnicity in a Colonial Asian Army: British Policy, War and the Indian Army, 1914–18', in D. C. Ellinwood and Cynthia Enloe, eds, *Ethnicity and the Military in Asia* (New Brunswick, NJ, 1981), pp.89–144; Julia Brown, 'War and the Colonial Relationship: Britain, India and the War of 1914–18', in Foot, ed. *W&S*, pp.85–106; S. D. Pradhan, 'Indians in the East African Campaign: A Case Study of Indian Experience in the First World War', in D. C. Ellinwood and S. D. Pradhan, eds, *India and World War I* (Manohar, India, 1978), pp.69–74; T. A. Heathcote, *The Military in British India: The Development of British Land Forces in South Asia, 1600–1947* (Manchester, 1995), pp.224–8; Tan Tai-Yong, 'An Imperial Home Front: Punjab and the First World War', *JMilH* 64 (2000), pp.371–410.

8. C. L. Joseph, 'The British West Indies Regiment, 1914–1918', *Journal of Caribbean History* 2 (1971), pp.94–124; Beckett, 'Nation in Arms', p.14; Glenford Howe, 'West Indian Blacks and the Struggle for Participation in the First World War', *Journal of Caribbean History* 28 (1994), pp.27–62; Michael Summerskill, *China on the Western Front: Britain's Chinese Work Force in the First World War*

(London, 1982); N. J. Griffin, 'Britain's Chinese Labor Corps in World War I', *MA* 40 (1976), pp.102–8; A. Philip Jones, *Britain's Search for Chinese Co-operation in the First World War* (New York, 1986), pp.103–30, 160–94; B. P. Willan, 'The South African Native Labour Contingent in France, 1916–1918', *JAH* 19, 1978, pp.61–86; G. W. T. Hodges, 'African Manpower Statistics for British Forces in East Africa, 1914–1918', *JAH* 19, 1978, pp.101–16; David Killingray and James Matthews, 'Beasts of Burden: British West African Carriers in the First World War', *Canadian Journal of African Studies* 13 (1979), pp.6–23; R. T. Edgar, 'Lesotho and the First World War: Recruiting, Resistance and the South African Native Labour Corps', *Mohlomi* 3–5, (1981), pp.94–108; Donald Savage and J. Forbes Munro, 'Carrier Corps Recruitment in the British East Africa Protectorate, 1914–18', *JAH* 7 (1966), pp.313–432.

9. Geoffrey Hodges, *The Carrier Corps: Military Labor in the East African Campaign, 1914–1918* (New York and Westport, CT, 1986), pp.99–108, 110–11,130–4, 207–8; idem, 'African Manpower Statistics', p.113; idem, 'Military Labour in East Africa and its Impact on Kenya', in Melvin E. Page, ed., *Africa and the First World War* (London, 1987), pp.137–51; Melvin E. Page, 'Black Men in a White Man's War', ibid., pp.1–27; Albert Grundlingh, 'The Impact of the First World War on South African Blacks', ibid., pp.54–80; Bernard Waites, 'Peoples of the Underdeveloped World', in Liddle, ed., *Facing Armageddon*, pp.603, 608–9.

10. Waites, 'Peoples of the Underdeveloped World', p.603; Marc Michel, *L'Appel à l'Afrique: Contributions et Réactions à l'effort de Guerre en AOF, 1914–1919* (Paris, 1982), pp.73–95, 117–34, 239–60, 403–24; idem, 'Mythes et réalités du concours colonial: soldats et travailleurs d'Outre-mer dans la guerre française', in Becker and Audoin-Rouzeau, eds, *Les sociétés européennes*, pp.393–410; C. M. Andrew and A. S. Kanya-Forstner, 'France, Africa and the First World War', *JAH* 19, (1978), pp.11–23; Gilbert Meynier, 'Les Algériens en France, 1914–18', *Revue d'Histoire Maghrebine* 5, (1976), pp.47–58; Myron J. Echenberg, 'Paying the Blood Tax: Military Conscription in French West Africa, 1914–29', *Canadian Journal of African Studies* 9 (1975), pp.171–92; Nouzille, 'Campagne de Cameroun', pp.9–20; Frederick Quinn, 'The Impact of the First World War and its Aftermath on the Beti of Cameroun', in Page, ed., *Africa and First World War*, pp.171–85; Joe Lunn, 'Les Races Guerrières: Racial Preconceptions in the French Military about West African Soldiers during the First World War', *JCH* 34 (1999), pp.517–36; Tyler Stovall, 'The Color Line behind the Lines: Racial Violence in France during the Great War', *AHR* 103 (1998), pp.737–69.

11. Stockwell, 'War and British Empire', p.37; Stephen Constantine, 'Britain and the Empire', in Constantine, Kirby and Rose, eds, *First World War in British History*, p.262; Andrews, *Anzac Illusion*, p.64; Waites, 'Peoples of Underdeveloped World', p.598; K. G. Sainie, 'The Economic Aspects of India's Participation in the First World War', in Ellinwood and Pradhan, eds, *India and World War I*, pp.141–76.

12. Gammage, *Broken Years*, p.283.

13. Waites, 'Peoples of Underdeveloped World', pp.604–6, 609; Anne Summers and R. W. Johnson, 'World War I Conscription and Social Change in Guinea', *JAH* 19 (1978), pp.25–38; Michael Crowder, 'Blaise Diagne and the Recruitment of African Troops for the 1914–18 War', in Michael Crowder, ed., *Colonial West Africa: Collected Essays* (London, 1978), pp.104–21; Michel, *L'Appel à l'Afrique*, pp.100–12, 223–35; Page, 'Black Men in a White Man's War', pp.1–27; Akinjide Osuntokun, *Nigeria in the First World War* (London, 1979), pp.100–33; Peter McLaughlin, 'The Legacy of Conquest: African Military Manpower in Southern Rhodesia during the First World War', in Page, ed., *Africa in First World War*, pp.115–36; idem, 'Victims as Defenders: African Troops in the Rhodesian Defence System, 1890–1980', *Small Wars and Insurgencies* 2 (1991), pp.240–75; Lewis J. Greenstein, 'The Nandi Experience in the First World War', ibid., pp.81–94; Hodges, *Carrier Corps*, pp.189–97, 205–6; Albert Grundlingh, 'Black Men in a White Man's War: The Impact of the First World War on South African Blacks', *W&S* 3 (1985), pp.55–82; idem, 'Impact of First World War on South African Blacks', pp.54–80; James Matthews, 'Reluctant Allies: Nigerian Responses to Military Recruitment, 1914–18', in Page, ed., *Africa and First World War*, pp.95–114; idem, 'World War I and the Rise of African Nationalism: Nigerian Veterans as Catalysts of Change', *Journal of Modern African Studies* 20 (1983), pp.493–502.

14. Peter Yearwood, 'Great Britain and the Repartition of Africa, 1914–19', *JICH* 18 (1990), pp.316–41; Waites, 'Peoples of Underdeveloped World', p.602; Judith Brown, 'War and the Colonial Relationship: Britain, India and the War of 1914–1918', in Ellinwood and Pradhan, eds, *India and World War I*, pp.19–47 [also in Foot, *War and Society*, pp.85–106]; Omissi, *Sepoy and Raj*, p.162.

15. S. E. Katzenellenbogen, 'Southern Africa and the War of 1914–18', in Foot, ed., *War and Society*, pp.107–21; Constantine, 'British Empire', pp.265–7; Gammage, *Broken Years*, pp.277–8; Robertson, *Anzac and Empire*, pp.259–61; Andrews, *Anzac Illusion*, pp.3, 52, 60–3, 214–16; L. L. Robson, 'The Australian Soldier: Formation of a Stereotype', in Michael McKernan and M. Browne, eds, *Australia: Two Centuries of War and Peace* (Canberra, 1988), pp.313–37; Joan Beaumont, 'The Anzac Legend', in Beaumont, ed., *Australia's War*, pp.149–80; D. A. Kent, 'The Anzac Book and the Anzac Legend: C. E. W. Bean as Editor and Image-maker', *HS* 21 (1985), pp.376–90; K. J. Fewster, 'Ellis Ashmead-Bartlett and the Making of the Anzac Legend', *Journal of Australian Studies* 10, (1982), pp.17–30; Alistair Thomson, *Anzac Memories: Living with a Legend* (Melbourne, 1994), pp.46–72; idem, ' "Steadfast unto Death"?: C. E. W. Bean and the Representation of Australian Military Manhood', *Australian Historical Studies* 23 (1989), pp.462–78; idem, 'The Anzac Legend: Exploring National Myth and Memory in Australia', in Raphael Samuel and Paul Thompson, eds, *The Myths We Live By* (London, 1990), pp.73–82; Ken Inglis, 'C. E. W. Bean: Australian Historian', in Lack, ed., *Anzac Remembered*, pp.63–96.

16. Andrews, *Anzac Illusion*, pp.102–17, 140–2; Joan Beaumont, 'Australia's War', in Beaumont, ed., *Australia's War*, pp.1–34; Stephen Harris, 'From Subordinate to Ally: The Canadian Corps and National Autonomy, 1914–18', *RIHM* 51 (1982), pp.109–30; Brown, 'Borden and Canada's War Aims', pp.55–66; Desmond Morton, 'Exerting Control: The Development of Canadian Authority over the Canadian Expeditionary Force, 1914–19', in Tim Travers and C. Archer, eds, *Men at War: Politics, Technology and Innovation in the Twentieth Century* (Chicago, 1982), pp.7–19; idem, ' "Junior but Sovereign Allies": The Transformation of the Canadian Expeditionary Force, 1914–18', in Norman Hillmer and Philip Wigley, eds, *The First British Commonwealth: Essays in Honour of Nicholas Mansergh* (London, 1980), pp.56–67; A. M. J. Hyatt, 'Sir Arthur Currie and Politicians: A Case Study of Civil–Military Relations in the First World War', in Adrian Preston and Peter Dennis, eds, *Swords and Covenants* (London and Totowa, NJ, 1976), pp.147–63.

17. Andrews, *Anzac Illusion*, pp.131–3, 198–204; G. L. Cook, 'Sir Robert Borden, Lloyd George and British Military Policy, 1917–18', *HJ* 14 (1971), pp.371–5; Harris, 'From Subordinate to Ally', pp.109–18; Constantine, 'British Empire', pp.263–4; W. Roger Louis, *Great Britain and Germany's Lost Colonies, 1914–18* (Oxford, 1967), pp.41–50; 78–86, 97–9, 121–3, 133–6; idem, 'Australia and the German Colonies in the Pacific', *JMH* 4 (1966), pp.407–21; David Lowe, 'Australia in the World', in Beaumont, ed., *Australia's War*, pp.125–48.

18. Stockwell, 'War and Empire', pp.47–9; Brown, 'Borden and Canada's War Aims', pp.63–4; Andrews, *Anzac Illusion*, pp.204–5; L. F. Fitzhardinge, 'Hughes, Borden, and Dominion Representation at the Paris Peace Conference', *CHR* 49 (1968), pp.160–9; Constantine, 'British Empire', pp.270–7; Lowe, 'Australia in World', pp.125–48.

19. Waites, 'Peoples of Underdeveloped World', pp.598–602; Gerd Hardach, *The First World War, 1914–18* (London, 1973), pp.277–80.

20. Waites, 'Peoples of Underdeveloped World', pp.598, 606–7; Osuntokun, *Nigeria*, pp.21–63; Michael Crowder and Jide Osuntokun, 'The First World War and West Africa', in J. F. Ade Ajayi and Michael Crowder, eds, *A History of West Africa*, 2nd edn (London, 1987), II, pp.546–77; David Killingray, 'Repercussions of World War I in the Gold Coast', *JAH* 19, (1978), pp.39–60; idem, 'Military and Labour Policies in the Gold Coast during the First World War', in Page, ed., *Africa in First World War*, pp.152–70; Andrews, *Anzac Illusion*, pp.71–3, 128–30, 196–7; Marnie Haig-Muir, 'The Economy at War', in Beaumont, ed., *Australia's War*, pp.93–124; John Robertson, 'Australia and the Great War, 1914–18', in International Commission of Military History, *Acta 10* (Freiburg, 1986), pp.178–9; Hardach, *First World War*, pp.272–6, 280–9; Offer, *First World War*, p.372; Mary B. Rose, 'Britain and the International Economy', in Constantine, Kirby and Rose, eds, *First World War in British History*, pp.240–3.

21. Stockwell, 'War and Empire', p.41; Waites, 'Peoples of Underdeveloped World', pp.610–11.

22. Alan Palmer, *The Lands Between* (London, 1970), pp.120–33; Dragon Zivojinevic, 'Serbia and Montenegro: The Home Front, 1914–18', in Király and Dreisziger, eds, *East Central European Society*, pp.239–59.

23. F. A. K. Yasamee, 'Ottoman Empire', in Wilson, ed., *Decisions for War*, pp.229–68; Ulrich Trumpener, *Germany and the Ottoman Empire, 1914–1918* (Lexington, KT, 1970), pp.21–61; idem, 'Turkey's entry into World War I: An Assessment of Responsibilities', *JMH* 34 (1962), pp.369–80; Y. T. Kurat, 'How Turkey drifted into World War I', in Kenneth Bourne and Donald Cameron Watt, eds, *Studies in International History: Essays presented to W. Norton Medlicott* (London, 1967), pp.291–315; Feroz Gred Ahmad, 'Ottoman Armed Neutrality and Intervention, August–November 1914', in Sinan Kuneralp, ed., *Studies on Diplomatic History* (Istanbul, 1990), IV, pp.41–69; A. D. Harvey, *Collision of Empires: Britain in Three World Wars, 1793–1945* (London, 1992), p.222; F. Celiker, 'Turkey in the First World War', *RIHM* 46 (1980), pp.163–203.

24. Eliezer Tauber, *The Arab Movements in World War I* (London, 1993), pp.1–9, 35–82, 114, 244–59; Rashid Khalidi, 'The Arab Experience of the War', in Cecil and Liddle, eds, *Facing Armageddon*, pp.642–55; Brian Porter, 'Britain and the Middle East in the Great War', in Peter Liddle, ed., *Home Fires and Foreign Fields: British Social and Military Experience in the First World War* (London, 1985), pp.159–74; D. M. McKale, *War by Revolution: Germany and Britain in the Middle East in the Era of World War I* (Kent, OH, 1998), pp.69–96, 170–99. On Middle Eastern campaigns generally, see Paul K. Davis, *Ends and Means: The British Mesopotamian Campaign and Commission* (Cranbury, NJ, 1994); A. J. Barker, *The Neglected War: Mesopotamia, 1914–18* (London, 1967); and David Bullock, *Allenby's War: The Palestine–Arabian Campaigns, 1916–18* (London, 1988).

25. Bosworth, *Italy and Approach of War*, pp.80–1, 83–7, 121–41; William A. Renzi, *The Shadow of the Sword: Italy's Neutrality and Entrance into the Great War, 1914–15* (New York and Berne, 1987), pp.137–61, 253; John A. Thayer, *Italy and the Great War: Politics and Culture, 1870–1915* (Madison, WI, 1964), pp.290, 300, 307–70; John Gooch, 'Italy during the First World War', in Millett and Murray, eds, *Military Effectiveness*, pp.158, 160; idem, *Army, State and Society in Italy, 1870–1915* (London, 1989), pp.156–70; John Whittam, 'War Aims and Strategy: The Italian Government and High Command, 1914–19', in Hunt and Preston, eds, *War Aims and Strategic Policy*, pp.85–104; idem, *The Politics of the Italian Army, 1861–1918* (London, 1976), pp.178–88; Harvey, *Collision of Empires*, pp.228–31; John Stevenson, *The First World War and International Politics* (Oxford, 1988), pp.47–58; Simon Jones, 'Antonio Salandra and the Politics of Italian Intervention in the First World War', *European History Quarterly* 15 (1985), pp.157–73; H. J. Burgwyn, 'A Diplomacy Aborted: Italy and Romania go their Separate Ways in May 1915', *EEQ* 21 (1987), pp.305–18; Z. A. B. Zeman, *A Diplomatic History of the First World War* (London, 1971), pp.1–48.

26. Peter Opacic, 'On Some Questions concerning War Policy and Strategy of Serbia between 1914 and 1918', in ICMH, *Acta 10*, pp.338–40; Keith Robbins, 'British Diplomacy and Bulgaria, 1914–15', *Slavonic and East European Review* 49 (1971), pp.560–85; Simeon Damianov, 'Bulgaria's Decision to Enter the War: Diplomatic Negotiations, 1914–15', in Király and Dreisziger, eds, *East Central European Society*, pp.157–69; Stilyan Noykov, 'The Bulgarian Army in World War I', ibid., pp.403–15; Stevenson, *First World War and International Politics*, pp.58–61; W. W. Gottlieb, *Studies in Secret Diplomacy during the First World War* (London, 1957). For the pre-war period, see Richard Hall, *Bulgaria's Road to the First World War* (New York, 1997).

27. G. E. Torrey, 'Romania and the Belligerents, 1914–16', *JCH* 1 (1966), pp.171–91 [also in G. E. Torrey, *Romania and World War I* (Iasi, Romania, 1998), pp.9–28]; idem, 'Romania's Decision to Intervene: Bratianu and the Entente, June–July 1916', in Király and Dreisziger, eds, *East Central European Society*, pp.205–27 [also in Torrey, *Romania*, pp.95–120]; idem, 'The Romanian Campaign of 1916: Its Impact on the Belligerents', ibid., pp.528–46 [also in *Slavic Review* 39 (1980), pp.27–43]; idem, 'Romania in the First World War: The Years of Engagement, 1916–18', *IHR* 14 (1992), pp.462–79 [also in Torrey, *Romania*, pp.212–30]; idem, 'The Redemption of an Army: The Romanian Campaign of 1917', *W&S* 12 (1994), pp.23–42 [also in Torrey, *Romania*, pp.269–90]; idem, 'Romania leaves the War: The decision to sign an Armistice', *EEQ* 23 (1989), pp.283–92 [also in Torrey, *Romania*, pp.291–300]; idem, *Romania*, pp.29–94, 121–93, 231–68, 301–11; V. N. Vinogradov, 'Romania in the First World War: The Years of Neutrality, 1914–16', *IHR* 14 (1992), pp.452–61; Ilie Ceausescu, 'The Romanian High Command's Relations with the Allies in World War I', in ICMH, *Acta 10*, pp.273–86; Stefan Paslaru, 'The Strategic Impact of Romania's Entry into the First World War', *RIHM* 77 (1992), pp.33–45; Stevenson, *First World War and International Politics*, pp.61–4.

28. George B. Leontaritis, *Greece and the First World War: From Neutrality to Intervention, 1917–18* (New York, 1990), pp.3–80, 251–86; E. Goldstein, 'Great Britain and Greater Greece, 1917–20', *HJ* 32 (1989), pp.339–56; Richard Clogg, *Modern Greece* (London 1981), pp.19, 22–4; David Dutton, 'The Deposition of King Constantine of Greece, June 1917: An Episode in Anglo-French Diplomacy', *Canadian Journal of History* 12 (1978), pp.325–45; Domna Dontas, 'Troubled Friendship: Greco-Serbian Relations, 1914–18', in Dimitrije Djordjevic, ed., *The Creation of Yugoslavia, 1914–18* (Santa Barbara, CA, 1980), pp.37–50; Erwin A. Schmidl, 'The International Operation in Albania, 1913–14', *International Peacekeeping* 6 (1999), pp.1–10. See also George Leon, *Greece and the Great Powers, 1914–17* (Thessaloniki, 1974); and Christos Theodoulou, *Greece and the Entente, August 1, 1914–September 15, 1916* (Thessaloniki, 1971).

29. J. Vincent Smith, 'Britain, Portugal and the First World War, 1914–16', *European Studies Review* 4 (1974), pp.206–38; Harvey, *Collision of Empires*, pp.234–7.

30. Ian Nish, 'Japan', in Wilson, ed., *Decisions for War*, pp.209–28; idem, 'Japan, 1914–18', in Millett and Murray, eds, *Military Effectiveness*, p.238; Kiyoshi

Ikeda, 'The Impact of the European War in the Far East and the Japanese Decision to enter the War', in ICMH, *Acta 10*, pp.191–9; John Fisher, '"Backing the Wrong Horse": Japan in British Middle Eastern Policy, 1914–18', *JSS* 21 (1998), pp.60–74; Jehuda Walloch, *Uneasy Coalition: The Entente Experience in World War I* (Westport, CN, 1993), p.37. On Anglo-Japanese relations generally, see Ian Nish, *Alliance in Decline: A Study in Anglo-Japanese Relations, 1908–23* (London, 1972). On von Spee's squadron, see Peter Overlack, 'The Force of Circumstance: Graf Spee's Options for the East Asian Cruiser Squadron in 1914', *JMilH* 60 (1996), pp.657–82; and Keith Yates, *Graf Spee's Raiders: Challenge to the Royal Navy* (London, 1995).

31. Hardach, *First World War*, pp.258–66; Alan S. Milward, *The Economic Effects of Two World Wars on Britain*, 2nd edn (London, 1984), pp.57–8.

32. Robertson, *Anzac and Empire*, pp.19–21, 23–5; Keith Robbins, *The First World War*, 2nd edn (Oxford, 1993), p.112; Andrews, *Anzac Illusion*, pp.130–1; Lowe, 'Australia in World', pp.125–48.

33. Hermann J. Hiery, *The Neglected War: The German South Pacific and the Influence of World War I* (Honolulu, 1995); idem, 'West Samoans between Germany and New Zealand, 1914–21', *W&S* 10 (1992), pp.53–80; Robert Aldrich, *The French Presence in the South Pacific, 1842–1940* (Honolulu, 1990), p.191; Jean Guiart, 'Les Evénements de 1917 en Nouvelle Calédonie', *Journal de la Société d'Océanie* 26 (1970), pp.265–82.

34. Hardach, *First World War*, pp.262–6; Stevenson, *First World War and International Politics*, pp.133–5, 173–5; Zhitian Luo, 'National Humiliation and National Assertion: The Chinese Response to the Twenty-one Demands', *Modern Asian Studies* 27 (1993), pp.297–319; Summerskill, *China on Western Front*, pp.17–27; Stephen Craft, 'Angling for an Invitation to Paris: China's Entry into the First World War', *IHR* 16 (1994), pp.1–24; Jones, *Britain's Search for Chinese Co-operation*, pp.244–61; D. K. Wyatt, *Thailand: A Short History* (New Haven, CN, 1984), pp.230–2.

35. David M. Kennedy, *Over Here: The First World War and American Society* (New York, 1980), pp.12, 46–7; Edward P. Crapol, 'From Anglophobia to Fragile Rapprochement: Anglo-American Relations in the Early Twentieth Century', in Hans-Jürgen Schröder, ed., *Confrontation and Co-operation: Germany and the United States in the Era of World War I, 1900–1924* (Providence, RI, 1993), pp.13–32; Daniel Smith, *The Great Departure: The United States and World War I, 1914–20* (New York, 1965), pp.10–14. On the transition from neutrality to intervention generally, see Ernest R. May, *The World War and American Isolation, 1914–17* (Cambridge, MA, 1959); and Robert H. Ferrell, *Woodrow Wilson and World War I* (New York, 1985)

36. The best guide to the evolution of maritime law and its relationship to Anglo-American relations is John W. Coogan, *The End of Neutrality: The United States, Britain and Maritime Rights, 1899–1915* (Ithaca, NY, 1981). See also Hardach,

First World War, pp.11–13; Offer, *First World War*, pp.229–32, 235–9, 264–84; C. P. Vincent, *The Politics of Hunger: The Allied Blockade of Germany, 1915–19* (Athens, OH, 1985), pp.27–50.

37. May, *World War and Isolation*, pp.8–33; 81–9, 433–4; Coogan, *End of Neutrality*, pp.154–63, 216–20, 245–7, 272–3.

38. Coogan, *End of Neutrality*, pp.179–81, 193, 249–51, 272–3. For the more traditional view that Wilson maintained strict neutrality, see Arthur S. Link, *Wilson*, 5 vols (Princeton, NJ, 1947–65), while benevolent neutrality is stressed by May, *World War and Isolation*, pp.34–53.

39. August Heckscher, *Woodrow Wilson: A Biography* (New York, 1991), pp.361–70, 373–6, 380–2; May, *World War and Isolation*, pp.137–59, 184–6. On Bryan, Lansing and House, see Smith, *Great Departure*, pp.15–24.

40. May, *World War and American Isolation*, pp.191–4; Heckscher, *Wilson*, p.385; Reinhard R. Doerries, 'Promoting Kaiser and Reich: Imperial German Propaganda in the United States during World War I', in Schröder, ed., *Confrontation and Co-operation*, pp.135–66.

41. Ragnhild Fiebig-von Hase, 'The United States and Germany in the World Arena, 1900–17', and Jörg Nagler, 'German Imperial Propaganda and the American Homefront in World War I: A Response to Richard R. Doerries', both in Schröder, ed., *Confrontation and Co-operation*, pp.33–68, 167–76; Trevor Wilson, 'Lord Bryce's Investigation into Alleged German Atrocities in Belgium, 1914–15', *JCH* 14 (1979), pp.369–83; idem, *Myriad Faces of War*, pp.182–91.

42. M. H. Forster, 'US Intervention in Mexico: The 1914 Occupation of Vera Cruz', *Military Review* 57 (1977), pp.88–96; R. K. Kolb, 'Restoring Order South of the Border', *US Naval Institute Proceedings* 110 (1984), pp.56–61; Friedrich Katz, 'Pancho Villa and the Attack on Columbus, New Mexico, 1916', *AHR* 83 (1978), pp.101–39.

43. Harvey, *Collision of Empires*, p.238; Maldwyn A. Jones, *The Limits of Liberty: American History, 1607–1992*, 2nd edn (Oxford, 1995), pp.414–15, 423–4; Stephen Hartley, *The Irish Question as a Problem in British Foreign Policy, 1914–18* (London, 1987), pp.58–70; May, *World War and American Isolation*, pp.72–89, 347–70; Patrick Devlin, *Too Proud to Fight: Woodrow Wilson's Neutrality* (New York, 1975), pp.217–82.

44. Jones, *Limits of Liberty*, pp.420–2; Heckscher, *Wilson*, pp.433–41; May, *World War and Isolation*, pp.416–33; Stevenson, *First World War and International Politics*, pp.84–5; Ragnhild Fiebig-Hase, 'Der Anfang vom Ende des Krieges: Deutschland, die USA und die Hintergründe des amerikanischen Kriegseintritts am 6 April 1917', in Michalka, ed., *Erste Weltkrieg*, pp.125–58.

45. A. O. Saldanha da Gama, 'The European War and the Brazilian Decision to enter the War', in ICMH, *Acta 10*, pp.186–90.

46. Bill Albert, *South America and the First World War: The Impact of the War on Brazil, Argentina, Peru and Chile* (Cambridge, 1988), pp.37–121, 180–305; Hardach, *First World War*, pp.266–73; Emily Rosenberg, 'Anglo-American Economic Rivalry in Brazil during World War I', *Diplomatic History* 2 (1978), pp.131–52.

47. Hardach, *First World War*, pp.13–30; Göran Rystad, 'Oberste Heeresleitung, Auswärtiges Amt and the German Monroe Docrine for the Baltic', in ICMH, *Acta 10*, pp.85–7; Fritz Wille, 'Probleme der Schweizerischen Neutralitätspolitik während des Ersten Weltkrieges', ibid., pp.110–17; M. Farrar, 'Le système de blocus suisse, 1914–18', *Revue d'Histoire Moderne et Contemporaine* 21 (1974), pp.591–622; Marc Frey, 'Trade, Ships and the Neutrality of the Netherlands in the First World War', *IHR* 19 (1997), pp.541–62; Har Schmidt, 'Dutch and Danish Agricultural Exports during the First World War', *Scandinavian Economic History Review* 44 (1996), pp.161–82; Carsten Due-Nielsen, 'Denmark and the First World War', *Scandinavian Journal of History* 10 (1984), pp.62–74; Hans A. Schmitt, ed., *Neutral Europe between War and Revolution, 1917–23* (Charlottesville, VA, 1989), especially H. K. Meier, 'The Swiss National General Strike of November 1918', pp.66–86; Olaf Riste, *The Neutral Ally: Norway's Relations with Belligerent Powers in the First World War* (Oslo, 1965), pp.89–119, 191–212.

48. Jean-Marc Delaunay, '1914: Les espagnols et la guerre', in Becker and Audoin-Rouzeau, eds, *Les soiétés européennes*, pp.117–34; G. H. Meaker, 'A Civil War of Words: The Ideological Impact of the First World War on Spain', in Schmitt, ed., *Neutral Europe*, pp.1–65.

49. Kennedy, *Over Here*, pp.296–347; Hardach, *First World War*, pp.254–8.

50. Kathleen Burk, *Britain, America and the Sinews of War, 1914–18* (Boston, MA, 1985), pp.54–76, 77–96, 195–220; eadem, 'Great Britain and the United States, 1917–18: The Turning Point', *IHR* 1 (1979), pp.228–45; eadem, 'The Mobilisation of Anglo-American Finance during World War I', in N. F. Dreiziger, ed., *Mobilising for Total War* (Waterloo, 1981), pp.23–42; Milward, *Economic Effects*, pp.63–5; Ferguson, *Pity of War*, pp.326–9.

51. Kennedy, *Over Here*, pp.296–347; Hardach, *First World War*, pp.254–8.

52. Hardach, *First World War*, pp.138–50; 249–50; 283–94; Milward, *Economic Effects*, pp.11–16; Rose, 'Britain and International Economy', pp.243–8.

CHAPTER FIVE

Westerners and Easterners

The steady enlargement of the number of belligerents made grand strategy a pressing issue for military and political leaderships alike since it confronted them increasingly with the need to make difficult strategic choices. Grand strategy is the appropriate employment of a state's armed forces and resources in order to achieve particular national political objectives. It follows that strategic objectives should match the desired political objectives and that there should be consistency between strategic means and political ends so that both strategic and political objectives are equally achievable. Thus, the objectives must be commensurate with the resources available to achieve them.

In practice, however, such a strategy/policy match may well be difficult to achieve, either through lack of resources or, more frequently, because of disagreement between and/or within the military and political leadership over objectives. Indeed, what may appear feasible or rational from a military point of view may not appear relevant or possible from the political point of view and vice versa. In the Great War, the interplay of war aims and grand strategy, and of competing civil and military hierarchies within belligerent states and, especially, within coalitions was exceedingly complex.

Civil–military relations

The traditional view of wartime strategic decision-making in Britain and, to a lesser extent in France and Germany, has been that of the clash between 'Westerners' and the 'Easterners'. In Britain it was an image that was relentlessly cultivated in the so-called battle of the memoirs in the 1920s and 1930s.[1]

Briefly stated, the traditional argument is that, once deadlock occurred on the Western Front in the autumn of 1914, politicians in Britain and France were motivated to seek a new strategy to break that deadlock. Their earlier easy transference of control over strategy in August 1914 to the soldiers now rebounded since the latter were unwilling to divert manpower from the Western Front to other theatres. Soldiers regarded the latter as side-shows irrelevant to the main effort. Indeed, to use the oft-repeated phrase of defenders of Sir Douglas Haig's strategy as Commander-in-Chief of the British Expeditionary Force from December 1915 onwards, the war could not be won without 'engaging the main body of the main enemy in a continental war'.[2] Soldiers like Haig and Sir William Robertson, the Chief of the Imperial General Staff (CIGS) between December 1915 and February 1918, therefore, were 'Westerners'. Politicians like Churchill and David Lloyd George were 'Easterners', convinced of the desirability of finding an 'indirect approach' through such campaigns as the Dardanelles between February 1915 and January 1916 and that at Salonika from October 1915 onwards.

The strategic direction of the war in Britain was certainly punctuated by major civil–military disputes, not only over the sideshows, but also over the conduct of the two main British offensives on the Western Front: the Somme between July and November 1916 and the Third Battle of Ypres – popularly known as Passchendaele – between July and November 1917. The adoption of a strategy of attrition in the summer of 1916, however, spelled the end of what David French has argued was the real alternative strategy in British policy circles. This was one associated principally with the Chancellor of the Exchequer, Reginald McKenna, and the president of the Board of Trade, Walter Runciman.

McKenna and Runciman saw no advantage in raising a large army, believing that the best way to sustain the Entente would be by continuing to bankroll it and to maintain the economic blockade through capitalising on Britain's maritime strength. A strategy of 'limited liability' or 'business as usual', it promised maximum advantage at minimum cost. Rather bitterly, Robertson described it as 'to find out what is the smallest amount of money & smallest number of men with which we may hope, some day, to win the war, or rather not to lose it'.[3]

A limited liability strategy had been intended though, as Hew Strachan has remarked, this should not be confused with limited effort in terms of the naval contribution to the war and the conflict outside Europe. It was, however, increasingly untenable. Naval blockade could not result in any swift German economic collapse and intensification of the blockade would risk alienating the United States. Intensification also required the neutralisation of the German High Seas Fleet. This was desirable in any case, but was difficult to achieve when the Germans declined on most occasions to contest a naval battle in the North Sea. As a result, there was a greater possibility of the British losing the war through naval action than by winning it. The raising of the New Armies also effectively undermined a strategy of 'business as usual' predicated on minimum social and economic mobilisation. Bankrolling the Entente and raising the New Armies made Britain increasingly dependent upon American money and materials.

McKenna and Runciman drew their inspiration of a 'British way in warfare' from the period of the eighteenth century when, supposedly, Britain had acquired its empire and defeated France by using the Royal Navy to impose a blockade and utilising the army to seize colonies. In reality, Britain had only been able to prevail with the assistance of allies. The only war lost was that for America, when Britain was without a continental ally. It had also been necessary to despatch sizeable forces to fight on the continent. Unfortunately, Germany was far less vulnerable to blockade than France had been in the past. Britain itself was less self-sufficient and, thus, more vulnerable to counter-economic warfare than in the past. Moreover, Germany's colonies were of little consequence.[4]

In France, too, there was a strategic aspect to the dispute between Joffre, who remained Commander-in-Chief until December 1916, and Aristide Briand, a former French prime minister, who accepted the justice ministry in the Viviani government in June 1914 and was then prime minister again himself from October 1915 to March 1917. By contrast, in Imperial Germany, the Westerners and Easterners debate could be interpreted largely in terms of the differences between Falkenhayn, who remained Chief of General Staff until August 1916, and the dual military leadership on the Eastern Front, Hindenburg and Ludendorff. Ultimately, Hindenburg replaced Falkenhayn as Chief of Staff, with Ludendorff becoming First Quartermaster General. Subsequently, OHL (General Headquarters) under Hindenburg and Ludendorff exerted its influence over all aspects of German policy-making, undermining Bethmann and forcing his resignation as chancellor in July 1917.

Elsewhere, civil–military disputes were less products of strategic debate than a reflection either of the same willingness, as in Britain and France, to entrust too much power to the military or, as in Germany, of the existing power of the military in decision-making. Pre-war arrangements in Russia had vested wartime authority in the person of the supreme commander, the assumption from 1903 onwards being that the Tsar himself would exercise that authority. In the event, the Tsar was persuaded to appoint Grand Duke Nicholas as supreme commander in August 1914. This led to considerable friction between the Grand Duke and the War Minister, Sukhomlinov, and between Stavka (Russian General Headquarters) and the civil authorities within the widely designated theatre of operations. Rivalries within the High Command exacerbated the difficulties, Sukhomlinov having mano-euvred his supporters into a number of key appointments prior to the war. While Sukhomlinov was dismissed in June 1915, the problem was only really resolved when the Tsar took the supreme command himself on 1 September 1915, the Grand Duke being sent to the Caucasus command. In Portugal, where military dictatorship was a very recent memory, war-time governments tried to avoid criticism of the military. Opposition groups, however, made capital from atrocities in the ongoing campaign to subjug-ate Angola in 1915 and Portuguese military failures against Lettow-Vorbeck in Mozambique in 1916.

Only Serbia, Japan and the United States among the more significant powers did not experience major civil–military friction during the war. In Serbia, civil–military harmony derived from the close friendship between prime minister Pasic, and the Chief of General Staff, Field Marshal Radomir Putnik. The king was too old to intervene actively in strategic policy-making and the regent, Alexander, too young and inexperienced to exercise the role of supreme commander. It was not uncommon for there to be friction be-tween the rival clans controlling the Japanese army and navy but, since the services often controlled the government as a whole, actual civil–military friction was generally avoided.

In the United States, Wilson maintained the principle of strict political control of the armed forces to the extent that he had disapproved even of war planning. In practice, however, there were few real mechanisms for effective civil–military co-ordination and, believing in the separation of civil and military affairs, Wilson allowed his military and naval commanders in the European theatre, General John Pershing and Admiral William Sims, respectively, considerable latitude. The one substantial dispute between Wilson and Pershing arose only in October 1918, when Pershing favoured imposing far harsher armistice terms than Wilson.[5]

Where civil–military disputes were experienced, they were often exacer-bated by the lack of an adequate machinery for strategic decision-making. As already indicated, the intention in Russia was that the Tsar would em-body both military and political authority, directly linking Stavka to the Council of Ministers. The appointment of Grand Duke Nicholas broke this anticipated close relationship between Stavka and the Council since he was determined to exercise his viceregal powers over the rear areas to their fullest extent. Indeed, even a new Supreme Council established by the Tsar was virtually powerless to intervene, with the result that there was little political and strategic co-ordination until September 1915. The Grand Duke had courted the political opposition but, with the appointment of Alekseev as Chief of Staff, Stavka became more functional and apolitical, an effect heightened by the appointment of the technocrat, Shuvayev, to the war ministry.[6]

Rather similarly, King Victor Emmanuel was Italian Commander-in-Chief and politicians were wary of infringing his prerogatives by establishing any more formal defence machinery. Equally, however, they had not consulted their military advisers with respect to either the decision to remain neutral in August 1914 or the decision to enter the war in May 1915. Once Italy's war began, however, Cadorna as Chief of Staff was given effective control of strategy and succeeded both in negating the influence of the government's official representative at Comando Supremo (Supreme Command) and also in defeating a proposal for a new defence council in early 1916.

Cadorna managed to remove the War Minister, General Vittorio Zupelli, in February 1916 by threatening to resign himself, but came close to dismissal in May when it looked likely that the Austro-Hungarian army would break into Lombardy. In the event, Salandra hesitated to dismiss Cadorna and resigned himself in June 1916 amid dissatisfaction with his own war leadership. Cadorna persuaded the new prime minister, Paolo Boselli, to exclude ministers from visiting the war zone and, in September, removed one of his corps commanders, Luigi Capello, whom some saw as a possible alternative as Chief of Staff. In the wake of Caporetto, which resulted in Cadorna's dismissal and the fall of Boselli's government, a war committee was established on 15 December 1917. This comprised Boselli's successor, Vittorio Orlando, and six of his ministers, with the professional heads of the army and navy in attendance. Nonetheless, as John Gooch has expressed it, the army 'remained masters of the front' and Cadorna's successor, Armando Diaz, only succumbed to government pressure for a new offensive in October 1918.[7]

In Britain, the pre-war Committee of Imperial Defence (CID) had been a useful mechanism for strategic decision-making, but the War Council, which emerged from it in November 1914, proved unsatisfactory. No memoranda were circulated, there was no regular agenda, meetings were infrequent, and there was no proper record kept of decisions. In theory, the War Council's decisions were not binding on the Cabinet, but the latter was in effect bypassed by Asquith's reliance upon Churchill, Lloyd George and Field Marshal Lord Kitchener, who had been appointed Secretary of State for War on 5 August 1914. As one junior minister remarked in March 1915, the only real difference between War Council and the Cabinet was Kitchener, Churchill and Lloyd George dominating proceedings in front of 'a different set of spectators'.[8]

When war broke out, Kitchener was on home leave from Egypt, where he was British Agent and Consul-General. Grown increasingly autocratic and secretive in his overseas appointments, however, Kitchener had little time for the niceties of Cabinet debate and did not feel obliged to discuss his decisions with either politicians or subordinates. Kitchener had genuine strategic insight but, rather aptly, Lloyd George characterised him as 'one of those revolving lighthouses which radiate momentary gleams of revealing light far out into the surrounding gloom and then suddenly relapse into complete darkness'.[9]

Such a situation left the initiative within the War Council in the hands of those whom John Gooch has termed 'strategic entrepreneurs', namely Churchill, Lloyd George and the increasingly influential secretary to the CID and now the War Council, Maurice Hankey. The result was the Dardanelles expedition. This rested on too many assumptions about the possibility of knocking Turkey out of the war and its likely consequences. The latter appeared to include opening a new supply route to Russia through the Black Sea; creating a new Balkan League, which would draw Italy, Greece, Romania and even Bulgaria into the Entente; and increasing pressure upon Austria-Hungary and, in turn, upon Germany.[10]

The failure of the naval and military campaigns at the Dardanelles, coupled with Admiral Lord Fisher's resignation as First Sea Lord, the impact of the publicity given the British Expeditionary Force's shortage of shells on the Western Front, and other domestic political events resulted in Asquith forming a coalition government on 19 May 1915. The War Council now gave way to the Dardanelles Committee, originally comprising six former members of the War Council and five Unionists, but without serving officers other than Kitchener. In theory, its responsibilities were confined to strategy and diplomacy in the eastern Mediterranean and it met less frequently than the Cabinet. In November 1915, following Unionist pressure on Asquith to refine the machinery, the Dardanelles Committee begat the five-man War Committee, comprising Asquith, Lloyd George, McKenna, and the Unionists Arthur Balfour and Andrew Bonar Law. The Chief of Imperial General Staff and First Sea Lord customarily attended and minutes produced by Hankey in the form of 'conclusions' were circulated.

Failure at the Dardanelles also prompted a reconstitution of the general staff in September 1915. In December, as part of the wider reconstruction of the High Command, consequent upon declining confidence in both Kitchener and Sir John French, French was succeeded by Haig on 19 December 1915. Robertson became Chief of the Imperial General Staff (CIGS), four days later. Robertson's terms were that the CIGS should be regarded as sole military adviser to the War Committee, but he discontinued detailed briefings to ministers, substituting a weekly summary, which Hankey, for one, considered 'an insult to the intelligence of the War Committee and the Cabinet'. Kitchener, already shorn of responsibility for munitions by the creation of a new ministry under Lloyd George in May 1915, was confined to administrative matters until his death by drowning in June 1916, when HMS *Hampshire*, carrying him on a mission to Russia, struck a German mine off the Orkneys.[11]

The extent of Robertson's power was clear to Lloyd George when he succeeded to the War Office on Kitchener's death. Robertson himself was not averse to veiled references in his private correspondence to the benefits of military dictatorship but, unlike the situation in Germany, the British military leadership did not aspire to the control of anything other than strategic policy.[12] When Lloyd George became prime minister in December 1916, his ability to impose his own strategic views was circumscribed through the weakness of his political position and lack of any majority support within parliament.

Accordingly, Lloyd George resorted to subterfuge in attempting to out-manoeuvre Haig and Robertson and to force one or both to resign. This was despite the establishment of a five-man War Cabinet, which in theory offered him far more influence over decision-making. The War Cabinet had a permanent secretariat under Hankey and, eventually, increased to seven members. In addition, Lloyd George established his own secretariat – the 'Garden Suburb' – as a further independent source of advice. In practice, however, Lloyd George often scrapped the War Cabinet's agenda at short notice and, despite Hankey's efforts, its meetings were far from businesslike. In October 1917, for example, one observer commented to Robertson that the meeting he had attended had not proved very edifying, to which Robertson retorted, 'They were very good today. You should see them after an air raid'. In fact, it strongly resembled the War Committee, albeit with clearer overall authority.[13]

Curiously, the direction of naval affairs by 1917 presented almost the exact opposite of the problem with Haig and Robertson. Churchill and Fisher, who was recalled as First Sea Lord when Prince Louis of Battenberg was forced from office in October 1914 for alleged German sympathies, were equally autocratic and their wartime relationship was a stormy one. Fisher, however, had a keen sense of the need for professional subordination to politicians and, therefore, had not made his views on the Dardanelles public. Neither of Fisher's successors, Admirals Sir Henry Jackson and Jellicoe, who succeeded to the post in November 1916, had any real drive and neither of Churchill's immediate successors wished to interfere in naval matters until Sir Eric Geddes, who had already exercised authority over naval shipbuilding as Controller of the Navy, was appointed in July 1917. Jellicoe was dismissed in December 1917.

The collapse of the Italian army at Caporetto in October 1917 finally enabled Lloyd George to divert troops from France, and on 7 November the Entente conference at Rapallo agreed on the establishment of a Supreme

War Council (SWC) at Versailles. It proved a formal counterweight to the CIGS. In February 1918, a dispute over the control of an Allied reserve enabled Lloyd George to trap Robertson into either remaining CIGS with reduced powers or going to Versailles as British representative. Refusing both posts, Robertson resigned on 16 February 1918 and was replaced by Sir Henry Wilson, although Haig and his French counterpart, Philippe Pétain, were able to block the creation of a general reserve.

The prospect of the British and French armies being split apart by the German offensive finally forced Haig to accept the appointment of Ferdinand Foch as Allied Supreme Commander at the Doullens conference on 26 March 1918, though Haig and Pétain retained tactical control over their own troops. Moreover, the offensive enabled Lloyd George to establish a new 'X' committee consisting of himself, Wilson and Lord Milner, who had become Secretary of State for War in April 1918, to discuss strategy prior to meetings of the War Cabinet. Like the War Policy Committee before it, the 'X' committee took decisions without reference to the War Cabinet. Haig's position remained insecure but there was no acceptable alternative and, by the summer, the Entente was on the offensive, although no one expected the war to be won in 1918.[14]

In France, there had been a long history of friction between the Third Republic's politicians and its professional soldiers. On 2 August 1914, however, since it was assumed that the war would be short, Joffre received 'absolute liberty' of action for the execution of operations while a state of siege was declared in the eight *départements* within the 'zone of the armies'. The latter was extended to thirty-three *départements* on 10 August and Joffre's power was increased further when the government left Paris for the safety of Bordeaux on 3 September: it did not return until 7 December 1914. Joffre communicated direct with President Poincaré rather than through either prime minister or Minister of War and his position was strengthened by the ready acquiescence in his decisions of the latter, Alexandre Millerand. Both the press and the parliamentary commission on military affairs were in effect excluded from the Grand Quartier Général (GQG; General Headquarters) and from the zone of armies.

Politicians were wary of the kind of political interference in military affairs which had weakened the army in the past. Joffre's prestige after the victory on the Marne in 1914 equally warded off much overt criticism. The perennial governmental instability within the Third Republic also strengthened Joffre's hand, since ministers feared that questioning the conduct of the war would result in their own political demise.[15]

Briand, however, was an early convert to an alternative strategy. Joffre resisted the government's decision to participate in the Dardanelles campaign, but was undermined by the political need to find a significant command for the radical Republican general Maurice Sarrail, whom he had removed from the Third Army in July 1915. Sarrail, who would have succeeded Joffre as Chief of Staff in the autumn of 1914 if the war had not broken out, received the command of an 'Army of the Orient' in August, but Joffre continued to refuse to release men for the Dardanelles. Ultimately, Sarrail's army was committed to Salonika in October 1915. There was some improvement in the discussion of strategy, however, when the Conseil Supérieur de la Défense Nationale (Supreme Council for National Defence) was established in August 1915: it comprised Poincaré, Joffre, Millerand, the Foreign Minister Théophile Delcassé, and the Minister of Marine, Victor Augagneur. It had a permanent secretariat and functioned as a means of co-ordinating military and political policy, although it was only summoned at the request of either Joffre or Millerand.[16]

The failure at the Dardanelles and of Joffre's own offensives played a part in the fall of the Viviani ministry in October 1915, Delcassé initiating the governmental crisis by resigning in opposition to further Balkan adventures at Salonika. Galliéni, already senior in the military hierarchy to Joffre, became Minister of War in Briand's new ministry. Initially, the attempt by Galliéni and Briand to reduce Joffre's power, through creating an Allied co-ordinating council, failed. Indeed, Joffre was elevated to commander-in-chief of all French armies in December 1915, albeit largely to ensure that he took Salonika seriously, since he would now be ultimately responsible for its success. Galliéni had favoured becoming supreme commander himself, but this was vetoed by Briand and Poincaré while Galliéni's health failed in February 1916. His successor, General Pierre Roques, was equally critical of Joffre's handling of the battle for Verdun, which opened that same February. In June 1916, the first secret parliamentary session of the war concluded that there had been a failure to fortify Verdun adequately and a second session in December called for Joffre's replacement. That same month, Briand created a new small War Cabinet and replaced Roques as War Minister with the pro-consular figure of General Louis-Hubert-Gonzalve Lyautey. Briand also persuaded Joffre to accept the purely nominal post of technical adviser to the government. When the new Commander-in-Chief, Robert Nivelle, ignored his advice, Joffre resigned on 26 December 1916.[17]

The controversy over Nivelle's own plans, coupled with the fall of Serbia, led to Briand's resignation in March 1917. Neither the new prime minister, Alexandre Ribot, nor his Minister of War, Paul Painlevé, were convinced of the likely success of Nivelle's planned offensive and it was given only half-hearted approval. Painlevé had already attempted to re-establish ministerial control by appointing Foch as Chief of Staff at the Ministry of War, and the failure of the offensive led to Nivelle's replacement by Pétain on 15 May 1917. This marked the effective reassertion of political control over French strategy although, in any case, there was general agreement over Pétain's more limited strategic objectives. Indeed, a defensive strategy became regarded as suitably 'Republican', given that most advocates of the offensive such as Foch, Noël de Castelnau and Charles Mangin were known as ardent Catholics, unsympathetic to Republican ideals.

In November 1917, with the fall in rapid succession of both Ribot and a short-lived Painlevé administration, Georges Clemenceau assumed near-dictatorial powers. One casualty was Sarrail, whom Clemenceau removed in December 1917: Sarrail had alienated both the Italians and the Greeks through his attempts to dabble in the affairs of Albania. As far as the soldiers were concerned, Clemenceau's influence was only curtailed by the appointment of Foch as Allied Supreme Commander in April 1918, since he was answerable to the Supreme War Council rather than Clemenceau.[18]

There was little doubt in Imperial Germany over the efficacy of handing over strategic control to the professionals. Indeed, the revival of the Prussian Law of Siege of 1851 in August 1914 in effect handed over all local administration to twenty-four Deputy Commanding Generals responsible only to the Kaiser. The Deputy Commanding Generals were subordinated to the new Kriegsamt (Supreme War Office) in October 1916, but they retained much of their independence until October 1918. From the beginning, the army also became involved in such key policy areas as provision of raw materials, food supplies and manpower.

In fact, there was no adequate mechanism for overall strategic decision-making and, even within the army, the Chief of General Staff could be challenged (at least in theory) by the rival power structures represented by the Prussian ministry of war and the Kaiser's Military Cabinet. There was equally little co-ordination within the navy, Tirpitz having discouraged the development of the Admiralty staff, lest it challenge his own strategic ideas. Nor was there much contact between army and navy, while the astonishing total of forty army and eight naval officers had the right of direct access to the Kaiser.[19]

By the end of 1914, Falkenhayn did not believe that a decisive victory was possible. Thus, believing that France and, especially, Britain represented the greater threat to German interests, Falkenhayn was prepared to countenance seeking terms with Russia and resisted sending further troops to the Eastern Front. In the west, Falkenhayn would seek a result through *Ermattungsstrategie* (attritional strategy) coupled with unrestricted submarine warfare. By contrast, Hindenburg and Ludendorff, whose cause was promoted in Berlin by the influential Major Hans von Haeften, still believed decisive victory possible and that it would be won in the east.

Aware of the danger posed to his position by the combination of Hindenburg and Ludendorff, Falkenhayn attempted to have Ludendorff transferred to the Carpathians in January 1915. Hindenburg persuaded the Kaiser to allow Ludendorff to remain and Falkenhayn survived an attempt in turn by Hindenburg to have him dismissed. Falkenhayn was compelled, however, not only to reinforce the east in order to bolster the Austro-Hungarian front, but also to give up the post of Prussian Minister of War, which he had retained since succeeding Moltke. Falkenhayn's offensive against Verdun in February 1916 again highlighted his belief that the west was of more significance than the east.

With both the Kaiser and Chancellor Bethmann losing confidence in his strategy, Falkenhayn attempted in July 1916 to prevent the appointment of Hindenburg as supreme commander on the Eastern Front in response to the Russian Brusilov offensive. Falkenhayn anticipated that the suggestion of Hindenburg as supreme commander would push Conrad, whose own position was under threat, too far, while the Kaiser, who distrusted Hindenburg, had also previously rejected it. The attempt failed, however, when the Austro-Hungarians conceded in August that command unity was desirable in face of the Russian offensive. The very success of Brusilov in breaking the Austro-Hungarian front was also attributed to Falkenhayn's failure to reinforce the east. Romania's entrance into the war then sealed Falkenhayn's fate. Falkenhayn was unpopular in the army owing to his comparative youth and his cold and sarcastic manner; few regretted his dismissal on 29 August 1916.[20]

Bethmann appears to have believed that Falkenhayn's removal would end military interference in policy-making. In reality, the appointment of Hindenburg and Ludendorff dramatically increased OHL's interference in all aspects of policy. The military domination of strategic policy was epitomised not only by the reintroduction of unrestricted submarine warfare in February 1917 in order to defeat Britain, but also by the continued emphasis given to the Eastern Front. Bethmann, who had never quite made up his mind whether to pursue total victory or a negotiated peace, was dismissed on the threat of resignation by Hindenburg and Ludendorff on 13 July 1917, following a Reichstag Peace Resolution.

OHL found his successor, Georg Michaelis, suitably 'weak, pliable and unwilling to stand up to the soldiers'. The campaign against Bethmann orchestrated by OHL within the Reichstag, however, had actually strengthened its sense of authority and, when Michaelis proved incapable of providing any degree of political leadership, the Kaiser replaced him on 1 November 1917 with the Bavarian Catholic Count Georg Hertling. Hertling was more resistant, but OHL still increased its hold over foreign policy. Hindenburg and Ludendorff again used the threat of their own resignation to remove, first, the chief of the Kaiser's civil Cabinet, Rudolf von Valentini, in January 1918 and then the Foreign Minister, Richard von Kühlmann, in June.

Ultimately, the failure of the German spring offensives and the Entente counter-attack in August 1918 undermined even military confidence in Ludendorff. Hertling was replaced by Prince Max of Baden on 3 October and the dismissal of Ludendorff himself followed on 24 October 1918.[21]

Archduke Friedrich was nominally Austro-Hungarian Commander-in-Chief, but his role was usurped by Conrad, and Armee-Oberkommando (AOK; or Army High Command) directed the war independently of emperor and government. Indeed, Conrad tried to extend the powers of the Kriegsüberwachungsamt (War Supervisory Office) over the government's domestic policy in the autumn of 1915. He was unable to prevail, however, against Tisza's authority in Hungary and was also resisted by the Austrian prime minister, Count Stürgkh, whose removal Conrad failed to engineer.

Conrad's resignation was refused by the emperor following the collapse against the Brusilov offensive in the summer of 1916 but he was forced to make full disclosure of military operations to ministers. Emperor Franz Joseph died, however, on 21 November 1916 and his successor and grand-nephew, Karl, moved to reduce Conrad's authority, becoming Commander-in-Chief himself with Archduke Friedrich as his deputy at AOK. Conrad was then dismissed on 27 February 1917, with the distinctly junior corps commander, Arz von Straussenburg, elevated to Chief of Staff. Conrad was sent to command in the Tyrol. He was dismissed from that command on 15 July 1918 following the failure of the last Austro-Hungarian offensive of the war against the Italians.[22]

The politics of coalition

While continuing tensions between civilians and soldiers were thus clearly evident, there were frequently other factors which were equally significant in shaping strategic decisions. One was the need to accommodate coalition partners, although some belligerents took their coalition responsibilities more seriously than others. In theory, it should have been easier for the Central Powers, consisting of only four members, to co-ordinate strategic policy than for the Entente, which (excluding the British dominions) eventually included twenty-eight states. As it happened, however, there was no more co-ordination between Germany and its partners than within the Entente since coalition warfare was, and remains, an inherently difficult enterprise: Sarrail once remarked that Napoleon had not been a great general since he had only achieved success against coalitions between 1799 and 1815. Every belligerent fought in order to win or, at least, not to lose and, therefore, there was an essential unity of purpose between coalition partners.

Each state, however, had its own reasons for entering the war and would have, or would develop, during the conflict, its own particular objectives, serving its own national interests.

Consequently, war aims within a coalition could conflict with those of allies. Indeed, as already noted in the previous chapter, territorial promises made to prospective partners by both the Entente and Central Powers in the hope of attracting their adherence were in themselves frequently contradictory. Some partners within the coalition were likely to be more powerful than others in terms of military or economic resources and in a better position to impose their own aims on the alliance although, in the case of the Entente, the balance of power was by no means static. Even if a common strategic aim could be agreed, however, it was still likely that national considerations would render operational co-ordination difficult since such issues as unity of command, amalgamation of forces, and pooling of material resources all implied at least a partial surrender of national sovereignty.[23]

Among the Central Powers, there was little equality in the relationship between Germany and Austria-Hungary, deriving principally from the frequent need on the part of the Germans to rescue Vienna's army. Indeed, Hoffmann remarked on one occasion that the latter 'are like a mouth full of bad teeth: every time there is a slight breeze, there's an ache somewhere'. The need to shore up the Austro-Hungarians had been apparent in Galicia as early as October 1914. The renewal of their offensive in the Carpathians in January 1915 proved disastrous, necessitating the despatch of substantial German reinforcements to the east. These helped to secure the major victory at Gorlice-Tarnow in May, but the effect was to make the Austro-Hungarians ever more dependent upon the Germans.

There was a joint offensive against Serbia in autumn 1915. It did not, however, improve the relationship between Conrad and Falkenhayn, who had met for the first time only in December 1914. The Brusilov offensive in 1916, which effectively ended Austria-Hungary as a great power, was itself evidence of the lack of real co-operation between AOK and OHL. In the wake of the disaster, German NCOs stiffened Austro-Hungarian units, while Conrad's opponents welcomed the appointment of Hindenburg as supreme commander in the east on 27 July 1916.

After Hindenburg's translation to Berlin, the Kaiser became supreme commander on all fronts with Hindenburg acting in his name. Only Archduke Karl's Army Group remained nominally independent but with a German, Hans von Seeckt, as its Chief of Staff. Significantly, the Germans did not feel it necessary to consult Vienna on the renewal of unrestricted submarine warfare in February 1917. Alliance with Germany was welcomed by the Magyars, but it increasingly concerned other groups within the Empire such as the Czechs and the southern Slavs. Moreover,

Austro-Hungarian ambitions with regard to Poland and Romania clearly rested on German largesse.[24]

Such realisations fuelled the desire for a separate peace, Emperor Karl attempting an approach to the Entente through his brother-in-law, Prince Sixte (or Sixtus) of Bourbon-Parma, a French national serving in the Belgian army, between December 1916 and June 1917. Yet, such a peace would have required concessions, especially to Italy, at which even Karl baulked. The revelation of Karl's role by Clemenceau in April 1918 resulted in the emperor's abject apology to the Germans and capitulation on 13 May to a binding political, military and economic alliance which committed Vienna to do Germany's bidding. Germany, therefore, proved Austria-Hungary's 'secret enemy' since the continued pursuit of expansion destroyed an empire anxious to make peace.[25]

Germany's formal alliance with Turkey was far more recent than that with Austria-Hungary, although German officers had been involved in training the Turkish army since the 1880s. Thus, while there was relatively close military co-operation during the war, the Germans were much less able to influence Turkish political and economic policy.

Even within the Turkish army, the Germans largely remained advisers. Indeed, five of the nine army commands remained in Turkish hands throughout the war, though Falkenhayn commanded one of the two army groups established in June 1917. In turn, the Turks sent seven divisions to other fronts in 1916, two to Galicia, three for service in Romania and two to the Macedonian front. There was a degree of friction on occasions, especially between Sanders and Enver, but these did not become serious until 1917. German control of Turkish naval operations, however, was considerable.[26]

In the case of Bulgaria, whose interests conflicted with those of Turkey, German military influence was strong and, although there was supposed to be equality between Bulgaria and Germany under the terms of the military convention of 6 September 1915, Bulgarian forces in effect acted under the directions of OHL. The Bulgarians were treated with condescension and some suspicion, and relations between the Bulgarian and Austro-Hungarian commands also deteriorated rapidly.[27]

By contrast, the Entente developed a relatively elaborate system of inter-Allied committees by the end of the war, numbering twenty-five in total. However, these were entirely absent initially and there was no formal machinery for strategic or political co-ordination beyond a few meetings between French, Joffre, Lanrezac and others during the first campaign of the war. Co-ordination was accordingly weak, as epitomised by the muddle over the defence of Antwerp in October 1914 when British, French and Belgian forces were in theory co-ordinated by Foch. Asquith and Viviani did not meet until 6 July 1915 while Kitchener met Joffre and Millerand only five times in the first twelve months of war. Coinciding with the first meeting of the British and French prime ministers, the first inter-Allied military conference was held at Chantilly on 7 July 1915.

Other conferences followed. Often, however, there was little co-ordination between the decisions reached at the military conferences and those at the political conferences.[28] The entry of the United States into the war brought new measures for inter-Allied co-operation such as an Inter-Allied Council for War Purchases and Finance working through an Allied Purchasing Commission, which formed a constituent part of the American War Industries Board. Similarly, after March 1918, blockade policy was co-ordinated by an Allied Blockade Committee and the Inter-Allied Trade Committees established in five European neutral capitals.[29]

The exercise of Allied command over different nationalities, however, remained difficult, compounded in some cases by ignorance of languages. Sir John French, who had experienced particular problems dealing with Lanrezac, admitted to his confidante, Winifred Bennett, in April 1915 that, 'Truly, I don't want to be allied with the French more than once in a lifetime.' Robertson in October 1916 also found allies 'a tiresome lot'. The French pressed the idea of a unified command on a number of occasions and, at Calais in July 1915, the British accepted in principle that Joffre should determine the force, objective and date of any joint offensives in France. Haig always resisted any joint command arrangements though he worked well enough with Pétain.

While a significant development, the Supreme War Council was by no means entirely satisfactory. Commanders-in-chief could attend but were not members and had no vote although the French, who would have preferred unity of command, solved the problem by making Foch's Chief of Staff, General Maxime Weygand, their military representative to the Council. In the crisis of the German spring offensive in 1918, supposed unity of command was forged at Doullens. Doullens, however, did not define Foch's responsibilities satisfactorily and, at Beauvais on 3 April, Foch got powers of strategic direction but tactical control remained with the component field commanders. Foch's authority was extended to the Italian front on 14 April but Diaz, the Italian Chief of Staff, strenuously resisted him.[30]

The Belgian army presented a particular problem, for King Albert was an active Commander-in-Chief and maintained the fiction that Belgium remained a neutral defending its territory without formal association with the Entente. Not unnaturally, Albert disliked the idea of major offensives being conducted on Belgian soil and wished both to achieve liberation by diplomacy and also to preserve the Belgian army to ensure a voice at a peace conference. The Belgians were excluded from the command arrangements established at Doullens but, in practice, Foch was permitted to co-ordinate

Belgian operations and, in September 1918, Albert was placed in command of a northern army group with a French Chief of Staff.[31]

Similarly, in naval matters, command in the Mediterranean proved problematic. The Anglo-French Naval Convention in August 1914 left the French with primary responsibility for the Mediterranean but each of the Entente powers with naval units there operated independently. The Allied Naval Council established in November 1917 made little difference, despite American efforts to act as honest broker, and the Italians also declined to accept the appointment of an Allied supreme naval commander. By contrast, no difficulties arose in Anglo-American identification of naval priorities in the Atlantic.[32]

As an 'associated power' rather than a full member of the Entente, the United States was determined to preserve the identity of the American Expeditionary Force (AEF), which was established formally as a separate army in August 1918. Thus, while tasked with co-operating with the British and French forces, Pershing was instructed to resist attempts to amalgamate his units into those of the Allies. In fact, the AEF was highly dependent upon its coalition partners for artillery, air and, especially, logistical support as well as initial transportation to Europe and training once they arrived. Pershing was prepared to place the AEF under Foch's authority in 1918. Like Haig and Pétain, however, he still vigorously fought his corner, persuading Foch to allow him to launch an independent American offensive at St Mihiel in September 1918. Under Admiral Sims, the United States Navy was more accommodating, postponing its capital ship development programme in order to provide the escort vessels needed to help win the battle for the Atlantic sealanes against German submarines.[33]

Turning to the impact of coalition politics on Entente strategy, David French has made clear that the supposed division between British Westerners and Easterners is somewhat artificial since there was much common ground between them, particularly with respect to the position of Britain within the Entente. Both soldiers and politicians recognised the importance of holding the Entente together in order to defeat Germany. They also intended to ensure that Britain would become the strongest partner in the coalition in order to be able to impose its own terms on enemy and allies alike. As Kitchener expressed it: 'our Army should reach its full strength at the beginning of the third year of the War, just when France is getting into rather low water and Germany is beginning to feel the pinch'. Britain was the strongest economic partner in the anti-German coalition until the entry of the United States and the strongest naval partner. Therefore, her part on land would be confined initially to blockading the Central Powers and bankrolling and supplying the French and Russians.[34]

In this light, it could be argued that the primary motivation behind the Dardanelles campaign was to assist the Russians, who appealed to Britain for assistance on 2 January 1915, in drawing Turkish forces away from the Caucasus. It was vital to keep Russia in the war lest its collapse release German and Austro-Hungarian troops for the west or, indeed, Turkey. Like other assumptions connected with the campaign, this begged the question of whether Russia could have been satisfactorily supplied with more war material in the event of the Black Sea route being opened.[35] In turn, the British decision to contest the Dardanelles impacted upon French strategy since the initial plan for a British naval assault appeared to challenge further the command arrangements in the Mediterranean when operations in defence of Egypt had already been excluded from French control.

The apparent British interest in striking at Alexandretta, the major entrepôt for Asia Minor, as well as the Dardanelles, also rang alarm bells in Paris, since the French had long coveted controlling the trade routes centring on the port and believed their intended post-war influence over Syria threatened. Under an agreement hammered out between Churchill and Augagneur, the French Navy Minister, the British gained control of the Dardanelles operations in return for dropping the idea of an expedition to Alexandretta.

Similarly, it could be argued that the British joined in the Salonika campaign because their participation was requested by the French and Russians rather than because there was any confidence that such a venture could assist Serbia. The Salonika campaign itself was, as David Dutton has commented, largely 'a function of the requirements of French politics' in finding a worthwhile command for Sarrail. The British continued to support it largely as a means of preserving Briand's ministry. At the same time, however, just as the French did not trust the British to act alone at the Dardanelles, the British could not afford to allow the French to act alone at Salonika. Ultimately, however, Salonika did not receive further British reinforcements as the campaign was seen in London to be in French rather than British interests.[36]

David French has also suggested that the adoption of a strategy of attrition on the Western Front, a touchstone of the post-war Westerners versus Easterners debate, was not originally intended to cost British lives but to conserve them, since the brunt of the continental war would fall on the French and Russians. What then went wrong was that the heavy losses suffered by the French and Russians in 1914–15, and the realisation that the Germans would not oblige by attacking in the West, made it increasingly clear that the future of the Entente depended upon Britain's readiness to play a major role in the continental land war. Indeed, the French and the Russians were increasingly less inclined to wait patiently and perhaps indefinitely for the British army to arrive when much of their national territory remained in German hands and their own manpower resources were depleted.

Thus, the British offensive at Loos in September 1915 was mounted primarily for the political purpose of sustaining French and Russian morale, especially in the light of the Russian defeat at Gorlice-Tarnow, Kitchener remarking that 'unfortunately we have to make war as we must, and not as we should like to'. Ultimately, Britain's increasing commitment to the land war was to be reflected in the length of the Western Front held by the British Expeditionary Force, which increased from the 24 miles held in November 1914 to 123 miles by February 1918.[37]

By April 1916, most of the British policy-makers were reluctantly convinced that the war might end in either an indecisive peace or possibly even a German victory if the British did not participate fully in the combined offensive planned by the Allied military representatives at Chantilly in December 1915. Thus, the ground was laid for the opening of the Somme campaign on 1 July 1916. It was chosen as a battlefield because this was where the British and French sectors of the front lines met and because Anglo-French co-operation appeared to offer the best chance of success. It was not, however, specifically intended to take pressure off Verdun, since the strategy had been agreed before the opening of the German offensive on Verdun, and the British effort was continued for four months after the Germans had ceased to attack. For a brief period in August and September 1916, attrition seemed to be working, with Haig claiming results on the Somme, the Italians claiming to have inflicted heavy losses on an Austro-Hungarian offensive, the Brusilov offensive in the east, and Romania's entry into the war. By November, hopes had been dashed by the failure of the Somme offensive and the swift crushing of Romania.[38]

In some respects, therefore, the reluctant agreement to allow the Passchendaele offensive to proceed in the summer of 1917 was partly founded in Haig's promise that this would bring a morale-boosting victory, but also in the belief that if the British stood idle, the spectre of defeatism would spread through the Entente. It was also justified – though primarily in retrospect – on the grounds of relieving pressure on the French following the near collapse of their army in the Nivelle offensive.

With the failure of the offensive, which he had never expected to prove a decisive blow, Lloyd George determined to husband remaining manpower resources and economic staying-power until the arrival of the Americans in force would enable a decisive effort to be mounted in 1919. In that way, the British army would not totally exhaust itself, preventing the military and political balance within the Entente swinging entirely in the favour of the

United States. In other words, the British would still have sufficient soldiers left alive to retain some diplomatic leverage in the peace talks.

In the event, following the failure of the German spring offensives in 1918, the Entente counter-attacked in the summer. In October, when the Germans appealed to Woodrow Wilson for an armistice on the basis of his Fourteen Points, it posed a serious challenge for the British in terms of whether it would be better to continue the war in the expectation of a more complete victory. Alternatively, however, if the war continued, then American influence would increase yet further, Smuts arguing cogently on 24 October 1918 that in an 'American peace', the United States 'will have taken our place as the first military, diplomatic and financial power of the world'. Accordingly, the British accepted the terms proposed only on the understanding that Wilson's demands for freedom of the seas, the future of German colonies and the question of indemnities would not be settled until the subsequent peace conference.[39]

Of all the Entente powers, it has been argued that Russia was the most responsive to its partners' demands and needs despite its own often significant problems. The Chantilly conference in December 1915 agreed co-ordinated Russian, French and Italian offensives but this was then upset by the German offensive at Verdun. As a result, the Russians advanced towards Lake Narotch near Vilna in Lithuania in March 1916 specifically to try to draw German pressure off Verdun and assist the Serbs. The heavy casualties sustained in the process had a paralysing effect on most Russian commanders thereafter. An exception was Alexei Brusilov, whose offensive was brought forward at the request of the Italians. Russian supplies reached the British and French forces at Salonika and four Russian brigades also fought with the French army on the Western Front, sent as Alekseev explained because 'we are so dependent on the French for war-material that the categorical refusal we should give is out of the question'.

It should be noted, however, that the Russians did not fulfil their promise to the Romanians under the terms of the military convention of 17 August 1916, of launching a renewed offensive in Galicia and Bukovina, and of using the Russian fleet to ensure the security of the mouth of the Danube and Constanta on the Black Sea. The Russians were undoubtedly unhappy that they did not receive the material assistance they expected from Britain, though, in fact, Britain did provide the machine tools, railway stock and raw materials that enabled Russian war industry to expand.[40]

Other major partners within the Entente were not integrated into any overall strategy. Japanese strategy was conducted entirely independently and Japan did not participate in the Supreme War Council. Italy also largely chose to wage its own war. Thus, the military convention signed with Russia in May 1915 had no practical effect on Italian strategy and there was no Italian co-operation with Serbia. Cadorna did attempt to co-ordinate the timing of his fifth Isonzo offensive with the British and French in order to try to alleviate German pressure on Verdun in March 1916 and, similarly, the eleventh Isonzo offensive was launched in August 1917 to attempt some relief for the Russians. However, despite British and French forces being rushed to Italy after Caporetto, Diaz proved even less willing to co-operate than Cadorna and refused two requests by Foch in the summer of 1918 to launch a new Italian offensive.

When the Romanians did enter the war in 1916, they were in effect sacrificed by the other Entente partners. Russia's collapse then so isolated the Romanians that they made the best terms they could in May 1918. Pressed by her partners to launch an offensive to coincide with those expected on the Italian and Russian fronts, Putnik argued in July 1915 that such action would not be in Serbia's interests given the hostility of Bulgaria. In turn, the Serbs did not receive the support promised them when attacked by Bulgaria, Germany and Austria-Hungary in October 1915, the British and French concentration at Salonika being completed only after the Serbs had been defeated.[41]

Strategy and war aims: the Entente

While the needs of coalition partners might or might not influence strategic decisions, each belligerent's own concept of its national interests most certainly did. In the case of a number of members of the Entente such as Belgium, France and Russia, the national interest dictated that national territory occupied by the enemy after the war's first campaigns must be retaken. Clemenceau, indeed, routinely ended speeches by reminding his audience that the Germans were still at Noyon within easy reach of Paris. However, this vital preliminary necessity did not prevent the pursuit of other wider national objectives.

Britain, France and Russia adopted a joint Declaration of London on 5 September 1914, which rejected concluding a separate peace and accepted the need for consensus in formulating peace terms. As the war continued, however, national war aims became an important means by which domestic morale could be sustained for further sacrifices. In the process, war aims became a maximum negotiating position but their use as bargaining counters in itself tended to lead to escalation of demands since no belligerent could be seen to accept lesser gains. In fact, aims were best kept fairly vague in order to avoid the possibility of failure to achieve them appearing as defeat. Unfortunately, vagueness might suggest to domestic opinion that the gain was not worth the sacrifice: as Michael Howard has nicely expressed it: 'The flower of British and French manhood had not flocked to the colours in 1914 to die for the balance of power.'[42]

While Russia's immediate objective was to resist Germany and Austria-Hungary in Poland and Galicia, St Petersburg still hoped to fulfil its traditional objective of controlling the Dardanelles, the lifeline of Russian commerce, as well as moving the western frontier to the Vistula. By March 1915 the Russians had compiled an extensive list of Turkish territories for annexation, extending beyond Constantinople and the Dardanelles to southern Thrace. In terms of Austria-Hungary, the Russians favoured an independent Bohemia, an enlarged version of Serbia, and a semi-autonomous Poland. Such objectives necessitated the destruction of both Ottoman Turkey and Austria-Hungary and implied a division of effort between the main Eastern Front and the Caucasus front.

Nonetheless, as early as August 1914 the Russians conceded a degree of post-war autonomy to a Poland created from German, Austrian and Russian territory. Indeed, Grand Duke Nicholas issued proclamations promising Polish union as well as the liberation of Slavs within the Austro-Hungarian Empire. An autonomous Armenia was also promised by another Russian military proclamation.

In September 1914, Sazonov included the Polish proposal in his Thirteen Points presented to Britain and France, who both eventually announced their agreement to Polish reunification in November 1916, following a promise of Polish independence given by the Central Powers. Ultimately, the Russian Provisional Government also offered Poland independence in March 1917 in a military union with Russia. The Russians favoured leaving the Czechs within a post-war tripartite monarchy of Austria, Hungary and Bohemia. However, their indication in October 1914 that they would support the Romanian claim to Transylvania made any subsequent negotiation with Austria-Hungary exceedingly difficult.[43]

Serbia's initial aim was to survive the opening Austro-Hungarian onslaught, but its early success led to a declaration by the Serbian parliament on 7 December 1914 of the intention to liberate and unite all Serbs, Croats and Slovenes within the Austro-Hungarian Empire. The Serbs came under increased pressure from the Entente, however, to make concessions to Bulgaria but would not do so unless given some guarantee of a greater Serbia for the southern Slavs (or Yugoslavs).

With the exception of the Russian provisional government, the Entente did not officially accept Serbian war aims throughout the war and had promised much of the projected greater Serbia to Italy and Romania. Indeed, the Serbian government even contemplated the possibility of a separate peace deal, a factor leading to the government's purge of the Black Hand in 1916: 'Apis' was arrested and subsequently executed in June 1917. The Serbian participation in the eventual Allied offensive from Salonika in the autumn of 1918, however, reintroduced Serbian forces to Serbia and Montenegro and paved the way for the creation of the Kingdom of Serbs, Croats and Slovenes (later Yugoslavia) established on 1 December 1918. King Nikita had always opposed the inclusion of Montenegro in such a creation, but his people supported it.[44]

Belgium and France were both focused on the need to preserve territorial integrity. Belgium sought, first, the recovery of occupied territory, but then a more defensible frontier, which would also take in those areas with which there was an historic affinity such as Eupen and Malmédy. Some Belgians also coveted Luxemburg and Limburg but there was a recognition of the danger of incorporating a substantial German minority. Further afield, the Belgians were by no means happy simply to give Britain a free hand in disposing of Germany's African colonies. Indeed, conscious that the British and French might yield the Belgian Congo to Germany in any compromise peace, King Albert was prepared to entertain his own negotiations with Germany in 1915 and 1916, seeking territorial compensation for the abandonment of the neutrality which Belgium still claimed to maintain.[45]

For France, the recovery of Alsace-Lorraine was an obvious aim. The French also wished to be compensated for war losses and to ensure future security against German and, specifically, 'Prussian militarism'. Generally, however, the French were cautious in their stated aims, primarily for fear of upsetting the sometime fragile domestic political truce within France. The political turmoil in itself also meant that war aims emerged from a ferment of ideas from varying interlocking interests groups rather than from agreed policy.

Joffre certainly believed that he could not remain inactive when French soil was in the hands of the Germans. The result was a series of offensives that cost France dear in casualties and, in the process, as Douglas Porch has noted, fulfilled the strategic goals of the Germans rather than those of the French. Ultimately, the near-collapse of the French army in 1917 compelled the adoption of Pétain's more limited strategy intended to preserve the army and French influence within the Entente.

At the same time, Pétain served another national interest in shifting the focus of French strategic attention to the lost provinces of Alsace-Lorraine, since it was feared that the absence of any overt attempt to recover them by force of arms might result in failure to acquire them after the war. Some within the French government also discussed with the Russians their willingness to accept Russian control of the Straits and of Poland in return for Russian acceptance of French expansion into the Rhineland to control the left bank of the Rhine.

Others believed that Luxemburg must be annexed by either France or Belgium but, preferably, by France. The colonial interest was also active in pressing for a redrawing of colonial frontiers in Africa, an interim agreement being reached with Britain for the future of Togo and Kamerun in the spring of 1917. Still others saw advantage for France in the break-up of both the Ottoman and the Austro-Hungarian Empires and the provisional Sykes–Picot agreement with Britain in January 1916 divided up the Middle East. It was followed by a tripartite agreement with Russia over the division of Anatolia in April 1916.[46]

A number of French economic interests envisaged wider advantages accruing from German defeat, although some groups feared that the return of Lorraine's industrial resources would actually damage existing French enterprises. Ideas included acquisition of the Saar coalfields, which had not been French territory since 1814, and to ensure post-war penetration of the German market by French steel producers. Such an outcome would redress the economic balance between France and Germany and increase Germany's dependence upon French iron ore, though still leaving France dependent upon German coking coal, which the Saar did not produce. Similarly, acquisition of the left bank of the Rhine would bring France parts of the industrial Ruhr.

Economic aims were also evident in the French interest in the Salonika expedition, which offered great opportunities in Syria, Asia Minor and Persia. As a result of the promises made her, Italy would be a major economic regional player after the war, necessitating further protection for French trading interests. Thus, Sarrail carefully advanced French economic aims, ensuring that 75 per cent of the imports reaching Salonika's 250,000 inhabitants were French.

Similarly, it was the French who initiated an Entente economic conference in Paris in June 1916, designed to minimise German trade competition after the war. In the event, French difficulties during 1917 somewhat modified the public declaration of French war aims and, beyond a stated determination for recovering Alsace-Lorraine, Clemenceau was studiously vague.[47]

Italy could only fulfil her territorial ambitions by defeating Austria-Hungary, and Cadorna identified the seizure of Vienna as the only strategic objective that would bring about Austro-Hungarian recognition of defeat. Accordingly, despite the geographical constraints of the mountainous Italian theatre, Cadorna committed himself to a series of eleven offensives across the Isonzo between June 1915 and September 1917 and rejected other possible strategies such as co-operating more fully with Serbia or, indeed, amphibious operations against Turkey. Cadorna, however, had generally miscalculated in believing that Austro-Hungarian forces could not be released from the Eastern Front to meet the initial Italian effort and, when this offensive failed, he resorted to sheer attrition. By the autumn of 1917, Cadorna's armies had advanced just eighteen miles into Austria-Hungary at a cost of 1 million dead or wounded, the Italians' suffering certainly equalling, if not exceeding, that endured by the British on the Somme and at Passchendaele, or by the French and Germans at Verdun.

Salandra and Sonnino had not been sufficiently careful in negotiating the Treaty of London to spell out wider Italian interests beyond the recovery of *Italia irredenta*. In any case, in the knowledge that the Italians could barely hold a few garrisons against the Senussi in Libya, Sonnino did not support some of the wilder dreams of expansion into central and eastern Africa. Consequently, discovery at the end of 1916 of the Sykes–Picot agreement and the concession of the Straits to Russia revealed Italy to have been disadvantaged. In April 1917, therefore, Sonnino secured some recognition of Italian interests within the Ottoman Empire. Equally, the Italians firmly opposed any deal with Austria-Hungary along the lines proposed during the Sixte affair. The loss of Russia in 1917, however, made Italian desires to exclude Russian imperialism from the Adriatic less necessary and, without the agreement of Sonnino, who had remained Foreign Minister, Orlando permitted the convening in Rome of a Congress of Oppressed Nationalities in April 1918. He hoped to ally Italy with some of the subject nationalities within the Austro-Hungarian Empire by renouncing some Italian aspirations in Dalmatia. The Pact of Rome gave tacit Italian support for the establishment of a post-war Yugoslavia although, in the event, Italian troops seized Fiume, part of Austria-Hungary, in November 1918 and Orlando's administration appeared intent on enforcing the Treaty of London in full.[48]

The most obvious early British war aim was the restitution of Belgium, although adherence to the Entente also implied acquiescence in general French and Russian aims, which served British interests less well than safeguarding the Channel ports. The question of precisely what else Britain was fighting to achieve was raised systematically for the first time only amid the fleeting optimism of August and September 1916. It was soon clear, however, that the rather vague expression of a war being fought to destroy Prussian militarism, a theme used by Asquith in his speech on war aims at the Guildhall on 9 November 1914, masked differences of perception.

On the part of the soldiers, there was a determination to inflict a sufficiently clear military victory on Germany to deter future aggression. At the same time, there was a certain ambivalence towards what might be termed total victory since, as Haig put it in January 1918, 'few of us feel that the democratising of Germany is worth the loss of a single Englishman'. Indeed, the British military leadership as a whole believed that nothing would be gained by stripping Germany of her colonies or imposing crippling economic indemnities in view of the need to re-establish an effective post-war balance of power in Europe.

On the other hand, both Colonial Office and Admiralty were keen to take German colonies to ensure the future security of the Empire. The Foreign Office shared some of the army's views with respect to Germany but favoured a degree of self-determination extending to an independent Poland and was generally more favourable towards comprehensive German disarmament. Generally, politicians sought a more total victory in order to be able to restructure Germany, the crusade against Prussian militarism becoming a major theme of British wartime propaganda. Nonetheless, most British policy-makers recognised that, after the war, Germany would be required to balance France and, especially, Russia. The Russian collapse in 1917 saw a modification of attitudes towards the balance of power, with a renewed sense of the need to strengthen France, since Russian defeat suggested greater opportunities for Germany to increase its own post-war power.[49]

Austria-Hungary was hardly regarded as an opponent at all and, while no one was especially committed to its preservation, it was seen as a useful barrier to Germany's eastern ambitions. Thus, it was only belatedly, with the failure to detach Vienna from Berlin, that Britain came round to the view of allowing self-determination to prevail although some elements within the Foreign Office had been hostile to Austria-Hungary from the beginning.

The collapse of Russia simplified matters and there were additional hopes of raising Polish and Czech forces to continue the war in the east. Consequently, Britain edged towards recognition of the Polish National Committee on 15 October 1917 and the Czech National Committee on 2 August 1918, but only as official national organisations. The war ended before the Yugoslav Committee could receive British recognition, by which time British approval was largely academic. If Austria-Hungary did not arouse much passion outside the Foreign Office, there was similarly little animosity towards Bulgaria, whose territorial claims were actually generally supported. British 'Bulgarophilism', however, sat uneasily with the claims of Romania and Serbia.[50]

Of greater importance was the future security of the Empire and, in this context, the break-up of Turkey was increasingly seen as desirable. Middle Eastern oil resources were vital for a Royal Navy now fuelled by oil rather than coal. It was the need to secure Persia and to deflect Russian interest from acquiring German or Austro-Hungarian territory – yet keeping Russian military effort concentrated on the Eastern Front rather than the Caucasus – that persuaded the British government to allow the Russians the post-war control of Constantinople and the Straits in the Straits Agreement on 12 November 1914.

Similarly, Britain could not afford France's acquiring Syria without adequate compensatory protection for British interests in Egypt and Mesopotamia. Thus, a limited demonstration by the Indian army was mounted in November 1914 to occupy Basra in the Persian Gulf to reassure the Gulf rulers of British protection against the Turks, the Indian government having despatched the force to Bahrein even before Turkey entered the war. Fighting alongside the French and Russians did not automatically extinguish older imperial rivalries, and winning the war for Britain meant increasing security against both current enemies and current allies.[51]

Imperial considerations were evident in the negotiations opened with Sharif Hussein of Mecca in October 1914 as a means both of encouraging revolt against the Turks and of securing British influence over the Red Sea coast. French suspicions led to the Sykes–Picot agreement, whereby any post-war Arab kingdom would be divided into British and French spheres of influence. In the same way, the British support for Zionist aspirations, as evinced by the Balfour Declaration on 2 November 1917, promised the further establishment of British influence through a co-operative Jewish population in post-war Palestine. The problem, however, as Sir Henry Wilson remarked in June 1919, was that the British had made 'so many promises to everybody in a contradictory sense that I cannot for the life of me see how we can get out of our present mess without breaking our word to somebody'.[52]

The desire to ensure British prestige in Muslim eyes encouraged extension of the campaign in Mesopotamia to an advance upon Kut in June 1915 with an inadequate force. The advance to Kut became one on Baghdad in November 1915 but, within two days, the over-extended expedition was forced to retreat to Kut, where, surrounded, it was compelled to surrender in April 1916. Saving face after such a disaster was an additional stimulus for the renewed British offensive towards Baghdad in the spring of 1917, but this was also accelerated by fears that the Russians intended to move on Baghdad through Persia. The British offensive into Palestine in the spring of 1917 aroused both French and Italian suspicions of British aims. In turn, this encouraged publication of the Balfour Declaration whereby, as David French has remarked, the advance 'could be presented as a campaign of liberation, and Britain's post-war presence could be cloaked as a necessary step towards self-determination'.[53]

Public declaration of war aims was speeded by the German announcement on 12 December 1916 that they were willing to discuss peace terms. In turn, this prompted the intervention of the United States on 20 December 1916. The British rightly judged the German approach an attempt to split the Entente but could not afford outright rejection, which might strengthen German support in the United States. In response, therefore, the

British and French called for the restoration of Belgium and Serbia, the evacuation of German-occupied territory, indemnities for war damages, and self-determination for subject nationalities within the Austro-Hungarian and Ottoman Empires. They also accepted Wilson's proposal for a post-war League of Nations. Additional pressure was exerted by the collapse of the Tsarist government in Russia in March 1917 and by the call by the new Provisional Government in May for a peace without annexations or indemnities.

By the summer of 1917, the Russian defection, the French mutinies and the challenge of German unrestricted submarine warfare placed Britain and the Entente in a precarious position. Thus, though the Austro-Hungarian overtures for a separate peace were eventually rejected, the War Cabinet, which had previously rejected the idea of peace without victory, resolved in August 1917 that they would negotiate if the Germans evacuated Belgium.[54]

Passchendaele, which was held out by Haig as the victory that domestic morale sorely needed in the summer of 1917, also represented a lingering survival of the pre-war 'Belgian option' and, indeed, of Britain's concern to keep the Channel coast out of hostile hands.[55] It was waged, however, against the background of the Reichstag Peace Resolution, calling for a settlement based upon no annexations or indemnities, to which the British responded by a demand for democratisation of Germany in advance of any negotiations. Papal mediation was also rejected later in August, as was a further German approach in September.

Nonetheless, in response to the publication of a letter on 29 November 1917 by the former Unionist Foreign Secretary, Lord Lansdowne, calling for peace, Lloyd George suggested on 5 January 1918 a certain willingness to compromise. Italy's claims on Austria-Hungary would not be supported unless justified and, while Belgium, Serbia and Romania should all be restored, there should not be an automatic expansion of states in the Balkans despite the need to recognise self-determination within the Austro-Hungarian and Ottoman Empires.

Self-determination was a two-edged sword for the British in view of the situation in Ireland but, with great imperial proconsuls like Milner and Lord Curzon in the War Cabinet, and many of Milner's disciples within government, it was always evident that Turkey would be dismembered in the interests of what Paul Guinn has characterised as a 'new imperialism' at the heart of British politics. At the same time, the establishment of preferential tariffs over the expanded Empire would strengthen Britain's future economic position. Moreover, viewing the prospect of the war continuing into 1919, some, like Henry Wilson and Leo Amery, argued that Britain could act on the defensive in the west and seize the initiative in the east, expanding British influence to the Caucasus, Armenia and the Caspian as an appropriate buffer zone between a German-dominated eastern Europe and a British-dominated Asia and Middle East.[56]

When the United States entered the war, it was clear that the Americans had a strategy rather similar to that of Britain in 1914 in intending to dictate the peace. Wilson was prepared to accept the strategic assumptions of his allies but there were limitations to American attachment to the Entente. Significantly, indeed, the United States did not sign up to the 1914 Declaration of London precluding a separate peace. Thus, the American Expeditionary Force was committed to the Western Front precisely because this was identified as the decisive theatre, in which an independent American army launching its own major offensive would make a recognisable contribution to victory. Pershing remarked, indeed, that 'when the war ends our position will be stronger if our army acting as such will have played a distinct and definite part'.

The insistence on maintaining a separate army was integral to wider American war aims although some compromises had to be made in the spring of 1918 in order to ensure that the Entente was not defeated before the arrival of the bulk of the American Expeditionary Force. Since the British army was nearing exhaustion, the political price the Americans could extract was considerable. Indeed, once it was clear in August 1918 that the German offensives were over, the British reduced the shipping available to convey American troops to Europe for there was little advantage either in increasing American leverage or in sacrificing British export trade to do so.

Wilson maintained the concept of a war fought for democracy, which precluded territorial gains on the part of the Entente. Nor did Wilson show much interest in restoring a balance of power within Europe. Thus, Wilson was somewhat embarrassed by the negative response by his partners to the intervention of Pope Benedict XV in August 1917 since the Papal note reflected many of his own ideas, although Wilson could not accept the restoration of the status quo also implied by the note. In the autumn, Wilson had his special adviser, Colonel Edward House, convene a wide-ranging academic enquiry into a future peace settlement. When House's mission to Europe failed to get Lloyd George and Clemenceau to agree on a general statement of war aims, therefore, Wilson issued his Fourteen Points unilaterally on 8 January 1918. Rejecting secret diplomacy, Wilson endorsed freedom of the seas, free trade, reduction of armaments, restoration of occupied territories, self-determination, and a League of Nations. In effect, Wilson promised autonomy only for the Czechs and southern Slavs at this stage, though he did endorse an independent Poland. Three subsequent declarations refining Wilson's war aims were also issued unilaterally and he made little effort to co-ordinate his policy with that of his allies.[57]

With the negotiation of the Treaty of Brest Litovsk between Germany and the Bolsheviks in March 1918, matters looked black for the Entente and tentative negotiations were opened by Britain with both Austria-Hungary and Turkey. With the opening of the German spring offensive on the Western Front, however, these negotiations speedily collapsed. The British had extended some assistance to those within Russia likely to continue the war against the Germans at the end of 1917 in order to keep the Ukraine out of German hands and thus blunt the threat to British interests elsewhere. Neither Britain nor France had many troops to spare, however, and they therefore pressed Wilson and the Japanese to intervene in Russia. The revolt against the Bolsheviks in May 1918 by the Czech Legion, recruited by the Russians from former Austro-Hungarian prisoners of war, provided a useful opportunity, since the Czechs were distributed along the trans-Siberian railway and had seized the port of Vladivostock.

Wilson was apprehensive of such an enterprise but was persuaded by July 1918 that the Germans must be forced to retain large numbers of troops inside Russia for fear of tilting the balance in the west before the Americans could arrive in force. As a result, 7,000 American troops were landed at Vladivostock in August 1918, together with 70,000 Japanese. British troops had earlier landed at Murmansk in March 1918 and had penetrated Transcaspia from Mesopotamia and Persia. British, French and American troops also landed at Archangel in August 1918. The American role, however, was restricted to protecting the supply bases at the ports and extricating the Czechs.[58]

Strategy and war aims: the Central Powers

German strategy was in many respects ordained prior to the war by such factors as her landlocked position, the inept pre-war diplomacy that had confronted Germany with the likelihood of a war having to be fought on two fronts simultaneously, and the military primacy over the civilians. An additional complicating factor was the wide war aims with which Germany entered the war, as epitomised by the September Programme of 9 September 1914.

Whatever the interpretation put upon the origins of the September Programme, its reach was comprehensive. In terms of *Mittelafrika*, the wish list included acquisition of Angola, northern Mozambique, the Belgian Congo, much of French Equatorial Africa, part of Senegal, and, if Britain entered fully into the war, part of Nigeria. In terms of *Mitteleuropa*, outright annexations were limited to what was regarded as indispensable from military or industrial perspectives, but with indirect control extended over much of Europe through a customs union embracing Austria-Hungary, Belgium, Denmark, France, the Netherlands and Poland, with the possible addition of Italy, Norway and Sweden.

In addition to becoming economically dependent, France would be disarmed and lose the industrial region of Longwy-Briey and, conceivably, her Channel ports. Belgium would lose Liège and Antwerp, while Luxembuig would be incorporated within the Reich. In the east, Russia would be opened to German imports and weakened by a degree of self-determination for some of the subject nationalities such as the Poles, a solution to be preferred to annexation since the latter would merely increase the Polish presence within the Reich. On a number of occasions, Bethmann proclaimed that the Germans were fighting a war for the liberation of non-Russian nationalities such as the Ukrainians and the Finns. Within occupied Belgium, the *Flamenpolitik* (Flemish policy) encouraged Flemish separatism, nominal Flemish 'independence' being declared in January 1918. Similarly, it was intended to stimulate nationalism in India, Egypt, Morocco, Ireland and among the Turkomans within Persia.[59]

The September Programme was heavily influenced by economic interests such as the Kriegszielbewegung (War Aims Movement), a group forged by the director of Krupps and president of the Union of Ruhr Concerns, Alfred Hugenberg, in co-operation with the Alldeutscher Verband (Pan-German League). This did not mean that *Mitteleuropa* appealed to all German business interests since neither government nor business spokesmen consulted ordinary businessmen. It was not welcomed by German agrarianists, who feared competition from central Europe. Nor was *Mitteleuropa* seen as a substitute for possible exclusion from other world markets. Therefore, it would require some recognition from the Entente in any post-war settlement in order to work since it could not substitute for loss of British and American markets. Nonetheless, business leaders continued to press for expansion. After Bethmann's removal in July 1917, heavy industrialists told his successor Michaelis that they would fight another ten years to acquire Longwy-Briey while, in the east, others envisaged detaching buffer regions such as Courland and populating them with German settlers. Even the Bavarians had their own aims, seeking to incorporate Alsace into Bavaria.

The German Navy had equally extensive aims, extending control not only to the Belgian and Baltic coasts but to the Faeroe Isles and acquiring naval bases at Dakar or the Cape Verde islands, Valona in Albania, the Azores, Tahiti, Madagascar and in the Dutch East Indies. Indeed, the insistence of naval and economic interests in annexing much of Belgium remained an acute stumbling block to any negotiated peace. The Brest

Litovsk settlement imposed on the Bolsheviks in 1918 was to detach Finland, the Ukraine, the Crimea and the Transcaucasus from Russia. Poland, which was granted a nominal independence in November 1916 largely in the hope of attracting Polish recruits for the German army, was to be ruled by an Austro-Hungarian archduke and the Baltic states were to be closely linked to Germany itself.

In this way, the industrial and agricultural resources of the Caucasus and the Ukraine would be acquired for Germany, offsetting the Entente's intended post-war economic bloc. However, just as Egmont Zechlin has argued that the September Programme was a short-term reaction to British entry into the war, so Georges-Henri Soutou has argued that it was not actually in Germany's commercial interests to erect further trade barriers in Europe and that *Mitteleuropa* was only seriously pushed as a measure of economic self-defence after the Paris economic conference in June 1916. Indeed, he regards the Entente's economic war aims as a more significant challenge than *Mitteleuropa* to a post-war liberal international economic order, hence Woodrow Wilson's emphasis on a global economic 'open door' policy.[60]

Initial Austro-Hungarian war aims were to incorporate Serbia, Bosnia-Hercegovina and Dalmatia within the empire, though leaving Montenegro nominally independent. Albania would be partitioned between Austria-Hungary, Greece and Bulgaria and the 1866 frontier with Italy re-established to give a more 'natural boundary'. Austro-Hungarian defeats led to a greater emphasis upon the survival of the existing empire but with some additional strategic gains on the frontiers still sought, including the annexation of Montenegro and a protectorate in Albania.

Poland was especially significant for Austria-Hungary, since a fully independent Poland would be too great a focus of loyalty for Polish subjects remaining within Austrian Galicia. Simply partitioning Russian Poland would cause tensions within both Germany and Austria-Hungary. The 'Austrian solution' put forward in August 1915 was to unify Russian Poland and Austrian Galicia as an autonomous kingdom with a Habsburg sovereign. Bethmann supported this to a degree but, in April 1916, countered with an autonomous Poland linked directly to Germany. In August, Berlin and Vienna agreed to a public commitment to a post-war independent monarchy in Russian Poland, its proclamation on 5 November 1916 finally ruling out any prospect of a separate peace with an undefeated Russia.

In discussions at Kreuznach in May 1917, however, Germany accepted a proposal allocating Romania to Austria-Hungary (though with a substantial German interest in Romania's oil fields) while Poland would be ceded to Germany with the intention of pushing the Polish frontier far to the east. Subsequently, Vienna revived its interest in Poland but, at another conference at Kreuznach in October 1917, OHL demanded part of Austrian

Silesia as the price for accepting this as well as guarantees for German economic access to a Poland. The agreement in effect completed Polish and Austro-Hungarian military and economic integration within the Reich, a process Vienna had delayed as long as possible. Vienna also angered the Poles by ceding Cholm to the Ukraine as the price for securing grain supplies for Hungary in the first treaty of Brest Litovsk in February 1918.

Poles themselves fought in the German, Austro-Hungarian and Russian armies. Initially, indeed, the future Polish head of state, Joseph Pilsudski, supported the Central Powers, before switching sides in July 1917, following the fall of the Tsar and in the belief that the Germans were not serious about Polish independence. He was arrested by the Germans and remained in detention until November 1918. By contrast, Pilsudki's main pre-war rival, Roman Dmowski, favoured the Entente from the start. The Polish forces raised by the Central Powers and the Russians had been dispersed by 1918, but the French had also raised a separate Polish army in June 1917.

Increasingly, too, attention had to be paid to internal demands for autonomy from other nationalities, especially after the Entente had committed itself to self-determination. Like the Poles, Czechs and Slavs were confronted with a potential dilemma as to whether it would be better to remain loyal to the Austro-Hungarian Empire or to hope for an Entente victory. Many Czechs were wary of Russian ambitions in 1914 and, while Thomas Masaryk opted to leave Austria-Hungary in December 1914 to campaign for Czech independence in Paris, others preferred an internal solution. In the face of German and Hungarian opposition, however, Emperor Karl could not make any firm response to the Czech Union, created in November 1916. As a result, when recalled in May 1917, the Austrian parliament or Reichsrat became a forum for Czech discontent. Czech units, often recruited from prisoners of war, fought for the French, Italians and the Russians. Their belligerency was sufficient to secure British and American recognition for the Czech National Committee.

Similarly, confronted by the concept of a Yugoslavian state, many Croats and Slovenes favoured remaining in the Empire, albeit within an autonomous federal system. Italian aspirations, however, played a large part in shaping a distinct Yugoslav programme both within and without the Empire. Thus, while the Yugoslav Committee emerged in the west, a Yugoslav declaration for autonomy within the Empire was voiced in May 1917 and a National Council of Austria's southern Slavs was proclaimed in Ljubljana in August 1918. Ultimately, however, Karl's announcement of a federal system in the Austrian half of the Empire on 16 October 1918 came far too late to satisfy national aspirations.[61]

Turkey, who was not well integrated within the Central Powers in a political sense, did have war aims, attempting three separate offensive endeavours against the Entente by striking at the Suez Canal, stirring the Senussi in Libya to attack Egypt, and advancing into the Caucasus. The Turkish advance on Egypt was easily repulsed in February 1915, but the Senussi were not suppressed by the British until March 1916. It was the Caucasus that Enver, Minister of War, regarded as most significant, in the expectation of inspiring revolt among Russia's Islamic peoples. The peoples of the region, however, had their own nationalist aspirations, not least the Kurds, many of whom deserted to the Russians.

The Russians also raised a division among Christian Armenians. The latter were regarded by the Turks as instruments of the Russians and had suffered previous Turkish repression. Consequently, the role of Armenian troops in the repulse of the Turkish offensive in December 1914 and January 1915 and the subsequent declaration of a provisional Armenian government in April 1915 provoked genocide by the Turkish authorities. An estimated 1.5 million Armenians died in both Anatolia and Transcaucasia as a result of massacre, deportation to the Mesopotamian desert, starvation and disease, the majority by September 1915. After Russia's collapse, the Turks advanced into the Caucasus in February 1918 with the intention of regaining the territory lost in the Russo-Turkish War of 1877–78, compelling the Germans to commit forces themselves to secure Georgia. A British force defended the Centrocaspian Dictatorship against the Turks until withdrawing in September 1918. The Turks then took Baku in November 1918, but were forced to withdraw in turn.[62]

Germany began the war with just one strategy, based on confidence in the Schlieffen Plan winning the war quickly. Indeed, there was a belief that total war carried too great a risk in terms of the social fabric of Germany. A war of attrition must be avoided at all costs since raw materials and other supplies were relatively limited and, while the German economy was strong, its industrial base was not sufficient for prolonged war. When the great gamble failed on the Marne in 1914, Germany had little alternative but to stand generally on the defensive and to meet enemy offensives as they developed, with as much strength as possible for as long as possible. Indeed, on the Western Front in particular, the geographical strength of the positions taken up by German forces as they retreated and the fact that Germany remained in possession of much of Belgium and productive parts of France forced the Entente to take the initiative.

Equally, although its original purpose had been as a deterrent, the German navy had banked all on fighting a single decisive naval battle in the North Sea to annihilate the British Grand Fleet. Tirpitz had not considered any alternative should the Royal Navy simply resort to a long distance blockade by closing the Straits of Dover and the waters between Norway and Scotland. It was simply an article of faith that the Royal Navy must offer battle. In effect, the North Sea became, in the words of Holger Herwig, a 'dead sea' in strategic terms for the Royal Navy did not need to risk a decisive engagement in order to win the naval war, whereas the German High Seas Fleet did and yet could not risk doing so against British naval superiority.

Little consideration was given to the possibility of crushing the Russian Baltic Fleet, thus enabling a greater concentration against England. There was at least some initial success in commerce raiding on the part of the ten German vessels at sea when the war began but, with the exception of the *Goeben* and *Breslau*, the others had been lost by July 1915.

Subsequent German conversion to unrestricted submarine warfare from the naval point of view was a result of frustration. In 1914, Germany had only twenty-one U-boats capable of operating in the North Sea, of which only nine were diesel-powered craft capable of reaching the Atlantic. Nevertheless, Tirpitz's public advocacy of unrestricted submarine warfare struck a chord with public and politicians alike. Bethmann argued against it on the grounds that it would antagonise neutrals and possibly bring Italy and other Balkan states into the Entente, but his opposition was steadily eroded and the Chief of the Naval Staff, Admiral Hugo von Pohl, persuaded the Kaiser to agree to its introduction on 4 February 1915.

American reaction concerned Bethmann, while Falkenhayn's fear of the Dutch abandoning their neutrality led him to support the chancellor in pressing for the modification of the rules of engagement for the submarine campaign in the aftermath of the sinking of the *Lusitania* and the *Arabic*.[63]

Initially, Falkenhayn attempted to continue to break through in the west, but he concluded in November 1914 that this was now impossible. Moreover, he saw not France or Russia but Britain as the main opponent to Germany establishing its rightful position as a world power. Thus, he advocated reaching a compromise peace with the Russians. Bethmann agreed in principle with seeking an accommodation but wanted the approach to come from the Russians for fear that public opinion could be undermined by knowledge of a German peace offer. When the Russians were defeated at Gorlice-Tarnow in May 1915, Falkenhayn again suggested seeking a separate peace but, correctly, Bethmann doubted if the Tsar would act independently of his allies.

In selecting Britain as the main opponent, Falkenhayn recognised that it was the French army that was the main instrument of Britain's war, a logic of which Kitchener would have approved. Thus, over the winter of 1915–16, Falkenhayn resolved to strike at the French not in the expectation of breaking through, but of 'bleeding them white' in a 'meat grinder' since he would choose a point which the French must defend: 'The French General Staff would be compelled to throw in every man they have. If they do so, the forces of France will bleed to death – as there can be no question of a voluntary withdrawal – whether we reach our goal or not.' By destroying the French army he would destroy Britain's main weapon, and compel the French and British to negotiate. The chosen point of attack was Verdun, of symbolic significance to France as the last fortress to surrender to the Germans in the Franco-Prussian War. But Falkenhayn's intentions were too vaguely conveyed to the German field commander, Crown Prince Wilhelm of Fifth Army, who attempted to seize the French fortresses around Verdun rather than simply threaten them. Moreover, the offensive failed because such an attritional strategy had equal repercussions for both sides. Falkenhayn had expected a kill ratio in the Germans' favour of 5:2, but the reality was only 15:14 in the Germans' favour.[64]

Failure at Verdun, the success of the Brusilov offensive, and Romanian entry into the war resulted in Falkenhayn's dismissal in August 1916 and the summoning to Berlin of Hindenburg and Ludendorff. They were convinced that a decisive victory could be won against Russia, forcing the Russians to negotiate a separate peace, which would give Germany access to raw materials and food supplies from the Ukraine and thus avoid the consequences of the British naval blockade. A stable peace in the east would also allow Germany to transfer troops to the west to launch a major offensive in due course. Hindenburg and Ludendorff also subscribed to the wilder visions of German expansion. They compelled Bethmann, who was far from a moderate on war aims, to accept the Kreuznach Protocol in April 1917, which included provision for annexations in the Baltic, domination of Poland, occupation of the Belgian coast and Longwy-Briey, access to the Romanian oil fields, and occupation of Constanta. OHL also sponsored Tirpitz's extremist Vaterlandspartei (Fatherland Party), which claimed 1.25 million members by July 1918.[65]

Another consequence of Hindenburg and Ludendorff's success in effectively gaining control of the German governmental machine in August 1916 was renewed unrestricted submarine warfare. In some respects, it was not unlike the Schlieffen Plan in anticipating a victory in a short time. The assumption by Pohl's successor, Admiral Henning von Holtzendorff, was that Britain was particularly vulnerable to interdiction of wheat supplies and had at most 8 million tons of merchant shipping available to carry food supplies. This could be sunk at small cost and small risk at a rate of up to 667,000 tons a month. Since the 1916 harvest in the United States had proved poor and Britain largely depended upon American wheat, Britain could be brought to its knees within six to eight months.

In fact, the tonnage lost in the first six months of the campaign averaged 643,000 tons a month, but grain supplies were not sufficiently depleted to make it work. Bethmann managed to stave off an irrevocable decision being taken in March 1916, Tirpitz resigning as Navy Minister in consequence, but the *Sussex* pledge in May 1916 marked the end of the chancellor's success. Hindenburg and Ludendorff supported reopening unrestricted submarine warfare although they believed that victory should be secured over Romania first, thus freeing troops to mask the Netherlands and Denmark should they come into the war as a result of its reintroduction.

Bethmann, who likened such a course of action to a 'second decision for war' was further undermined by the Catholic Centre Party's support for the measure in October and the Entente's rejection of his tentative peace overtures in December, which persuaded the Kaiser that Germany must fight on. Accordingly, unrestricted submarine warfare was reintroduced from 1 February 1917. The political fallout in terms of the American entry into the war decisively tipped the balance against Germany, although the assumption was that the war could be won before the Americans arrived in sufficient numbers to make any difference.[66]

In fact, 1917 was Germany's best chance to make a successful negotiated peace but this was unacceptable to Hindenburg and Ludendorff, especially given the increasing turmoil in Russia. Initially, their response was cautious after the leftist leader of the Centre Party, Matthias Erzberger, suggested in a Reichstag speech on 6 July 1917 that the war could not be won, but the subsequent Reichstag Peace Resolution on 19 July led them to repudiate utterly the notion of negotiating a peace without annexations or indemnities. As it happens, the resolution was somewhat ambiguous in not excluding the possibility of other means than annexation to secure German influence in Europe. Hindenburg and Ludendorff tendered their resignations to the Kaiser, but so too did Bethmann, and it was the latter which was accepted.

With Russia successfully knocked out of the war in the autumn of 1917, assisted by OHL's agreement to allow the transportation of Lenin from Switzerland to the Baltic in the 'sealed train', OHL's true ambition was well illustrated by the draconian annexationist policies imposed on Russia at Brest Litovsk on 3 March 1918. The Bolsheviks yielded 90 per cent of Russia's coal mines, 54 per cent of its industry, 33 per cent of its railways, 32 per cent of its agricultural land and 34 per cent of its population.

Brest Litovsk was followed by similarly harsh terms imposed on Romania in the Treaty of Bucharest on 7 May 1918, which, among other provisions, ceded Romania's oil fields to German and Austro-Hungarian control for 99 years. The two treaties, however, had not exhausted OHL's territorial ambitions and, at the time of the armistice in November 1918, German forces were still advancing in the east. OHL was pursuing ideas of a German-sponsored puppet state in the Ukraine under Hetman Paul Skoropadsky, to counter Entente support for the Czechs; a similar Tartar republic in the Crimea; and increased German influence in Transcaucasia, where Georgia was taken under German protection in May 1918 to forestall Turkish ambitions. There was also considerable German interest in the Baltic provinces of Courland and Livonia, and Finland. Indeed, Germany formally allied itself with the Finns fighting the Bolsheviks in March 1918 and the Finns installed a German prince, Friedrich Karl of Hessen, as their monarch in October 1918.[67]

In many respects, Hindenburg and Ludendorff's approach was one of victory at whatever cost. The defeat of Russia certainly eased the pressure but it also held dangers in that both Austria-Hungary and Bulgaria might press for a negotiated peace. Turkey, too, was close to collapse and, while it was not clear what the consequences of Turkish defeat might be, they could not be favourable to Germany. Consequently, Ludendorff resolved to attack in the west to secure a victory before the Americans arrived in force. It must be stressed that he did not have to do so for he could still have negotiated, but Ludendorff wished to attack. Once again, it was an all-or-nothing gamble. At Spa in Belgium in July 1918, in a pause between the fourth and fifth German offensives, the German leadership in effect restated its longstanding war aims. While the Entente counter-attack caused some subsequent modification of aims in the west, it did not affect German ambitions in the east. Indeed, on 27 September 1918, Germany agreed the so-called supplementary treaties, a series of new agreements with the Bolsheviks, detaching Estonia and Livonia from Russia. The first of Germany's allies, Bulgaria, collapsed on the following day.

When the 1918 spring offensives failed, German strategy was in essence bankrupted but, in many respects, it had been so from the very beginning. With the weakening of the army on the Western Front through the late summer and autumn of 1918, even Ludendorff came to recognise that an armistice was necessary, though his intention was merely to win time in order to continue the war. When it became clear that the Entente would not grant terms which allowed such a breathing space, Hindenburg and Ludendorff proposed to fight on, but Prince Max threatened to resign as Chancellor and, on this occasion, it was the resignation of Ludendorff that was accepted by the Kaiser.[68]

The kind of free-ranging debate allowed within the German army at tactical and operational level was never permitted at strategic level. Moreover, the separation of the military and civilian spheres of government, the lack of administrative mechanism for the long-term discussion of strategic policy, and the underestimation of the resources of Britain and the United States all contributed to the incapacity of the German leadership to weigh the balance between short-term and long-term strategic risk. In that sense, the Entente's matching of strategy and policy, imperfect though it was, was far superior to that of Germany.

Notes and references

1. Ian Beckett, 'Frocks and Brasshats', in Bond, ed., *First World War and British Military History*, pp.89–112.

2. John Terraine, *The First World War*, 2nd edn (London, 1983), p.x; idem, 'British Military Leadership in the First World War', in Liddle, ed., *Home Fires and Foreign Fields*, p.49.

3. David French, *British Strategy and War Aims, 1914–16* (London, 1986), p.247.

4. French, *British Economic and Social Planning*, pp.98–120; Hew Strachan, 'The British Way in Warfare', in David Chandler and Ian Beckett, eds, *The Oxford Illustrated History of the British Army* (Oxford, 1994), pp.417–34; eidem, 'The British Way in Warfare Revisited', *HJ* 26 (1983), pp.447–61; eidem, 'The Battle of the Somme and British Strategy', *JSS* 21 (1998), pp.79–95; Michael Howard, *The British Way in Warfare* (London, 1975); idem, 'British Grand Strategy in World War I', in Kennedy, ed., *Grand Strategies*, pp.31–42; John Bourne, *Britain and The Great War, 1914–18* (London, 1989), pp.133–8; John Gooch, 'The Weary Titan: Strategy and Policy in Great Britain, 1890–1918', in Murray, Knox and Bernstein, eds, *Making of Strategy*, pp.278–306.

5. Filipe Ribeiro de Meneses, 'Too Serious a Matter to be Left to the Generals: Parliament and the Army in Wartime Portugal, 1914–18', *JCH* 33 (1998), pp.85–96; Opacic, 'Some Questions', p.330; Nish, 'Japan, 1914–18', pp.232–3, 236–9; J. Charles Schencking, 'Bureaucratic Politics, Military Budgets and Japana's Southern Adavance: The Imperial Navy's Seizure of German Micronesia in the First World War', *WH* 5 (1998), pp.308–26; Thomas K. Nenninger, 'American Military Effectiveness in the First World War', in Millett and Murray, eds, *Military Effectiveness*, pp.117–18, 128–9; Edward M. Coffman, 'The American Military and Strategic Policy in World War I', in Hunt and Preston, eds, *War Aims and Strategic Policy*, pp.67–84; David F. Trask, *The AEF and Coalition Warmaking, 1917–18* (Lawrence, KS, 1993), pp.11–13, 156–8.

6. Brian R. Sullivan, 'Caporetto: Causes, Recovery, and Consequences', in George J. Andreopoulos and Harold E. Selesky, eds, *The Aftermath of Defeat: Societies, Armed Forces, and the Challenge of Recovery* (New Haven, CN, 1994), pp.71–2; Jones, 'Imperial Russia's Forces at War', pp.291–5; Stone, *Eastern Front*, pp.191–3.

7. Gooch, 'Italy during First World War', pp.159–61; Whittam, *Politics of Italian Army*, pp.198–203; Brian Sullivan, 'The Strategy of the Decisive Weight: Italy, 1882–1922', in Murray, Knox and Bernstein, eds, *Making of Strategy*, pp.336–7; H. James Burgwyn, *The Legend of the Mutilated Victory: Italy, the Great War and the Paris Peace Conference, 1915–19* (Westport, CN, 1993), pp.51–67.

8. French, *British Economic and Strategic Planning*, pp.175–7; idem, *Strategy and War Aims*, pp.63–4; idem, '"A One-Man Show"? Civil–Military Relations in Britain

during the First World War', in Paul Smith, ed., *Government and the Armed Forces in Britain, 1856–1990* (London, 1996), pp.75–107; John Turner, 'Cabinets, Committees and Secretariats: The Higher Direction of War', in Burk, ed., *War and the State*, pp.57–83.

9. Gooch, *Plans of War*, pp.302–7; Lloyd George, *War Memoirs*, II, p.751; Keith Neilson, 'Kitchener: A Reputation Refurbished?', *CJH* 15 (1980), pp.207–27; George H. Cassar, *Kitchener: Architect of Victory* (London, 1977), pp.236–40, 245–6; Bourne, *Britain and Great War*, pp.139–45; Hew Strachan, *The Politics of the British Army* (Oxford, 1997), pp.128–30.

10. Gooch, *Plans of War*, p.299; French, *Strategy and War Aims*, pp.65–74; David R. Woodward, *Lloyd George and the Generals* (Newark, NJ, 1983), pp.27–45; Wilson, *Myriad Faces of War*, pp.108–21.

11. Gooch, *Plans of War*, pp.314–30; French, *Strategy and War Aims*, pp.160–3; Turner, 'Higher Direction', pp.59–62; Woodward, *Lloyd George and Generals*, pp.80–2; Paul Guinn, *British Strategy and Politics, 1914–18* (Oxford, 1965), pp.113–14.

12. Woodward, *Lloyd George and Generals*, p.81; idem, *The Military Correspondence of Field Marshal Sir William Robertson, Chief Imperial General Staff, 1915–18* (London, 1989), pp.40–1.

13. Turner, 'Higher Direction', pp.62–7; idem, 'Lloyd George, the War Cabinet, and High Politics', in Peter Liddle, ed., *Passchendaele in Perspective: The Third Battle of Ypres* (London, 1997), pp.14–29; David R. Woodward, *Field Marshal Sir William Robertson, Chief of the Imperial General Staff in the Great War* (Westport, CN, 1998), pp.97–110; French, 'One-man Show', pp.81–4; Trevor Wilson and Robin Prior, 'British Decision-making 1917: Lloyd George, the Generals and Passchendaele', in Cecil and Liddle, eds, *Facing Armageddon*, pp.93–102; eidem, *Passchendaele: The Untold Story* (New Haven, CT, 1996), pp.31–42, 141–56, 185–93; David French, *The Strategy of the Lloyd George Coalition, 1916–18* (Oxford, 1995), pp.124–32; Keith Neilson, *Strategy and Supply: The Anglo-Russian Alliance, 1914–17* (London, 1984), pp.265, 272–3; Woodward, *Lloyd George and Generals*, pp.116–30, 138–56, 160–86, 190–9; idem, 'Britain in a Continental War: The Civil–Military Debate over the Strategic Direction of the War of 1914–18', *Albion* 12 (1980), pp.37–65; Keith Grieves, 'Haig and the Government', in Brian Bond and Nigel Cave, eds, *Haig: A Reappraisal 70 Years On* (Barnsley, 1999), pp.107–27.

14. Turner, 'Higher Direction', pp.69–76; French, *Strategy of Lloyd George Coalition*, pp.161–70, 214–28; idem, 'One-man Show', pp.93–7, 101–5; S. W. Roskill, 'The Dismissal of Admiral Jellicoe', *JCH* 1 (1966), pp.69–93; John Gooch, 'The Maurice Debate, 1918', in Gooch, ed., *Prospect of War*, pp.146–63; Woodward, *Lloyd George and Generals*, pp.206–16, 221–47, 253–78, 282–305; idem, 'Did Lloyd George Starve the British Army of Men prior to the German Offensive of 21 March 1918?', *HJ* 27 (1984), pp.241–52; idem, *Robertson*, pp.187–204; Guinn, *British Strategy and Politics*, pp.259–62.

15. J. C. King, *Generals and Politicians: Conflict between France's High Command, Parliament, and Government, 1914–18* (Berkeley, CA, 1951), pp.3–4, 16, 45–7, 53–62; Porch, 'French Army', pp.192–3; M. M. Farrar, *Principal Pragmatist: The Political Career of Alexandre Millerand* (New York, 1991), pp.136–7, 172–80; idem, 'Politics versus Patriotism: Alexandre Millerand as French Minister of War', *French Historical Studies* 11 (1980), pp.577–609.

16. George H. Cassar, *The French and the Dardanelles: A Study of Failure in the Conduct of War* (London, 1971), pp.35–40, 151–80; J. K. Tannenbaum, *General Maurice Sarrail, 1856–1929: The French Army and Left-wing Politics* (Chapel Hill, NC, 1974), pp.55–74; King, *Generals and Politicians*, pp.70–88; David Ralston, 'From Boulanger to Pétain: The Third Republic and the Republican Generals', in Bond and Roy, eds, *War and Society*, pp.178–201; David Dutton, *The Politics of Diplomacy: Britain and France in the Balkans in the First World War* (London, 1998), pp.17–48.

17. King, *Generals and Politicians*, pp.82–6, 89–139; David Dutton, 'The Fall of General Joffre: An Episode in the Politico-military Struggle in Wartime France', *JSS* 1 (1978), pp.338–51; idem, 'The Union Sacrée and the French Cabinet Crisis of October 1915', *ESR* 8 (1978), pp.411–24.

18. King, *Generals and Politicians*, pp.13–16, 50–6, 150–9, 163–76; Dutton, *Politics of Diplomacy*, pp.116–42, 167–85; Ralston, 'Boulanger to Pétain', pp.178–201.

19. Herwig, 'Dynamics of Necessity', pp.81–2, 90–1; Martin Kitchen, 'Civil-military Relations in Germany during the First World War', in Adams, ed., *Great War*, pp.38–9, 41; idem, *The Silent Dictatorship: The Politics of the German High Command under Hindenburg and Ludendorff, 1916–18* (London, 1976), pp.45–63.

20. Karl-Heinz Janssen, *Der Kanzler und der General: Die Führungskrise um Bethmann Hollweg und Falkenhayn* (Göttingen, 1966), pp.68–79; Ekkehart Guth, 'Des Gegensatz zwischen dem Oberbefehlshaber Ost und dem Chef des Generalstabes des Feldheeres 1914–15: Die Rolle des Major v. Haeften im Spannungsfeld zwischen Hindenburg, Ludendorff und Falkenhayn', *MM* 35 (1984), pp.113–39; Ritter, *Sword and Sceptre*, III, pp.41–56, 179–206.

21. Kitchen, 'Civil–military Relations', pp.43–6, 53–7, 59–61; idem, *Silent Dictatorship*, pp.19–41, 127–37, 149–51; Herwig, *First World War*, pp.373–5; Ritter, *Sword and Sceptre*, III, pp.288–343; idem, IV, pp.28–49, 297–315; Konrad Jarausch, *The Enigmatic Chancellor: Bethmann Hollweg and the Hubris of Imperial Germany* (New Haven, CN, 1973), pp.264–307.

22. Rothenberg, *Army of Francis Joseph*, pp.177–8, 192, 198–9, 202–3; Herwig, *First World War*, pp.108–9, 232–3, 242–3.

23. Jehuda L. Wallach, *Uneasy Coalition: The Entente Experience in World War I* (Westport, CN, 1993), pp.1–5, 169–73; B. F. Cooling, 'Some Considerations of Allied Operational Co-operation in World War I', *RIHM* 63 (1985), pp.141–54.

24. Herwig, *First World War*, pp.135–64, 204–17, 242–3; Rothenberg, *Army of Franz Joseph*, pp.185, 189–91, 212; Norman Stone, 'The Austro-German Alliance, 1914–18', in Keith Neilson and Roy Prete, eds, *Coalition Warfare: An Uneasy Accord* (Waterloo, 1983), pp.19–28; Gerard Silberstein, *The Troubled Alliance: German–Austrian Relations, 1914–17* (Lexington, KY, 1970), pp.251–74, 308–23; F. R. Bridge, 'The Foreign Policy of the Monarchy, 1908–18', in Mark Cornwall, ed., *The Last Years of Austria-Hungary: Essays in Political and Military History, 1908–18* (Exeter, 1990), pp.7–30; Gordon A. Craig, 'The World War I Alliance of the Central Powers in Retrospect: The Military Cohesion of the Alliance', *JMH* 37 (1965), pp.336–44.

25. Herwig, *First World War*, pp.369–70; E. P. Keleher, 'Emperor Karl and the Sixtus Affair', *EEQ* 26 (1992), pp.163–84; Wolfdieter Bihl, 'La mission de médiation des Princes Sixte et Xavier de Bourbon-Parma en faveur de la paix', *GMCC* 170 (1993), pp.31–76; Ritter, *Sword and Sceptre*, III, pp.373–98; Stephen Verosta, 'The German Concept of Mitteleuropa, 1916–18 and Its Contemporary Critics', in Kann, Király and Fichtner, eds, *Habsburg Empire*, pp.203–20; Mark Cornwall, 'The Dissolution of Austria-Hungary', in Cornwall, ed., *Last Years of Austria-Hungary*, pp.117–42; G. W. Shanafelt, *The Secret Enemy: Austria-Hungary and the German Alliance, 1914–18* (Boulder, CO, 1985), pp.97–192.

26. Ulrich Trumpener, 'Suez, Baku, Gallipoli: The Military Dimensions of the German–Ottoman Coalition, 1914–18', in Neilson and Prete, eds, *Coalition Warfare*, pp.31–51 [also in Király and Dreisziger, eds, *East Central European Society*, pp.381–400]; idem, *Germany and Ottoman Empire*, pp.62–139, 167–99, 200–351; Fahri Geliker, 'Die Beziehungen des türkischen Oberkommandos zu seiner Regierung und dem deutschen Oberkommando: Wirkungen auf die türkische Kriegspolitik und den Kriegsverlauf an den türkischen Fronten', in ICMH, *Acta 10*, pp.307–17; Frank Weber, *Eagles on the Crescent: Germany, Austria and the Diplomacy of the Turkish Alliance, 1914–18* (Ithaca, NY, 1970), pp.136–58; Silberstein, *Troubled Alliance*, pp.99–128; Muzaffer Erendil, 'The Ottoman Empire in World War I: The Home Front and Military Affairs', in Király and Dreisziger, eds, *East Central European Society*, pp.369–80.

27. Robbins, *First World War*, p.106; Ilia Iliev, 'Problèmes de l'art militaire Bulgare pendant la Première Guerre mondiale', in ICMH, *Acta 10*, pp.318–29; Silberstein, *Troubled Alliance*, pp.150–78.

28. William J. Philpott, *Anglo-French Relations and Strategy on the Western Front, 1914–18* (London, 1996), pp.30–46; David Dutton, 'The Calais Conference of December 1915', *HJ* 21 (1978), pp.143–56; Cassar, *French and Dardanelles*, pp.187–92; Guinn, *British Strategy and Politics*, pp.165–9; Wallach, *Uneasy Coalition*, pp.76–88, 181–2; Neilson, *Strategy and Supply*, pp.225–45.

29. Trask, *Captains and Cabinets: Anglo-American Naval Relations, 1917–18* (Columbia, MS, 1972), pp.212–16; Burk, *Britain, America and Sinews of War*, pp.99–106, 147–56; Heckscher, *Wilson*, pp.442–8; Marion C. Siney, 'The Allied Blockade

Committee and the Inter-Allied Trade Committee: The Machinery of Economic Warfare, 1917–18', in Bourne and Watt, eds, *Studies in International History*, pp.330–44.

30. John Gooch, 'Soldiers, Strategy and War Aims in Britain, 1914–18', in Hunt and Preston, eds, *Wars Aims and Strategic Policy*, p.27; Philpott, 'Kitchener and the 29th Division: A Study in Anglo-French Strategic Relations, 1914–15, *JSS* 16 (1993), p.400; idem, *Anglo-French Relations*, pp.15–50, 93–111, 150–60; idem, 'Britain and France go to War: Anglo-French Relations on the Western FRont, 1914–18', *WH* 2 (1995), pp.43–64; Woodward, *Lloyd George and Generals*, pp.253–5, 258–78, 287–90, 293–6, 312–14, 320–2; R. A. Prete, 'Joffre and the Question of Allied Supreme Command', *Proceedings of the Annual Meeting of the Western Society for French History* 16 (1989), pp.329–38; French, 'One-man Show', pp.103–5; Wallach, *Uneasy Coalition*, pp.46–53, 62–3, 91–7, 103–17; Burgwyn, *Legend of Mutilated Victory*, pp.171–92.

31. Philpott, *Anglo-French Relations*, pp.19–21, 159; idem, 'Britain and France go to War', pp.43–64; idem, 'Britain, France and the Belgian Army', in Brian Bond, ed., *Look to Your Front: Studies in the First World War* (Staplehurst, 1999), pp.121–36; Ferro, *Great War*, pp.133–4.

32. Porch, 'French Army', p.205; Gooch, 'Italy during First World War', p.169; Trask, *Captains and Cabinets*, pp.177–80, 225–82, 362; Paul Halpern, *The Naval War in the Mediterranean, 1914–18* (London, 1987), pp.457–87; Lawrence Sandhaus, *The Naval Policy of Austria-Hungary, 1867–1918: Navalism, Industrial Development and the Politics of Dualism* (West Lafayette, IN, 1994), p.329; Burgwyn, *Legend of Mutilated Victory*, pp.171–92.

33. Nenninger, 'American Military Effectiveness', pp.124–8; Charles R. Schrader, '"Maconochie's Stew": Logistical Support of American Forces with the BEF, 1917–18', in Adams, ed., *First World War*, pp.101–31; Trask, *AEF and Coalition Warmaking*, pp.36–42, 50–5, 76–9, 102–9; idem, *Captains and Cabinets*, pp.77–101.

34. French, 'Allies, Rivals and Enemies', pp.24–5; idem, 'The Meaning of Attrition, 1914–16', *EHR* 103 (1988), pp.385–405; Sir George Arthur, *The Life of Lord Kitchener* (London, 1920), III, p.244; Neilson, *Strategy and Supply*, pp.7–11.

35. French, *Strategy and War Aims*, pp.xii–xiii, 80–5; idem, 'The Origins of the Dardanelles Campaign Reconsidered', *History* 68 (1983), pp.210–24; Neilson, *Strategy and Supply*, pp.59–65.

36. Cassar, *French and Dardanelles*, pp.48–60, 70–82; William J. Philpott, 'Kitchener and the 29th Division', pp.375–407; idem, *Anglo-French Relations*, pp.70–81; Guinn, *British Strategy and Politics*, pp.57–64, 132; Dutton, *Politics of Diplomacy*, pp.49–115, 143, 197; idem, 'The "Robertson Dictatorship" and the Balkan Campaign in 1916', *JSS* 9 (1986), pp.64–78; Neilson, *Strategy and Supply*, pp.108–10; idem, *Britain and the Last Tsar: British Policy and Russia, 1894–1917* (Oxford, 1995), pp.343–50.

37. French, *British Economic and Strategic Planning*, pp.151–3; idem, 'Meaning of Attrition', pp.385–405; idem, *Strategy and War Aims*, pp.111–12; Cassar, *Kitchener*, p.389; Rhodri Williams, 'Lord Kitchener and the Battle of Loos: French Politics and British Strategy in the Summer of 1915', in Lawrence Freedman, Paul Hayes and Robert O'Neill, eds, *War Strategy and International Politics: Essays in Honour of Sir Michael Howard* (Oxford, 1992), pp.117–32; Keith Simpson, 'The British Soldier on the Western Front', in Liddle, ed., *Home Fires and Foreign Fields*, p.141.

38. French, 'Allies, Rivals and Enemies', pp.28–9; idem, 'Meaning of Attrition', pp.385–405; idem, *Strategy and War Aims*, pp.181–5, 200–5, 220–3; Philpott, *Anglo-French Relations*, pp.112–28; Elizabeth Greenhalgh, 'Why the British were on the Somme in 1916', *WH* 6 (1999), pp.147–73; Woodward, *Robertson*, pp.29–48.

39. French, *Strategy of Lloyd George Coalition*, pp.260–85; idem, 'Who Knew What and When? The French Army Mutinies and the British Decision to Launch the Third Battle of Ypres', in Freedman, Hayes and O'Neill, eds, *War, Strategy and International Politics*, pp.133–53; idem, 'Watching the Allies: British Intelligence and the French Mutinies of 1917', *Intelligence and National Security* 6 (1991), pp.573–92; Woodward, *Robertson*, pp.127–54.

40. Jones, 'Imperial Russia's Forces at War', pp.290, 295; Stone, *Eastern Front*, pp.220, 232, 246; Dumitru Preda, 'Romania's Political and Military Relations with the Entente, August–September 1916', *RIHM* 77 (1992), pp.46–58; Woodward, *Lloyd George and Generals*, pp.62–6; Guinn, *British Strategy and Politics*, pp.150–5; Neilson, *Strategy and Supply*, pp.314–18; idem, *Britain and Last Tsar*, pp.350–7; idem, 'The Break-up of the Anglo-Russian Alliance: The Question of Supply in 1917', *IHR* 3 (1981), pp.62–75.

41. Nish, 'Japan, 1914–18', pp.238–40; Ceausescu, 'Romanian High Command's Relations with Allies', pp.273–87; Opacic, 'Some Questions', p.340; Gooch, 'Italy during First World War', pp.158, 168–9; Sullivan, 'Caporetto', pp.64–6; Torrey, *Romania*, pp.137–93, 231–90.

42. Strachan, *First World War*, pp.9–10; Stevenson, *First World War and International Politics*, pp.87–8; Stone, *Eastern Front*, p.218; Robbins, *First World War*, pp.103–4; Michael Howard, *Studies in War and Peace* (London, 1970), pp.104–5.

43. Jones, 'Imperial Russia's Forces at War', pp.285, 289–90; Paul Kennedy, 'Military Effectiveness in the First World War', in Millett and Murray, eds, *Military Effectiveness*, p.341; Stevenson, *First World War and International Politics*, pp.118–22; Stone, *Eastern Front*, p.218; Horst Günther Linke, *Das zarische Russland und der Erste Weltkrieg: Diplomatie und Kriegsziele, 1914–17* (Munich, 1982), pp.37–73, 129–67, 206–26; idem, 'Russlands Weg in den Ersten Weltkrieg und sie Kriegsziele, 1914–17', *MM* 32 (1982), pp.9–34 [also in Michalka, ed., *Erste Weltkrieg*, pp.54–93]; Kaiser, *Politics and War*, pp.341–2; William Renzi, 'Who Composed Sazonov's Thirteen Points: A Re-examination of Russia's War Aims of 1914', *AHR* 88 (1983), pp.347–57.

44. Opacic, 'Some Questions', pp.330–45; Milorad Ekmecic, 'Serbian War Aims', in Djordjevic, ed., *Creation of Yugoslavia*, pp.19–36; Alex Dragnich, 'The Serbian Government, the Army and the Unification of Yugoslavia', ibid., pp.37–50; M. Vojvodic, 'Serbia and the First World War: Political and Diplomatic Aspects', in B. Király and D. Djordjevic, eds, *East Central European Society and the Balkan Wars* (New York, 1987), pp.240–39; Zivojinovic, 'Serbia and Montenegro', pp.239–59.

45. Rune Johnson, *Small States in Boundary Conflict: Belgium and the Belgian–German Border, 1914–19* (Lund, 1988); Louis, *Britain and Germany's Lost Colonies*, pp.62–8; Ferro, *Great War*, pp.133–4; Fischer, *Germany's Aims*, pp.215–24.

46. David Stevenson, *French War Aims against Germany, 1914–19* (Oxford, 1982), pp.12–13, 23–7, 36–44, 48–56, 82–3, 139–40, 216–22; Dutton, *Politics of Diplomacy*, p.149; Porch, 'French Army in First World War', pp.201–4; idem, 'The Marne and After: A Reappraisal of French Strategy in the First World War', *JMilH* 53 (1989), pp.363–85; Christopher Andrew and A. S. Kanya-Forstner, 'The French Colonial Party and French Colonial War Aims, 1914–18', *HJ* 17 (1974), pp.79–106; idem, *France Overseas: The Great War and the Climax of French Imperial Expansion* (London, 1981); R. A. Prete, 'French Military War Aims, 1914–16', *HJ* 28 (1985), pp.887–99; F. W. Brecher, 'French Policy towards the Levant, 1914–18', *Middle Eastern Studies* 29 (1993), pp.641–64.

47. Douglas Johnson, 'French War Aims and the Crisis of the Third Republic', in Hunt and Preston, eds, *War Aims and Strategic Policy*, pp.41–54; Pierre Renouvin, 'Les buts de guerre du gouvernement française', *Revue historique* 235 (1966), pp.1–38; V. H. Rothwell, *British War Aims and Peace Diplomacy, 1914–18* (Oxford, 1971) pp.266–81; Stevenson, *French War Aims*, pp.32–5, 75–88, 94–114, 216–9; idem, 'French War Aims and the American Challenge, 1914–18', *HJ* 22 (1979), pp.877–94; David Dutton, 'France and the Commercial Exploitation of Greece during the Great War', *CJH* 14 (1979), pp.65–83; idem, 'The Balkan Campaign and French War Aims in the Great War', *EHR* 94 (1979), pp.97–113; idem, *Politics of Diplomacy*, pp.143–66; John McDermott, 'Total War and the Merchant State: Aspects of British Economic Warfare against Germany, 1914–16', *CJH* 21 (1986), pp.61–76; R. E. Bunselmeyer, *The Cost of War, 1914–19: British Economic War Aims and the Origins of Reparation* (Hamden, CN, 1975), pp.21–51.

48. Gooch, 'Italy during First World War', pp.165–7; Whittam, 'War Aims and Strategy', pp.93–7; Robbins, *First World War*, p.115; Sullivan, 'Strategy of Decisive Weight', pp.331–42; idem, 'Caporetto', pp.64–7.

49. French, *Strategy and War Aims*, pp.210–16, 227–8; idem, *Strategy of Lloyd George Coalition*, pp.32–8; Gooch, 'Soldiers, Strategy and War Aims in Britain', pp.21–40; Guinn, *British Strategy and Politics*, pp.123–5, 183–4; Rothwell, *British War Aims*, pp.18–19; David Stevenson, 'Belgium, Luxembourg and the Defence of Western Europe, 1914–20', *IHR* 4 (1982), pp.504–23; J. S. Galbraith, 'British

War Aims in World War I: A Commentary on Statesmanship', *JICH* 13 (1984), pp.25–45; Lorna Jaffe, *The Decision to Disarm Germany: British Policy towards Postwar German Disarmament, 1914–19* (Boston, MA, 1985), pp.3–60; H. I. Nelson, *Land and Power: British and Allied Policy on Germany's Frontiers, 1916–19* (London, 1963), pp.3–26; Louis, *Britain and Germany's Lost Colonies*, pp.56–76.

50. Rothwell, *British War Aims*, pp.75–87, 116–23, 158–71, 215–33; Kenneth J. Calder, *Britain and the Origins of the New Europe, 1914–18* (Cambridge, 1976), pp.4, 22, 85, 93–103, 108–213, 216.

51. Gooch, 'Soldiers, Strategy and War Aims', pp.27–8; Guinn, *British Strategy and Politics*, pp.43–4, 219–22; Stevenson, *First World War and International Politics*, pp.124–31, 176–82; French, *Strategy and War Aims*, pp.48–9, 136–8, 140–3, 146–8; idem, 'Allies, Rivals and Enemies', pp.28–32; Jukka Nevakivi, 'Lord Kitchener and the Partition of the Ottoman Empire, 1915–16', in Bourne and Watt, eds, *Studies in International History*, pp.316–29; S. A. Cohen, 'The Genesis of the British Campaign in Mesopotamia, 1914', *Middle Eastern Studies* 12 (1976), pp.119–30; C. Jay Smith, 'Great Britain and the 1914–15 Straits Agreement: The British Promise of November 1914', *AHR* 70 (1965), pp.1015–34; Geoffrey Paget, 'The November 1914 Straits Agreements and the Dardanelles–Gallipoli Campaign', *Australian Journal of Politics and History* 33 (1987), pp.253–60; Neilson, *Britain and Last Tsar*, pp.357–64.

52. Marion Kent, 'Great Britain and the End of the Ottoman Empire', in Marion Kent, ed., *The Great Powers and the End of the Ottoman Empire* (London, 1984), pp.172–205; J. E. Peterson, 'Southwest Arabia and the British during World War I', *Journal of South African and Middle Eastern Studies* 2 (1979), pp.18–37; Jehuda Reinharz, 'The Balfour Declaration and Its Maker: A Reassessment', *JMH* 64 (1992), pp.455–99; Leonard Stein, *The Balfour Declaration* (London, 1961), pp.117–46, 309–60, 533–604; Keith Jeffery, *The British Army and the Crisis of Empire, 1918–22* (Manchester, 1984), p.122.

53. David French, 'The Dardanelles, Mecca and Kut: Prestige as a Factor in British Eastern Strategy, 1914–16', *W&S* 5 (1987), pp.45–61; idem, *Strategy of Lloyd George Coalition*, pp.9–10; 133–5; Rothwell, *British War Aims*, pp.24–6, 28–30, 87–5, 123–42; idem, 'Mesopotamia in British War Aims, 1914–18', *HJ* 13 (1970), pp.273–94; Davis, *Ends and Means*, pp.15–48; Woodward, *Robertson*, pp.155–72; Matthew Hughes, *Allenby and British Strategy in the Middle East, 1917–19* (London, 1999), pp.23–42; J. S. Galbraith, 'No Man's Child: The Campaign in Mesopotamia, 1914–16', *IHR* 6 (1984), pp.358–85.

54. French, Strategy of the Lloyd George Coalition, pp.6–9, 40–62, 94–8, 103–9; idem, ' "Tous ces vagues discours de nous mènent à rien": La politique britannique et la paix avec l'Autriche-Hongrie, 1916–18', *GMCC* 170 (1993), pp.119–30; Guinn, *British Politics and Strategy*, p.247; Stevenson, *First World War and International Politics*, pp.80–4, 140–4; idem, 'The Failure of Peace by Negotiation, 1917', *HJ* 34 (1991), pp.65–86; W. B. Fest, 'British War Aims and German Peace Feelers during the First World War (December

1916–November 1918)', *HJ* 15 (1972), pp.285–308; Guy Pedronici, 'La France et les négociations secrètes de paix en 1917', *GMCC* 170 (1993), pp.131–40; Rothwell, *British War Aims*, pp.38–49, 59–66, 83–7.

55. Philpott, 'Strategic Ideas of Sir John French', pp.458–78; idem, *Anglo-French Relations*, pp.53–67; 129–49; idem, 'The Great Landing: Haig's Plan to invade Belgian from the Sea in 1917', *IWMR* 10 (1995), pp.84–9; Alf Peacock, 'The Proposed Landing on the Belgian Coast, 1917', *Gunfire* 11/12 (1988), pp.2–50, 3–56; Andrew Wiest, 'The Planned Amphibious Assault', in Liddle, ed., *Passchendaele in Perspective*, pp.201–14; Brian Bond, 'British War Planning for Operations in the Baltic before the First and Second World Wars', in S. Rystad, K.-R. Böhme and W. M. Carlgran, eds, *In Quest of Trade and Security: The Baltic in Power Politics, 1500–1990*, 2 vols (Lund, 1995) II, pp.107–38.

56. French, 'Allies, Rivals and Enemies', pp.31–5; idem, *Strategy of Lloyd George Coalition*, pp.62–4, 139–47, 171–8, 187–92, 199–206, 316–18; David Woodward, 'The Origins and Intent of Lloyd George's January 5 War Aims Speech', *Historian* 34 (1971/2), pp.22–39; idem, *Robertson*, pp.111–26; Guinn, *British Strategy and Politics*, p.193; Rothwell, *British War Aims*, pp.68–75, 145–55; Robbins, *First World War*, p.108; Stevenson, *First World War and International Politics*, pp.162–9, 189–93; Benjamin Schwarz, 'Divided Attention: Britain's Perception of a German Threat to her Eastern Position in 1918', *JCH* 28 (1993), pp.103–22; Bunselmayer, *Cost of War*, pp.21–51; Brian Bond, *The Pursuit of Victory: From Napoleon to Saddam Hussein* (Oxford, 1996), pp.109–11; B. Millman, 'Sir Henry Wilson's Mischief: Field Marshal Sir Henry Wilson's Rise to Power, 1917–18', *Journal of Canadian History* 30 (1995), pp.467–86.

57. Smith, *Great Departure*, pp.83–99; Trask, *AEF and Coalition Warmaking*, pp.6–8, 20–4; Hans-Jürgen Schröder, 'Demokratie und Hegemonie: Woodrow Wilson's Konzept einer Neuen Weltordnung', in Michalka, ed., *Erste Weltkrieg*, pp.159–77; David Esposito, *The Legacy of Woodrow Wilson: American War Aims in World War I* (Westport, CT, 1996); Edward Parsons, 'Why the British Reduced the Flow of American Troops to Europe in August to October 1918', *CJH* 12 (1977), pp.173–92; Victor S. Mamatey, *The United States and East Central Europe, 1914–18: A Study in Wilsonian Diplomacy and Propaganda* (Princeton, NJ, 1957), pp.153–317; Paula Fichtner, 'Americans and the Disintegration of the Habsburg Monarchy: The Shaping of an Historiographical Model', in Kann, Király and Fichtner, eds, *Habsburg Empire*, pp.221–34.

58. French, 'Allies, Rivals and Enemies', pp.32–5; idem, *Strategy of Lloyd George Coalition*, pp.195–9, 239–44, 246–53, 273–4; I. Flotto, 'Woodrow Wilson: War Aims, Peace Strategy and the European Left', in Arthur Link, ed., *Woodrow Wilson and a Revolutionary World, 1913–21* (Chapel Hill, NC, 1982), pp.127–36; Nenninger, 'American Military Effectiveness', pp.124–7, 131–2, 153; David Trask, *The United States in the Supreme War Council: American War Aims and Inter-allied Strategy, 1917–18* (Middletown, CT, 1961), p.74; idem, 'Woodrow Wilson contra the Allies, 1917–18', in ICMH, *Acta 10*, pp.261–72; Guinn, *British*

Strategy and Politics, pp.308–13; Rothwell, *British War Aims*, pp.158–84, 187–90; Stevenson, *First World War and International Relations*, pp.207–16; Z. A. B. Zeman, *The Break-up of the Habsburg Empire, 1914–18: A Study in National and Social Revolution* (Oxford, 1961), pp.198–216. On intervention in Russia generally, see J. Bradley, *Allied Intervention in Russia* (London, 1968); idem, 'L'Intervention alliée dans les Etats Baltes', *Revue d'Histoire Moderne et Contemporaine* 23 (1976), pp.236–57; M. J. Carley, 'The Origins of the French Intervention in the Russian Civil War, January–May 1918: A Reappraisal', *JMH* 48 (1976), pp.413–39; Eugene Trani, 'Woodrow Wilson and the Decision to Intervene in Russia: A Reconsideration', *JMH* 48 (1976), pp.440–61; and Michael Kettle, *Russia and the Allies, 1917–20: The Allies and the Russian Collapse, March 1917– March 1918* (London, 1981); idem, *Russian and the Allies, 1917–20: The Road to Intervention, March–November 1918* (London, 1988).

59. Fischer, *Germany's Aims*, pp.98–119, 122–46, 313–22, 359–60; idem, 'German War Aims', pp.98–108, 113–15; idem, *Kaiserreich to Third Reich*, pp.56–66; idem, *War of Illusions*, pp.439–58, 516–41; Ritter, *Sword and Sceptre*, III, pp.29– 40; Hans Wilhelm Gatzke, *Germany's Drive to the West: A Study of Germany's Western War Aims during the First World War* (Baltimore, MD, 1950), pp.7–62, 139–44; Stevenson, *First World War and International Politics*, pp.89–9; Sophie de Schaepdrijver, 'Occupation, Propaganda and the Idea of Belgium', in Roshwald and Stites, eds, *European Culture*, pp.281–92; Imanuel Geiss, *Der Polnische Grenzstreifen, 1914–18: Ein Beitrag zur Deutschen Kriegszielpolitik im Ersten Weltkrieg* (Lubeck, 1960), pp.41–95, 117–47.

60. Kitchen, *Silent Dictatorship*, pp.89–95; Holger Herwig, 'Admirals versus Generals: The War Aims of the Imperial German Navy, 1914–18', *CEH* 5 (1972), pp.208–33; Jarausch, *Enigmatic Chancellor*, pp.185–229; Fischer, *Germany's Aims*, pp.164–73, 179–83, 247–59, 271–9, 313–19; idem, 'German War Aims', pp.116–19; Kaiser, *Politics and War*, pp.335–41; Zechlin, 'Cabinet versus Economic warfare', pp.237–60; Georges-Henri Soutou, *L'Or et le sang: les buts de guerre économiques de la premiére guerre mondiale* (Paris, 1989); idem, 'Die Kriegsziele des Deutschen Reiches, Frankreichs, Grossbritanniens und der Vereinigten Staaten während des Ersten Weltkrieges: ein Vergleich', in Michalka, ed., *Erste Weltkrieg*, pp.28–53; idem, 'German Economic War Aims Reconsidered: The American Perspective', in Shröder, ed., *Confrontation and Co-operation*, pp.315–21.

61. Kitchen, *Silent Dictatorship*, pp.89–95, 105–7, 140–3, 189–95; Stevenson, *First World War and International Politics*, pp.95–9, 144–8; Ritter, *Sword and Sceptre*, III, pp.100–17, 209–35; idem, IV, pp.145–87, 237–43; Fischer, *Germany's Aims*, pp.236–44, 310–11, 353–6; Manfred Rauchensteiner, *Der Tod des Doppeladlers: Österreich-Ungarn und det Erste Weltkrieg* (Graz, 1994), pp.303–24; Imanuel Geiss, 'World War I and East Central Europe: A Historical Assessment', in Király and Dreisziger, eds, *East Central European Society*, pp.27–42; Victor S, Mamatey, 'The Czech Wartime Dilemma: The Habsburgs or the Entente?', ibid., pp.103–11; idem, 'The Union of Czech Political Parties in

the Reichsrat, 1916–18', in Kann, Király and Fichtner, eds, *Habsburg Empire*, pp.3–28; Janko Pleterski, 'The Southern Slav Question, 1908–18', in Cornwall, ed., *Last Years of Austria-Hungary*, pp.77–100; Bridge, 'Foreign Policy of Monarchy', pp.7–30; Zeman, *Break-up*, pp.65–94, 100–9, 122–7, 151–9, 177–98; R. A. Williams, 'The Czech Legion in Italy during World War I', in Williamson and Pastor, eds, *Essays on World War I*, pp.199–214; Josef Kalvoda, 'The Origins of the Czechoslovak Army, 1914–18', in Király and Dreisziger, eds, *East Central European Society*, pp.419–35; Segel, 'Culture in Poland', pp.60–8; Leonard Ratajczyk, 'The Evolution of the Polish Army, 1914–22', ibid., pp.439–53; Leslaw Dudek, 'Polish Military Formations in World War I', ibid., pp.454–70; Eligiusz Kozlowski, 'The Polnishe Wehrmacht, 1916–18', ibid., pp.471–85; M. Kamil Dziewanowski, 'Polish Society in World War I: Armed Forces and Military Operations', ibid., pp.486–99; Marian Leczyk, 'La genèse des formations militaires polonaises en France pendant la première guerre mondiale et leur participation aux combats sur le front franco-allemand', *RIHM* 63 (1985), pp.61–72; Mark Cornwall, 'The Experience of Yugoslav Agitation in Austria-Hungary, 1917–18', in Cecil and Liddle, eds, *Facing Armageddon*, pp.656–76; Clifford F. Wargelin, 'A High Price for Bread: The First Treaty of Brest Litovsk and the Break-up of Austria-Hungary, 1917–18', *IHR* 19 (1997), pp.757–88.

62. Keegan, *First World War*, pp.238–43; Martin Gilbert, *First World War*, 2nd edn (London, 1995), pp.166–7; Vahakn Dadrian, 'The Role of the Special Organisation in the Armenian Genocide during the First World War', in Panios Panayi, ed., *Minorities in Wartime: National and Racial Groupings in Europe, North America and Australia during the World Wars* (Oxford, 1993), pp.50–82. See also K. Ahmed, *Kurdistan in the First World War* (London, 1994); M. J. Somakian, *Empires in Conflict: Aremnia and the Great Powers, 1895–1920* (London, 1995); and V. N. Dadrian, *The History of the Armenian Genocide: Ethnic Conflict from the Balkans to Anatolia to the Caucasus* (Providence, RI, 1995).

63. Herwig, 'Dynamics of Necessity', pp.89–92; idem, *Luxury Fleet: The Imperial German Navy, 1888–1918* (London, 1980), pp.87–8; Ivo Lambi, *The Navy and German Power Politics, 1862–1914* (Boston, MA, 1984), pp.343, 355; Paul Kennedy, 'The Development of German Naval Operational Plans against England, 1896–1914', in Kennedy, ed., *War Plans*, pp.177–93; Offer, *First World War*, pp.324–30; Gary E. Weir, 'Tirpitz, Technology and Building U-boats, 1897–1916', *IHR* 6 (1984), pp.174–90; Michael Epkenhans, 'Der kaiserliche Marine im Ersten Weltkrieg: Weltmacht oder Untergang?', in Michalka, ed., *Erste Weltkrieg*, pp.319–40; Werner Rahn, 'Strategische Probleme der deutschen Seekriegführung, 1914–18', ibid., pp.341–65; May, *World War and American Diplomacy*, pp.113–36, 197–227; Ritter, *Sword and Sceptre*, III, pp.119–77, 288–343; Fischer, *Germany's Aims*, pp.287–93, 302–9.

64. Kitchen, 'Civil–military Relations', pp.43–4; Fischer, *Germany's Aims*, pp.189–208; Afflerbach, *Falkenhayn*, pp.300–5, 321–4, 451–6, 543–5; Klaus Epstein, *Matthias Erzberger and the Dilemma of German Democracy* (Princeton, NJ, 1959),

pp.209–18; L. L. Farrar, 'Peace through Exhaustion: German Diplomatic Motivations for the Verdun Campaign', *RIHM* 32 (1972–75), pp.477–94; Gerd Krumeich, '"Saigner la France"? Mythes et Réalitié de la stratégie allemande de la bataille de Verdun', *GMCC* 182 (1996), pp.17–30; Michael Salewski, 'Verdun und die Folgen: Eine militärische und geistesgeschichtliche Betrachtung', *Wehrwissenschaftliche Rundschau* 25 (1976), pp.89–96; Herwig, 'Strategic Uncertainties', p.271.

65. Kitchen, *Silent Dictatorship*, pp.99–107; Ritter, *Sword and Sceptre*, III, pp.416–36; idem, IV, p.16; Fischer, *Germany's Aims*, pp.342–51, 356–60; Herwig, *First World War*, pp.304–7; L. L. Farrar, *Divide and Conquer: German Efforts to Conclude a Separate Peace, 1914–18* (New York, 1978), pp.57–84; idem, 'Separate peace – general peace – total war: The Crisis in German policy during the spring of 1917', *MM* 20 (1976), pp.51–80; idem, 'Opening to the West: German Efforts to Conclude a Separate Peace with England, July 1917–March 1918', *CJH* 10 (1975), pp.73–90.

66. Kitchen, *Silent Dictatorship*, pp.111–24; Jarausch, *Enigmatic Chancellor*, p.281; Offer, *First World War*, pp.357–67; Herwig, *First World War*, pp.312–25; Holger Herwig and David F. Trask, 'The Failure of Imperial Germany's Undersea Offensive against World Shipping, February 1917–October 1918', *The Historian* 33 (1971), pp.611–36; May, *World War and American Isolation*, pp.228–52; 404–15; Stevenson, *First World War and International Politics*, pp.103–6; Raffael Scheck, 'Der Kampfe des Tirpitz – Krieses für den uneingeschränken U-Boot-Krieg und einen politischen Kurwechsel im deutschen Kaiserreich, 1916–17', *MM* 55 (1996), pp.69–91.

67. Kitchen, 'Civil–military Relations', pp.50–7; idem, *Silent Dictatorship*, pp.157–84, 189–207, 211–27, 231–44; Ritter, *Sword and Sceptre*, III, pp.399–407, 457–87; idem, IV, pp.5–16, 28–48, 69–117, 171–87, 244–56, 269–95; Fischer, *Germany's Aims*, pp.364–69, 399–404, 416–28, 475–523, 534–62; Farrar, *Divide and Conquer*, pp.96–101; Robbins, *First World War*, p.118; idem, 'German Policy in the Eastern Baltic Sea in 1918: Expansion or Anti-Bolshevik Crusade?', *Slavic Review* 32 (1973), pp.339–57; Klaus Epstein, *Matthias Erzberger and the Dilemma of German Democracy* (Princeton, NJ, 1959), pp.182–90, 203–4; P. W. Dyer, 'German Support of Lenin during World War I', *Australian Journal of Politics and History* 30 (1984), pp.46–55; Stevenson, *First World War and International Politics*, pp.198–205.

68. Kitchen, 'Civil-military Relations', pp.56–61; idem, *Silent Dictatorship*, pp.247–67; Fischer, *Germany's Aims*, pp.563–82, 609–13, 630–3; Helmut Otto, 'Die strategische Planung der dritten Obersten Heeresleitung 1916–18 in Spannungsfeld zwischen den Kriegszielen und dem Kriegspotential des deutschen Kaiserreiches', in ICMH, *Acta 10*, pp.35–46; Holger Afflerbach, 'Die militärische Planung des Deutschen Reiches im Ersten Weltkrieg', in Michalka, ed., *Erste Weltkrieg*, pp.280–318.

CHAPTER SIX

New Ways of War

The achievement of war aims and the success of strategy depended upon significant military victory, but it had become apparent by the end of 1914 that deadlock on the Western Front confronted belligerents with new problems. Asquith's reaction to various suggestions made by Maurice Hankey, in his 'Boxing Day' memorandum in December 1914, for developing new technological means for breaking the deadlock, was to find it curious that there might be a reversion to what he called medieval forms of warfare. In reality, science and technology were to be harnessed to the war effort to an extent that not only was the destructive impact of weaponry greatly increased, but also it became possible to more effectively target civilian populations. Indeed, Churchill was to write after the war that, 'When all was over, Torture and Cannibalism were the only two expedients that the civilised, scientific Christian societies had been able to deny themselves: and these were of doubtful utility.'[1]

Science and war

The popular reaction to science and technology was one of ambivalence. On the one hand, technological advance was welcomed as a means of transcending existing boundaries, although the loss of the *Titanic* in 1912 had certainly provided a corrective to unlimited faith in its capabilities. On the other hand, modernity and technology also offered frightening uncertainty. The development of aviation well illustrates the dual impact. Flying attracted considerable public interest before the war: in the year in which Louis Blériot made the first flight across the English Channel – 1909 – an estimated 250,000 people attended a flying meeting at Rheims. At the same time, however, the threat posed by the military use of aircraft and, especially, dirigibles caused considerable public apprehension.

In part, the pre-war 'Zeppelin panic' in Britain also derived from the ready incorporation of science into traditional 'invasion scare' literature. Most of the writers of such fiction had little scientific prescience and, in any case, the purpose of their publications was often avowedly propagandist. Nonetheless, some writers were more predictive than others. H. G. Wells, for example, not only predicted some aspects of the future air war in novels such as *Argonauts of the Air* (1895) and *The War in the Air* (1907), but also contributed a story to *The Strand* magazine in 1903, 'The Land Ironclads', which consciously offered a potential solution to the battlefield deadlock foreseen by Bloch, to whose work Wells briefly referred in the story.[2]

From the beginning of the war, the scientific communities within the belligerent states became involved in their respective war efforts. In France, the Academy of Sciences placed itself at the disposal of the government on 4 August 1914. Painlevé, the distinguished mathematician, who became Minister of Education in October 1915, at once established a board for defence-related inventions under another mathematician, Emile Borel, to integrate industrial innovation directly into the war effort.

Similarly, pressure by German scientists led to the establishment of the Kriegsrohrstoffabteilung (KRA; Raw Materials Section) of the Prussian War Ministry in September 1914 to try to provide synthetic and other substitutes for those raw materials lost through the Allied economic blockade. The German army also made early use of the Kaiser Wilhelm Institute for Physical and Electrochemistry at Berlin, whose director, Fritz Haber, graduated swiftly from developing an anti-freeze for vehicles operating on the Eastern Front to taking charge of the chemical warfare programme. Like other scientists before and since, Haber believed that harnessing science to war would save lives by ending the war more quickly. In 1916, a scientific commission was established within the Kriegsamt (Supreme War Office), and in January 1917 Haber and another leading chemist, Emil Fischer, established the Kaiser Wilhelm Foundation for the Science of War Technology. In Austria-Hungary, the Technische Hochschule (Technical High School) in Vienna was converted into a research institute in 1916 to improve the production of munitions, while the United States entered the war in April 1917 with two existing agencies established as a result of its observations of the war in Europe, the Naval Consulting Board and the National Research Council.[3]

In Britain, scientific involvement was somewhat slower to develop despite the existence of pre-war scientific advisory commissions such as that at the Royal Arsenal at Woolwich and the Royal Aircraft Factory at

Farnborough. Neither army nor Royal Navy, however, responded with any great alacrity to the offer by the Royal Society in October 1914 to establish advisory committees, primarily from the assumption that the war would be short. Indeed, it was not until July 1915 that the Admiralty Board of Invention and Research was established, while, in August 1915, Lloyd George set up the Munitions Inventions Department (MID). A third board, the Air Inventions Committee, became operational in May 1917. The boards were really established to shift the burden of dealing with unsolicited ideas for new weapons from the Admiralty and Ministry of Munitions, although it was also recognised that they would place research and development on a sounder basis.[4]

The ideas themselves were often quite ludicrous, such as the suggestion that cormorants with explosives fastened to them be trained to swoop on surfaced submarines, and others trained to peck away the mortar on the chimneys of the Krupps armaments factory in Essen. Consequently, a shift in emphasis was soon made to initiating worthwhile scientific research, such as the development of underwater detection methods, from November 1915 onwards. This laid the basis for the emergence of what was to become known as Asdic (Anti-Submarine Detection Investigation Committee), now sonar (sound, navigation and ranging). Similarly, research into anti-aircraft defence was to result in the development of some early prototypes of height and range finders by 1917.

The difficulty was that invention and development was not a rapid process and, in fact, sonar was not developed in time to be used on active service during the war itself. Thus, practical wartime developments tended to be on the smaller scale, such as the Stokes trench mortar developed by the Trench Warfare Department of the Munitions Inventions Department. However, with the encouragement of the Ministry of Munitions, advances were also made by industrial scientists in areas such as munitions production, synthetic substitution and new industrial processes. The Zionist, Dr Chaim Weizmann, made an invaluable contribution to British munitions output with a new production method for acetone. Moreover, a new department of state, the Department of Scientific and Industrial Research (DSIR) was established in 1916 to provide a more co-ordinated and coherent approach towards the integration of government and science: it was to survive into the post-war period.[5]

Under the pressure of war, science also contributed to advances in medicine, although it can be noted that physiologists contributed to the development of the offensive as well as the defensive aspects of research into gas warfare. War, indeed, stimulated medical research, which had previously been most advanced in terms of tropical medicine. In 1914, for example, British military doctors were confronted with outbreaks of meningitis in tented camps and a threat from typhoid, which had struck down some 60,000 French soldiers in the first six months of war. Trench warfare in the autumn introduced dangers from tetanus, gas gangrene infection and what became known as trench fever, caused by scratching of louse excreta. New antiseptics and anaesthetics were developed and new methods for the control and prevention of diseases such as enteric fever, nephritis, malaria, dysentery, and typhus.

The development of a British vaccine against dysentery has already been noted, while the prevalence of typhus on the Eastern and Balkan fronts prompted Austro-Hungarian pathologists to develop a means of early diagnosis. A new anti-typhoid vaccination introduced by the French in February 1915 reduced its incidence to less than 1 per cent within twelve months. In Mesopotamia, the problems of 'deficiency diseases' such as scurvy advanced acceptance of the vitamin theory, propounded just prior to the war as an alternative to the erroneous bacteriological explanation for such disease. Blood transfusion became widely established as a routine surgical measure and innovations were made in the preliminary 'surgical toilet' of wounds. The perception of an increased incidence of heart disease among soldiers, a condition known as soldier's heart, similarly led to pioneering research work at Colchester and Hampstead hospitals.

There were significant developments too in the production of artificial limbs. Far from being an invention of the Second World War, plastic surgery was first evolved by an ear, nose and throat surgeon, Harold Gillies, at the Queen's Hospital in Sidcup. In previous wars there had usually been about five deaths to disease for every one in battle but, between 1914 and 1918, if the effects of the influenza pandemic of 1918 are excluded, the average was only one death from disease to fifteen from battle. At the same time, however, it was the first war in which the wounded had a greater chance of living than dying from the effect of their wounds. Thus, while 44 per cent of those wounded during the American Civil War subsequently died, this was true of only 8 per cent of those wounded in the Great War.[6]

The exercise of command

The harnessing of science and technology to the war effort at least promised some solution to the newly emerged deadlock on the Western Front in the autumn of 1914. Indeed, once deadlock had occurred, soldiers in all armies were confronted with both new technical and managerial problems in coming to terms with the practical difficulties of trench warfare, the enormous increase in the size of armies and the scale of conflict. In every case, it required a considerable process of adjustment and learning on the part of commanders. As Sir John French was to write to a friend in December 1914, 'modern weapons and conditions have completely revolutionised war. It is quite different from anything which you and I have known. A battle is a siege on one side and a fortress defence on the other, but on a gigantic scale.'[7]

In many respects, the technical and managerial problems were intimately related. Thus, overcoming the managerial problems was arguably the key to achieving a solution to the technical difficulties, since it was often the traditional, hierarchical nature of armies which presented the most immediate obstacle to the necessary innovation. Some armies, however, adapted more quickly than others to the changed circumstances. The British were slower to adapt than the French or the Germans. Partly, this was a result of the small size of the regular army in 1914 and the extraordinary wartime expansion. At peak there were 3.9 million men in the British army in 1917, of whom 1.5 million served on the Western Front in 56 divisions formed into 17 corps and 5 armies. Such expansion necessitated an equivalent increase in the number of officers, but there were only 12,738 regular officers in 1914. By 1918, there was an estimated 12,000 officers in staff appointments, or almost as many as in the entire regular officer corps four years previously.[8]

Pre-war staff training had been deficient. The belated development of the general staff in Britain had resulted in a staff serving commanders rather than the system pertaining on the continent, in which the staff and not the commanders were the real centre of authority. Rigid demarcation in staffing terms also saw a division between those responsible for operations and intelligence, and those tasked with personnel and supply functions.

Such rigidity was compounded by a highly personalised system of promotion riddled with rivalries. Indeed, pre-war rivalries rather than incompetence *per se* was often the reason for the wartime removal of brigade and divisional commanders. It should be noted, however, that dismissals were by no means unusual: a total of 180 French general officers were *dégommé* (degummed) by December 1914 alone, including 3 army commanders and 24 corps commanders, while 217 Italian general officers were *silurato* (torpedoed) by Cadorna before his own dismissal. The Germans also removed 33 general officers after the failure of the 1914 campaign in the West including 2 army commanders.[9]

Few British regulars had handled large formations before the war. In 1914 the only corps headquarters in peacetime was that at Aldershot and, apart from Haig as its current incumbent, only French and Smith-Dorrien among serving soldiers had previously commanded there. By contrast, the French and German armies had 20 and 35 such peacetime corps commands, respectively. Moreover, command was not well understood in terms

of finding the essential balance between guidance and control of subordinates, something all the more necessary when the lack of modern communications made empowerment of subordinates vital.[10]

Unfortunately, this balance remained elusive. Haig, who succeeded French
as Commander-in-Chief of the British Expeditionary Force in December
1915, was well aware of the delicate balance to be struck between control
and guidance. In practice, however, Haig was inconsistent in his approach
to command, interfering in operational matters on some occasions while
failing to assert his authority on others.[11]

The pattern was set at Neuve Chapelle in March 1915 when Haig commanded First Army and Sir Henry Rawlinson commanded IV Corps. In
what would be the first major offensive launched from a defensive trench
system, Haig and Rawlinson favoured radically different lengths for the
opening bombardment. The uneasy compromise was 35 minutes. The same
occurred again in planning the Somme campaign, by which time Haig was
Commander-in-Chief and Rawlinson commander of Fourth Army. Neuve
Chapelle had convinced Rawlinson of the efficacy of a limited, step-by-step
advance, usually referred to as 'bite and hold'. He expected an opening
artillery bombardment of four to five days on a limited area to neutralise all
defences. By contrast, Haig, who had little understanding of artillery, suggested a short bombardment of only five or six hours over a much wider
area to effect an immediate breakthrough. The result was an artillery plan
and opening infantry assault geared to 'bite and hold' married to Haig's
wider expectations of rapid consolidation and cavalry exploitation. For this
the wide dispersion of guns and infantry was unsuitable, although the bombardment was ultimately extended over seven days owing to bad weather. In
the process, little thought was given to tactical considerations or artillery–
infantry co-operation, factors greatly contributing to the 57,470 casualties,
including 19,240 dead, suffered on 1 July 1916.[12]

The same confusion was reproduced in Haig's relationship with Sir Hubert
Gough, commanding Fifth Army, who assumed that he was intended to
break through the German lines in the Passchendaele campaign. Haig conceived of the offensive as having an attritional impact upon the German
army, but did not seem able to distinguish between the Belgian coast and
the Passchendaele ridge as the primary objective.[13]

The effects of Haig's alternating detachment from or interference in the
planning process, and his unhelpful views of the immutability of the struc-
tured nature of battle, were compounded by an atmosphere of fear engen-
dered by his demand for an absolute loyalty abrogating genuine discussion.[14]
Adding significantly to all these problems was the isolation of General Headquarters (GHQ) both physically and mentally from the remainder of the
army.

In a sense, 'chateau generalship' was an unavoidable by-product of the new managerial problems associated with the scale of war. Indeed, there were considerably worse cases of isolation, such as the example of Cadorna in the Italian army and Conrad in the Austro-Hungarian army. Moreover, just as there was no real alternative to the Western Front, there was no real alternative to Haig. As Churchill later remarked, Haig 'might be, surely he was, unequal to the prodigious scale of events; but no one else was discerned as his equal or his better'. That Haig was the best product of the system speaks volumes for the system itself: it had become increasingly bureaucratic, with what John Bourne has referred to as a 'rigid people-centred' structure of top-down line management.[15] Confusion in command existed not only at the highest level but also throughout the British army. Furthermore, control was not assisted by the often primitive state of communications until late into the war.[16]

Lack of consistency and doctrine was equally displayed at tactical level. Thus, it was simply not the case that British infantry universally went over the top on 1 July 1916 committed to walking slowly in linear formations towards the German front line: in several sectors, troops advanced in small groups and successfully reached the opposing front line in the south where the distances across No Man's Land were shorter and German defences weaker. It should be noted, however, that the pattern varied not just from one corps to another but also from one division to another, one brigade to another and even from one battalion to another.[17]

By 1918, however, younger men were increasingly reaching divisional command. This was significant, for divisions were increasingly recognised as the most appropriate level for tactical control of all-arms operations. Moreover, Haig had been compelled by the failure of Passchendaele to change personnel at GHQ and, either through choice or default, increasing freedom of action was accorded down the chain of command.[18]

In the Royal Flying Corps (RFC), which was part of the British army, the tensions between operational commanders and higher command were considerable. The Royal Navy did not suffer from quite the same problems since the Admiralty operated as a provider of resources rather than a central executive authority with no real overall direction of naval operations. Yet, few naval officers displayed much flexibility, unless in relatively small, independent commands such as Commodore Reginald Tyrwhit's Harwich Force of destroyers and light cruisers or Vice-Admiral Sir Reginald Bacon's Dover Patrol.

Partly, the need to accommodate new technology had thrown up technocrats lacking a sense of naval traditions although, paradoxically, the navy was equally hypnotised by other aspects of its past. Initiative was thus subordinated to excessive centralisation of authority and a blind obedience to superiors. In the Imperial German Navy, senior officers were somewhat resentful of the 'war of lieutenants' that developed in submarine warfare, where fewer senior officers were needed. U-boats also took away the most promising younger officers given the relative inactivity of the High Seas Fleet.[19]

By contrast, the German army had always recognised the need to surrender initiative to local commanders, the concepts of *Führung nach Direktive* (directive command) and *Auftragstaktik* (mission-oriented orders) being long established. In 1916, the realisation that it could take eight to ten hours for messages from headquarters to reach divisional commanders in the front line resulted in tactical control being largely devolved to divisional level, including control of sector artillery. In turn, this increased the role and responsibility of brigade and battalion commanders. At the same time, recognising the disparity of resources available to them, the Germans allowed tactics to be shaped by technology in order to maximise its potential, although they continued to rely upon technological enhancement rather than technological innovation: they embraced neither motorisation nor armoured warfare.[20]

The war on land

If there was little real improvement in the understanding of managerial problems in the British army, it was eventually more successful in coming to terms with the purely technical difficulties. For all the popular emphasis upon the machine gun, the really significant developments in the Great War were in artillery. In the Russo-Japanese War of 1904–05, it was calculated that only 10 per cent of casualties were caused by artillery fire but, in the Great War, it has been calculated that 67 per cent of all casualties were caused by artillery. In the case of the German army, 58.3 per cent of its wartime deaths were attributed to artillery compared with just 8.4 per cent in the Franco-Prussian War of 1870–71.

Once deadlock had occurred, artillery was certainly the key to overcoming increasingly powerful defences. Firstly, the ability of the attacker to protect his infantry as it crossed what soon became known as No Man's Land rested on his artillery and, secondly, the ability to enable the infantry to 'break in' the opposing defences equally rested on the use of artillery to break them down. Unfortunately, surprise was likely to be lost on the Western Front because it required a lengthy build-up of supplies and manpower in preparation for any attempt to attack. The ability to protect the attackers was limited to the range of the artillery, which could not be readily brought forward from its fixed positions behind the lines in order to extend any break made by the infantry. At the same time, while artillery could reach the opposing defences, initially it was not sufficiently powerful to destroy a defensive system totally. Even when heavier artillery was deployed, sufficient numbers of infantry invariably survived to break up an infantry attack through sheltering in deep dugouts and bunkers. Even if a break-in was achieved, a 'breakthrough' presented just as many difficulties of recognising and reinforcing success. As Nicholas Jones has commented, 'for surprise one surrendered mobility, and vice versa'.

As one might expect, the attacker was generally likely to lose more men than the defender in such conditions. Thus, in 1915, the French suffered 70.7 per cent of the total casualties sustained by both sides during their offensives in Champagne, the Russians 70.5 per cent of those sustained at Gorlice-Tarnow and the British 55.3 per cent of those sustained at Neuve Chapelle. Similarly, the British and French sustained 60.8 per cent of the casualties on the Somme in 1916 and the British 57.4 per cent of those sustained during the Passchendaele offensive in 1917. At Verdun in 1916, however, the defending French sustained 52.8 per cent of the casualties, although this also reflected their own subsequent counter-offensives, while the British sustained 55.6 per cent of the casualties in the German March offensive in 1918.

Unlike the relatively static offensives between 1915 and 1917, however, the March offensive is suggestive of an irony of the Great War. As Hew Strachan has noted, trench warfare conserved lives compared with more mobile warfare. Thus, while attrition at Verdun cost the lives of over 377,000 French and over 337,000 Germans, the French lost far more men in the open warfare of 1914 and 1918. Similarly, while Passchendaele cost the British over 65,000 casualties in August 1917, British losses in the mobile conditions of August 1918 reached over 113,000. Figures for the Canadian Expeditionary Force equally demonstrate that September 1918 was the second worst figure for Canadian casualties after April 1915, in terms of average casualties per division engaged, and that August 1918 was only marginally better than September 1916. As Bill Rawling has noted, 'Even in the last three months the evolving technology of war could not drastically reduce casualties; it could only change the ratio between losses and gains.'[21]

The first real British offensive aimed at breaking through the German front line was that at Neuve Chapelle on 10 March 1915. In many respects, it was a highly innovative experiment in terms of aerial reconnaissance of the German trenches and the co-ordination of artillery fire by timetable to fit the projected lines of advance. Over a narrow front of 2,000 yards, some 340 British guns fired their 35 minute bombardment, delivering the equivalent to 288 pounds of high explosive per yard of opposing trench. A break-in to the German lines was achieved, despite the breakdown of communications as soon as the British infantry left their trenches, and mist obscuring much of what was happening. The difficulties of reinforcing success and exploiting such a break-in so as to convert it into a breakthrough led to the ultimate failure of the offensive, the attack being broken off on 12 March 1915, with just 4,000 square yards gained at a cost of 12,000 casualties.

Unfortunately, the wrong lessons were drawn, since the initial impact had been that achieved by the concentration of heavy fire over a narrow frontage in a short time. The mistaken assumption was that a longer bombardment by more guns over a wider frontage would more thoroughly neutralise the defenders. In part, the assumption may have derived from a resistance to seek alternative solutions to simply resorting to what Tim Travers has characterised as a 'more and more' approach: Russian commanders in particular shared the belief that all would be well if more shells were available.

Prior to Loos on 24 September 1915, the British used 533 guns in a 48 hour bombardment over a frontage of 7,500 yards, but the impact was the equivalent of only 43 pounds per yard of trench. Similarly, in advance of the opening of the attack on the Somme on 1 July 1916, 1,431 British guns fired 1.7 million shells over 7 days on a 22,000 yard front but, again, the delivery impact was only about 150 pounds per yard, still significantly less than at Neuve Chapelle. Moreover, at least 30 per cent of British shells may not have exploded, reflecting the limitations of British manufacturing at this stage. Furthermore, the majority of the shells were shrapnel, which were of little use against entrenched troops and even failed to cut the wire through their poor quality.

Some formations used creeping barrage on 1 July, but this itself presented problems since it encouraged infantry linear formations. If the infantry could not keep up, the moving barrage could not easily be recalled given the absence of communications. It was, indeed, a war fought without effective voice control. Although telephone wires and cables were dug ever deeper, they were still cut by artillery fire and could only be extended into No Man's Land as the infantry advanced. It was exceedingly difficult, therefore, to know whether and where success had been achieved: on 1 July 1916, despite the receipt of 160 telegrams from corps headquarters, Rawlinson remained unaware of the real situation for over seven hours.

Moreover, reinforcing success was also problematic since reserves could not be held too close to the front line for fear that they would fall victim to counter-bombardment. At Vimy in May 1915, the success of Pétain's XXXIII Corps in breaking into the German front line could not be exploited since it took six and a half hours for reserves to be moved up. In a subsequent attack on Vimy by the French Tenth Army in September 1915, the reserves were held so far forward that they suffered heavy casualties from German counter-bombardment. In fact, it was a dispute between French and Haig over the placing of reserves at Loos that was ostensibly the reason for French's removal three months later.[22]

Verdun similarly demonstrated the difficulties presented by the modern battlefield. As on the Somme, it was the use of artillery that most obviously characterised the *Materialschlacht* (battle of material) of industrialised warfare. The British had anticipated that their troops would simply walk into the German front line after the opening bombardment on the Somme, and Falkenhayn, too, assumed that 'not even a mouse could survive' the German bombardment at Verdun. In reality, the bombardment was not sufficiently accurate, especially through the wear and tear of prolonged firing as the campaign continued. Nor was artillery decisive, the French forts around the city proving highly resilient to shells, and their tunnels providing the same kind of protection to the French infantry as the German dugouts on the Somme.[23]

The German army learned most from the Somme and Verdun although new ideas had already been developing through 1915. Colonel Hans von Seeckt had experimented in January 1915 with defensive firepower and infantry counter-attack. The German Third Army in Champagne had begun to develop a deeper defensive system in February 1915, and the Germans were also influenced by a document captured from the French in May 1915. They had suffered from the opening British bombardment on the Somme since, at this stage, they had clung to the fairly common concept of a firmly held front line.

Under the guidance of Fritz von Lossberg, the Germans developed the concept of 'elastic defence in depth' in the winter of 1916–17. Lossberg, however, was not the only contributor to the debate, and the codification of the new ideas, *Grundsätze für die Führung in der Abwehrschlacht im Stellungskrieg* (Basic Principles for the Conduct of the Defensive Battle in Position Warfare), published in December 1916, was the work of Colonel Max Bauer and Captain Hermann Geyer of OHL's operations section. A second publication, *Allgemeines über Stellenbau* (Principles of Field Construction) specified the arrangement of the defence in depth.

The new system thinned front line manpower but considerably deepened the defensive zone, to enable the possibility of surrendering ground in order to render the attackers vulnerable to a mobile counter-attack. In theory, the doctrine required the construction of three successive trench lines as outpost, battle and rear zones, with both artillery and machine guns fully integrated into the strongpoint-based defences. The defence would be conducted primarily in the battle zone – extending from 1,500 to 3,000 yards in depth – with specially designated *Eingriefdivisionen* (counter-attack divisions) poised to intervene as necessary, responsibility for their use being vested at divisional and even battalion level.

In all, five new defensive positions were prepared over the winter of 1916–17, comprising the Flanders, Wotan, Hunding (later Brunhild), Michel and Siegfried lines. The defence zone of the *Siegfriedstellung* (Siegfried position), popularly known as the Hindenburg Line, from Arras to Soissons extended to between 6,000 and 8,000 yards in depth, the Germans shortening their line by 25 miles by retreating to it between February and April 1917. It at once proved its worth against Nivelle's offensive, for the thinning of the front line saved casualties from French artillery fire and enabled fifteen divisions to be held back for counter-attack.

Following the British success at Messines on 7 June 1917, when Sir Herbert Plumer's Second Army took a ridge by detonating nineteen mines placed under the German line, Lossberg became Chief of Staff to the German Fourth Army in Flanders. As a result, further defensive lines were hastily prepared. On average, the German defences in Flanders extended to a depth from front to rear of 10,000–12,000 yards with an emphasis upon concrete pillboxes as strongpoints given the difficulty of digging deep into the waterlogged soil.[24]

Messines had been intended to prevent the Germans enfilading the British advance during the subsequent Passchendaele offensive. In essence, Passchendaele was an artillery battle. The Royal Artillery had improved immeasurably in terms of the development of sophisticated methods such as sound ranging, flash spotting, survey work and aerial reconnaissance and photography, which enabled a new accuracy in indirect and predicted fire and far more refined creeping barrages and counter-battery fire. The difficulty was that there was still a reluctance to trust entirely to the new methods and a preference for longer, old-style artillery bombardment. Among other failings, this cut up the ground and destroyed the drainage system in an area of high water tables in ways prejudicial to the subsequent movement of artillery forward in support of further advances.

On 31 July 1917, Fifth Army gained an average of 3,000 yards across a frontage of 13,700 yards, following a fifteen day preliminary bombardment involving some 3,036 British and French guns firing 4.3 million shells. Yet, the Fifth Army's bombardment was still insufficient to accomplish all the tasks set for the artillery, not least counter-battery work, while the intended depth of advance also lay beyond the range of artillery support. Moreover, as on the Somme, sufficient defenders survived because the delivery per yard of front did not reproduce the psychological and destructive impact of Neuve Chapelle.

Unfortunately, too, even though attacks by Second Army in September 1917 had considerably more artillery support, this was still insufficient to suppress German batteries. Difficulties of getting the guns forward amid deteriorating weather after September meant later attacks were mounted virtually without any artillery support. Thus, while Fifth Army suffered 86,000 casualties for the gain of three and a half miles in seven weeks, Second Army with its supposedly more methodical and limited attacks took 69,000 casualties for an advance in September and October 1917 of under 4,000 yards. The Canadian Expeditionary Force then suffered a further 12,000 casualties for perhaps 700 yards in the culminating operation around Passchendaele between 26 October and 10 November 1917. All that had been so painfully gained was simply abandoned in three days during the German spring offensive in 1918.[25]

Passchendaele was also a transitional experience for British infantry. As already remarked, infantry had not actually conformed to any uniform tactical pattern on 1 July 1916, though there was a certain penchant for successive linear waves to keep the momentum of attack going. This was an idea picked up from a French captain, André Laffargue, who believed this a means of achieving infiltration into an opposing front line. Written in August 1915, Laffargue's somewhat ambiguous pamphlet, *L'Étude sur l'Attaque* (Study of the Attack) was translated into English four months later. However, infantry still lacked weight of firepower of their own – compared with weight of equipment – to cross No Man's Land and the confidence to act without hugging a curtain of fire.

With the Germans ceasing to hold continuous positions, British divisions increasingly recognised the need to train for the 'dogfighting' semi-open phase of warfare when planned artillery support had ended. The Lewis gun, a light machine gun (technically, an automatic rifle), had appeared in July 1915 but no more than four were available for any battalion in July 1916 and it was primarily intended as a close-range weapon. By late 1916, however, British infantry were being trained to fight their own way forward in specialised platoons with increased firepower of their own. The Machine Gun Corps had been created as a kind of light artillery and a battalion now had 30 Lewis guns, 8 light Stokes mortars and at least 16 men armed with rifle grenades. Small groups of infantry now utilised looser formations and this immediate fire support to get forward.

Through the summer of 1917, Australian platoons were reorganised with Lewis gun, bomb and rifle grenadier sections while the Canadian Expeditionary Force's adoption of the new tactics was speeded by observation of the lessons of the latter stages of Verdun, Major-General Arthur Currie reporting on the French experience in February 1917. The results were apparent in the planning for the successful Vimy operation in April 1917 and by Currie's subsequent operation at Lens and Hill 60 in July 1917. As Bill Rawling has noted, however, even this careful preparation was still sufficient only to ensure that enough men survived the assault to hold on to captured positions. Where time was not available for preparation, as in the latter stages of Passchendaele, to which the Canadian Expeditionary Force was committed in October 1917, losses would still be heavy.

The tactical changes among British and dominion units were again apparent at Cambrai in November 1917, where tactical surprise was also achieved by the use of tanks and by the pre-registration of targets, which eradicated the need for preliminary bombardment. At the same time, the ability to communicate with infantry beyond its own front line was also improving, continuous wave wireless sets having been operated over a range of 8,000 yards at Vimy. Communications, however, remained poor to the end of the war and wireless was more useful in co-ordinating ground attacks by aircraft, being first used systematically for this purpose at Cambrai.

By July 1918, the emphasis on specialised platoons of Lewis gunners, rifle grenadiers and bombers had disappeared since sufficient supplies of weapons had become available to all sections. Thus, tactical flexibility and initiative reigned supreme. Indeed, British manuals, notably SS135 *Instructions for the Training of Divisions for Offensive Action* (December 1916) and SS143 *Instructions for the Training of Platoons for Offensive Action* (February 1917), were arguably equal to those of the Germans. In practice, it was still up to individual divisions how far they adopted the new tactical doctrine and some persisted in the use of linear wave formation in attack.

Continuing British failings can also be seen in the attempt to recreate a German-style defence in depth over the winter of 1917/18 in order to defend against the kind of tactics the British themselves had used at Cambrai and those then faced in the German counter-attack. Rather than matching the flexibility of the German system, the British tended to rely upon static defensive points with minimal counter-stroke capability. Matters were not assisted by the need to extend Fifth Army's line by 28 miles just six weeks before the German spring offensive began. The result was that the rear zone, in which the relatively few available reserves were to be held, hardly existed. In any case, the battle was fought not in the main battle zone, as intended, but in the forward zone, which should have been only lightly held.[26]

The Germans, too, had greatly refined infantry tactics by 1917, in response to their increasing belief that it was not possible to hold a forward zone against the combination of artillery and tanks, and that a successful defence depended upon resourceful infantry counter-attack. They had also benefited from French experience by capturing in the summer of 1916 either the pamphlet by Laffargue or, conceivably, a similar pamphlet published in November 1915 by Commandant Lachèvre. Tactical innovators such as Lossberg and Geyer also noted the French use of short bombardments in the later limited operations at Verdun and Brusilov's similar success against the Austro-Hungarians in June 1916.

The Russian army was not noted for tactical innovation and did not even issue a new infantry manual based on war experience until July 1916. Brusilov, however, was far more thorough, using aerial photography for the first time on the Eastern Front to locate enemy batteries. He also achieved tactical surprise, disguising his intended point of breakthrough with a series of four localised attacks. The plan was assisted by too many Austro-Hungarian troops being located in the front line and too many reserves kept close to the front. Ironically, however, the success was also owing to scarcity of Russian resources, forcing Brusilov to rely on a brief, but intense opening bombardment. The dispersion of Brusilov's assaults and the lack of reserves available – the offensive had been a diversion for the main effort elsewhere – curtailed the extent of Russian success. Brusilov subsequently became Commander-in-Chief of the Russian armies, but the revolution intervened before his methods could be more widely applied.[27]

In any case, the German army was well attuned to tactical inventiveness, as evinced by Falkenhayn's creation of an ad hoc motorised taskforce in Romania in 1916. Experimentation with new infantry tactics had begun as early as March 1915, with the creation of a *Sturmabteilung* (Storm Detachment) of pioneers supporting a new 37 mm light artillery piece, which was intended to neutralise obstacles to an advance by bringing direct fire to bear at close range. The unit was not initially a success but its tactics were progressively refined by Captain Wilhelm Rohr. Increased to a *Sturmbataillone* (Storm Battalion), Rohr's unit began training others. In October 1916, eighteen *Sturmbataillone* were formed, each including pioneers, machine gunners, light artillery and mortar crews, and flame-throwers. Training generally was reformed in accordance with 'Orders Concerning the Training of Infantry during the Current War' issued in January 1917, the new initiative allowed to NCOs and ordinary soldiers resulting also in the introduction of ideological indoctrination. The Italians had also experimented with an *arditi* (shock) company in October 1915, forming assault battalions in mid-1917 and assault divisions in September 1918, although their creation did little to change the rigidity of Italian tactics.[28]

Specially located *Sturmtruppen* (Stormtrooper) formations featured in the German counter-attack at Cambrai on 30 November 1917, which wiped out the gains made by the British with tanks ten days earlier. Stormtroopers were formed into small, self-sufficient groups armed with mobile mortars and Bergmann sub-machine guns, infiltrating between strongpoints to effect a break-in and to achieve maximum penetration at least as far as the defending artillery lines. Control of reserves was vested in the forward elements so that they would reinforce success rather than failure.

Allied to this was the artillery method devised by Colonel Georg Bruchmüller – partly in response to failing levels of shell production – to support the advance with rapid and accurate fire in a short hurricane bombardment. A liberal mix of high explosive and gas shells added to the disorienting effect, paralysing and disrupting the opposing command structure. It marked a movement towards 'neutralisation' as opposed to 'destruction' of an opponent with the barrage organised into different phases in order to achieve specific tactical effects. Bruchmüller had introduced the creeping barrage while serving with the Tenth Army at Lake Narotch in March 1916 and had then drawn up the artillery plan for Tarnopol in July 1916, including predicted fire based on aerial reconnaissance. His methods had then been used in the offensive by General Oskar von Hutier's German Eighth Army at Riga on 1 September 1917, taking the Russian garrison of 25,000 men in just three days. The method was repeated at Caporetto on 24 October 1917, when the Italians lost in just four days what they had taken thirty months to gain, before reproduction at Cambrai.

Codification came in *Der Angriff im Stellungskrieg* (The Attack in Position Warfare), written by Geyer and issued on 1 January 1918. On 21 March 1918, at the opening of the German spring offensive (Operation Michael) on the Western Front, in which the assault was led again by Hutier, now commanding Eighteenth Army, Bruchmüller used 6,608 guns in a 5 hours and 50 minutes' preliminary bombardment against the British Fifth Army. A total of 3.2 million rounds – one-third of them gas rounds – were fired in seven carefully prepared phases. The Germans also committed 52 of their 70 specially created attack divisions. In 1916, the Allies had painfully won 98 square miles on the Somme in 140 days at a cost of 1.5 million casualties; assisted by mist and fog, the Germans seized 140 square miles of the same area in just 24 hours at a cost of only 39,000 casualties.

It has been generally accepted that the Germans sacrificed strategy to tactics in the spring of 1918, Ludendorff remarking that he would simply punch a hole in the Entente lines and, 'For the rest, we shall see'. Nonetheless, there was also a tactical weakness in the failure to maintain the infiltration tactics after the initial breakthrough both on 21 March, and in the subsequent four offensives.

While the pace of advance achieved – amounting to 35 miles in just four days on the Aisne in May – was prodigious by previous standards, it still did not impart sufficient psychological paralysis to create strategic success. Moreover, the stormtroop divisions suffered very heavy casualties. Coupled with the heavy losses, the failure of the offensives damaged morale. Conceivably, too, elasticity in attack and defence encouraged the belief among German troops that ground was of little value once the Entente began to counterattack in July and August 1918.[29]

Given the way in which French methods influenced both British and German tactical doctrine, it is perhaps surprising to note the failure of the French themselves to discover a tactical solution to the problem of the Western Front. In fact, despite innovators such as Laffargue, the French were technically backward and as slow as the British to evolve new artillery techniques, depending largely upon a rigid form of infantry-heavy assault until 1917. Nivelle had certainly glimpsed some of the tactical lessons at Verdun, but he was too committed to pushing ahead with his disastrous offensive in April 1917 to hold back, despite the German withdrawal to the Hindenburg Line and intelligence reports regarding the nature of the new German defences.

In part, Nivelle's miscalculation stemmed from the continuing belief in the offensive, which those like Foch continued to advocate even after the disasters of 1917. Indeed, in April 1917 French formations vied with each other to deliver the fastest rolling barrage, with which few of the infantry could keep up. Pétain consciously attempted to adapt tactics to a greater reliance upon artillery and airpower but was not always successful in imposing flexibility: many commanders found it difficult to accept the concept of yielding ground in an 'elastic defence'. Consequently, in the words of Douglas Porch, the French never satisfactorily succeeded 'in reconciling flexibility with planning'. Some of these failings were apparent in those American Expeditionary Force formations trained by the French in the spring and summer of 1918.

The effectiveness of the Americans themselves was limited by piecemeal commitment and sheer inexperience. In many cases, the Americans were poorly equipped and poorly prepared, gas warfare being one of the most obvious areas of neglect. Moreover, Pershing ignored many of the lessons so painfully learned by the French and British in his preference for aggressive infantry with an emphasis upon the rifleman and rigid set-piece assaults conducted in strength on narrow fronts. Not surprisingly, American casualties were high at both St Mihiel on 12 September 1918 and Meuse–Argonne on 26 September.[30]

By this time, however, the Entente was nearing victory in the west assisted by the extraordinary amount of materiel resources now available, which compensated for declining manpower. The successful British assault on the Hindenburg Line on 29 September 1918, for example, saw a bombardment which delivered 126 shells per 500 yards of German line per minute for eight hours. In all, some 945,052 rounds (including 30,000 newly produced mustard gas shells) were fired. The British advanced to a depth of 6,000 yards as a result.[31]

It has been argued that the British rate of advance in the 'Hundred Days' of 1918 – approximately 28 miles a month – was greater than that of the Allies during the Italian campaign of 1943–45. What needs to be emphasised, however, is that no one solved the problem of converting a break-in into a breakthrough because the technical means to do so were never available for all the developments in artillery and communications. Indeed, the only arm of exploitation available remained cavalry.

Cavalry was rather more integrated within the British army than generally supposed. A genuine all-arms battlegroup of cavalry, engineers, armoured cars, machine guns and field artillery, for example, was intended to exploit any breakout at High Wood on the Somme on 14 July 1916. When, however, the 20th Deccan Horse and the 7th Dragoon Guards were brought, far too late, into the attack on High Wood, they were pinned down by machine gun fire. Similarly, at Arras on 11 April 1917, an attempted advance by two brigades of the 3rd Cavalry Division was halted before Monchy while, at Cambrai, the cavalry was unable to get across a canal once the Germans had blown the bridges. The 7th Cavalry Brigade performed relatively well at Amiens on 8 August 1918, despite failing to co-ordinate its advance with Whippet medium tanks.

There was still a role for cavalry in areas such as Palestine and on the Eastern Front. In Palestine, General Sir Edmund Allenby's cavalry displayed the benefits of its mobility both in the advance towards Jerusalem between October and December 1917, and the subsequent advance on Damascus and Aleppo in September 1918, culminating in the victory at Megiddo, characterised by Archibald Wavell as 'the greatest exploit in the history of horsed cavalry'.

Over 4,000 cavalry charges took place on the Eastern Front, including the shattering of the Austro-Hungarian Seventh Army by Russian cavalry at Gorodenko on 27–28 April 1915. Cavalry, however, could not reckon to cover more than five miles a day on campaign and the vaunted cavalry offensive into east Prussia in 1914 had been largely stillborn.[32]

The absence of a technical means of breaking deadlock did not mean that technical solutions were not attempted. Thus, gas was seen as a breakthrough weapon when first used by the Germans, and so was the *Flammenwerfer* (flame-thrower) at a tactical level. Developed before the war by a Berlin engineer, Richard Fiedler, the flame-thrower used gas pressure to shoot out inflammable oil over a distance of 65 feet. Some attempt appears to have been made to use the weapon against the French in the autumn of 1914, but its effective debut came at Hooge near Ypres on 29 July 1915, when six were used to dislodge the British 41st Brigade from Hooge crater. The proximity of the front lines, however, was an important factor and the weapon would not have the same impact again.

By contrast, gas had a more lasting impact although, in military parlance, its real function was as a 'force multiplier'. Irritants had been fired in shells by the Germans without effect around Neuve Chapelle in October 1914. Shells containing xylyl bromide gas fired against the Russians at Bolimov on 3 January 1915 were equally ineffective because the liquid froze in the low temperatures. However, following experiments by Haber, chlorine gas was then released from cylinders between Pilckem and Langemarck on 22 April 1915 to initiate the Second Battle of Ypres, the Germans maintaining that The Hague conventions applied only to deliberately poisoning food and water. The use of cylinders got around another provision banning use of poisoned projectiles. An 8,000 yard gap was torn in the French lines when French colonial troops fled from the gas (and concentrated artillery fire), but it was plugged by the Canadians using improvised gas masks.

Gas released from cylinders was a fickle weapon, as the British discovered when a change of wind blew it back on their own troops at Loos. The direction of the prevailing wind also made it difficult for the Italians to use gas against the Austro-Hungarians while, at Caporetto, the Germans were able to take advantage of the deep valleys to project concentrated chlorine and phosgene on to the Italian positions. Phosgene, an asphyxiating gas, had first been used by the Germans at Verdun, and it was also at Verdun that flame-throwers were used in large quantities and that German troops were also issued with the celebrated *Stahlhelm* (steel helmet).

Increasingly, gas was put into shells. Some sixty-three types were used during the war on all fronts, from acute lung irritants such as chlorine, to paralysants such as hydrocyanic acid, and vesicants such as dichlordiethyl sulphide (mustard gas). The latter was first used by the Germans in July 1917 after development by a chemist at the Bayer works and one of Haber's assistants at the Kaiser Wilhelm Institute: the French did not manage to manufacture it until June 1918 and the British two months later.

Early attempts at protection were rudimentary and consisted of little more than cotton or gauze pads soaked with appropriate chemical solutions. Helmets, masks and box respirators were then developed. Indeed, for all its apparently devastating impact, gas caused only an estimated 1.2 million casualties, of whom perhaps 91,000 were immediate fatalities (about 6 per cent). Soldiers were better protected from gas than from any other weapon during the war, provided masks were put on promptly and properly. The one exception was mustard gas, which attacked all moist parts of the body. It might be added that there were also civilian losses, not from direct attack but from accidents in factories while filling shells, as at Avonmouth and Chittening in Britain, and Amequin and Armentières in France.[33]

Gas on its own, therefore, was not a decisive weapon and rare indeed in being invented in one war and discarded in the next. More promising, in theory, was the tank. The idea of utilising the pre-war agricultural caterpillar-tracked tractors as a means of overcoming barbed wire had occurred to Hankey in December 1914, but it had also occurred to others such as the British official war correspondent in France, Colonel Ernest Swinton, whom Hankey credited with first alerting him to the potential in October 1914. A French officer, Colonel J. E. Estienne, also had a similar idea. Estienne was not able to interest Joffre until December 1915, but Churchill took up Hankey's idea in February 1915 by establishing an Admiralty Landships Committee, the Royal Naval Air Service (RNAS) having operated armoured cars from its first base at Ostend in August 1914 and, thereafter, from Dunkirk.

Under the guidance of the Committee's chairman, the Director of Naval Construction, Eustace Tennyson D'Eyncourt, and its consulting engineer, Colonel R. E. B Crompton, a prototype tank known as 'Little Willie' was built by William Tritton and Walter Wilson at the Foster Works in Lincoln. The next prototype, 'Big Willie', underwent trials at Hatfield Park in January and February 1916 and the first six of the production model Mark I, or 'Mother', reached France in August 1916.

Haig only dimly perceived the developments taking place in artillery but he was keen to use tanks, and 49 were deployed for a renewed attack on the Somme at Flers-Courcelette on 15 September 1916. However, of the 32 making the start line, only 9 spearheaded the attack, the rest breaking down: only 6 square miles of ground was taken. Nonetheless, a Tank Corps was formally established in July 1917, while the French had also put tanks manufactured by the firms of Renault, St Chamond and Schneider into production. Schneiders were used for the first time on 16 April 1917 on the Chemin des Dames; in a reproduction of the British pattern on the Somme, of 48 Schneiders used, 8 broke down and 32 were knocked out or abandoned.[34]

The chronic technical limitations were again illustrated by the first substantial use of the new British Mark IV at Messines in June 1917. Only 19 out of 68 tanks could keep up with the infantry advance, while, overall, a total of 48 became ditched or 'bellied' at some stage and 17 broke down. It was quickly concluded that tanks could make no real contribution to Passchendaele. But, in the scheme put forward by Third Army for an attack at Cambrai that autumn, it was felt that tanks could flatten the wire sufficiently for the infantry to get forward quickly, in order to take advantage of tactical surprise afforded by the new artillery methods of predicted fire and silent registration.

Ironically, then, the great tank attack on 20 November 1917 was not a result of Tank Corps proposals for large-scale tank 'raids'. Of 378 tanks available, only 92 remained serviceable within three days, and they were withdrawn from the battle on 27 November. At Amiens on 8 August 1918, where 414 tanks – mostly the improved Mark V – were used, only 38 started on 11 August and only 6 started on 12 August. Indeed, the operation's success rested far more on tactical surprise amid heavy mist, the artillery bombardment and the infantry's own firepower. Nor, as already indicated, were the Whippets able to operate successfully with cavalry, and the first experiment with 'armoured infantry' – machine gunners carried in a stretched version of the Mark V tank – was also disappointing. Not only were tanks vulnerable to mechanical problems, but also to artillery and anti-tank rifles, which the Germans soon introduced. In addition, crews suffered greatly from heat exhaustion and carbon monoxide poisoning.

The Germans had little interest in developing tanks of their own, although a few large and unwieldy A7Vs were brought into service, in the belief that, at best, it was an infantry support weapon. Following the first small tank versus tank battle at Villers-Bretonneux on 24 April 1918, the A7V was soon scrapped and use made of captured tanks.

As a result of the tank's limitations, there was little real agreement within the British Expeditionary Force on whether mechanical warfare truly offered a substitute for manpower. In that sense, tanks during the war remained what GHQ concluded in August 1918, a 'mechanical contrivance' with potential usefulness only as an adjunct to combined infantry and artillery assault.[35]

Another area where technology contributed to development was in intelligence. Human sources of intelligence were regarded as the most important, and considerable effort continued to be put into obtaining intelligence from trench raids, the capture of documents such as paybooks and the interrogation of prisoners. Similarly, agent networks were established, such as the British network successfully broken up by the Germans in Brussels in November 1914. In Mesopotamia the British similarly made use of Bedouin tribesmen, though most were considered worthless. In Palestine, by contrast, although originally sceptical of its value, the British made increasing use of the Jewish *Nezah Yisrael Lo Yeshakker* ('The strength of Israel shall not lie') or Nili organisation. Signals intelligence, however, became increasingly significant and was certainly the most reliable source available in the Middle East.[36]

Wireless telegraphy in itself was a significant advance but it was not secure and, in any case, for speed of communication, messages were frequently sent in clear rather than in cipher, as was the case with both the Russian and German armies prior to Tannenberg. While armies on the Eastern Front and in the Middle East continued to use radio for communication, armies in the western theatre turned to telegraph or telephone at the end of 1914.

Electrical currents from the cables could be intercepted through the earth, however, by such devices as the German 'Moritz' listening set. By 1916, therefore, armies in the west had reverted to radio. Consequently, there was a constant struggle between encryptors and codebreakers and no code remained safe for long, especially as carelessness was commonplace. The Austro-Hungarian army, which alone among major armies had possessed a signals intelligence service prior to 1914, had several successes in breaking Russian and Italian codes. Both Britain and France also had increasing success in breaking ciphers.

Signals security was therefore crucial. A wireless deception plan was used for the first time by the British before the Messines operation and by the Germans before Caporetto. The most successful use of signals intelligence, however, was in the Middle East. In Mesopotamia and Palestine, respectively, General Sir Stanley Maude's offensive towards Baghdad between January and March 1917 and Allenby's successful direction of the Third Battle of Gaza, beginning on 31 October 1917 were guided by interception of Turkish signals. Surprise was further achieved by Allenby at Gaza by the more traditional deception methods of planting false documents to be picked up by the Turks.[37]

It was still important to interpret intelligence correctly. Preconceptions might hinder correct interpretation. Clearly, too, mistakes could be made. There was a failure to predict the German retreat to the Hindenburg Line in February 1917, when the Germans successfully deceived the British into believing they were about to mount an offensive in Flanders. Similarly, there was a failure to predict accurately the timing and location of the expected German offensive in March 1918. Further afield, the whole of the Dardanelles campaign was a noticeable Entente intelligence failure.[38]

What, then, contributed to the Entente's final victory on land? The ability to deploy artillery, aircraft, infantry and tanks in relatively close co-operation through technical advances in communications by late 1917 had led to the emergence of a primitive all-arms doctrine and a distinctly 'modern' style of warfare. This was crucial to victory in 1918, but there were other factors.

Dominick Graham is surely right to note the emergence of a tougher and younger core of natural leaders among surviving British officers, and of a young conscript army, which seemingly rekindled some of the enthusiasm of the Kitchener volunteers and who certainly died even more numerously. There is a need, too, to consider the greater co-ordination of Entente effort after March 1918, the abandonment of wider strategic objectives in favour of limited localised attacks and, perhaps above all, the failure of the Germans to maintain the momentum of their own spring offensives. Moreover, it is generally accepted that final victory owed much to the overwhelming weight of Entente *matériel*. In the last analysis, the Entente had greater manpower resources, which was just as well given the greater effectiveness of the Germans in inflicting losses. One calculation, indeed, is that the Germans killed at least 35 per cent more men than they lost, and captured between 25 and 38 per cent more men than were captured off them.[39]

The war at sea

In March 1918 the Germans used long-range artillery to bombard Paris, compelling an estimated 500,000 people to flee the city. Similarly, the German High Seas Fleet had bombarded West Hartlepool, Scarborough and Whitby on 16 December 1914, causing 133 civilian deaths. Naval bombardment of civilian targets was not repeated but other developments at sea equally provided means of striking at the will of a civilian society to sustain the war effort.

The Entente imposed a naval blockade on the Central Powers primarily by means of patrols and mines but the Imperial German Navy resorted to submarine warfare. The German submarine *U-21* became the first submarine to sink a ship in action at sea when sinking HMS *Pathfinder* in the Firth of Forth on 3 September 1914, the only previously successful submarine attack, in the American Civil War, having been inside a harbour. The first merchantman to fall victim was the SS *Glitra* to *U-17* on 20 October, while HMS *Birmingham* became the first vessel to sink a submarine by ramming *U-15* in the North Sea on 9 August 1914.

One of the most significant demonstrations of the potential of the submarine was the loss of three old British vessels of the 7th Cruiser Squadron – HMS *Aboukir*, HMS *Cressy* and HMS *Hogue* – cruising the Broad Fourteens off the Dutch coast to *U-9* within 47 minutes on the morning of 22 September 1914. As a result, Admiral Sir John Jellicoe moved the Grand Fleet to Lough Swilly off Ireland until the defences of Scapa Flow could be improved.

In turn, British submarines were successful in penetrating both the Baltic and the Sea of Marmara during the war. Submarine successes spurred development of bulges added to ships as underwater protection and, by 1917, it was possible for naval vessels to survive torpedo attack. Paravanes also reduced the effectiveness of mines, an area of warfare in which the Royal Navy was itself generally somewhat deficient.[40]

Prior to the introduction of unrestricted submarine warfare in February 1915, only 10 British merchant ships had been lost to submarine attack, compared with 14 to mines and 51 to surface commerce raiders. It should be noted, however, that the first submarine campaign was largely waged using surface gunfire, since U-boats carried few torpedoes and submerged in order to approach vessels undetected and then to evade detection themselves. Submarines continued to attack vessels in the Mediterranean with impressive results and, therefore, full unrestricted submarine warfare was revived in February 1917.

Compared with 1915, when the Germans had only possessed 22 seagoing U-boats, by 1917 there were 121 available – of which 41 would always be at sea – with enhanced underwater capabilities and more torpedoes. A dramatic increase in Entente shipping losses resulted, rising from 464,599 tons in February 1917 to 507,001 tons in March and 834,549 tons in April 1917. Indeed, the damage was sufficient for Jellicoe, now First Sea Lord, to give his support in June for what became the Passchendaele campaign as a means of breaking through to the German submarine bases at Ostend and Zeebrugge. In reality, the submarine menace had been lessened by then and the real naval challenge was the threat to Channel shipping from German destroyers stationed at the Belgian ports. Ultimately, the Royal Navy raided Zeebrugge on 22/23 April 1918 and Ostend on 9 May 1918 to try to close the ports. The submarine campaign might have been even more effective had Admiral Holtzendorf not repeatedly rejected proposals for creating what in the Second World War would become known as wolf packs, in the belief that covering all sea approaches to Britain with individual submarines would force the British to disperse their escort vessels.[41]

A number of methods were initially utilised against the submarine such as decoy ships or Q-ships – heavily armed vessels disguised as harmless merchantmen. Minefields and nets were also used, as in the Dover Barrage, to try to close off the U-boat route into the Channel, and the Otranto Barrage in the Adriatic. However, the solution to unrestricted submarine warfare was a revival of the method well known to the age of sail, namely the convoy. Convoys had been used from the beginning of the war to protect troop ships and, in February 1917, were successfully introduced for the coal trade between Britain and France and, in April 1917, for the Scandinavian trade. They had also been used for vessels sailing to neutral Holland.

The Admiralty, however, resisted the general introduction of convoys in the belief that the desirable ratio of escorts to merchantmen would be as high as 2:1. Merchant captains also protested that they could not keep station in convoys, which would be reduced to the speed of the slowest ship, and that they would therefore present a wealth of targets. Ships in convoy, it was further argued, would not be able to zigzag as did single ships, while the arrival of a convoy might lead to congestion in ports. Maurice Hankey, together with Commander Reginald Henderson, however, pressed for convoys on the grounds that they would be as hard to locate at sea as a single ship, that the concentration of vessels made escort duties easier, and that convoys could be routed away from danger areas. Convoy duty was also far less wasteful of resources being squandered on ineffective anti-submarine patrols.

As a result of support from Lloyd George and from the American naval commander in the Atlantic, Sims, an experimental convoy was run from Gibraltar to Plymouth on 10 May 1917 without loss. American entry to the war in itself removed fears of a lack of escort vessels. By October 1917, a total of 99 homeward bound convoys had reached harbour safely and only 10 vessels had been lost. In all, British shipping losses in the last quarter of 1917 of 702,779 tons (235 ships) were only just over half the peak figure of 1,315,496 tons (413 ships) lost in the second quarter of the year.

By November 1917, the convoy system was fully operational and U-boats were forced to attack under water and largely in coastal waters. Escorts were now more successful using prototype hydrophones to detect them and equally newly developed depth charges. By 1918, sonar had been developed and the French had developed echo ranging. Airships, flying boats and towed balloons had also all been introduced in anti-submarine roles. In effect, however, the U-boats had already been defeated and, of 391 deployed by the Germans during the war, 178 were lost: construction had barely kept pace with losses.

Apart from sonar, other scientific developments also assisted the anti-submarine war. The Admiralty's celebrated Room 40 played a major role by deciphering German naval codes, although the Admiralty did not always make best use of its intelligence. The work was initially assisted by the capture by the Russians of the codebooks of SMS *Magdeburg* after it ran aground on the Estonian coast in August 1914, but Room 40 had to start afresh with new German codes in 1916 and 1917. Apart from its work in tracking German surface and submarine movements, Room 40 also intercepted the Zimmermann telegram. Another development was the ability to communicate between ships by wireless. It should be noted, however, that naval wireless transmitted messages only in Morse, involving a loss in 'real time' intelligence. Thus, tactical signalling in the heat of battle was still carried out by flag, with all its attendant problems of visibility. Indeed, one of the reasons for the rigidity of Grand Fleet battle tactics was the lack of communications.[42]

The appearance of submarine and mines ensured that the Great War was the last in which the battleship would be regarded as the main instrument of seapower. Yet another threat to the capital ship was the torpedo boat, the Italians in particular enjoying some success with these in the Adriatic, accounting for Austro-Hungarian battleships in December 1917 and June 1918. Another was lost to a prototype Italian midget submarine in

November 1918. The vulnerability of the capital ship contradicted prevailing contemporary belief, encompassed in the work of the American naval theorist Alfred Thayer Mahan, that a culminating fleet action would alone confer the command of the sea. Indeed, the naval war was to fit rather better with the ideas of the British theorist Sir Julian Corbett, who stressed that seapower and naval battle in itself could not bring victory. For Corbett, the proper and most significant naval role was to protect the home base and to secure and maintain the use of the sea for strategic purposes.[43]

The significance of Mahanian battle had apparently been proven by the distinctly old-fashioned encounter between the Russian and Japanese navies at Tsushima in May 1905, fought at relatively short range and resulting in the destruction of the Russian Baltic Fleet. As with the military lessons of the war, the naval lessons were not necessarily clear-cut. Some observers noted, indeed, that the loss of the flagship of the Russian Far Eastern Fleet, the *Petropavlovsk*, to a mine in April 1904 had exposed the vulnerability of the capital ship. So it proved, for a single line of mines was sufficient to wreck the Anglo-French attempt to force the Dardanelles by naval action alone on 18 March 1915, when three capital ships were lost and a fourth badly damaged. The loss of HMS *Audacious* to a mine in October 1914 had proved a particular shock to the Royal Navy and, indeed, its loss was kept secret until the end of the war. In consequence of the twin threat from mine and submarine, as Arthur Balfour noted, the North Sea was commanded by neither the British nor German battle fleets but was in a condition of 'joint occupation' by each sides' submarines.

In terms of capital ships themselves, the Royal Navy's launching of the revolutionary HMS *Dreadnought* in 1906, combining big guns with oil-burning turbine engines, had actually destroyed its own naval superiority although, as Trevor Wilson, has noted, Britain was also establishing 'a new margin of superiority before other countries could get in ahead of it'. In 1914, Britain possessed 24 dreadnoughts with a further 13 laid down. By comparison, Germany had 13 with a further 10 laid down. By October 1914, however, *Audacious* had been lost and other dreadnoughts were under repairs, reducing the number to 19 compared with the 16 now available to Germany.

Moreover, while forcing the pace of innovation can be advantageous in strategic and even, in the long run, in financial terms, it can be risky initially in the event of technological teething problems. Indeed, the naval war was fought at a time when, to quote Colin White, 'technical advantages were often nullified by continuing limitations in other fields'. By comparison with British ships, German boilers were smaller and more efficient and German dockyard facilities more modern. Fire direction and control became crucial, and in these areas, too, Germany had a lead. In the Royal

Navy, an adequate fire direction system developed by Captain Percy Scott had begun to be installed just prior to the war. However, the fire control system associated with a civilian businessman, Arthur Pollen, to ensure range and bearing were constantly adjusted had been rejected in favour of a cheaper system devised by Commander F. C. Dreyer, which proved ineffective in poor visibility.

German range-finders and fire control systems were superior, hence the success of Spee's cruisers, SMS *Scharnhorst* and SMS *Gneisenau* in sinking two elderly cruisers of Rear-Admiral Sir Christopher Craddock's South American squadron at Coronel on 1 November 1914. A more powerful force, including the modern battle cruisers, HMS *Inflexible* and HMS *Invincible*, then destroyed Spee at the Falkland Islands on 8 December 1914. At the Falklands, however, British guns achieved only one hit per gun every 75 minutes and only a 7 per cent hit rate overall in a high-speed battle fought at long range, which necessitated rapid change of range calculations.

It had been assumed before the war that ships would engage in battle in long, relatively static parallel lines, an assumption informing the lack of British development in fire control. Had the German cruisers *Goeben* and *Breslau* not been allowed to escape through the Dardanelles in October 1914 by ambiguous orders and lack of initiative, it is conceivable that they, too, would have inflicted considerable damage on the pursuing British Mediterranean squadron.

Admiral Sir David Beatty's battle cruiser squadron was largely successful in the action off the Dogger Bank on 24 January 1915, in which the German cruiser SMS *Blücher* was sunk, but the remaining German vessels escaped as Beatty took precautions against the threat of submarine and mine. Despite the loss of the *Blücher*, the German shooting had been much more accurate. Excluding the *Blücher* from calculation, 22 shells (2.1 per cent) out of 976 fired, hit Beatty's ships. The British ships fired 1,150 shells, of which only 6 (0.5 per cent) registered hits. Moreover, the Germans learned the lesson from the near loss of SMS *Seydlitz* that shell bursts on gun turrets could transmit fire down the ammunition hoists to the magazines. By contrast, only slight improvements were made to the British fire direction system and nothing was done to guard against the risk of fire in the magazines.[44]

The only sustained clash between the Grand and High Seas Fleets came at Jutland on 31 May–1 June 1916, following the determination of the new German fleet commander, Vice-Admiral Reinhard Scheer, to adopt a more positive role. Scheer's plans of trapping part of the Grand Fleet was almost assisted by failures in the Admiralty to pass on information from Room 40's interception of German signals. Beatty's ship, HMS *Lion*, nearly suffered the fate so narrowly averted by the *Seydlitz* at Dogger Bank, but its magazine was just flooded in time. HMS *Invincible*, however, was not as lucky and was lost to flash ignition of its magazine. It is assumed the same occurred in the two other battle cruisers lost, *Queen Mary* and *Indefatigable*. Beatty's squadron had a far greater weight of broadside than the battle cruisers of Vice-Admiral Franz Hipper's scouting force but landed only 6 hits to the 25 of the Germans in the first phase of the action.

Overall, the High Seas Fleet fired 3,597 shells during the action as a whole and achieved 120 hits (3.33 per cent) compared with the Grand Fleet's discharge of 4,598 shells, of which 100 hit (2.17 per cent). Subsequent investigation attributed the British failures largely to poor shells but, while this was a factor, German gunners were better trained and the Dreyer fire control system proved incapable of dealing with rapid changes of range. It was also the case that the British battle cruisers were inadequately armoured: as Beatty memorably remarked after the loss of the *Queen Mary*, 'There seems to be something wrong with our bloody ships to-day.'

The British also lost three cruisers and eight destroyers. German losses were one battleship, another old pre-dreadnought battleship, four cruisers and five destroyers. The balance of loss in the Germans' favour in terms of tonnage was 111,980 tons to 62,230, and the loss in terms of casualties, 6,945 to 2,921. Jellicoe had been cautious, intending to fight in line of battle at long range. He chose not to pursue the High Seas Fleet for fear of torpedo attack from German destroyers. Once night fell on 31 May, it transpired that the Germans were also better equipped for night action just as Scheer had demonstrated considerable seamanship in twice executing the difficult 'battle turn-away' manoeuvre when Jellicoe ships had crossed his 'T' during the main fleet action. British shells had also frequently failed to penetrate the German armour, a failing not experienced by the Germans.

While Jutland was inconclusive on the relative merits of British and German naval construction, in the wider context, it made no significant difference to the Royal Navy's strategic advantage: as one journalist famously remarked, the High Seas Fleet had succeeded only in assaulting its gaoler before returning to goal. Conceivably, a more complete Royal Navy victory at Jutland might have opened new strategic opportunities for the Entente in the Baltic, but it is unlikely that these would have been decisive or contributed to the survival of the Tsar.[45]

Corbett's theories of seapower laid emphasis upon the need for amphibious capability but little was seen of amphibious operations. The Royal Navy's own plans for landing on the German Baltic coast or on islands such as Borkum and Heligoland were ruled out owing to the dangers of exposing capital vessels to submarines, mines, torpedo boats and coastal defences in confined waters. The Dardanelles campaign was the kind of amphibious operation demanded by a 'British way in warfare', although the original concept had been of a naval campaign only.

Unfortunately, there had been little co-operation between army and navy prior to the war but, whatever the differing strategic perspectives, inter-service co-operation was far better at operational level for all that the actual machinery for co-ordination was rudimentary. The landings on Gallipoli in April 1915 had to be improvised in the absence of any specialised landing craft, and naval delayed action high explosive shells were not ideal for fire support. Once the troops were landed, the navy continued to service the campaign logistically, while having to fend off attack: the battleship HMS *Goliath* was lost to a torpedo boat on 12/13 May 1915 and another battleship, HMS *Triumph*, to *U-21* on 25 May.

Many of the lessons, not least the need for specialised craft, were applied to the plan to mount an amphibious assault on the Belgian coast in support of the Passchendaele offensive in 1917. The latter proved abortive but Gallipoli was not the only example of co-operation between army and navy, or of naval effects upon land campaigns. Monitors had been used to bombard the German forces at Nieuport on the Belgian coast in the autumn of 1914 and the Dover Patrol was directly responsible for the security of the lines of communication to the British Expeditionary Force across the Channel. The Mesopotamia campaign also saw the advance of the army supported by a flotilla of gunboats on the Tigris and the Royal Navy provided an advisory mission to help defend Serbia against Austro-Hungarian gunboats on the Danube. After the war, however, inter-service co-operation lapsed in Britain once more and lessons had to be relearned in the Second World War. Elsewhere the Russians mounted a number of amphibious operations in the Black Sea, taking Trabzon in 1916.[46]

Yet another challenge to the capital ship was airpower, a German guard ship being the first sunk from the air when attacked by Japanese aircraft at Tsingtao in October 1914. Mines were also laid from the air in the Baltic and an air torpedo attack attempted at the Dardanelles in March 1915. During the same campaign, HMS *Triumph* became the first ship to fire on another it could not see using aerial spotting over the Sea of Marmara on 25 April 1915. This was not done by wireless telephony, which was not available in aircraft until 1917, but by dropping messages. Similarly, a seaplane was used to direct naval bombardment of Gaza and al-'Arish in Palestine that same month, landing close to the ships to relay information. The first capital ship sunk from the air was a Russian pre-dreadnought in April 1916.

Despite some opposition to developing airpower within the Royal Navy, on 3 November 1915, a conventional aircraft, a Bristol Scout C piloted by Flight Commander Bernard Fowler, was successfully flown off an impro-vised flight-deck on HMS *Vindix*. The first to land successfully – a Sopwith Pup – was flown on to HMS *Furious* on 2 August 1917, although its pilot,

Squadron Commander E. H. Dunning, drowned trying to repeat the feat five days later. In July 1918, seven Sopwith Camels successfully flew off the *Furious* to bomb a Zeppelin base at Tondern and there was an abortive plan to use air-launched torpedoes against the High Seas Fleet in Wilhelmshaven.

Increasingly, too, aircraft were used to escort convoys, albeit within the limitations of range, but dirigibles had a much longer range and were used fairly successfully. HMS *Ark Royal*, a converted steamer, was used as a seaplane carrier at the Dardanelles but, in October 1918, the world's first true aircraft carrier, HMS *Argus*, was commissioned. However, it was not to see service in the war and had been a converted liner. The first vessel specifically designed as an aircraft carrier, HMS *Hermes*, was laid down in 1917 but not put into commission until 1923.[47]

The war in the air

Airpower had great potential in terms of bringing war directly to the civilian population: naval blockade or submarine warfare could only do so indirectly. Aircraft had been used in the Italo-Turkish War (1911–12) and, to a limited extent, in the Balkan Wars (1912–13), proving that there was a military potential. Initially, aircraft were regarded only as reconnaissance machines, as in the opening campaign of the war. In fulfilling the reconnaissance function, however, airmen began to experiment with improvised weapons to bring down opponents in the attempt to ensure unimpeded reconnaissance.

Three Royal Flying Corps (RFC) machines became the first to force down an opponent on 25 August 1914. The RFC also undertook its first acrial spotting for artillery on 13 September, although, at this stage, aircraft were unable to communicate directly with the ground. Aerial wireless carried in a balloon was first used to direct artillery fire at Aubers Ridge on 9 May 1915 and aircraft were utilised to monitor the progress of an attack at St Julien on 25 April 1915 during the Second Battle of Ypres. Aerial photography was first attempted by the RFC on 15 September 1914, although the first suitable camera was developed only in the following year. By 1918, however, photographic images could be taken as high as 15,000 feet.

Once wireless was available, aerial spotting was further refined. Indeed, by 1917, 90 per cent of the Canadian Corps's counter-battery fire was directed from the air. Arguably, aerial reconnaissance and observation remained the most important contribution of airpower to the war. Aerial resupply was also attempted in the case of the British garrison besieged in Kut in Mesopotamia in 1916.[48]

By 1917–18, too, the ground attack role, in which the RFC in particular had become adept, was of increasing significance. The Germans, for example, employed 730 aircraft against the British Fifth and Third Armies on 21 March 1918, of which half were fighters or specially developed, partially armoured close-support machines. In response, the RFC fired almost 200,000 rounds in the first four days of the German offensive and contributed to the slowing of the German advance. German and RFC losses were both heavy but, by this stage, the RFC was better able to supply replacement men and machines.

Ground attack also played its part in the Allied victory in 1918: at Amiens on 8 August, British machines dropped 1,563 bombs and fired 122,150 rounds in support of the ground attack. On 12 September 1918, the American attack at St Mihiel was supported by an astonishing 1,476 Entente aircraft. Similarly, Allenby used airpower extensively in a tactical role. Seven British squadrons destroyed a Turkish column at Wadi el Far'a in Palestine on 21 September 1918, albeit largely through the effect on morale rather than physical damage to the Turks. Pétain was also a keen advocate of tactical airpower, urging the expansion of the French airforce and issuing a new tactical directive for a ground attack role in July 1917.[49]

Air superiority thus became increasingly recognised as a necessary adjunct to ground operations. It was assumed by early airpower theorists such as Frederick Sykes, however, that most air battles would only take place by mutual consent and that aircraft could literally hide in the vast expanse of the sky. Indeed, it appeared difficult to win command of the air without seeking constant battles that an opponent could choose to avoid. Consequently, for much of the war, the RFC's policy, as established by its General Officer Commanding (GOC) in the field from August 1915 to December 1917, Hugh Trenchard, was one of 'strategic offensive' to win command of the air over German lines. Trenchard's policy was one of continued standing patrols maintained regardless of the tactical situation on the ground. The Germans, meanwhile, could choose to concentrate aircraft to gain local superiority as desired. Inevitably, this resulted in losses not only from German aircraft but also from the failure of damaged machines to make their way back to Allied lines against the prevailing westerly winds.

During the Somme campaign, while successfully establishing superiority over the battlefield, British losses in the air were far higher than those of the Germans. Indeed, the RFC lost more pilots (499) and aircraft (782) than the numbers available at the beginning of the offensive (410 pilots and 426 aircraft). The loss of superiority over the Somme forced the Germans to reorganise their air arm with an autonomous air headquarters under General Erich von Höppner and squadrons that could be combined into larger flights. It was a lesson also absorbed from Verdun, which was arguably the first campaign to demonstrate the value of achieving air superiority. The development was sealed with the creation of *Jagdgeschwader* (fighter groups) in June 1917, the most famous being *Jagdgeschwader* I, popularly known as Richthofen's 'Flying Circus' after its commander, Manfred, Baron von Richthofen (the 'Red Baron').

The success of the fighter groups was reflected by losses sustained by the RFC, especially among reconnaissance aircraft, during the Arras operations in April 1917. A total of 151 RFC machines were lost in 'Bloody April', with 238 aircrew dead and 105 wounded, reducing the average number of hours flying time of an RFC pilot before becoming a casualty to 92 hours from the 295 hours a year previously.

The RFC's difficulties were compounded by the lack of progress made prior to the war in developing a British aviation industry comparable to those in France and Germany. Consequently, there was over-reliance on the Royal Aircraft Factory, which trailed behind the Germans in technical efficiency, not least in engine development. Secondly, there was the refusal to adopt parachutes on the grounds that they were unreliable, too bulky and might lead airmen to abandon aircraft too readily – all demonstrably untrue. Indeed, both fixed and free-fall parachutes were available before the war, but no British order was placed for free-fall parachutes until September 1918, although agents were dropped behind German lines by such means. Attrition rates among aircrew were also increased by accident: between 1914 and 1918, while 6,166 British pilots died in action, some 8,000 were lost in accidents.[50]

Early in the war RFC machines on the offensive had forced down a German aircraft in August 1914 while a Russian pilot, P. N. Nesterov, simply rammed an Austro-Hungarian aircraft in September 1914 at the cost of his own life. A French sergeant, Joseph Frantz, flying a Voisin 'pusher' (with engine and propeller at the back) succeeded in shooting down a German aircraft on 5 October 1914 with a machine gun mounted in the front cockpit. Such a practice, however, was risky in a normal 'puller' aircraft if a machine gun was fired forward through the propellor. Accordingly, two other Frenchmen, Roland Garros and Raymond Saulnier, who had been experimenting since November 1914, fixed steel plates to their propellers in February 1915 in the hope that they would deflect the 7–10 per cent of their own bullets which they expected to hit them.

On 1 April 1915 Garros successfully downed a German machine and did so twice more within seventeen days. However, the Dutch-born Anthony Fokker invented an interrupter gear based on a pre-war Swiss design and close inspection of Garros's machine after it was forced down in turn. Improved interrupter gears, better sights and machine guns with increased rates of fire were subsequently introduced by both sides, but the Fokker monoplane, the *Eindecker*, was the first true fighter aircraft. Making its first appearance in July 1915, the Fokker had an effect vastly exceeding its numbers and actual performance. Indeed, the 'Fokker fodder' produced by the Royal Aircraft Factory prompted a judicial enquiry in Britain. In reality, the real ascendancy of the Fokker was only between October 1915 and May 1916. Yet, it ushered in the era of aces such as Oswald Boelcke and Max Immelmann (the 'Eagle of Lille'), who flew the first two Fokkers.

Many aces followed, including Richthofen, who had shot down 80 Allied aircraft by the time of his death in April 1918. In fact, personalised air-to-air duel was a short-lived phenomenon as formation flying became the norm in 1916 and there was little of the 'knights of the air' chivalry suggested by wartime propaganda. Indeed, aerial warfare became as much a war of attrition and mass as that on the ground.

Despite the initial poor quality of British machines, new models constantly evolved on both sides with higher speed and higher rate of climb to present new challenges. The leadtimes in aircraft production, indeed, were sometimes measured only in weeks. As a whole, airframe and engine technology was greatly advanced by the war.[51]

At the same time that the effectiveness of airpower was established in relation to ground operations, including the use of tactical bombing, the first wartime experiments also took place with strategic bombing. Technically, aerial attack was prohibited by The Hague conventions of 1899 and 1907 but, since Germany had not signed them, any prohibition was not operative, for it applied only to conflicts between signatories. In any case, since the wording of the conventions was obscure with regard to aerial warfare, most states assumed that bombing was legitimate.

On 22 September 1914, the Royal Naval Air Service (RNAS), which had a more wide-ranging view of the potential of airpower than the Royal Flying Corps, carried out the first genuine strategic bombing mission on a military target by attacking Zeppelin sheds at Dusseldorf and Cologne. German Zeppelins undertook the first attack on ships at sea on 25 December 1914, ironically intercepting the British naval force launching the first seaborne air attack – by seaplanes – on the Zeppelin sheds at Cuxhaven. The first air raids on civilian targets were those by Zeppelins on French and Belgian Channel ports on 21 August 1914 followed by a raid on Paris on 30 August. Great Yarmouth became the first British town attacked on 19 January 1915, with London attacked for the first time on 31 May 1915.

Two years later, on 25 May 1917, the first German strategic air raid using conventional aircraft – Gotha G.IV bombers based at Ghent – rather than dirigibles, was launched on Folkestone. The campaign then extended to London by day and night, one daylight raid on 13 June 1917 by fourteen Gothas causing 162 deaths and near-panic in the East End. This raid and the appearance of 21 Gothas over London in daylight on 7 July, which resulted in riotous attacks on allegedly German-owned property in the East End, played a decisive role in the establishment of the Smuts Committee. It also persuaded King George V to change his dynastic name from Saxe-Coburg-Gotha to Windsor.

Smuts first recommended a reorganisation of home air defence with more and better aircraft. In a second report on 17 August 1917, Smuts recommended retaliation directed by an authority independent of army and naval rivalries. Following further raids, an Air Ministry and air staff were established in January 1918 with the Independent Force, Royal Air Force (RAF), coming into independent existence on 1 April 1918. The RNAS had carried out thirteen bombing raids on some German towns from Lexeuil near Belfort between July 1916 and March 1917, but the Admiralty's enthusiasm for extending the campaign had been opposed by Haig, who believed the resources better devoted to support of ground operations. The RAF was tasked on 6 June 1918 with retaliatory attacks on the German homeland. Sykes, now Chief of Air Staff, calculated that 80 per cent of Germany's chemical industry lay in range of British bombers using French bases.

Sykes had made a virtue of the difficulty of obtaining command of the air to argue that aircraft could deliberately avoid opposing aircraft and thus overcome the deadlock on land. It was a view also taken by the Italian theorist of airpower Guilio Douhet. However, Trenchard, who now commanded the RAF, preferred to target airfields and railways. In any case, he believed that the most effective defence of London from the air would be to force the Germans on the defensive in the skies over France and Flanders. Some 242 raids were carried out on Germany and 543 tons of bombs dropped, at the cost of 109 aircraft lost and 243 wrecked. The tonnage was too small to do much damage and, as early as June 1918, it was concluded that only 23.5 per cent of bombs were falling within the designated target area. The raids resulted in 797 German dead, 380 wounded and an estimated 15 million marks' worth of damage. The new Handley Page V-1500 bomber, with a 126 foot wing-span and a bomb load of 3,500 kilograms, was not ready until the end of the war, being poised to make the first raid on Berlin on the day the armistice was signed.

The Italians and Austro-Hungarians also carried out strategic bombing attacks. Indeed, the Italians were in the forefront of the use of airpower for strategic purposes, Gianni Caproni having developed the first true strategic bomber in 1913. By 1916, Italy had 40 of Caproni's massive three-engined triplanes with a 98 foot wing-span, a bomb load of 1,500 kilograms and fuel for a seven hour flight. Douhet had also begun to develop his theories of strategic airpower, although he was director of the Italian army's aviation section only from 1913 to 1914 and returned to it briefly in 1918 – indeed, it has been suggested that he never learned to fly. While Austro-Hungarian aircraft raided Verona, Venice, Padua and Milan, the Italians struck at Adriatic ports, but the Italian air offensive did not become of any significance until 1918. Paris was also subjected to aerial bombardment, 267 people being killed in Zeppelin or Gotha raids during the war compared with 256 killed by the long-range artillery bombardment during the German spring offensive in 1918.[52]

German raids resulted in 1,413 of the 1,570 wartime civilian deaths in Britain through enemy action. Little thought had been given to co-ordinating air defence prior to the war and inter-service rivalry continued to bedevil its evolution. A blackout or rather 'dim out' was introduced for defended harbours in August 1914 and was extended to other designated areas. Zeppelin attacks on inland targets such as Burton-on-Trent and Walsall in early 1916 forced a more general extension. The Gotha raids then compelled the introduction of an official air raid warning system in July 1917, policemen on bicycles issuing warnings and Boy Scouts sounding the 'all clear'. London was ringed with 353 searchlights, 266 anti-aircraft guns with 159 day fighters and 123 night fighters for additional protection. The problem was that air defence proved highly ineffective – in 397 sorties the Germans lost only 24 Gothas over England – while tying up over 300 British machines, although another 37 Gothas were lost in accidents. Moreover, it was calculated that the anti-aircraft guns had needed to fire 14,540 rounds to bring down one aircraft.

It was concluded that there was no effective anti-aircraft defence against the bomber. Zeppelins, however, could be caught through their slow rate of climb. Flight Sub-Lieutenant Rex Warneford successfully dropped bombs on one on 6 June 1915 over Ghent and Lieutenant W. Leefe Robinson shot down a similar Schütte Lanz dirigible with new incendiary bullets over Cuffley in Hertfordshire on 2/3 September 1915. Moreover, poor wireless security on the part of Zeppelin crews greatly assisted British signals intelligence. In all, Germany lost 17 airships in combat with 21 lost in accidents.

Bombers operating in daylight did not use wireless. But, even given forewarning, without adequate radar or ground-to-air communications, air defence fighters were initially groping for contact with the Gothas and the heavier *Riesenflugzeuge* bombers introduced by the Germans in late 1917. Improved range-finding and sound location devices became available, but the fighters themselves were technically limited. Thus, neither the Gotha raids nor those of the RAF either proved or disproved the evolving theories of strategic airpower in which both sides had invested so much hope.[53]

Looking at the contribution of technology as a whole, the emergence of the aircraft carrier HMS *Argus* at the very end marks the nature of the

Great War. It was a new kind of conflict in that tanks, manned aircraft and aircraft carriers all emerged, but their potential lay in the future. Indeed, much that occurred was traditional in terms of the line of battle at Jutland or the cavalry charges that took place on the Eastern Front and in Palestine. In that sense, therefore, it was a transitional conflict in military terms. This was not the case with respect to states and societies, upon which the war's impact was rather more total.

Notes and references

1. Michael Brock and Eleanor Brock, eds, *H. H. Asquith: Letters to Venetia Stanley* (Oxford, 1982), p.346; Winston S. Churchill, *The World Crisis, 1911–18*, 6 vols (London, 1923), I, pp.10–11.

2. Michael Paris, *Winged Warfare: The Literature and Theory of Aerial Warfare in Britain, 1859–1917* (Manchester, 1992), pp.16–59, 124–46; Stephen Kern, *The Culture of Time and Space, 1880–1918* (Cambridge, MA, 1983), pp.242–7; I. F. Clarke, *Voices Prophesying War, 1789–1984*, 2nd edn (London, 1970), pp.64–106; Paul Harris, *Men, Ideas and Tanks: British Military Thought and Armoured Forces, 1903–19* (Manchester, 1995), pp.4–8; Tim Travers, 'Future Warfare: H. G. Wells and British Military Theory, 1895–1916', in Bond and Roy, eds, *War and Society* I, pp.67–87; John Buckley, *Air Power in the Age of Total War* (London, 1999), pp.22–41. On the impact of aviation, see also Dominick Pisano, *Legend, Memory and the Great War in the Air* (Seattle, WA, 1992); Robert Wohl, *A Passion for Wings: Aviation and the Western Imagination, 1908–18* (New Haven, CT, 1994); Peter Fritzsche, *A Nation of Fliers: German Aviators and the Popular Imagination* (Cambridge, MA, 1992); Alfred Gollin, *The Impact of Air Power on the British People and their Government, 1909–14* (Stanford, CA, 1989); idem, *No Longer an Island: Britain and the Wright Brothers, 1902 1909* (Stanford, CA, 1984).

3. Guy Hartcup, *The War of Invention: Scientific Developments, 1914–18* (London, 1988), pp.29–37; Henry Harris, 'To Serve Mankind in Peace and the Father-land at War: The Case of Fritz Haber', *German History* 10 (1992), pp.24–38.

4. Hartcup, *War of Invention*, pp.21–9; Keith Vernon, 'Science and Technology', in Constantine, Kirby and Rose, eds, *First World War in British History*, pp.81–105; Michael Pattison, 'Scientists, Inventors and the Military in Britain, 1915–19: The Munitions Inventions Department', *Social Studies of Science* 13 (1983), pp.521–68; idem, 'Scientists, Government and Invention: The Experience of the Inventions Boards, 1915–18', in Liddle, ed., *Home Fires and Foreign Fields*, pp.83–100; J. K. Gusewelle, 'Science and the Admiralty during World War I: The Case of the Board of Invention and Research', in G. Jordan, ed., *Naval Warfare in the Twentieth Century, 1900–45* (London, 1977), pp.105–17; R. M. MacLeod and E. K. Andrews, 'Scientific Advice in the War at Sea, 1915–17: The Board of Invention and Research', *JCH* 6 (1971), pp.3–40.

5. Hartcup, *War of Invention*, pp.44–68; I. Varcoe, 'Scientists, Government and Organised Research: The Early History of the DSIR, 1914–16', *Minerva* 8 (1970), pp.192–217; R. M. MacLeod and E. K. Andrews, 'The Origins of DSIR: Reflections on Ideas and Men, 1915–16', *Public Administration* 48 (1970), pp.23–48.

6. Steve Strudt, 'War as Experiment: Physiology, Innovation and Administration in Britain, 1914–18: The Case of Chemical Warfare', in Roger Cooter, Mark Harrison and Steve Sturdy, eds, *War, Medicine and Modernity* (Stroud, 1998), pp.65–84; Joel D. Howell, ' "Soldier's Heart": The Redefinition of Heart Disease and Speciality Formation in Early Twentieth Century Great Britain', ibid., pp.85–105; Hartcup, *War of Invention*, pp.168–80; J. S. Haller, 'Treatment of Infected Wounds during the Great War, 1914–18', *Southern Medical Journal* 85 (1992), pp.305–13; J. D. C. Bennett, 'Medical Advances consequent to the Great War, 1914–18', *Journal of the Royal Society of Medicine* 83 (1990), pp.738–42; Nick Bosanquet, 'Health Systems in Khaki: The British and American Medical Experience', in Cecil and Liddle, eds, *Facing Armageddon*, pp.451–65; Mark Harrison, 'The Fight against Disease in the Mesopotamia Campaign', ibid., pp.475–89; Andrew Bamji, 'Facial Surgery: The Patient's Experience', ibid., pp.490–501; Ian Whitehead, 'Third Ypres – Casualties and British Medical Services: An Evaluation', in Liddle, ed., *Passchendaele in Perspective*, pp.191–2; Roxanne Panchasi, 'Reconstructions: Prosthetics and the Rehabilitation of the Male Body in World War I France', *Differences* 7 (1995), pp.109–40; G. Noon, 'The Treatment of Casualties in the Great War', in Griffith, ed., *British Fighting Methods*, pp.87–112; B. Király, 'Elements of Limited and Total Warfare', in Kann, Király and Fichtner, eds, *Habsburg Empire*, pp.135–56. For French anti-typhoid figures, see *Gunfire* 15 (1990), p.60.

7. Towle, 'Russo-Japanese War and British Military Thought', pp.64–8.

8. Keith Simpson, 'The Officers', in Beckett and Simpson, eds, *Nation in Arms*, pp.64–96; Bond, *Victorian Army and Staff College*, pp.299–329; Peter Scott, 'The Staff of the BEF', *Stand To* 15 (1985), pp.44–61; John Bourne, 'British Generals in the First World War', in G. D. Sheffield, ed., *Leadership and Command: The Anglo-American Experience since 1861* (London, 1997), pp.93–116.

9. Bidwell and Graham, *Firepower*, pp.44–6; Dominick Graham, 'Observations on the Dialectics of British Tactics, 1904–45', in Ronald Haycock and Keith Neilson, eds, *Men, Machines and War* (Waterloo, 1988), pp.51–73; idem, 'Sans Doctrine: British Army Tactics in the First World War', in Travers and Archer, eds, *Men at War*, pp.69–92; Bond, *Victorian Army and Staff College*, pp.299–329; Tim Travers, 'The Hidden Army: Structural problems in the British Officer Corps, 1900–18', *JCH* 17 (1982), pp.523–44; Harvey, *Collision of Empires*, p.310; Gooch, 'Italy during First World War', p.176; Herwig, 'Dynamics of Necessity', p.94.

10. Ian Beckett, *Johnnie Gough, VC: A Biography of Brigadier-General Sir John Edmund Gough* (London, 1989), pp.148–9.

11. Travers, *Killing Ground*, pp.85–97; idem, 'A Particular Style of Command: Haig and GHQ, 1916–18', *JSS* 10 (1987), pp.363–76; Dominick Graham, *Against Odds: Reflections on the Experience of the British Army, 1914–45* (London, 1999), pp.31–47; Gerard De Groot, 'Educated Soldier or Cavalry Officer?: Contradictions in the Pre-1914 Career of Douglas Haig', *W&S* 4 (1986), pp.51–69; Tim Travers, 'The Army and the Challenge of War, 1914–18', in Chandler and Beckett, eds, *Oxford Illustrated History of British Army*, pp.215–40.

12. Travers, *Killing Ground*, pp.101–18, 127–46, 152–90; Robin Prior and Trevor Wilson, *Command on the Western Front: The Military Career of Sir Henry Rawlinson, 1914–18* (Oxford, 1992), pp.25–35, 68–73, 137–53, 171–3, 193–5, 222–3, 227–32; Bidwell and Graham, *Firepower*, pp.73–87.

13. Anthony Farrar-Hockley, *Goughie: The Life of General Sir Hubert Gough* (London, 1975), pp.223–4; Prior and Wilson, *Passchendaele*, pp.108–10; Travers, *Killing Ground*, pp.203–17; idem, *How the War Was Won: Command and Technology in the British Army on the Western Front, 1917–18* (London, 1992), pp.11–19; Andrew Wiest, 'Haig, Gough and Passchendaele', in Sheffield, ed., *Leadership and Command*, pp.77–92; Peter Simkins, 'Haig and his Army Commanders', in Bond and Cave, eds, *Haig*, pp.78–106.

14. Travers, *Killing Ground*, pp.220–43; idem, *How the War Was Won*, pp.56–64; idem, 'Particular Style of Command', p.368; Gerard De Groot, ' "We Are Safe Whatever Happens": Douglas Haig, the Reverend George Duncan and the Conduct of the War, 1916–18', in N. Macdougall, ed., *Scotland and War, AD 79 to 1918* (Edinburgh: 1991), pp.193–211; idem, 'The Reverend George S. Duncan at GHQ, 1916–18', *Military Miscellany I* (Stroud, 1996), pp.266–436.

15. Gerard De Groot, *Douglas Haig, 1861–1928* (London, 1988), pp.117–18, 130, 140–1, 217–19, 240–1, 294–5; Winston S. Churchill, *Great Contemporaries*, rev. edn (London, 1938), p.230; Martin van Creveld, *Command in War* (Cambridge, MA, 1985), pp.156, 186, 262; Bourne, *Britain and Great War*, pp.171–2; Gooch, 'Italy in First World War', p.175.

16. Ian Beckett, 'Hubert Gough, Neill Malcolm and Command on the Western Front', in Bond, ed., *Look to Your Front*, pp.1–12; Travers, *How the War Was Won*, pp.50–109; idem, 'Command and Leadership Styles in the British Army: The 1915 Gallipoli Model', *JCH* 29 (1994), pp.403–42.

17. Prior and Wilson, *Command*, pp.158–61.

18. Travers, *How the War Was Won*, pp.149, 175–82; Prior and Wilson, *Command*, pp.394–8; John Bourne, 'British Generals', pp.93–116; idem, 'British Divisional Commanders during the Great War: First Thoughts', *Gun Fire* 29 (1993), pp.22–31; idem, 'The BEF's Generals on 29 September 1918: An Empirical Portrait with some British and Australian Comparisons', in Peter Dennis and Jeffrey Grey, eds, *1918: Defining Victory* (Canberra, 1999), pp.96–113; Peter Simkins, 'Co-stars or Supporting Cast? British Divisions in the "Hundred Days", 1918', in Griffith, ed., *British Fighting Methods*, pp.50–69.

19. John Gooch, 'The Armed Services', in Constantine, Kirby and Rose, eds, *First World War in British History*, pp.192–3, 199–200; Paul Kennedy, 'Britain in the First World War', in Millett and Murray, eds, *Military Effectiveness*, p.52; Herwig, 'Dynamics of Necessity', pp.99–100; Arthur J. Marder, *From the Dreadnought to Scapa Flow: The Royal Navy in the Fisher Era, 1904–1919*, 5 vols (Oxford, 1961– 70), V, pp.302, 305–6, 313–29; Malcolm Cooper, 'A House Divided: Policy, Rivalry and Administration in Britain's Military Air Command, 1914–18', *JSS* 3 (1980), pp.178–201.

20. Bourne, *Britain and Great War*, pp.172–3; G. C. Wynne, *If Germany Attacks: The Battle in Depth in the West* (London, 1940), pp.125–6; Martin Samuels, *Command or Control? Command, Training and Tactics in the British and German Armies, 1888– 1918* (London, 1995), pp.10–33; idem, 'Directive Command and the German General Staff', *WH* 2 (1995), pp.22–42; Geyer, 'German Strategy', pp.541–5; Herwig, 'Dynamics of Necessity', pp.94, 97; Creveld, *Command in War*, pp.169– 72.

21. Guy Pedronici, 'L'Évolution des idées stratégiques françaises', in ICMH, *Acta 10*, p.24; Jones, 'Imperial Russia's Forces at War', p.308; Herwig, *First World War*, pp.191–2; Jay Winter, *The Experience of World War I* (London, 1988), pp.124, 140, 154; R. W. Whalen, *Bitter Wounds: German Victims of the Great War* (Ithaca, NY, 1984), pp.42–3; Strachan, *First World War*, p.22; idem, *European Armies*, pp.138–9; Bill Rawling, *Surviving Trench Warfare: Technology and the Canadian Corps, 1914–18* (Toronto, 1992), pp.215, 219–21; idem, 'A Resource Not to be Squandered: The Canadian Corps on the 1918 Battlefield', in Dennis and Grey, eds, *1918*, pp.43–71.

22. Prior and Wilson, *Command*, pp.84–5, 98, 110–13, 167–9, 182–3, 191–2, 233–4; Bidwell and Graham, *Firepower*, pp.73–87; Wilson, *Myriad Faces of War*, pp.258–60, 319–21; Strachan, *European Armies*, p.138; P. A. Pedersen, 'The AIF on the Western Front: The Role of Training and Command', in McKernan and Browne, eds, *Australia*, p.173; Jones, 'Imperial Russia's Forces at War', pp.306, 311–12; Bourne, *Britain and Great War*, pp.59–67; Tim Travers, 'Learning and Decision-making on the Western Front, 1915–16: The British Example', *CJH* (1983), pp.87–97; Bailey, 'British Artillery', pp.23–49; Keegan, *First World War*, pp.336–42; Gary Sheffield, 'Blitzkrieg and Attrition, 1914– 45', in McInnes and Sheffield, eds, *Warfare in the Twentieth Century*, pp.53–4; Peter Bryant, 'The Recall of Sir John French', *Stand To* 22/23/24 (1988), pp.25–9, 32–8, 22–6, resp.

23. Herwig, *First World War*, pp.183–4, 191–2; Afflerbach, *Falkenhayn*, p.361; Ferro, *Great War*, pp.76–8.

24. Herwig, *First World War*, pp.165, 250–1; Bruce Gudmundsson, *Stormtroop Tactics: Innovation in the German Army, 1914–18* (New York, 1989), pp.30–2; Heinz Hagenlücke, 'The German High Command', in Liddle, ed., *Passchendaele*, pp.45–58; Gooch, 'Italy in First World War', pp.171–4, 178–9; Sullivan, 'Caporetto', pp.59–78; Porch, 'French Army', pp.219, 223; Wynne, *If Germany*

Attacks, pp.85, 92–9, 121–31, 138–9, 150–61, 168–82, 199–214, 277–80, 313–15; Timothy Lupfer, *The Dynamics of Doctrine: The Change in German Tactical Doctrine during the First World War* (Leavenworth, KS, 1981), pp.1–30; Samuels, *Command or Control*, pp.161–97; Prior and Wilson, *Passchendaele*, pp.71–3 Strachan, *European Armies*, pp.140–2.

25. Sir Lawrence Bragg, A. H. Dowson and H. H. Hemming, eds, *Artillery Survey in the First World War* (London, 1971), pp.9–40; Peter Chasseaud, 'Field Survey in the Salient: Cartography and Artillery Survey in the Flanders Operations in 1917', in Liddle, ed., *Passchendaele in Perspective*, pp.117–39; Hartcup, *War of Invention*, pp.68–76; Bidwell and Graham, *Firepower*, pp.89–91, 101–11; Prior and Wilson, *Passchendaele*, pp.55–7, 61–3, 82–7, 115–19, 121, 128, 131, 161–2, 166–7, 199–200; Ian Beckett, 'Operational Command: The Plans and the Conduct of the Battle', in Liddle, ed., *Passchendaele in Perspective*, pp.111–12; Paddy Griffith, 'The Tactical Problem: Infantry, Artillery and the Salient', ibid., pp.61–72.

26. Prior and Wilson, *Command*, pp.158–61, 311; Bidwell and Graham, *Firepower*, pp.113–15, 117–28, 141–4; Graham, 'Sans Doctrine', pp.69–92; Peter Scott, 'Mr Stokes and his Educated Drainpipe', *The Great War* 2 (1990), pp.80–94; Paddy Griffith, 'The Lewis Gun Made Easy: The Development of Automatic Rifles in the Great War', *The Great War* 3 (1991), pp.108–15; idem, *Battle Tactics on the Western Front: The British Army's Art of Attack, 1916–18* (New Haven, CT, 1994), pp.54–8, 76–9, 95–100, 129–34, 193–5; idem, 'The Extent of Tactical Reform in the British Army', in Griffith, ed., *British Fighting Methods*, pp.1–22; Andrew Whitmarsh, 'The Development of Infantry Tactics in the British 12th (Eastern) Division, 1915–18', *Stand To* 48 (1997), pp.28–32; Gary Sheffield, 'The Indispensable Factor: The Performance of British Troops in 1918', in Dennis and Grey, eds, *1918*, pp.72–95; Pedersen, 'AIF on Western Front', pp.178–83; Rawling, *Surviving Trench Warfare*, pp.89–95, 114–31, 142, 208; A. M. J. Hyatt, *General Sir Arthur Currie: A Military Biography* (Toronto, 1987), pp.63–7; Ian M. Brown, 'Not Glamorous but Effective: The Canadian Corps and the Set-piece Attack, 1917–18', *JMilH* 58 (1994), pp.421–44; Bourne, *Britain and Great War*, pp.91–2; John Lee, 'Some Lessons of the Somme: The British Infantry in 1917', in Bond, ed., *Look To Your Front*, pp.79–88; Peter Simkins, 'Somme Reprise: Reflections on the Fighting for Albert and Bapaume, August 1918', ibid., pp.147–62.

27. Griffith, *Battle Tactics*, pp.230–1, n.33; Rothenberg, *Army of Francis Joseph*, pp.196–7; Stone, *Eastern Front*, pp.223, 229–30, 237–41, 249–52; Jones, 'Imperial Russia's Forces at War', pp.306–7, 312.

28. James S. Corum, *The Roots of Blitzkrieg: Hans von Seeckt and German Military Reform* (Lawrence, KS, 1992), pp.7–11; Martin Samuels, *Doctrine and Dogma: German and British Infantry Tactics in the First World War* (Westport, CN, 1992), pp.7–96; idem, *Command or Control*, pp.88–93; Gudmundsson, *Stormtroop Tactics*, pp.43–53, 91–104; Lupfer, *Dynamics of Doctrine*, pp.27–9, 37–49; Geyer,

'German Strategy', pp.546–7; Herwig, *First World War*, pp.252–4; Harvey, *Collision of Empires*, p.352; Gooch, 'Italy in First World War', p.180; Strachan, *European Armies*, pp.144–5.

29. Geyer, 'German Strategy', p.552; Herwig, *First World War*, p.400, 409–10; idem, 'Dynamics of Necessity', pp.100–3; Lupfer, *Dynamics of Doctrine*, pp.37–54; Helmut Otto, 'Strategisch-operative Planungen des deutschen Heeres für die Frühjahsoffensive 1918 an der Westfront', *MM* 17 (1978), pp.463–80; Gudmundsson, *Stormtroop Tactics*, pp.109–21, 125–37, 139–52, 155–68; Samuels, *Command or Control*, pp.235–45; Travers, *How the War Was Won*, pp.86–8, 99, 155; Wynne, *If Germany Attacks*, pp.294–5; Bourne, *Britain and Great War*, p.89; David Zabecki, *Steel Wind: Colonel Georg Bruchmüller and the Birth of Modern Artillery* (Westport, CN, 1994), pp.33–57, 63–97; idem, 'Colonel Georg Bruchmüller and the Birth of Modern Artillery Tactics', *Stand To* 53 (1998), pp.5–11.

30. Porch, 'French Army', pp.212, 214–17, 219–23; Nenninger, 'American Military Effectiveness', pp, 134–8, 142–6; Trask, *AEF and Coalition Warmaking*, pp.171–4; Charles E. Heller, *Chemical Warfare in World War I: The American Experience, 1917–18* (Leavenworth, KS, 1984), pp.135–59; Gregory Martin, 'German Strategy and Military Assessments of the American Expeditionary Force (AEF), 1917–18', *WH* 1 (1994), pp.160–96.

31. Prior and Wilson, *Command*, pp.363–6, 368; eidem, 'What Manner of Victory? Reflections on the Termination of the First World War', *RIHM* 72 (1990), pp.80–96; Travers, *How the War Was Won*, p.169.

32. Griffith, 'Extent of Tactical Reform', p.18; idem, *Battle Tactics*, pp.161–2; Stephen Badsey, 'Cavalry and the Development of Breakthrough Doctrine', in Griffith, ed., *British Fighting Methods*, pp.138–74; John Singleton, 'Britain's Military Use of the Horse, 1914–18', *P&P* 139 (1993), pp.178–203; Terry Norman, *The Hell Called High Wood* (London, 1984), pp.81–2, 96–101; Archibald Wavell, *Allenby: A Study in Greatness* (London, 1940), p.245; Jonathan Newell, 'Allenby and the Palestine Campaign', in Bond, ed., *First World War and British Military History*, pp.189–226; idem, 'Learning the Hard Way: Allenby in Egypt and Palestine, 1917–18', *JSS* 14 (1991), pp.363–87; Jones, 'Imperial Russia's Forces at War', pp.299–300.

33. Edward Spiers, *Chemical Warfare* (London, 1986), pp.13–33; idem, 'Chemical Warfare in the First World War', in Bond, ed., *Look To Your Front*, pp.163–78; L. F. Haber, *The Poisonous Cloud: Chemical Warfare in the First World War* (Oxford, 1986), pp.22–40, 83–105, 117, 207–38, 243–9; Ulrich Trumpener, 'The Road to Ypres: The Beginnings of Gas Warfare in World War I', *JMH* 47 (1975), pp.460–80; Herwig, *First World War*, p.189; Simon Jones, 'Gas Warfare: The British Defensive Measures: The Second Battle of Ypres', *Stand To* 14 (1985), pp.15–23; idem, 'Under a Green Sea: The Defensive British Responses to Gas Warfare', *The Great War* 1/2 (1989/90), pp.126–32, 14–21; Donald Richter, 'The Experience of the British Special Brigade in Gas

Warfare', in Cecil and Liddle, eds, *Facing Armageddon*, pp.353–64; Hartcup, *War of Invention*, pp.94–117; Tim Travers, 'Allies in Conflict: The British and Canadian Official Historians and the Real Story of Second Ypres (1915)', *JCH* 24 (1989), pp.301–25; Heller, *Chemical Warfare*, pp.6–34.

34. Hartcup, *War of Invention*, pp.80–91; Bidwell and Graham, *Firepower*, pp.135–8; Hubert C. Johnson, *Breakthrough: Tactics, Technology and the Search for Victory on the Western Front* (Novato, CA, 1994), pp.170–3; Harvey, *Collision of Empires*, p.383; Paul Harris, *Men, Ideas and Tanks: British Military Thought and Armoured Forces, 1903–39* (Manchester, 1996), pp.9–39, 62–7; idem, 'The Rise of Armour', in Griffith, ed., *British Fighting Methods*, pp.113–37; idem, 'Haig and the Tank', in Bond and Cave, eds, *Haig*, pp.145–54.

35. Harris, *Men, Ideas and Tanks*, pp.99–113, 123–5, 146–51, 159–89; Bidwell and Graham, *Firepower*, pp.137–9; Pedersen, 'AIF on Western Front', pp.186–8; Tim Travers, 'The Evolution of British Strategy and Tactics on the Western Front in 1918: GHQ, Manpower and Technology', *JMilH*, 54 (1990), pp.173–200; idem, 'Could the Tanks of 1918 have been War-winners for the British Expeditionary Force?', *JCH* 27 (1992), pp.389–406; idem, *How the War Was Won*, pp.36–49, 110–27, 140–44; Prior and Wilson, 'What Manner of Victory', pp.80–96; Griffith, *Battle Tactics*, pp.164–9.

36. David French, 'Sir John French's Secret Service on the Western Front, 1914–15', *JSS* 7 (1984), pp.423–40; Eliezer Tauber, 'The Capture of the Nili Spies: The Turkish Version', *Intelligence and National Security* 6 (1991), pp.701–10; Richard Popplewell, 'British Intelligence in Mesopotamia, 1914–16', in Michael Handel, ed., *Intelligence and Military Operations* (London, 1990) pp.139–72.

37. Hartcup, *War of Invention*, pp.76–8; Showalter, *Tannenberg*, pp.170, 230; David French, 'Watching the Allies', pp.573–92; John Ferris, 'The British Army and Signals Intelligence in the Field during the First World War', *Intelligence and National Security* 3 (1988), pp.23–48; idem, *The British Army and Signals Intelligence during the First World War* (Stroud, 1992), pp.1–24, 340–5 n.3, 347–8 n.19; William Friedman, *Solving German Codes in World War One* (Laguna Hills, CA, 1977), pp.79, 112–4, 126; Herbert O. Yardley, 'Achievements of the Cipher Bureau MI-8 during the First World War', *Cryptologia* 8 (1984), pp.62–74; Yigal Sheffy, *British Military Intelligence in the Palestine Campaign, 1914–18* (London, 1998), pp.69–73, 82–3, 128–133, 159–67, 219–56, 269–86; idem, 'Institutionalised Deception and Perception Reinforcement: Allenby's Campaigns in Palestine, 1917–18', in Handel, ed., *Intelligence and Military Operations*, pp.173–238; David Kahn, 'Codebreaking in World War I and II', *HJ* 23 (1980), pp.617–40; Michael Occleshaw, *Armour Against Fate: British Military Intelligence in the First World War* (London, 1989), pp.72–109, 111–22, 129–34, 196–200, 325–64.

38. David French, 'Failures of Intelligence: The Retreat to the Hindenburg Line and the March 1918 Offensive', in Dockrill and French, eds, *Strategy and Intelligence*, pp.67–95; Peter Morris, 'Intelligence and its Interpretation:

Mesopotamia, 1914–16', in Christopher Andrew and Jeremy Noakes, eds, *Intelligence and International Relations, 1900–1945* (London, 1987), pp.77–102.

39. Jonathan Bailey, 'The First World War and the Birth of the Modern Style of Warfare', *Strategic and Combat Studies Institute Occasional Paper* 22 (1996), pp.13–21; Bidwell and Graham, *Firepower*, p.117; Ferguson, *Pity of War*, pp.294–303, 445; Robin Prior and Trevor Wilson, 'Winning the War', in Dennis and Grey, eds, *1918*, pp.33–42.

40. Hartcup, *War of Invention*, pp.140–4; Richard Hough, *The Great War at Sea, 1914–18*, 2nd edn (Oxford, 1986), pp.61–2, 171–2, 180–6; Kennedy, 'Britain', pp.53–4; Bryan Ranft, 'The Royal Navy and the War at Sea', in Turner, ed., *Britain and First World War*, pp.53–69.

41. Wilson, *Myriad Faces of War*, pp.91, 94, 427–9, 630–2; Herwig, *Luxury Fleet*, pp.228–9; Geoffrey Till, 'Passchendaele: The Maritime Dimension', in Liddle, ed., *Passchendaele in Perspective*, pp.73–87.

42. Hartcup, *War of Invention*, pp.123–35; Hough, *Great War at Sea*, pp.303–11; Marder, *Dreadnought to Scapa Flow*, II, pp.349–66; idem, IV, pp.69–88, 115–66, 256–92; Wilson, *Myriad Faces of War*, pp.433–8; Patrick Beesley, *Room 40: British Naval Intelligence, 1914–18*, 2nd edn (Oxford, 1984), pp.204–24, 252–70, 307–15; Nicholas Hiley, 'The Strategic Origins of Room 40', *Intelligence and National Security* 2 (1987), pp.245–73; John Ferris, 'Before Room 40: The British Empire and Signals Intelligence, 1898–1914', *JSS* 12 (1989), pp.431–57; Alberto Santoni, 'The First Ultra Secret: The British Cryptanalysis in the Naval Operations of the First World War', *RIHM* 63 (1985), pp.99–110; Heinrich Walle, 'Die Anwendung der Funktelegraphie beim Einsatz deutscher U-Boote im Ersten Weltkrieg', ibid., pp.111–38; Christopher Andrew, *Secret Service: The Making of the British Intelligence Community* (London, 1987), pp.139–85; Andrew Gordon, *The Rules of the Game: Jutland and British Naval Command* (London, 1997), pp.354–5; Kennedy, 'Britain', pp.57–8, 60–1; Keegan, *First World War*, pp.282–3; Herwig, 'Failure of Imperial Germany's Undersea Offensive', pp.611–36; idem, *First World War*, pp.319, 325; Stephen Roskill, *Hankey: Man of Secrets*, 3 vols (London, 1970) I, pp.355–9; Halpern, *Naval War in Mediterranean*, pp.243–63, 276–84, 386–94.

43. Renato Sicurezza, 'Italy and the War in the Adriatic', in Cecil and Liddle, eds, *Facing Armageddon*, pp.180–92; D. M. Schurman, *The Education of a Navy: The Development of British Naval Thought, 1867–1914* (London, 1965), pp.60–82; Paul Kennedy, *The Rise and Fall of British Naval Mastery* (London, 1976), pp.2–9; Philip A. Crowl, 'Alfred Thayer Mahan: The Naval Historian', in Paret, ed., *Makers of Modern Strategy*, pp.444–80; Jon Sumida, 'British Naval and Operational Logistics, 1914–18', *JMilH* 57 (1993), pp.447–80.

44. Philip Towle, 'The Effect of the Russo-Japanese War on British Naval Policy', *Mariner's Mirror* 60 (1974), pp.383–94; idem, 'The Evaluation of the Experience of the Russo-Japanese War', in Brian Ranft, ed., *Technical Change and British*

Naval Policy, 1860–1939 (London, 1977), pp.65–79; Colin White, 'The Navy and the Naval War Considered', in Liddle, ed., *Home Fires and Foreign Fields*, pp.115–34; Hough, *Great War at Sea*, pp.63–4, 79–80, 137–8, 141; William H. McNeill, *The Pursuit of Power* (Oxford, 1983), pp.294–9; Jon Tetsuro Sumida, *In Defence of Naval Supremacy: Finance, Technology and British Naval Policy, 1889–1914*, 2nd edn (London, 1993), pp.xvii, 77–100, 115–38, 163–76, 196–256, 297–9; idem, 'British Capital Ship Design and Fire Control in the Dreadnought Era: Sir John Fisher, Arthur Hungerford Pollen, and the Battle Cruiser', *JMH* 51 (1979), pp.205–30; idem, ed., *The Pollen Papers: The Privately Circulated Works of Arthur Hungerford Pollen, 1901–16* (London, 1984), p.334; Marder, *Dreadnought to Scapa Flow* I, pp.43–70, 395–7; idem, II, pp.20–41, 101–29, 156–75; James Goldrick, *The King's Ships were at Sea: War in the North Sea, 1914–15* (Annapolis, MD, 1984), pp.260–78; Hartcup, *War of Invention*, pp.10–14, 118–22; Kennedy, *Rise and Fall of Naval Mastery*, p.245.

45. Wilson, *Myriad Faces of War*, pp.79–80, 288–99; Beesley, *Room 40*, pp.151–68; Marder, *Dreadnought to Scapa Flow*, III, pp.80–5, 116–17, 167–71, 174–6; idem, V, pp.310–11; Kennedy, *Rise and Fall of Naval Mastery*, pp.246–9; Sumida, *In Defence of Naval Supremacy*, pp.299–305; Hough, *Great War at Sea*, pp.204–7, 275–85, 295–7; Paul Halpern, *A Naval History of World War I* (Annapolis, MD, 1994), pp.419–20; N. J. M. Campbell, *Jutland: An Analysis of the Fighting* (Annapolis, MD, 1986), pp.337–404; V. E. Tarrant, *Jutland: The German Perspective* (London, 1995), pp.264–72.

46. Geoffrey Till, 'Brothers in Arms: The British Army and Navy at the Dardanelles', in Cecil and Liddle, eds, *Facing Armageddon*, pp.160–79; Halpern, *Naval War in Mediterranean*, pp.47–83; Arthur J. Marder, *From the Dardanelles to Oran: Studies of the Royal Navy in War and Peace, 1915–40* (Oxford, 1974), pp.1–32; Wiest, 'Great Landing', pp.84–9; idem, 'Planned Amphibious Assault', pp.201–14; Peacock, 'Proposed Landing', pp.2–50; White, 'Navy and Naval War', pp.128–31.

47. Sheffy, *British Military Intelligence in Palestine*, pp.94–6; Marder, *Dreadnought to Scapa Flow*, IV, pp.10–24; Jack Bruce, 'The War in the Air: The Men and Their Machines', in Cecil and Liddle, eds, *Facing Armageddon*, pp.193–205; John Bullen, 'The Royal Navy and Air Power: The Projected Torpedo-bomber Attack on the High Seas Fleet at Wilhelmshaven in 1918', *IWMR* 2 (1987), pp.71–7; Lee Kennett, *The First Air War, 1914–18* (New York, 1991), pp.187–206; Buckley, *Air Power*, pp.56–8; Harvey, *Collision of Empires*, pp.390–1; Hough, *Great War at Sea*, pp.186–9, 317–18.

48. Michael Paris, 'The First Air Wars: North Africa and the Balkans, 1911–13', *JCH* 26 (1991), pp.97–109; S. F. Wise, 'The Strategic Use of Airpower in the Context of the Evolution of the Air Weapon in the First World War', in ICMH, *Acta 10*, pp.225–40; Hartcup, *War of Invention*, pp.154–6; Occleshaw, *Armour against Fate*, pp.55–71; Harvey, *Collision of Empires*, p.390; Buckley, *Air Power*, pp.46–50.

49. Bidwell and Graham, *Firepower*, pp.143–5; Buckley, *Air Power*, pp.53–6; Wilson, *Myriad Faces of War*, pp.608–17; Wise, 'Strategic Use of Airpower', p.227; Brereton Greenhous, 'Aircraft versus Armor: Cambrai to Yom Kippur', in Travers and Archer, eds, *Men at War*, pp.93–118; Harvey, *Collision of Empires*, p.409; Malcolm Cooper, *The Birth of Independent Air Power* (London, 1986), pp.146–51; P. Mead, *The Eye in the Air: The History of Air Observation and Reconnaissance for the Army, 1785–1945* (London, 1983), pp.117–20; Kennett, *First Air War*, pp.23–40; Porch, 'French Army', pp.218–19; Guy Pedronici, *Pétain, général en chef, 1917–18* (Paris, 1974), pp.59–60, 207–10.

50. Malcolm Smith, 'The Tactical and Strategic Allocation of Air Power on the Western Front', in Liddle, ed., *Home Fires and Foreign Fields*, pp.53–67; idem, *British Air Strategy Between the Wars* (Oxford, 1984), pp.13–43; Paris, *Winged Warfare*, pp.188–90; Cooper, *Birth of Independent Airpower*, pp.15–16, 71–81; idem, 'The Development of Air Policy and Doctrine on the Western Front, 1914–18', *Aerospace Historian* 28 (1981), pp.38–51; idem, 'British Flying Operations on the Western Front, July 1917: A Case Study of Trenchard's Offensive Policy in Action', *Cross and Cockade* 23 (1982), pp.354–70; Kennett, *First Air War*, pp.71–3; Harvey, *Collision of Empires*, pp.412–13; John Morrow, *German Air Power in World War One* (Lincoln, NE, 1982), p.91; idem, *The Great War in the Air: Military Aviation from 1909 to 1921* (Shrewsbury, 1993), pp.132–5, 149–53, 173, 215–16, 234–5, 317–18; Arthur Gould Lee, *No Parachute*, 2nd edn (London, 1969), pp.298–312; Denis Winter, *The First of the Few: Fighter Pilots in the First World War* (London, 1982), p.36.

51. Keegan, *First World War*, p.386; Hartcup, *War of Invention*, pp.145–50, 152–6; Cooper, *Birth of Independent Air Power*, pp.30–1; John H. Morrow, 'Knights of the Sky: The Rise of Military Aviation', in Frans Coetzee and Marilyn Shevin-Coetzee, eds, *Authority, Identity and the Social History of the Great War* (Providence, RI, 1995), pp.305–24; idem, *Great War in Air*, pp.64, 81, 92, 105–63, 174–5; Buckley, *Air Power*, pp.62–6; Paris, *Winged Warfare*, p.184.

52. Paris, *Winged Warfare*, pp.164–9, 188–90; idem, 'First Air Wars', pp.97–109; Smith, *British Air Strategy*, pp.15–22; Morrow, *Great War in Air*, pp.68, 81, 246–50; idem, 'Aviation Technology and Strategic Air Power in World War I: The English, French and Italian Experiences', *RIHM* 63 (1985), pp.89–98; John Sweetman, 'The Smuts Report of 1917: Merely Political Window Dressing?', *JSS* 4 (1981), pp.152–74; Cooper, *Birth of Independent Airpower*, pp.63–5, 97–107, 115–25, 134–6; S. F. Wise, 'The Royal Air Force and the Origins of Strategic Bombing', in Travers and Archer, eds, *Men at War*, pp.151–8; idem, 'Strategic Use of Airpower', pp.232–9; Corum, *Roots of Blitzkrieg*, p.17; Joachim Kuropka, 'Die britische Luftkriegskonzeption gegen Deutschland im Ersten Weltkrieg', *MM* 27 (1980), pp.7–25; Lee Kennett, *A History of Strategic Bombing* (New York, 1982), pp.29–32, 55; Harvey, *Collision of Empires*, pp.394–5, 397.

53. Hartcup, *War of Invention*, pp.157–64; Gilbert, *First World War*, pp.171–2, 289–90; Alfred Gollin, 'A Flawed Strategy: Early British Air Defence

Arrangements', in Adams, ed., *First World War*, pp.31–7; Cooper, *Birth of Independent Airpower*, pp.42–53; Marian C. McKenna, 'The Development of Air Raid Precautions in World War I', in Travers and Archer, eds, *Men at War*, pp.173–95; Paris, *Winged Warfare*, p.176; John Ferris, ' "Airbandit": C3I and Strategic Air Defence during the First Battle of Britain, 1915–18', in Dockrill and French, eds, *Strategy and Intelligence*, pp.23–66.

CHAPTER SEVEN

Nations in Arms

Governments and armed forces had anticipated a short war. They were then forced to confront the realities not only of massive casualties but also of competing demands for manpower between the armed forces, industry and agriculture, as the conflict became one in which it was just as vital to out-produce as to out-fight the enemy. Not surprisingly, the manpower pool available to most armies rapidly declined, with ever more desperate efforts to comb out every possible fighting man from the civilian population.

In continental Europe, mobilisation meant calling up trained reserves to join the standing army, consisting of conscripts currently under arms and the regular cadre. Although in theory universal, conscription was in practice always selective. There were always men exempted by virtue of physical fitness, occupation, or even nationality in the case of some minorities. There were also those eligible for military service who were not called up, since only a portion of the available manpower could usually be accommodated in any one year. Indeed, wide disparities existed between European states in terms of the proportion of eligible manpower usually required to serve.

It is not possible to calculate precise figures, but between 15 and 19 million men were mobilised in Europe in August 1914. By 1918, conceivably over 65 million men had been mobilised world-wide.[1] While many continental Europeans had previously experienced conscripted military service, this was certainly not true for others. British and American wartime soldiers and many of those drawn from European colonies had not undertaken such service in peacetime. Few, however, were prepared for the kind of war they would now experience.

All armies, whether professional long-service forces enlisted by voluntary means, or dependent upon conscription, would naturally attempt to divest soldiers of civilian values and 'recreate them in the army's image' by inculcating appropriate military values.[2] This was quite feasible for long-service volunteers, but conscripts could only be exposed to such influences for the two or three years of the initial training period and occasional periods of reserve liability thereafter. Under conditions of rapid and continuous wartime expansion, it was far harder to separate the temporary soldier from civilian values. The new nations in arms, therefore, were truly citizen armies. While the war clearly exposed men to experiences very different from those at home, it could never sever their link with civilian life, nor could it eradicate the social or regional diversity that had existed in civilian society. Thus, as Hew Strachan has remarked, 'the corollary of the creation of a nation in arms was that the army's ills were the nation's, and the nation's were the army's'.[3]

Conscription and manpower

The conscription systems of the major continental powers and the impact of wartime demands upon them were very similar. In Russia, it had not been anticipated that there would be a need to call up many more than 5 million men for a short war so mobilisation involved the active army, comprising those conscripts called up between 1911 and 1913, and the 'first-class' reserve of men who had served between 1904 and 1910. The term of service introduced in 1906 was three years with the colours at the age of 21, seven years in the first-class reserve and eight years in the second-class reserve, before further liability up to the age of 43 in the *opolchentsky* (territorial units).

General N. N. Golovin later claimed that 96 per cent of mobilised conscripts reported for duty in 1914. It is clear, however, that mobilisation was accompanied by disturbances in many rural areas, one estimate being that 49 out of 101 provinces in European Russia and Asia were affected. The disturbances were exacerbated by poor administration but clearly suggest that many peasants, and especially those with families, were less than willing to serve.[4]

Wastage from all causes was soon running at between 300,000 and 400,000 men a month. As a result, it was necessary not only to call up the first- and second-class reserves stretching back to those who had first served in 1896 but also, in effect, to mortgage the military future by calling up cohorts early.

The Tsarist system, however, was ramshackle, with accurate records of population and military liability often lacking. Existing exemptions were also generally maintained so that, as Norman Stone has commented, a situation arose of 'grandfathers and grandsons leaving for the front, being waved off by the middle, exempted, generation'. By the end of 1916, the Russians had suffered 3.6 million dead and a further 2.1 million men had been captured by the Germans or Austro-Hungarians. At least 600,000 men remained in war-related industries and a further 600,000 men had to be released from military service to industry. As a result, the army was increasingly one of rural peasants, with concomitant effects on peasant unrest and the army's morale. Indeed, in the crisis months of early 1917, the concentration of older, unwilling conscripts in large training centres around St Petersburg and Moscow was to contribute to the collapse of the Tsarist state.[5]

With far fewer manpower resources than Russia, Germany actually ended by mobilising more men: 13.2 million (or 41.4 per cent of the male population) compared with 13 million (or 17.4 per cent of the male population) in Russia. Initially, in similar anticipation of a short war, about 2 million German reservists were not recalled in August 1914. Additionally, there were perhaps 5.4 million men of military age, who had not previously been trained through past exemption.

After 1893, Germany had a basic two-year term of military service at the age of 20, followed by five years in the reserve, five years in the *Landwehr* (militia) and further service to the age of 45 in the secondary militia force known as the *Landsturm*. By contrast with the reluctance to come forward in Russia, there were an estimated 308,000 *Kriegsfreiwillige* (wartime volunteers) in Germany at the start of the war, who did not wait to be conscripted.

Casualties and the evolution of a war economy, however, increasingly resulted in manpower problems similar to those in Russia. Similar measures were applied but, after the launching of the Hindenburg Programme to boost war production in August 1916, industrial requirements had a greater priority and skilled men frequently had to be returned from army to industry. Thus, it became largely a question of pressing convalescents back into service early as well as mortgaging the future.

The defeat of Russia in 1917 did enable men to be transferred to the west in 1918 so that about 4 million were available, with 1 million men remaining in the east. However, it has been estimated that at least 10 per cent of those transferred from east to west deserted en route and there was little confidence on the part of German commanders in those who had been repatriated after being prisoners of the Russians. Consequently, there was an attempt to claw back men from industry. Resorting to conscription for strikers in January 1918, however, did little to increase the commitment of such men to the war. Possibly as many as 1 million German soldiers were also in effect 'shirkers' participating in a so-called *verdecker Militärstreik* (undercover military strike) in rear areas during the last few months of the war.[6]

Austria-Hungary had a small peacetime army relative to size of population, representing only about 0.9 per cent of the Empire's population. Indeed, the Austro-Hungarian army fielded fewer infantry battalions in 1914 than it had in the Austro-Prussian War of 1866.[7] The term of service for the Kaiserlich und Königliche Armee (Imperial and Royal Army) or 'common' army, was three years followed by two years in the reserves, known respectively as the *honvéd* (Hungary), the *Landwehr* (Austria) and the *domobran* (Croatia). Some of those not called up were sent to the *Ersatzreserve* (second reserve) for a mere six weeks' annual training, but there were also wide exemptions.

Like much else in the Empire, the common army was hampered by problems of nationality. In 1914, by one calculation, 26.7 per cent of the army was German, 22.3 per cent Hungarian, 13.5 per cent Czech, 8.5 per cent Polish, 8.1 per cent Ruthenian, 6.4 per cent Romanian, 6.7 per cent Croat or Serb, 3.8 per cent Slovak, 2 per cent Slovene and 1.4 per cent Italian. Non-German units were stiffened by German officers and NCOs and, overall, over 78 per cent of all officers were German, resulting in considerable problems when officer casualties proved heavy.

Other than Germans, the Croats, Slovenes and Bosnian Muslims were deemed most reliable and, proportionally, the latter were the most conscripted during the war. Not all nationalities, however, were equally committed to the war effort and the list of those regarded as unreliable steadily increased. One Czech regiment unfurled the Bohemian flag upon mobilisation in Prague in August 1914 and another surrendered en masse to the Russians in April 1915. It soon became the practice to station Italian units in the Balkans or on the Eastern Front. Croats, Slovenes and Serbs, however, were generally content to fight the Italians. By 1917, men were increasingly being mixed rather than allowed to serve in separate national units.

After the collapse of Russia, some 500,000 Austro-Hungarian prisoners were repatriated but, though relatively few had volunteered to fight for the Entente, they were all regarded with considerable suspicion and kept under close supervision, causing further resentment. In June 1918, indeed, former prisoners of war were involved in a mutiny in a Slovak regiment at Kragujervac in Serbia, resulting in the execution of 44 mutineers. There were also an estimated 200,000 former prisoners of war and deserters roaming in 'green cadres' in areas of Bosnia, Moravia and Galicia. In fact, a belated effort was mounted in late 1917 to introduce patriotic instruction. Yet, the army as a whole remained effective until the summer of 1918. In all, Austria-Hungary appears to have mobilised about 31.5 per cent of its male population.[8]

Conscription in Italy, where a two-year term had been introduced in 1910, was less rigorously applied than elsewhere in continental Europe. Evasion of military service had become common, although the high rates of evasion recorded also reflected the failure by officials to take account of those Italians who had emigrated. In 1914, an estimated 10.4 per cent of conscripts failed to report for military service, not far short of the all-time record for absenteeism set in 1863. Actual wartime mobilisation in 1915 resulted in an absenteeism rate of 12.1 per cent, which was the highest since unification. The real rate was considerably less, with at least 78 per cent of the overall total of 470,000 wartime absentees actually emigrants.

Conscription policy was fairly indiscriminate, but war-related industries attracted most exemptions. Since such industries were heavily concentrated in the urban north rather than the rural south, the effect was to perpetuate Italy's north–south divide. Moreover, northern conscripts were generally better educated and tended to be posted to the artillery and engineers, leaving the infantry mostly composed of southern peasants. Since an adequate system of reliefs, to enable men to return to assist with sowing and harvest, was not organised until 1917, southern peasants could easily imagine themselves being sacrificed for a northern urban oligarchy. This increased ordinary soldiers' contempt for *imboscati* (shirkers), not least well-paid munitions workers. The problem was compounded by the conscription of striking workers from Turin munitions factories in August 1917, creating an unstable situation which contributed to the collapse of the army at Caporetto.[9]

The Turks also had a somewhat inefficient conscription system. Non-Muslims had traditionally been exempted on payment of a fine and many wealthier Muslims had also taken advantage of the provision. The Balkan Wars had resulted in the loss of some of the most developed regions of the Ottoman Empire, containing almost 4 million people. As a result, the burden of war service fell primarily upon the peasants of Anatolia. Losses were heavy, especially at Gallipoli, and the Turks had to conscript Iraqi and Syrian Arabs, whom they considered inferior soldiers. Poorly paid, fed and clothed, the Turkish armies reversed the normal trend of the war by losing seven times as many men to disease as to battle. With desertion reaching some 500,000 men by 1918, Turkish manpower shortages were acute.

The expectation in France was that between 5 and 13 per cent of men would not appear upon mobilisation. In the event only 1.5 per cent were absentees. A three-year term of military service had been introduced in 1913, two years having been the norm since 1905. Thus, the cohorts of 1911 to 1913 were serving when the war broke out. Some 80 per cent of all French males between the ages of 18 and 46 had been called up by the spring of 1915. France eventually mobilised about 45 per cent of its male population, a greater proportion than any other of the major belligerents although, taking all belligerents into account, Bulgaria mobilised the greatest proportion.[10]

Like the British, the United States army was an exception to the continental model in that it was enlisted in peacetime by voluntary means. The United States regular army was approximately 100,000 strong in April 1917. Conscription was immediately applied through the Selective Service Act of May 1917 largely, it would appear, in an attempt to prevent 'random' and unplanned volunteering. However, men were encouraged to register voluntarily to an extent that almost amounted to voluntarism. Indeed, Woodrow Wilson spoke of making 'a selection from a nation which has volunteered in mass', although it might be added that the names of those who registered voluntarily were widely publicised to pressure others who had not. The legislation provided for the call up of those aged 21 to 30 (later 18 to 45). Some 24 million men were registered, of whom approximately 3 million were eventually inducted. In all, the draft provided about two-thirds of the mobilised strength of the American forces, since the introduction of conscription also stimulated voluntary enlistment into the regular army.

In theory, each state of the union should have provided an equal proportion of its males of military age. But as many as 2.5 million men awaiting American citizenship were exempted, increasing the burden in those eastern urban areas where immigrants were concentrated. It was still the case that as many as one in five of all those conscripted were foreign born, while some 25 per cent of all those inducted were illiterate. Additional difficulties surrounded the conscription of black males, a greater proportion of whom (36 per cent) were inducted by comparison to eligible white males (25 per cent). Blacks, however, were then confined largely to non-combat duties, the only black combat division, the 92nd (Colored) Division, being quickly withdrawn from the Argonne after one of its regiments broke.

There were also ambiguities in the definition of conscientious objection and at least 20,000 claiming exemption on these grounds were inducted. By one means or another, some 16,000 of them were persuaded to undertake combat duties. Only 175,000 Americans had been sent to France by the end of 1917. The pace of transportation then picked up dramatically and some 2 million Americans arrived by the end of 1918, approximately 1.5 million of them in the last six months of the war. Yet, even the American Expeditionary Force experienced shortages of trained replacements as casualties mounted over the summer of 1918. Up to 3 million Americans failed to register and an estimated 337,000 of those called up 'dodged the draft', leading to the first 'slacker raids' in urban areas in March 1918: in New York in September 1918, over 50,000 men were detained, of whom 16,505 were deemed to be draft dodgers.[11]

The voluntary spirit and its limits

The existence of conscription did not prevent men from volunteering for military service, but it was in Britain that the voluntary spirit was most evident through the absence of conscription until 1916. Between August

1914 and November 1918, 4.9 million men were enlisted, of whom 2.4 million were volunteers and 2.5 million conscripts. That yielded a wartime total of 5.7 million men in the army at one time or another, approximating to 22.1 per cent of the male population of the United Kingdom.[12] The effort between 1914 and 1918 compares to 19.4 per cent of the male population serving in the armed forces as a whole during the Second World War (in which 4.6 million men served). Thus, with the possible exception of the almost 23 years of continuous warfare between December 1792 and June 1815, the Great War represents the greatest degree of military participation Britain ever experienced.[13]

Overwhelmingly English in nationality, the regular army was also largely urban in origin, with unskilled labourers the largest single category of pre-war recruit. There was in effect what Field Marshal Lord Nicholson in 1906 called a 'compulsion of destitution' about recruitment with the burden of military service falling wholly unequally.[14] Behind the regulars stood the small army and special reserves and the part-time Territorial Force. While embracing middle-class elements, the Territorials were largely dependent for recruits upon the working class, albeit skilled manual workers in receipt of regular wages rather than the casually employed found in the ranks of the army.[15]

The greater proportion of the British Expeditionary Force would have to be found upon mobilisation from the reserves and these would also make up wastage for the first six months. Thereafter, the Territorials would be the means of expansion, but they were only liable for overseas service if they chose to take the so-called imperial service obligation. In 1914, just over 18,000, or only some 7 per cent, had done so although at least the County Territorial Associations (CTAs) provided a ready-made machinery for wartime expansion.[16]

Whatever assumptions had been made prior to the war, however, all were set aside by the appointment of Kitchener as Secretary of State for War. Kitchener had not served at home since 1883 and was wholly unfamiliar with any pre-war arrangements.[17] The Unionist politician Leo Amery aptly described him as a 'great improviser but also a great disorganiser'.[18] This was particularly seen in Kitchener's distaste for the Territorials, whom he regarded as amateurs and a 'town clerk's army'. His attitude in effect spelt the end of any pre-war plans to expand through the County Territorial Associations, as Kitchener resolved to raise his 'Kitchener' or 'New' Armies through the War Office.

Nevertheless, there was more to Kitchener's reasoning than simple prejudice. There were no practical plans for expansion through the Associations and Kitchener believed they would be swamped by having to train and recruit simultaneously. Similarly, Kitchener was reluctant to put pressure on married men to volunteer for service abroad. Most significant of all was his preoccupation with possible German invasion, against which the Territorials were the principal defence. Indeed, two regular divisions were initially kept back from the British Expeditionary Force for home defence.[19]

Kitchener was eventually reluctantly persuaded to allow Territorials to 'fill the gap' in France and Flanders in the winter of 1914/15 before his New Armies were ready to do so. Meanwhile, the failure to utilise the County Territorial Associations clearly resulted in duplication of effort and competition, both in recruitment and in finding equipment, damaging to both Territorials and New Armies.[20] Unfortunately, it was also the case that the raising of the New Armies was almost entirely haphazard in the absence of any coherent manpower policy. Kitchener himself had no clear idea of how many men might be needed.[21]

The pattern of military participation, as a result of voluntary enlistment, was quite arbitrary. The traditional interpretation has been one of an overwhelming patriotic rush to the colours in August 1914 with recruiting offices across Europe besieged by young men engaged, like so many lemmings, in a collective rendezvous with death. The *kriegsfreiwillige* (volunteers) in Germany, for example, have been characterised as being motivated not only by a mixture of patriotism and adventure, but also with a highly idealistic commitment to re-establishing a sense of *Volksgemeinschaft* (national community). It has been argued that this was a conscious attempt to escape from modernity, the 'bondage' of class and status and the 'unnatural' constraints of the marketplace.[22]

In Britain, 15 per cent of all wartime enlistments did indeed take place in the first two months but the rush to the colours was not immediate and it has been almost precisely dated to the period between 25 August and 9 September 1914. Initial confusion was not assisted by a lack of news from France until the publication of the sensational 'Amiens despatch' on 30 August by two journalists reporting the retreat from Mons. German atrocity stories had also surfaced, and on 24 August the Earl of Derby approached the War Office with a suggestion to raise 'Pals' battalions of men from the same communities, factories and so on. The idea had actually originated in the War Office as early as 14 August and the Stockbrokers Battalion of the Royal Fusiliers had begun to recruit on 21 August.[23]

Together, these factors seem to have accounted for the great increase. Only 51,647 men had enlisted in Britain prior to 15 August 1914, but 174,901 were enlisted between 30 August and 5 September. The most fruitful recruiting period was over by 9 September as the news from France improved and there were increasing rumours that recruits were suffering discomfort in improvised accommodation. It also appeared that men were no longer required, deferred enlistment having been introduced in view of the accommodation problems and with the War Office also trying to regulate the flow by arbitrary variations in age and physical requirements.[24]

It is also clear that the process of enlistment was exceedingly complex with wide regional and local variations. Much remains obscure, although the availability of the surviving personnel records of the British army for the Great War will in due time result in a greater understanding.[25] Of course, patriotism played its part and, as John Bourne has argued, there was more than one kind of patriotism, deriving from a complex web of individual loyalties. Other factors were equally important. One was certainly family situation, and inefficiency by the War Office in paying out adequate separation allowances discouraged married men from enlisting. Others with dependants also took time to put their domestic affairs in order. Equally, there were those only too glad to escape family or, indeed, humdrum routine.

The propaganda effort of the Parliamentary Recruiting Committee and similar organisations had some effect, as did women handing out white feathers. Detailed studies of cities such as Bristol, Birmingham and Leeds show a particular link with employment. Possibly as many as 480,000 men lost their jobs in Britain by the end of August 1914 and many others were placed on half-time in the prevailing economic uncertainty at the outbreak of war. Significantly, enlistment dropped away rapidly once large government contracts were placed in the autumn for clothing, boots, munitions and other war essentials.[26]

Within British industry, wage rates as such do not appear to have been a major factor in determining enlistment but the response from industry did reflect the age structure of the labour force in differing sectors as well as purely local factors. Thus, in Gwynedd in Wales, some slate quarry owners refused to keep open the places of those who enlisted, while other owners threatened men with dismissal if they did not enlist. Faced with such uncertainties, increasing numbers of quarrymen simply took up employment vacancies in the railways, docks and mines. By contrast, both the North Eastern and Cardiff Railway Companies encouraged enlistment by inducements such as guarantees of post-war employment and welfare assistance to dependants. From the beginning, there was also a degree of protectionism for key workers such as railwaymen and Admiralty employees.[27]

Others enlisted under the peer influence of what has been called social inheritance, joining because their friends had done so. The most obvious manifestation of this was the success of the Pals battalions, of which 115 were raised including the Hull Commercials, the Accrington Pals and the Glasgow Corporation Tramways Battalion. Interestingly, what might be termed private enterprise, with similar kinds of locally raised battalions, was also attempted in Canada as a means of reviving recruitment in 1915. Here, however, it resulted in an even more ruinous competition than was evident between the Kitchener formations and the Territorials in Britain. Some reasons why men enlisted simply defy categorisation. Some, indeed, may simply have enlisted on impulse.[28]

Whatever the reasons for enlistment, the effect of what occurred in August and September 1914 was that certain groups were far more willing to enlist than others. Wales and Scotland certainly increased the proportion of their males under arms to a level largely matching that of England, with Scotland actually producing the largest proportion of recruits under voluntary enlistment within the United Kingdom. In Scotland, vestiges of traditional clan loyalties played a part in the Highlands and, at least, a belief that some commitment had been made of a post-war redistribution of land to crofters and cottars, leading to considerable post-war unrest when this proved illusory. In the case of the Welsh and Irish, Kitchener's distrust of the possible politicisation of a proposed Welsh Army Corps and of the offers to raise units from the pre-war Ulster Volunteer Force (UVF) and the rival nationalist Irish National Volunteers (INV) put something of a blight upon enlistment.

Political factors were clearly involved in the lack of response from Ireland with an active anti-recruiting campaign by some nationalists. Yet, historical judgements should not become imprisoned by a knowledge of Ireland's future, which contemporaries did not possess in 1914. Ireland was a sparsely populated, largely rural country in which lack of employment opportunities had encouraged emigration. This left a smaller reservoir of potential recruits than on the mainland. If agricultural occupations are excluded, then Ireland conforms approximately to the enlistment pattern in Britain. There is little evidence to suggest that Catholics were reluctant to enlist and, indeed, to quote David Fitzpatrick, 'the readiness of individuals to join the colours was largely determined by the attitudes and behaviour of comrades – kinsmen, neighbours, and fellow-members of organisations and fraternities'. Economic, religious and political factors were of less significance. Rather similarly, it is difficult to identify any specific Scottish or Welsh service 'experience' substantially different from that of the remainder of the army.[29]

Seen from the perspective of sectoral distribution of occupation, some groups in Britain bore a proportionally high share of the military effort. By February 1916, sampling surveys of the Board of Trade, although not entirely reliable, suggest that whereas 40 per cent of those engaged in the professions, entertainment, finance and commerce had enlisted, less than 30 per cent of those in industry as a whole, agriculture or transport had done so. Thus, as Jay Winter has remarked, 'men engaged in commercial or distributive trades were in uniform and at risk for longer periods and in relatively larger numbers than were industrial workers, transport workers or agricultural workers'.[30]

The effective limit of volunteers was reached by December 1915, by which time it was clear that conscription must follow through a process of exhaustion. Technically, the first Military Service Act in January 1916 conscripted all single men and childless widowers between the ages of 18 and 41. The Military Service Act (No. 2) of June 1916 then extended conscription to all men between these ages; the age range was extended to those between 18 and 50 in April 1918 by the Military Service (No. 2) Act. The same legislation in 1918 also provided for the conscription of men up to the age of 56 if the need arose, and for the extension of conscription to Ireland. Ultimately, the former was deemed unnecessary and the latter politically impossible.[31]

In theory, conscription should have equalised the burden after 1916 but, as elsewhere, conscription was applied selectively. The steady evolution of a war economy and of a manpower policy, for example, pushed the army to the bottom of the list of priorities. Indeed, in January 1918 the production of timber, iron ore, food, merchant shipping, aeroplanes and tanks all took priority over the army.[32]

Moreover, medical boards exempted over 1 million men in the last twelve months of the war when there was some pressure on doctors to lower rejection rates. Partly, this was owing to suspect criteria of what constituted fitness: physical ability was too readily equated with stature. Partly, however, it was also social prejudice. Jews and, especially, Russian Jews were automatically rejected as inferior. Coloured recruits were also generally rejected until the colour bar was lifted in June 1918.[33] Again, while often perceived to be unduly influenced by military demands, the exemption tribunals applied widely differing standards. In October 1918, by which time many exemptions had been removed, there were still 2.5 million men in reserved occupations.[34]

Undoubtedly, too, there were evasions leading to the unedifying spectacle of official round-ups of likely looking men at railway stations, parks and cinemas in the summer and autumn of 1916, at least 93,000 men failing to appear.[35] Conscientious objection, however, has received somewhat disproportionate attention considering that only 16,500 claims for exemption were made on such grounds.[36]

The cumulative effect of the way in which conscription was applied meant that there was no material change in the social composition of the British army after 1916. The sampling surveys of the Board of Trade show each of the occupational sectors remained in approximately the same relationship to one another with regard to the proportion of manpower enlisted in 1918 as in 1916.[37] Thus, the British army was no more representative of society as a whole under conscription than it had been before its introduction.

The experience of military service

Conscription had been a major break with pre-war expectations in Britain but, in theory, the wartime experience of military participation as a whole had enormous social and institutional implications. For the first time in a century, very large numbers of troops were permanently visible to British society and, with the delay in providing hutted accommodation in the autumn of 1914, in close proximity to civilians. Reactions varied on both sides but, in many cases the influx of men from different classes and from different regions was undoubtedly a cultural shock for householders on whom they were billeted in what was a markedly parochial society prior to 1914.[38]

Increasingly, many householders became disillusioned with the military presence.[39] It should also be noted, however, that the presence of troops could also be beneficial, Welsh seaside resorts actually competing to attract military camps during the slack autumn period of 1914. The conflicting efforts of War Office, County Territorial Associations, corporations and individuals to equip units also benefited business, as did the erection of the many army camps that sprang up. Official contractors made handsome profits although local contractors also did well by undercutting them.[40]

It was a question not just of becoming aware of one's own country but of foreign countries as well. The exposure of the British soldier to the French and Belgian civilian and vice versa had its own revelations. British soldiers often commented adversely on the perceived lack of hygiene among French and Belgian civilians, the mercenary ways of these civilians, and their own resentment at being made to feel unwelcome in countries they had come to defend. Civilians naturally felt resentful of damage to crops, destruction of property and the frequent petty theft and looting. Prostitution was a severe trial to the British military authorities. In 1916, some 19.2 per cent of all British army hospital admissions were for venereal disease. It was also claimed that the numbers incapacitated by it were equivalent to a division a day by 1918 though, in fact, 50 per cent of the troops had contracted the disease in England rather than France. The incidence was still higher among dominion forces, Australian cases of venereal disease in 1917 running at 144 per 1,000 men and Canadian cases at 158 per 1,000 in 1918 compared with the average of 34 per 1,000 men in the British army as a whole.[41]

In the case of dominion forces, the relationship might be not just with the French and Belgian population but with that of Britain itself. Much of the Australian Imperial Force (AIF) sent to the Western Front spent several months in British training camps. Many had been born in Britain, initial impressions were usually favourable and the AIF was given a warm welcome.

The heroic image surrounding the Australians deteriorated rapidly, however. From the point of view of British civilians, Australians were associated with prostitution, venereal disease, bigamous marriages and boisterous trouble-making. In turn, Australian soldiers disliked the class distinctions observed in British civil and military life and resented the increasing wariness with which they were treated. Coupled with the publicity given the 'bush ethos' of Australians, despite the fact that only about 14 per cent had been employed in agricultural occupations before enlistment, the experience tended to reinforce what was rapidly becoming the accepted national self-image among the men of the AIF.[42]

If Australians, who largely thought of Britain as home, could cause concern to military and civil authorities, this was even more so with regard to Asian or African servicemen arriving in Britain or France, when contact might lead to sexual relations between colonial troops and white women. Indian troops serving in France, or convalescing in Britain after wounds, were kept under surveillance as far as possible and restricted in their off-base activities, since such sexual relations were deemed 'detrimental to the prestige and spirit of European rule' in India. Initially, the War Office had hoped to keep Indian wounded in France and its objection to allowing white nurses to tend them in English hospitals went all the way to the Cabinet. The sepoys themselves appear to have formed a largely favourable impression of Europe and, especially, of London and Paris. Indeed, in some cases, they began to question some of their own social and religious customs.

Those French colonial troops serving on the Western Front were also kept isolated in special camps when out of the line and discouraged from contacts with civilians. Here, however, it was paternalism rather than racism which motivated the French military authorities. Colonial troops wintered in the Midi, were given special diets of familiar foods and, if Muslim, were instructed by their own clerics. Nonetheless, any sexual contacts between French women and colonial troops were regarded as a perversion of the natural order liable to taint the latter.[43]

The arrival of the 1.8 million men of the American Expeditionary Force in 1917 resulted in the exposure of the French to different values from those projected by the British forces. The Americans acted very much as tourists in France since the majority served there longer in peacetime than during wartime since they remained some months after the armistice. As Mark Meigs has remarked, for the American Expeditionary Force 'battle and tourism had become experiential neighbours'. Pershing himself was anxious that his soldiers should see Paris and the YMCA was tasked with finding useful leisure pursuits for off-duty servicemen. The process continued after the armistice with the establishment of an American Expeditionary Force 'university' at Beaune.

There was an air of modernism about the Americans, who helped to spread the popularity of jazz in France. An effective campaign of 'dissuasion and prophylaxis', which had been begun in army camps in the United States, kept down American venereal rates to 126 per 1,000 between August 1917 and August 1918. However, there were also frequent inter-marriages between American servicemen and French women: accounting, for example, for between 19 and 37 per cent of total marriages in the Nantes and Saint Nazaire regions in 1918–19. The image of soldier as tourist also applied to the Australian Imperial Force in its first overseas posting to Egypt in December 1914, though racial attitudes towards Egyptians marred the experience and ultimately led to a notorious Australian riot in Cairo's brothel district in April 1915.[44]

The impact of army life upon those who enlisted would vary as much as the impact upon those civilian communities exposed to a military presence. However, there are distinct dangers in generalisation about the experience of military service, since there was no typical experience.[45] It should certainly not be accepted that a handful of well-known sensitive intellectual, or otherwise literary-minded, wartime officers like Siegfried Sassoon, Wilfred Owen, Robert Graves or, in the case of the German army, the playwright and novelist Carl Zuchmayer, and the author Franz Schauwecker, were in any way representative of their armies as a whole. The British army was certainly not one which universally carried Palgrave's *The Golden Treasury* in its knapsacks, let alone the literary agent's contract. As John Bourne has commented, the army was 'essentially the British working man in uniform'.[46]

Cultural historians have tended to assume from the literary evidence that there was a universality of experience linking officers and men in a common community of spirit bred in the trenches. This is sometimes expressed as the concept of a 'war generation' or 'front generation'. It is argued, from this largely post-war literary invention, that the kind of high expectations supposedly shared by the German volunteers doomed them to disillusionment under the stress of 'machine-age' warfare. Trench warfare thus produced men with a 'defensive personality', lacking aggression and indifferent to the traditional virtues of sacrifice they had once espoused. Unable to come to terms with the stark difference between the realities of the front line and the failures of those at home to comprehend those realities, such men were prone to war neuroses. Thus, the introspection of the trenches created a kind of idealised community in which officers and men alike shared both during and after the war.[47]

The question of veterans is addressed again in Chapter Eleven (pp.411–16). Reliance on literary sources or the subsequent careers of a few high-profile individuals such as Harold Macmillan or the BBC's first 'disc jockey',

Christopher Stone, however, tends to perpetuate the idea that there were no divisions within armies. It also assumes that the front line and the home front were quite separate spheres.[48]

As is suggested later, the notion of separate spheres has been exaggerated, while the reality was that divisions within armies were profound. Not least there were divisions between officers and men, to an extent to suggest that, if a war generation did exist, as David Englander and Richard Bessel have expressed it, it did so 'only for so long as it remained under fire'.[49] There were wide differences between service on different fronts and in different sectors. Indeed, it is too often forgotten that the Great War was not fought solely on the Western Front. Campaigning conditions on the Eastern Front, where the war was always more fluid, in Mesopotamia or East Africa were quite different from those in France and Flanders.

Even the Western Front was not a theatre of unrelieved terror, deprivation, disillusionment and futility. There were considerable differences between trench warfare in the flat, waterlogged fields of Flanders, on the chalk downs of the Somme uplands, or the forested slopes of the Vosges. Some sectors were considered quiet and others active. The Christmas Truce of 1914 is invariably remembered but a 'live and let live' system existed in many sectors of the front. In any case, it was simply not the case that soldiers spent their entire service in the front line.

The nature of modern warfare was such that the ratio of combatant and non-combatant troops altered considerably during the war as more and more men were required to supply the materials needed to keep an army fighting. The British army did not use its manpower very intelligently, but the ratio of combatant to non-combatant troops still changed from 83.3:16.6 in 1914 to 64.8:35.1 by 1918. In the same way, it can be noted that 1.4 million Austro-Hungarian soldiers were serving on Austro-Hungarian soil rather than at the front in January 1918, while only about 25 per cent of the 2.3 million men serving in the field were actually in combatant rather than non-combatant roles. Some 35 per cent of the Russian army's strength was also in garrison or support roles.[50]

Using the British army as an example, at the front itself, there were divisions between officers in fighting units and staff officers, between the different arms and branches of service, and between specialists such as machine gunners and ordinary infantry. There were differences between divisions, some being regarded as holding formations and others as assault divisions. Above all, there were differences between regulars, Territorials and New Army volunteers. As the war continued so the distinctions blurred as any pretence to draft men from a particular area to a particular unit was sacrificed to the military necessity of making losses good, a reduction in identity particularly resented among Territorial and Irish units.[51]

But, even if these earlier divisions blurred as units were increasingly fed from the same pool of manpower, there remained a distinction between those who had volunteered and those who had been conscripted after 1916. The universal impression of the conscript among contemporaries was a being of progressively declining intelligence, physique and ability. As with all gener- alisations, too much should not be read into the stereotyped contemporary view of the conscript. There is certainly no evidence, as alleged at the time, of conscripts having a greater propensity towards indiscipline. Indeed, as already suggested, one of the factors in the army's eventual success in 1918 was arguably the supply of younger conscripts who, to quote Shelford Bidwell and Dominick Graham, 'ignorant and easily killed though they often were, blended with surviving natural leaders to keep the show going'.[52]

What can be said of the experience of soldiers is that the welcome afforded new arrivals in a unit varied widely and the conditioning of men depended almost entirely upon the unit in which they served. That might not always be the same unit, for there was a constant change of personalities. Most units would steadily lose any connection with the particular locality or social group from which they might have been raised. From case studies undertaken, it is apparent that no one British battalion was quite like any other.[53]

Much the same could be said for the German soldier. Military service did not change existing pre-war social divisions or suspicion of national minorities within the Reich. Jews, who had not been commissioned in the army since 1885, were now permitted to receive commissions up to the rank of captain and Jewish chaplains allowed the same rights as those for other religions, but it made little real difference to existing anti-Semitic attitudes. Similarly, Alsace-Lorrainers and Poles continued to be posted as far away as possible from their homelands. Treated throughout as poten- tially treacherous, it was not perhaps surprising that there was a large-scale mutiny of Alsace-Lorrainers at Beverloo in Belgium in May 1918.[54]

Those German university students called up, or who had volunteered in 1914, found the hostility they experienced from NCOs and men of different social classes especially dispiriting.[55] Divisions between officers and men were also apparent with officer's privileges, especially better food, coming under increasing attack. Indeed, the Reichstag Committee of Inquiry into the Causes of the German Collapse held after the war paid particular attention to the evidence of 'abuses' of officers' privileges and the sense of loss of rights among ordinary soldiers, who did not have recourse to an adequate complaints procedure for their grievances. The problem was exacerbated by the rigid seniority for promotion within the army and the lack of oppor- tunities afforded good NCOs to advance. Earlier in the war, the excellent cadre of German NCOs had been a strength of the army.[56]

By contrast, in the Russian army, the lack of good NCOs widened divisions between officers and men. Indeed, it has been argued that Russian regiments in essence reproduced the nature of peasant society, with a unbridgeable gulf between the officer/landlord and soldier/peasant.[57]

The French army was also characterised by divisions between officers and men. This resulted largely from the bureaucratic approach of French officers to military life, and the steady decline in officer quality through the war. The indifference of many officers to the conditions endured by their men could hardly fail to increase the likelihood of disciplinary problems. Certainly, French trench journalism suggests little evidence of there being a war generation or a fraternity within the trenches, except under exceptional circumstances.[58]

Morale and discipline

Many soldiers were exposed to colleagues from widely differing social backgrounds, and military service clearly broadened horizons. For working-class recruits, however, the army might not be far different from the regimentation of the factory, and one explanation for the maintenance of British morale on the Western Front is that men were used to the subordination and tedium commonplace in industrial society. Most armies in the Great War comprised men equally exposed to hardship in civilian life, be they industrial workers from Germany or peasants from Russia and France.[59] It could be argued, therefore, that the majority of soldiers would not have recognised the disillusionment said to have been experienced by those of literary sensitivities, who embarked upon war with high expectations in 1914.

Industrialised warfare certainly increased the degree to which men were exposed to concussion and sensory deprivation, derived from heavier and more prolonged artillery bombardment. The battlefield had also become progressively more 'empty' as the range of weapons increased, thus further distancing soldiers from a ready identification of the enemy. In turn, these newer pressures undoubtedly heightened the impact of those experienced by soldiers in earlier wars, such as the effects of sleep deprivation and exhaustion, the fear of mutilation or death, the guilt fears of survivors and anxieties felt for friends or family. Morale could equally be damaged by a range of other factors such as insufficient motivation, poor training, boredom, lack of creature comforts such as adequate food and quarters, the debilitating effects of climate or disease, and lack of confidence in officers.

Nonetheless, whatever the increased pressures of the modern battlefield, morale and fighting spirit could still be built upon traditional military remedies: the appeal to patriotism, religion, regiment, or honour; good leadership;

discipline; rewards such as medals; accurate information; good medical arrangements; adequate leave arrangements; efficient administration; realistic training; rest; and palliatives like alcohol or cigarettes in appropriate measure. In addition, the cultivation of the 'primary group' – a small group of individuals bonded together by their service – was of inestimable value in maintaining morale under any circumstances. Moreover, as Niall Ferguson has argued, some men enjoyed the experience of war, and, in central and eastern Europe, men fought on long after the armistice. Indeed, a kind of fatalism kept men inured to violent death.[60]

Not unexpectedly, the maintenance of morale was of crucial significance to military leaderships and all armies undertook extensive monitoring. The British Expeditionary Force's GHQ tended to use the relatively crude indices of the incidence of trench feet, shell shock and crime.[61] Trench journalism was also monitored. There were over 100 such newspapers circulating among the British and dominion units in France and Flanders, over 400 among French troops, and others among the Belgians.[62] Trench journals, however, appear mainly to have been the work of junior subalterns and middle-class NCOs and to have been largely self-censored. Moreover, even claimed circulation figures are small and, in the words of David Englander, the 'documented readership remains elusive'.

Consequently, military authorities were likely to derive more useful information on the state of morale from surveying the results of censorship of the extraordinary quantities of service mail common to all armies. In the case of the British army, this amounted to 12.5 million letters a week, while the German field postal service, not effectively censored until 1917, carried 2 billion items during the war. Some problems also arise with the use of censorship reports since, as David Englander has again remarked, the balance in men's letters between self-censorship and self-expression is unknowable. Unfortunately, few British reports based on this material have survived, but they have proved a fruitful source for the French, Russian and British Indian armies.[63]

All armies suffered morale problems. In the British army, military crime invariably rose after heavy casualties with particular problems during the first winter of the war, following the near destruction of the old regular army during First Battle of Ypres, and during the winter of 1917/18 following Passchendaele. Absence without leave and drunkenness remained relatively high throughout the war.

There were also some instances of collective indiscipline, the best known being at the Etaples base camp in September 1917, although it has been much exaggerated in popular accounts. There was also something of a collapse of morale within the British Fifth Army during the opening of the German spring offensive on the Western Front in March 1918, although the figures available for sickness, crime and discipline for Fifth Army between April 1917 and the start of the German offensive show little signs of any serious morale problem.[64]

Other than the disintegration of an army under the pressure of enemy action, the most obvious sign of military collapse is desertion, surrender, mutiny or widespread collective indiscipline. With the exception of the Turkish army, desertion was relatively small overall and, more often than not, was more a case of lateness in returning from leave until the final collapse of the Russian army in 1917 and that of the German and Austro-Hungarian armies in 1918. As Niall Ferguson has suggested, surrender could be a distinctly dangerous practice given the propensity of soldiers to kill rather than take prisoners, but it became an increasing factor in the collapse of the Russian army in 1917 and the German army in the summer and autumn of 1918. A substantial proportion of Italian and Austro-Hungarian wartime losses were also in the form of prisoners of war.

In many instances, mutiny is not necessarily an appropriate description of forms of collective disobedience towards military authority. Some might be better characterised as strikes, particularly when involving citizen soldiers. In fact, while military authorities readily ascribe mutinies to external influences, most result from long-term mundane, grievances concerning pay, leave or conditions. Often these are exacerbated by poor administration and a failure of communications between officers and men. Not only do armies truly march on their stomachs, as Napoleon once observed, but soldiers are perennially interested in defending or acquiring privileges.[65]

There is usually little evidence of the kinds of political motivations alleged by the authorities. Two mutinies involving British colonial contingents are typical examples. It has been argued that a mutiny among West Indian troops at Taranto in Italy in December 1918 was an early manifestation of indigenous nationalism. It arose, however, primarily from unfavourable comparisons with the pay of British troops and from the use of the West Indians as dock labour. The mutiny among the men of the 5th (Native) Light Infantry of the Indian army at Singapore in February 1915, which resulted in the death of 32 Europeans and the public execution of 37 mutineers, was blamed on Sikh Ghadarite subversion, and the influence of German prisoners of war from the cruiser *Emden* and other internees held on the island. In reality, while rumours of the regiment's impending despatch to fight in Mesopotamia provided the trigger, internal divisions between Indian officers and men lay at the root of the mutiny. The situation was compounded by poor rations and the strained relationship between the commanding officer and the other British officers.

The events at the 'Bull Ring' at Etaples between 9 and 15 September 1917 were also due to poor food and accommodation, and the failure of elderly officers to keep in check NCOs, who subjected new drafts and men returning from convalescence alike to an unnecessarily brutal training re-gime. Rather similarly, those disturbances affecting Australian units in the autumn of 1918 were the result either of sheer exhaustion or of a high *esprit de corps*, since units bitterly resented proposals of disbandment and amalga-mation. The mutiny in the 49th Brigade of the British 16th (Irish) Division in April 1918 was also a result of being broken up to reinforce other bri-gades. Generally, indeed, it might be noted that morale and discipline in Irish formations was little different from that of the rest of the British Army. Thus, the 'Indianisation' of the 10th (Irish) Division in the Middle East in 1918 was due both to the need for experienced soldiers in France and also to the high rate of malarial disease within the division. It was not due to any perceived fears of political unreliability.[66]

The most widespread mutinies occurred in the French army in the spring of 1917, following the collapse of Nivelle's offensive launched on 16 April, and coinciding with strikes in Paris, St Étienne and other industrial areas. Between 30,000 and 40,000 men were involved with incidents in 68 of the army's 112 divisions, 5 divisions being badly affected and a further 15 seriously affected. The first cases occurred on 17 April and there were sporadic incidents until as late as January 1918, although the worst was over by August 1917. The mutinies were blamed on external factors such as the influence of agitators and degenerates supposedly meeting troops going on leave at Paris railway stations, the influence of the revolution in Russia, and the widely publicised establishment of soviets by the Russian brigade ser-ving with the French army. There were also varying rumours that Annamese workers, or French colonial troops employed in policing women's strikes, were raping conscripts' wives.

Of more significance was the impact of the casualties suffered during the offensive, the disturbances being largely confined to the Soissons region from which it had been launched. There were also more mundane griev-ances which had contributed to the unrest. In particular, pay, leave and rations exercised the minds of French soldiers. In theory, they should have enjoyed seven days' leave every three months, but commanding officers rarely respected this policy. Moreover, leave had been reduced in prepara-tion for the offensive. Food and accommodation was often poor and, while munitions workers received between one and fifteen francs a day, French soldiers received just 25 centimes a day.

Significantly, Pétain, who succeeded Nivelle as Commander-in-Chief on 15 May 1917 acted, firstly, to improve the material conditions of his troops. Secondly, he modified the nature of military operations, since it was clear to him that the mutinies did not represent a refusal to fight *per se* but a disinclination to pursue an offensive style of warfare. At the same time, disciplinary action was taken against those mutineers identified as 'leaders', with 554 death sentences passed, of which approximately 49 (or 8 per cent) were carried out. The erroneous idea that decimation was practised, with one man in ten shot, probably arose from the selection by lot in some cases of those sent for court martial.[67]

In his seminal study of the mutinies, Guy Pedronici concluded that they occurred for broadly 'military' reasons and involved no political aspects. More recently, Leonard Smith has argued that it was largely Pétain's willingness to negotiate, and the crucial mediating role played by sympathetic junior officers, that prevented the mutinies from becoming more politicised. Indeed, he argues that this negotiation was part of an ongoing 'dialogue' between French soldiers and their commanders, which was political in the sense of representing a power relationship within the army. It is arguable that, like conclusions drawn from literary evidence, this kind of interpretation attributes too much sophistication to ordinary soldiers. In any case, as Smith acknowledges, there were no clear political demands beyond a peace, which would somehow include a restoration of Alsace-Lorraine: that was all but impossible without military victory.[68]

There were also some instances of collective indiscipline in the French forces serving at Salonika in 1918 and among those committed to the Allied intervention in Russia in 1918–19. At Salonika, the demand for peace appears to have been related principally to the fact that the men had already been there for twenty months. It is impossible to assess whether political, and specifically Bolshevik, influences were of any account among French troops in Russia. What may be of more significance was the better pay enjoyed by the British and, especially, American troops serving alongside the French.[69]

It has been suggested by John Keegan that a major crisis of morale such as that represented by the French mutinies or the collapse of the British Fifth Army tended to occur in all armies, except that of the Germans, between two and a half and three years after real entry into the war. If Britain's baptism of fire is counted from the battle of Loos in September 1915, when New Army divisions were first used, then March 1918 fits well. Equally, Keegan argues that, with the exception of Germany, there is a correlation between the occurrence of collapse and the total number of combat deaths equalling the number of fighting infantry, such an occurrence signifying that the odds of individual survival had passed from possibility to probability of death.[70] Again, March 1918 fits well, while the French mutinies fit both of Keegan's criteria. He argues that the Germans were an exception owing to their eastern victories in 1917. Yet, unlike the armies of France, Italy and Russia in 1917 and, ultimately, even Germany in late 1918, the British did not suffer total or near total collapse. A comparison of the British and French armies is therefore instructive.

Soldiers of both armies shared similar privations but, in theory, the French were better motivated by being in defence of their homeland, although, admittedly, this could affect adversely those whose homes lay behind German lines. There is no evidence that the British were better fed than the French, who were allowed more leave, particularly after Pétain's reforms in 1917, while dominion contingents received better pay than British soldiers. The French were not harassed behind the lines while 'at rest' in quite the way that British troops were – although the French still complained of such harassment – and the French were spared 'bull' (an obsession with spit and polish, i.e. the external evidence of parade ground soldiering), of which British trench newspapers routinely complained. Nor did the French pursue the 'active front' policy of British trench raiding, which did have some beneficial impact provided raids were well planned, but a negative one if not.[71]

Yet, clearly, there were differences between the British and French which contributed to the greater stability of the British. Drill and coercion clearly assisted and so, too, did regimental tradition and the local identity of units. Divisional loyalty also became marked in at least some parts of the British army: surprisingly, it would appear not to have extended to the Irish divisions. British medical care was superior to that of the French and the French officer showed none of the concern for his men's welfare so inculcated in the British system.

Working-class soldiers both accepted and expected the imposition of discipline because, in British society, deference, which was not regarded as subservience, was routinely extended by the working class to social superiors in return for paternalism. Paternalism tended to create something of a culture of dependency among British soldiers, but also mitigated the harsher aspects of the disciplinary code.[72]

The French had *marraines de guerre* (literally, wartime godmothers), but did not have the extensive British welfare network of divisional and regimental canteens, YMCA, Church Army and comfort funds: 800,000 parcels were reaching the British Expeditionary Force each week by April 1917. The cinemas, the military and civilian concert and bathing parties so often mentioned in British memoirs do not figure in those of the French. In Britain, troop entertainment was organised by the YMCA and, from 1917, by the Navy and Army Canteen Board. Overseas, the YMCA was responsible and the army itself. Nor do the divisional sports meetings, the boxing tournaments, horse shows, football and cricket matches which, incidentally, provided men with an opportunity to embarrass officers without incurring penalties.[73]

Much may come down to national character. French soldiers appear to have been motivated primarily by what Audoin-Rouzeau has called national sentiment – a kind of defensive patriotism that transcended class and sectional loyalties – coupled with the expectation of peace, and an attitude of dutiful resignation. Hopes for peace did not mean peace at any price and it is argued that the sense of duty prevailed because so many social and political issues for ordinary French soldiers hung on the outcome of victory or defeat. Thus, in so far as any interest was aroused by the Russian revolution among ordinary French soldiers, it was largely in terms of the likely impact on the war in the west. Similarly, if there was any sense of pacifism within the army, it was a result of war-weariness and not ideology. Certainly, French soldiers had consistently more hatred for the Germans than did British soldiers. A feeling of fidelity to the dead also motivated the *poilu* (ordinary soldier), as did the individualised sense of responsibility inculcated for over forty years by republican ideology.[74]

The same kind of stoicism, in the expectation of peace, appears to have been kindled increasingly in the German army. It is significant that the failure of the German offensive in March 1918 revived earlier problems within the army, since it had clearly held out hope of swift victory and peace. It also resulted in the loss of many of the best remaining officers among the specially trained attack divisions. OHL had introduced 'patriotic instruction' in the summer of 1917, but the refusal of Hindenburg and Ludendorff to embrace any form of political and social reform undermined this from the beginning. The ultimate failure of the Brusilov offensive in the summer of 1916 had a similar adverse effect on the Russian army and the pattern was repeated with the failure of the Austro-Hungarian offensive in Italy in June 1918.[75]

In the British and dominion forces, national character is clearly of some significance. The Anzac myth was predicated upon a supposed bush ethos deriving from ideas of 'mateship' and egalitarianism. It was certainly the case that Australian soldiers generally had a jaundiced view of the British army, and that the view that Australians were undisciplined was equally widespread among the British military leadership. Nonetheless, the Australian Imperial Force did have the advantage of maintaining rigorous physical standards and the reasonable familiarity with firearms resulting from the introduction of compulsory military training before the war. Moreover, the AIF did undoubtedly draw strength from a notion of being different from the British.[76]

British citizen soldiers, as John Bourne has noted, 'were not social blanks waiting for the army to write its will upon them'. There was a predisposition in British working-class popular culture which made light of hardship. It might be characterised either as a phlegmatic acceptance of fate or sheer bloodymindedness, but was commonly observed with a sardonic, vulgar humour. A sense of community and social cohesiveness was well engrained through the shared experience of adversity and a spirit of mutual support epitomised by such organisations as the friendly societies. This factor ideally complemented the significance of the small 'primary group' in maintaining morale. In the same way, the increasing division of the army into specialisms reproduced the small-scale nature of much of British industry, where even larger enterprises routinely divided men into work gangs. Men were used to making life bearable and were well suited to the challenges of war, relying on civilian values and not those of the army to see them through.[77]

There were large numbers of trade unionists in the British army's rank and file but they rarely figured in wartime disturbances. It is significant in this regard that the list of grievances in the twelve-point petition drawn up by the Soldiers and Workers Council established among units stationed at Tonbridge Wells in Kent in June 1917 – the only other such councils were at Birmingham and Swansea – was not only almost entirely concerned with the mundane issues of daily military life, but also equated grievances with the rights of the citizen. It has been described, indeed, as displaying 'preeminently the voice of the respectable working man'.[78]

Both Army Council and War Cabinet recognised in September 1917 that those disturbances which had occurred in the British army had resulted from issues such as pay and leave. Some attention had been given in earlier years to using chaplains and the YMCA to begin a kind of low-level patriotic instruction. A more formal educational scheme was authorised in February 1918, although not finally implemented until August, by which time the restoration of mobile warfare limited both its effect and its necessity.[79]

Where trade unionists did emerge much more prominently was in the post-war demobilisation disturbances of January 1919. Many of those serving in the base camps affected were specially enlisted volunteer tradesmen, who had been enjoying a regime that became a model for post-war civil labour relations.[80] Compared with trade unionists, survivors of the regular army continued to appear prominently in wartime disturbances and suffered a disproportionate number of wartime executions.[81]

Under the provisions of the British Army Act, a total of 361 men were executed during the war, of whom 291 were serving with British regiments, 25 with Canadian and 5 New Zealand; the remainder were foreign labourers. Taking into account all executions up to the suspension of the death penalty in 1924 and including those civilians and prisoners of war executed for various offences, the total comes to 438. The United States army executed 35 men between April 1917 and June 1919, only 10 of whom committed offences in France, while the Belgians executed 18 soldiers and the Germans supposedly 48 soldiers. In some respects, therefore, the application of discipline was harsher in the British than other armies, but at least 750 Italian soldiers were executed during the war, some by lot. Indeed, 141 Italians were executed in November 1917 alone in the effort to arrest collapse after Caporetto. Figures are uncertain for the French army and unknown for the Austro-Hungarian and Russian armies.

It needs to be borne in mind, however, that only 10.8 per cent of death sentences actually imposed by British courts martial on white soldiers were confirmed, compared to 76.9 per cent in the case of the Chinese Labour Corps. Nearly 40 of those executed had previously been sentenced to death and 2 of them twice previously. Others had previously served, or had had suspended, sentences of imprisonment for capital offences. Although it has been argued that the process was biased against Irishmen, colonial labourers and those deemed mentally degenerate or 'worthless', it should also be noted that standards in the conduct of courts martial differed little from those in pre-war civil courts.[82]

Disproportionate attention has been devoted in Britain to the relatively minor matter of wartime executions, largely through the popular perception that those executed must all have been suffering from shell shock, a term coined by Dr (later Lieutenant-Colonel) Charles Myers in *The Lancet* in February 1915. In fact, similar psychological disorders had been observed in previous wars. However, there was no agreed theory, diagnosis or therapy relating to the condition among medical practitioners, who were divided between physiological and psychological concepts of mental health. Ironically, Myers had no qualifications in psychiatry, medical or experimental psychology.

The predominant medical view was that of the practitioners of biological, deterministic medicine rather than those of the relatively new and controversial fields of psychiatry and psychology. The similarity of the condition with the kind of hysteria normally associated with female mental disorders in itself contributed to the coining of the term 'shell shock'. There was also a tendency to regard it as a matter of class and character, officers suffering from shell shock and other ranks from varying manifestations of hysteria. In view of the widely divergent medical views, it was relatively easy for the military authorities to associate the condition with cowardice and malingering.[83]

Ultimately, shell shock became a usable political issue, which meant different things to different people. It was recognised formally as a condition by the post-war War Office Committee of Enquiry into Shell-Shock but, dominated by conservative practitioners such as Sir Frederick Mott, the Committee produced a report which was ambiguous in its findings. It should be noted, however, that the Committee was satisfied that only 186 men were sentenced to death for cowardice, the offence usually associated with shell shock, and only 18 of these men actually executed.[84]

Judging by the lack of disciplinary disturbances in the British army until demobilisation, most wartime servicemen simply wished to return to civilian life as soon as possible. Thoughts of home were equally important to soldiers of other armies because they had never really ceased to be civilians. The separation of the front from civilian society is something of a misconception: David Englander has argued, indeed, that it is a 'modernist myth'.[85]

There was certainly widespread criticism of civilians by soldiers, even the most radical servicemen and ex-servicemen believing implicitly in the existence of the 'shirker' at home. Thus, British soldiers frequently showed their dislike for strikers.[86] Yet, criticism of civilians did not imply a rejection of civilian society. The hostility to shirkers common to most soldiers in most armies often reflected, as John Horne has expressed it, a disguised rural and lower middle class resentment of the privileges enjoyed by the urban working class in war. The enormous volume of mail between front and home provided a vital bridge, so that it was more a question of interaction than alienation. Separation was also limited by the constant movement during the war between front and home, as men were released to or recalled from war-related industries.

Moreover, it has also been argued recently by Eric Schneider, on the basis of the reports sent back to grieving relatives in Britain by the British Red Cross Wounded and Missing Enquiry Bureau, that civilians were not shielded as much as usually suggested from the more harrowing aspects of life at the front by a 'conspiracy of silence'. Indeed, they displayed a 'morbid curiosity about the exact circumstances surrounding their loved ones' deaths'. Certainly, there was little real attempt to hide the extent of casualties until at least the end of 1916 so far as the national press was concerned. The provincial press continued to publish full casualty lists throughout the war, as well as news of local servicemen.

The same was true of other armies. French soldiers displayed the same dislike of strikers and *embusqués* (shirkers) but were intensely 'home-centred'. While alienated from the *bourage de crâne* (eye-wash) peddled by the politicians and press, therefore, they continued to view themselves as civilians. Thus, there was never any true separation of front and rear, and French soldiers never considered themselves a separate caste. Despite dilution and the extensive employment of women and prisoners of war, German soldiers were still needed to help with the harvest and civil tasks. In fact, 2.4 million German soldiers were detached from the army on industrial or agricultural tasks in 1918.[87] The question of national as opposed to military morale is treated in a later chapter but the two were intimately related. In the case of the Russian and German armies, military collapse triggered political collapse, removing any real division between front and home front.[88]

Viewing the military experience in the Great War as a whole, it could be argued that for those not actually maimed physically or mentally by the war, wartime service had neither an overtly positive nor an overtly negative impact. Moreover, although the legacy of war is addressed in a later chapter, it can be noted that the British army's post-war recruitment was buoyant, which provides little evidence of any immediate revulsion against matters military.[89]

If the impact of the war upon the individual was not as great as has been supposed, it is certainly clear that, in the case of the British army, expansion had little impact on the army as an institution.[90] It might be concluded, therefore, that, while wars may change societies, they change those societies more than the armies that defend them. Or, to put it another way, it is continuity and not discontinuity which is most apparent about the institutional military experience of the Great War. Issues of continuity and discontinuity are equally relevant to wider questions concerning the effect of the war on states and societies.

Notes and references

1. Kennedy, *Rise and Fall*, p.274; Ferro, *Great War*, p.227.

2. John Bourne, 'The British Working Man in Arms', in Cecil and Liddle, eds, *Facing Armageddon*, p.337.

3. Stéphane Audoin-Rouzeau, 'The French Soldier in the Trenches', in Cecil and Liddle, eds, *Facing Armageddon*, p.222; Hew Strachan, 'The Morale of the German Army, 1917–18', ibid., p.393.

4. Jones, 'Imperial Russia's Forces at War', p.274; A. K. Wildman, *The End of the Russian Imperial Army: The Old Army and the Soldiers' Revolt, March to April 1917* (Princeton, NJ, 1980), pp.97–104; Dittmar Dahlmann, 'Russia at the Outbreak of the First World War', in Becker and Audoin-Rouzeau, eds, *Les sociétés européennes*, pp.53–64.

5. Stone, *Eastern Front*, pp.212–17; Wildman, *End of the Russian Imperial Army*, pp.94–9; Jones, 'Imperial Russia's Forces at War', pp.272–84.

6. Jones, 'Imperial Russia's Forces at War', pp.278–9; Kennedy, *Rise and Fall*, p.269; Chickering, *Imperial Germany*, pp.178, 195; Herwig, *First World War*, pp.33, 119, 248, 293, 325, 344, 397, 425; Herwig, 'Dynamics of Necessity', p.83; Whalen, *Bitter Wounds*, pp.38–43; Strachan, 'Morale of German Army', pp.393–5; Wilhelm Deist, 'The German Army, the Authoritarian Nation-state and Total War', in John Horne, ed., *State, Society and Mobilisation in Europe during the First World War* (Cambridge, 1997), pp.160–72; Richard Bessel, *Germany after the First World War* (Oxford, 1993), pp.5–6, 45–7.

7. Herwig, 'Imperial Germany', p.71.

8. Norman Stone, 'Army and Society in the Habsburg Monarchy, 1900–14', *P&P* 33 (1966), pp.95–111; Rotheberg, 'Habsburg Army', pp.73–86; Herwig, *First World War*, pp.129, 230–1, 234–5, 353, 359–60; Tibor Hajdu, 'Army and Society in Hungary in the Era of World War I', in Király and Dreisziger, *East Central European Society*, pp.112–23; Janos Decsy, 'The Habsburg Army on the Threshold of Total War', ibid., pp.280–8; Richard Plaschka, 'The Army and Internal Conflict in the Austro-Hungarian Empire, 1918', ibid., pp.338–53; idem, 'Contradictory Ideologies: The Pressure of Ideological Conflicts in the Austro-Hungarian Army of World War I', in Kann, Király and Fichtner, eds, *Habsburg Empire*, pp.105–19; Spence, 'Yugoslav Role', pp.354–65; Rudolf Jerabek, 'The Eastern Front, 1914–18', in Cornwall, ed., *Last Years of Austria-Hungary*, pp.101–16; Geoffrey Wawro, 'Morale in the Austro-Hungarian Army: The Evidence of Habsburg Army Campaign Reports and Allied Intelligence Officers', in Cecil and Liddle, eds, *Facing Armageddon*, pp.399–412; Mark Cornwall, 'Morale and Patriotism in the Austro-Hungarian Army, 1914–18', in Horne, ed., *State Society and Mobilisation*, pp.173–2; Chickering, *Imperial Germany*, p.195.

9. John Gooch, 'Italy before 1915', in May, ed., *Knowing One's Enemies*, pp.219–20; idem, 'Italy during First World War', pp.181–3; idem, 'Morale and Discipline in the Italian Army, 1915–18', in Cecil and Liddle, eds, *Facing Armageddon*, p.436; Whittam, 'War and Italian Society', pp.144–61; idem, *Politics of Italian Army*, pp.196–7; Sullivan, 'Caporetto', pp.59–78.

10. Erik Zürcher, 'Little Mehmet in the Desert: The Ottoman Soldier's Experience', in Cecil and Liddle, eds, Facing Armageddon, pp.230–41; idem, 'Between Death and Desertion: The Experience of the Ottoman Soldier in World War I', *Turcica* 28 (1996), pp.235–58; Ferro, *Great War*, p.8; Porch, 'French Army', pp.198–9; Chickering, *Imperial Germany*, p.195; Adrian Gregory, 'Lost Generations: The Impact of Military Casualties on Paris, London, and Berlin', in Winter and Robert, eds, *Capital Cities*, p.67.

11. Nenninger, 'American Military Effectiveness', pp.122–4, 130, 137, 148; Trask, *AEF and Coalition Warmaking*, p.15; Kennedy, *Over Here*, pp.147–8, 150, 155–7, 162–9, 188; Ronald Schaffer, *America in the Great War: The Rise of the War Welfare State* (New York, 1991), pp.17, 87, 175–7. See also Edward M. Coffman, *The War to End All Wars: The American Military Experience in World War I*, 2nd edn (Madison, WI, 1986).

12. *Statistics of the Military Effort of the British Empire during the Great War* (London, 1922), pp.30, 156–9, 363–4.

13. Central Statistical Office, *Fighting with Figures: A Statistical Digest of the Second World War* (London, 1995), pp.38–9; Alex Danchev, 'The Army and the Home Front, 1939–45', in Chandler and Beckett, eds, *Oxford History of British Army*, pp.309–14; Clive Emsley, *British Society and the French Wars, 1793–1815* (London, 1979), pp.133, 169; M. Greenwood, 'British Loss of Life in the Wars of 1794–1815 and 1914–18', *Journal of the Royal Statistical Society* 105 (1942), pp.1–16.

14. Beckett, 'Nation in Arms, 1914–18', pp.6, 10; Edward Spiers, 'The Regular Army', ibid., pp.39–41, 44–6; Beckett, 'British Army', p.102.

15. Ian Beckett, 'The Territorial Force' in Beckett and Simpson, *Nation in Arms*, pp.128–30; idem, 'The Territorial Force in the Great War', in Liddle, ed., *Home Fires and Foreign Fields*, pp.21–2; idem, *The Amateur Military Tradition, 1558–1945* (Manchester, 1991), pp.217–22.

16. Beckett, *Amateur Military Tradition*, p.222.

17. Peter Simkins, 'Kitchener and the Expansion of the Army', in Beckett and Gooch, eds, *Politicians and Defence*, pp.96–7.

18. Lloyd George, *War Memoirs*, II, p.751; Leo Amery, *My Political Life*, 2 vols (London, 1953), II, p.23.

19. Beckett, 'Territorial Force', pp.130–1; idem, *Amateur Military Tradition*, pp.226–8; Simkins, 'Kitchener and the Expansion of the Army', pp.87–90, 97–100; idem, *Kitchener's Army: The Raising of the New Armies, 1914–16* (Manchester, 1988), pp.31–46.

20. Beckett, *Amateur Military Tradition*, pp.228–31; idem, 'Territorial Force', pp.131–7.

21. Beckett, 'Nation in Arms', p.12; French, 'Rise and Fall of Business as Usual', pp.7–31; F. W. Perry, *The Commonwealth Armies: Manpower and Organisation in Two World War* (Manchester, 1988), pp.9–10.

22. Thomas Rohkrämer, 'August 1914: Kriegsmentalität und ihre Voraussetzungen', in Michalka, ed., *Erste Weltkrieg*, pp.759–77; Eric Leed, *No Man's Land: Combat and Identity in World War I* (Cambridge, 1979), pp.40; Robert Wohl, *The Generation of 1914* (London, 1980), p.208.

23. Beckett, 'Nation in Arms', pp.7–8; Simkins, *Kitchener's Army*, pp.49–75, 83–4; Clive Hughes, 'The New Armies', in Beckett and Simpson, eds, *Nation in Arms*, pp.100–7.

24. Beckett, 'Nation in Arms', pp.8–9; Simkins, *Kitchener's Army*, pp.104–33.

25. Ian Beckett, 'The Soldier's Documents of the Great War and the Military Historian', *Archives* 23 (1998), pp.63–7; Doron Lamm, 'British Soldiers of the First World War: Creation of a Representative Sample', *Historical and Social Research* 13 (1988), pp.55–98; Simkins, *Kitchener's Army*, pp.165–87; idem, 'The Four Armies, 1914–18', in Chandler and Beckett, eds, *Oxford History of British Army*, pp.241–62.

26. Bourne, *Britain and Great War*, p.219; Beckett, 'Nation in Arms', pp.9–11; idem, 'British Army', pp.102–4; Roy Douglas, 'Voluntary Enlistment in the First World War and the Work of the Parliamentary Recruiting Committee', *JMH* 42 (1970), pp.564–85; J. M. Osborne, *The Voluntary Recruiting Movement in Britain, 1914–16* (New York, 1982), pp.106–29, 138–44; Simkins, *Kitchener's Army*, pp.107–8.

27. P. E. Dewey, 'Military Recruiting and the British Labour Force during the First World War', *HJ* 27 (1984), pp.199–224; Simkins, *Kitchener's Army*, pp.108–12; Hughes, 'New Armies', pp.102, 120.

28. Beckett, 'British Army', p.104; Brown and Loveridge, 'Unrequited Faith', pp.59–62; Simkins, *Kitchener's Army*, pp.79–100.

29. Simkins, *Kitchener's Army*, pp.94–9, 112–16; Edward Spiers, 'The Scottish Soldier at War', in Cecil and Liddle, eds, *Facing Armageddon*, pp.314–35; G. Urquhart, 'Negotiations for War: Highland Identity under Fire', in Bertrand Taithe and Tim Thornton, eds, *War: Identities in Conflict, 1300–2000* (Stroud, 1998), pp.159–72; Ewen Cameron and Iain Robertson, 'Fighting and Bleeding for the Land: The Scottish Highlands and the Great War', in Catriona M. M. Macdonald and E. W. McFarland, eds, *Scotland and the Great War* (East Linton, 1999), pp.81–100; Patrick Callan, 'British Recruitment in Ireland, 1914–18', *RIHM* 63 (1985), pp.41–50; idem, 'Recruiting for the British Army in Ireland during the First World War', *Irish Sword* 17 (1987/88), pp.42–56; Terry Denman, *Ireland's Unknown Soldiers: The 16th (Irish) Division in the Great War, 1914–18* (Dublin, 1992); idem, 'Sir Lawrence Parsons and the Raising of the 16th Irish Division', *Irish Sword* 17 (1987/88), pp.90–103; idem, 'The 10th (Irish) Division, 1914–15: A Study in Military and Political Interpretation', *Irish Sword* 17 (1987/88), pp.16–24; idem, 'The Catholic Irish Soldier in the First World War: The Racial Enviroment', *Irish Historical Studies* 27 (1991), pp.352–65; D. and J. Howie, 'Irish Recruiting and the Home Rule Crisis of August–September 1914', in Dockrill and French, eds, *Strategy and Intelligence*, pp.1–22; David Fitzpatrick, 'Militarism in Ireland, 1900–22', in Thomas Bartlett and Keith Jeffery, eds, *A Military History of Ireland* (Cambridge, 1998), pp.379–406; idem, 'The Logic of Collective Sacrifice: Ireland and the British Army, 1914–18', *HJ* 38 (1995), pp.1017–30; idem, *Politics and Irish Life, 1913–21: Provincial Experience of War and Revolution*, 2nd edn (Cork, 1998), pp.93–4; Nick Perry, 'Politics and Command: General Nugent, the Ulster Division and Relations with Ulster Unionism, 1915–17', in Bond, ed., *Look To Your Front*, pp.105–20; Tim Bowman, 'The Irish Recriting and Anti-recruiting Campaigns, 1914–18', in Bertrand Taithe and Tim Thornton, eds, *Propaganda: Political Rhetoric and Identity, 1300–2000* (Stroud, 1999), pp.223–38; Clive Hughes, 'New Armies', pp.114–22; Gervase Phillips, 'Dai Bach Y Soldiwr: Welsh Soldiers in the British Army, 1914–18', *Llafur* 6 (1993), pp.94–105.

30. Jay Winter, 'Britain's Lost Generation of the First World War', *Population Studies* 31 (1977), pp.449–66; Beckett, 'British Army', pp.104–6; Dewey, 'Military Recruiting', pp.201–2.

31. Beckett, 'Nation in Arms', pp.12–13; Simkins, *Kitchener's Army*, pp.138–58; R. J. Q. Adams and R. Poirier, *The Conscription Controversy in Britain, 1900–18* (London, 1987), passim; A. J. Ward, 'David Lloyd George and the Irish Conscription Crisis', *HJ* 17 (1974), pp.107–29.

32. Keith Grieves, *The Politics of Manpower, 1914–18* (Manchester, 1988), pp.149–80; idem, 'Total War: The Quest for a British Manpower Policy, 1917–18', *JSS* 9 (1986), pp.79–95.

33. Jay Winter, 'Military Fitness and Civilian Health in Britain during the First World War', *JCH* 15 (1980), pp.211–44; idem, *The Great War and the British People* (London, 1985), pp.25–64; Mathew Thomson, 'Status, Manpower and Mental Fitness: Mental Deficiency in the First World War', in Cooter, Harrison and Sturdy, eds, *War, Medicine and Morality*, pp.149–66; Harold Pollins, 'Jews in the British Army in the First World War', *The Jewish Journal of Sociology* 37 (1995), pp.100–11; Barry A. Kosmin, Stanley Waterman and Nigel Grizzard, 'The Jewish Dead in the Great War as an Indicator for the Location, Size and Social Structure of Anglo-Jewry in 1914', *Immigrants and Minorities* 5 (1986), pp.181–92; David Killingray, 'All the King's Men: Blacks in the British Army in the First World War, 1914–18', in R. Lotz and I. Pegg, eds, *Under the Imperial Carpet* (Crawley, 1986), pp.164–81; idem, 'Race and Rank in the British Army in the Twentieth Century', *Ethnic and Racial Studies* 10 (1987), pp.276–90.

34. Ian Beckett, 'The Real Unknown Army: British Conscripts, 1916–19', in Becker and Audoin-Rosseau, eds, *Les sociétés européennes*, pp.339–56 [an extended version can be found in *The Great War* 2 (1989), pp.4–13]; Winter, 'Military Fitness and Civilian Health', pp.211–44; K. R. Grieves, 'Military Tribunal Papers: The Case of Leek Tribunal in the First World War', *Archives* 16 (1983), pp.145–50; idem, 'The "Recruiting Margin" in Britain: Debates on Manpower during the Third Battle of Ypres', in Liddle, ed., *Passchendaele in Perspective*, pp.390–405; Ian Beckett, 'Aspects of a Nation in Arms: Britain's Volunteer Training Corps in the Great War', *RIHM* 63 (1985), pp.27–39.

35. Beckett, 'Real Unknown Army', pp.342–3; Wilson, *Myriad Faces of War*, p.400.

36. John Rae, *Conscience and Politics: The British Government and the Conscientious Objector to Military Service, 1916–19* (Oxford, 1970), pp.22–67, 94–133; T. C. Kennedy, *The Hound of Conscience: A History of the No-Conscription Fellowship* (Fayetteville, AK, 1981), pp.89–105; Keith Robbins, 'The British Experience of Conscientious Objection', in Cecil and Liddle, eds, *Facing Armageddon*, pp.691–706.

37. Dewey, 'Military Recruiting and British Labour Force', p.205.

38. Simkins, *Kitchener's Army*, pp.231–52; idem, 'Soldiers and Civilians: Billeting in Britain and France', in Beckett and Simpson, *Nation in Arms*, pp.165–192.

39. Beckett, 'Nation in Arms', pp.18–20; Simkins, 'Soldiers and Civilians', pp.175–6.

40. Clive Hughes, 'Army Recruitment in Gwynedd, 1914–16', unpub. MA thesis, Wales, 1983, pp.75–6; Beckett, 'Nation in Arms', pp.19–20.

41. Beckett, 'Nation in Arms', p.19; Simkins, Billeting, pp.178–86; Suzann Buckley, 'The Failure to Resolve the Problem of Venereal Disease among the Troops

in Britain during World War One', in Bond and Roy, eds, *War and Society*, pp.65–85; Mark Harrison, 'The British Army and the Problem of Venereal Disease in France and Egypt during the First World War', *Medical History* 39 (1995), pp.133–58; Andrews, *Anzac Illusion*, pp.183–4.

42. McKernan, *Australian People and Great War*, pp.116–49; Robson, 'Origin and Character of First AIF', pp.741–5; Andrews, *Anzac Illusion*, pp.179–88; John Fuller, *Troop Morale and Popular Culture in the British and Dominion Armies, 1914–18* (Oxford, 1991), pp.149, 168–74.

43. Omissi, *Sepoy and Raj*, pp.64–6, 122–3; idem, *Indian Voices of the Great War: Soldiers' Letters, 1914–18* (London, 1999), pp.1–22; Jeffrey Greenhut, 'Race, Sex, and War: The Impact of Race and Sex on Morale and Health Services for the Indian Corps on the Western Front, 1914', *MA* 1981, pp.71–4; idem, 'Imperial Reserve', pp.54–73; Michel, 'Mythes et Réalitiés du Concours Colonial', pp.401–9; Waites, 'Peoples of the Undeveloped World', p.604; J. H. Lunn, 'Kande Kamara Speaks: An Oral History of the West African Experience in France, 1914–18', in Page, ed., *Africa and First World War*, pp.28–53.

44. Mark Meigs, *Optimism at Armageddon: Voices of American Participants in the First World War* (London, 1997), pp.69–142, 189–97; André Kaspi, 'Les soldats américains et la société française', in Becker and Audoin-Rouzeau, eds, *Les sociétés européennes*, pp.323–31; Thomas Camfield, 'The US Army Troop Morale Program of World War I', *MA* 41 (1977), pp.125–8; William H. Kenney, 'Le Hot: The Assimilation of American Jazz in France, 1917–40', *American Studies* 25 (1984), pp.5–24; James Cooke, 'The American Soldier in France, 1917–19', in Cecil and Liddle, eds, *Facing Armageddon*, pp.242–55; Donald Smythe, 'Venereal Disease: The AEF's Experience', *Prologue* 26 (1994), pp.119–31; Edward H. Beardsley, 'Allied against Sin: American and British Responses to Venereal Disease in World War I', *Medical History* 20 (1976), pp.189–202; Kennedy, *Over Here*, pp.205–6, 213, 220; Schaffer, *America in Great War*, pp.100–7; R. White, 'The Soldier as Tourist: The Australian Experience of the Great War', *W&S* 5 (1987), pp.63–77; idem, 'Europe and the Six-Bob-a-Day Tourist: The Great War as Grand Tour, or Getting Civilised', *Australian Studies* 5 (1991), pp.122–39; Suzanne Brugger, *Australians and Egypt, 1914–1919* (Melbourne, 1980), pp.30–47, 145–7.

45. Among the better 'popular' accounts are: John Ellis, *Eye-deep in Hell: The Western Front, 1914–18* (London, 1976); Denis Winter, *Death's Men: Soldiers of the Great War* (London, 1978); and Peter Liddle, *The Soldier's War* (London, 1988), which has the merit of looking beyond the Western Front to other theatres.

46. John Bourne, 'British Working Man in Arms', pp.336–52.

47. E. J. Leed, 'Class and Disillusionment in World War I', *JMH* 50 (1978), pp.680–99; idem, *No Man's Land*, pp.105–14; Wohl, *Generation of 1914*, pp.203–37; G. D. Sheffield, 'The Effect of The Great War on Class Relations in Britain: The Career of Major Christopher Stone', *W&S* 7 (1989), pp.87–105.

48. David Englander, 'People at War; France, Britain and Germany, 1914–18 and 1939–45', *European History Quarterly* 18 (1988), p.234.

49. Richard Bessel and David Englander, 'Up from the Trenches: Some Recent Writing on the Soldiers of the Great War', *ESR* 11 (1981), pp.387–95; Bessel, *Germany after First World War*, pp.8, 258, 271; Schaffer, *America in Great War*, pp.193–7.

50. Simpson, 'British Soldier', pp.141–6; P. Doyle and M. Bennett, 'Geology and Warfare on the Western Front', *Stand To* 49 (1997), pp.34–8; Malcolm Brown and Shirley Seaton, *Christmas Truce: The Western Front, December 1914* (London, 1984); Tony Ashworth, 'The Sociology of Trench Warfare, 1914–18', *British Journal of Sociology* 19 (1968), pp.407–23; Beckett, 'British Army', pp.110–12; David Englander, 'Manpower in the British Army', in *Les Fronts Invisibles: Actes du Colloque International sur la Logistique des Armées au Combat pendant la Première Guerre Mondiale* (Nancy, 1984), pp.93–102; Herwig, *First World War*, p.360; Wildman, *End of Russian Imperial Army*, I, p.105.

51. Beckett, 'Nation in Arms', pp.21–3; idem, 'Territorial Force', pp.137–8, 146–8, 150–1; idem, 'British Army', pp.110–12; Nicholas Perry, 'Nationality in the Irish Infantry Regiments in the First World War', *W&S* 12 (1994), pp.65–95; idem, 'Maintaining Regimental Identity in the Great War: The Case of the Irish Infantry Regiments', *Stand To* 54 (1998), pp.5–11; K. W. Mitchinson, 'The Reconstitution of 169 Brigade, July to October 1916', *Stand To* 29 (1990), pp.8–11; idem, 'The Transfer Controversy: Parliament and the London Regiment', *Stand To* 33 (1991), pp.29–32; Graham Stewart, 'County and Regiment: An Analysis of Recruitment and the Northumberland Fusiliers, 1914–18', *Stand To* 49 (1997), pp.27–32.

52. Beckett, 'Real Unknown Army', pp.346–51; Bidwell and Graham, *Firepower*, p.117; David Englander, 'Mutiny and Myopia', *Bulletin of the Society for the Study of Labour History* 52 (1987), pp.5–7; idem, 'People at War', pp.229–38.

53. Beckett, 'British Army', pp.109–10.

54. Chickering, *Imperial Germany*, p.98; Christhard Hoffmann, 'Between Integration and Rejection: The Jewish Community in Germany, 1914–18', in Horne, ed., *State, Society and Mobilisation*, p.94; Alan Kramer, '*Wachess* at War: Alsace-Lorraine and the Failure of German Mobilisation, 1914–18', ibid., pp.105–21.

55. Bernd Ulrich, 'Die Desillusionierung der Kriegsfreiwilligen von 1914', in Wolfram Wette, ed., *Der Krieg des Kleinen Mannes: Eine Militärgeschichte von Unten* (Munich, 1992), pp.110–26.

56. Wolfgang Kruse, 'Krieg und Klassenheer: Zur Revolutionierung der deutschen Armee im Ersten Weltkrieg', *Geschichte und Gesellschaft* 22 (1996), pp.530–61; Wilhelm Deist, 'The Military Collapse of the German Empire: The Reality Behind the Stab-in-the-Back Myth', *WH* 3 (1996), pp.186–207; idem, 'Le moral des troupes allemandes sur le front occidental à la fin de l'année 1916',

in Becker, Winter, Krumeich, Becker and Audoin-Rouzeau, eds, *Guerre et Cultures*, pp.91–102; Strachan, 'Morale of German Army', pp.388–91; Benjamin Ziemann, 'Fahnenflucht im deutschen Heer, 1914–18', *MM* 55, 1996, pp.93–130; idem, 'Verweigerungsformen von Frontsoldaten in der deutschen Armee, 1914–18', in Andres Gestrich, ed., *Gewalt im Krieg: Ausübung, Erfahrung und Verweigerung von Gewalt in Kriegen des 20. Jahrhunderts* (Munster, 1996), pp.99–122.

57. John Bushnell, 'Peasants in Uniform: The Tsarist Army as a Peasant Society', *Journal of Social History* 13 (1979/80), pp.565–76; Stone, *Eastern Front*, pp.166–71, 224–5; Wildman, *End of the Russian Imperial Army*, pp.91–4, 106–7.

58. Porch, 'French Army', pp.222–3; Stéphane Audoin-Rouzeau, *Men at War, 1914–18: National Sentiment and Trench Journalism in France during the First World War* (Oxford, 1992), p.52.

59. P. Joyce, *Work, Society and Politics* (Hassocks, 1980), pp.29–41; Bourne, *Britain and Great War*, pp.220–1.

60. Ferguson, *Pity of War*, pp.357–66, 388–94. On morale generally, see Elmer Dinter, *Hero or Coward: Pressures Facing the Soldier in Battle* (London, 1985), Richard Holmes, *Firing Line* (London 1985); Anthony Kellett, *Combat Motivation* (Ottawa, 1980); F. M. Richardson, *Fighting Spirit: A Study of Psychological Factors in War* (London 1978). John Baynes, *Morale: A Study of Men and Courage* (London, 1967) looks specifically at the Cameronians at Neuve Chapelle in March 1915. For a revisionist view of the significance of religion, see Rich Schweitzer, 'The Cross and the Trenches: Religious Faith and Doubt among some British Soldiers on the Western Front', *W&S* 16 (1998), pp.33–58.

61. J. Brent Wilson, 'The Morale and Discipline of the BEF, 1914–18', unpub. MA thesis, New Brunswick, 1978, pp.66–117.

62. Fuller, *Troop Morale and Popular Culture*, p.7; Audoin-Rouzeau, *Men at War*, p.8.

63. Audoin-Rouzeau, *Men at War*, pp.9–10; idem, Les soldats français et la nation de 1914 à 1918, d'après les journaux des tranchées', *Revue d'Histoire Moderne et Contemporaine* 34 (1987), pp.66–86; David Englander, 'Soldiering and Identity: Reflections on the Great War', *WH* 1 (1994), pp.304, 310; idem, 'Military Intelligence and the Defence of the Realm: The Surveillance of Soldiers and Civilians in Britain during the First World War', *Bulletin of the Society for the Study of Labour History* 52 (1987), pp.24–32; idem, 'The French Soldier, 1914–18', *French History* 1 (1987), pp.49–67; Annick Cochet, 'Les Paysans sur le front en 1916', *Bulletin du Centre d'Histoire de la France Contemporaine* 3, 1982, pp.37–48; J. N. Jeanneney, 'Les archives des commissions de contrôle postal aux armées, 1916–18: Une source précieuse pour l'histoire contemporaine de l'opinion et des mentalités', *Revue Histoire Moderne et Contemporaine* 15 (1968), pp.209–33; J.-P. Devos and P. Waksman, 'Le moral à la 3e Armée en 1918, d'après les archives de la justice militaire et du contrôl postal', *RIHM* 37 (1977), pp.89–101; Irina Davidian, 'The Russian Soldier's Morale from the

Evidence of Tsarist Military Censorship', in Cecil and Liddle, eds, *Facing Armageddon*, pp.425–33; Omissi, *Sepoy and Raj*, pp.114–23.

64. Wilson, 'Morale and Discipline', pp.67–117, 212–62; David Englander and James Osborne, 'Jack, Tommy and Henry Dubb: The Armed Forces and the Working Class', *HJ* 21 (1978), pp.593–62; David Englander, 'Discipline and Morale in the British Army, pp.117–18', in Horne, ed., *State, Society and Mobilisation*, pp.132–6. On Etaples, see D. Gill and G. Dallas, 'Mutiny at Etaples Base, 1917', *P&P* 69 (1975), pp.88–112 reprised in their monograph, *The Unknown Army: Mutinies in the British Army in World War One* (London, 1985), pp.63–80; Julian Putkowski, 'Toplis, Etaples and the "Monocled Mutineer"', *Stand To* 18 (1986), pp.6–11.

65. Ferguson, *Pity of War*, pp.344–5, 367–88; C. J. Lammers, 'Strikes and Mutinies: A Comparative Study of Organisational Conflicts between Rulers and Ruled', *Administrative Science Quarterly* 14 (1969), pp.558–72.

66. W. F. Elkins, 'A Source of Black Nationalism in the Caribbean: The Revolt of the British West Indies Regiment at Taranto, Italy in 1918', *Science and Society* (1970), pp.99–103; Ian Beckett, 'The Singapore Mutiny of February 1915', *JSAHR* 62 (1984), pp.132–53; Gammage, *Broken Years*, pp.228–9; Timothy Bowman, 'The Discipline and Morale of the BEF in France and Flanders, 1914–18 with particular reference to Irish Units', unpub. PhD thesis, Luton, 1999, pp.384–7, 391–3, 410–22.

67. Guy Pedronici, *Les mutineries de 1917* (Paris, 1967), pp.194, 198–207, 215, 281–8; Pedronici, 'Une crise exceptionnelle: les refus collectifs d'obeissance en 1917', *Revue Historiques de l'Armée* 4 (1967), pp.75–84; Audoin-Rouzeau, *Men at War*, p.11.

68. Leonard Smith, *Between Mutiny and Obedience: The Case of the French Fifth Infantry Division during World War I* (Princeton, NJ, 1994), pp.203–14; idem, 'The French High Command and the Mutinies of Spring 1917', in Cecil and Liddle, eds, *Facing Armageddon*, pp.79–92; idem, 'War and "Politics": The French Army Mutinies of 1917', *WH* 2 (1995), pp.180–201; idem, 'The Disciplinary Dilemma of French Military Justice, September 1914–April 1917: The Case of the 5e Division d'Infanterie', *JMilH* 55 (1991), pp.47–68; idem, 'Remobilising the Citizen-soldier through the French Army Mutinies of 1917', in Horne, ed., *State, Society and Mobilisation*, pp.144–59; Charles-Henri Taufflich, 'Les Mutineries de 1917: L'Example du 37e Corps d'Armée', *GMCC* 182 (1996), pp.123–38.

69. P. Facon, 'La crise du moral en 1917 à l'armée française d'orient', *Revue Historiques des Armées* 4 (1977), pp.93–114; idem, 'Les mutineries dans le corps expeditionnaire français en Russe septentrionale, 1918–19', *Revue d'Histoire Moderne et Contemporaine* 24 (1977), pp.455–74.

70. John Keegan, *The Face of Battle* (Harmondsworth, 1978), pp.276–7; idem, *First World War*, p.372.

71. Tony Ashworth, *Trench Warfare, 1914–18: The Live and Let-live System* (London, 1980), pp.176–203.

72. Gary Sheffield, 'Officer–Man Relations, Morale and Discipline in the British Army, 1902–22', unpub. PhD thesis, London, 1994, pp.102, 162–70, 335; idem, 'Officer–Man Relations, Discipline and Morale in the British Army in the Great War', in Cecil and Liddle, eds, *Facing Armageddon*, pp.413–24; idem, 'The Operational Role of British Military Police on the Western Front, 1914– 18', in Griffith, ed., *British Fighting Methods*, pp.70–86; K. R. Grieves, '"Lowther's Lambs": Rural Paternalism and Voluntary Recruitment in the First World War', *Rural History* 4 (1993), pp.55–75; John Lee, 'The British Divisions at Ypres', in Liddle, ed., *Passchendaele in Perspective*, pp.224–5; Bowman, 'Discipline and Morale', p.406.

73. Alan Wilkinson, *The Church of England and the First World War* (London, 1978), pp.109–35, 153–68; Beckett, 'Nation in Arms', pp.23–5; Fuller, *Troop Morale and Popular Culture*, pp.81–113; Englander, 'Discipline and Morale', p.130. L. J. Collins, *Theatre at War, 1914–18* (London, 1998), pp.100–76.

74. Annick Cochet, 'Les soldats français', in Becker and Audoin-Rouzeau, eds, *Les sociétés européennes*, pp.357–66; Audoin-Rouzeau, 'French Soldier in Trenches', p.228; John Horne, 'Soldiers, Civilians and the Warfare of Attrition: Representations of Combat in France, 1914–18', in Coetzee and Shevin-Coetzee, eds, *Authority*, pp.223–49; Englander, 'French Soldier', pp.58, 60, 67; Audoin-Rouzeau, *Men at War*, pp.163–84; Fuller, *Troop Morale and Popular Culture*, pp.38–40; Smith, 'Remobilising the Citizen-soldier', p.159.

75. Anne Lipp, 'Friedenssehnsucht und Durchhaltebereitschaft: Wahrnehmungen und Erfahrungen deutsches soldaten im Ersten Weltkrieg', *Archiv für Sozialgeschichte* 36 (1996), pp.279–92; Strachan, 'German Morale', p.390; Deist, 'Military Collapse of German Empire', pp.186–207; idem, 'German Army, Authoritarian Nation-state and Total War', pp.160–72; Davidian, 'Russian Soldiers' Morale', p.431; Mark Cornwall, 'Morale and Patriotism in the Austro-Hungarian Army, 1914–18', in Horne, ed., *State, Society and Mobilisation*, p.188.

76. Robertson, *Anzac and Empire*, pp.259–61; Dawes and Robson, *Citizen to Soldier*, pp.6, 90–166; 168–99; Gammage, *Broken Years*, pp.230–63, 280–3; Andrews, *Anzac Illusion*, pp.40–6; 103–8, 149–54, 165–6, 172–7.

77. Fuller, *Troop Morale and Popular Culture*, pp.118–59; Bourne, *Britain and the Great War*, pp.218–21; idem, 'British Working Man', pp.336–52.

78. Englander and Osborne, 'Jack, Tommy and Henry Dubb', p.605; David Egan, 'The Swansea Conference of the British Council of Soldiers' and Workers' Delegates, July 1917', *Llafur* 1 (1975), pp.162–87.

79. Beckett, 'Real Unknown Army', p.341; S. P. Mackenzie, *Politics and Military Morale: Current Affairs and Citizenship Education in the British Army, 1914–50* (Oxford, 1990), pp.3–31; idem, 'Morale and the Cause: The Campaign to Shape

the Outlook of Soldiers of the BEF, 1914–18', *CJH* 25 (1990), pp.215–31; Englander, 'Discipline and Morale', pp.140–1.

80. Dallas and Gill, *Unknown Army*, pp.63–81; Andrew Rothstein, *The Soldiers' Strikes of 1919* (London, 1980); Desmond Morton, 'Kicking and Complaining: Demobilisation Riots in the Canadian Forces, 1918–19', *CHR* 5 (1980), pp.334–60. See also Julian Putkowski, *The Kinmel Park Camp Riots, 1919* (Clwyd, 1989).

81. Anthony Babington, *For the Sake of Example* (London, 1983); Julian Putkowski and Julian Sykes, *Shot at Dawn* (Barnsley, 1989); Gerard Oram, *Death Sentences passed by Military Courts of the British Army, 1914–24* (London, 1998).

82. Putkowski and Sykes, *Shot at Dawn*, pp.16–18; Pedronici, *Les mutinieries*, p.201; Gooch, 'Italy in First World War', p.181; Sullivan, 'Caporetto', pp.68–71; A. B. Godefroy, 'Executions in the Canadian Expeditionary Force, 1914–18', *Stand To* 52 (1998), pp.19–24; Christopher Pugsley, *On the Fringe of Hell: New Zealanders and Military Discipline in the First World War* (Auckland, 1991); Peter Scott, 'Law and Orders: Discipline and Morale in the British Armies in France, 1917', in Liddle, ed., *Passchendaele in Perspective*, pp.349–68; Harvey, *Collision of Empires*, p.439; Gerard Oram, *Worthless Men: Race, Eugenics and the Death Penalty in the British Army during the First World War* (London, 1998), pp.17–18, 28–31, 60–73, 84–112; Bowman, 'Discipline and Morale', pp.109–67; John Peaty, 'Capital Courts-martial during the Great War', in Bond, ed., *Look To Your Front*, pp.89–104; idem, 'Haig and Military Discipline', in Bond and Cave, eds, *Haig*, pp.196–222.

83. P. J. Lynch, 'The Exploitation of Courage: Psychiatric Care in the British Army, 1914–18', unpub. MPhil., London, 1977, pp.84, 93, 180–3, 221; Leed, *No Man's Land*, pp.163–6, 181–3; Martin Stone, 'Shell Shock and the Psychologists', in W. T. Bynum, R. Porter and M. Shepherd, eds, *The Anatomy of Madness*, 2 vols (London, 1985), pp.242–71; Harold Merskey, 'Shell Shock', in G. E. Berrios and H. L. Freemand, eds, *150 Years of British Psychiatry 1841–1991* (London 1991), pp.245–67; J. E. Talbott, 'Soldiers, Psychiatrists and Combat Trauma', *Journal of Interdisciplinary History* 27 (1997), pp.437–54; Schaffer, *America in Great War*, pp.199–212; Elaine Showalter, 'Rivers and Sassoon: The Inscription of Male Gender Anxieties', in Margaret Higonnet, Jane Jenson, Sonya Michel and Margaret Collins, eds, *Behind the Lines: Gender and the Two World Wars* (New Haven, CT, 1987), pp.61–9; Roger Cooter, 'Malingering in Modernity: Psychological Scripts and Adversarial Encounters during the First World War', in Cooter, Harrison and Sturdy, eds, *War, Medicine and Modernity*, pp.125–48; P. Lerner, 'Psychiatry and Casualties of War in Germany, 1914–18', *JCH* 35 (1), (2000), pp.13–28; Joanna Burke, 'Effeminacy, Ethnicity and the End of Trauma: The Sufferings of "Shell-shocked" Men in Great Britain and Ireland, 1914–39', ibid., pp.57–70.

84. Ted Bogacz, 'War Neurosis and Cultural Change in England, 1914–22: The Work of the War Office Committee of Enquiry into "Shell-Shock"', *JCH* 24

(1989), pp.227–56; Keith Simpson, 'Dr Dunn and Battle Stress: The Experiences of a Regimental Medical Officer of 2nd Royal Welch Fusiliers, 1915–18', *The Great War* 3 (1991), pp.76–86; idem, 'Dr James Dunn and Shell-shock', in Cecil and Liddle, eds, *Facing Armageddon*, pp.502–22; E. D. Brown, 'Between Cowardice and Insanity: Shell Shock and the Legitimation of the Neuroses in Great Britain', in E. Mendelsohn, M. R. Smith and P. Weingart, eds, *Science, Technology and the Military* (New York, 1988), pp.323–45; Joanna Bourke, *Dismembering the Male: Men's Bodies, Britain and the Great War* (London 1996), pp.76–123.

85. Englander, 'Soldiering and Identity', p.317.

86. David Englander, 'Troops and Trade Unions in 1919', *History Today* 37 (1987), pp.8–13; Englander and Osborne, 'Jack, Tommy and Henry Dubb', p.619.

87. John Horne, 'Mobilising for "Total War", 1914–18', in Horne, ed., *State, Society and Mobilisation*, p.12; Eric F. Schneider, 'The British Red Cross Wounded and Missing Enquiry Bureau: A Case of Truth-telling in the Great War', *WH* 4 (1997), pp.296–315; Bourne, *Britain and Great War*, pp.205–6; Becker, *Great War and French People*, pp.116, 138–9, 195; Englander, 'People at War', pp.235–6; idem, 'French Soldier', pp.62, 67; Audoin-Rouzeau, *Men at War*, pp.109–43, 151–2; Nikolaus Buschmann, 'Der Verschwiegene Krieg: Kommunikation zwischen Front und Heimatfront', in Hirschfeld, Krumeich, Langewiesche and Ullman, eds, *Kriegserfahrungen*, pp.208–24; Anne Lipp, 'Heimatwahrnehmung und Soldatisches "Kriegserlebnis"', ibid., pp.225–42.

88. Strachan, *First World War*, p.29.

89. Keith Jeffery, 'The Post-war Army', in Beckett and Simpson, eds, *Nation in Arms*, pp.211–34.

90. Keith Simpson, 'The Officers', in Beckett and Simpson, eds, *Nation in Arms*, pp.70, 76–83, 88; Simkins, *Kitchener's Army*, pp.212–30.

CHAPTER EIGHT

War and the State

Over the past twenty years or so, historians have come increasingly to recognise the often pivotal role played by war and conflict in historical development. The concept of total war has become generally familiar as a means of describing the nature of the two world wars of the twentieth century and also as a means of differentiating them from other conflicts. The term 'total war' was used by Ludendorff in his memoirs in 1919 and, again, in his polemic in 1935, *Der Totale Krieg*. Similarly, it was used by the right-wing French writer, Léon Daudet in 1918, echoing Clemenceau's reference to *guerre intégrale* in July 1917 as a link between home and front. The former stormtrooper, Ernst Jünger, wrote of total mobilisation in 1930 and the phrase 'total war' was also used in a ritualistic fashion in the Second World War by individuals as varied as Josef Goebbels and Winston Churchill.[1]

In its modern sense, total war conveys a linkage between war and social change and is associated with the analytical framework postulated by Arthur Marwick, beginning with his study of Britain in the Great War, *The Deluge*, in 1965, although the linkage had been made in the 1950s by others such as Richard Titmuss and Stanislas Andrzejewski. Four 'modes' outlined by Marwick in 1968 as a framework for gauging and comparing the degree of change effected by war became a four-tier 'model' six years later. For Marwick, total war implied, firstly, enhanced destruction and disruption on an unprecedented scale; secondly, the emergence of a testing challenge to the existing social and political structures of states and societies; thirdly, greater participation in the context of the total mobilisation of a state's resources; and fourthly, a cataclysmic socio-psychological impact upon existing attitudes and values. When combined, the cumulative effect would result in real and enduring social change.

Marwick's model was offered only as a rough tool, but it is undeniable that the idea of total war as a determinant of major change had a profound impact. From the beginning, some historians were more cautious. Some have rejected the concept entirely, Trevor Wilson criticising the use of the term for the Great War 'when all that is meant is something like a "bloody big war"'. Wilson goes too far but, in part, the more justifiable caution was owing to Marwick's interpretation of the Great War as an event marking a significant discontinuity with the past. As remarked in Chapter 1, historians increasingly emphasise continuity rather than change. Moreover, 'total war' is a relative concept since, as an absolute akin to Clausewitz's concept of absolute war, it was unrealisable in the Great War and for much of the Second World War through the lack of instantaneously destructible weapons. In any case, no state has yet been able to subordinate all civilian needs totally to those of the military. Wartime mobilisation, like 'universal conscription', is always necessarily partial.[2]

Marwick himself further clarified his ideas in the 1980s and 1990s, the four-tier model being recast as four 'dimensions' and social change being more explicitly characterised as including changes in social geography, economics, technology, social structure, social cohesion, social welfare, social policy, material conditions, customs, behaviour, artistic, intellectual and cultural ideas and practices, family relationships and the role and status of women, and social and political values. Moreover, Marwick more closely defined participation, in an echo of Andrzejewski, as involving that of hitherto 'under-privileged' social groups. At the same time, Marwick made more explicit his view that servicemen under discipline are far less likely to benefit from military participation in war than those on the home front, who enjoy greater opportunities from civil participation in the war effort.[3]

As Marwick has stated, longer-term evolutionary, ideological and structural trends need to be borne in mind in assessing the degree to which war either accelerated or, conceivably, hindered changes that would have occurred anyway in the course of time. Some social and other trends can be measured, since modern states have increasingly collected statistical information, albeit that aggregate measurements have their own limitations. The calculation of change in perceptions and values, however, is even more problematical. The most dramatic long-term change will be more likely apparent in states that are defeated, occupied or newly created as a result of war. Moreover, through accidents of location, some states are likely to suffer far more disruption than others, in terms not only of loss of population, but also of the very economic structure of the state.

Thus, Serbia, Belgium and Poland were arguably the states worst affected in the Great War in terms of material damage. Belgium is said to have lost over 100,000 houses (about 6 per cent) with 240,000 acres of agricultural land rendered unfit for cultivation through shelling. Indeed, an area 600 kilometres long and between 10 and 20 kilometres wide, including 3 major towns and over 60 villages, had been totally flattened in addition to the coastal area inundated in 1914. Similarly, in north-east France, communities and even the very terrain in which they were situated had been erased. In the *département* of the Meuse, for example, 334 out of 586 communes had been seriously if not totally devastated. In the single canton of Charny near Verdun, 9 villages with a pre-war population of 2,569 had completely disappeared by 1918. As late as 1982, only 5 of the villages were reinhabited with a combined population of just 63 people, 48 of whom lived in one village.

Over 90 per cent of Poland had been fought over, beginning with the Russian depradations in Galicia, as well as east Prussia, in August and September 1914. In all, during the war Poland saw an estimated 1.8 million buildings (10 per cent of national property) destroyed, 11 million acres rendered unfit for cultivation and 710,000 hectares of forest out of its pre-war total of 2.3 million hectares felled. A by-product of the latter was the extinction of the 400 or so remaining beasts of the once-extensive Lithuania bison herd. War damage in Serbia amounted to an estimated Ffr4.7 billion.[4]

States which emerge victorious have less inclination to change and are more likely to revert to pre-war practices. Nonetheless, in terms of the impact of the Great War upon states, in the short-term, all the major belligerents witnessed increasing state control and intervention. Clearly, Germany, Austria-Hungary and Russia were already autocratic states to greater or lesser extents, but the war had a similar impact upon mature liberal democracies such as Britain, France and the United States. Moreover, precedents had been established and many features of the wartime state between 1914 and 1918 would be reproduced in the response by governments to economic depression in the 1920s and 1930s, as well as during the Second World War.

The growth of government

The first indication of the enhancement of state power was the spate of emergency legislation enacted or revived across Europe in 1914 such as the Prussian Law of Siege of 1851, which provided for the suspension of all those sections of the German constitution guaranteeing civil liberties. Indeed, until December 1916 the Deputy Commanding Generals had the power to imprison individuals without trial and to expel individuals from their districts. Moreover, under the *Burgfrieden* (fortress truce), both employers and unions in Germany agreed to suspend industrial disputes for the duration of the war, while the Reichstag also passed enabling legislation to allow the government to pass those laws deemed necessary without parliamentary consent. The Reichstag surrendered its legislative functions to the upper house or Bundesrat.

Similar siege laws dating from 1849 and 1878 were revived in France on 2 August 1914, with both Chamber of Deputies and Senate adjourning indefinitely, although parliamentary scrutiny was resumed in December 1914. In Austria, parliament – the Reichsrat – had been prorogued in March 1914 owing to obstructionist tactics by Czech deputies and it was not recalled until May 1917. The Hungarian parliament sat throughout the war, albeit postponing the elections due in 1915 for the duration. Two imperial decrees based on a law of 1869 also suspended civil rights and handed much of civil jurisdiction to a new Kriegsüberwachungsamt (War Supervisory Office). While not applying to Hungary, the emergency regulations continued in operation in Austria until July 1917. In Italy, where support for the war was slight, the conservative instincts of Salandra and Sonnino made the Italian response to war more akin to that of the Central Powers than the Entente. A series of decrees in May 1915 severely limited civil liberties. Their scope was progressively widened, especially after Caporetto in October 1917.

In Britain, the Defence of the Realm Act (DORA), which became law on 8 August 1914, gave government sweeping powers. Its provisions were extended on 18 August and 27 November 1914 and again in both 1915 and 1916. An effective electoral truce was also declared, with any subsequent vacancies in parliamentary seats to be filled by the sitting party in the constituency without by-election. A general election should have occurred by 1915, but the life of the existing parliament was extended twice in 1915 and again in August 1916. The House of Commons gave up its right to scrutinise naval and military estimates and Asquith made no statement on the progress of the war in the House until March 1915. Contentious legislation on Irish Home Rule and Welsh disestablishment was placed on the statute book in 1914, but immediately suspended for the duration.

Similarly, Australia passed the War Precautions Act in August 1914, enabling the introduction of censorship, the curtailment of civil liberties, and the control of aliens, which included the effective removal of the protection even from naturalised Australians. Subsequently, the Unlawful Associations Act of December 1916 enabled the Australian prime minister Hughes to move against groups regarded as subversive, such as Australian members of the American syndicalist movement, the Industrial Workers of the World, popularly known as the Wobblies. In the course of the suppression of the Wobblies, British, Irish and American agitators were deported.

In many respects, the emergency legislation enacted in the United States, such as the Espionage Act of June 1917 and the Sedition Act of May 1918, was even more sweeping in its scope. The former, for example, authorised the Postmaster-General, Albert S. Burleson, to prevent the circulation of mail by suspect groups such as organised labour, political parties and ethnic organisations. There were over 2,200 wartime prosecutions under the American emergency legislation, of which 1,055 resulted in convictions.[5]

In most belligerent states, railways were swiftly taken under state control in August 1914. In Britain this did not mean nationalisation *per se* since the individual rail companies were guaranteed the same level of profits they had enjoyed in 1913 and the rail system was pointedly administered not by the government but for the government. Indeed, since control was initially intended to last for just one week, this necessitated renewal of the requisition measure every seven days for the duration. Control of railways was followed in Britain and France by that of the mines and shipyards. Precisely the same pattern occurred in the United States in 1917, where the railways came under the direction of the Secretary of the Treasury, William McAdoo, in December 1917. Of course, the assumption in 1914 was that intervention would not be necessary for long. It should be noted, moreover, that the progressive extension of state intervention was largely in response to circumstances rather than as a result of any coherent plan. Indeed, DORA regulations were so carelessly defined that the British government's lawyers had myriad difficulties, especially in terms of compensation claims made in respect of requisitions.[6]

State intervention was most marked by the appearance of new government ministries, departments and agencies. More often than not, these appeared in the key areas such as food, manpower policy and munitions as a result of the incapacity of existing organisations in both public and private sectors to meet new demands. In Britain, Lloyd George pressed for the passing of a Defence of the Realm (Amendment No. 2) Act in March 1915, which gave government powers over engineering, as a first step in placing the country on a total war footing: firms could now be forced to take government work if they had the plant to do so. The shell shortage then enabled Lloyd George to wrest control of munitions from the War Office, the Ministry of Munitions appearing in May 1915 with its own sweeping powers under the Munitions of War Act to control all armaments factories as felt necessary.

Under Lloyd George, the Ministry of Munitions developed a highly innovative approach in such areas as managerial organisation, cost accounting, welfare provision for labour, electrification and automation. The ministry commandeered raw materials, centralised foreign purchases and dealt in the import market. There were eventually over 25,000 employees in 50 departments and, by 1918, the ministry directly managed 250 government factories and supervised another 20,000 'controlled' establishments.[7]

New committees also proliferated and, after Lloyd George became prime minister, new ministries of Labour, Shipping, and Food were created together with a Department of National Service. In all, the number of national government employees in Britain almost doubled between 1911 and 1921 and the number of local government employees increased by one-third. It should not be assumed, however, either that intervention had not occurred in these areas already, or that expansion automatically improved government administration. The Ministry of Shipping, for example, was merely an extension of a web of shipping controls established in 1915 and 1916, while the Ministry of Munitions was a merger between the existing War Office Armament Output Committee and the Treasury Munitions of War Committee.[8]

The most marked change after December 1916 was Lloyd George's determination to strengthen central control over departments. Interestingly, however, the Treasury lost much of its former centralising influence. One reason was simply the exigencies of war: Lloyd George, while still Chancellor, told the War Office in October 1914 that it did not need to seek Treasury approval for war purchases. A second reason was that many of the new ministries were never subjected to Treasury control, the legislation establishing them giving them control over their own staffs.[9]

The same kind of transformation occurred elsewhere. In the United States, little had been done prior to April 1917 to intervene in the economy. Many elements within Wilson's Democratic Party instinctively distrusted federal power. Coming on top of orders already placed by the Entente, the sudden demands by the War Department plunged American industry into chaos. In response, a variety of new agencies emerged, but the administration preferred incentive to outright control, with the result that industrial mobilisation was by no means centralised. The pre-war 'preparedness' movement had thrown up a Council of National Defense and a Civilian Advisory Commission in August 1916, intended to prepare for integration of government and business in the event of American entry to the war. It provided some basis for the new agencies. In particular, the advisory commission suggested establishing the War Industries Board (WIB) in July 1917, as a means of bringing order to the government's purchasing system. From March 1918 the War Industries Board was headed by the Wall Street banker, Bernard Baruch.

Other wartime creations included the National War Labor Board under a former president, W. H. Taft; the War Labor Practices Board, War Finance Board, and the Food Administration, which was headed by Herbert Hoover, an engineer who had been leading the London-based Commission for the Relief of Belgium. As in Britain, new creations were not automatically successful, the Emergency Fleet Corporation achieving little before the war ended, while the Fuel Administrator, Harry Garfield, proved unequal to a fuel crisis in the winter of 1917–18. Indeed, Garfield's decision to shut all factories east of the Mississippi for four days in January 1918 prompted an attempt by congressional critics to vest war direction in a three-man war cabinet excluding Wilson. Wilson countered with legislation passed in May 1918 to authorise him to reorganise government agencies without consulting Congress.[10]

With no political party having any particular ideological commitment to intervention, there was little state involvement in French industry prior to 1914. The initial tendency was to allow existing industrial organisations such as the ironmasters' trade association, the Comité des Forges, virtually a free hand in war production. Indeed, the association secured the monopoly over iron and steel imports in May 1916 and became sole distributor of French production of crude iron and steel in July 1918. An autonomous Ministry of Armament and War Production was created in December 1916 under the direction of Albert Thomas, a socialist deputy who had originally been appointed Under-Secretary of War for Artillery and Munitions within the War Ministry in May 1915. Thomas had some power over the munitions industry in the sense that the state was its only customer but, unlike the situation in Britain, firms retained the right to refuse government contracts. By November 1915, contracts were being more carefully scrutinised and more financial controls introduced. Nonetheless, escalating military demands ensured that industrialists, acting through *groupes de fabrication* (production cartels), largely maintained the prices they had fixed in 1914.

While Thomas was responsible for military production, co-ordination of non-military production was assumed by the Ministry of Commerce and Industry, headed, after October 1915, by Etienne Clémentel. A more radical socialist than Thomas, Clémentel had a clearer vision of what might be termed state capitalism. What enabled Clémentel to begin to realise some of his aims was British pressure on the French to reduce wastage of resources, Britain having economic leverage through its control of credit and shipping. Thus, Clémentel established an Exemptions Committee to resolve what products were essential, marginal or dispensable. The so-called consortium system to allocate resources to industry followed in October 1917. With Clemenceau's revival of centralised executive authority after November 1917, Clémentel and Louis Loucheur, who had replaced Thomas in September 1917, were able to increase the pace of state intervention in industry. Clémentel's wider vision, however, was still not realised by the time the war ended.[11]

To an even greater extent than in France, industrial mobilisation in Italy was left in the hands of the private sector. The resulting lack of overall government control enabled industry to pass on its costs to the state with long-term disadvantages in terms of inflation. Even in Italy, however, the number of government ministries increased from 12 to 22 during the course of the war. In terms of state supervision, General Alfredo Dallolio, appointed as Under-Secretary for Arms and Munitions in June 1915, created Mobilitazione Industriale (MI; Industrial Mobilisation) three months later to oversee war production. The use of the army as an instrument of state intervention signified that the military represented one of the stronger components of the Italian state. Typically, however, while MI controlled overall economic planning, industrialists ran MI's important regional committees, although these were staffed by the War Ministry and chaired by servicemen. In June 1917, Dallolio became first head of a new Ministry of Arms and Munitions.[12]

Germany faced crippling deficiencies of such vital raw materials as cotton, oil, hemp, manganese, copper, rubber and phosphates. Little had been done to address such deficiencies since both public and private sectors in Germany were largely indifferent to economic planning for war. Some raw materials could be provided by the manufacture of artificial substitutes, but others could not. It was the attempt to ease the intense competition for dwindling supplies between army, the Ministry of Interior, the Deputy Commanding Generals and heavy industry, therefore, that led to the early creation of the Kriegsrohstoffabteilung (KRA; Raw Materials Section) on 13 August 1914. Later in 1914, a Central Purchasing Commission was also established to handle neutral trade and prevent industry competing in neutral markets.[13]

The constituent states of Imperial Germany enjoyed considerable autonomy and the federal structure was a significant weakness in terms of co-ordination, while the administration of the Deputy Commanding Generals was based upon military districts that bore no relation either to geography or to existing regional and state boundaries. One illustration of the haphazard evolution of management is in food supply. While the Ministry of the Interior rejected the idea advanced by Hugenberg and another leading industrialist, Hugo Stinnes, to reduce demand by forcing up the price of wheat, the Ministry of Finance accepted it, establishing the War Wheat Corporation in November 1914 to try to stabilise food stocks. Subsequently, the splendidly named Imperial Potato Office was created in October 1915 to attempt similar stabilisation of another staple. It failed manifestly to persuade either Bavaria or the Deputy Commanding Generals to yield food stocks to the centre. As a result, the Kriegsernährungsamt (KEA; War Food Office) emerged in May 1916, led by Wilhelm Groener, former head of the field railways section of the German General Staff, and Adolf Freiherr von

Batocki-Friebe. The KEA marked the army's intervention into food policy, although Groener was the only soldier in it. Unfortunately, however, the KEA did not have the authority to compel other agencies to do its bidding and food agencies continued to proliferate.

Military intervention in manpower policy was characterised by new creations such as the Abteilung für Zurückstellungswesen (AZS; Exports and Exemptions Section) stabilised under Richard Sichler in 1915 and in munitions procurement by the Waffen und Munitionsbeschaffungsamt (WUMBA; Weapons and Munitions Procurement Office), established by the Prussian War Minister, General Adolf Wild von Hohenborn, in September 1916. WUMBA was partly intended to strengthen Wild's position in the light of OHL's intervention in the economy under Hindenburg and Ludendorff. The latter reached its apogee in the creation of the Kriegsamt under Groener on 1 November 1916. This incorporated all existing agencies such as the KRA, KEA, AZS and WUMBA and also subordinated the Deputy Commanding Generals. Technically, the Kriegsamt was placed under the authority of the Prussian War Ministry, but Groener simultaneously became Deputy War Minister and Wild was replaced by the more compliant General Hermann von Stein. As needs dictated, further new agencies were formed within the Kriegsamt such as the Ständige Ausschuss für Zusammenlegungen (SAZ; Standing Committee on Consolidations) to advise on factory closures in December 1916.

In practice, internal co-ordination of the various agencies remained weak. After Groener's dismissal in August 1917, power reverted to the Prussian War Ministry and a new Reichswirtschaftsamt (RWA; Imperial Economic Office) was created, assuming some Kriegsamt functions such as those of SAZ.[14]

In Austria-Hungary, there was little initial interference in civilian control of industry, although a law dating from 1912 gave the state the ability to requisition industry and labour. As a result, a series of 91 ad hoc agencies or *zentralen* were established with general oversight of production. Some were only belatedly created such as the Kriegsgetreideverkehrsanstalt (Agency for Wartime Grain Traffic) in early 1916. In Austria in March 1917 the Trade Ministry's General Commissariat for the War Economy and a new interdepartmental War and Transitional Economy Commission were joined in administering the war economy by supervisory trade councils from the private sector. In Hungary, some 263 firms had been placed under martial law by October 1915, principally mines, railways, flour mills and food processing companies. By 1918, however, the number of firms under military supervision had increased to over 900, employing 500,000 workers.[15]

Generally, in response to greater state intervention in the economy, there was a movement of businessmen into government. In Britain, Kitchener appointed a number of businessmen to the War Office Ordnance Department, one of whom was George Booth. Lloyd George continued the process at the Ministry of Munitions, making over ninety appointments from among the 'men of push and go' and extended it when he became prime minister. Indeed, Lloyd George especially sought 'leading hustlers' who had proved capable of improvisation. Thus, the shipowner Sir Joseph Maclay became Minster of Shipping; the coal owner Lord Rhondda succeeded Devonport, himself owner of a retail grocery chain, as Minister of Food, and a railway executive, Sir Eric Geddes, previously in the Ministry of Munitions, became successively Director-General of Transportation in the British Expeditionary Force, Controller of the Navy and, in July 1917, First Lord of the Admiralty. Not least of Geddes's achievements was to reorganise the logistic infrastructure of the British Expeditionary Force in such a way as to render it capable of sustaining successive offensives in 1917 and to meet the challenges of the return to mobile warfare in 1918. His brother, Auckland, became Minister of National Service. Not all businessmen were necessarily efficient administrators and there was certainly resentment from Whitehall insiders of businessmen, in the words of Keith Grieves, 'working as unpaid organisers beyond existing hierarchical forms of control'.

In turn, however, business came to question the degree to which government appeared to bow to labour demands. The war therefore marked the beginning of a more confrontational approach to labour on the part of business, as characterised by the breakdown of the National Industrial Conference called by Lloyd George in February 1919. In a sense, business also lost its belief in the ability of government to bring about constructive change in industrial relations.[16]

Prior to the war, the Wilson administration in the United States had proved generally favourable towards big business. In some respects, creation of the War Industries Board was intended to deflect criticism that co-operation with government was enabling business to evade anti-trust legislation. Business generally was induced to co-operate with the administration by incentives such as service on wartime regulatory agencies, which enabled businessmen to gain information on commercial rivals, and to influence policy. Indeed, the 'dollar a year' men, who entered government on a token salary, were not always impartial in the allocation of contracts, resulting in a draft bill in 1918 to replace them with full-time civil servants, although it never reached the statute book. Generally, government guaranteed wartime prices in the belief that this maximised production, and 'new capitalists' emerged who saw the benefit of entering partnership with the state.[17]

Canadian manufacturers similarly served on a Shell Committee, established in 1914 to handle War Office orders from Britain. Production delays, however, resulted in the Ministry of Munitions setting up an Imperial Munitions Board as its Canadian agent in November 1915. The Board was led by a financier and meat packer, Joseph Wesley Flavelle, who largely kept the Canadian government, and some of the more venal politicians seeking contracts for associates, at arm's length. Only two national factories were established, Flavelle relying largely on private contractors to fulfil orders.[18]

In Germany, the industrialist Walther Rathenau of AEG, inspired the creation of the Raw Materials Section (KRA). He was joined in it by another AEG executive, Wichard von Moellendorf. A Jewish businessman, Rathenau faced many difficulties and his attempt to fix prices was resisted strongly by the Ministry of the Interior, the Deputy Commanding Generals, other industrialists, and the authorities in states such as Bavaria. Nonetheless, the KRA was successful in developing various alternatives, such as synthetic fixation of nitrogen – invented by Fritz Haber – and extraction of oil lubricants from coal tar. Rathenau's agency also combed Germany for recoverable materials and secured raw materials from neutrals, operating through 25 'corporations' or cartels established for each commodity and organised as joint stock companies. Through such means, Germany did not suffer a serious shell shortage.

Rathenau resigned in April 1915 but Richard Merton was another industrialist who became involved in government, joining the Kriegsamt as Chief Social Adviser. As a light industrialist from an aluminium concern, however, Merton fell foul of heavy industrialists. The heavy industrialists themselves had an increasing influence over OHL while the KRA's big industrial cartels in essence regulated their own prices, awarding contracts to themselves, supplying raw materials to favoured customers at below cost prices, and overcharging the government for their products. Profits were certainly made – those of munitions companies quadrupled between 1913 and 1916 – but these were eroded by inflation and, overall, were relatively modest. Nonetheless, as Gerald Feldman has commented, German industrialists were largely characterised by the 'desire to keep their stock of skilled workers, maximise their profits, and maintain their social power'.[19]

There was no real partnership between government and business in France although Clemenceau introduced businessmen as well as technicians into his administration: Loucheur had also been a successful entrepreneur before joining Thomas's ministry in December 1916. Bureaucrats were ill equipped to negotiate with industrialists and some consortia successfully manipulated the system to their commercial advantage, while the members of the Comité des Forges used its influential position to undermine commercial competition from independent metallurgists. Generally, too, French industry benefited from state investment in new plant. A tax on war profits was introduced in February 1917, but it applied only to a small proportion of actual profits. Citroën, for example, became the largest private shell producer, making a profit of Ffr6.1 million between 1914 and 1917, and paying just Ffr60,000 in profit taxation.

Enforcement of anti-trust legislation also lapsed. The French state did attempt to dictate production conditions on occasions, but the attempt to create a national arsenal at Roanne near Lyon was strongly opposed by industrialists. Indeed, it became a noted scandal, the Ffr203 million spent on it by September 1918 resulting in production worth only Ffr15 million.[20]

Whatever the precise new structures established within belligerent states, most faced similar challenges in terms of the management of the war economy, particularly the need to organise industrial mobilisation and to maintain food supply. In turn, a greater role in such areas drew states into increased intervention in further areas such as industrial relations and welfare provison, especially as it became increasingly necessary to sustain the national will and morale of the population in order for the state to survive at all.

Economic management

Financial policy proved a particular problem for the belligerents when the costs of war escalated alarmingly, the initial assumption being that war costs could be recouped through post-war reparations. One estimate is that the war cost the Entente powers US$147 billion and the Central Powers US$61.5 billion in terms of increased public expenditure. Figures vary, but total war expenditure for Britain may have been US$43.8 billion; US$13.4 billion for Austria-Hungary; US$14.7 billion for Italy; US$28.2 billion for France; and US$47 billion for Germany. Just eighteen months' involvement may have cost the United States US$36.2 billion.[21]

Even in peacetime, only a portion of public expenditure could realistically be covered by taxation revenue, whether direct or indirect, with the remainder coming from government borrowing. The balance between direct and indirect taxation varied. Britain had a well established progressive income tax system, so that direct taxation accounted for 39 per cent of government revenue in 1913. By contrast, the German and Austro-Hungarian central governments were dependent upon indirect taxation within a federalised fiscal system. The balance between direct and indirect taxation changed in Britain with direct taxation accounting for 79.5 per cent of tax revenues by 1918–19. The standard rate of British income tax was increased from 1s.2d in the pound to 3s.6d in September 1915 and to 6s.0d in the pound in April 1918. In Germany it was only in 1916 that a new federal tax was introduced to help pay for the war in the form of an indirect value added tax upon war profits. Meanwhile, indirect taxation revenue declined, through the absence of imported goods on which to levy duties, and falling levels of consumption through scarcity of other goods subject to taxation such as alcohol.

Peacetime patterns were largely maintained, however, in the sense that Britain raised only between 23 and 26 per cent of wartime public expenditure from taxation, Italy some 23 per cent, France about 24 per cent and Germany between 16 and 18 per cent. Printing more money and borrowing, therefore, remained the principal means of war finance. This was achieved through selling war bonds at home and, if possible, overseas. Germany floated nine successive war loans, France four, Britain three, and the United States five. Considerable efforts were put into selling war bonds, which were not always successful. The fourth German loan in March 1916 attracted 5.2 million savers, but the fifth in September 1916 attracted only 3.8 million and the ninth was undersubscribed by 39 per cent. By contrast, Britain raised over £1 billion in war bonds between October 1917 and September 1918, a spectacular 'ruined village' erected in Trafalgar Square helping to draw in £29 million from Londoners in just eight days in October 1918. It is estimated that 100,000 people still hold war loan stock in Britain since, although it was devalued in 1932, it has no maturity date and pays a fixed interest rate.

The level of national debt increased in all belligerents between 1914 and 1919: France by a factor of five, Germany by a factor of eight and Britain by a factor of eleven (from £650 million to £7.4 billion). Indeed, in the event of victory, both Germany and Austria-Hungary needed to impose reparations on their opponents in order to clear war debts. In the case of Britain, by 1918, the national debt was increasing every four months by more than the total debt incurred during the entire period of British participation in the French Revolutionary and Napoleonic Wars between 1792 and 1815. Since interest rates had been increased to attract investment, the war also left Britain with a far larger burden of debt service than before the war. Seen in terms of the level of debt prior to the war, however, while historians have often characterised the German reliance upon war loans rather than taxation as damagingly inflationary, Niall Ferguson has pointed out that the real increase in the British national debt was twice that of Germany. Indeed, he has argued that, if war expenditure is directly related to casualties, it cost the Entente over three times as much to kill an individual Central Powers serviceman than vice versa.[22]

Inflationary pressures were considerable for all belligerents, the rise in the circulation of paper currency between 1913 and 1918 being 504 per cent in Italy; 532 per cent in France; 1,141 per cent in Germany; and 1,154 per cent in Britain, where the one pound note or 'Bradbury' (named after the Bank of England official who signed them) and the ten shilling note made their first appearance. Total money supply in the United States increased by about 75 per cent between 1916 and 1920. Since more paper money did not mean more goods to purchase, despite varying degrees of control, prices in most states at least doubled.

Some care needs to be exercised with regard to price and cost of living indices, particularly when based on a notional basket of consumables. Items priced might vary in quantity and quality over time, not least through wartime substitution, and official statistics might distort the reality. Moreover, different social groups might have different concepts of their basic requirements and different minimum forms of expenditure. At best, therefore, indices demonstrate general trends. The Board of Trade's overall cost of living index for the British working class rose from its theoretical base 100 in July 1914 to 145 by July 1916, the food index rising in the same period from 100 to 161. In France, the food price index at base 100 in 1914 rose to 174 by 1917, and in Italy to 184. In the United States, speculative demand pushed up the price index 14 points between March and April 1917 alone. In Germany prices trebled, but, in Belgium and Austria-Hungary, prices increased by over 1,000 per cent. Further afield, Australian wholesale prices rose by 166 per cent between 1914 and 1918, retail prices by 87.1 per cent and the cost of living by 53 per cent.[23]

As might be expected, the volume of export trade declined for most belligerents and imports increased, resulting in greater balance of trade deficits, which, in the case of the Entente, largely meant with the United States. In peacetime, trade deficits might be partially covered by invisible earnings from overseas investment and shipping hire, but these were also likely to be much reduced in wartime.

Inevitably, in the longer term, the trading position of the Central Powers declined compared with that of the Entente, as a result of the economic blockade. German trade with neutrals continued, but at least 60 per cent of Germany's overseas investments were confiscated by her enemies and the value of her foreign trade declined from US$5.9 billion in 1913 to just US$800 million by 1917. In the event, however, some compensation derived from contributions imposed on occupied Belgium and from the price controls imposed in Germany, which enabled wartime wages to be kept down. In 1918, therefore, Germany still had £112 million worth of gold, which was used after the armistice to purchase food supplies.[24]

War and industrial mobilisation

One measure of the transition to modern, industrialised 'total' war was that it became as important to out-produce as to out-fight an opponent. In this respect, the Entente had a built-in advantage in terms of its overwhelming superiority in industrial and manufacturing capacity. Britain's intervention alone doubled the Entente's percentage of total industrial potential over that of the Central Powers and, if Russia's resources were lost in 1917, the addition of those of the United States more than restored the advantage. Thus, based on 1913 figures, whereas Germany and Austria-Hungary possessed only 68 per cent of the industrial potential of Britain, France and Russia combined, they possessed only 37 per cent of that of Britain, France and the United States combined.[25] This did not make the war any shorter, since the Central Powers' possession of interior lines, initial relative self-sufficiency, and early military successes, facilitating a degree of economic exploitation of occupied territories, compensated for overall material weakness. In the longer term, however, greater resources would tell as all belligerents endeavoured to increase the degree of economic mobilisation.

Generally, production levels across Europe fell through economic dislocation, resulting from trade disruption, shortages of raw materials, manpower problems, and, for some, occupation. British production fell by about 10 per cent between 1914 and 1917 and German production by some 25 per cent. The effects varied from industry to industry so that, while British coal production declined by 20 per cent between 1913 and 1918, steel production rose by 25 per cent. In the case of the Scottish jute industry based on Dundee, wartime demand for sandbags and the need for sacks for food distribution resulted in large profits, which more than compensated for lost export markets. After the war, however, prices collapsed and the removal of restrictions on transporting Indian jute production brought renewed competition.

Inevitably, the concentration on war production involved a reduction in consumer production. Thus, in Germany, while there was a growth rate of 170 per cent over a four-year period in the chemical industry and 49 per cent in mechanical engineering and electrical industries, there was a 59 per cent decline in building construction and 58 per cent in textiles. In Britain at least, this process did not result in any great degree of privation, since less essential trades were curtailed first and the pressure of demand in a situation of labour shortage stimulated greater efficiency in consumer production. Nonetheless, the drift of labour to war production generally altered regional employment patterns: Saxony, for example, lost an estimated 10 per cent of its population as a result of labour migration between 1910 and 1917. Wars also naturally tended to strengthen larger production units at the expense of smaller ones.[26]

One crucial sector was that of munitions. As it happened, however, most states' armaments industries had been generally more sophisticated and innovative than other sectors of industry prior to the war. Thus, although

Britain faced a shell shortage, shortfalls were the product of the extra-ordinary additional orders placed with private firms by government in 1914 without regard for capacity, rather than of unrealistic expectations on the part of industry itself. Indeed, by 1916, the Ministry of Munitions could produce in just three weeks what had been a year's production of eighteen-pounder shells in 1914; a year's pre-war production of medium shells took eleven days and a year's pre-war production of heavy shells just four days.[27]

The increase in French industrial capacity was even more remarkable given the loss of so much to the Germans in 1914. Moreover, initial mobil-isation had also closed down 52 per cent of France's industrial plants: by the end of August 1914 only just over one-third of skilled men remained outside the army. The fact that much of the armaments industry had to be improvised from scratch assisted in the introduction of large assembly lines and a more flexible labour force.

It has been claimed, indeed, that France produced more weapons and munitions during the war than Britain and was far more of an 'arsenal of democracy' than the United States. French coal production had recovered to 71 per cent and steel production to 42 per cent of pre-war levels by 1917. The French also produced twice as many aero engines as either Britain or Germany put together and more aircraft. French industrial recovery, how-ever, was largely predicated on British and American capital loans and imports of coal, coke, pig-iron, steel and machine tools using British ships.[28]

Even Italian industry, beset by crippling shortages of raw materials and lack of manufacturing capacity, responded sufficiently to raise war produc-tion by the end of 1916. Indeed, in the process, the stimulus given to the iron and steel industry by the war began the conversion of Italy from an agrarian to a genuinely industrial economy.[29]

Germany faced considerable industrial difficulties and, when Hindenburg and Ludendorff assumed power, they faced a serious munitions crisis, caused in no small way by the insistence of heavy industry on continuing to export steel through Switzerland. The heavy industrialists insisted that if exports were to be restricted then there must be a large-scale armaments pro-gramme to compensate for lost profits, hence the Hindenburg Programme of 31 August 1916 intended to increase artillery and machine guns by one-third and to double ammunition and mortar production. Aircraft produc-tion, which had already been substantially increased, was to be expanded yet further to 1,000 aeroplanes a month. This target was then subsequently doubled by adoption of the Amerikaprogramme (America Programme) in June 1917, which was intended to prepare for competition with United States aircraft production.

The Hindenburg Programme's principal architect was Colonel Max Bauer, the artillery expert in OHL. Unfortunately, no one had satisfactorily worked out whether such a programme was feasible. Moreover, it was constructed on the assumption that munitions production could be increased without reference to the economy as a whole. The programme required massive investment in infrastructure, and a large increase in industrial manpower and working hours, which would be difficult to achieve. Moreover, the production quotas were set entirely arbitrarily according to a military timetable.

The result was that production fell rapidly, particularly when major shortages were experienced in coal production over the winter of 1916–1917. Difficulties were compounded by an escalating transport crisis on the railways and freezing of waterways. Steel production in February 1917 was less than that in August 1916 and 252,000 tons short of the target set by the programme. The goal of 1,000 aircraft a month was attained by June 1917, but the America Programme targets were well beyond the capacity of the German air industry. As a result, the maximum monthly production attained was 1,600 aeroplanes in July 1918. By March 1918, German production levels were only 57 per cent of those achieved in 1913, although it again needs to be stressed that German forces were never seriously affected by shortages of war material. Indeed, Germany produced more ammunition in 1918 than at any time during the Second World War.[30]

Austria-Hungary had only limited industrial capacity in 1914 and confronted shortages of raw materials of all kinds. Recourse was had to such expedients as reopening abandoned mines, and melting down church bells and pots and pans. These measures, and drawing emergency supplies from Germany, could never alleviate the shortages. Moreover, a lack of manpower planning had denuded the industrial labour force and closed factories: over 24,000 enterprises shut down either from lack of military contracts or from restricted sales. As a result, while the number of firms involved in war production increased steadily, Austro-Hungarian industry never produced more than limited numbers of trench mortars, flame-throwers and light machine guns. Austria-Hungary was also short of rail transport with which to carry war production or, indeed, anything else. The situation was exacerbated by coal shortages, which further reduced not only production of engines and rolling stock, but the ability to keep the rail system running.

Bulgaria and Turkey had no domestic armaments industries and were dependent upon German supplies. What industry there was in Bulgaria, however, was largely militarised, the number of enterprises taken over by the state increasing from 92 in July 1916 to 141 by the end of 1917. As elsewhere, there had been little thought of long-term war planning and many of the larger commercial enterprises had been forced to close through mobilisation of the labour force. By the end of 1917, however, Bulgarian industry had attained about 65 per cent of its pre-war production levels.[31]

Certain sectors of belligerents' economies were stimulated by the particular demands of modern war. In turn, pre-war trends could be further distorted by new demand, as in Britain, where coal, shipping and heavy industry, all previously in decline, were revitalised. However, the war also stimulated the growth of industries little established before the war. The loss of German imports of optical instruments, for example, seriously affected production of such vital equipment as range-finders, prompting the Ministry of Munitions to provide British firms with capital investment and scientific and technical assistance sufficient to boost production. The four tons of optical glass being produced each month by 1918 was equivalent to twice the world's peacetime consumption four years earlier. Not all state intervention, however, produced satisfactory results: government investment in British production of soluble cellulose acetate, the weatherproofing applied to the linen fabric used for aircraft skins, resulted in a financial scandal.[32]

The need to ensure war-related production inevitably gave government a greater role in determining manpower policies. The introduction of such policies was not always easy given the prevailing assumptions in 1914 that the war would be short, and the failure in consequence to control the movement of skilled manpower into the armed forces.

The net effect was to compel the search for alternative sources of labour such as the unskilled and women. The introduction of new sources of labour then raised the difficulties of dilution, whereby the restrictive practices of the pre-war skilled unions had to be tackled head on. The British government fought shy of compulsory labour direction, and a voluntary national registration programme was introduced in June 1915. The National Service Scheme to release young and fit men from industry, by providing substitutes from non-essential work, was again voluntary when introduced in February 1917. Some 206,000 men registered but, since most were engaged on essential work, only 388 were actually moved to new employment.

Only in December 1917 was a War Cabinet Committee on Manpower established. This finally effected a coherent manpower policy, subordinating military demands to an overall assessment of priorities: merchant-shipbuilding and the production of aircraft, tanks, iron ore, food and timber all took precedence over army manpower. Yet, it can be noted that even in June 1918, rather than impose labour conscription the government preferred to call skilled workers previously exempted from military service to register voluntarily as war munitions volunteers, albeit on pain of losing the exemption. The opposition was such that the scheme was abandoned.[33]

In France, as elsewhere, the growth of some sectors was achieved at the expense of others considered less significant to the war effort, such as textiles and construction. Thus, the labour force in war industries increased by 40 per cent, rising from 50,000 in 1914 to 1.7 million by September 1917, while that of non-war industries declined by 44 per cent. In Italy, those involved in war-related production grew from 20 per cent of the labour force in 1915 to 64 per cent by 1918.[34]

Manpower policy in Germany was initially characterised by the usual competition between industry, army and Deputy Commanding Generals. In pursuit of the production goals of the Hindenburg Programme, OHL then attempted to introduce total labour conscription. In the event, the *Hilfsdienstgesetz* (Auxiliary Service Law) of 5 December 1916, which was partly modelled on the British Munitions of War Act, conscripted males aged between 17 and 60 rather than those aged between 15 and 60 as originally contemplated. The price of getting the law through the Reichstag was some concession to organised labour, not least rights of assembly on the shopfloor, workers' councils for firms with over fifty employees, and the ability of workers to move freely for increased pay upon appeal. In February 1917, however, Groener issued a decree prohibiting workers in key industries from leaving on penalty of conscription and, in March, many exemptions were cancelled. The growing fuel crisis then forced the release of 40,000 miners from the army in May 1917 at a time when OHL was resistant to demands for more manpower to be returned to industry.[35]

Essential workers remained largely protected from conscription and the use of prisoners of war and foreign workers as well as women meant that, by 1918, the civilian labour force was only 7 per cent smaller than in 1914. Indeed, as part of the general exploitation of occupied territories, an estimated 87,000 Poles and Belgians had been engaged 'voluntarily' for labour in Germany by mid-1916. At the same time, all non-war production in French and Belgian industry under German occupation was halted and raw materials ruthlessly stripped for German consumption.

In October 1916, forced labour deportations began from Belgium, Hindenburg and Ludendorff having demanded that 200,000 workers be found. Ironically, so many were deported to Germany that they could not be adequately employed and, in any case, the physical condition of the Belgian population was such that little could be expected of them. Representations from the Netherlands resulted in the deportations being suspended in February 1917, by which time about 62,000 Belgians had been taken. Forced labour was also applied in occupied France, where men from labour camps were forced to help construct the Hindenburg Line over the winter of 1916–17.

By 1918, an estimated 700,000–800,000 Polish workers had also been deported to Germany, in addition to those forced into labour battalions in Poland itself. At least half of the 2.5 million prisoners of war held by the

Germans were also employed in some way. Foreign labour and prisoners were used not only in Germany itself, but also in the mines and industries which the Germans had occupied in France in 1914, although the amounts extracted and produced fell well short of pre-war levels.[36] In Austria-Hungary, manpower planning was equally haphazard, allowing industry to be denuded of key skilled workers in August 1914.[37]

Government's determining of manpower policies, in turn, led to its direct involvement in labour relations. War distorted the normal working of the labour market, in effect restructuring it in complex ways. The position of labour generally improved through the premium put on skilled manpower, and trade union membership rose in most belligerent states. At the same time and as a consequence of labour's increased bargaining position, after initial periods of industrial truce, industrial militancy grew. It did so to the extent that government in both Britain and the United States contemplated conscripting strikers, those groups being considered for this being Midlands engineering workers in Britain in July 1918 and machinists in Connecticut in October 1918.

In Britain, the first agreement on dilution – the Crayford Agreement – was directly negotiated in November 1914 between the Engineering Employers Federation and the unions. In March 1915, however, the government itself negotiated the Shells and Fuses Agreement. Subsequently, the Treasury Agreements were reached with 35 unions to prevent workers taking advantage of their strengthened position: the Agreements outlawed strikes, introduced more flexible working practices, permitted dilution on war work, and referred industrial disputes to official arbitration. Under the first Agreement, employers had promised not to use dilution as a means of reducing employment or wages after the war and, by the second, promised restraint of business profits.

These voluntary agreements were incorporated in the statutory provisions of the Munitions of War Act in June 1915, which also in effect tied workers to their place of employment, by preventing them from working for six weeks unless they first obtained a leaving certificate from an employer. While there was some suspicion that the legislation might be used to impose working conditions upon men, it provided for appeals to a munitions tribunal. Moreover, the Act also in effect nominated trade union leaderships as the means through which government would negotiate for dilution and changes in working practices. However, rising food prices, high rents, restricted labour mobility and wartime profiteering all contributed to growing discontent on the factory floor which could not be controlled by the union hierarchies.[38]

The increasing significance of shopfloor collective action organised by shop stewards was enhanced by the proliferation of government departments in the running of the economy, since there was little overall co-ordination and employers were generally encouraged to buy their way out of difficulties. The power of shop stewards was illustrated by the role of the Clyde Workers Committee (CWC) in orchestrating unrest in the Clyde shipyards and engineering works through the winter of 1915/16.[39]

Ultimately, the concession of rent controls eroded the pressures deriving from housing shortages in an area suffering from worker migration. It isolated the Clyde Workers Committee; enabling the government to break it in March 1916 by the arrest and deportation of ten of its leaders. The fact that the engineers as a whole were isolated within the labour movement by being widely perceived as an elite also enabled the government to act. By contrast, Lloyd George had readily conceded national pay bargaining to the leaders of the south Wales miners, who had gone on strike in July and August 1915. Like employers, unions increasingly viewed the intervention of the state in industrial relations as something to be avoided. Thus, in 1917, the proposals of the Whitley Committee, to establish widespread joint employer–labour consultative procedures, were ignored by both sides of industry.

The government's intention to impose dilution upon non-war production helped to provoke widespread unofficial strikes in April and May 1917, involving as many as 200,000 engineering workers and resulting in an estimated loss of 1.5 million working days. Once more, a union leadership was unable to control shop stewards, even after substantial concessions were made on the conscription of skilled men. Engineering workers were again on strike in April 1918 at the height of the German spring offensive. It was, however, the blunting of the offensive at a time when the leaving certificates – abolished in August 1917 – were reintroduced which brought renewed engineering strikes in Coventry and Birmingham in July 1918. The strike ended with the threat of the conscription, although there was also an enquiry, which once more abandoned leaving certificates.

Overall, Britain had by far the worst rate of militancy of any belligerent, with longer strikes and from an earlier date than elsewhere. Figures vary slightly, but one estimate is that there were 3,227 strikes in Britain between 1915 and 1918, involving 2.6 million strikers and costing the loss of 17.8 million working days. By comparison, France suffered 1,608 strikes, involving 520,000 strikers with the loss of 2.7 million working days, in the same period; and Italy suffered 1,801 industrial strikes, involving 575,000 strikers. Yet, there was far less industrial militancy in Britain than between 1910 and 1914: over 8,000 awards made by arbitration tribunals during the war were accepted without protest.[40]

Just as the industrial labour force in Britain experienced a degree of 'war collectivism' in terms of the intervention of the state in industrial relations, so too did the French labour movement. The latter, however, developed a more benevolent view of the role of the state in regulating employment and protecting the interests of the worker as a consumer since French industrialists had greater scope than their British counterparts in imposing wages and conditions. Indeed, pre-war legislation specifying a maximum ten hour day and one day off per week was suspended between August 1914 and July 1917. In the interests of maximum productivity, Thomas was resistant to controls on industry. He was also supportive, however, of increased application to French industry of the 'scientific management' and employer welfare paternalism associated with the American theorist Frederick Winslow Taylor.

Thomas established *commissions mixtes* of employer and labour representatives in April 1916 to advise on the wages and welfare of munitions workers and, in 1917, he encouraged the emergence of *délégués d'atelier* (shop stewards), limited to only a few firms before the war. Few industrialists welcomed the extension of such a system but Thomas wanted to draw the CGT (General Labour Confederation) into a more meaningful collaboration with the state in terms of munitions production.

Equally, as the labour force generally expanded so fewer workers were mobilised soldiers under military discipline and strikes in national defence industries were declared illegal in January 1917. At the same time, however, Thomas introduced compulsory arbitration, and minimum wages were attained in some areas with provision for regular mandatory wage rises. To some extent, concession to labour changed with Clemenceau's accession to the premiership. But, whatever the public rhetoric, in practice Clemenceau did not maintain quite such an uncompromising line towards labour in negotiation after the collapse of strikes in Paris and Lyon and in the Loire and the Cher between January and May 1918, to which the government responded with selective arrests and recall of mobilised strikers.[41]

In Italy, MI (Industrial Mobilisation) in effect brought the labour force under military supervision in 1915, its responsibilities eventually extending to over 1,900 firms employing 903,000 workers. About 40 per cent of the male labour force was formally militarised and required to wear uniform, though this varied from sector to sector. Under military control, strike action was forbidden and workers were unable to leave their place of employment for any reason although, paradoxically, there was an increase in labour mobility through assignment by state employment agencies. Existing labour contracts on conditions and wages were suspended for the duration, although arbitration was permitted through regional committees with appeals to the MI's Central Committee. Arbitration, however, did not apply to work organisation or to disciplinary matters, and all workers, including women and children, were subject to the military penal code. Even limited arbitration involving labour representatives represented a modernisation of Italian industrial relations, as did the enforced movement of labour from smaller to larger enterprises. Moreover, the very rigidity of MI, in maintaining that wages should not vary in response to the labour market, meant uniform rates for overtime and a set ten hour day, which undoubtedly benefited labour in smaller industries.

Industrialists were sufficiently critical of Dallolio's intervention to get him removed as head of MI in May 1918. At the same time, however, given the importance now attached by the state, as well as commentators like Antonio Gramsci and Mussolini, to the role of labour, workers themselves began to develop a new awareness. Consequently, the war established collective bargaining on a much wider scale.[42]

Across the Atlantic, the powerful American Federation of Labor (AFL) led by Samuel Gompers endorsed entry to the war in the expectation of making gains. American labour was able to do so through the government seeking to maximise uninterrupted war production by conceding high wages and improved working conditions. In effect, the National War Labor Board set both an unofficial minimum wage and an eight hour day. The pattern of labour relations was set almost at once through the construction of army camps in 1917. In order to obtain co-operation from employers and unions, the government indemnified contractors against rising labour costs while establishing a commission to arbitrate in labour disputes. Such labour commissions were then extended to other sectors, although arbitration was voluntary and depended upon economic incentive to the unions and indemnification of employers.

The federal government, however, refused to countenance the continuance of the closed shop. Concession to labour was also not intended to alter the normal peacetime relationship between capital and labour, and the government's response to strike action was ambivalent. The 4,450 disputes in 1917 was the highest total yet experienced in the United States. The copper mines in Montana and Arizona were especially badly hit, resulting in vigilante action by county authorities and employers. In the case of the timber industry in the Pacific North-west, the government itself broke up the Industrial Workers of the World movement ('Wobblies') in September 1917, sending troops to work in the industry and organising a new union under military supervision. Ultimately, too, in the autumn of 1918 the administration threatened to conscript striking machinists in Connecticut.[43]

Significantly, compared with other belligerents, trade union membership declined in Germany. Moreover, there were far fewer strikes than in Britain, totalling some 1,469 disputes between 1915 and 1918 involving 1.1 million strikers, and resulting in the loss of 3.5 million working days. Some 24.2 per cent of strikers were located in the Berlin region between 1915 and

1918, with 17.3 per cent in the Rhineland and 11.5 per cent in Westphalia. Nonetheless, industrial disputes rose sharply on pre-war levels and, confronting clothing and food shortages, the German union leadership was less willing to co-operate with government. However, union leaders were losing control of their members. Large-scale demonstrations resulted, such as that by 55,000 metalworkers in Berlin in June 1916 and that by over 300,000 workers in Berlin and Leipzig in April 1917.

Heavy industry, notably the Association of German Iron and Steel Industrialists, was intensely suspicious of Groener and, especially, Merton. Thus, a proposal by the latter in August 1917 for greater control of profits brought about the dismissal of both men, Groener being relegated to a divisional command. Yet, even Groener had been urging a crackdown on industrial militancy, especially, the newly formed Unabhängige Sozialdemokratische Partei Deutschlands (USPD; German Independent Social Democratic Party). Indeed, Groener famously branded strikers in April 1917 as *hundsfott* (curs).

In the light of the continuing disturbances, Chancellor Bethmann promised post-war reform of the Prussian franchise in February 1917. The Kaiser was also persuaded to make the same commitment in April, a suffrage bill being signed on 12 July 1917 following the Reichstag Peace Resolution. In the event, it failed to reach the final stage for approval until October 1918 as OHL delayed the legislation. Similarly, OHL reversed Groener's conciliatory policies towards labour after August 1917. Its attempt to strengthen the Auxiliary Service Law did not succeed, but strikes in January and February 1918 were ruthlessly suppressed by force. In March 1918, Ludendorff proposed reducing wages and, in June, Hindenburg demanded that all workers be placed under direct military supervision. Ultimately, the lack of real concession was not sufficient to win labour support. Ironically, once Imperial Germany had collapsed, industrialists and unions were able to reach the Stinnes–Legien agreement on 15 November 1918 to ensure an ordered transition to a peacetime economy through the establishment of a joint committee.[44]

Food supply

While labour disputes and strikes might take on an increasingly political hue as the war progressed, most were in essence about the relationship between wages and prices. Relatively little research has been undertaken into the movement of wartime public opinion, largely owing to the absence of reliable sources. In the case of France, however, information available for a number of regions suggests that there was comparatively little interest in events at the front. What mattered most were economic conditions, especially the price of food. In this respect, urban areas were more vulnerable than rural areas, especially through the migration of additional population attracted by wartime employment opportunities or, in the case of many French urban areas, refugees. Accordingly, prices were likely to increase at a greater rate in major urban centres than elsewhere.

Food shortages created increasing unrest, food riots occurring in Vienna as early as May 1915 and 'butter' riots in Berlin in October 1915. Bread cuts in April 1917 sparked the major strikes in Berlin and Leipzig and there were food riots again in July 1917. Widespread strikes in January 1918, involving at least 350,000 in Berlin alone, were again prompted by food shortages amid harsh winter weather. Over 600,000 strikers protested against the reduction of the flour ration in Austria in January 1918 and food shortages also contributed to a naval mutiny at the Austro-Hungarian naval base at Cattaro in February 1918.

Similarly, there were food demonstrations in France and riots in Italy in 1917. Some 10,000 came out on the streets of Paris in May 1917, rising to 100,000 workers on strike in the Paris region by June. At least 50 died in food riots in Turin in August 1917. Yet, while governments invariably recognised the importance of increasing industrial prediction, many neglected agricultural production to the detriment of the overall war effort.[45]

European agricultural production was badly affected by the war, especially in the east. The land was stripped not only of labour, but also of the horse, which provided the main source of power for most agricultural communities. The farm machinery that did exist often fell into disrepair through a lack of spare parts and available engineers, while blacksmiths were also often scarce. The supply of fertilisers and foodstuffs was equally curtailed. The result was that continental agricultural production fell by about one-third, representing a serious deficiency when it is considered that no food could be stored cheaply, or for long before it deteriorated. Indeed, while both Britain and Germany considered stockpiling or other measures to safeguard food supplies prior to the war, there was actually little that could be practicably achieved.[46]

Germany in theory produced almost 90 per cent of its own food requirements before the war, but home production of particular commodities was uneven and all depended upon imported fertiliser and fodder, and foreign seasonal labour. The Eltzbacher Commission concluded in December 1914 that 19 per cent of the calories consumed in Germany were imported, 27 per cent of the protein and 42 per cent of the fats. Imports were maintained for a time, but as the blockade tightened so supplies from the Netherlands and Denmark were reduced. Romania was another source until it joined the Entente but supplies were resumed once the country was overrun. In all, therefore, Romania provided about 1.8 million tons of food and fodder to Germany between 1914 and 1918. Even this, however, added only about 6 per cent annually to the declining German grain harvest.

One problem was that German agriculture was organised on too small a scale. The pre-war assumption was that rye and potatoes could substitute for wheat, while agricultural production could be maintained and yields even increased by reclamation of wasteland and the greater application of fertilisers. In the event, while potash as a fertiliser was abundant, the lack of nitrates proved crippling. The agricultural labour force also declined by about 60 per cent although foreign labour (particularly from Poland) and prisoners of war were pressed into service.

Acreage under crops declined by 15 per cent and, depending upon area, agricultural production fell by between 50 per cent and 70 per cent between 1913 and 1917. Moreover, there had been a considerable miscalculation of the need for fodder. Pig producers, for example, had relied upon imported Russian barley for fodder and, when this supply was cut off, resorted to using potatoes. The need to ensure a potato supply for human consumption therefore prompted a compulsory slaughter – the *schweinemord* – of 9 million pigs (35 per cent of the total) in January 1915, resulting in a short-term glut but a long-term increase in pork prices.

Official attempts to shift consumption by market pricing so that grain was more attractive than meat led to meat shortages and a flourishing black market in livestock. This brought requisition parties combing farms in 1917 and 1918, to the great resentment of the farming community. As prices were fixed by local authorities so merchants shifted supplies to where controls had not yet been applied, while farmers shifted production to commodities not yet controlled. As transportation problems also increased, so it became increasingly difficult to feed the growing urban population. The consequence was increasing tensions between urban and rural communities, and between producers and retailers on the one hand and consumers on the other. The failure to comprehend the delicate balance of the agricultural market was compounded by the Hindenburg Programme affording agriculture no priority at all.

As indicated earlier, the KEA (War Food Office) began to impose a more systematic rationing system, bread being the first commodity rationed in January 1915, followed by fats, milk, meat and butter. General rationing was introduced in 1916 while food was also increasingly reduced in quality such as *K-Brot* (short for *Kriegsbrot* or war bread) made with potato flour; egg substitute made from ground maize; and meat soup cubes made from flavoured brine. Over 11,000 different ersatz products were manufactured, including 837 different varieties of meatless sausage.

The winter of 1916–17, generally known as *Kohlrübenwinter* (turnip winter), since the potato crop fell victim to fungus disease, forced the establishment of new war economy bureaux in December 1916 and January 1917 to ensure procurement of men, horses, machinery and fertiliser. It had been hoped that the annexation of the Ukraine would ease bread supplies but the 1917 harvest was poor and the Ukrainians themselves proved uncooperative. Consequently, in June 1918 the bread ration was again reduced.[47]

Yet, while the German food supply clearly declined, the effect was variable depending upon the proximity of a given location to agricultural areas. It is often claimed that over 762,000 Germans died from malnutrition during the war, the majority in 1917–18, but there is little evidence to support this contention. Excluding the effects of the influenza pandemic, the excess of civilian deaths over the pre-war level was somewhere between 250,000 and 424,000. One careful contemporary wartime study of Leipzig suggested that the caloric content of the average diet in the city in 1917–18 remained comparable to peacetime nutrition levels, although it was deficient in protein and fat. Other studies suggest average calorie intake did not fall more than 5 per cent below the norm after the winter of 1917–18, although the wartime norm was below pre-war consumption levels and based upon reduced wartime body weights.

Despite the difficulties and the undoubted fact that they were often hungry, Germans did not starve. The overall effect on civilian mortality rates was a reversion to the level of 1901–05: as Avner Offer has remarked, 'the war at worst caused the loss of not much more than a decade of public health progress'. Similarly, though the Allied blockade continued after the armistice, conditions in Germany were no worse than during the war. In a sense, however, it was the psychological perception of starvation that made the greatest impact.[48]

Austria-Hungary appeared largely self-sufficient in food and made no preparations in advance of the war. Supply depended, however, upon Hungarian-grown agricultural produce, exchanged in peacetime for Austrian manufactured goods under protective tariffs excluding foreign competitors. Unfortunately, the 1914 and 1915 harvests were poor and, with the best Austrian agricultural areas in Russian-occupied Galicia, prices rose sharply.

Bread rationing was introduced in Austria in April 1915, followed by coffee, fats, milk and sugar. By 1916, even potatoes were in short supply, the harvest being less than half that of 1914, and the calculated deficit in bread grain by October 1916 was 10.5 million metric quintals. In Hungary, milk rationing was introduced in November 1915 and bread rationing in January 1916. As in Germany, all manner of substitutes were introduced while horses were slaughtered for meat. The Austrian government's intention to raise the maximum prices for bread and flour had to be abandoned in January 1916 in the face of public opposition, while rising prices caused rioting in Vienna in May and September 1916.

The announcement of further flour reductions in January 1918 brought widespread strikes drawing in an estimated 600,000 workers and contributing to the Cattaro naval mutiny. The Germans protested vigorously when grain convoys en route from Romania to Germany were seized by the Austro-Hungarian army in April 1918. Civilian unrest was also fuelled by increasing requisition of crops by the army, especially as it became apparent that some nationalities were being targeted more than others, such as Slavs and Poles in Austria and Czechs in Hungary.[49]

Bulgaria established a Public Foresight Committee as early as March 1915 to ensure adequate distribution of food and to fix prices for commodities prohibited from export. In effect, the prices fixed legitimised rises of over 25 per cent in the cost of grain and bread and the Committee was dissolved within four months. It was revived in October 1915, but only as a means of cereal collection. With even this work duplicated by various requisitioning commissions, a Central Committee for Economic Welfare and Public Foresight was created in July 1916, with wider powers to oversee cereal purchase and distribution. A Board of Economic Welfare and Public Foresight with yet more powers appeared in April 1917. Private merchants still contrived to compete with the official authorities for grain supplies and, by October 1917, military requisitioning had replaced attempts at purchase. Compulsory sowing of crops and what was in effect a compulsory plough policy had been introduced in 1916 but farmers consistently ignored unrealistic crop quotas. Even the diversion of troops and refugees to agricultural labour and the use of military draught animals could not improve the rapidly declining food situation.[50]

Like Germany, France had been largely self-sufficient in foodstuffs but agricultural production declined by between 30 per cent and 50 per cent during the war. Indeed, by 1917, oats production was down 37 per cent, wheat by 60 per cent and sugar beet by 67 per cent. The loss of men and horses to the army and the neglect of production of fertiliser and farm machinery led to a crisis when a particularly bad harvest occurred in 1917, forcing up prices and reducing the French army to just two days' worth of grain stocks before American grain was hastily transported in British ships to avert the crisis. Price controls were introduced for basic foods in 1916, but it was only under American and British pressure that France moved towards rationing in June 1918, sugar, bread and flour being the first commodities affected.

Italy's pre-war agricultural imports accounted for 80 per cent of the food essential to the diet, especially grain, which comprised 57 per cent of all imports. As elsewhere, price controls were applied in 1916 and rationing in

1917. What made the situation more difficult, however, was poor distribution and a law which prevented foodstuffs being transported from one province to another. In 1917, a poor harvest exacerbated food shortages in urban areas, where the population had grown as a result of industrialisation. Bread rations were reduced to less than 200 grams a day in some cities, hence the unrest in Milan and, especially, in Turin, although the latter was also linked to peace demands occasioned by a visit of a delegation from the Petrograd Soviet. In the countryside, too, there was increasing unrest, often led by women.[51]

British agriculture similarly faced difficulties, with farms expected to produce more food with fewer workers and fewer horses. Women, schoolchildren and soldiers made up some of the deficiency: subsequently, some 30,000 prisoners of war were also employed. Moreover, British agriculture was both comparatively overstocked with horses and more mechanised than continental agriculture. Thus, while switching to war production such as munitions, agricultural machinery suppliers maintained a sufficient level of normal production. Increasingly, too, tractors were imported from the United States, the war marking their large-scale adoption in Britain. Supplies of fertiliser and animal feedstuffs were more problematic, but had not caused serious problems as late as 1916.

Britain imported about 60 per cent of its food requirements before the war, but had certain in-built advantages over continental states in its pattern of land tenure, principally tenants occupying large farms as opposed to small units occupied by peasant owner-occupiers in much of Europe.[52]

Initially, in common with the 'business as usual' approach, there was little intervention in agriculture, although controls were introduced to secure the continued importation of commodities such as sugar, grains and meat. Nonetheless, other interventionist policies were rejected, including a suggestion to encourage more domestic cereal production through guaranteeing minimum prices for wheat and a compulsory plough policy. The latter was felt too radical a break with existing practice.

The poor North American wheat harvest in 1916, however, forced a re-evaluation and a Food Production Department of the Board of Agriculture was instituted in January 1917 to intervene directly in terms of allocation of resources at home. Subsequently, the Corn Production Act of August 1917 guaranteed minimum prices for wheat, oats and potatoes for six years to encourage investment by farmers, as well as guaranteeing minimum wages. Under what now became a compulsory plough policy, an additional 2.1 million acres were cultivated, the tillage acreage in 1918 being the highest achieved between 1886 and 1942. By 1918, the wheat and potato crops were 40 per cent above pre-war averages and reliance upon imports was reduced.

Yet, the achievement was modest: it has been calculated that the percentage of home-grown food increased by barely 1 per cent. Britain could feed itself for an additional 30 days a year by 1918, domestic grain output now satisfying 16 weeks of the year's need. Overall British production now represented an estimated 47 per cent of the calories consumed in Britain compared with 41 per cent before the war. Nonetheless, the essential stability in production meant that the calorie level of the average British diet had declined by only 3 per cent, although the protein intake had declined by 6 per cent.[53]

Coupled with the attempt to increase food production was the effort to control consumption. Self-regulation of business was much preferred to price-fixing, and a modest public education programme and encouragement of allotments was preferred to either wage increases or rationing. Appointed as first Food Controller of the new Ministry of Food in January 1917, Lord Devonport extended the food economy campaign and prepared for the introduction of rationing, the two themes being linked by encouragement of a voluntary rationing scheme in February 1917. Under continuing pressure, not least from the War Emergency Workers' National Committee (WEWNC), his successor, Lord Rhondda, introduced a bread subsidy in September 1917, together with a relaxation on brewing restrictions and a range of price controls: the cost of a four-pound loaf was reduced from 1s.0d to 9d. A joint enterprise of the Labour Party, unions and co-operative societies, the WEWNC made food prices one of its central concerns, as did the parliamentary committee of the Trades Union Council (TUC) and Labour-inspired local Food Vigilance Committees.

It was intended to bring in sugar rationing in the autumn of 1917, but difficulties were encountered in establishing a workable system. Price controls also proved unpopular when they were set higher than the public wished, while some overseas traders took commodities to other markets. The only solution was compulsory rationing, a policy long advocated by the Food Ministry's second Secretary, William Beveridge. Prompted by some local authorities taking matters into their own hands, nationwide sugar rationing was introduced on 31 December 1917 followed by meat and fats in London and the home counties in February 1918. Rationing was then extended nationwide in April. It achieved not so much a general reduction of consumption as, in the words of Margaret Barnett, 'a levelling of consumption of essential foodstuffs'. The result of the government's food policies overall, however, was that there was no serious food shortage and the supply of energy in the national diet remained adequate throughout the war.[54]

The extent to which British consumers were shielded from real hardship caused some difficulties with Britain's continental allies and, after April 1917, increasing pressure was brought to bear by the United States Food

Administration under Hoover to force more pooling of resources. The Grain Corporation, established by Hoover in August 1917, eventually became the effective clearing house for all wheat grown throughout the Americas, while his Sugar Equalisation Board bought up the entire sugar crops of the United States, Cuba, the West Indies and the Philippines in 1918–19.[55]

Hoover was determined to avoid domestic rationing. Thus, his policy was primarily to curtail consumption through educational campaigns and voluntary rationing. The high minimum price set by the Grain Corporation encouraged more production in the Mid West and, following the poor harvest in 1917, there were record harvests in 1918 and 1919. In a voluntary agreement, Hoover also persuaded meat-packing firms to offer a minimum price for pork and pork products. This resulted in such a large pork surplus that Hoover unsuccessfully tried to induce the Entente to accept it when it wanted wheat.[56]

State welfare

Inevitably, the increase in state intervention affected individuals to a far greater extent than before, and in many different ways. At a minor level, the British experienced greater control of licensing laws in 1914, the average closing hour of public houses being brought forward from 12.30a.m. to 10.00p.m. Similarly, British Summer Time was introduced in May 1916. Both were ostensibly to improve levels of production, although the advocacy of liquor control by Lloyd George in early 1915, including weakening of spirits and beer, was primarily a device to move Liberals generally towards state control. In the event, state purchase of the liquor trade was not implemented but licensed premises were actually taken over by the state in Enfield Lock, Carlisle and Gretna: these state-owned public houses were sold off only in the 1970s and licensing laws relaxed only in 1985. DORA's many restrictions included prohibition on public clocks chiming between sunset and sunrise, on whistling for taxi cabs between 10p.m. and 7a.m. and on loitering under railway arches. At a more significant level, of course, war brought the imposition of conscription.[57]

But, if there was greater regulation of individuals' lives, there were also potential longer-term benefits in the shift in emphasis from pre-war *laissez-faire* attitudes to an acknowledgement that government should provide not only the resources for, but also control over the provision of services previously left to charitable organisations. Prior to the war, British labour had been particularly suspicious of state welfare provision, cherishing the self-help mechanisms of the friendly and co-operative societies and demanding of the state only the right to work for adequate wages. Indeed, the tradition of voluntary organisations and self-help continued to be evident in the readiness to support war charities of all kinds, no less than 18,000 new such funds springing up during the war to join established charities such as the Red Cross, which collected over £22 million in Britain during the war.

In many respects, state intervention during the war was also unwelcome to labour in terms of dilution and manpower control. A kind of moral economy therefore dictated that sacrifice required, firstly, a measure of control over profits and perceived inequalities, equating to the kind of conscription of riches advocated by the WEWNC and adopted officially as a policy by the Trades Union Council in September 1916. Secondly, it demanded an appropriate reward rather than simply a restoration of the pre-war status quo. In the process, the social cohesion of the 'home front' might be strengthened. The emergence of what has been characterised as a war welfare state, however, confronted more coercive governments with the dilemma of contemplating reforms which might endanger the very system on which the state was based. At the same time, there was a certain paradox, even in liberal democracies, in that the kinds of change anticipated required a continuing role on the part of the state when, after the experience of war, many people wanted a diminution of state intervention.[58]

Of course, there had been measures of welfare provision in Britain before 1914. The war, however, extended both state and private welfare provision, while also bringing novel intrusions by the state into the lives of the working class as consumers through such means as liquor control, rationing and rent control.

The Factory Acts were waived for the duration, but the Health of Munitions Workers Committee of the Ministry of Munitions was empowered to inspect working premises. Over 900 factory canteens were established from the proceeds of the excess profits tax. The Ministry also set up cloakrooms, washing facilities and day nurseries. It led the way in providing facilities for its own employees and spent some £4.3 million on housing for its workers, building 10,000 permanent homes on 38 sites such as the Well Hall estate in Woolwich and at Gretna.

Local authorities were encouraged to maintain milk supplies for mothers and babies and, in 1916, women working in the production of TNT (trinitrotoluene) were provided with a free daily pint of milk in the (mistaken) belief that it nullified its toxicity. Building upon the pre-war interest in infant and maternal welfare, the permissive Notification of Births Act 1907 was amended in July 1915 to require compulsory registration of births within 36 hours, thus proving local authorities with information on which to act to ensure child health. Midwifery training also came under greater scrutiny in 1916.

The Maternity and Child Welfare Act of August 1918, again building on the pre-war system, required local authorities to establish formal committees to provide services for mothers and infants under five years of age. The new concerns were characterised by the national Baby Week in July 1917. Older children benefited equally from the extension in the provision of school meals for the needy for the whole calendar year. In the words of Jay Winter, child welfare in wartime was an area where 'collective virtue and national interest clearly coincided'. Similarly, the Rents and Mortgage Interest (Rent Restriction) Act of December 1915, which was the principal victory of the unrest on the Clyde, has been characterised by Winter as a major contribution to the standards of working-class life, although there was no actual penalty for contravening its provisions and it was frequently evaded. Problems with evictions experienced where there was a change of landlords subsequently brought the Increase of Rents and Mortgages (Amendment) Act in April 1918.[59]

In educational terms, it had been intended to bring forward new legislation had the war not broken out in 1914, since there was a general consensus on the need to improve education in view of the greater efficiency of German schools and the fact that 75 per cent of British children left school at 14. Greater numbers of working-class children attended fee-paying secondary schools during the war, but, by 1917, an estimated 600,000 children had also left school early to take up wartime employment. Wartime juvenile delinquency also added to public concern. Accordingly, the President of the Board of Education, H. A. L. Fisher, sought to encourage greater secondary provision, ending the practice of half-timing, raising the leaving age from 12 to 14, and improving teaching as a career. His legislation ran out of time in 1917 when opposition arose to perceived over-centralisation. Employers were also concerned at the potential loss of cheap labour through ending half-timing. Amended legislation was introduced in March 1918 but, with the onset of post-war economic difficulties, the continuation classes Fisher had envisaged for those between the ages of 14 and 18 never materialised. The number of free places at secondary schools remained limited and there was no acceptance of the principle of universal secondary education.[60]

A similar pattern of enhanced welfare provision was experienced elsewhere. Employer welfare schemes were well established in the United States before the war but these were now greatly extended, over four hundred firms introducing new welfare measures such as medical facilities, restrooms and leisure clubs. Like the British Ministry of Munitions, the Emergency Fleet Corporation in the United States began a public housing programme for its workers, constructing over 8,000 houses and 850 apartments, while the United States Housing Corporation housed 6,000 families and over 7,000 individuals. One measure intended to improve health was prohibition.

Initially, the sale of liquor was prohibited near military bases but manu-facture of alcohol was then stopped to conserve grain. In the longer term, prohibition, as introduced by the Eighteenth Amendment to the Constitu-tion in December 1917 and ratified in 1919, resulted in a significant post-war increase in criminality after its implementation in January 1920.

State housing was also provided for workers in France, and employers were encouraged to provide an appropriate range of facilities and leisure activities. Family allowances were paid for workers in the railways, mines and some metal industries, while 'equalisation funds' were provided in other trades to compensate for disparities in family allowances paid in specific regions. Thomas also endeavoured to give some protection to female work-ers, through such means as restricting their working hours on nightshifts, while an Under-Secretariat of State for Health established in 1915 set up clinics, restaurants, canteens and shelters. Nursing rooms were introduced by law in August 1917, although only a minority of firms complied with the legislation and the increasing emphasis on pro-natalism saw many sub-sequently closed. Rent controls were introduced in 1914 and there were restrictions on alcohol consumption, absinthe being controlled from March 1915 and all alcohol but wine, beer and cider being prohibited in factories from March 1917.

In Italy, by contrast, the state took only a limited role in welfare, relying upon local communes which, in turn, depended upon local voluntary organ-isations or *fasci* (branches). The state, however, did promote the establish-ment in 1916 of the General Commissary for Civilian Relief and Internal Propaganda followed, in 1917, by the creation of the Ministry for Military Relief and War Pensions. A limited subsidy was paid to the families of servicemen but this was withheld from those in possession of property, widowed mothers where wives were already receiving it, and boys over 12 years of age. Unmarried cohabitants of the dead were eventually given pensions in 1918, but the purchasing power of Italian war widows' pensions generally declined through the war.[61]

It was a measure of the failure of the German state that it could not get welfare policy right. The benefit system, introduced as a result of the desire to encourage women into work, actually discouraged them from doing so. Separation allowances coupled with rent controls and payments often made by firms to the families of former employees meant that many women were better off than in peacetime. Moreover, the state did not feel inclined to compel women in *Kriegerfamilien* (warrior families) to work.

By contrast, German war widows and orphans were identified as a particular problem in 1915. The standard pension rates dating from 1907 were altered to reflect the pre-war wage of the deceased, with the intention of maintaining the family's status. However, while separation allowances were raised twice in 1916, widows' pensions were not and there was no general increase until June 1918. Despite the efforts of voluntary organisations such as the National Foundation for Dependants of Fallen Soldiers, therefore, life became increasingly difficult for German war widows.

Nonetheless, the Women's Department and Frauenarbeitszentrale (Women's Labour Office) in the Kriegsamt and the National Ausschuss für Frauenarbeit im Kriege (National Committee for Women's War Work) established a network of welfare organisations for female industrial workers, notably the provision of factory nurses. Pro-natalism was just as marked as in Britain and France. Maternity benefits had been discretionary before the war but became mandatory for soldiers' wives in December 1914, while efforts were also made to improve midwifery and infant-feeding practices in an attempt to lower infant mortality to compensate for a declining birth rate. The pre-war child care research institute known as the Kaiserin August Viktoria-Haus disseminated much of the propaganda material and sponsored infant care clinics, milk depots and local associations for mothers and infants. Financial restrictions, however, curtailed wider reforms. Similarly, the moral health of young workers between 18 and 21 was protected by the development from March 1916 onwards of the *Sparzwang*, a compulsory savings plan based on wage deductions, which was intended to reduce conspicuous consumption by youths.

While welfare provision was being extended, however, the failure of rationing and the growth of the black market undermined the very legitimacy of the German state. A decree against excessive prices had been promulgated in July 1915 and *Preisprüfungsstellen* (price examination agencies) created in September 1915 to determine an appropriate and just level for prices. Various organisations also came together to create the War Committee for Consumer Interests to influence government and price agencies but it proved all impossible to determine 'just' prices, further discrediting what might be regarded as state socialism. It is possible that between one-third and a half of the country's food supplies were traded on the black market. In December 1917 it was revealed that Neükollen's municipal council in the Berlin suburbs was itself trading on the black market. This, however, was not unusual and other civic authorities and large firms bought supplies for their own outside official circles. Thus, as Avner Offer has commented, black marketeering 'forced every citizen into breaking the law', with concomitant consequences for the respect in which the state was held.[62]

The perceived failures of state mobilisation in Germany and Italy informed and shaped aspects of fascist ideology in the inter-war period. Much of the rhetoric of fascism mirrored that of wartime mobilisation so that what ideally should have been created in the war would be established in peace. Indeed, while Industrial Mobilisation (MI) in Italy had been quickly dismantled, in 1922 Mussolini established the similar Board of Civil Mobilisation headed by none other than MI's former head, Dallolio.[63] Generally, too, while wartime controls were divested by belligerents immediately after the war, the precedents set were to be revived during the Second World War.

It had been intended to continue some wartime controls in Britain in the expectation that Germany would remain an economically powerful enemy. The sudden and unexpected collapse of the Central Powers in 1918 removed much of this justification, especially undermining the plans of the Ministry of Reconstruction, created in 1917. Moreover, the piecemeal way in which controls had been applied during the war meant there was a lack of any coherent doctrine of collectivisation to justify their retention.[64]

The creation of the War Cabinet, and especially the Cabinet Secretariat was a radical change in government practice although, as John Turner has commented, the difference between Asquith and Lloyd George in terms of administrative reform was more a matter of politics in that Lloyd George was better able to rid himself of internal opposition. The Cabinet Secretariat survived, although it was not until the 1930s that it was routinely staffed by civil servants as opposed to regular servicemen and 'irregular' civilians. Some of the new ministries also survived to be joined by the ministries of Health and Transport in 1919.

It has been suggested, however, that the reassertion of Treasury controls over departmental staffing and public expenditure in 1919–25 rendered the impact of war on central government null and void. However, the machinery had been overhauled and, in many cases, had become more professional in such areas as labour and health policy.[65]

Lloyd George had hoped that, in the interests of British industrial competitiveness, trade union restrictive practices would not be revived and the co-operative spirit of the Whitley Councils would be continued. Trade unions, however, urged restoration of pre-war practices and, as shown by the failure of the National Industrial Conference, neither unions nor employers wished to maintain wartime consensus. Indeed, 'Whitleyism' survived only in newer industries or those where labour organisation had been previously weak.

Ration coupons expired in May 1919 and food controls lapsed by 1920, although both were reintroduced amid the post-war price boom, and the lessons of the Great War in respect of food control were to be reimposed during the Second World War. Moreover, government expenditure continued to grow with the continued general acceptance of the assumption of the war years that the state should take a more proactive role in social policies. In the process, the relationship between government and the plethora of pre-war voluntary agencies was permanently altered.

Thus, rent controls were retained and there were extensions in unemployment insurance and other health insurance benefits, although these, and an increase in pensions, were less than the cost of living. The principle of benefit without contribution was incorporated in the Unemployment Insurance Act in 1920, which was a major advance. On the other hand, the wage controls introduced for munitions workers in 1916 and agricultural workers in 1917, outlining a minimum wage, lasted only for eighteen months after the war.

What condemned the minimum wage was the reassertion of Treasury control. Much else was curtailed by post-war economic retrenchment, not least expectations of housing construction. The war had seen the introduction of housing subsidies, the latter prompted by the need to provide housing for the expanded munitions labour force when the war was driving up costs and bringing a halt to building. A housing programme was pushed forward under the Housing and Town Planning Act of July 1919, but, in the event, plans to build 500,000 houses on pre-war garden city lines were stymied by financial difficulties in July 1921. Wartime plans for a Ministry of Health did come to fruition, but without control over some areas of health provision, such as the factory inspectorate, and with wide powers left in the hands of local authorities, who generally lacked enthusiasm for action. There was post-war legislation on transport, land acquisition, forestry, electricity supply and industrial courts, but it was less than had been intended.

While it was the reduction of government expenditure that chiefly accounted for the end of reconstruction in 1921, reconstruction itself was a term open to differing interpretations. For some, it implied transformation, but for others it meant the restoration of the pre-war status quo. Nevertheless, many of those involved in reconstruction planning like Addison, Beveridge and Tawnay would re-emerge during the Second World War and, at the very least, as Arthur Marwick has noted, the post-war legislation 'set new standards of expectation in social welfare'.[66]

In France, wartime laws and decrees were revoked in October 1919. Legislation was passed on an eight hour day in April 1919. There was also a new housing Act in 1922, the pre-war unemployment fund was made permanent, and family allowances and cash subsidies to arrest the declining birth rate. Shop stewards, however, were largely eliminated and the expectations on the part of labour of institutionalised collective bargaining was not realised.

A Ministry of Hygiene and Social Assistance and Protection was established in 1920 but there was no national social insurance scheme or public housing policy until the 1930s. The French government did retain a role in mining concessions and in hydroelectric power. Similarly, while control of the railways was relinquished in October 1921, it was on condition that the rail companies should have a common board of directors and be guided by the Railway Council. The onset of economic depression, however, which came later to France than to other European states, saw the revival of import and price controls after 1931. Moreover, the nationalisation policies introduced by the Popular Front between 1936 and 1938 went well beyond those enacted during the war and reflected ideological considerations rather than the non-doctrinaire practical approach adopted during the war. The outline plans for economic mobilisation adopted in July 1938 rationalised the lessons of the Great War and were further extended by the Vichy regime after June 1940.[67]

Only a few wartime agencies survived in the United States. In fact, the war had little touched the country and there were no great pressures for change. Some business interests wanted some of the creations to remain and certainly wanted continuing relaxation of anti-trust laws. The unions similarly wanted the state to continue to control the railroads, McAdoo's Railroad Administration having proved beneficial to them. However, the War Industries Board had been wound up by the end of November 1918 and the railroads had returned to civil control by March 1920.

The precedents remained, however, to be utilised in the face of economic depression. Thus, the War Finance Corporation was revived as the Reconstruction Finance Corporation by President Hoover in 1932 and Hoover also revived the Food Administration in the form of the Federal Farm Board. Under President Franklin D. Roosevelt, who had been Secretary of the Navy in Wilson's wartime administration, the Civilian Conservation Corps resembled the American Expeditionary Force while the National Recovery Administration of 1933 bore a close resemblance to the War Industries Board. In effect, the war had presaged increasing federal power through the inter-war years, albeit in response to the depression, while, at the same time, marking a shift towards corporatism in government.[68]

Generally, the war resulted in advances in mothers' allowances for dependent children, introduced in 39 countries by 1919, workmen's compensation and private pension schemes. There was post-war housing legislation in Austria, Belgium and the new Czechoslovakia; and social insurance legislation in Austria, Bulgaria, Czechoslovakia and the new Yugoslavia. Clearly, therefore, the war had changed concepts of the role of the state within society, although similar advances were also made in countries which had remained neutral such as Sweden and Switzerland.[69]

Management of morale

What drove the tentative beginnings of war welfare was the recognition that the maintenance of national morale was a crucial component in national survival. Successful political leadership in wartime therefore required astute manipulation of public opinion. While liberal democracies like Britain, France and the United States entered the war with greater legitimacy in the eyes of their population than more coercive political systems, much still depended upon the ability and authority of politicians. The situation was rather different in Germany, but it has been argued that the 'silent dictatorship' of Hindenburg and Ludendorff was bonapartist in the sense that it was plebiscitary, the notion of its standing apart from the constitution depending upon a wide degree of popular identification with their aims for Germany.[70]

In dealing with public opinion and what might be termed home management, political leaderships were conscious of a range of potential weapons enabling them to influence wartime public opinion. Initially, there was often more than sufficient support for the war in the major belligerent states, the appeal to patriotic nationalism being reinforced by the shared values, political and cultural forms, symbols and rituals which underpinned the concept of nation and state. As a result, there was almost a process of 'self-mobilisation' and attempts to manipulate the public were often indirect and even superficial.

As the war continued, however, governments were increasingly concerned to maintain the national will to win. Indeed, it has been argued that, in the face of growing war-weariness and the revolution in Russia, there was a concerted attempt to remobilise public opinion in 1917 in Britain, France, and Germany as characterised by the establishment, respectively, of the National War Aims Committee (NWAC), the Union des Grandes Associations contre la Propagande Ennemie (UGAPE; Union of Associations against Enemy Propaganda), and the Fatherland Party. Even the Italian government, which had made little previous effort to 'sell' the war to its people, established the Opere Federate di Assistenza e di Propaganda Nazionale (Federated Society for Assistance and National Propaganda) in the wake of Caporetto. The targets of this more co-ordinated effort, which was often concentrated on the projection of war aims, were primarily domestic opponents of the war, principally pacifists and socialists. Generally, the state sought to project ideals of duty, sacrifice and solidarity within the civilian population while, at the same time, dealing with perceived injustices undermining civilian resolve such as war profiteering and shirking.

In seeking to stimulate or revive national morale and damage that of the enemy, whether external or internal, propaganda was the most obvious tool. Propaganda, however, was not just a matter of what appeared in the press. It could also embrace the efforts of a range of official and unofficial groups and organisations, including the Church, and extend into the classroom and popular leisure such as cinema, gramophone and music hall. It could involve use of a variety of popular forms from graphic art such as pictorial postcards and cartoons to souvenirs. In Germany it has been estimated that 9 million postcards were printed every month during the war and 'iron-nail memorials' in the form of iron crosses, swords or U-boats became popular. In Britain, media for propaganda included porcelain figures of Kitchener, and the crested china busts, binoculars, artillery, shells and tanks produced by the Goss factory in Stoke-on-Trent and similar firms. In France, the *images d'Epinal*, the popular cheap comic-strip-style posters published since the 1830s by the Pellerin firm at Epinal and traditionally sold by itinerant pedlars, served a similar purpose. War-related jigsaw puzzles, parlour games and toy soldiers all fulfilled similar purposes for children throughout Europe. Even commercial advertisements could reflect the impact of the war.[71]

Certainly, there was an eagerness to be informed in wartime, circulation figures for the press generally increasing: those of German newspapers rose by 69.9 per cent during the war. The infant cinema also increased its audience. The leading German newsreel producer, Oskar Messter, claimed the weekly wartime newsreel audience in Germany and Austria was 15.5 million. In Britain there were some 4,500 cinemas by 1914 with an estimated weekly audience of 7 million, rising to 21 million by 1917. The United States had over 12,000 cinemas. Even in occupied Belgium, some 50 million tickets were sold in over 1,500 cinemas between June 1916 and June 1917. In eastern Europe, too, the cinema increased its appeal.[72]

Censorship was applied by all belligerents although this was initially military rather than political censorship. In Britain, the Defence of the Realm Act (DORA) gave the government sweeping powers in this regard. On the rare occasions, however, when maverick correspondents like Ellis Ashmead-Bartlett on Gallipoli, did not observe discretion, the newspaper proprietors and editors themselves operated a self-censorship far more effective than that of the official Press Bureau.

The British national and provincial press was overwhelmingly hostile to Germany, its customary outrage at what was generally very light censorship being immediately muted when the victims were socialist or pacifist journals, a number of which were suppressed. Overall, censorship appears to have had little effect in changing the ways in which the British press operated and was far less significant than reductions in advertising revenues and increase in the price of paper. Indeed, Nicholas Hiley has argued that the government was forced into becoming a 'news agency' largely through its inability to control the means available for dissemination of news.[73]

The pattern was reproduced elsewhere. In Canada the Emergency War Measures Act of 1914 established censorship, the main aim being to target anti-British material coming into Canada from the United States. A Press

Bureau emerged in France in August 1914 and the Oberszensurstelle (Central Censor's Office) in Germany in February 1915 followed by the Kriegspresseamt (War Press Office) under OHL control in October 1915. In practice, the implementation of German censorship lay in the hands of the Deputy Commanding Generals, resulting in wide variations. In addition, newspapers from neutral countries were available and no prohibition was ever placed on printing Entente military communiqués. Similarly, Austria had its Kriegspressequartier (War Press Bureau) keeping journalists under close control while their reports were also submitted to the Kriegsüberwachungsamt (War Supervisory Office).

As in Britain, continental military censorship soon shaded into political censorship. The latter was extended to a careful surveillance of even popular entertainment such as theatre, cabarets and popular fiction. Indeed, in Germany after August 1916, anything regarded as undermining confidence in the military was prohibited. Even a patriotic drama on Frederick the Great was banned in 1917 for fear that the depiction of the pre-emptive attack on Saxony in 1756 might be too reminiscent of August 1914. Coupled with the introduction of patriotic instruction for the army, OHL increased its domestic propaganda effort from July 1917. Its only success, however, appears to have been in terms of that part of the civil and military programme providing entertainment through provision of films or suitably Germanic theatre such as works by Schiller and Kleist. Hindenburg was also promoted as a symbolic figure, revered through the erection of wooden statues of him in many cities, into which nails could be hammered upon donation to war charities or war bonds.[74]

In France, censorship increased notably in September 1914, Millerand issuing more detailed instructions that prohibited sensational headlines and the shouting of headlines by news vendors. Clemenceau's *L'Homme libre* was suspended when he declined to accept censorship, as was his successor paper, *L'Homme enchaîné*. The French pacifist journal *Bonnet Rouge* was censored 1,076 times in fifteen months, although none of the European belligerents approached the severity of the controls imposed in the United States under the Sedition Act.

The ability of the press to bring down government was more limited than sometime supposed, although press criticism of government could be of significance and both political and military leaders were not averse to using the press for their own ends. It was press criticism of the Admiralty at the height of the U-boat campaign, for example, which enabled Lloyd George to force through changes there. Similarly, Northcliffe waged a press campaign against Kitchener in 1915 over the shells scandal with the assistance of Sir John French. Subsequently, Northcliffe waged a press campaign against both Asquith in 1916 and against Lloyd George in 1918. In

Germany, the decision by Ludendorff to lift prohibition on the discussion of war aims in November 1916, supposedly on the grounds that it would be good for morale, was actually intended to put pressure on Bethmann.[75]

The general tendency of a patriotic press to 'play the game' with respect to domestic news consumption meant that most British government propaganda targeted opinion overseas. There were initial attempts to explain the war to the British public through such means as the University of Oxford History Faculty's *Why We Are at War: Great Britain's Case*, known as the Red Book, but the Foreign Office's domination of the British propaganda effort often led to the neglect of the home front, unless there was a specific need to be addressed such as a new issue of war bonds. In the United States, George Creel's Committee on Public Information claimed to have distributed 75 million leaflets by the end of the war, the Committee using basic advertising techniques, and operating through other organisations such as the Friends of German Democracy in an effort to disguise the impression of state involvement.

Like the press, the British public needed little tuition in anti-German sentiment and the pre-war spy scare persisted until at least 1915. Increasingly, the public demanded internment of aliens and subjected actual or supposed Germans to harassment after such events as air raids on London. There were at least seven deaths in East End riots in May 1915 following the loss of the *Lusitania* and even dachshunds were stoned in the streets on occasions. There were large-scale demonstrations against enemy aliens in a number of cities in 1918, a petition with 1.2 million signatures being handed in to Downing Street that August. One prominent victim of hysteria was the First Sea Lord, Prince Louis of Battenberg, hounded from office in October 1914, after which the family name was changed to Mountbatten. Jews also came under physical attack, however, in East London in 1917 in the belief that they were evading conscription.

Similarly, Germans came under suspicion in Australia. Indeed, German-Australians were disenfranchised in 1917, the government's anti-German drive being a deliberate strategy to rally public support for the war. Deep wounds were also opened by the ill feeling whipped up by groups like the All British Association, which equally attacked those perceived to be opposed to the war effort such as Irish and Catholics. Germans, Hungarians and Ukrainians all came under suspicion in Canada. Similarly, in the United States over 250,000 Americans were recruited into the Justice Department-sponsored American Protective League, dedicated to searching out dissent. Almost half the states of the Union prohibited the use of the German language and there was one notorious incident in Maryville, Illinois, in which Roger Prager, a harmless German-born drifter, was lynched in April 1918. The same concept of an 'enemy within' played its part in the wartime persecution of Jews in central and eastern Europe and of Armenians in Turkey. Indeed, prior assumptions about the inclusiveness of national identity were widely challenged in a war fought on such a scale.[76]

Official agencies found little difficulty in persuading writers and intellectuals to produce propaganda material for them. Among many, Charles Masterman's War Propaganda Bureau at Wellington House in London enlisted Rudyard Kipling, Sir Arthur Conan Doyle, Thomas Hardy, Arnold Bennett, John Galsworthy and H. G. Wells. John Buchan became head of the Department of Information, which succeeded Wellington House in December 1916.

In Germany, Thomas Mann set out an elaborate defence of German culture by contrast to the general decadence of that in Britain and France in his polemic, *Betrachtungen eines Unpolitischen* (Reflections of a Non-political). Similarly, *Der Aufruf an die Kulturwelt* (The Appeal to the Civilised World) appeared on 4 October 1914. It was drafted by the Jewish playwright Ludwig Fulda, and reworked by the playwright Hermann Sudermann and a Berlin politcian, Georg Reicke. A total of 93 academics and intellectuals signed it, including the scientist who had developed quantum theory, Max Planck; the philosopher, Wilhelm Windelband; the composer, Englebert Humperdinck; the artist, Max Liebermann, and the inventor of X-rays, Wilhelm Roentgen. Its defence of German culture, however, had only a negative impact abroad. In July 1915 a total of 1,347 German intellectuals similarly signed the *Intellektuelleneingabe* (Intellectuals' petition) demanding more expansive war aims. There were also attempts to ban foreign works in Germany but, generally, this was relaxed provided the author or composer had died before 1914: an exception was made for George Bernard Shaw's 'John Bull's Other Island' on the grounds that its anti-English stance preserved its 'objectivity'.

In turn, French intellectuals such as the historian and director of the Ecole Normale Supérieure, Ernest Lavisse, and the permanent secretary of the Académie Française, Etienne Lamy, responded to the German challenge. The theories of Immanuel Kant became a particular philosophical battleground in France while there was a revival of classicism and an endeavour to promote French as opposed to German scientific concepts. Some eighty musicians including Charles Camille Saint-Saëns signed a petition to urge the prohibition of the performance of works by German and Austrian composers, though Joseph Maurice Ravel declined to do so.

Similarly, Austro-Hungarians rallied to the cause. The celebrated *Hassgesang gegen England* (Hymn of Hate against England) of August 1914 was the work of a German-born Jewish writer based in Vienna, Ernst Lissauer. Ludwig Wittgenstein joined up in Austria while the composer Arnold Schoenberg was rejected on medical grounds. The poet Richard von Schaukal was ennobled for his contribution to war propaganda.

Intellectuals were equally important in sustaining concepts of national identity. This was true of the Bulgarian poets Ivan Vazov and Kiril Hristov, but especially of Belgian and Romanian intellectuals after their countries were overwhelmed by the Germans. Thus, the journal, *România*, sustained the army and nation in its Moldavian exile, while *La Libre Belgique* was the most prominent of a number of clandestine newspapers circulated in occupied Belgium, often featuring the satirical cartoons of Dutch-born artist Louis Raemaekers.[77]

Church and religion played their part in reinforcing the state, and the use of religious iconography was a common propaganda device, suggesting the continuing recognition of the significance of at least a secular Christianity. The Archbishop of Canterbury would not sanction the use of the pulpit for recruiting, but Church of England clergy were active outside of it, not least the Bishop of London A. F. Winnington-Ingram, who pushed the concept of a holy war. Anglican clergy saw an opportunity for spiritual renewal in Australia and openly supported the recruiting drive and, later, conscription. Australian Catholic clergy, who regarded themselves as an alienated minority, chose to seek integration through patriotism, notably condemning the Easter Rising in Dublin in uncompromising terms. They were placed in a difficult position by the conscription referenda, mostly supporting conscription in the first vote, then switching sides in the second, as it had become apparent that most of their congregations opposed it.

In France, where the clergy were an important influence in local life, the role of religion was more equivocal, given the traditional hostility between the secular Republic and the Catholic Church. Papal neutrality was unacceptable to many French Catholics, while the government refused to allow the public prayers for peace for which Benedict XV had called in January 1915. The French Catholic Church itself did its best to counter allegations by anti-clerical groups that it was unpatriotic, seeking to use the war as a means of restoring the Church's position at the centre of national life. Certainly, the war brought an increase in attendances at mass and communion although, as elsewhere, this did not necessarily equate to a religious revival in terms of faith. Both Catholic and Protestant Churches in Germany supported the war effort, the Protestant Churches strongly emphasising a war against Catholic France and Orthodox Russia and the apostate Protestants of England. As elsewhere, Catholics in Germany wished to demonstrate their loyalty to the state. German Jews were also initially accepted within the *Burgfrieden* (fortress truce) though allegations of war profiteering and evasion of military service soon appeared.[78]

Education was another ideological battleground. Australian state primary schools already preached the virtues of empire and imperial citizenship before the war. Efforts to raise money and provide goods for soldiers, such as shirts and gloves, became institutionalised. In Sydney, senior boys were used also as strike breakers on the railways in August 1917. Rather as the Jacobins had consciously used education to prepare the child for further military service during the French Revolutionary Wars, so the French Ministry of Education refashioned the syllabus in a patriotic light. Significantly, the UGAPE originated in the Ligue de l'Enseignement (The Teaching League), a voluntary organisation supporting the state primary school system. French schools were also made the focus for collections towards war charities and war loans, although it would appear that there was less emphasis upon the war by 1917. It was also hoped that an anti-alcohol campaign in schools would have some impact upon parents.

In the same way, Italian schools were co-opted to encourage a national mobilisation in terms of voluntary charitable organisation. Teachers were invariably involved in the Committees for Civilian Assistance, set up in municipalities in May 1915 and eventually numbering over 4,500. Teachers were given a formal role both in the care of war orphans and also in the enhanced propaganda effort of 1917–18, co-ordinated by the Commissariat for Civilian Assistance and Propaganda.

German teachers were also propaganda agents. They organised the collection of materials such as scrap metals and performed administrative tasks such as distributing ration cards. In the United States, where education was decentralised, pressure from a variety of national and local groups ranging from the National Education Association to rotary clubs ultimately forced the administration to draw up war issues courses for schools. The process extended to post-secondary education, with most able-bodied male students enrolled in the Students' Army Training Corps.[79]

Whatever the source, propaganda followed similar themes in every belligerent. In many ways, the Germans themselves did much to make the work of Entente propagandists easier. In October 1915, for example, they executed the British nurse Edith Cavell for helping Allied servicemen to escape from Belgium to the Netherlands. In July 1916, they executed Captain Charles Fryatt of the British steamer *Brussels* for trying to ram a U-boat attacking his vessel. The issue by a German firm of a medal commemorating the sinking of the *Lusitania*, intended as a satirical statement on British hypocrisy in allegedly carrying munitions on a liner, was equally turned against the Germans.

German gifts to the Entente's propaganda did not prevent fabrication such as the photograph of three German cavalrymen seemingly loaded down with loot in Belgium, which appeared in the *Daily Mirror* on 20 August 1914; it was actually a photograph which had appeared in a Berlin newspaper in June 1914 of the three winners of a cavalry competition holding their trophies. The German factory allegedly turning the corpses of their own soldiers into lubricating oils and fertiliser was another wartime fabrication of long duration.

Subsequently, and especially after the United States entered the war, British propaganda targeted opinion in Austria-Hungary and Germany. By this time, Lloyd George had succumbed to demands for a more overtly active propaganda arm and had turned the machine over to the press barons Beaverbrook and Northcliffe. One result was the establishment of Northcliffe's Enemy Propaganda Department, served by opponents of the preservation of Austro-Hungarian rule such as R. W. Seton-Watson and Lewis Namier. Rather similarly, the Germans circulated propaganda newspapers in occupied Poland, Belgium and France. The French circulated newspapers in Alsace and Lorraine and subsidised others in Italy, Switzerland, Greece, Romania and, in 1918, even in Germany. Anxious to counter German promotion of Flemish separatism, the exiled Belgian government also consciously attempted to influence neutral opinion as well as that in occupied Belgium itself through newspapers.[80]

There is considerable debate as to the effect of wartime propaganda in general and its particular contribution to the collapse of the Central Powers. Clearly, military victory and not propaganda was the most significant factor. Even in terms of domestic propaganda, famous recruiting posters such as Alfred Leete's 'Kitchener Wants You', an image first published in Britain on 5 September 1914 did not arrest the decline in recruitment. Moreover, while the Parliamentary Recruiting Committee eventually printed over 5.7 million posters and 14.2 million leaflets at a total cost of £24,000, this was less than Rowntree's of York had spent on advertising a brand of cocoa in 1911–12.

In France, soldiers on leave were by far the most significant agents in opinion-forming, and in France and Germany soldiers regularly returned to industry and agriculture. In domestic terms, propaganda arguably had its greatest impact upon children too young to contribute to the war effort directly – in Germany, it was those too young to have fought who were most affected by the myth of the front generation. Germans, including Hitler, certainly made much of the success of British propaganda in undermining German domestic morale. To some extent this conveniently served the promotion of the *dolchstoss* (stab in the back), but it can be noted that the German authorities were consistently concerned to refute Entente propaganda.[81]

An interesting development was the manipulation of a medium in its infancy, namely the cinema. Rather as in the case of the recruiting poster campaign, however, films directly related to the war represented only a small proportion of the total produced, amounting perhaps to no more than 10 per cent in Britain. A war tax imposed on cinema admissions in 1916 also reduced the potential audience and closed perhaps one thousand cinemas.

In August 1914, a number of British film companies attempted to get cameramen out to the front. However, photographers as well as newsmen were expelled by the War Office, which even wanted to ban the export of newsreel on grounds of security. The French, by contrast, permitted filming at least in rear areas from May 1915 onwards, while the Germans established a special film unit at the start although OHL was suspicious of allowing cameramen too close to the front. Indeed, a suitably edited version of a German war newsreel was shown at a London cinema, the Scala, in May 1916 and, in the absence of any British newsreel covering the war, others showed French film.

Wellington House was increasingly frustrated with the lack of film. The main press agencies would not co-operate with the restrictive conditions laid down by the War Office for any relaxation of the prohibition, so Wellington House turned to the cinema newsreel firms, which in March 1915 had established a consortium known as the Topical Committee of Film Manufacturers' Association. The Topical Committee had already been in contact with the War Office and an official film unit was agreed sometime between March and July 1915. By 1918, over 700 films of one kind or another had been made, including that sponsored by the National War Aims Committee, *The National Film*, a somewhat tawdry drama filmed in Chester with British troops drafted in as extras to play brutal and licentious Germans.

Meanwhile the Topical Committee had sent two cameramen, Geoffrey Malins and Teddy Tong, to France in November 1915 to begin making a series of newsreels behind the lines. Tong fell ill and was replaced by J. B. McDowell in June 1916. Technical limitations remained acute. Indeed, they placed an undue emphasis on the dramatic scenes provided by heavy artillery behind the lines firing at distant targets. As a result, it has been argued by Stephen Badsey that it was as much the limitations of the camera as the nature of warfare that 'produced a film record of monstrous guns and strange landscapes, the sinister "empty battlefield" of the twentieth century, in an unusually exaggerated form'. Thus, the camera's limitations 'reinforced the shapelessness of war, and the helplessness of individuals in war'. It was somewhat ironic, therefore, that the attempt to record reality was marked by adding faked scenes to the celebrated film produced of the Somme offensive in July 1916.

The Battle of the Somme opened in thirty-four London cinemas on 21 August 1916. It caused a sensation and, although no overall viewing figures are extant, it has been suggested that 1 million saw it in the first week and 20 million saw it in the first six weeks. Strictly speaking, it was not a propaganda film since it had been made at very short notice and was assembled from film not intended to provide a continuous narrative. Nor was there any particular conception of an enemy since Germans appeared only as prisoners or bodies.

Some 13 per cent of the footage was devoted to the wounded and the dead and, although the total of British casualties was never revealed, there was no attempt to hide the physical destruction of a battlefield. The response evoked in the audiences was generally a mixture of pity and horror. This was especially so of the faked scenes, which were taken as genuine. Those who had lost relatives in the war particularly seemed to feel that it helped them. Indeed, as Nicholas Reeves has suggested, the film may have fulfilled its purpose in bridging the chasm between front and home and suggesting that the sacrifice was worthwhile, for the film was 'incorporated within the audience's own existing ideology'. The depiction of death, in the sense of seeing falling soldiers as opposed to dead bodies, was not repeated in other British wartime film and no more were made after 1917 since it was believed that the novelty of battle films had worn off and the public was jaded.[82]

The German authorities were so impressed by the film's impact that they had their own Somme film, *Bei Unseren Helden an der Somme* (With Our Soldiers on the Somme), produced. It premiered on 17 January 1917. Much of it was staged in training areas, however, and it was widely condemned in Germany for not looking sufficiently authentic. Despite OHL's suspicion of film, Ludendorff eventually recognised the potential of film for domestic propaganda purposes, authorising the establishment of a new umbrella organisation for film production known as the Universum-Film-Aktiengesellschaft (Ufa; Universal Film Joint Stock Company), in December 1917. Cinemas were then given priority for coal stocks. All foreign films had been prohibited in Germany in September 1914 and, just as censorship had affected *Schundliteratur* (trash literature), a ban had also been placed on domestic production of *Schundfilms* (trash films) such as detective films. A 'field grey' genre emerged and the Germans produced fictional features such as *Das Tagebuch des Dr Hart* (The Diary of Dr Hart), depicting the work of a German doctor in occupied Poland. Indeed, it has been argued that the entertainment films shown to troops behind the lines were probably the only effective part of the patriotic instruction programme introduced in 1917. Similarly, the popular actresses Henny Porten and Danish-born Astra Nielsen promoted war loans.

Ufa had taken over both Messter's Berlin-based production company and the Austrian Sascha film company. The latter had produced its own newsreels, benefiting from the access of its founder, Count Alexander Kolowrat-Krakowsky, to army headquarters. Sascha also produced patriotic 'shorts' to be shown alongside its feature films, which were themselves mostly comedies with an underlying propaganda message.[83]

Hollywood was also mobilised for the war effort, the newly formed National Association of the Motion Picture Industry (NAMPI) co-operating closely with Creel's Committee on Public Information. It did so largely for its own purposes, recognising opportunities to establish its respectability, and to avoid any question of being starved of resources if regarded as non-essential. In fact, Hollywood's war-related output was small, amounting to only 23 per cent of current films in release in October 1918. Some, however, made a considerable impact, such as Cecil B. De Mille's *Joan the Woman* (1916). Starring Geraldine Farrar, it helped make Joan of Arc a role model for American women despite the inconvenient reality that she had been burned at the stake by English machinations. D. W. Griffith's *Hearts of the World* (1918), made with the co-operation of Canadian troops, was seen by an estimated 742,000 cinema-goers in New York alone between April and October 1918, while another popular De Mille film was the Mary Pickford vehicle *The Little American* (1917). The latter's anti-German theme fell foul of the film censor in Chicago, necessitating a court case to get it released there, as did George Kleine's *The Unbeliever* (1918), in effect a recruiting film for the US Marine Corps.

Charlie Chaplin's comedy *Shoulder Arms*, opening just two weeks before the armistice, also proved immensely popular despite the risks involved in cinema-going from influenza, which led to widespread cinema closures. As in Germany, stars like Farrar, Pickford, Chaplin and Douglas Fairbanks were extensively used to help sell liberty bonds: indeed, the latter three drew 30,000 people to one war bond rally in New York in April 1918. Similarly, the Four Minute Men organisation used intermissions as a platform for patriotic speeches: Creel estimated that over 755,000 such speeches were made during the war to a total audience in excess of 314 million. Film-makers also assisted Hoover in establishing a motion picture division of the War Food Administration to push food economies.[84]

In France, newsreels remained the responsibilty of private companies until January 1917, though under War Ministry supervision. Thereafter, an Army Cinema Section produced an official weekly newsreel. A French film of the Somme, however, had only limited screenings. Some of the most extensive war output by a film industry was that by Italian cinema, which even produced a feature dealing with the execution of Edith Cavell.[85]

The use of the cinema was another example of the transitional nature of the war, for film's greatest impact lay in the future. At the same time, however, it also illustrates how the exigencies of war compelled the state to intervene even in the public's leisure activities. Indeed, there were few areas in which the role of the state was not greatly enhanced. Thus, whatever the ideological or other attitudes towards state intervention prior to 1914, virtually all belligerent governments were compelled to take a major role in the management of industry and agriculture within the context of an emerging war economy. Such a role invariably involved the formulation of specific policies with regard to such matters as labour relations and welfare, contributing in turn to the identification between the people and the national cause. Wartime changes in the role of the state did not endure in every case but, at least in the short term, the impact of the war upon society was inescapable.

Notes and references

1. Beckett, 'Total War', pp.1–3; John Horne, 'Introduction: Mobilising for "Total War"', 1914–18', in Horne, ed., *State, Society and Mobilisation*, pp.3–5, 242 n.10; Hans-Ulrich Wehler, '"Absoluter" und "totaler" Krieg: Von Clausewitz zu Ludendorff', *Politische Vierteljahresschrift* 10 (1969), pp.220–48.

2. Stanislas Andrzejewski, *Military Organisation and Society*, 2nd edn (London, 1963), pp.6–29; Richard Titmuss, 'War and Social Policy', in Richard Titmuss, ed., *Essays on the Welfare State* (London, 1958), pp.75–87; Wilson, *Myriad Faces of War*, p.669; Arthur Marwick, *The Deluge: British Society and the First World War* (London, 1965 and Harmondsworth, 1967); idem, *Britain in Century of Total War*, pp.11–17; idem, *War and Social Change*, pp.11–14; idem, 'Problems and Consequences of Organising Society for Total War', in Dreisziger, ed., *Mobilisation for Total War*, pp.3–21; Bond, *War and Society*, pp.168–9; Richard Bessel, 'Mobilisation and Demobilisation in Germany, 1916–19', in Horne, ed., *State, Society and Mobilisation*, pp.221–2; Deist, 'German Army, Authoritarian Nation-state and Total War', p.160; Roger Chickering, 'Total War: The Use and Abuse of a Concept', in Boemeke, Chickering and Förster, eds, *Anticipating Total War*, pp.13–28.

3. 'Introduction', in Arthur Marwick, ed., *Total War and Social Change* (London, 1988), pp.x–xxi; A. Marwick, 'Introduction – War and Social Change in Twentieth Century Britain', *The Deluge*, 2nd edn (London, 1991), pp.11–48.

4. D. H. Aldcroft, *From Versailles to Wall Street, 1919–29* (Harmondsworth, 1977), p.19; Mark Derez, 'A Belgian Salient for Reconstruction: People and Patrie, Landscape and Memory', in Cecil and Liddle, eds, *Facing Armageddon*, pp.439, 444; Schaepdrijver, 'Occupation', pp.267–94; Antony Polansky, 'The German Occupation of Poland during the First and Second World Wars: A Comparison', in Roy A. Prete and A. Hamish Ion, eds, *Armies of Occupation* (Waterloo, 1984), pp.97–142; Jan Molenda, 'Social Change in Poland during World War One', in Kiràly and Dreisziger, eds, *East Central European Society*, pp.187–201; Dragan Zivojinovic, 'Serbia and Montenegro: The Home Front, 1914–18', ibid., pp.239–59; Jean-Paul Amat, 'L'Inscription de la Guerre dans les Paysages Ruraux du Nord-est de la France', in Becker and Audoin-Rouzeau,

eds, *Les sociétés européennes*, pp.411–37; Simon Schama, *Landscape and Memory*, 2nd edn (London, 1996), pp.65–6.

5. Kitchen, *Silent Dictatorship*, pp.50–4; Marwick, *Deluge*, pp.36–9; John Horne, 'A Parliamentary State at War: France, 1914–18', in A. Cosgrove and J. I. McGuire, eds, *Parliament and Community* (Belfast, 1983), pp.211–35; Harvey, *Collision of Empires*, p.442; Cameron Hazlehurst, *Politicians at War, July 1914 to May 1915: A Prologue to the Triumph of Lloyd George* (London, 1971), pp.138–40; Bourne, *Britain and Great War*, p.106; Robbins, *First World War*, pp.137, 145; Peter Pastor, 'The Home Front in Hungary, 1914–18', in Király and Dreisziger, *East Central European Society*, pp.124–34; Galántai, *Hungary*, pp.80–84; Paul Corner and Giovanna Procacci, 'The Italian Experience of "Total" Mobilisation, 1915–20', in Horne, ed., *State, Society and Mobilisation*, pp.223–40; Beaumont, 'Politics of Divided Society', pp.35–63; Pam Maclean, 'War and Australian Society', in Beaumont, ed., *Australia's War*, pp.64–92; Kevin Fewster, 'The Operation of State Apparatuses in Times of Crisis: Censorship and Conscription, 1916', *W&S* 3 (1985), pp.37–54; Frank Cain, 'The Industrial Workers of the World: Aspects of its Suppression in Australia, 1916–19', *Labour History* 42 (1982), pp.54–62; Schaffer, *America in Great War*, pp.13–20; Kennedy, *Over Here*, pp.26–7, 75–81; Neil A. Wynn, *From Progressivism to Prosperity: World War I and American Society* (New York, 1986), pp.41–61.

6. Wilson, *Myriad Faces*, p.215; Shaffer, *America in Great War*, pp.37–8; G. R. Rubin, *Private Property, Government Requisition and the Constitution, 1914–27* (London, 1994), pp.23–38, 71–92.

7. French, 'Rise and Fall of Business as Usual', pp.22–5; Chris Wrigley, 'The Ministry of Munitions: An Innovatory Department', in Burk, ed., *War and State*, pp.32–56; R. J. Q. Adams, *Arms and the Wizard: Lloyd George and the Ministry of Munitions, 1915–16* (London, 1978), pp.64–8; Hazlehurst, *Politicians at War*, pp.196–200; Nicholas J. Griffin, 'Scientific Management and the Direction of Britain's Military Labour Establishment during World War I', *MA* 42 (1978), pp.197–201; Harvey, *Collision of Empires*, p.293; Peter Dewey, *War and Progress: Britain, 1914–45* (London, 1997), p.27.

8. Keith Neilson, 'Managing the War: Britain, Russia and ad hoc Government', in Dockrill and French, eds, *Strategy and Intelligence*, pp.96–118; Rodney Lowe, 'Government', in Constantine, Kirby and Rose, eds, *First World War in British History*, pp.29–50; L. Margaret Barnett, *British Food Policy during the First World War* (Boston, MA, 1985), pp.69–75; Trebilcock, 'War and Failure of Industrial Mobilisation', p.155; Sir Llewellyn Woodward, *Great Britain and the War of 1914–18*, 2nd edn (London, 1972), pp.489–91.

9. Rodney Lowe, 'The Ministry of Labour, 1916–19: A Still, Small Voice?', in Burk, ed., *War and State*, pp.108–34; Kathleen Burk, 'The Treasury: From Impotence to Power', ibid., pp.84–107; Wrigley, 'Ministry of Munitions', p.43; Turner, 'Higher Direction', pp.64–5.

10. Nenninger, 'American Military Effectiveness', pp.120–1; Schaffer, *America and Great War*, pp.31–63; Wynn, *Progressivism to Prosperity*, pp.65–82, 86–108; Valerie Connor, *The National War Labor Board: Stability, Social Justice and the Voluntary State in World War I* (Chapel Hill, NC, 1983), pp.18–34; Robert Cuff, 'Herbert Hoover, the Ideology of Voluntarism and War Organisation during the Great War', *Journal of American History* 64 (1977), pp.358–72; P. A. C. Koistinen, 'The Industrial–Military Complex in Historical Perspective', *BHR* 41 (1967), pp.378–403.

11. John F. Godfrey, *Capitalism at War: Industrial Policy and Bureaucracy in France, 1914–18* (Leamington Spa, 1987), pp.29–37, 47–52, 64–81, 85–99, 181–91, 289–93, 296; Porch, 'French Army', p.197; Gerd Hardach, 'Industrial Mobilisation in 1914–18: Production, Planning and Ideology', in Patrick Fridenson, ed., *The French Home Front, 1914–18* (Providence, RI, 1992), pp.57–88; Alain Hennebicque, 'Albert Thomas and the War Industries', ibid., pp.89–132.

12. Corner and Procacci, 'Italian Experience', pp.223–40; Luigi Tomassini, 'The Home Front in Italy', in Cecil and Liddle, eds, *Facing Armageddon*, pp.577–95; Douglas J. Forsyth, *The Crisis of Liberal Italy: Monetary and Financial Policy, 1914–22* (Cambridge, 1993); Gooch, 'Italy in First World War', p.163; Harvey, *Collision of Empires*, p.296.

13. G. D. Feldman, *Army, Industry and Labor in Germany, 1914–18* (Princeton, NJ, 1966), pp.45–52; idem, 'Hugo Stinnes and the Prospect of War before 1914', in Boemeke, Chickering and Förster, eds, *Anticipating Total War*, pp.77–95; Herwig, 'Strategic Uncertainties', p.267.

14. Wilhelm Deist, 'Voraussetzungen innenpolitischen Handelns das Militär im Ersten Weltkrieg', in Wilhelm Deist, ed., *Militär, Staat und Geseelschaft Studien zur preussisch-deutschen Militärgeschichte* (Munich, 1991), pp.103–52; Feldman, *Army, Industry and Labor*, pp.31–4, 73–116, 168–90, 253–66, 291–300, 385–404, 407–9, 420–5; Martin Schumacher, *Land und Politik: Eine Untersuchung über politische Parteien und agrarische Interessen, 1914–23* (Dusseldorf, 1978), pp.60–2.

15. Harvey, *Collision of Empires*, p.27; Hardach, *First World War*, pp.74–5; Herwig, *First World War*, pp.236–42; Pastor, 'Home Front in Hungary', pp.124–34.

16. Jonathan Boswell and Bruce Johns, 'Patriots or Profiteers? British Businessmen and the First World War', *Journal of European Economic History* 11 (1982), pp.423–45; John Turner, *British Politics and the Great War: Coalition and Conflict, 1915–18* (New Haven, CN, 1992), pp.336–63, 373–87; idem, 'The Politics of Organised Business in the First World War', in John Turner, ed., *Businessmen and Politics* (London, 1984), pp.33–4; Peter Cline, 'Eric Geddes and the "Experiment" with Businessmen in Government, 1915–22', in K. D. Brown, ed., *Essays in Anti-Labour History* (London, 1974), pp.74–104; Keith Grieves, 'Improvising the British War Effort: Eric Geddes and Lloyd George, 1915–18', *W&S* 7 (1989), pp.40–55; idem, 'The Transportation Mission to GHQ, 1916', in Bond, ed., *Look To Your Front*, pp.63–78; Ian Brown, *British Logistics on the Western Front, 1914–18* (Westport, CN, 1998), pp.139–74; John McDermott,

'"A Needless Sacrifice": British Businessmen and Business as Usual in the First World War', *Albion* 21 (1989), pp.263–82; Rodney Lowe, 'The Failure of Consensus in Britain: The National Industrial Conference, 1919–21', *HJ* 21 (1978), pp.647–75.

17. Shaffer, *America and Great War*, pp.47–63; Kennedy, *Over Here*, pp.126–33, 139–40; Ferro, *Great War*, p.172.

18. Michael Bliss, 'War Business as Usual: Canadian Munitions Production, 1914–18', in Dreisziger, ed., *Mobilisation for Total War*, pp.45–53.

19. James Joll, 'Walther Rathenau: Intellectual or Industrialist?', in Berghahn and Kitchen, eds, *Germany in Age of Total War*, pp.46–62; Wolfgang Michalka, 'Kriegsrohstoffbewirtschaftung, Walther Rathenau und die "kommende Wirtschft"', in Michalka, ed., *Erste Weltkrieg*, pp.485–505; D. G. Williamson, 'Walther Rathenau and the KRA, August 1914–March 1915', *Zeitschrift für Unternehmensgeschichte* 23 (1978), pp.118–36; Wolfgang J. Mommsen, 'Society and War: Two New Analyses of the First World War', *JMH* 47 (1975), pp.52–38; Gabriel Kolko, *Century of War: Politics, Conflicts and Society since 1914* (New York, 1994), p.71; Ferro, *Great War*, p.172; McNeill, *Pursuit of Power*, p.324; Kocka, *Facing Total War*, pp.30–9.

20. Godfrey, *Capitalism at War*, pp.60–4, 127–42, 150–79, 200–88; Hardach, 'Industrial Mobilisation', pp.76–8; Morrow, *Great War in the Air*, p.146; James M. Laux, 'Gnôme et Rhône: An Aviation Engine Firm in the First World War', in Fridenson, ed., *French Home Front*, pp.135–52; Robert O. Paxton, 'The Calcium Carbide Case and the Decriminalisation of Industrial Ententes in France, 1915–26', ibid., pp.153–80; Hew Strachan, 'Economic Mobilisation', in Hew Strachan, ed., *The Oxford Illustrated History of the First World War* (Oxford, 1998), p.144.

21. Hardach, *First World War*, pp.150–5; Dewey, *War and Progress*, pp.28–9; Theo Balderston, 'War, Finance and Inflation in Britain and Germany, 1914–18', *EcHR* 42 (1989), pp.222–44; Kennedy, *Rise and Fall*, pp.267–8; idem, 'Britain in First World War', p.33; Ferguson, *Pity of War*, pp.322–3.

22. Ferguson, *Pity of War*, pp.118–35, 322–6, 331–8; Harvey, *Collision of Empires*, p.274; Chickering, *Imperial Germany*, pp.103–8; Hardach, *First World War*, pp.156–66, 168–9; Marwick, *Deluge*, p.176; Herwig, *First World War*, pp.257–9; Woodward, *Great Britain and War*, pp.457–8, 514–20; Wilson, *Myriad Faces*, pp.646–7; G. D. Feldman, *The Great Disorder: Politics, Economics and Society in the German Inflation, 1914–24* (New York, 1993), pp.37–51; C.-L. Holtfrerich, *The German Inflation, 1914–23: Causes and Effects in International Perspective* (New York, 1986), pp.108–9; Manfred Zeidler, 'Die deutsche Kriegsfinanzierung 1914 bis 1918 und ihre Folgen', in Michalka, ed., *Erste Weltkrieg*, pp.415–33; Sullivan, 'Strategy of Decisive Weight', p.340; Bessel, 'Mobilisation and Demobilisation', pp.217–18; Robert Winnett, 'Cash in on Great War Investments', *Sunday Times* 24 Jan. 1999, p.7; James E. Cronin, *The Politics of State Expansion: War, State and Society in Twentieth Century Britain* (London, 1991), p.76.

23. Jonathan Manning, 'Wages and Purchasing Power', in Winter and Robert, eds, *Capital Cities*, pp.255–85; Hardach, *First World War*, pp.98, 169–73; Ferguson, *Pity of War*, pp.329–31; Ferro, *Great War*, pp.171–2; Peter Dewey, 'Nutrition and Living Standards in Wartime Britain', in Richard Wall and Jay Winter, eds, *The Upheaval of War: Family, Work and Welfare in Europe, 1914–18* (Cambridge, 1988), p.201; idem, *War and Progress*, pp.27, 31–2; Haig-Muir, 'Economy at War', p.109.

24. Ferguson, *Pity of War*, pp.252–4; Offer, *First World War*, p.65; Dewey, *War and Progress*, pp.43–5; Hardach, *First World War*, pp.31–4; Vincent, *Politics of Hunger*, p.49; Martin Horn, 'External Finance in Anglo-French Relations in the First World War', *IHR* 17 (1995), pp.51–77.

25. Kennedy, *Rise and Fall*, pp.258, 271; Ferguson, *Pity of War*, pp.248–9, 444.

26. Ferguson, *Pity of War*, pp.249–50, 254–9; Jay Winter, 'Some Paradoxes of the Great War', in Wall and Winter, eds, *Upheaval of War*, pp.9–42 [also in Becker and Audoin-Rouzeau, eds, *Les sociétés européennes*, pp.453–91]; Clive H. Lee, 'The Scottish Economy and the First World War', in Macdonald and McFarland, eds, *Scotland and Great War*, pp.11–35; Richard Bessel, *Germany After the First World War* (Oxford, 1993), p.17; Wolfgang J. Mommsen, 'The Social Consequences of World War I: The Case of Germany', in Marwick, ed., *Total War and Social Change*, pp.25–44.

27. Clive Trebilcock, 'The British Armaments Industry, 1890–1914: False Legends and True Utility', in Best and Wheatcroft, eds, *War, Economy and Military Mind*, pp.89–107; idem, 'War and Failure of Industrial Mobilisation', pp.155–8; Kennedy, 'Britain in First World War', pp.35, 44; Adams, *Arms and Wizard*, pp.53–4, 172–3; Peter Dewey, 'The New Warfare and Economic Mobilisation', in Turner, ed., *Britain and First World War*, pp.70–84.

28. Kennedy, *Rise and Fall*, pp.265–6; Challenor, *French Theory of Nation in Arms*, p.93; McNeill, *Pursuit of Power*, pp.319–22; Porch, 'French Army', pp.195–6; Ferguson, *Pity of War*, pp.250–1, 265–7; Hardach, 'Industrial Mobilisation', p.61; Laux, 'Gnôme et Rhône', pp.149–50; Godfrey, *Capitalism at War*, pp.64–81, 187; Buckley, *Air Power*, pp.62–6.

29. Gooch, 'Italy in First World War', p.163; Giovanna Procacci, 'A "Late-comer" in War: The Case of Italy', in Coetzee and Shevin-Coetzee, eds, *Authority*, pp.3–27.

30. Feldman, *Army, Industry and Labor*, pp.149–67, 253–83; Kitchen, *Silent Dictatorship*, pp.38–9, 48–9, 67–85; idem, 'Militarism and the Development of Fascist ideology: The Political Ideas of Colonel Max Bauer, 1916–18', *CEH* 8 (1975), pp.199–220; Morrow, *German Air Power*, pp.73–120, 189; idem, *Great War in the Air*, pp.222–33; Michael Geyer, *Deutsche Rüstungspolitik, 1860–1980* (Frankfurt, 1984), pp.90–105; Kennedy, *Rise and Fall*, p.272; McNeill, *Pursuit of Power*, p.340; Winter, 'Some Paradoxes', p.40.

31. Rothenberg, *Army of Francis Joseph*, p.193; Hardach, *First World War*, pp.74–7; Morrow, *German Air Power*, pp.167–85; Herwig, *First World War*, pp.237–42, 357; J. Robert Wegs, 'Transportation: The Achilles Heel of the Habsburg War Effort', in Kann, Kiràly and Fichtner, eds, *Habsburg Empire*, pp.121–34; idem, 'The Marshalling of Copper: An Index of Austro-Hungarian Economic Mobilisation during World War I', *Austrian History Yearbook* 12/13 (1976/77), pp.189–202; Ljuba Berov, 'The Bulgarian Economy during World War I', in Kiràly and Dreisziger, eds, *East Central European Society*, pp.170–83.

32. Dewey, *War and Progress*, pp.25–6; Roy MacLeod and Kay MacLeod, 'War and Economic Development: Government and the Optical Industry in Britain, 1914–18', in Winter, ed., *War and Economic Development*, pp.165–203; D. C. Coleman, 'War, Demand and industrial Supply: The "Dope Scandal", 1915–19', ibid., pp.205–27.

33. Dewey, 'Military Recruiting', pp.199–24; idem, 'New Warfare and Economic Mobilisation', pp.70–84; Grieves, *Politics of Manpower*, pp.40–60, 63–86, 90–114, 149–76; idem, 'Total War', pp.79–95; idem, 'The "Recruiting Margin" in Britain: Debates on Manpower during the Third Battle of Ypres', in Liddle, ed., *Passchendaele in Perspective*, pp.390–405; Adams and Poirier, *Conscription Controversy*, pp.171–82, 205–24, 241–4; Woodward, *Great Britain and War*, p.464; David Greasley and Les Oxley, 'Discontinuities in Competitiveness: The Impact of the First World War on British Industry', *EcHR* 49 (1996), pp.82–100.

34. Godfrey, *Capitalism at War*, p.186; Hardach, 'Industrial Mobilisation', pp.57–88; Marwick, *War and Social Change in Twentieth Century*, p.65; Ferro, *Great War*, p.120.

35. Feldman, *Army, Industry and Labor*, pp.73–96, 197–249, 301–16; idem, 'The Political and Social Foundations of Germany's Economic Mobilisation, 1914–16', *Armed Forces and Society* 3 (1976), pp.121–46; Gunther Mai, 'Burgfrieden und Sozialpolitik in Deutschland in der Anfangsphase des Ersten Weltkrieges', *MM* 22 (1976), pp.21–50; Ferguson, *Pity of War*, p.267; Ritter, *Sword and Sceptre*, III, pp.345–58; Herwig, *First World War*, p.260.

36. Ritter, *Sword and Sceptre*, III, pp.358–72; Bessel, *Germany after First World War*, pp.22–3; Polansky, 'German Occupation of Poland', pp.97–142; Molenda, 'Social Change in Poland', pp.187–201; François Roth, 'Lorraine Annexée et Lorraine Occupée, 1914–18', in Becker and Audoin-Rouzeau, eds, *Les sociétés européennes*, pp.289–309; Annette Becker, 'Life in an Occupied Zone: Lille, Roubaix, Tourcoing', in Cecil and Liddle, eds, *Facing Armageddon*, pp.630–41; Schaepdrijver, 'Occupation', p.272; Helen McPhail, *The Long Silence: Civilian Life under the German Occupation of Northern France, 1914–18* (London, 1999), pp.158–83; Richard B. Speed, *Prisoners, Diplomats, and the Great War: A Study in the Diplomacy of Captivity* (New York, 1990), pp.63–80; Fischer, *Germany's Aims*, pp.260–71, 593–8; D. Heal, 'Luxembourg in the Great War', *Stand To* 46 (1996), pp.29–32.

37. Herwig, *First World War*, p.280.

38. John Turner, '"Experts" and Interests: David Lloyd George and the Dilemmas of the Expanding State, 1906–19', in Roy MacLeod, ed., *Government and Expertise in Britain, 1815–1919* (Cambridge, 1988), pp.203–23; G. R. Rubin, *War, Law and Labour: The Munitions Acts, State Regulation and the Unions* (Oxford, 1987), p.203; Chris Wrigley, 'The First World War and State Intervention in Industrial Relations, 1914–18', in Chris Wrigley, ed., *A History of British Industrial Relations, 1914–39* (Brighton, 1987), pp.23–70; idem, 'Trade Unions and Politics in the First World War', in Ben Pimlott and Chris Cook, eds, *Trade Unions in British Politics*, 2nd edn (London, 1991), pp.69–87; idem, 'The Impact of the First World War on the British Labour Movement', in Dockrill and French, eds, *Strategy and Intelligence*, pp.139–59; idem, *David Lloyd George and the British Labour Movement* (Hassocks, 1976), pp.149–63, 180–204; idem, The State and the Challenge of Labour in Britain, 1917–20', in Chris Wrigley, ed., *Challenges of Labour: Central and Western Europe, 1917–20* (London, 1993), pp.262–88; Adams, *Arms and Wizard*, pp.80–9; Alistair Reid, 'Dilution, Trade Unionism and the State in Britain during the First World War', in S. Tolliday and J. Zeitlin, eds, *Shop Floor Bargaining and the State* (Cambridge, 1985), pp.46–74; idem, 'The Impact of the First World War on British Workers', in Wall and Winter, eds, *Upheaval of War*, pp.221–33; Bernard Waites, *A Class Society at War: England, 1914–18* (Leamington Spa, 1987), pp.184–93, 201–16.

39. Joseph Melling, 'Whatever Happened to Red Clydeside? Industrial Conflict and the Politics of Skill in the First World War', *International Review of Social History* 35 (1990), pp.3–32; John Foster, 'Strike Action and Working-class Politics on Clydeside, 1914–19', ibid., pp.33–70; J. Hinton, 'The Clyde Workers Committee and the Dilution Struggle', in Asa Briggs and John Saville, eds, *Essays in Labour History, 1886–1923* (London, 1971), pp.152–85; R. K. Middlemas, *The Clydesiders: A Left-wing Struggle for Parliamentary Power* (London, 1965), pp.58–113.

40. Ferguson, *Pity of War*, pp.274–5; Ferro, *Great War*, pp.178–9; Harvey, *Collision of Empires*, pp.431–2; I. G. Gerber, 'Corporatism in Comparative Perspective: The Impact of the First World War on American and British Labour Relations', *BHR* 62 (1988), pp.93–127; Henry Pelling, *Popular Politics and Society in Late Victorian Britain* (London, 1968), pp.147–64.

41. Patrick Fridenson, 'The Impact of the First World War on French Workers', in Wall and Winter, eds, *Upheaval of War*, pp.235–48; Martin Fine, 'Albert Thomas: A Reformist's Vision of Modernisation, 1914–32', *JCH* 12 (1977), pp.545–64; Hardach, 'Industrial Mobilisation', p.62; G. C. Humphreys, *Taylorism in France, 1904–20: The Impact of Scientific Management on Factory Relations and Society* (New York, 1986), pp.145–224; Thierry Bonzon, 'The Labour Market and Industrial Mobilisation, 1915–17', in Winter and Robert, eds, *Capital Cities*, pp.164–95; H. Lagrange, 'Strikes and the War', in L. H. Haimson and C. Tilly, eds, *Strikes, Wars and Revolutions in International Perspectives: Strike Waves in the Late Nineteenth and Early Twentieth Centuries* (Cambridge, 1989), pp.473–99; John Horne, *Labour at War: France and Britain, 1914–18* (Oxford,

1991), pp.59–60, 67–75, 176–96; idem, 'The State and the Challenge of Labour in France, 1917–20', in Wrigley, ed., *Challenge of Labour*, pp.239–61; idem, 'The Comité d'Action (CGT–Parti Socialiste) and the Origins of Labour Reformism, 1914–16', in Fridenson, ed., *French Home Front*, pp.241–79; Gilbert Hatry, 'Shop Stewards at Renault', ibid., pp.219–37.

42. Corner and Procacci, 'Italian Experience', pp.223–40; Procacci, 'Latecomer', pp.3–27; idem, 'Popular Protest and Labour Conflict in Italy, 1915–18', *Social History* 14 (1989), pp.31–58; idem, 'State Coercion and Worker Solidarity in Italy, 1915–18: The Moral and Political Context of Social Unrest', in L. Haimson and G. Sapelli, eds, *Strikes, Social Conflict and the First World War: An International Perspective* (Milan, 1991), pp.145–78; Luigi Tomassini, 'Industrial Mobilisation and State Intervention in Italy in the First World War: Effects on Labour Unrest', ibid., pp.179–212; idem, 'Industrial Mobilisation and the Labour Market in Italy during the First World War', *Social History* 26 (1991), pp.59–87; idem, 'Home Front in Italy', pp.577–95.

43. Kennedy, *Over Here*, pp.27–9, 73–4, 258–70; Maurine Weiner Greenwald, *Women, War, and Work: The Impact of World War I on Women Workers in the United States*, 2nd edn (Ithaca, NY, 1990), pp.48–53; Connor, *National War Labor Board*, pp.50–67, 89–125.

44. Feldman, *Army, Industry and Labor*, pp.73–96, 116–35, 316–61, 373–404, 409–42, 477–93; idem, 'Das deutsche Unternehmertum zwischen Krieg und Revolution: Die Entstehung des Stinnes-Legien-Abkommens', in G. D. Feldman, ed., *Vom Weltkrieg zur Weltwirtschaftskrise: Studien zur deutschen Wirtschafts und Sozialgeschichte, 1914–32* (Göttingen, 1984), pp.100–27; idem, 'War Economy and Controlled Economy: The Discrediting of "Socialism" in Germany during World War I', in Schröder, ed., *Confrontation and Co-operation*, pp.229–52; Friedhelm Boll, 'Le problème ouvrier et les grèves: l'Allemagne, 1914–18', in Becker and Audoin-Rouzeau, eds, *Les sociétés européennes*, pp.257–78; Harvey, *Collision of Empires*, p.431; Martin Kitchen, 'Hindenburg, Ludendorff and the Crisis of German Society, 1916–18', in Travers and Archer, eds, *Men at War*, pp.21–48; Kocka, *Facing Total War*, pp.46–8, 67–75.

45. Becker, *Great War and French People*, pp.113–49, 205–12, 325; Flood, *France, 1914–18*, pp.147–65; Thierry Bonzon and Belinda Davis, 'Feeding the Cities', in Winter and Robert, eds, *Capital Cities*, pp.305–41; Godfrey, *Capitalism at War*, p.120; Herwig, *First World War*, pp.361–5, 376–9; Stephen Bailey, 'The Berlin Strike of January 1918', *CEH* 13 (1980), pp.158–74.

46. Offer, *First World War*, pp.223–5, 338–47; French, *British Economic and Strategic Planning*, pp.51–3, 55–8.

47. Joe Lee, 'Administrators and Agriculture: Aspects of German Agricultural Policy in the First World War', in Winter, ed., *War and Economic Development*, pp.229–38; Lothar Burchardt, 'The Impact of the War Economy on the Civilian Population of Germany during the First and Second World Wars', in Wilhelm Deist, ed., *The German Military in the Age of Total War* (Leamington

Spa, 1985), pp.40–70; Alyson Jackson, 'Germany, the Home Front: Blockade, Government and Revolution', in Cecil and Liddle, eds, *Facing Armageddon*, pp.563–76; Ferro, *Great War*, p.121; R. G. Moeller, 'Dimensions of Social Conflict in the Great War: The View from the German Countryside', *CEH* 14 (1981), pp.142–68; N. P. Howard, 'The Social and Political Consequences of the Allied Food Blockade of Germany, 1918–19', *German History* 11 (1993), pp.161–88; Vincent, *Politics of Hunger*, pp.124–51; George Yaney, *The World of the Manager: Food Administration in Berlin during World War I* (New York, 1994), pp.21–44, 49–72, 99–141; Offer, *First World War*, pp. 25–6, 61–4; Bessel, *Germany after First World War*, pp.35–7; Belinda Davis, 'L'État contre la société: nourir Berlin, 1914–18', *GMCC* 183 (1996), pp.47–62; Keith Allen, 'Sharing Scarcity: Bread Rationing and the First World War in Berlin, 1914–23', *Social History* 32 (1998), pp.371–93.

48. Ferguson, *Pity of War*, pp.276–8; Harvey, *Collision of Empires*, p.299; Offer, *First World War*, pp.31–8, 45–53, 56–9, 66–7, 390; Peter Loewenberg, 'Germany, the Home Front: The Physical and Psychological Consequences of Home Front Hardship', in Cecil and Liddle, eds, *Facing Armageddon*, pp.554–62; Howard, 'Social and Political Consequences', pp.161–88; Strachan, *First World War*, p.18; Bessel, *Germany After First World War*, pp.40–2; Vincent, *Politics of Hunger*, pp.157–65.

49. Rothenberg, *Army of Francis Joseph*, p.193; Ferguson, *Pity of War*, p.252; Herwig, *First World War*, pp.272–9, 361–5; Horst Haselsteiner, 'The Habsburg Empire in World War I: Mobilisation of Food Supplies', in Király and Dreisziger, eds, *East Central European Society*, pp.87–102; Daniel Szabo, 'The Social Basis of Opposition to the War in Hungary', ibid., p.139; Plaschka, 'Army and Internal Conflict', pp.338–53.

50. Berov, 'Bulgarian Economy', pp.170–83.

51. Kennedy, *Rise and Fall*, p.266; Marwick, *War and Social Change in Twentieth Century*, p.54; Thierry Bonzon, 'La société, l'état et le pouvoir local: l'approvisionnement à Paris, 1914–18', *GMCC* 183 (1996), pp.11–28; Hardach, *First World War*, pp.111, 131–2; Procacci, 'Latecomer', pp.16–19; Luigi Tomassini, 'Approvisionnement, protestations et propagande en Italie pendant la première guerre mondiale', *GMCC* 183 (1996), pp.63–82; idem, 'Home Front in Italy', pp.577–95.

52. P. E. Dewey, *British Agriculture in the First World War* (London, 1989), pp.1–4, 7, 11–12, 36–56, 60–6, 69–77, 120–7, 139–42, 148–60, 164–9; idem, 'Agricultural Labour Supply in England and Wales during the First World War', *EcHR* 28 (1975), pp.100–12; idem, 'Government Provision of Farm Labour in England and Wales, 1914–18', *Agricultural History Review* 27 (1979), pp.110–21; Barnett, *British Food Policy*, pp.3–4.

53. Dewey, *British Agriculture*, pp.23–34, 91–103, 201–9, 227, 239–42; idem, 'Food Production and Policy in the United Kingdom, 1914–18', *Transactions of Royal Historical Society* 30 (1980), pp.71–89; idem, 'Nutrition and Living Standards',

pp.201–10; McNeill, *Pursuit of Power*, p.343; Barnett, *British Food Policy*, pp.20–34, 48–66, 193–207; Kathleen Burk, 'Wheat and the State during the First World War', in Dockrill and French, eds, *Strategy and Intelligence*, pp.119–38.

54. Barnett, *British Food Policy*, pp.35–40, 69–91, 125–57, 212, 216; José Harris, 'Bureaucrats and Businessmen in British Food Control, 1916–19', in Burk, ed., *War and State*, pp.135–56; R. Harrison, 'The War Emergency Workers' National Committee', in Briggs and Saville, eds, *Essays in Labour History*, pp.211–59; J. M. Winter, *Socialism and the Challenge of War* (London, 1974), pp.184–233; Horne, *Labour at War*, pp.219–34; Julia Bush, *Behind the Lines: East London Labour, 1914–19* (London, 1984), pp.35–68, 139–62; Bonzon and Davis, 'Feeding Cities', p.330; Jonathan Manning, 'La guerre et la consommation civile à Londres, 1914–18', *GMCC* 183 (1996), pp.29–46; French, 'Rise and Fall of Business as Usual', p.20; Burk, 'Wheat and the State', pp.119–38; Wrigley, 'Impact of First World War and Labour', pp.151–3; Dewey, 'Nutrition and Living Standards, pp.202–4, 210; Waites, *Class Society at War*, pp.211–13, 224–31.

55. Barnett, *British Food Policy*, pp.170–89, 211; Hardach, *First World War*, p.98.

56. Offer, *First World War*, pp.376–81; Kennedy, *Over Here*, pp.117–23.

57. John Turner, 'State Purchase of the Liquor Trade in the First World War', *HJ* 23 (1980), pp.589–615; M. Rose, 'The Success of Social Reform? The Central Control Board (Liquor Traffic), 1915–21', in Foot, ed., *War and Society*, pp.71–84; McNeill, *Pursuit of Power*, p.335.

58. Horne, 'Introduction', pp.1–18; idem, ' "L'Impôt du Sang": Republican Rhetoric and Industrial Warfare in France, 1914–18', *Social History* 14 (1989), pp.201–23; idem, 'État, société et "économie morale": l'approvisionnement des civils pendant la guerre de 1914–18', *GMCC* 183 (1996), pp.3–10; Jean-Louis Robert, 'The Image of the Profiteer', in Winter and Robert, eds, *Capital Cities*, pp.104–32; Thierry Bonzon, 'Transfer Payments and Social Policy', ibid., pp.286–302; Cronin, *Politics of State Expansion*, pp.37–48; Bernard Waites, 'The Government of the Home Front and the "Moral Economy" of the Working Class', in Liddle, ed., *Home Fires and Foreign Fields*, pp.175–93; K. Burgess, 'The Political Economy of British Engineering Workers during the First World War', in Haimson and Tilly, eds, *Strikes, Wars and Revolutions*, pp.289–320; Simon Fowler, 'War Charity Begins at Home', *History Today* 49 (1999), pp.17–23.

59. Turner, *British Politics*, pp.29, 38–40, 379; Dewey, *War and Progress*, p.37; Martin Pugh, *The Making of Modern British Politics, 1867–1939*, 2nd edn (Oxford, 1993), pp.113–21, 200–4; Gerber, 'Corporatism in Comparative Perspectice', pp.93–127; Noel Whiteside, 'Industrial Welfare and Labour Regulation in Britain at the Time of the First World War', *International Review of Social History* 25 (1980), pp.307–31; idem, 'Welfare Legislation and the Unions during the First World War', *HJ* 23 (1980), pp.857–74; idem, 'The British Population at War', in Turner, ed., *Britain and First World War*, pp.85–

98; A. Ineson and D. Thom, 'TNT Poisoning and the Employment of Women Workers in the First World War', in Paul Weindling, ed., *A Social History of Occupational Health* (London, 1985), pp.89–107; Deborah Thom, *Nice Girls and Rude Girls: Women Workers in World War I* (London, 1998), pp.122–39, 164–87; Angela Woollacott, 'Maternalism, Professionalism and Industrial Welfare Supervisors in World War I Britain', *Women's History Review* 3 (1994), pp.29–56; Wilson, *Myriad Faces of War*, pp.800, 805–9; Adams, *Arms and Wizard*, pp.129–31; M. Swenarton, *Homes Fit for Heroes: The Politics and Architecture of Early State Housing in Britain* (London, 1981), pp.48–66; Gail Braybon and Penny Summerfield, *Out of the Cage: Women's Experiences in Two World Wars* (London, 1987), p.95; Deborah Dwork, *War is Good for Babies and Other Young Children: A History of the Infant and Child Welfare Movement in England, 1898–1918* (London, 1987), pp.88–90, 211–14; J. M. Winter, 'The Impact of the First World War on Civilian Health in Britain', *EcHR* 30 (1977), pp.487–507; idem, *Great War and British People*, pp.167–78, 188–211, 240–3; Susanna Magri, 'Housing', in Winter and Robert, eds, *Capital Cities*, pp.374–417; Richard A. Soloway, 'Eugenics and Pronatalism in Wartime Britain', in Wall and Winter, eds, *Upheaval of War*, pp.369–88.

60. Marwick, *Deluge*, pp.124–5; Wilson, *Myriad Faces*, pp.814–19; Rex Pope, *War and Society in Britain, 1899–1948* (London, 1991), p.60.

61. Greenwald, *Women, War and Work*, p.53; Schaffer, *America in Great War*, pp.64–74, 96–108; Fridenson, 'Impact of War on French Workers', pp.240–1; Mathilde Dubesset, Françoise Thébard and Catherine Vincent, 'The Female Munitions Workers of the Seine', in Fridenson, ed., *French Home Front*, pp.183–218; Procacci, 'Latecomers', pp.3–27; Catherine Rollet, 'The "Other War" I: Protecting Public Health', in Winter and Robert, eds, *Capital Cities*, pp.421–55; Francesca Lagorio, 'Italian Widows of the First World War', in Coetzee and Shevin-Coetzee, eds, *Authority*, pp.175–98.

62. Ute Daniel, 'The Politics of Rationing versus the Politics of Subsistence: Working Class Women in Germany, 1914–18', in Roger Fletcher, ed., *Bernstein to Brandt: A Short History of German Social Democracy* (London, 1987), pp.89–95; eadem, 'Women's Work in Industry and Family: Germany, 1914–18', in Wall and Winter, eds, *Upheaval of War*, pp.267–96; Paul Weindling, 'The Medical Profession, Social Hygiene and the Birth rate in Germany, 1914–18', ibid., pp.417–37; Eve Rosenhaft, 'Restoring Moral Order on the Home Front: Compulsory Savings Plans for Young Workers in Germany, 1916–19', in Coetzee and Shevin-Coetzee, eds, *Authority*, pp.81–109; Ewald Frie, Vorbild oder Spiegelbild? Kriegsbeschädigtenfürsorge in Deutschland, 1914–19', in Michalka, ed., *Erste Weltkrieg*, pp.563–80; Young-Sun Hong, 'The Contradictions of Modernisation in the German Welfare State: Gender and the Politics of Welfare Reform in First World War Germany', *Social History* 17 (1992), pp.251–70; Bessel, *Germany After First World War*, pp.41–2; Marwick, *War and Social Change in Twentieth Century*, pp.41–2; Kocka, *Total War*, p.157; Karin Haussen, 'The German Nation's Obligation to the Heroes' Widows', in

Higonet, Jenson, Michael and Weitz, eds, *Behind the Lines*, pp.126–40; Offer, *First World War*, pp.58–9.

63. Corner and Procacci, 'Italian Experience', pp.223–40; Tomassini, 'Industrial Mobilisation', pp.86–7.

64. R. H. Tawney, 'The Abolition of Economic Controls, 1918–21', *EcHR* 12 (1943), pp.1–30; P. Abrams, 'The Failure of Social Reform, 1918–20', *P&P* 24 (1963), pp.43–64; Peter Cline, 'Winding Down the War Economy: British Plans for Peacetime Recovery, 1916–19', in Burk, ed., *War and State*, pp.157–81; Rodney Lowe, 'The Erosion of State Intervention in Britain, 1917–24', *EcHR* 31 (1978), pp.270–86.

65. Turner, 'Higher Direction', pp.75–8; Burk, 'Treasury', pp.97–102; Lowe, 'Ministry of Labour', pp.119–31; idem, 'Government', pp.29–50.

66. Wrigley, 'Ministry of Munitions', pp.47–52; Lowe, 'Erosion of State Intervention', pp.270–86; idem, 'Government', pp.29–50; Barnett, *British Food Policy*, pp.212–17; Swenarton, *Homes Fit for Heroes*, pp.67–135; L. F. Orbach, *Homes for Heroes: A Study of the Evolution of British Public Housing, 1915–21* (London, 1977), pp.9–33; 68–88, 126–38; M. Kirby, 'Industry, Agriculture and Trade Unions', in Constantine, Kirby and Rose, eds, *First World War in British History*, pp.51–80; Paul Barton Johnson, *Land Fit for Heroes: The Planning of British Reconstruction, 1916–19* (Chicago, IL, 1968), pp.59–67, 107–17, 175–218, 487–9, 502–5; G. R. Rubin, 'Law as a Bargaining Weapon: British Labour and the Restoration of Pre-war Practices Act, 1919', *HJ* 32 (1989), pp.925–45; Abrams, 'Failure of Social Reform', pp.43–65; B. B. Gilbert, *British Social Policy, 1914–1939* (London, 1970), pp.51–161; Waites, *Class Society at War*, pp.216–21; Cronin, *Politics of State Expansion*, pp.72–8, 87–92; idem, 'The Crisis of State and Society in Britain, 1917–22', in Haimson and Tilly, eds, *Strikes, Wars and Revolutions*, pp.457–73; Joshua Cole, 'The Transition to Peace, 1918–19', in Winter and Robert, eds, *Capital Cities*, pp.196–226; Marwick, *Deluge*, pp.258–65, 296–308; ibid., 2nd edn, p.33.

67. Godfrey, *Capitalism at War*, pp.237, 297–300; Horne, 'Comité d'Action', pp.241–79; idem, *Labour at War*, pp.350–94; Marwick, *War and Social Change in Twentieth Century*, pp.66, 90.

68. Schaffer, *America and Great War*, pp.213–17; Kennedy, *Over Here*, pp.140–2, 245–58; Wynn, *Progressivism to Prosperity*, pp.196–221; William E. Leuchtenburg, 'The New Deal and the Analogue of War', in John Braemen, Robert Bremner and Everett Walters, eds, *Change and Continuity in Twentieth Century America* (Columbus, OH, 1964), pp.81–143.

69. Marwick, *War and Social Change in Twentieth Century*, pp.89–90, 214–15; Arthur Marwick and Bill Purdue, 'The Debate over the Impact and Consequences of World War I', in Henry Cowper, Clive Emsley, Arthur Marwick, Bill Purdue, David Englander, eds, *World War I and its Consequences* (Buckingham, 1990), pp.98–100.

70. Gordon Craig, 'The Political Leader as Strategist', in Paret, ed., *Makers of Modern Strategy*, pp.482–91; Kitchen, *Silent Dictatorship*, pp.271–8.

71. L. L. Farrar, 'Nationalism in Wartime: Critiquing the Conventional Wisdom', in Coetzee and Shevin-Coetzee, eds, *Authority*, pp.133–51; Horne, 'Introduction', pp.1–18; idem, Remobilising for "Total War": France and Britain, 1917–18', in Horne, ed., *State, Society and Mobilisation*, pp.195–211; idem, 'Social Identity in War: France, 1914–18', in T. G. Fraser and Keith Jeffery, eds, *Men, Women and War* (Dublin, 1993), pp.119–35; Walter L. Adamson, 'The Impact of World War I on Italian Political Culture', in Roshwald and Stites, eds, *European Culture*, pp.308–17; Flood, *France, 1914–18*, pp.147–65; Jay Winter, *Sites of Memory, Sites of Mourning: The Great War in European Cultural History* (Cambridge, 1995), pp.82–5, 122–31; idem, *Experience of World War I*, pp.230–3; idem, 'Nationalism, the Visual Arts and the Myth of War Enthusiasm in 1914', *History of European Ideas* 15 (1992), pp.357–62; George L. Mosse, *Fallen Soldiers: Reshaping the Memory of the World Wars* (New York, 1990), pp.126–44; Heike Hoffmann, '"Schwarzer Peter im Weltkrieg": Die deutsche Spielwarenindustrie, 1914–18', in Hirschfeld, Krumeich, Langewiesche and Ullman, eds, *Kriegserfahrungen*, pp.323–35; Harriet Rudolph, 'Kultureller Wandel und Krieg: Die Reaktion der Werbesproche auf die Erfahrung des Ertsen Weltkriegs am Bespiel von Zeitungsanzeigen', ibid., pp.283–301.

72. J. M. McEwen, 'The National Press during the First World War: Ownership and Circulation', *JCH* 17 (1982), pp.459–86; Ferguson, *Pity of War*, pp.241–6; Alice Goldfarb Marquis, 'Words as Weapons: Propaganda in Britain and Germany during the First World War', *JCH* 13 (1978), pp.467–98; David Welch, 'Cinema and Society in Imperial Germany, 1905–18', *German History* 8 (1990), pp.28–45; Nicholas Hiley, 'The News Media and British Propaganda, 1914–18', in Becker and Audoin-Rouzeau, eds, *Les sociétés européennes*, pp.175–81; Schaffer, *America in Great War*, p.12; Schaepdrijver, 'Occupation', pp.276–7; Guido Convents, 'Cinema and German Politics in Occupied Belgium', in Karel Dibbets and Bert Hogenkamp, eds, *Film and the First World War* (Amsterdam, 1995), pp.171–8; Jerzy Toeplitz, 'The Cinema in Eastern and Central Europe before the Guns of August', ibid., pp.17–27.

73. Colin J. Lovelace, 'British Press Censorship during the First World War', in George Boyce, James Curran and Pauline Wingate, eds, *Newspaper History: From the Seventeenth Century to the Present Day* (London, 1978), pp.307–19; Philip Towle, 'The Debate on Wartime Censorship in Britain, 1902–14', in Bond and Roy, eds, *War and Society*, pp.103–16; D. Hopkins, 'Domestic Censorship in the First World War', *JCH* 4 (1970), pp.151–69; J. M. McEwen, '"Brass-Hats" and the British Press during the First World War', *CJH* 18 (1988), pp.43–67; Keith Grieves, 'War Correspondents and Conducting Officers on the Western Front from 1915', in Cecil and Liddle, eds, *Facing Armageddon*, pp.719–35; Hiley, 'News Media', pp.175–81; idem, 'La bataille de la Somme et les médias de Londres', in Becker, Winter, Krumeich, Becker and Audoin-Rouzeau, eds, *Guerre et Cultures*, pp.193–206; Stephen Badsey and Philip Taylor,

'Images of Battle: The Press Propaganda and Passchendaele', in Liddle, ed., *Passchendaele in Perspective*, pp.371–89.

74. J. A. Keshen, *Propaganda and Censorship during Canada's Great War* (Edmonton, 1996); Flood, *France, 1914–18*, pp.25–6; Wilhelm Deist, 'Censorship and Propaganda in Germany during the First World War', in Becker and Audoin-Rouzeau, eds, *Les sociétés européennes*, pp.199–210; Gary D. Stark, 'All Quiet on the Home Front: Popular Entertainment's, Censorship and Civilian Morale in Germany, 1914–18', in Coetzee and Shevin-Coetzee, eds, *Authority*, pp.57–80; Marilyn Shevin-Coetzee, 'Popular Nationalism in Germany during World War I', *History of European Ideas* 15 (1992), pp.369–75; Kurt Kosyk, 'La bataille de Somme dans la presse des Puissances centrales', in Becker, Winter, Krumeich, Becker and Audoin-Rouzeau, eds, *Guerre et Cultures*, pp.207–20; Martin Creutz, 'Les journalistes et la censure dans l'Empire allemand pendant la Grande Guerre', ibid., pp.221–8; Mark Cornwall, 'News, Rumours and the Control of Information in Austria-Hungary, 1914–18', *History* 77 (1992), pp.50–64; Harvey, *Collision of Empires*, p.478.

75. Stéphane Audoin-Rouzeau, '"Bourrage de Crâne" et Information en France en 1914–18', in Becker and Audoin-Rouzeau, eds, *Les sociétés européennes*, pp.163–74; Becker, *Great War and French People*, pp.42–63; French, 'One-man Show', pp.78–9; J. M. McEwen, 'Lloyd George and Northcliffe at War, 1914–18', *HJ* 24 (1981), pp.651–72; idem, 'The Press and the Fall of Asquith', *HJ* 21 (1978), pp.863–83.

76. Bourne, *Britain and Great War*, pp.231–2; Cate Haste, *Keep the Home Fires Burning: Propaganda in the First World War* (London, 1977), pp.108–39; Eberhard Demm, 'Propaganda and Caricature in the First World War', *JCH* 28 (1993), pp.163–92; idem, 'The Battle of the Cartoonists: German, French and English Caricatures in World War I', in Haim Shamir, ed., *France and Germany in an Age of Crisis, 1900–60: Studies in Memory of Charles Bloch* (Leiden, 1990), pp.127–44; Philip Dutton, '"Geschäft über Alles": Notes on Some Medallions inspired by the Sinking of the Lusitania', *IWMR* 1 (1986), pp.30–42; Robbins, *First World War*, p.139; David French, 'Spy Fever in Britain, 1900–1915', *HJ* 21 (1978), pp.355–70; Panikos Panayi, *The Enemy in Our Midst: Germans in Britain during the First World War* (New York, 1991), pp.153–83, 199–200, 223–58; idem, 'Anti-German Riots in London during the First World War', *German History* 7 (1989), pp.184–203; idem, 'Germans in Britain during the First World War', *Historical Research* 64 (1991), pp.63–76; idem, 'An Intolerant Act by an Intolerant Society: The Internment of Germans in Britain during the First World War', in David Cesarani and Tony Kushner, eds, *The Internment of Aliens in Twentieth Century Britain* (London, 1993), pp.53–78; Catriona M. M. Macdonald, 'May 1915: Race, Riot and Representations of War', in Macdonald and McFarland, eds, *Scotland and Great War*, pp.145–72; David Saunders, 'Aliens in Britain and Empire during the First World War', in Frances Swyripa and John Herd Thompson, eds, *Loyalties in Conflict* (Edmonton, 1983), pp.99–124; John Herd Thompson, *The Harvests of War* (Toronto,

1978), pp.73–94; Desmond Morton, 'Sir William Otter and Internment Operations in Canada during the First World War', *CHR* 55 (1974), pp.32–58; David Englander, 'Public Order in Britain, 1914–18', in Clive Emsley and Barbara Weinberger, eds, *Policing Western Europe: Politics, Professionalism and Public Order, 1850–1940* (New York, 1991), pp.90–138; McKernan, *Australian People and Great War*, pp.150–77; Maclean, 'War and Australian Society', pp.84–8; Oliver, *War and Peace*, pp.61–84; Stephen Vaughan, *Holding Fast the Inner Lines: Democracy, Nationalism and the Committee on Public Information* (Chapel Hill, NC, 1980), pp.3–22, 61–82, 98–140, 214–32; David Kennedy, 'Rallying Americans for War, 1917–18', in James Titus, ed., *The Home Front and War in the Twentieth Century: The American Experience in Combative Perspective* (Washington DC, 1982), pp.47–56; M. Levene, 'Frontiers of Genocide: Jews in the Eastern War Zones, 1914–20 and 1941', in Panayi, ed., *Minorities in Wartime*, pp.83–117; Jörg Nagler, 'Victims of the Home Front: Enemy Aliens in the United States during the First World War', ibid., pp.191–215; Gerhard Fischer, 'Fighting the War at Home: The Campaign against Enemy Aliens in Australia during the First World War', ibid., pp.263–86; David Cesarani, 'An Embattled Minority: The Jews in Britain during the First World War', in T. Kushner and K. Lunn, eds, *The Politics of Marginality: Race, the Radical Right and Minorities in Twentieth Century Britain* (London, 1990), pp.61–81; M. S. Seligmann, 'The First World War and the Undermining of the German Jewish Identity as seen through American Diplomatic Eyes', in Taithe and Thornton, eds, *War*, pp.193–202; Pam Maclean, 'Control and Cleanliness: German–Jewish Relations in Occupied Eastern Europe during the First World War', *W&S* 6 (1988), pp.47–69; Aviel Roshwald, 'Jewish Cultural Identity in Eastern and Central Europe during the Great War', in Roshwald and Stites, eds, *European Culture*, pp.89–126.

77. D. G. Wright, 'The Great War, Government Propaganda and English "Men of Letters"', *Literature and History* 7 (1978), pp.70–100; Steven W. Siak, '"The Blood that is in our Veins comes from German Ancestors": British Historians and the Coming of the First World War', *Albion* 30 (1998), pp.221–52; Stuart Wallace, *War and the Image of Germany: British Academics, 1914–18* (Edinburgh, 1988), pp.29–42, 58–73, 167–90; Peter Buitenhuis, *The Great War of Words: Literature as Propganda, 1914–18 and After* (London, 1989), pp.37–53; Gary Messinger, *British Propaganda and the State in the First World War* (Manchester, 1992), pp.24–52, 85–98, 225–34; Schaffer, *America in Great War*, pp.109–48; Martha Hanna, *The Mobilisation of Intellect: French Scholars and Writers during the Great War* (Cambridge, MA, 1996), pp.79–208; Wolfgang J. Mommsen, 'German Artists, Writers and Intellectuals and the Meaning of War, 1914–18', in Horne, ed., *State, Society and Mobilisation*, pp.21–38; Peter Jelavich, 'German Culture in the Great War', in Roshwald and Stites, eds, *European Culture*, pp.42–7; Steven Beller, 'The Tragic Carnival: Austrian Culture in the First World War', ibid., pp.139–46; Evelina Kelbetcheva, 'Between Apology and Denial: Bulgarian Culture during World War I', ibid., pp.223–8; Bucur, 'Romania', ibid., pp.259–64; Schaepdrijver, 'Occupation', ibid., pp.271–3; Ivan

Sanders, 'Hungarian Writers and Literature in World War I', in Király and Dreisziger, eds, *East Central European Society*, pp.145–54; Robert A. Kann, 'Trends in Austro-German Literature during World War I: War Hysteria and Patriotism', in Kann, Király and Fichtner, eds, *Habsburg Empire*, pp.159–83; Eva S. Balogh, 'The Turning of the World: Hungarian Progressive Writers on the War', ibid., pp.185–201; Wilson, *Myriad Faces*, p.402; Jean-François Sirinelli, 'Les intellectuels français et la guerre', in Becker and Audoin-Rouzeau, eds, *Les sociétés européennes*, pp.145–61; Eberhard Demm, 'Les intellectuels allemands et la guerre', ibid., pp.183–97; Robbins, *First World War*, p.157.

78. Wilkinson, *Church of England*, pp.32–90, 251–5; John Wolfe, *God and Greater Britain: Religion and National Life in Britain and Ireland, 1843–1945* (London, 1994), pp.236–53; Schweitzer, 'Cross and Trenches', pp.33–58; McKernan, *Australian People and Great War*, pp.14–42; Maclean, 'War and Australian Society', pp.73–4; James McMillan, 'French Catholics: Rumeurs Infâmes and the Union Sacrée, 1914–18', in Coetzee and Shevin-Coetzee, eds, *Authority*, pp.113–32; Becker, *Great War and French People*, pp.178–91; Flood, *France, 1914–18*, pp.96–107; Gerhard Besier, 'Les Églises Protestantes en Allemagne, en Grande-Bretagne, en France, et le Front Intérieur, 1914–18', in Becker and Audoin-Rouzea, eds, *Les sociétés européennes*, pp.211–35; Annette Becker, *War and Faith: The Religious Imagination in France, 1914–30* (Oxford, 1998); pp.7–17; Robbins, *First World War*, p.158; J. A. Moses, 'State, War, Revolution and the German Evangelical Church, 1914–18', *Journal of Religious Studies* 17 (1992), pp.47–59; Kurt Meier, 'Evangelische Kirche und Erster Weltkrieg', in Michalka, ed., *Erste Weltkrieg*, pp.691–724; Heniz Hürten, 'Die katholische Kirche im Ersten Weltkreig', ibid., pp.725–35; Clemens Picht, 'Zwischen Vaterland und Volk: Das deutsche Judentum im Ersten Weltkrieg', ibid., pp.736–56; Hoffmann, 'Between Integration and Rejection', pp.89–104.

79. McKernan, *Australian People and Great War*, pp.43–64; Becker, *Great War and French People*, pp.150–60; Andrea Fava, 'War, "National Education" and the Italian Primary School, 1915–18', in Horne, ed., *State, Society and Mobilisation*, pp.53–69; S. Audoin-Rouzeau, 'Children and the Primary Schools of France, 1914–18', ibid., pp.39–52; idem, 'Die mobilisierten Kinder: Die Erziehung zum Krieg an französischen Schluen', in Hirschfeld and Krumeich, eds, *Keiner fühlt sich hier als Mensch*, pp.151–74; idem, '"L'enfant héroïque" en 1914–18', in Becker, Winter, Krumeich, Becker and Audoin-Rouzeau, eds, *Guerre et Cultures*, pp.173–182; idem, 'French Children as Target for Propaganda', in Cecil and Liddle, eds, *Facing Armageddon*, pp.767–79; S. Audoin-Rouzeau and A. Becker, 'Violence et consentement, la culture de guerre du premier conflit mondial', in J. P. Rioux and J. P. Sirinelli, eds, *Pour une histoire culturelle* (Paris, 1997), pp.251–71; Flood, *France, 1914–18*, pp.84–96; Eberhard Demm, 'German Teachers at War', ibid., pp.709–18; Kennedy, *Over Here*, pp.53–9.

80. Michael Sanders and Philip M. Taylor, *British Propaganda during the First World War, 1914–18* (London, 1982); Michael Sanders, 'Wellington House and British Propaganda during the First World War', *HJ* 18 (1975), pp.119–46; Philip

Taylor, 'The Foreign Office and British Propaganda during the First World War', *HJ* 23 (1980), pp.875–88; Ruth Harris, 'The "Child of the Barbarian": Rape, Race and Nationalism in France during the First World War', *P&P* 141 (1993), pp.170–206; Wilson, *Myriad Faces*, pp.743–7; Michelle Shaver, 'Roles and Images of Women in World War I Propaganda', *Politics and Society* 5 (1975), pp.469–86; Harold D. Lasswell, *Propaganda Technique in World War I*, 2nd edn (Cambridge, MA, 1971), pp.77–101, 161–84, 206; E. Demm, 'Les thèmes de la propagande allemande en 1914', *GMCC* 150 (1984), pp.3–16; Jean-Claude Montant, 'L'Organisation Centrale des Services d'Informations et de Propagande du Quai d'Orsay pendant la Grande Guerre', in Becker and Audoin-Rouzeau, eds, *Les sociétés européennes*, pp.135–43; Michel Dumoulin, 'La propagande belge dans les pays neutres au début de la première guerre mondiale', *Revue Belge d'histoire Militaire* 22 (1977), pp.246–59.

81. Simkins, *Kitchener's Army*, pp.122–3; Hiley, 'News Media and British Propaganda', pp.175–81; idem, 'Sir Hedley Le Bas and the Origins of Domestic Propaganda in Britain, 1914–17', *Journal of Advertising History* 10 (1987), pp.34–40; idem, ' "Kitchener Wants You" and "Daddy, What did you do in the War?" The Myth of British Recruiting Posters', *IWMR* 11 (1997), pp.40–58; Englander, 'People at War', pp.235–6; P. Renouvin, 'L'Opinion publique et la guerre en 1917', *Revue d'Histoire Moderne et Contemporaine* 15 (1968), pp.4–23; Nicoletta F. Gullace, 'Sexual Violence and Family Honor: British Propaganda and International Law during the First World War', *AHR* 102 (1997), pp.714–47; Marquis, 'Words as Weapons', pp.467–98; Ferguson, *Pity of War*, pp.212–14, 223–5, 227–9, 231–5; Bessel, *Germany After First World War*, p.259.

82. Nicholas Reeves, *Official British Film Propaganda during the First World War* (London, 1986), pp.44–81, 125–32, 142–5, 157–69, 189–219, 222–48; idem, ' "The Real Thing at Last": The Battle of the Somme and the Domestic Cinema Audience in the Autumn of 1916', *The Historian* 51 (1996), pp.4–8; idem, 'Film Propaganda and its Audience: The Example of Britain's Official Films during the First World War', *JCH* 18 (1983), pp.463–94; idem, 'Through the Eye of the Camera: Contemporary Cinema Audiences and their "Experience" of War in the Film, Battle of the Somme', in Cecil and Liddle, eds, *Facing Armageddon*, pp.780–98; idem, 'Official British Film Propaganda', in Michael Paris, ed., *The First World War and Popular Cinema: 1914 to the Present* (Edinburgh, 1999), pp.27–50; Roger Smither, ' "A Wonderful Idea of the Fighting": The Question of Fakes in "The Battle of the Somme" ', *HJFRT* 13 (1993), pp.1499–68; S. D. Badsey, 'Battle of the Somme: British War Propaganda', *HJFRT* 3 (1983), pp.99–115; Gary Messinger, 'An Inheritance Worth Remembering: The British Approach to Official Propaganda during the First World War', *HJFRT*, 13 (1993), pp.117–28.

83. Rainier Rother, 'Bei Unseren Helden an der Somme (1917): The Creation of a "Social Event" ', *HJFRT* 15 (1995), pp.525–42; idem, 'The Experience of the First World War and the German Film', in Paris, ed., *First World War and Popular Cinema*, pp.217–46; Franz Marksteiner, 'Where is the War? Some

Aspects of the Effects of World War One on Austrian Cinema', ibid., pp.247–60; Welch, 'Cinema and Society', pp.28–45; Jay Winter and Blaine Baggett, *1914–18: The Great War and the Shaping of the Twentieth Century* (London, 1996), p.143; Stark, 'All Quiet on Home Front', pp.67–75; Wolfgang Mühl-Benninghaus, 'German Film Censorship during World War I', *Film History* 9 (1997), pp.71–94; Jelavich, 'German Culture', pp.36–42; Ramona Curry, 'How Early German Film Stars Helped Sell the War(es)', in Dibbets and Hogenkamp, eds, *Film and First World War*, pp.139–48.

84. Leslie Midkiff DeBauche, *Reel Patriotism: The Movies and World War I* (Madison, WI, 1997), pp.27, 35, 37–41, 48, 63–71, 81–4, 111–34, 147–57; idem, 'The United States' Film Industry and World War One', in Paris, ed., *First World War and Popular Cinema*, pp.138–61; idem, 'Mary Pickford's Public on the Home Front', in Dibbets and Hogenkamp, eds, *Film and First World War*, pp.149–59; Robin Blaetz, 'Joan of Arc and the War', ibid., pp.116–24; Tim Travers, 'Canadian Film and the First World War', in Paris, ed., *First World War and Popular Cinema*, pp.96–114.

85. Pierre Sorlin, 'France: The Silent Memory', in Paris, ed., *First World War and Popular Cinema*, pp.115–37; Giovanni Vitelleschi, 'The Representation of the Great War in Italian Cinema', ibid., pp.172–91.

CHAPTER NINE

War and Society

In further refining his interpretation of the relationship between war and social change, Arthur Marwick suggested differentiating 'society at war' from 'society not at war' as more meaningful than considering 'war and society' as two distinct variables. This is helpful in recognising that war is not separate from society but that, from time to time, societies engage in war in a way which adds wartime processes to existing agents of change as part of a continuum between the peacetime and wartime experience.[1]

This does not necessarily make the assessment of the impact of war any easier. It can assist differentiation between long-term 'unguided' structural changes, such as those deriving from demographic pressures or the processes of industrialisation and urbanisation, and shorter-term 'guided' changes such as the kinds of institutional decision made by governments and dealt with in the previous chapter. Nonetheless, it may still be difficult to judge the relative significance of guided and unguided factors in stimulating any given change. There is also the operation of what Marwick has described as 'contingency', in other words sheer chance.

Some trends can be measured in modern states, but others must remain a matter of speculation. Indeed, the calculation of changes in perceptions and attitudes is qualitative rather than quantitative and, therefore, problematical. Moreover, a society embraces a multitude of individuals interrelating in complex, overlapping and changing patterns, according to a variety of determinants both within and beyond their control. While class is usually regarded as the primary social relationship, war often has a greater impact upon the relationship between men and women, and between young and old, since individuals' experience of war is determined more by age and gender than by class. Societies are not uniform in their development and the likely effect of war will also vary depending both upon the nature of a particular society and the intensity of its war experience. It renders gener-alisation exceptionally hazardous.[2]

Life and death

Questions of mortality and life expectancy provide a ready example of the difficulties of assessing war's true impact. Clearly, there was immense loss of life in the short term. In the long term, however, the war may not have made any substantial difference in demographic terms, and there is a con-siderable debate as to its impact upon civilian health. Indeed, the war cut across demographic trends in complicated ways, when some states such as France were experiencing a declining birth rate before the war and others population growth.

Precise figures of war losses are all but impossible to determine. The general assumption is that the war resulted in 9–10 million military dead worldwide. This is not the same as total war dead or war-related dead, an even more difficult figure to calculate through such distortions as wartime and post-war refugees, post-war redrawing of frontiers, and continuing con-flict in Russia. In any case, as with other statistics, those of demography are difficult to interpret. It is easier to determine female life expectancy than male life expectancy, which is greatly distorted by wartime service. Material conditions varied widely while the mobility of population in wartime also ensured the mixing of different demographic profiles.

Accordingly, there is little agreement on what might be termed the 'demographic deficit'. One calculation for Britain, France, Germany and Austria-Hungary yields a civilian death toll of 3.7 million and a birth deficit of 15.3 million. Another suggests between 20 and 24 million. It is virtually impossible, however, to compute the total of war losses, war-related losses and losses of potential births. Moreover, these kinds of calculation exclude both the estimated 1.5 million Armenian victims of the Turks, and also the victims of the influenza pandemic of 1918. The latter, indeed, may have cost well over 21 million lives.[3]

The exact relationship between the war and 'Spanish influenza' – so-called owing to the mistaken belief that it was brought by seamen to the Spanish peninsula from Asia – is hard to determine. The traditional explana-tion was that wartime privation created conditions conducive to the conver-sion of the outbreak from an epidemic to a pandemic, while also facilitating its transmission. It did begin in crowded army camps in the United States in March 1918. Yet, the soldiers first affected had not yet gone overseas and the United States experienced little wartime privation. Moreover, between

12 and 16 million deaths were in India, which was not directly affected by the war. Similarly, it killed an estimated one-quarter of the population of the South Pacific islands. Neutral states were just as badly afflicted. Nor did influenza take any account of class, equally attacking those whose better nutritional levels should have assisted resistance. Specifically, it struck young adults rather than more vulnerable groups such as the elderly and, among adults, women rather than men, probably owing to the greater number of women in urban areas prior to military demobilisation.

The influenza was not regarded as significant when the first cases appeared in the United States, but it spread rapidly to Europe through the American Expeditionary Force's disembarkation ports. While waning within a few months, influenza impacted upon the conduct of the war by the way in which it weakened the German army during Ludendorff's ongoing western offensives. British troops carried the disease to Murmansk in Russia in June 1918 and, through commerce on the high seas, it had reached the Far East and Australasia by July. Sometime in August 1918, for reasons still not fully understood, the virus mutated with more virulent outbreaks in Freetown in Sierra Leone, Brest in France and Boston in Massachusetts. By June 1919, an estimated 675,000 Americans had died from the disease, of whom perhaps 550,000 would not otherwise have died.

One of the best known of the 166,000 French victims was the poet, Guillaume Appollinaire, who survived a severe head wound in 1917 only to die of influenza two days before the armistice. Britain lost perhaps 228,000 to influenza, including Leefe Robinson, who had shot down the first Zeppelin over England. Germany lost about 174,000 to the disease. Possibly 300,000 Africans died, South Africa being especially hit since the Cape was a major shipping route. There was one final bout of influenza in early 1920 but this was far less virulent.[4]

Rather more directly war-related, the classic 'military disease' of typhus was widespread in eastern Europe at the end of the war though unknown on the Western Front. It caused between 135,000 and 160,000 deaths in Serbia over the winter of 1914–15, and an estimated 1.5 million deaths in Russia by 1920. Cholera was also rife on the Italian front in early 1915.[5]

War dead may be interpreted in differing ways. In terms of the individual impact of war dead, the shadow was arguably cast most across France, which suffered about 1.3 million dead, representing 16.8 per cent of those mobilised and 13.3 per cent of the male population aged between 15 and 49. This was primarily because the French birth rate was already lower than that of most other European states. Germany lost more men – approximately 2 million dead – but this represented a smaller proportion of those mobilised (15.4 per cent) and a smaller proportion of males between 15 and 49 (12.5 per cent). While Germany recorded the largest number of military dead, Serbia lost the largest proportion both of those mobilised (37.1 per cent) and of males aged 15 to 49 (22.7 per cent).[6]

In the case of Britain, military dead numbered approximately 722,000. It represented a loss of about 11.8 per cent of those mobilised and 6.3 per cent of males aged between 15 and 49. It has been argued by Jay Winter that the effect was dysgenic, in that some sectors of society had volunteered in greater proportion to others, while many working-class men had been physically unfit for military service through the level of pre-war deprivation in urban areas. Moreover, officers suffered proportionally more dead than other ranks. Thus, there was an element of truth in the post-war concept of a 'lost generation' among the potential future socio-political elite, although, as Winter has remarked, the greater fertility among poorer classes and the greater availability of contraception to their social superiors equally affected the vitality of traditional elites.[7]

The demographic gain in Britain, as elsewhere, outweighed the demographic loss since the British population grew by some 2 million between 1911 and 1921, albeit with a reduced growth rate compared with that between 1901 and 1911. Men over military age appear to have experienced improved chances of survival during the war and, generally, there was 'an absolute and a relative improvement in the survival chances of manual workers'. Female health also improved, although there was an increase in tuberculosis against the general trend, conceivably from the greater migration of wartime population to urban centres coupled with the deterioration in housing conditions under pressure of population. Having fallen by some 7 per cent between 1905 and 1913, infant mortality declined by a further 20 per cent between 1913 and 1919, despite an increase in infant disease in 1915. The only exception to the trend was in illegitimate births.

As suggested in the previous chapter, much was due to the improvement in the nutrition of mothers and children, enhanced concerns for infant and maternal welfare seen in better medical care, and increases in family income through separation allowances and wages keeping pace with inflation. Generally, the British working class was better fed and clothed during the war than before it. Even the acute housing shortage, by compelling children to remain with their mothers and thus keeping the size of households large, contributed to greater income for individual households and thus to the overall improvement in the living standards. State liquor control also had its effect through lowering the incidence of neglect from parental alcoholism. Rationing may also have improved diets in some cases.[8]

It is argued that these paradoxically higher living standards were not eroded by post-war economic depression, particularly as families remained smaller. The social scientist A. L. Bowley concluded in 1924 that there was only half as much poverty in Britain as there had been in 1913. In general, too, the concept of poverty was subtly changing as a result of increasing wartime expectations, from a measurement of subsistence to an assessment of relative deprivation in terms of goods and service enjoyed by other working-class families.

In any case, the war did not substantially alter existing demographic trends. Thus, while there was an increase in marriages at the beginning and at the end of the war, female celibacy rates did not increase. Nor did the average age differential between husbands and wives, although the war did mark a change in that more of the population married than before and at an earlier age, and more divorced. The difficulty is to judge whether more marriages were directly related to the war, in terms perhaps of making men and women more willing and more adventurous in marrying, or whether there were other quite imponderable factors.

Increased nuptiality, however, did not lead to an increase in the birth rate. The birth rate declined sharply during the war but, by the 1920s, had reverted to its pre-war pattern of a more gradual decline. In turn, the declining birth rate cancelled out the general increase in life expectancy. In short, in demographic terms, the loss of life in Britain was not large and was made good relatively quickly.[9]

Winter's figures for increasing British wartime health have been disputed, since his 'life data' are based on mortality rates rather than morbidity rates and may disguise wide regional variations. Other statistics have been suggested as demonstrating more continuity with pre-war trends, especially with respect to children, such as height measurements. It is also argued that modern epidemiology has suggested that increases in tuberculosis could as easily be due to malnutrition as overcrowding and that this was recognised by some wartime medical opinion. Winter's further research, however, has established the general value of aggregate life table data, demonstating that the war had a positive effect on civilian health in Britain and France, a negative impact in Belgium and Germany and, as might be expected, no significant effect on Sweden. While acknowledging the contribution that malnutrition might make to tuberculosis, Winter has also pointed out that it represented only 6 per cent of total mortality and was easily outweighed by improvements in other previous fatal conditions.

Winter has now modified his earlier conclusions with regard to at least London in view of some of the contradictions of female mortality apparent from his later research. Generally, it would appear that the elderly and young adults fared worse, and children best. Common to at least Paris, London and Berlin was a rise in deaths among illegitimate children and the elderly, while there was a general upward trend in tuberculosis among young women. Those historians who have criticised Winter, however, have themselves indicated that there was still considerable continuity between pre-war and post-war trends, again suggesting little demographic impact since the trends were towards long-term diminution in mortality rates and improved infant health.[10]

In France, despite some variations amongst differing population groups and the large losses, life expectancy after 1918 was broadly the same, as if no war had occurred. As in Britain, men over military age increased their life expectancy, suggesting a similar general improvement in civilian health. With the exception of 1918, when female deaths increased dramatically as a result of influenza, female mortality rates differed little from the pre-war period. Compensation for the absence of war dead came from increased male immigration into France from southern Europe and the French Empire, increased rates of marriage and remarriage, and French women marrying younger men than would have been normal prior to the war. The birth rate, which had been declining steadily prior to the war, continued to do so, with only 313,000 declared births in 1916. There was then a substantial increase, with over 833,000 declared births in 1920 and over 811,000 in 1921, assisted by the active pro-natalism campaign and the prohibition of advice on abortion and birth control in July 1920. As in Britain, the divorce rate also increased after the war.[11]

German military war dead were naturally also predominantly young. Some 39.9 per cent were between the ages of 20 and 25 and 68.8 per cent were single. In addition, however, there was the effect of the blockade. Reference has already been made in the previous chapter to estimates of the resulting additional civilian deaths as being between 250,000 and 424,000. Female mortality certainly increased, with a substantial rise in deaths from tuberculosis. Civilian life expectancy was reduced significantly between 1916 and 1918, but with an upward trend of infant deaths already occurring by 1915.[12]

Just as Germany demonstrates the war's demographic impact differently from Britain and France, so do the figures available for Belgium, although these are distorted by the German occupation and the near-famine conditions existing by 1917–18. It is clear that both male and female civilian mortality increased, with perhaps 240,000 war-related deaths. Having lost much of its population as refugees, the Belgian birth rate declined by 40 per cent. Infant mortality also increased in 1916–17.[13]

Further afield, the demographic pattern accorded more with the British experience. Men outnumbered women in every age group in pre-war Australia. Consequently, although Australia's 60,000 war dead reduced the ratio of males to females in the 20–24 and 25–29 age groups, nuptial rates were reduced by only 3–4 per cent. Moreover, post-war male immigration speedily compensated for war losses and the war made little difference to the long-term demographic trend.[14]

Yet, the impact of the war was also felt over a longer term, both through dependants left widows or orphans, and through prolongation or even delay of suffering. In 1928, with many dependants either no longer needing support or having been declared ineligible for it, the German government calculated that, in addition to over 820,000 disabled servicemen, there were still 1.6 million dependants to provide for, including over 359,000 widows and over 787,000 fatherless children or orphans, the balance being made up of aged parents. Some 18 per cent of the Weimar government's expenditure was devoted to war-related pensions by 1929, taking up as much as 30 per cent of those funds available to the federal authorities once reparations and subsidies to states had been deducted.

In Britain, over 192,000 widows' pensions had been granted by 1921 including provision for over 344,000 children. In 1921, some 1.1 million men were in receipt of disability pensions, 36,400 men being considered to have 100 per cent disability, although this figure had climbed to 2.4 million by 1929. According to the British Legion in November 1927, over 4,000 ex-servicemen had developed epilepsy as a result of war service and over 42,000 had contracted tuberculosis. There were still 3,000 limbless survivors of the war in Britain in 1977 and still 27,000 men living in receipt of disability pensions in 1980. Some 11,501 American servicemen were still undergoing treatment for various war-related conditions in veterans' hospitals or domiciliary care in 1940, 9,305 of them for neuropsychiatric illnesses. Around 1 million Frenchmen were in receipt of invalidity pensions after 1918. Of these, 120,000 were amputees or otherwise mutilated and 50,000 men had 100 per cent disability. In all, perhaps 280,000 British, French and German ex-servicemen were permanently disfigured, the *gueles cassées* (broken faces).[15]

The sense of loss could also hit harder when those originally listed as missing were subsequently found to be dead, as with some 25 per cent of the 28,000 bodies of British soldiers found for the first time between 1921 and 1928, at which point the memorials to the missing in France and Flanders alone contained over 268,000 names. There were still 100,000 Germans unaccounted for in 1933. Bodies are still regularly discovered in France and Flanders. To give but one example, three soldiers of the 13th Battalion, Royal Fusiliers – two identifiable and one unknown – killed at Monchy near Arras in April 1917 and discovered during new building work eighty years later, were reinterred in April 1998.[16]

Class

Turning to the war's impact upon the structure of society, it is especially difficult to quantify class, especially as individuals' own perception of their

status was liable to be subjective, and the opportunities for vertical or hori-
zontal social mobility might vary considerably. Social structure is not uniform,
which makes it difficult to generalise in terms of suggesting, for example,
that the middle classes suffered most in Europe and the industrial working
class did best. Moreover, eastern European society was not comparable to
that in western Europe.

Within the pattern of an overall trend, a high degree of social mobility
might be in operation as some individuals seized opportunities to move
upwards while the position of others declined. Clearly, there were winners
and losers in the wartime distortion of the normal market relationship
between capital and labour. The most obvious winners were likely to be
those involved in war production, some businessmen and traders. The likely
losers were those in non-essential employment, those on fixed incomes and
marginal groups such as the elderly. In the process, socio-economic differentials were likely to be narrowed, but older inequalities would remain
alongside newer divisions thrown up by war.[17]

There is some evidence of a compression and simplification of the class
structure existing in Britain as a result of the war, although this should not
be pressed too far. Cutting across the existing structure, the war imposed
a degree of equality, not least through the increase in the numbers paying
income tax from 1.5 million in 1914, when the starting point was annual
income of £160, to 7.7 million by 1918, the threshold being lowered to
£130 in 1916. Indirect taxation also increased dramatically on commodities such as beer, spirits, tobacco, matches, sugar, cocoa, coffee and motor
vehicles, increasing the average burden on a family from 6 per cent of
income to 10 per cent of income.

While other wartime financial changes hit many in the middle class, to
varying degrees, the working class benefited from increasing wages and
transfer payments such as separation allowances. In the process, there was
a narrowing of the gap between the working class and the middle class. This
was also true within the working class, which had been highly com-
partmentalised, not least in the division between the skilled and unskilled.[18]

The old British landed elite had already been badly affected by the
agricultural depression at the end of the nineteenth century and the Liberal
government's pre-war taxation policies. The burden was increased by wartime taxes and death duties, which increased to 40 per cent on estates over
£2 million in 1919. Many heirs to estates were also lost on active service.
There had been pre-war land sales but nothing on the scale of the sale of
between 6 and 8 million acres in England and Wales, including perhaps
one-quarter of all cultivated land in Britain, between 1918 and 1922. Land
sales released capital for investment elsewhere at a time when land values had
risen more than rents. Yet, it was still the case that, in 1925–26, the net income

of the two wealthiest groups in society – those earning above £2,000 a year in 1913–14 – was some 60 per cent less than it had been before the war.

Moreover, the landed tended to withdraw after 1918 from traditional social and political leadership in county communities in what F. M. L. Thompson has characterised as 'self-liquidation'. The land itself passed mostly to former tenant farmers. Arguably, there were bigger losses of land among the gentry since more aristocratic families survived with at least a nucleus of their former estates. Moreover, the traditional elite had never been a caste but a relatively open society and new money moved into land ownership, Lloyd George creating 98 new peers between 1917 and 1921. Thus, the composition of the landed class changed without any essential transformation of its relationship with other classes.

Elsewhere, particularly where the aristocracy had been of a different nationality from the peasant population, as in the Baltic states, Slovakia and Romania, the traditional elite was weakened by the appearance of new post-war states. In eastern Europe and the Baltic states, land confiscation undermined the position of the old elite, while revolution removed it altogether in Russia. Conceivably, some 60 million acres changed hands in eastern and central Europe as peasants either received or seized land. Monarchy, too, crumbled in Russia, Germany and Austria-Hungary and those states created from Russia and Austria-Hungary, although it survived in Bulgaria. In Britain, by contrast, it was considerably strengthened by the anglicisation of the dynastic name and the image of the Royal Family sharing the people's privations.[19]

In terms of the middle class, the proportion of white-collar workers in the British labour force rose from 1.7 million to 2.7 million between 1911 and 1921, representing an increase from 12 per cent to 22 per cent of the population in work. In itself, this suggests some of the narrowing of differentials as more aspired to the status of salaried. As with other sectors of society, however, there were many subtle variations in situation, status and experience within the middle class. Some businessmen undoubtedly did well through the expansion of industry, some traders benefited from the black market, and some retailers from the enhanced purchasing power of the working class. On the other hand, there was rising taxation, the fall of rentals, a collapse of traditional safe investment, and the loss of purchasing power deriving from the declining value of fixed incomes. The Professional Classes War Relief Council claimed to be assisting 10,000 British families by July 1918 with expenses such as school fees. In the medium-term, however, middle-class finances recovered relatively rapidly through the government's post-war deflationary policies.[20]

More is said of the position of labour later in this chapter, but it has been argued that the erosion of differentials between skilled and unskilled during the war made the working class more homogeneous than previously. Skill had become less important in a machine age and, as Bernard Waites has remarked, the term 'artisan' dropped from usage after the war. Through increased unionisation and greater self-assertiveness borne of the enhancement of its status in wartime, Waites argues, the British working class became more prone to class conflict, especially when it was fuelled by common detestation for profiteering.

By contrast, Alistair Reid has argued that the pre-war gap between skilled and unskilled has been exaggerated and a concentration on evidence from the engineering industry has also masked the degree to which the gap between skilled and unskilled genuinely narrowed. Thus, the working class shared 'not an increasingly homogeneous class position but rather a common experience of institutional changes'. Wartime competition for wage rises had clearly exacerbated older skill demarcation disputes in some cases. There had been winners as well as losers within the working class as well as the division between those who had fought and those who had not.

In any case, greater class awareness did not mean the emergence of a revolutionary working class, as evinced by the failure of the Labour Party to win working class political support after the war. Both Waites and Reid, moreover, agree that those gains made by the working class derived from the increased bargaining position of 'constitutional' labour in relation to the state rather than from any change in social relationships between classes. In other words, while much poverty had been eliminated, national income redistributed to a degree, differentials eroded and opportunities expanded, most groups advanced together in broadly the same relationship as before. In Britain, therefore, to quote Waites, the war 'did not fundamentally disturb those processes of social differentiation which are generic to a capitalist market society'.[21] The same has been said of Australia, where the war did not result in any major break in the existing pattern of class relationships, partly as a result of the insulation of distance from the main theatres of war, and partly from a less rigid class structure.[22]

In the case of Germany, it has been argued by Jürgen Kocka that class divisions intensified during the war, not only between entrepreneurs and the rest of society, but also within the *Mittelstand* (middle class). In the latter, the division was between white-collar workers on the one hand, and the *Handwerker* (skilled artisans) and *Kleinhändler* (small retailers) on the other. Kocka also argues that the German working class did well only in the context of losing less than other social groups. In particular, however, the war hit retailers, artisans and white-collar workers as well as civil servants, all of whose status had rested on the respectability of salaried non-manual labour and their autonomy within society *vis-à-vis* both entrepreneurs and working class. Retailers were hit by the depression of consumer expenditure.

The middle classes generally suffered from the loss of investments in worthless government bonds and the decline in the value of fixed incomes, including rentals, in the face of wartime inflation. Indeed, while there was an attempt to maintain the wages of public sector manual workers, this was not true of their salaried colleagues.

As calculated by the Imperial Statistical Office, real income of officials fell by between 47 and 70 per cent according to grade, the worst affected being the best educated upper echelons. Similarly, one organisation of white-collar workers, the Deutscher Handlungsgehilfen-Verband (DHV; German Clerks Association), calculated that the average wages of its 123,000 members had increased by only 18.2 per cent by December 1917 compared with an average rise in the cost of living of 185 per cent. The proportion of self-employed also dropped significantly. Interestingly, however, while all Germans found less to purchase, class consumption patterns remained generally much the same throughout the period between 1902 and 1928.

Kocka argues that, while the *Mittelstand* as a whole was radicalised, there was increasing 'class polarisation' within it. The 'old' *Mittelstand* of higher civil servants, artisans and small retailers became more aligned with industrialists in recognition of their mutual hostility towards both organised labour and also the increasing intervention of the state in the economy. The 'new' *Mittelstand* of white-collar workers found increasingly common ground in adversity with organised labour, though lower civil servants generally were less politicised than others.

Taken with other tensions within the Reich such as the divisions between urban and rural communities and between regions, these class tensions added to the hostility towards the state. It can be argued, therefore, that the collapse of Germany was a movement directed against the state, and OHL in particular, rather than against capital. Indeed, the Stinnes-Legien Agreement in October 1918 suggests not only that the position of labour had been strengthened but that so too had the degree of mutual interest between capital and labour in opposition to state intervention.

Together with the continuing support of much of the German middle class for expansive war aims, this might explain why the German working class was not by nature revolutionary. Certainly, it is noticeable that the collapse of Germany was engineered by mutinies among servicemen who were better fed and paid than most Germans. Notwithstanding the 'stab in the back' myth, it was only after the military and naval collapse that the German home front imploded. Equally, however, the perceived decline of the traditional middle strata of society provided a significant element in what Wolfgang Mommsen has characterised as the 'seedbed for extreme nationalism'. Rather similarly, Charles Maier has seen the post-war rise of fascism in Germany and Italy as a defensive response on the part of embattled 'bourgeois' society to the collaboration of industry and organised labour.[23]

Labour

There was a substantial increase in the size of the labour force in most belligerents. Not surprisingly, there was also a dramatic decrease in unemployment as war economies developed although, initially, there was considerable additional unemployment owing to the prevailing economic uncertainty at the outbreak of war. In the process of expansion, trade unions generally increased in strength and, through the need of the state to ensure war production, the position of labour within society generally improved in the short term. Wartime gains, however, were not always sustained.

In Britain the numbers in trade unions increased from about 4.1 million in 1913 to 8.3 million by 1920. Where trade unions were already strong, they increased their strength but considerable gains were also made in areas where unions had previously been weak, such as agriculture and white-collar occupations and among the unskilled. Moreover, the number of trade unionists formally affiliated to the Trades Union Council increased from 2.2 million in 1913 to 4.5 million by 1918.

At the same time, the war stimulated amalgamation among unions, the Iron and Steel Trades Confederation coming into existence in 1917 and six other federated unions in early 1918. Increased unionisation and federation, the latter often prompted by the rank and file, again suggests a greater sense of solidarity and social consciousness within the working class. The subsequent decline in union membership in the midst of the depression in the 1920s might also suggest that members saw them only as a means to an end in acquiring greater bargaining power and not as an expression of class cohesion or solidarity.[24]

United States trade union membership grew from 3.1 million in 1917 to 4.2 million in 1919, although it was the stronger unions within the American Federation of Labor (AFL) that most improved their position. War also encouraged the creation in August 1918, under the AFL's aegis, of a National Committee for Organising Iron and Steel Workers to penetrate an industry from which unions had been largely excluded since the 1890s, and which was characterised by the employment of largely unskilled immigrant labour. In the event, not only was a large-scale steel strike in September 1919 broken by the employers, but the collapse of an industrial conference convened by Woodrow Wilson in January 1920 effectively limited labour's wartime gains. Wartime wage increases were also soon eroded by continuing inflation and there was no guarantee on the part of government for labour's right of collective bargaining.[25]

A similar pattern of wartime increase in union membership was duplicated elsewhere, as in France, where the increase was from 2 to 3 million. The CGT had represented only some 6 per cent of French labour in 1914, with some 237,000 members. Its membership declined initially but, through the recruitment of younger entrants to employment, it had 576,000 members by 1918 and 1.2 million by 1920. In Hungary, there was a sevenfold increase in union membership during the war. In Australia, too, union membership increased from 523,271 to 581,755, with the proportion of the labour force that was unionised rising from 27.9 per cent in 1911 to 51.6 per cent by 1921. As elsewhere, the war also stimulated the emergence of fewer, larger unions through amalgamation.[26]

Germany proved something of an exception. In 1914, the 'free' trade unions linked with the SPD (Social Democratic Party), as opposed to the 'yellow' trade unions sponsored by employers, had some 2.5 million members. Conscription increasingly denuded the active union membership, 64 per cent of all trade unionists being in the army by 1916. Some ground was then regained, although often through the recruitment of women or juveniles, but the total membership of the SPD unions had still reached only 1.6 million by 1918. There was, however, a massive increase in unionisation after the armistice, taking the total to 5.4 million in 1919.[27]

The need for government to ensure the continuance of production generally resulted in lower working hours and higher wages in most states. In Britain, it is estimated that, between 1914 and 1918, average working hours fell from 50 hours per week to between 44 and 48 hours per week, and the average wage rose from £51 per week in 1911 to £103 per week in 1924. Higher wages in monetary terms, however, did not necessarily equate to higher wages in real terms since what mattered to the individual was the purchasing power of wages in relation to wartime inflation, and the amount of disposable income available.

All statistics, however, need to be treated with care because averages tend to hide considerable differences between one industry and another, and there could be wide variations even within the same industry. They also hide the initial downturn in wages through economic uncertainties in 1914. Generally, wage differentials narrowed between skilled and unskilled labour, between men and women, and between older and younger workers although, again, there were wide variations. As might be expected, those employed in war industries generally did better than those employed in occupations more marginal to the war effort. By 1917, for example, while average wages in Britain had risen by 55 per cent, those in the cotton industry had risen by only between 14 and 20 per cent. At that date, the largest increases had been secured by miners, unskilled engineering workers, iron ore miners, blast-furnacemen and iron and steel millmen.

Wage data are equally difficult to calculate given the additional complication of piece-rates, time-rates, bonuses, overtime payments and other variations. Practices varied, so that while the skilled were paid on piece-rates (i.e. by results) and the unskilled on time-rates (i.e. by the hour) in wartime Paris, the opposite was true in Berlin. Similarly, in Britain unskilled engineering workers were paid on piece-rates and the skilled by the hour, whereas the reverse was true in steel and shipbuilding. In the past, a presumption was made that skilled men paid by the hour would not benefit to the same extent as semi-skilled or unskilled men paid by piece-work rates. This ignored, however, the widespread official and unofficial bonuses and incentives provided for skilled labour although flat-rate bonuses, which were increasingly negotiated nationally, would tend to add a greater percentage to lower wages.[28]

In Britain, much of the earlier interpretation of the effect of dilution and the narrowing of differentials within and between differing sectors of industry was based on the engineering industry. The experience of labour employed in other sectors such as shipbuilding was very different. Differentials between the skilled and unskilled were certainly eroded since labour rather than skill was what was predominantly required. Indeed, dilution did tend to prove that skilled men were less necessary than imagined, especially with the advances of wartime automation techniques. Similarly, arbitration on the part of wartime tribunals tended to advantage the unskilled since flat wage rises were often the result. In engineering, the general improvement of the unskilled in relation to the skilled was in the order of 14 per cent, but it averaged less than 7 per cent in other heavy industries such as mining and shipbuilding.

Wartime 'winners' included engine drivers, railway platelayers and railway porters, while wartime 'losers' included textile workers and male shop assistants. While, however, it can be argued that the greatest gains were made by those who, before the war, had been the most poorly paid, it does not mean that the skilled were actually losers. Even in engineering, dilution most often meant that the skilled would be moved to supervisory roles. Moreover, the skilled remained in a sufficiently strong bargaining position to recover any temporary loss both during and after the war.[29]

In calculating the extent of labour's gains, much depends upon the relationship of wages to prices. On average about 75 per cent of household expenditure had been devoted to food, fuel and housing in pre-war Britain. Ministry of Food calculations suggest that total weekly expenditure by working-class families on food increased by about 60 per cent between 1914 and 1918. Increased earnings, transfer payments such as separation allowances, and changes in consumption patterns generally offset some of the effects of inflation.

In any case, inflation did not affect all commodities uniformly, food and clothing prices rising far faster than those for fuel. Housing was often in short supply but rents were controlled and increasing expenditure on tobacco more-or-less cancelled out decreasing expenditure on controlled liquor. Clothing prices probably represented the most significant additional financial burden but economies could be made on clothing, so that a greater proportion of working-class income was available for food than prior to the war. Yet, an average increase in retail prices of perhaps 25 to 30 per cent a year still represented a considerable break from the pre-war experience of increases of only 1 or 2 per cent.[30]

Wages in real terms did keep ahead of inflation in Britain overall although they did not actually catch the cost of living until the very end of the war. This was far from the case in Germany or Austria-Hungary. In the former, both wages and employment were hit at the outbreak of war, but unemployment fell below the pre-war average in June 1915 and wages also began to increase. Real wages, however, declined. From a nominal base 100 in 1914, while the cost of living (excluding black market prices) stood at 304 in 1918, average monetary wages stood at 234 and average real wages at only 73.

Again there were wide variations both regionally and between industries, with men in the electrical and chemical industries benefiting the most and those in food production the least. In the process, wage differentials between skilled and unskilled were distorted. In Bavaria, the differential diminished in civil industries and increased in war industries, but in the Rhineland, it was the differential between the skilled and the unskilled in war industries which diminished with the skilled paid by the hour and the unskilled by piece-rates. As in Britain, inflation was a psychological shock when the pre-war economy had been stable. Already by the end of 1915, it is estimated that one-quarter of all German households were in receipt of war-related family-support.[31]

There is a natural tendency to concentrate upon the experience of the industrial working class familiar in western societies but, of course, peasants made up the majority of the working population in much of central and eastern Europe. It has been argued that something of a transformation in peasant societies was already under way prior to 1914 and that this was accelerated during the war. Certainly, peasants benefited at least in theory from the land redistribution, which accompanied the appearance of new creations such as the Baltic states, and the restructuring of older states such as Romania, where Magyar and Russian landowners were displaced. Peasant parties also emerged in many states and peasant interests were more strongly represented. In many cases, however, declining agricultural income and pressure of population undermined the apparent gains.[32]

Women

It is well known that there were substantial increases in the number of women in employment during the war. Traditionally, it has been said that this wartime participation enhanced the status of women to the extent that, in Britain, they received the vote in 1918. The crucial question, however, is whether there was such a change in women's status within society and, if so, whether such a change would have occurred anyway and was merely accelerated by the war. It also needs to be borne in mind that contemporaries had a different perception of emancipation than is now common: in 1914 it simply meant equal rights in the public sphere.[33]

The perceived role of women in much initial wartime propaganda was traditional, with emphasis upon supporting recruiting. In some cases, this involved handing out white feathers but, more usually, women were expected to provide material comforts for servicemen and, at most, take on a role in nursing. The heroism of women such as Dr Elsie Inglis of the Scottish Women's Hospital in Serbia – whose original offer to form an ambulance unit had been met with the memorable response at the War Office, 'My good lady, go home and sit still' – equally served traditional perceptions of the woman's role. Indeed, propaganda reasserted feminisation and the traditional feminine role. Significantly, Belgium was represented in feminine terms in British propaganda, and the fate of Belgian women at the hands of rapacious German troops was an early propaganda theme. Paradoxically, at the same time, there was both more than a hint of sexual reward in the depiction of women's role in recruiting efforts and a concern with the exposure of vulnerable young recruits to prostitution.

Ultimately, with the expansion of war industry, the emphasis changed. This was especially so in Britain when there was something of a labour shortage in munitions work in 1916–17. Indeed, it became almost fashionable for even middle-class and upper-class women to contemplate becoming a 'munitionette', although no more than perhaps 9 per cent of them were from these classes. Not only did women become more visible in industrial employment, but they clearly ran the risks of TNT poisoning, from which 109 women died in Britain during the war, and of industrial accidents. An explosion at the national filling factory at Barnbow killed 35 women in December 1916 while many women were among the 69 fatalities in an explosion at Silvertown in east London in January 1917; 35 women died in another at Chilwell in July 1918.[34]

Britain provides a good example of the subsequent militarisation of women's roles. Initially, middle- and upper-class women responded to appeals to undertake voluntary efforts, such as assisting the 200,000 Belgian refugees who reached Britain in the autumn of 1914. This was an acceptable extension of traditional social service and a variety of support groups and comforts funds were created for refugees, servicemen, prisoners and those working-class women laid off in 1914. Upper- and middle-class women also undertook the morality patrols by the Women's Police Service and the Women's Patrols Committee of the National Union of Women Workers in the vicinity of army camps, an activity then extended to factories by agreement with the Ministry of Munitions in July 1915.

Quasi-military organisations were also created under the patronage of titled women, although even they aroused suspicion through donning quasi-military uniform, which appeared to take them beyond acceptable feminine roles. Traditionally, indeed, the British army had only employed women as nurses prior to 1914. There was considerable reluctance to use women in any other capacity, but their work in the munitions industry forced the army to reconsider. In April 1915, therefore, the Army Council authorised the employment of women as cooks and waitresses in Britain in Lady Londonderry's Women's Legion, which received official recognition in February 1916. It eventually numbered some 6,000 women. If women could replace men at home, then there was no logical reason why they should not do so overseas and, in March 1917, the first cooks of the new Women's Army Auxiliary Corps (WAAC) arrived in France. The 41,000 women who served in the WAAC – renamed Queen Mary's Army Auxiliary Corps in April 1918 – were mostly working or lower middle class. Consequently, there was a tendency to view them as lacking the more altruistic patriotic motivations perceived in their social superiors.

Patriotism was not incompatible with wanting to earn better money, experience different work, escape domestic service or see a different country. The WAAC, however, quickly earned an unjustified reputation for immorality. Class had as much to do with this as fears of the consequences of women in uniform usurping masculine roles. Hostility to the WAAC also derived from resentment on the part of those men behind the lines employed as clerks, cooks, drivers and storemen, who were now combed out for service at the front. The military as a whole never quite came to terms with the concept of women in uniform and their status within the army remained ambiguous. The corps was disbanded in 1920, not being revived until the creation of the Auxiliary Territorial Service (ATS) in 1938. A Women's Royal Naval Service (WRNS) also came into existence in January

1918, followed by the Women's Royal Auxiliary Air Force (WRAAF) in April, but they did not attract quite the same hostility as the WAAC.[35]

It has been suggested that those women who did serve close to the front developed a different concept of gender from those women who remained at home. Proximity to combat, especially for nurses, evinced 'a solidarity or comradeship with [men] that overrode all distinctions'. In one sense, however, this merely reinforced post-war gender barriers, by emphasising the desire of feminists to distance themselves from masculine concepts of war. Moreover, it has been suggested that the essential division between men, who fought, and women, who did not, also widened the gender gap. As might be expected, there was a class distinction in perceptions of the war experience among women themselves.[36]

In Germany and Austria-Hungary, too, many women fulfilled an entirely traditional role during the war. Middle-class and upper-class German women joined the various organisations brought under the umbrella of the National Women's Service. In Mannheim, for example, there were no less than 72 charitable organisations which came under its auspices. The Germans established a Rear Area Women's Auxiliary Programme in 1917, but women were employees of the army rather than serving soldiers. A Women's Signal Corps was also formed in May 1918 but its training had not been completed by the time of the armistice.

In Russia, by contrast, between 5,000 and 6,000 women had been enlisted for combat by November 1917. The best known unit was the so-called Battalion of Death raised by the provisional government and led by Maria Botchkareva, known as Yashka. Elsewhere, some women disguised themselves as men to enlist, such as the British woman Flora Sandes who served with the Serbian army. A number of Polish women served with the Austro-Hungarian army. Others had joined the pre-war military units established to fight for Polish independence, and successors to these units eventually fought with the new Polish army against Russian and Ukrainian incursions in 1919–20.[37]

Australian women were largely deprived of the kinds of opportunity to develop their role experienced in Europe. Although women already had the vote in Australia they were still seen as having largely a domestic role in society. The Anzac myth and its post-war rituals in themselves celebrated masculine values and a degree of direct wartime participation which Australian women could not share. It was unusual for Australian women to remain in employment after marriage and those that did work earned less than half the wages of men undertaking the same work. The number of women employed did increase from 24 per cent of the Australian labour force in 1914 to 37 per cent by 1918 but, in the absence of any real munitions industry, largely through entering traditional areas such as textiles and clothing in greater numbers. To the extent that women's wartime profile was raised within Australian society it was through voluntary and, specifically, middle-class effort. Overall, therefore, as Michael McKernan has noted, the war was 'not the watershed for Australian women as it was for women in other societies'.[38]

Primarily, it was entry to the war economy by working-class women rather than voluntary activity on the part of middle- and upper-class women which, at least in theory, provided the greatest opportunity to change the perception of women's role in society. In the peasant societies of continental Europe, women had always played an important role in the rural economy. This intensified as men were mobilised, as in France, where the pre-war female agricultural labour force may already have amounted to 3.2 million. Little changed, therefore, in the lives of most French peasant women and, in the long term, it was mechanisation rather than the war that made a difference. In Italy, the absence of husbands similarly forced women into a new relationship with the state and its bureaucracy, to which they were often vulnerable, though some found support from deserters and draft dodgers.

Women had largely ceased to be a significant element in the British pre-war agricultural labour force. Accordingly, there was a quasi-military aspect to the attempt to recruit more women to undertake agricultural work. In March 1917, a Women's Land Army emerged, with the intention of providing a permanent skilled and mobile female labour force for work on farms and in forestry, although a separate Women's Forestry Corps continued to be administered by the Board of Trade. Significantly, its members were paid less than unskilled male agricultural labourers, although an elaborate welfare network was created for them. The Board of Trade estimated that there were still only about 148,000 women employed in agriculture in 1918, but it is possible that the true figure was closer to 263,000.[39]

Before the war the most common employment for women in Britain had been in domestic service, which employed 1.6 million women in 1911 or approximately one-quarter of the female workforce. Relatively large numbers had also been employed in millinery, dressmaking, pottery, weaving and light industrial work in the north and Midlands. Many women were employed casually in 'sweated trades', childminding, taking in washing and in agricultural work, but such 'invisible' employment was not recorded in the census returns. About 90 per cent of the women employed before the war were single and working class. Even among the working class, the expectation was that most women would cease employment upon marriage, although married women were common in the northern cotton industry.

With the outbreak of war there was a steady expansion in the female workforce as men enlisted. It should be noted, however, that, in the first twelve months, while some 400,000 women came into employment, so did

1 million men since the first recourse of employers was to unemployed men. Indeed, positive recruitment of women came only after the establishment of the Ministry of Munitions and, especially, after the introduction of conscription. Moreover, women had been worse hit than men by the initial increase in unemployment, with possibly 44.4 per cent of the female labour force out of work in September 1914. Thus, official statistics tend to imply a larger increase in women's employment than was actually the case.

Figures vary. One contemporary commentator, A. W. Kirkaldy, estimated that 1.6 million more women were employed in Britain in 1918 than in 1914, the total rising from 3.2 million to 4.8 million. Kirkaldy, however, omitted those in domestic service and other groups such as the self-employed, women employed by their husbands, and those involved in small-scale dressmaking. Alternatively, it is suggested that, taking all these other categories into account that the number of women in paid employment rose from 5.9 million to 7.3 million, representing a slightly smaller wartime increase of 1.4 million.

Approximately half of the women brought into employment to substitute for men in uniform were employed in commerce rather than industrial occupations. Indeed, the number of women employed in industry increased only from 2.1 million to 2.9 million, representing an increase from 26.1 per cent of the total labour force to 36.1 per cent. It might be noted, however, that the increases in some areas were attained as a result of decreases elsewhere as the better pay available in war industries lured women from traditional and 'invisible' employment. Thus, the numbers employed in domestic service declined by 400,000 and the number in the clothing industry by 76,000. At the Gretna national cordite factory, some 80 per cent of the female labour force had been previously employed, with 36 per cent having been in domestic service. Similarly, 71 per cent of the female labour force at Armstrong Whitworth had been previously employed, with 20 per cent coming from domestic service.[40]

Wartime propaganda exaggerated the extent of dilution, especially in the munitions industry, as did the greater visibility of women in public transport. Unions and employers alike resisted dilution and women were employed for very specific functions. In many cases, women did not supplant skilled male labour for, in practical terms, dilution was not substitution *per se* but a reorganisation of working practices so that the unskilled could perform more tasks. Indeed, it is calculated that only about 23 per cent of the women who came into the munitions industry were actually doing men's work.

It is also the case that the majority of the 'new' women who entered employment during the war were either working-class women entering the workforce earlier than might have been the case previously, or married women returning to employment. In a sense, therefore, wartime work was not a novel experience for many women and, whatever the financial rewards they received, would not have had a particularly liberating effect. Nonetheless, the disquieting flight of women from domestic service, the increased purchasing power available to 'munitionettes', and their working-class origins resulted in accusations of selfishness and extravagance.[41]

War work was probably more liberating for the minority of middle-class women who came forward and enjoyed a degree of economic independence as a result. Whether middle or working class, however, many women may not have regarded wartime employment as permanent. Accordingly, they may have returned relatively willingly to domesticity, where they already held much influence within the family, despite often appreciating the opportunities that employment had given them. In many cases, wartime employment had been a necessity rather than a desire.

It had certainly not meant equal pay, which government and unions alike had resisted. Indeed, while a Ministry of Munitions circular, L2, of October 1915 had appeared to suggest that women should get the same pay as men, this was only a requirement where women did not require supervision. It was largely intended as a sop to unions, who feared dilution might be used as a means of lowering the rate for particular jobs. Moreover, it was common to pay women on time-rates rather than the piece-rates to which equality had been applied by the regulation. Only in munitions work had women's pay kept pace with inflation but it was still less than that of men. On average, women's wages in Britain rose from 13s.6d a week in 1914 to 35s.0d by 1918, but this only represented an increase from about half men's earnings to about two-thirds.

The general conclusion must be that there was little difference in the lives of most working women before and after the war. Female employment during the war was seen, as Gerard De Groot has emphasised, as a cheap source of easily exploitable labour which could be dispensed with in peacetime. Indeed, not only did the end of wartime demand reduce women's employment prospects in Britain but the general wartime increases in their wage levels had made them less cheap than previously.[42]

In Germany, the female labour force rose from 1.5 million in 1914 to 2.3 million in 1918, or from 22 per cent to 35 per cent of the total industrial labour force in enterprises with over ten employees. Overall, however, the number of compulsorily insured women workers in the labour force increased by only 17 per cent from 3.5 million to 4.1 million. Moreover, it is clear that the general increase in women's employment during the war was modest compared with previous periods of growth such as between 1889 and 1913. Generally, indeed, there was some reluctance to employ women when prisoners of war, foreign labour or men recalled from the army might be available. Some women also delayed entering employment until family allowances or widows' pensions proved inadequate. It was, therefore, only really after the passing of the Auxiliary Service Law that there was any concerted attempt to bring women into industry.

Again, it was a question of women moving into war industries from domestic service and the food and clothing industries. Of over 90,000 women employed in Bavarian war industries between March and August 1917, between 41 and 46 per cent had previously worked in factories, 18 per cent had been employed in domestic service, with only 28 per cent previously not employed.

Some war industries saw dramatic increases in female employment as part of the redistribution. Krupps at Essen moved from a position where no women were employed at all in 1914 to over 30,000 female workers by 1918. Similarly, there was a marked overall increase of 38 per cent in female employment in Berlin, embracing a 116 per cent increase of women in metalworking by 1917 and a 279 per cent increase in machine tools. There was, however, also an increase in the number of home workers as those women unable to contemplate factory work, through the need to maintain their dependants, took on the production of items such as uniforms and sandbags within their own homes.

The wages earned by German women differed according to the employment. At the same time, the wage differential between men and women was reduced, although women continued to receive far less than men for the same task. Average women's wages increased by 186 per cent in war industries and by 102 per cent in non-war industries compared with the 152 per cent and 81 per cent, respectively, of men. In relation to men's wages, however, this represented an average increase from only 46 per cent of the men's wages in 1914 to 52 per cent by 1918.[43]

As in Germany, Austro-Hungarian employers tried to avoid using women, preferring to use prisoners of war when it was felt that women's true role was in the home. About 1 million Austrian women came into the labour force during the war, increasing the size of the female labour force by 40 per cent. By 1916, the female portion of the labour force in Vienna's metal and machine industries had increased to 42.5 per cent and, in some factories, it was said to be as high as 78 per cent. As elsewhere, while women's wages rose, they still earned only between one-third and one-half of male wages. Indeed, some employers deliberately kept women on reduced piece-work rates to restrict their earning potential.[44]

In Italy, there was resistance to female employment until 1916. It derived both from social perceptions of the appropriate role for women and from male workers, who feared they might be conscripted as a result of their replacement by women. As elsewhere, it became a question of adapting manufacturing processes for women and a series of modest welfare measures was also introduced, including the prohibition of night work and theoretical equality of pay for equal work. The number of women and children employed by Industrial Mobilisation (MI) increased from almost 76,000 in December 1916 to 258,000 by August 1918. Overall, women were about 22 per cent of the Italian labour force by 1918, but with wide variations within industry and by region.[45]

As in Britain, many French women found themselves unemployed in the summer of 1914. Consequently, there was the same process of redistribution in the female labour force, as well as the return of married women to employment. Although there was a relatively high proportion of women in paid employment before the war – about 38.2 per cent of the total labour force – there was opposition to more coming into industry. Not least this was through the perceived need to maintain the birth rate and the conception of the mother's role as patriotic in itself. In this regard, the promotion of the *marraine de guerre* in January 1915 as a surrogate mother 'adopting' a soldier appeared to provide women with an additional, acceptable role in support of the war effort. Misgivings arose, however, concerning the potential sexual connotations of the relationship between soldier and *marraine*. The same ambiguity was apparent in French attitudes towards wartime prostitution, which might also threaten the recovery of the birth rate through the competition between wives and prostitutes and the spread of venereal disease.

Those women who did enter industry were again confined largely to poorly paid, low-skill tasks, although they shared in general wartime wage increases. Precise figures are uncertain but, in general terms, the proportion of women employed in the industrial labour force rose only from 29.8 per cent in 1914 to 37.1 per cent by 1917, which was when the demand for female labour peaked. As elsewhere, averages hide wide variations. The most marked increase in female employment was in commerce, banking and insurance, but, in all, the number of women in the labour force increased only from 7.7 million in 1906 to 8.6 million by 1921. Women's pay varied greatly from sector to sector but, generally, differentials between men and women narrowed before widening once more after 1918: in the Paris metal industry, for example, the differential narrowed from 45 per cent in 1914 to 16 per cent in 1916, only to rise again to 21 per cent by 1921.[46]

While there were two and a half times more women employed in industry in the United States in 1918 than in 1917 – about 1 million – the majority were, again, either single women moving from other employment, such as domestic service which lost 253,000 women between 1910 and 1920, or married women returning temporarily to work. Moreover, the overall female labour force increased by only half a million or 6.3 per cent between 1910 and 1920. Much of the increase in female employment was in those areas which women had already entered. Thus, of 70,385 women who entered railroad employment between 1917 and 1918, 72 per cent did so in clerical or semi-clerical positions. Women, however, did become streetcar conductors for the first time.

Many American unions were opposed to female employment, fearing both dilution and changes in work practices. Similarly, male workers were often hostile, especially if women competed for promotion and, as else-where, women workers were portrayed as immoral and working only to purchase frivolous goods. Thus, female reformers brought into the US Army Ordnance Department and the US Railroad Administration, in the spirit of Taylorism, to maximise the efficient use of women workers failed to achieve equality of pay or security of employment for women. Indeed, health and other regulations affecting women were widely flouted and it was estimated that only 9 per cent of women employed in New York received the equal pay to which they were entitled. Female medical personnel volunteering for war service also failed to achieve commissioned status.[47]

A parallel can also be drawn in the United States with another previously disadvantaged group, the black population. The war resulted in a significant switch of that population from the rural south to the urban and industrial north. Indeed, between 1910 and 1920, with the movement of some 333,000 blacks northwards or westwards, the black population of the north and west grew by some 748,000. Urban population generally increased in all belligerents as population followed new employment opportunities, but the move of the American black northwards opened the theoretical possibility of some escape from poverty through a measure of economic independence. In many cases, however, blacks were being recruited as strike breakers and faced hostility from northern trade unionists. Consequently, there were serious racial clashes in East St Louis, Missouri, in July 1917 and in Chicago in July 1918. In 1919, there were over twenty serious race riots, the worst again in Chicago, where 38 people were killed, including 23 blacks.

Black women had been heavily concentrated in agriculture or domestic service prior to the war. A colour line still existed in terms of white-collar work but the war resulted in an even larger increase in blacks in domestic service as white women moved into other employment. Black women, however, were also able to move into areas such as food processing and the clothing industry for the first time.[48]

In entering wartime employment, women also joined trade unions, contributing significantly to the overall rise in membership in Britain. Overall, women trade unionists increased from 437,000 in 1914 to 1.2 million by

1918. Although 383 British unions accepted women, others such as the Amalgamated Society of Engineers and the Amalgamated Society of Carpenters and Joiners declined to admit them.

The French Federation of Metal Workers, founded in April 1916, recruited well among women and the unskilled although, by 1918, less than 12 per cent of French female munitions workers were unionised compared with 25 per cent of men. Some 397,000 American women were also unionised by 1920, especially in the clothing, textile and shoe industries. Similarly, the number of women trade unionists associated with Social Democratic Party unions in Germany increased from 230,000 in 1913 to 423,000 by 1918, the proportion increasing from 8 per cent of the overall membership to 25 per cent. Women also accounted for half the wartime increase in union membership in Australia.

In becoming unionised, women were also increasingly prominent in strike action, as they were in food riots, through their greater awareness of the effect of inflation upon household budgets. Many German women became increasingly resistant to the leadership of the state although, in the longer term, they were no more inclined to become directly involved in politics than before. It was also the case that, in industrial situations in states like Italy and Hungary, women were less inhibited by the likely application of military discipline than men. Their strikes also tended to be more sudden and shorter than those of men. In Italy, the proportion of strikers in industry who were women rose from 15.1 per cent in 1914 to 64.2 per cent in 1917.

Striking dressmakers in Paris secured a half-day on Saturdays and, in general, women assisted in the campaign for the institution of the eight hour day achieved in 1919. In the United States, women telephonists used their power to cripple the activities of the American Telephone and Telegraph Company (AT&T), when a strike erupted in Wichita, Kansas, in December 1918 over the dismissal of a supervisor who had called for increased pay. It spread rapidly to New England, where higher wages were conceded in April 1919, and then to the southern states, the Midwest and Far West though with less success. In Britain, most women's industrial unrest initially surrounded welfare issues but equal pay became more of an issue in 1918.[49]

At the end of the war, however, the numbers of women employed in industry began to decline rapidly. In Britain, some 750,000 women were made redundant by the end of 1918 alone, the press notably changing abruptly from praise for women workers to hostility towards them. Two-thirds of those who had entered employment during the war had left it by 1920. The decline was even greater in more traditional areas such as the textile industry and domestic service. In the latter case, former munitions workers in particular refused to contemplate a return to what they regarded as servile labour. By contrast, the number of women increased in newer industries such as chemicals and light engineering. To some extent, women also maintained their wartime position in white-collar work though, in so far as white-collar occupations had become recognised as women's work, the status of the occupation declined.

It was assumed that women would return to the home and, in Britain, wartime regulations were changed so that women visiting labour exchanges would find it difficult to insist on industrial or even office employment on pain of losing unemployment benefit: married women were excluded entirely from benefit by 1922. Even a traditional woman's occupation such as the laundry trade was opened to disabled soldiers and there was considerable government propaganda to reinforce the desirability of domesticity and the concept of a marriage bar. Indeed, the Sex Disqualification (Removal) Act 1919, intended to prevent sex or marriage from being a bar to civil and judicial employment, was interpreted selectively by the courts.

The achievement of the franchise tended to fragment the women's movement and left women without an effective political voice, while unionisation proved of little assistance in defending women's employment. Women did gain a degree of equality in terms of divorce and custody of children through the Matrimonial Causes Act 1923 and the Guardianship of Infants Act (1921), but these were of more relevance to middle- and upper-class women than to the majority of working-class women.[50]

There were also fewer women employed in French industry in 1926 than in 1906, the war beginning a long-term decline in the number of women employed. The government encouraged the process by offering a bonus to those women who left employment by 5 December 1918. In many cases, women were simply made redundant. In the process, however, there were also some permanent changes in female employment patterns. There were small increases in the numbers employed in agriculture and a reduction from 34.3 per cent of the industrial labour force in 1906 to 28.6 per cent by 1926. As in the war itself, this hid large variations. The number of women employed in domestic service also declined from 930,000 in 1911 to 784,000 by 1926. More significantly, however, the proportion of women employed in 'liberal' professions, such as teaching, commerce and administration, dramatically increased from 27,000 in 1911 to 276,000 by 1921.

In Germany, where there was also an increasing pro-natalist campaign, women were also displaced from employment in 1918. Some found new jobs in the inflationary boom of 1921–22, albeit in more traditional areas of employment. Overall, however, from a position where 30.5 per cent of German women had been employed in 1907, the percentage was still only 35.6 per cent in 1925.

A Woman's Bureau was established in the US Department of Labor after the war but, by 1920, women were a smaller percentage of the workforce than in 1910. Indeed, while women streetcar conductors won the right to remain employed in Detroit in March 1919, although most had by then already left, the union in Cleveland had succeeded in forcing women out. By 1930, only 17 out of 35,697 streetcar conductors remained women. In short, American women workers found themselves weak in the face of 'managerial rationalisation strategies, on the one hand, and the hostility of male workers, anxious to maintain their own decreasing margins of craft integrity and job security, on the other'.[51]

The question of how women's contribution to the war effort related to the achievement of the franchise in Britain and elsewhere is a difficult one. Arthur Marwick has argued that the war did accelerate the process, through giving women a greater sense of their own value and breaking down male prejudice after the controversies of the pre-war suffragette campaign. By contrast, Martin Pugh has pointed to the war's emphasis upon masculine values and the considerable resistance to the threat to male employment posed by female dilution. As Pugh has noted, few politicians 'actually advocated women suffrage on the grounds of the work they had performed during the war, though all paid the necessary tribute to it'. Most politicians however, were in favour of electoral reform and the Representation of the People Act of February 1918 should be seen as a war measure and not a women's measure.

The argument for electoral reform was the potential disenfranchisement of men who had lost their residence qualification of twelve months' continuous occupation through service overseas; the need to reward those without the vote who had fought for their country; and the need to allow all those who had contributed to the victory to determine the future. The Speaker's Conference held on electoral reform in 1916 had been far from unanimous on female enfranchisement and wished to enfranchise only stable, mature women. Such women were more likely to identify politically with their husbands than the predominantly young, single, working-class munitionettes, who, as Martin Pugh has remarked, appeared 'an unstable and disturbing element'. The eventual legislation enfranchised some 7 million women over the age of 30 in 1918, who were either ratepayers or married to ratepayers, balancing the extension of the franchise simultaneously to the 40 per cent of British males who had also not voted prior to 1914. With some 5 million women over the age of 21 excluded from the new franchise, the terms ensured that women would not be a majority of the electorate although, as it happened, women often acted as proxy for absent male voters in 1918.

Having lost the political initiative through the effective suspension of the issue when they might have been close to success in 1914, the women's movement accepted what was on offer, which in itself was no more than had been proposed in legislation lost on a parliamentary technicality in 1912.[52]

American women in eleven states already had the vote by 1917 and the National American Woman Suffrage Association (NAWSA), which pledged its full support for the war effort, hoped to use the opportunity to advance its cause further. In the event, NAWSA was undermined by the more militant Women's Party, which picketed the White House for eighteen months from January 1917. It is not apparent, however, whether the latter had much impact although Wilson declared that extending the franchise was 'vital to the winning of the war'. The Nineteenth Amendment to the Constitution was duly passed by the House of Representatives in January 1918, although it only passed the Senate in 1919 and was not ratified until 1920. Nonetheless, although an achievement, in the words of David Kennedy, the extension of the suffrage 'proved far less consequential in women's lives than its proponents had long believed'. Similarly, the subsequent campaign by women's groups resulting in the Sheppard–Towner Act in 1921, which provided federal support for maternal and infant health care, 'aimed not to breach the walls of industry for women but to make women more secure in their traditional environs, the home and the nursery'.[53]

Women also got the vote in Canada, Germany, the Soviet Union, the Baltic states, the new states carved from Austria-Hungary, and Sweden. In France, however, where there was already universal male suffrage, it was not to be. It had been widely anticipated, particularly among leading feminists, that the vote would be granted in recognition of women's contribution to the war effort. In the event, although the Chamber of Deputies overwhelmingly voted for female suffrage in May 1919, the Senate rejected it in November 1922, largely on the grounds that it would increase clerical influence. Women had been given the right during the war to vote in rural communes but this, and other wartime concessions, such as the rights of a mother to exercise paternal authority, were removed in 1918, although women could still become legal guardians. Women did not receive full legal capacity in France until 1938 or achieve the vote until 1944.[54]

Social mores and leisure pursuits

It has been argued that women's real contribution to the war was in the traditional role of keeping home fires burning and raising children in the absence of fathers. In so doing, they dealt not only with deprivation and separation, but also the possibility and reality of untimely widowhood. Thus, the wartime and post-war emphasis on motherhood and pro-natalism, as De Groot puts it, 'reflected a popular will, it did not create that will'. Certainly, the difficulty faced by many women in feeding their families in conditions of rising prices and shortage of foodstuffs and their own full-time employment should not be underestimated. Indeed, Ute Daniel has also made the point that it did not follow that, because women did not work in industry or agriculture, they were not working within the home.

It is also suggested that British family ties were strengthened by the war. Family and household patterns do not appear to have changed substantially even in the absence of servicemen, although individual family situations would depend upon different circumstances. If family ties were strengthened, however, the increase in state intervention and, indeed, the post-war appearance of more estate council housing, tended to weaken pre-war mutualist concepts of what might be termed 'neighbourly duties' as epitomised by the pre-war charitable and co-operative societies.[55]

As suggested by the establishment of female morality police in Britain, sexual mores in particular were often those which most concerned contemporaries. Prostitution and venereal disease were of perennial concern to the military authorities and the supposed 'khaki fever' displayed by young women in 1914 aroused particular alarm. As Sylvia Pankhurst expressed it after the war: 'Alarmist morality mongers conceived most monstrous visions of girls and women, freed from the control of fathers and husbands who had hitherto compelled them to industry, chastity and sobriety, now neglecting their homes, plunging into excesses, and burdening the country with swarms of illegitimate children.'

Contemporary perceptions do not necessarily correspond with reality. In theory at least, more women were aware of contraception, as were soldiers issued, sometimes reluctantly by the authorities, with wartime prophylactics. Indeed, while the wartime illegitimacy rate in Britain rose by 30 per cent, it needs to be borne in mind that, since the overall birth rate declined, fewer women were actually having illegitimate children. Similarly, an official enquiry established in February 1918 to investigate the widespread accusations of immorality aimed at the Women's Army Auxiliary Corps (WAAC) found that only 21 pregnancies had occurred among 6,023 WAAC serving in France (0.5 per cent), two of whom were married and nearly all of whom had been pregnant before they went overseas. In addition, there had been just 12 cases of venereal disease in the Corps.

Nonetheless, there was a perceived change in attitudes among women as evidenced by the appearance in female fashion of shorter hairstyles, more makeup, lighter fabrics and shorter skirts, of which the Northcliffe press particularly disapproved. The same changes in fashion were apparent in France. More women had also taken up smoking and alcohol although, in the case of alcohol, this went against a more general trend. Generally, there was a change in patterns of wartime consumption assisted by inflation. Alcohol consumption had already declined before the war and continued to do so at much the same rate irrespective of the new licensing laws and other restrictions such as increased prices. Smoking, however, increased.[56]

In Germany, too, it was widely believed that sexual immorality flourished during the war although, as elsewhere, female adultery and prostitution at home – a careful watch was kept on prisoners of war – was regarded as more significant than the army's promotion of officially sponsored brothels at the front. The percentage of German illegitimate births increased from 10 to 13 per cent of the increase in population during the war. As in Britain, women were said to be extravagant, especially 'war wives'. The reality amid the rising cost of living was more often of women undertaking foraging expeditions into the countryside for food, female crime increasing by 14.5 per cent overall by 1917 and female crime against property by a staggering 75.6 per cent.

Citation of female adultery as grounds for divorce increased from 10 per cent of cases in France in 1914 to 18 per cent by 1918, while the French illegitimacy rate climbed from a pre-war average of around 9 per cent of births to around 14 per cent during the war, before subsiding to pre-war patterns in 1920.[57]

While the war obviously made a distinction between men and women in the sense that it was overwhelmingly men who fought, the same factor also made distinctions between young and old or, more specifically, between those eligible for military service and those either too old or too young to fight. While the very elderly became something of a marginal group, those over military age could still contribute to the war effort. In Britain they did so through service in the special constabulary and the Volunteer Training Corps (VTC), later the Volunteer Force, given formal status in November 1914 through the fears of possible German invasion of East Anglia.[58]

In some respects, however, the sharpest distinction was between the war generation and those too young to fight. The war tended to widen the generation gap, not least between fathers and children. Relationships were affected both through wartime absence and, indeed, through wartime presence. Thus, on the one hand, fathers might return strangers, or disabled, or not at all; on the other, if fathers had not seen service, there were possible consequences from the pervasive messages of recruiting posters such as the celebrated 'What did you do in the war, Daddy?'

In Italy, there was a significant increase in juvenile delinquency among those between 9 and 13 years of age, varying from aggressive begging to gang vandalism, while there was also concern at the increase in smoking among both boys and women. Generally, there was fear of adolescents slipping out of parental control while also suffering from interrupted schooling through working or even queuing for food. In Germany, indeed, between 250,000 and 300,000 youths aged from 14 to 17 were in war industries to the detriment of their education. Fears of the corrupting influence of high earnings led to the compulsory youth savings schemes.

Juvenile delinquency certainly increased. In Germany, among those aged between 15 and 18, for example, crime increased by 57.4 per cent between 1913 and 1917 although this was considerably less than the increase among women aged between 18 and 50. Moreover, it has been argued that the combination of absence of fathers and wartime deprivation contributed to the later attraction of the Nazi youth movement and the surrogate father figure of Hitler. In Britain, juvenile delinquency particularly increased among those aged 11 to 13, for which many blamed the cinema, though the National Council of Public Morals pointed more to the social and economic pressures of the war. Juvenile delinquency also increased in the United States.[59]

Leading on from juvenile delinquency, it can be noted that, while 'ordinary' crime declined, there were new crimes such as failure to observe the blackout as well as increased fraud and profiteering. Like other statistics, however, crime figures are open to differing interpretations, especially when it was by no means the case that all crime was recorded.[60]

Public leisure was also inevitably affected by war, although initially horse racing and football continued in Britain until 1915. The University Boat Race was also abandoned in 1915 and the Whitsun and August Bank Holidays cancelled in 1916. Professional and, thereby, working-class sport generally, was particularly adversely affected, professionals coming under pressure to enlist in 1914 when it was perceived that they were not coming forward as much as their amateur colleagues. In fact, as the Football Association pointed out, of some 5,000 professional footballers in Britain in 1915, 2,000 had already enlisted and 2,400 were married, so that only 600 could be considered as genuinely shirking. Moreover, almost 500,000 men had come forward from amateur football organisations. Horse racing also came under pressure and organised meetings ceased in May 1915.

There was similar criticism of professional sportsmen in Australia, particularly in the avowedly working-class sports of boxing, football and rugby league. Much of the country's spectator and participant sport had been voluntarily cancelled by the end of 1915 and government curbs were introduced in September 1917, although football continued in Sydney and Melbourne.

While sport was affected, this did not appear to apply to holidays. Holiday resorts in England and Wales were able to recoup losses in the autumn of 1914 by accommodating formations of the New Army. Blackpool, which had continued with its illuminations – started only in 1912 – in the autumn of 1914 had over 10,000 troops in the town over the 1914–15 winter. In any case, the holiday trade survived remarkably well throughout the war. Generally, however, holidaymakers were less boisterous than before the war. Much the same was true elsewhere, there being little discernible change in attendance at German spas and holiday resorts.[61]

In Britain, there were measurable increases in dancing, with American jazz and ragtime the basis for the development of popular new dances, the foxtrot and the Charleston, which became the rage amid fears of cultural pollution. Attendance at the infant cinema, equally dominated by American imports, increased in Britain up to around 20 million a week, embracing both middle- and upper-class audiences for the first time. In the same way, theatres which had been frequented primarily by the middle and upper classes became popular with the working class. Music halls remained immensely popular with artists such as Harry Lauder, George Robey and Harry Tate prominent in raising war funds. Among more classical artists, Clara Butt and May Whitty also did much to try and increase the audience for serious music and theatre. Indeed, the Music in Wartime Committee aimed to be musically propagandist as well as to entertain. Museum and gallery visiting also continued to the extent that the closure of those in London in 1916, largely as an economy measure, was partially rescinded, though objects of major value were removed to other parts of the country as a precaution against air raids. War exhibitions of one kind or another were often mounted, but also those with a more subtle contribution to public information such as exhibitions on health and hygiene aimed at housewives. Museums in London, Norwich, Newcastle, Bristol, Salford and Belfast, for example, all put on 'War on Houseflies' exhibitions in 1915.

Nevertheless, the imposition of new taxes upon places of entertainment in May 1916 had some effect on leisure patterns, the additional halfpenny on cinema tickets up to 2d and one penny on seats up to 6d pushing the wealthier patrons into cheaper seats and pricing out many working-class patrons. Licensing restrictions also had an effect, probably contributing to greatly increased sales of gramophone records, which had reached 6 million a year by 1918. Escapism had much to do with the determination to maintain such leisure pursuits and with the popularity of plays such as *Peter Pan*, musicals such as Oscar Asche's *Chu Chin Chow* and *The Maid of the Mountains*, revues such as *The Bing Boys Are Here*, and the comedy film shorts of Charlie Chaplin. Chaplin was immensely popular with the troops, and Harry Lauder also entertained thousands of soldiers during his tour of the front in June 1917. Similarly, Ivor Novello's popular song, *Keep the Home Fires Burning*, supposedly composed because his mother was tired of hearing Jack Judge's *It's a Long Way to Tipperary*, was first performed by a travelling professional concert party at Rouen in 1915. *Tipperary* and many other ballads, ditties and parodies became part-and-parcel of British military and civilian culture. In effect, British popular culture became a unifying force at home as well as at the front, helping to establish a more homogenised 'nationalisation of taste' which, ironically, undermined many of the older local and regional loyalties from which that popular culture had drawn its vitality and strength.[62]

In continental Europe, cinema was also the principal means of escapism from war or, in the case of Poland, Romania and Belgium, from occupation. Indeed, where foreign imports were no longer available, local production was stimulated. The first indigenous Bulgarian and Croatian feature films appeared during the war while the Hungarian film industry expanded under the leadership of directors such as Sándor Korda and Mihály Kertész, both to become better known subsequently as Alexander Korda and Michael Curtiz. Alongside film, older popular forms of entertainment also flourished: in Austria, Franz Léhar wrote several new operettas and Leo Fall enjoyed enormous success with *Die Rose von Stambul* (The Rose of Constantinople). Traditional *szopa* puppetry was revived in Poland, where it took on a satirical edge under German occupation. Cabaret and variety shows were almost universally popular across metropolitan societies. So, too, were the kinds of dramatic *tableaux vivantes* put on by the Taunzien Palast theatre in Berlin, or the recreation of the battle of Verdun staged in a Paris theatre.

By contrast, the rituals of rural peasant communities were seemingly little changed by war and, amid the stimulus given to all manner of nationalisms, rural cultural traditions were often consciously promoted, as in Bulgaria and Hungary, where Béla Bartók turned to creating folk ballets. Gypsy music was prominent in Hungary and Romania, although in France jazz had overtaken folksong in popularity by the end of the war. Where some traditional pastimes were no longer practicable, other pursuits were substituted. Thus, in Belgium, the Germans seized and melted down musical instruments for their copper, putting an end to the popular pre-war brass bands. Pigeon racing had also been popular and this, too, was ended as the Germans slaughtered homing pigeons on grounds of security. Belgians, therefore, took up alternatives such as pelota and cycling while attendance at religious services, which were the only form of organised public meeting allowed, increased substantially.[63]

While many wartime pursuits continued after the war, church attendance appears to have declined across Europe. There is little quantitative evidence available to judge, however, whether the war accelerated or arrested secularism. The war increased religious observance if not religious belief and, in France at least, there was a spirit of wartime ecumenism, particularly among soldiers. At the same time, however, it also stimulated what can only be described as superstition: even British soldiers who were not Catholics regularly asked the nuns of Albert on the Somme for medals, crucifixes and pocket rosaries, while French trenches often had horseshoes hung next to crucifixes. Moreover, the war resulted in a rapid growth in secular spiritualism as the bereaved turned to spiritualists in order to try to communicate with the dead. Similarly, both British and especially French soldiers reported spiritualist phenomena, and the return of the dead was to feature in art, literature and cinema well after the war.

Despite the controversies of Papal intervention in search of a negotiated peace, the Catholic Church did enjoy something of a revival, negotiating new accords with most of the continental states in the early 1920s. The effect on Protestant Churches was more ambiguous as a result of the greater fragmentation of national Churches, a factor creating renewed interest in ecumenism. Further afield, the Russian and, especially, the Greek Orthodox Churches went into decline, the authority of the Greek patriarch at Constantinople affected by the post-war defeat of Greece by a resurgent Turkey, and that of the Russian patriarch in Moscow by revolution.[64]

In conclusion, then, a conflict as widespread and disruptive as the Great War could not have failed to generate wartime changes of varying kinds and to have had a significant wartime impact upon the societies engaged in it. What the historian must then judge is how far changes survived the immediate wartime situation which generated them and, indeed, how far those changes which did take place were merely accelerated by the war and would have occurred anyway over the course of time. As Marwick has expressed it: 'the comparison one has to make is not simply between post-war and pre-war society, but between post-war society and the situation that society would have reached at the same point in time had there been no war.'[65]

In general, it would appear that, while the reach of the state was undoubtedly extended, the war had remarkably little long-term impact upon society in many of the belligerents. There were more continuities than discontinuities between the pre-war and post-war periods and the war was not as significant in this regard as were long-term structural trends. In the case of Britain, as Jay Winter has noted, many who had previously had little to do with the state would discover that 'the tentacles of the political realm stretched further than ever before' and the size and power of economic units of production had also increased. There was also that 'nationalisation of taste' in popular culture. Yet, as De Groot has memorably commented: 'If war is the locomotive of history, the rolling stock in this case was typically British: slow, outmoded and prone to delay and cancellation.'[66] However, as indicated earlier, greater changes were likely to occur in defeated states. That leads to the link between war and revolution, for political events generated by the war most changed the nature of states and societies in Europe.

Notes and references

1. Marwick, *Deluge* (1991), pp.16–17; idem, *Total War and Social Change*, pp.xiv–xv.

2. Richard White, 'War and Australian Society', in McKernan and Browne, eds, *Australia*, pp.391–423.

3. Jean-Louis Robert and Jay Winter, 'Conclusions: Towards a Social History of Capital Cities at War', in Winter and Robert, eds, *Capital Cities*, pp.536–41; Whalen, *Bitter Wounds*, p.38; Chickering, *Imperial Germany*, p.195; Nicole Pietri, 'L'Evolution des populations d'Autriche-Allemande pendant la Grande Guerre', in Becker and Audoin-Rouzeau, eds, *Les sociétés européennes*, pp.311–22; Roberts, *Europe*, pp.368–74.

4. Winter, *Great War and British People*, pp.119–21; Wilson, *Myriad Faces*, pp.650–1; Gilbert, *First World War*, p.508; Alfred W. Cosby, *America's Forgotten Pandemic: The Influenza of 1918*, 2nd edn (Cambridge, 1989), pp.5–6, 17–29, 37–40, 60–1, 159, 189–94, 206–7, 298–306; Debauche, *Reel Patriotism*, p.147; K. David Patterson, 'The Influenza Epidemic of 1918–19 in the Gold Coast', *JAH* 24 (1983), pp.485–502; idem, 'The Diffusion of Influenza in Sub-Saharan Africa during the 1918–19 Pandemic', *Social Science and Medicine* 17 (1983), pp.1299–1307; Geoffrey Rice and Linda Bryder, *Black November: The 1918 Influenza Epidemic in New Zealand* (Wellington, 1988); Linda Bryder, 'Lessons of the 1918 Influenza Epidemic in Auckland', *New Zealand Journal of History* 16 (1982), pp.97–121; I. D. Mills, '1918–19 Influenza Pandemic: The Indian Experience', *Indian Economic and Social History Review* 23 (1986), pp.1–40; Sandra M. Tomkins, 'The Failure of Expertise: Public Health Policy in Britain during the 1918–19 Influenza Epidemic', *Social History of Medicine* (1992), pp.435–54; eadem, 'The Influenza Epidemic of 1918–19 in Western Samoa', *Pacific Historical Review* 27 (1992), pp.181–97; Catherine Rollet, 'The "Other War" II: Setbacks in Public Health', in Winter and Robert, eds, *Capital Cities*, pp.456–86.

5. Zivojinovic, 'Serbia and Montenegro', p.243; Kolko, *Century of War*, p.105; Gilbert, *First World War*, pp.186, 204.

6. Winter, *Great War and British People*, pp.74–5; Becker, *Great War and French People*, pp.330–3; Whalen, *Bitter Wounds*, pp.38–40.

7. Jay Winter, 'Some Aspects of the Demographic Consequences of the First World War in Britain', *Population Studies* 30 (1976), pp.539–52; idem, 'Britain's Lost Generation', pp.449–66; idem, *Great War and British People*, pp.65–99.

8. Winter, 'Impact of First World War on Civilian Health', pp.487–507; idem, *Great War and British People*, pp.103–53, 240–5; idem, 'Aspects of the Impact of the First World War on Infant Mortality in Britain', *Journal of European*

Economic History 11 (1993), pp.713–38; idem, 'Some Paradoxes', pp.12–16; Jay Winter, Jon Lawrence and J. Ariouat, 'The Impact of the Great War on Infant Mortality in London', *Annales de démographie historique* 9 (1993), pp.329–53; Gordon Phillips, 'The Social Impact', in Constantine, Kirby and Rose, eds, *First World War in British History*, pp.107–11; Rollet, 'Other War I', pp.421–55; idem, 'Other War II', pp.456–86; Dewey, 'Nutrition and Living Standards', pp.197–220; Whiteside, 'British Population at War', pp.85–98.

9. Winter, *Great War and British People*, pp.250–73; Wilson, *Myriad Faces*, pp.763–8; Richard Wall, 'English and German Families and the First World War, 1914–18', in Wall and Winter, eds, *Upheaval of War*, pp.44–53, 65–93; Phillips, 'Social Impact', pp.107–11, 121–6; Marwick, *Deluge*, pp.328–9.

10. Linda Bryder, 'The First World War: Healthy or Hungry?', *HWJ* 24 (1987), pp.141–57; Bernard Harris, 'The Demographic Impact of the First World War: An Anthropometric Perspective', *Journal of the Society for the Social History of Medicine* 6 (1993), pp.343–66; Jay Winter, 'Public Health and the Political Economy of War', *HWJ* 26 (1988), pp.163–73; idem, 'Some Paradoxes', pp.9–42; idem, 'Surviving the War: Life Expectation, Illness and Mortality Rates in Paris, London, and Berlin, 1914–19', in Winter and Robert, eds, *Capital Cities*, pp.487–523; H. J. Voth, 'Civilian Health during World War I and the Causes of German Defeat: A Re-examination of the Winter Hypothesis', *Annales de démographie historique* 11 (1995), pp.291–307; Rollet, 'Other War II', pp.456–86.

11. Winter, *Great War and British People*, pp.256, 260; idem, 'Some Paradoxes', pp.10, 16–24; Jules Maurin, 'Effets de la mobilisation française sur la population, 1914–18', *RIHM* 63 (1985), pp.73–88; Patrick Festy, 'Effets et répercussions de la première guerre mondiale sur la fécondité française', *Population* 39 (1984), pp.977–1010.

12. Gregory, 'Lost Generations', p.77; Jay Winter and J. Cole, 'Fluctuations in Infant Mortality Rates in Berlin during and after the First World War', *European Journal of Population* 9 (1993), pp.235–63; Winter, 'Some Paradoxes', pp.27–32; Bessel, *Germany after First World War*, pp.9–10; Ferguson, *Pity of War*, p.277; Ute Daniel, *The War From Within: German Working-class Women in the First World War* (Oxford, 1997), pp.129–38.

13. Winter, *Experience of World War I*, p.179; idem, 'Some Paradoxes', pp.24–7; Peter Scholliers and Frank Daelemans, 'Standards of Living and Standards of Health in Wartime Belgium', in Wall and Winter, eds, *Upheaval of War*, pp.139–58.

14. White, 'War and Australian Society', pp.415–16.

15. Hausen, 'German Nation's Obligation', pp.126–40; Françoise Thébaud, 'La guerre et le deuil chez les femmes françaises', in Becker, Winter, Krumeich,

Becker and Audoin-Rouzeau, eds, *Guerre et Cultures*, pp.103–10; Winter, *Great War and British People*, pp.273–8; idem, 'Kinship and Remembrance in the Aftermath of the Great War', in Jay Winter and Emmanuel Sivan, eds, *War and Remembrance in the Twetieth Century* (Cambridge, 1999), pp.40–60; Bourke, *Dismembering the Male*, pp.31–75; Peter Leese, 'Problems Returning Home: The British Psychological Casualties of the Great War', *HJ* 40 (1997), pp.1055–67; F. W. Hirst, *The Consequences of the War to Great Britain* (Oxford, 1934), pp.298–9; Lyn MacDonald, *The Roses of No Man's Land* (London, 1980), pp.303–4; Schaffer, *America in Great War*, pp.199–212; Michael Geyer, 'Ein Vorbote des Wohlfahrtsstaates, die Kriegsopferversorgung im Frankreich nach dem ersten Weltkrieg', *Geschichte und Gesellschaft* 9 (1983), pp.230–77; Ewald Frie, 'Vorbild oder Spiegelbild? Kriegsbeschädigtenfürsorge in Deutschland, 1914–19', in Michalka, ed., *Erste Weltkrieg*, pp.563–80; Robbins, *First World War*, p.153; Englander, 'People at War', pp.233–4; Winter and Baggett, *1914–18*, p.364; Whalen, *Bitter Wounds*, pp.69–81, 155–65; Seth Koven, 'Remembering and Dismemberment: Crippled Children, Wounded Soldiers and the Great War in Britain', *AHR* 99 (1994), pp.1167–1202.

16. Simpson, 'British Soldier on Western Front', p.137; *War Graves of the Empire* (London, 1928), pp.35–40; Bourke, *Dismembering the Male*, pp.228–35; J. M. Winter, 'Communities in Mourning', in Coetzee and Shevin-Coetzee, eds, *Authority*, pp.325–55.

17. Bernard Waites, 'The Effect of the First World War on Class and Status in England, 1910–20', *JCH* 11 (1976), pp.27–48; idem, *Class Society at War*, pp.17–29, 34–75; Robert and Winter, 'Conclusions', pp.545–7; Marwick, *Deluge*, pp.18–21.

18. Marwick, *Deluge*, pp.19, 327; idem, *Britain in Century of Total War*, pp.170–1; Kolko, *Century of War*, pp.100–1; R. C. Whiting, 'Taxation and the Working Class, 1915–24', *HJ* 33 (1990), pp.895–916; Waites, *Class Society at War*, pp.105–13; idem,' Effect of First World War', pp.27–48.

19. Wilson, *Myriad Faces*, p.772; Waites, *Class Society at War*, pp.85–90, 93–6, 234–5; F. M. L. Thompson, 'English Landed Society in the Twentieth Century: I, Property: Collapse and Survival', *Transactions of the Royal Historical Society*, Fifth Series 40 (1990), pp.1–24; idem, 'English Landed Society in the Twentieth Century: II, New Poor and New Rich', *Transactions of the Royal Historical Society*, Sixth Series 1 (1991), pp.1–20; idem, *English Landed Society in the Nineteenth Century* (London, 1963), pp.322–3; Whiteside, 'British Population at War', p.97; Roberts, *Europe*, p.375.

20. Waites, *Class Society at War*, pp.25–6, 47–54, 81 5, 96–7, 245–64; Jon Lawrence, 'Material Pressures on the Middle Classes', in Winter and Robert, eds, *Capital Cities*, pp.229–54; Cronin, *Politics of State Expansion*, p.74.

21. Waites, *Class Society at War*, pp.30–3, 160–78, 279–80; idem, 'Effect of First World War', pp.44–5; Alistair Reid, 'The Impact of the First World War on British Workers', in Wall and Winter, eds, *Upheaval of War*, pp.221–33; idem,

'World War I and the Working Class in Britain', in Marwick, ed., *Total War and Social Change*, pp.16–24; idem, 'Dilution, Trade Unionism and the State', pp.46–74; Wilson, *Myriad Faces*, pp.768–9; Phillips, 'Social Impact', pp.118–19; De Groot, *Blighty*, pp.123–6, 294–304.

22. White, 'War and Australian Society', pp.397–401.

23. Kocka, *Facing Total War*, pp.84–113, 115–40, 155–61; Ferguson, *Pity of War*, pp.277–81; Lawrence, 'Material Pressures', pp.229–54; Hardach, *First World War*, p.203; Burchardt, 'Impact of War Economy', pp.40–70; Wolfgang Mommsen, 'Society and War: Two New Analyses of the First World War', *JMH* 47 (1995), pp.529–38; idem, 'Social Consequences of World War I', pp.25–44; Feldman, *Army, Industry and Labor*, pp.519–41; Armin Triebel, 'Variations in Patterns of Consumption in Germany in the Period of the First World War', in Wall and Winter, eds, *Upheaval of War*, pp.159–95; Herwig, *First World War*, pp.258, 293; Charles Maier, *Recasting Bourgeois Europe: Stabilisation in France, Germany and Italy in the Decade after World War I* (Princeton, NJ, 1975), pp.579–93.

24. Wrigley, 'Impact of First World War on British Labour', pp.141–2; Marwick, *Deluge*, pp.299–300; Waites, *Class Society at War*, pp.213–14; Dewey, *War and Progress*, p.37; Horne, *Labour at War*, p.397; Bourne, *Britain and Great War*, p.195; De Groot, *Blighty*, p.123.

25. Schaffer, *America in Great War*, pp.69–70; Kennedy, *Over Here*, pp.270–9.

26. Marwick, *War and Social Change*, p.74; Horne, *Labour at War*, pp.10, 176, 397; Fridenson, 'Impact of War on French Workers', pp.243–4; Pastor, 'Home Front in Hungary', p.127; Kolko, *Century of War*, p.109; Haig-Muir, 'Economy at War', pp.93–124.

27. Hardach, *First World War*, p.176; Kocka, *Facing Total War*, p.66.

28. Phillips, 'Social Impact', pp.111–19; Bessel, *Germany after First World War*, pp.25–6; Ferguson, *Pity of War*, pp.271–5; Hardach, *First World War*, pp.204–9; idem, 'Industrial Mobilisation', pp.57–88; Reid, 'Impact of War', pp.221–33; Winter, *Great War and British People*, pp.230–40; Dewey, *War and Progress*, p.41; Marwick, *War and Social Change*, p.74; Horne, *Labour at War*, p.395; Manning, 'Wages and Purchasing Power', pp.255–85; Waites, *Class Society at War*, pp.127–48, 194–201.

29. Winter, *Great War and British People*, pp.230–40; Waites, Effects of First World War on Class and Status', pp.27–48; idem, *Class Society at War*, pp.148–59; Phillips, 'Social Impact', pp.111–19; Reid, 'Impact of War', pp.221–33; idem, 'World War I and Working Class', pp.19–21.

30. Winter, *Great War and British People*, pp.218–30; Dewey, *War and Progress*, pp.31–2; Armin Triebel, 'Coal and the Metropolis', in Winter and Robert, eds, *Capital Cities*, pp.342–73; Magri, 'Housing', pp.374–417; Phillips, 'Social Impact', pp.126–31; De Groot, *Blighty*, pp.204–6.

31. Feldman, *Army, Industry and Labor*, pp.117, 471–2; Burchardt, 'Impact of War Economy', pp.40–70; Hardach, *First World War*, pp.197–204; Kocka, *Facing Total War*, pp.17–21; Bessel, *Germany after First World War*, pp.26–7, 30–5; Elizabeth H. Tobin, 'War and the Working Class: The Case of Düsseldorf, 1914–18', *CEH* 18 (1995), pp.257–98; Herwig, *First World War*, p.282.

32. Norman Stone, *Europe Transformed, 1878–1919* (London, 1983), pp.127–8.

33. James F. McMillan, 'World War I and Women in France', in Marwick, ed., *Total War and Social Change*, pp.2–3.

34. Martin Pugh, *The Making of Modern British Politics, 1867–1939*, 2nd edn (Oxford, 1993), p.188; Susan Kingsley Kent, 'Love and Death: War and Gender in Britain, 1914–18', in Coetzee and Shevin-Coetzee, eds, *Authority*, pp.153–74; Braybon and Summerfield, *Out of Cage*, pp.61–4, 75, 84–6; Nicoletta F. Gullace, 'White Feathers and Wounded Men: Female Patriotism and the Memory of the Great War', *JBS* 36 (1997), pp.178–206; Shaver, 'Roles and Images', pp.469–86; Arthur Marwick, *Women at War, 1914–18* (London, 1977), pp.68–9, 107–10; idem, *Deluge*, p.94; Angela Woollacott, *On Her Their Lives Depend: Munition Workers in the Great War* (Berkeley, CA, 1994), pp.79–88; Wilson, *Myriad Faces*, p.237; Gilbert, *First World War*, p.345.

35. Shaver, 'Roles and Images', pp.469–86; Wilson, *Myriad Faces*, pp.158, 775; Peter Calahan, *Belgian Refugee Relief in England during the Great War* (New York, 1982), pp.176–7; Anne Summers, *Angels and Citizens: British Women as Military Nurses, 1854–1914* (London, 1988), pp.238–43, 250–70; Marwick, *Women at War*, pp.21–2, 36–42, 81–94, 168–9; Jenny Gould, 'Women's Military Service in First World War Britain', in Higonet, Jenson, Michel and Weitz, eds, *Behind the Lines*, pp.114–25; Elizabeth Crosthwait, 'The Girl Behind the Man Behind the Gun: The Women's Army Auxiliary Corps, 1914–18', in Leonore Davidoff and Belinda Westover, eds, *Our Work, Our Lives, Our Words* (Totowa, NJ, 1986), pp.161–81; Diana Shaw, 'The Forgotten Army of Women: The Overseas Service of Queen Mary's Army Auxiliary Corps with the British Forces, 1917–21', in Cecil and Liddle, eds, *Facing Armageddon*, pp.365–79; Nancy L. Goldman and Richard Stites, 'Great Britain and the World Wars', in Nancy L. Goldman, ed., *Female Soldiers: Combatants or Non-combatants* (Westport, CT, 1982), pp.21–46; eadem, pp.49, 64, 67; Philippa Levine, '"Walking the Streets in a Way No Decent Woman Should": Women Police in World War I', *JMH* 66 (1994), pp.34–78; Woollacott, *On Her Their Lives Depend*, pp.170–9; Janet Watson, 'Khaki Girls, VADs, and Tommy's Sisters: Gender and Class in First World War Britain', *IHR* 19 (1997), pp.32–51; Krisztina Robert, 'Gender, Class and Patriotism: Women's Paramilitary Units in First World War Britain', ibid., pp.52–65; Henriette Donner, 'Under the Cross – Why VADs Performed the Filthiest Tasks in the Dirtiest War: Red Cross Women Volunteers, 1914–18', *Journal of Social History* 30 (1997), pp.687–704.

36. Kent, 'Love and Death', p.165; Sandra M. Gilbert, 'A Soldier's Heart: Literary Men, Literary Women and the Great War', in Higonet, Jenson, Michel

and Weitz, eds, *Behind the Lines*, pp.197–226; Braybon, 'Women and War', pp.144, 161–4; Sharon Ouditt, 'Tommy's Sisters: The Representation of Working Women's Experience', in Cecil and Liddle, eds, *Facing Armageddon*, pp.736–51; Angela Woollacott, 'Sisters and Brothers in Arms: Family, Class and Gendering in World War I Britain', in Miriam Cooke and Angela Woollacott, eds, *Gendering War Talk* (Princeton, NJ, 1993), pp.128–47; eadem, *On Her Their Lives Depend*, pp.162–6.

37. Marsha Rozenblit, 'For Fatherland and Jewish People: Jewish Women in Austria during the First World War', in Coetzee and Shevin-Coetzee, eds, *Authority*, pp.199–220; Chickering, *Imperial Germany*, p.118; Herwig, *First World War*, p.273; Margaret Darrow, 'French Volunteer Nursing and the Myth of War Experience in World War I', *AHR* 101 (1996), pp.80–106; Robert M. Ponichtera, 'Feminists, Nationalists, and Soldiers: Women in the Fight for Polish Independence', *IHR* 19 (1997), pp.16–31.

38. Maclean, 'War and Australian Society', pp.64–92; McKernan, *Australian People and Great War*, pp.65–93; White, 'War and Australian Society', pp.407–17.

39. Kolko, *Century of War*, p.96; McMillan, 'World War I and Women in France', pp.3–4; Anna Bravo, 'Italian Peasant Women and the First World War', in Paul Thompson and N. Burcharat, eds, *Our Common History: The Transformation of Europe* (London, 1982), pp.157–70; Dewey, *British Agriculture*, pp.51–6, 127–36; Marwick, *Women at War*, pp.79–81, 101; Braybon and Summerfield, *Out of Cage*, p.45.

40. Gail Braybon, *Women Workers in the First World War* (London, 1981), pp.24–50; eadem, 'Women and the War', in Constantine, Kirby and Rose, eds, *First World War in British History*, pp.141–67; Woollacott, *On Her Their Lives Depend*, pp.17–24; Winter, *Great War and British People*, p.46; Wrigley, 'Impact of First World War on British Labour', pp.144–5; Marwick, *Women at War*, pp.12–22, 51–60, 68–75, 166; Braybon and Summerfield, *Out of Cage*, pp.11–29, 31–44; Deborah Thom, 'Women and Work in Wartime Britain', in Wall and Winter, eds, *Upheaval of War*, pp.297–326; eadem, *Nice Girls and Rude Girls*, pp.24–49; Dewey, *War and Progress*, pp.38–9; Wall, 'English and German Families', pp.54–8; Martin Pugh, *Women and the Women's Movement in Britain, 1914–59* (London, 1992), pp.18–21; Strachan, *First World War*, p.32; Adams, *Arms and the Wizard*, p.126; Buckley, *Air Power*, pp.62–6; Pope, *War and Society*, p.21; Horne, *Labour at War*, p.401; S. J. Hurwitz, *State Intervention in Great Britain: A Study of Economic Control and Social Response, 1914–19* (New York, 1949), pp.35, 132.

41. Reid, 'World War I and Working Class', pp.17–19; Walls, 'English and German Families', p.58; Watson, 'Khaki Girls, pp.32–51; Braybon, *Women Workers*, pp.50–7, 60–90; eadem, 'Women and War', p.149; Deborah Thom, 'Tommy's Sister: Women at Woolwich in World War I', in Raphael Samuel, ed., *Patriotism: The Making and Unmaking of British National Identity*, 2 vols (London, 1989),

II, pp.144–57; eadem, 'Women and Work in Wartime Britain', pp.303–5; eadem, *Nice Girls and Rude Girls*, pp.5–6, 144–60; Woollacott, *On Her Their Lives Depend*, pp.124–33, 143–52.

42. De Groot, *Blighty*, pp.132, 139, 304–8; Hurwitz, *State Intervention*, p.136; Bourne, *Britain and Great War*, p.197; Hardach, *First World War*, p.207; Marwick, *Women at War*, p.56; Braybon and Summerfield, *Out of Cage*, pp.47–56; Susan Kingsley Kent, 'The Politics of Sexual Difference: World War I and the Demise of British Feminism', *JBS* 27 (1988), pp.232–53; eadem, 'Gender Reconstruction after the First World War', in Harold Smith, ed., *British Feminism in the Twentieth Century* (London, 1990), pp.68–81; Braybon, *Women Workers*, pp.96–109, 113–7, 131–49; eadem, 'Women and War', pp.160–6; Rosemary Thacker, 'Women in the Tramway Industry, 1914–19', *The Historian* 58 (1998), pp.22–5; Woollacott, *On Her Their Lives Depend*, pp.48–79, 113–17, 188–216; Wilson, *Myriad Faces*, pp.720, 728–30.

43. Daniel, *War From Within*, pp.24–5, 37–80, 88–9, 94–8; idem, 'Women's Work in Industry and Family', pp.267–96; idem, 'Der Krieg der Frauen, 1914–18: Zur Innenansicht des Ersten Weltkriege in Deutschland', in Hirschfeld and Krumeich, eds, *Keiner fühlt sich hier als mensch*, pp.131–49; idem, Fiktionen, Friktionen und Fakten: Frauenlohnarbeit im Ersten Weltkrieg', in Michalka, ed., *Erste Weltkrieg*, pp.530–62; Kocka, *Facing Total War*, pp.17–19; Wall, 'English and German Families', pp.59–62; Chickering, *Imperial Germany*, pp.114–20; Bessel, *Germany after First World War*, pp.16, 18–19; Winter, *Experience of World War I*, p.175; Bonzon, 'Labour Market and Industrial Mobilisation', p.188; Hardach, *First World War*, p.203; Herwig, *First World War*, pp.293–5.

44. Robert Wegs, *Die Österreichische Kriegswirtschaft, 1914–18* (Vienna, 1979), pp.95–7; Herwig, *First World War*, pp.279–81; Reinhard J. Sieder, 'Behind the Lines: Working-class Family Life in Wartime Vienna', in Wall and Winter, eds, *Upheaval of War*, pp.109–38.

45. Tomassini, 'Industrial Mobilisation', pp.59–87.

46. Ferro, *Great War*, p.170; Becker, *Great War and French People*, pp.22, 268; Jean-Louis Robert, 'Women and Work in France during the First World War', in Wall and Winter, eds, *Upheaval of War*, pp.251–66; Marie-Monique Huss, 'Pronatalism and the Popular Ideology of the Child in Wartime France: The Evidence of the Picture Postcard', ibid., pp.329–67; McMillan, 'World War I and Women in France', pp.1–15; Susan R. Graysel, 'Mothers, Marraines, and Prostitutes: Morale and Morality in First World War France', *IHR* 19 (1997), pp.66–82; Horne, *Labour at War*, pp.100–13, 401; Patrick Fridenson, 'A New View of France at War', in Fridenson, ed., *French Home Front*, p.7; Hardach, 'Industrial Mobilisation', pp.57–88; Dubesset, Thébaud and Vincent, 'Female Munition Worker', pp.183–218; Flood, *France 1914–18*, p.75; Judith Still, 'The Reserve Army of Labour? French Women in the First World War', in Michael Scriven and Peter Wagstaff, eds, *War and Society in Twentieth Century France* (New York, 1990), pp.34–48.

47. Kennedy, *Over Here*, pp.284–7; Greenwald, *Women, War, and Work*, pp.5–22, 46–8, 57–86, 93–106, 120–5, 141–2, 146–53, 190, 236–9; Wynn, *Progressivism to Prosperity*, pp.133–52; Connor, *National War Labor Board*, pp.142–57; Kimberly Jensen, 'Physicians and Citizens: US Medical Women and Military Service in the First World War', in Cooter, Harrison and Sturdy, eds, *War, Medicine and Modernity*, pp.106–24.

48. Marwick, *War and Social Change*, pp.77–9; Schaffer, *America in Great War*, pp.75–7; Kennedy, *Over Here*, pp.279–84; Greenwald, *Women, War, and Work*, pp.22–7; James Grossman, 'Citizenship and Rights on the Home Front during the First World War: The Great Migration and the "New Negro"', in Panayi, ed., *Minorities in Wartime*, pp.169–90; Wynn, *Progressivism to Prosperity*, pp.108–24, 170–91.

49. Braybon and Summerfield, *Out of Cage*, p.73; Braybon, *Women Workers*, pp.60–90; De Groot, *Blighty*, p.136; Thom, 'Women and Work in Wartime Britain', pp.311–13; eadem, *Nice Girls and Rude Girls*, pp.94–118; Woollacott, *On Her Their Lives Depend*, pp.101–5; Tomassini, 'Industrial Mobilisation', pp.59–87; Pastor, 'Home Front in Hungary', p.127; Haig-Muir, 'Economy at War', pp.93–124; Daniel, *War From Within*, pp.246–50, 283–94; Becker, *Great War and French People*, pp.203–19; Dubesset, Thébaud and Vincent, 'Female Munition Worker', pp.183–218; Kocka, *Facing Total War*, pp.66–7; Belinda Davis, 'Food Scarcity and the Empowerment of the Female Consumer in World War I Berlin', in Victoria de Grazia and Ellen Furlough, eds, *The Sex of Things: Gender and Consumption in Historical Perspective* (Berkeley, CA, 1996), pp.287–310; Greenwald, *Women, War, and Work*, pp.39–41, 185–6, 207–31; Herwig, *First World War*, pp.176, 274, 363.

50. De Groot, *Blighty*, pp.262–5; Braybon, *Women Workers*, pp.173–210, 216–27; eadem, 'Woman and War', pp.153–60; Bourne, *Britain and Great War*, p.197; Reid, 'World War I and Working Class', p.18; Rubin, 'Law as Bargaining Weapon', pp.925–45; Marwick, *Women at War*, pp.149–52, 162–3; Waites, *Class Society at War*, pp.242–3; Whiteside, 'British Population at War', pp.92–3; Susan Pederson, 'Gender, Welfare and Citizenship in Britain during the Great War', *AHR* 95 (1990), pp.983–1006; Braybon and Summerfield, *Out of Cage*, pp.119–29, 138, 145; Thom, *Nice Girls and Rude Girls*, pp.187–99.

51. Maurin, 'Effets de la mobilisation', pp.82–3; Robert, 'Women and Work in France', pp.263–5; Steven C. Hause, 'More Minerva than Mars: The French Women's Rights Campaign and the First World War', in Higonet, Jenson, Michel and Weitz, eds, *Behind the Lines*, pp.99–113; Bessel, *Germany after First World War*, p.164; Cornelie Usborne, '"Pregnancy is the Women's Active Service": Pronatalism in Germany during the First World War', in Wall and Winter, eds, *Upheaval of War*, pp.389–416; Daniel, *War From Within*, pp.103–6, 152–60, 276–83; Kennedy, *Over Here*, pp.284–7; Greenwald, *Women, War, and Work*, pp.128–36, 159–72, 180–4, 243.

52. Marwick, *Women at War*, pp.22–32, 152–8; Wilson, *Myriad Faces*, p.726; David H. Close, 'The Collapse of Resistance to Democracy: Conservatives, Adult Suffrage and Second Chamber Reform, 1911–28', *HJ* 20 (1977), pp.893–918; Martin Pugh, *Electoral Reform in War and Peace, 1906–18* (London, 1978), pp.17–44, 70–86, 136–54; idem, 'Politicians and the Women's Vote, 1914–18', *History* 59 (1974), pp.358–74; idem, *Women's Suffrage in Britain, 1867–1928* (London, 1980), pp.30–5; Sandra Stanley Holt, *Feminism and Democracy: Women's Suffrage and Reform Politics in Britain, 1900–18* (London, 1986), pp.116–50; Kent, 'Politics of Sexual Difference', pp.232–53.

53. Schaffer, *America in Great War*, pp.92–5; Kennedy, *Over Here*, pp.284–7.

54. Hause, 'More Minerva than Mars', pp.99–113; McMillan, 'World War I and Women in France', pp.1–15; idem, *Housewife or Harlot: The Place of Women in French Society, 1870–1940* (Brighton, 1981), pp.178–82.

55. De Groot, *Blighty*, pp.223–5; Daniel, 'Women's Work', p.267; Wall, 'English and German Families', pp.65–98; Soloway, 'Eugenics and Pronatalism', pp.369–88; Bourne, *Britain and Great War*, p.235; Marwick, *Women at War*, pp.137–43; Braybon and Summerfield, *Out of Cage*, pp.97–107; Phillips, 'Social Impact', pp.132–8; Braybon, *Women Workers*, pp.117–31, 154–70, 185–204.

56. Braybon and Summerfield, *Out of Cage*, pp.107–13; Sylvia Pankhurst, *The Home Front* (London, 1932), p.98; Wilson, *Myriad Faces*, pp.390, 641–2, 724–5; Woollacott, *On Her Their Lives Depend*, pp.143–52, 188–216; eadem, 'Khaki Fever and its Control: Gender, Class, Age and Sexual Morality on the British Home Front in the First World War', *JCH* 29 (1994), pp.325–48; Lutz D. H. Sauerteig, 'Sex, Medicine and Morality during the First World War', in Cooter, Harrison and Sturdy, eds, *War, Medicine and Modernity*, pp.167–88; Bourne, *Britain and Great War*, pp.235–6; De Groot, *Blighty*, pp.231–7.

57. Maurin, 'Effets de la mobilisation', pp.86–7; Marwick, *Deluge*, p.278; Daniel, *War From Within*, pp.138–47, 182–5, 189–207; Chickering, *Imperial Germany*, pp.119–20; Herwig, *First World War*, p.282; Sieder, 'Behind the Lines', pp.109–38.

58. Beckett, 'Aspects of Nation in Arms;', pp.27–39; idem, 'Nation in Arms', 15–17; idem, *Amateur Military Tradition*, pp.236–43; J. M. Osborne, 'Defining their Own Patriotism: British Volunteer Training Corps in the First World War', *JCH* 23 (1988), pp.59–75; K. W. Mitchinson, 'The National Reserve, 1910–19', unpub. ms., pp.24–37.

59. White, 'War and Australian Society', pp.417–20; Tomassini, 'Home Front in Italy', pp.586–8; Bessel, *Germany after the First World War*, pp.24–5; Daniel, *War From Within*, pp.160–71; Herwig, *First World War*, p.295; Chickering, *Imperial Germany*, pp.120–6, 150; Jürgen Reulecke, 'Männerbund versus the Family: Middle-Class Youth Movements and the Family in Germany in the period of the First World War', in Wall and Winter, eds, *Upheaval of War*,

pp.439–52; Peter Loewenberg, 'The Psychohistorical Origins of the Nazi Youth Cohort', *AHR* 76 (1971), pp.1457–502; Marwick, *Deluge*, pp.125–7; Wynn, *Progressivism to Prosperity*, pp.154–5.

60. Chickering, *Imperial Germany*, pp.147–51; De Groot, *Blighty*, pp.140–3.

61. Wilson, *Myriad Faces of War*, pp.164, 403–4, 512; De Groot, *Blighty*, pp.226–31; Jack Williams, 'Cricket and the Great War', *Stand To* 51 (1998), pp.5–9; Edmund McCabe, 'Rugby and the Great War', *Stand To* 52 (1998), pp.26–9; C. Veitch, ' "Play Up! Play Up! and Win the War": Football, the Nation and the First World War, 1914–15', *JCH* 20 (1985), pp.363–78; Bruno Cabanes, 'Culture de guerre, loisirs ouvriers: contacts et oppositions en Angleterre pendant la première guerre mondiale', in Becker, Winter, Krumeich, Becker and Audoin-Rouzeau, eds, *Guerre et Cultures*, pp.165–72; James Walvin, *Leisure and Society, 1830–1950* (London, 1978), pp.129–32; Michael McKernan, 'Sport, War and Society: Australia, 1914–18', in R. Casman and M. McKernan, eds, *Sport in History: The Making of Modern Sporting History* (St Lucia, 1979), pp.1–20; idem, *Australian People and Great War*, pp.94–115; John K. Walton, 'Leisure Towns in Wartime: The Impact of the First World War in Blackpool and San Sebastian', *JCH* 31 (1996), pp.603–17; Winter, *Experience of World War I*, p.178; Kolko, *Century of War*, p.100.

62. Marwick, *Deluge*, pp.150–6, 321–2; De Groot, *Blighty*, pp.239–40, 242–3; Collins, *Theatre at War*, pp.35–64, 66–70; Gaynor Kavanagh, *Museums and the First World War: A Social History* (Leicester, 1994), pp.22–51, 65–81, 99–102; Nicholas Hiley, 'The British Cinema Auditorium', in Dibbets and Hogenkamp, eds, *Film and First World War*, pp.160–70; Smith, 'War and British Culture', pp.180–2; Jay Winter, 'British National Identity and the First World War', in S. J. D. Green and R. C. Whiting, eds, *The Boundaries of State in Modern Britain* (Cambridge, 1995), pp.261–77; idem, 'Popular Culture in Wartime Britain', in Roshwald and Stites, eds, *European Culture*, pp.330–48; John Ferguson, *The Arts in Britain in World War I* (London, 1980), pp.62–7.

63. Segel, 'Culture in Poland', pp.72–85; Beller, 'Tragic Carnival', pp.154–9; Claire Nolte, 'Ambivalent Patriots: Czech Culture in the Great War', in Roshwald and Stites, eds, *European Culture*, pp.169–75; Joseph Held, 'Culture in Hungary during World War I', ibid., pp.177–81; Marc Ferro, 'Cultural Life in France, 1914–18', ibid., p.415, n.28; Andrew Wachtel, 'Culture in the South Slavic Lands, 1914–18', ibid., pp.195–7, 202–4, 207–9; Kelbetcheva, 'Between Apology and Denial', pp.217–22; M. Bucer, 'Romania: War, Occupation, Libersation', ibid., pp.243–5, 253–4, 258–9; Schaepdrijver, 'Occupation', pp.275–8; Adamson, 'Impact of World War I on Italian Political Culture', pp.311–13, 327; Mosse, *Fallen Soldiers*, pp.145–6.

64. Étienne Fouilloux, 'Première guerre mondiale et changement religieux en Europe' in Becker and Audoin-Rouzeau, eds, *Les sociétés européennes*, pp.439–52; Becker, *War and Faith*, pp.32–61, 96–113; idem, 'La foi aux États-Unis

pendant la première guerre mondiale', in Becker, Winter, Krumeich, Becker and Audoin-Rouzeau, eds, *Guerre et Cultures*, pp.183–92; Wilkinson, *Church of England*, pp.230–93; Winter, *Sites of Memory*, pp.54–77.

65. Marwick, *War and Social Change*, p.222.

66. Winter, 'Popular Culture', p.346; De Groot, *Blighty*, p.311.

CHAPTER TEN

War, Politics and Revolution

Industrial militancy was by no means uncommon in belligerent states during the Great War but, in most cases, it sprang from bread-and-butter issues. This was quite literally true in the case of the widespread strikes in both France and Italy in 1917 caused primarily by food shortages. Perceived wartime deprivations of any kind, however, followed general pre-war experience of relative prosperity. Militancy also stemmed from the changing nature of the industrial workforce, not least its greater mobility, and the changing conditions imposed upon it. Since the state was expected to maintain food supplies and had also taken upon itself the functions formerly associated with employers, it was the state that was increasingly regarded as the obstacle to the achievement of wider aspirations.

To some extent, the growth of trade unionism assisted the containment of militancy since unions received a new measure of recognition and respectability. At the same time, however, the strengthened position of labour brought a growing realisation that the strike was a particularly effective political weapon in wartime, especially where the leadership of organised labour was compromised by co-operation with government. There were movements opposed to the war in most belligerents and, certainly by 1917, war-weariness was sufficiently common for governments to attempt to organise a wider mobilisation of public opinion. It still required, however, a substantial breakdown in the functioning of the state and in the capacity of political leaderships to convert militancy into social and political collapse.[1]

Leadership

Successful political leadership was a vital component in national survival, but it required astute manipulation of public opinion. Politicians, however, already faced other challenges. Generally, as already noted, politicians had surrendered considerable authority to the military in terms of strategic policy and thereafter spent much of the war trying to wrest back what they had yielded. At the same time, the war often promoted the emergence of new governmental coalitions and the incorporation of those previously excluded from government such as the socialists, who entered government for the first time in both Britain and Italy.[2]

While liberal democracies like Britain, France and the United States entered the war with greater legitimacy in the eyes of their population than more coercive political systems such as that of Germany, much still depended upon the ability and authority of politicians. It took the willpower of a Clemenceau in France to re-establish political control over the war in November 1917. In Germany, Chancellor Bethmann was not sufficiently robust to prevent the military steadily increasing influence over all aspects of policy, a process marked by the effective assumption of power by Hindenburg and Ludendorff in August 1916 and Bethmann's own dismissal in July 1917.

In Britain, it could be argued that Asquith was too used to seeking compromise and consensus to be an effective war leader. A diffident and lethargic figure, Asquith largely counted upon the desire of his Liberal colleagues to cling to office and, in creating the coalition in May 1915, upon the desire of the Unionist leader, Bonar Law, to avoid an election. The pre-war political situation in Britain had been marked by internal divisions within both Unionists and Liberals and it has been argued that, while Asquith wished to avoid an election that might split the Liberals, Law wished to do so for fear of losing control over the Unionists.

Lloyd George was an altogether tougher proposition, favouring strong executive control at the centre, but even he never succeeded in overcoming the consciousness of his weak political position. Therefore, he also used the threat of an election to sustain his coalition. Both Asquith and Lloyd George were assisted by the uncertainties as to the outcome of fighting an election on an electoral register increasingly out of date and when local constituency organisation had been weakened by the enlistment of many party agents. Indeed, MPs found it difficult to retain much contact with their constituents, especially as many had themselves received wartime commissions: Josiah Wedgwood commented in August 1914 that Churchill had given so many naval commissions to MPs that the War Office 'in sheer self-defence, had to do the same'. In fact, 184 MPs, 139 of them Unionists, were serving with the armed forces by January 1915.[3]

The relative powerlessness of individual MPs did not prevent the resurgence of British party politics when the war proved of longer duration than expected. Thus, back-benchers were a significant factor in the making of administrations in both May 1915 and December 1916. Indeed, there was significant Unionist restlessness with the truce in face of the apparent drift of war policy. This was especially so with the occurrence in May 1915 of both the reported shell shortage, publicised in *The Times*, and the resignation of Fisher as First Sea Lord over the Dardanelles campaign. Having told the Commons as recently as 10 May 1915 that a coalition was not under contemplation, Asquith reconstructed the government as such on 17 May.[4]

Disputes between Unionists and Liberals over possible reform of the franchise opened new wounds in the early summer of 1916, forcing the establishment of the Speaker's Conference on electoral reform. The failure of the Somme campaign and Lansdowne's advocacy within Cabinet of peace negotiations in November 1916 led to demands by the Unionists for a more vigorous prosecution of the war. Manoeuvring by Law, Sir Edward Carson, leader of the Ulster Unionists, and Lloyd George forced Asquith's resignation on 5 December 1916. Lacking sufficient support from his own party and unable to command the support of the Liberal majority, Law declined to form a government, but Lloyd George accepted the invitation to construct a new coalition on 7 December.[5]

Unionist back-bench pressure had pushed Law into supporting Asquith's removal, and Lloyd George's survival depended upon a degree of military success. Ironically, the same back-benchers would not countenance the change in High Command that Lloyd George deemed necessary to secure that success. Moreover, it was always possible that a dissident Unionist minister among those excluded from the War Cabinet might seek to enlist wider support.

Nonetheless, few MPs were willing to risk an election. Indeed, there was some fear that, with no clear victory in sight, a demand for peace on the part of those Liberal and Labour back-benchers outside the coalition might prove all too attractive a political rallying cry for the electorate, particularly in the light of Lansdowne's public demand for peace in November 1917. The prolongation of the coalition, in what was increasingly an election campaign from July 1918 onwards, was intended to control the pace of political change and preserve stability in the face of the emerging challenges of organised extra-parliamentary interests such as labour and business. Indeed, John Turner has argued that the Lloyd George coalition represented a 'counter-revolutionary' political force.[6]

In France, the virtual abdication of responsibilities by the Chamber of Deputies and Senate in August 1914 handed considerable power to the government. When parliament reassembled in December 1914, ordinary French politicians began to reassert control over the executive by means of the revival of parliamentary commissions. It was the pressure of the army commissions of Senate and Chamber, for example, that forced the establishment of the Under-Secretariat for Artillery and Munitions in May 1915 and, in many respects, ushered in the Briand ministry in October 1915. The commissions were less dominant after June 1916, but the subsequent secret sessions of Chamber and Senate, such as those held on Verdun, intensified the pre-war trend towards 'controlling governments through harassment'.

Secret sessions resulted in the fall of Briand administrations in both November 1916 and March 1917 and the resignation of Lyautey as War Minister. It was, similarly, a parliamentary vote of no confidence that forced out the Painlevé administration in November 1917. In reverting to government by executive decree, however, the authoritarian Clemenceau, who had previously made the Senate Army Commission a personal political platform, effectively ended parliamentary influence over government policy.[7]

Despite the suspension of normal political activities in Germany in 1914, the Reichstag did increase its powers to some extent. A parliamentary Food Advisory Board was established in August 1914 and, in October 1916, the budget committee became the main standing committee of the Reichstag. The debate on the Auxiliary Service Law in the autumn of 1916 and the Peace Resolution in July 1917 also demonstrated that there was some scope for parliamentary influence. This was primarily a result of the coalescing of a new coalition grouping around the Majority Social Democratic Party (SPD), the Catholic Centre Party, the Progressive Party and some National Liberals.

The fall of Michaelis as Chancellor following the Reichstag's vote for reform of the Prussian franchise in October 1917, and Michaelis's attempt to censure the USPD (Independent Social Democratic Party) for its alleged role in a short-lived naval mutiny at Wilhelmshaven in August, marked the apogee of Reichstag influence. Its limitations were then shown by its inability to commit Michaelis's successor, Hertling, to its political programme. Thereafter, it was only the collapse of Germany that propelled the Reichstag coalition into office under Prince Max of Baden in October 1918.

Wider reform was impossible given the nature of socio-economic and political power in the Reich. Indeed, it might be argued that it was the lack of parliamentary support for the state and the essentially non-parliamentary system of government that most contributed to the failure to adapt sufficiently to the demands of the war. Victory had been intended to compensate for wartime privations and the lack of political reform. When it was not forthcoming, therefore, political tension increased, with no authoritative political figure to counter it.[8]

In Austria-Hungary, the Common Council of Ministers met only about forty times during the war and, for all practical purposes, the Austrian and Hungarian administrations operated entirely separately in managing political issues. The Hungarian parliament sat throughout the war. Parliamentary opposition to Prime Minister Tisza coalesced around the issue of the extension of the suffrage. Indeed, ultimately, it was the suffrage issue that cost Tisza his office when Emperor Karl forced his resignation in May 1917. Tisza retained a parliamentary majority, however, and his resistance continued to frustrate his successors. Consequently, only a limited franchise reform was passed in July 1918, which increased the size of the electorate to just 13 per cent of adult males.[9]

In Austria, the Reichsrat remained prorogued until 1917. Count Stürgkh attempted to rule by decree for fear that parliamentary recall would open a can of worms. Stürgkh, however, was assassinated in October 1916 by Fritz Adler, the son of the Austrian socialist leader. As suggested in Chapter Five (pp.139–40), the subject nationalities increasingly saw a solution to their aspirations outside the Empire. Thus, upon its recall by Emperor Karl, the Reichsrat became a forum for Czech and then Yugoslav demands.[10]

Opposition

Political developments in Germany and Austria-Hungary are a reminder that opposition to the war was increasingly being experienced in many states by 1917, but it had been there from the beginning. Of course, the expectation of many European socialists that war could be prevented through international solidarity had been frustrated. Not expecting the July Crisis to develop into war, socialist leaders, many of whom had attended an emergency session of the International Socialist Bureau (ISB) – in effect the secretariat of the Second International – at Brussels on 29–30 July 1914, had generally adopted a cautious, 'wait and see' attitude. In the words of Georges Haupt, they had become 'disoriented spectators . . . submerged by the wave of nationalism'. Indeed, socialist movements had largely split on the war issue. In each case, the majority of socialists supported their national war efforts, arguing that the war was one of defence and liberty, in which the working class had as much interest in victory as anyone else, while denouncing foreign socialists for voting for war credits.

Thus, in France, the 'majoritaires', characterised by Jouhaux of the CGT (General Labour Confederation), found themselves opposed by the 'minoritaires' such as Alphonse Merrheim, the secretary of the metalworkers' union, the Fédération des Métaux. The anti-war articles of the novelist Romain Rolland began to appear in a Swiss journal in September 1914 under the general title of *Au-dessus de la mêlée* (Above the Fray). Ironically, Rolland's articles, inspired by the German sack of Louvain and addressed to the German playwright Gerhart Hauptmann, became widely known only through criticism by his opponents in the spring of 1915. They were not published in book form until November 1915. Indeed, only a small group of 'Vitalist' intellectuals followed Rolland's lead, including Georges Sorel and the Belgian Emile Verhaeren. A number of French pacifist or anti-war journals were published such as Henri Guilbeaux's *Demain*. Other than *Bonnet Rouge*, however, many of them were of short duration and often confined to small circulating workers' libraries.

The Labour Party in Britain was similarly split, with Ramsay MacDonald resigning as chairman of the Parliamentary Labour Party (PLP) in opposition to the war. Most members of MacDonald's Independent Labour Party followed a similar anti-war course. Opposition to the war, however, remained a minority activity for some time. In September 1915, only 7 out of 607 delegates to the Trades Union Council conference opposed a pro-war resolution. Support for a negotiated peace gained considerable ground by early 1917, but Entente success rallied London Trades Council support for the war in the summer and autumn of 1918 although that in Birmingham split on the issue.[11]

While most German socialists, including Friedrich Ebert and Carl Legien, supported the *Burgfrieden* from the beginning as a necessary defensive war against Tsardom, elements within the SPD had made their opposition to the war known. While fourteen SPD dissidents were persuaded not to vote against war credits in the Reichstag in August 1914, Karl Liebknecht did so in December 1914. Subsequently, others abstained on further war credit votes but it was not until December 1915 that Hugo Haase and nineteen others voted against the fifth war credits bill. In March 1916, eighteen deputies including Haase, who were expelled from the parliamentary party after voting against the sixth bill, formed the SPD Arbeitsgemeinschaft (Working Group). Liebknecht meanwhile formed the International Group with Rosa Luxemburg, Franz Mehring and Klara Zetkin. In January 1916, the International Group was renamed the Spartacists, taking its name from the slave who had led a revolt against Rome in 73 BC. Radical anti-war sentiment was growing in a number of centres including Berlin, Leipzig and Dusseldorf, and it was Liebknecht's arrest in June 1916 which led to widespread strikes.

Both Spartacists and Arbeitsgemeinschaft attended an opposition socialist conference in Berlin in January 1917, to which the SPD leadership responded by declaring all opposition socialists expelled from the party. Under the leadership of Haase, therefore, the USPD was formally established in April 1917 on a platform of peace. The SPD thus became the Majority SPD in terms of its parliamentary representatives. Actual party membership, however, declined from just over 1 million in 1914 to 243,000 by 1917, although this was partly a result of conscription. By contrast, the USPD claimed to have 100,000 members by 1918 with over 100 local branches concentrated in industrial centres. In turn, the Spartacists, who had joined the USPD, eventually broke away to form Kommunistischen Partei Deutschlands (KPD; German Communist Party) in December 1918.

As elsewhere, a few intellectuals opposed the war, just 141 signatures appearing on a petition opposing war aims in July 1915. Thomas Mann's brother Heinrich was one of the more prominent critics of the war, while, in Austria-Hungary, the playwrights Stefan Zweig and, especially, Karl Kraus, also opposed the war.[12]

Understandably, governments were sensitive to the possibility of anti-war opposition and surveillance of actual and potential dissidents was common. In Germany, this extended to regular letter inspection, and special attention being paid to conversations in railway carriages and to graffiti on toilet walls, by a network of paid informers. Similarly, in Austria-Hungary, the responsibilities of the War Supervisory Office went beyond merely censoring press reports. In Britain, the military authorities were sufficiently worried by the prospect of 'British Bolshevism' to recast home defence plans in 1917–18. By 1917, MI5 had 250,000 report cards and 27,000 personal files on potential dissidents, well in excess of the 70,000 or so resident aliens in Britain. The head of Special Branch, Sir Basil Thomson, began a series of fortnightly reports on pacifism, revolutionary organisations in the United Kingdom and morale abroad in early 1918. Nonetheless, Thomson's own assessment in 1920 was that the number of revolutionaries in Britain was 'ridiculously small'.[13]

Dissenters were frequently prosecuted. Thus, Liebknecht received a two and a half years sentence in May 1916, increased on appeal to four years and one month. Rosa Luxemburg was arrested for sedition in July 1917. Among the many prosecuted in the United States, one of the leading 'Wobblies', W. D. Haywood, received a prison sentence of twenty years and the leader of the socialists, Eugene V. Debs, who had contested the presidency in 1912, got ten years. Notoriously, the film-maker Robert Goldstein also received ten years for what were regarded as anti-English scenes in his film, *The Spirit of '76*, set in the War of Independence. Almost twenty academics were sacked for not being sufficiently pro-war, the most prominent being James McKean Cattrell, a psychologist at Columbia University.

As already noted, the leaders of the Clyde Workers Committee were deported from the Clyde in March 1915 and one Clydeside leader, John

Maclean, received eight years' imprisonment, of which he served 22 months, for incitement to sedition. The British philosopher Bertrand Russell was fined £100 in June 1916 for anti-conscription activities and lost his lectureship at Trinity College, Cambridge, as a result. In May 1918 he was given six months' imprisonment for 'statements likely to prejudice' relations with the United States, having alleged that American troops would be used as strike breakers in Britain as they had been in America. Court cases, however, gave Russell a public platform, the prosecution in the first case being bungled: the same was true of the trial of the assistant secretary of the teacher's union, Hélène Brion, who received a three month suspended sentence in France in March 1918. Two other leading British pacifists were also jailed, Clifford Allen being held from August 1916 to December 1917 and E. D. Morel given six months in August 1917.[14]

Pacifism in Britain had suffered a blow in August 1914 from the fact that the chairman of the Peace Society, J. A. Pease, chose not to resign from Asquith's Cabinet. New politically motivated groups, however, soon emerged. The junior minister who did resign from the government, Charles Trevelyan, formed the Union of Democratic Control (UDC) with MacDonald, Norman Angell and Morel on 5 August 1914. In theory, like MacDonald himself, the UDC, which had eventually 10,000 members, was not opposed to national defence and wished to effect a negotiated peace and to assert the right of 'the people' to control policy made in its name, primarily by creating a different kind of post-war world. Other Independent Labour Party (ILP) members had different views. The suffrage movement was also divided, Sylvia Pankhurst of the Women's Suffrage Federation (WSF) breaking from her mother and sister to oppose the war and seeking to send delegates to a peace congress at The Hague in April 1915.

Conscription was a major issue for the British peace movement and the No Conscription Fellowship (NCF) was formed by Fenner Brockway and Clifford Allen on 3 December 1914 for those of military age. In all, 843 'absolutists' spent two or more years in prison, with 17 given death sentences later commuted to life imprisonment and 142 given life sentences; 10 died while imprisoned.

What might be termed British Bolshevism, however, was mostly concerned with the issues of dilution and erosion of differentials. Thus, a call to form soldiers' and workers' councils in every town, emanating from a conference convened by the UDC, ILP, trade unions and other socialist groups, including the small British Socialist Party (BSP), at Leeds in June 1917 in celebration of the Tsar's abdication fell on deaf ears. The London Trades Council, which had sent delegates, declined to act on the resolution while the dockers' union denounced the conference as a bogus, middle-class affair. Those meetings which attempted to create such councils were invariably broken up.

Lansdowne's call for more moderate war aims and the Labour Party's own declaration of non-expansionist war aims in December 1917 did cause the government some difficulties. Lloyd George, however, successfully outflanked the anti-war movement by his war aims speech in January 1918, shifting Britain's publicly stated war aims to a vague idea of democratic peace. The fact that the Bolsheviks then signed up to Brest Litovsk in March 1918 cut even more ground from under the peace movement with the wide recognition that peace in the east freed German resources to pursue a decisive victory in the west. However, what was of far more concern for the government than pacifism was the Metropolitan Police pay strike in August 1918.[15]

The greatest wartime challenge to the authority of the British government was arguably the Easter Rising in Dublin in April 1916. Whatever its long-term consequences, however, it posed little real threat at the time. It appears to have had virtually no impact upon Irish servicemen in France and Flanders. The Home Rule bill had been put on the statute book in September 1914 but its operation suspended for the duration. In response to John Redmond's support for the war effort, the Irish Volunteers had split, a rump of 13,000 or so, often now called Irish National Volunteers (INV), being opposed to assisting the British. Plans for an insurrection begun by the Irish Republican Brotherhood (IRB) in 1915 depended upon both the participation of the INV and German assistance. The former British diplomat and Irish Protestant nationalist Sir Roger Casement went to Germany but recruited only 55 men for his 'Irish Brigade' among Irish prisoners of war held by the Germans.

Casement himself was arrested after landing at Tralee Bay from the *U-19* on 21 April 1916. The rising on Easter Monday, 24 April 1916, was staged by fewer than 2,000 men and women drawn from the more radical sections of the INV, led by Patrick Pearse, and James Connolly's Irish Citizen Army. Some 258 civilians, 132 soldiers and police, and 64 rebels died before the self-proclaimed Provisional Government of the Irish Republic surrendered on 29 April 1916. Fifteen rebels were subsequently shot between 3 and 12 May before United States pressure halted the executions, while Casement was hanged in August 1916. The rising forced the British government to recognise the likelihood of partition as a long-term solution. The executions swayed public opinion in Ireland itself, the nationalist Sinn Féin (Ourselves Alone) winning five by-elections in 1917 and 1918 and 73 seats at the general election in 1918.[16]

The greatest threat to national resolve in France was from war-weariness. This certainly contributed to the widespread mutinies in the French army in the spring of 1917. However, there was rarely any political element in the mutinies and they came down to issues of pay and leave. Confidence had already been shown by not arresting socialist leaders under the Carnet B in 1914. The French anti-war movement and those branded as *défaitistes* (defeatists) also lacked the organisation and leadership to sustain a challenge to government.

Clovis Andrieu, a skilled metalworker and leading pre-war syndicalist militant, who was arrested in May 1918 for his role in the increased industrial militancy in the Saint Étienne region, was more revolutionary than most in his opposition to the war. In the event, most French workers remained convinced of the need for France to prevail. French national morale dipped lowest in May to June 1917, but never even reached a crisis point in rural areas. Conceivably, the loss of Russia to the Entente would have had a greater impact had there not been a year's interval between the overthrow of the Tsar and the peace treaty between the Bolsheviks and the Germans.[17]

By contrast, extra-parliamentary opposition became increasingly significant in Germany. Pacifism in terms of non-socialist opposition to the war had been weak in 1914, the German Peace Society being small and ineffectual. The strikes in Berlin in June 1916 after Liebknecht's arrest marked a new politicisation. The privations of the 'turnip winter' of 1916–17 and the attempt by Hindenburg and Ludendorff to impose full labour mobilisation through the Auxiliary Service Law in December 1916 exacerbated difficulties, making union membership more receptive to the kind of sedition being advocated by radical elements. In turn, strikes and disturbances played a greater role in forcing the promised reform of the suffrage than did parliamentary action.

As the food crisis worsened, in January 1918, even more overtly political strikes occurred in Berlin and elsewhere involving at least 400,000 workers. They led to demands by the elected councils of the strikers for peace without annexations or reparations, workers' participation in peace negotiations, democratisation of the Prussian franchise, abolition of the Auxiliary Service Law, an amnesty for political prisoners, and improvements in the supply of food.[18]

The war was always likely to put pressure on Austria-Hungary's ramshackle multinational organisation, in which the practice of divide and rule meant that only an overriding loyalty to the Emperor guaranteed protection against other nationalities' demands. With food supplies dwindling in 1917, industrial militancy increased and the halving of the flour ration in January 1918 resulted in strikes through much of the empire and the emergence of workers' councils. Military censors had noted the support for the strikes within the army and undeniably political aspects also began to emerge in some of the military disturbances which occurred in May 1918.[19]

Negotiated peace had become a metaphor for wider opposition to the war by 1917 and, alongside the growing demands for such a peace there was something of a revival of the pre-war hopes of international socialism among the anti-war socialist minorities. In the event, however, this proved illusory. A call to an international conference in Copenhagen in January 1915 was rejected by the French General Labour Confederation (CGT) and socialists, who went to an alternative meeting in London. Generally, indeed, the Second International, which moved its headquarters from Brussels to The Hague in December 1914, was virtually powerless. More significant was the gathering of 38 assorted socialist delegates of twelve nationalities, including Lenin, at Zimmerwald in Switzerland in September 1915. The delegates wanted immediate peace, but the majority, including Merrheim, rejected Lenin's 'revolutionary defeatism', which implied the necessity of defeating one's own government as a prerequisite for peace, and his call for the establishment of a Third International. Another meeting of 43 delegates from eight states was held at Kienthal, also in Switzerland, in April 1916, with similar results.

In April 1917 the International Socialist Bureau called for a new peace conference. The demand was taken up by the Petrograd Soviet in May 1917 and a joint appeal was issued in July for a conference at Stockholm, which it was hoped would bring a negotiated peace. The Russian provisional government lent its support and delegations were formed in most states. Significantly, these were mostly from pro-war majority groups who, though sceptical of the chances of peace, generally believed that war aims should be non-expansive and, in the case of those from Entente states, also hoped to keep Russia in the war. There was also a belief that they could convert progressive elements within the Central Powers to their own agenda. In the event, the French government withheld passports from the French socialist delegation and British seamen refused to transport the British socialist delegation. The Stockholm conference, therefore, did not take place although more radical elements, including the USPD (Independent Social Democratic Party) and the Bolsheviks, held a preliminary conference, which called for an international mass struggle for peace.[20]

Revolution

War-weariness manifested itself most obviously in Russia. If, as J. A. S. Grenville memorably expressed it, Italy, Austria-Hungary and Russia were 'racing each other to collapse' by 1917, then it was Russia that was always likely to win the race through the enormous additional pressure placed on the Tsarist system by the challenge of war.[21]

Russia had already experienced considerable social, economic and political pressures as a result of defeat in the Russo-Japanese War. In the aftermath of revolution, a nominal constitutional monarchy had emerged with a Council of Ministers headed by a president and an elected assembly or Duma, marking a distinct change in a state without democratic tradition. Reform had also been begun in agriculture with the abolition of communes. In 1908, too, plans were announced for the progressive extension of universal primary education by 1922. Stimulated by the rearmament programme for both army and navy, industry grew, especially in metallurgy, engineering and shipbuilding. The generally liberal-minded middle classes, too, expanded in wealth and numbers.

Modernisation, however, was not without its costs. In the countryside, the impact of reform was limited and it had not diminished the desire for land redistribution. Rapid industrialisation came at the cost of concentrating the industrial workforce in a few key areas such as Moscow, Riga and St Petersburg (renamed Petrograd in August 1914 in reaction against its Germanic sounding name). In the case of St Petersburg, the industrial workforce rose from 158,000 in 1908 to 216,000 by 1913. Such rapid industrialisation and accompanying urbanisation put considerable strains on housing and there was already growing industrial militancy before the war.

As yet, however, the revolutionary movement was too fractured to fully exploit militancy, the Marxists of the Social Democratic Workers Party having split into Bolsheviks (partisans of the majority) and Mensheviks (partisans of the minority) in 1903. The Socialist Revolutionaries (SRs), founded in 1901, were also divided over revolutionary tactics. While also divided, middle-class liberals were thwarted by the change in the franchise in 1907, which had resulted in the return of a more conservative Duma and an end to expectations of further reform. Moreover, there was increasingly less support for the Tsar and neither the Orthodox Church nor an army badly affected by mutiny in 1905 were quite the bulwarks of autocracy they had proved to be in the past.

In many respects, it might be argued that the Great War cut across reforms which would otherwise have enabled the Tsarist system to survive in the longer term. Indeed, there was little real evidence of any immediate revolutionary challenge to the state, but divisions were clearly widening. The problems created by the attempt to wage the war, however, proved far too great for the government to survive.[22]

The war led to a considerable food crisis. In the past this was attributed to declining production, as a result of conscription of the agricultural labour force and the greater mobility of the remaining rural labour force seeking new opportunities in industry. In fact, agricultural production actually increased with good harvests. In the case of cereals, output increased by 10 per cent despite the lack of fertiliser and the loss of over 2 million horses to the army. In theory, even taking account of the demands of the army, it has been calculated that the 1917 harvest produced a grain surplus over all requirements of at least 520 million puds (approximately 8.4 million tons).

The real difficulty, however, was one of transportation, although it was not the case, as sometimes imagined, of grain chasing trains but, as Norman Stone has argued, of trains chasing grain. Food was not a transport priority and track maintenance had declined, but the whole pre-war system had been geared to taking bulk supplies from larger producers. Wartime increase in production took place among smaller producers, thus requiring longer rail journeys and more trains. Indeed, such were the difficulties of marketing that many peasants either resorted to feeding surplus to livestock or reverting to subsistence agriculture.

As a result, by 1917, despite some 2.5 billion roubles being spent on the rail network, St Petersburg was receiving not much more than half its daily requirement of grain and Moscow only one-third. Bread and flour rationing were introduced in Moscow on 11 March 1917. Significantly, the revolution erupted in St Petersburg in March 1917 on the back of food disturbances compounded by fuel shortages and severe winter weather, which exacerbated the transport crisis. Ironically, crowds on the streets were swelled once the disturbances began by a sudden improvement in the weather, which encouraged people to go outside after several months' confinement.[23]

In a similar way to there being abundant food available, although in the wrong places, it has been sometimes assumed that Russian industry simply collapsed under the strain of wartime production. Initially, it was certainly affected by mobilisation and by the loss of Poland in 1915, one-fifth of coal and one-tenth of iron ore resources being lost to the Germans. Moreover, as elsewhere, Russia suffered a shell shortage in 1915. The government itself declined to believe that its industry could cope, with the result that it ordered large amounts of munitions from Britain and the United States. In any case, the government took the view that resources would be better spent on purchasing shells overseas than developing new factories, which would be idle in peacetime.

In the event, overseas manufacturers, already struggling to fill orders from their own governments, failed to match Russian expectations. By November 1916, foreign suppliers had delivered only 7.1 million of the 40.5 million shells ordered. Even if they did arrive, there was still the problem of transporting them. The northern ports were closed by ice for much of the year and the trans-Siberian railway was capable of handling only 280 wagons a day. Little was done to sort out the chaos that developed at Archangel in northern Russia and, while a railway connecting the port to Petrograd was completed in 1917, the development of Murmansk as an ice-free port was not usefully completed until 1923. By March 1917, American boot manufacturers had resorted to sending their products by parcel post.

Russia's own industrialists led the demand to be allowed to reorganise the war economy. In the wake of the retreat from Galicia and the shell shortage, the Special Council of Defence was established by industry and the Duma in May 1915 on the model of the British Ministry of Munitions. It was intended to encourage amalgamation and consolidation of industrial units and to channel government finance to key areas such as munitions and railways. Alongside encouragement of existing munitions production by the usual small coterie of trusted firms around St Petersburg, the government also increased state production of munitions. In all, the Special Council, which was divided into four bodies after August 1915, dealing with defence, fuel, transport and food, spent some 15 million roubles between 1914 and 1917, representing about one-third of all government expenditure.

The prices charged by private enterprise, however, increased significantly and there was both inefficiency and corruption. Attempts were made to prevent prices being pushed up, not only by the cartels traditionally represented within Russian industry – Prodameta for metals, Prodvagon for railway manufacturers and Produgol for coal – but also by competition between government departments. One later Soviet calculation was that, by 1916, profits among 21 larger enterprises had increased by 431 per cent over those of 1913.

In the process, the labour force in heavy industry quadrupled between 1914 and 1916. In state factories alone the workforce expanded from 120,000 in 1914 to 400,000 by 1917. The number of miners doubled, the numbers in the building trade increased by one-third, and those employed in the oil industry increased to 0.5 million. Indeed, the total urban population increased from 22 million in 1914 to 28 million by 1916. Industrial output as a whole was up by 17 per cent by 1916, doubling in the chemical industry, increasing by 30 per cent in the coal industry and almost fivefold in engineering. Overall, Russia's economy grew by 21.6 per cent between 1913 and 1916. It could be argued, therefore, that the increasing economic crisis was born of over-rapid growth.[24]

The problem was that industrial expansion had again been based on a few areas such as St Petersburg and Moscow, which were precisely those most affected by the food shortages. Between 1914 and 1917, the St Petersburg labour force increased from 242,000 to 391,000 and in Moscow from 153,000 to 205,000. With municipal authorities forced to compete for food supplies on the open market, prices rose. Inflation was also encouraged by the amount of money the government had to raise in loans since it was reluctant to incur unpopularity by increasing taxes.

The money in circulation rose from 2.3 billion roubles in July 1914 to 7.9 billion by October 1917, or by 1,102 per cent. The government had also chosen to enact prohibition, so losing one-third of its revenue on top of the loss of customs duties from the end of the export trade through the Baltic and the Dardanelles. Moreover, the amount of gold backing the currency progressively declined, so decreasing the value of the currency abroad. Even when greater direct taxation and an excess profits tax were introduced in 1916, the proceeds were so small that they did not cover a weekend's expenditure on the war. The government's six war loans, followed by a seventh attempted by the provisional government, also failed to generate sufficient revenue to cover the cost of war, which stood at US$11.7 million by August 1917.

There was little check on inflation. A price index for St Petersburg set at 100 in December 1914 would have reached 192 by December 1916 while a similar index of 100 set in Moscow in December 1913 would have reached 361 by January 1917. Prices rose even more rapidly between March and November 1917. In effect, while wages had increased by between 50 per cent and 200 per cent depending upon the industry, all prices had increased by at least 100 per cent and, in some cases, by 500 per cent. Only the wages of metal- and chemical workers appear to have kept pace with inflation.

Not unexpectedly, strikes increased steadily, from 1,946 in 1915 to 2,306 in 1916, with 751 in the first two months of 1917. Initially, as elsewhere, strikes were motivated primarily by economic conditions, as in the case of the first significant wave of industrial action between April and August 1915. Moscow was as prominent as Petrograd in the wartime strikes, but it was in Petrograd that strikes became increasingly politicised. The same sense of 'moral economy', demanding equality of sacrifice, emerged as elsewhere in wartime Europe. Nonetheless, it was only in the first two months of 1917 that political strikes predominated.[25]

The government itself did not cope well with the war's demands. There had been a spirit of patriotic union in the Duma in August 1914 similar to the *Burgfrieden* or *Union Sacrée*, war credits being voted with no conditions attached. Indeed, only 21 deputies in the Duma voted against the war: 5 Bolsheviks, 6 Mensheviks and 10 Trudoviks (Labour Party). The political truce ended, however, with the military failures in 1915 and the continued resistance of the government to reform. Prorogued in January 1915, the Duma was recalled in July, with a new political alliance emerging within it in August.

This alliance was the so-called Progressive Bloc, orchestrated by Paul Miliukov of the Kadets (Constitutional Democrats), a radical party representative of small businesses. The alliance included 235 out of the 422 members of the Duma and comprised six groups. Apart from the Kadets, it also embraced the Octobrists (Conservative-Liberals), led by A. I. Guchkov, a wool manufacturer, and largely representing the larger industrial concerns; and the Progressists, founded in 1912 by Moscow-based textile manufacturers to seek a wider political role for industry as a whole.

Within a few weeks, however, the Duma was prorogued ostensibly for six months as the Tsar left for the front, taking up quarters with Stavka in Mogilev to the south-west of Moscow until December 1916. In some respects, the Tsar's decision was sensible. It removed the tension that had arisen in civil–military relations, but it consigned government in St Petersburg to the autocratically minded Empress Alexandra, who was increasingly influenced by Grigorii Rasputin.

In all, there were four presidents of the Council (prime ministers), three War Ministers, three Foreign Ministers and six Ministers of the Interior between the Tsar's departure for the front and March 1917. The Bloc maintained a presence as a kind of rump parliament after the suspension of the Duma, but the Tsar declined to offer even the moderate concessions sought by Miliukov.[26]

In some respects, much day-to-day administration increasingly fell into the hands of so-called voluntary or public organisations such as the All Russian Union of Zemstvos (rural councils), headed by a liberal monarchist, Prince George L'vov, and the Union of Municipalities. Both emerged in August 1914, initially to organise relief of the sick and wounded. In June 1915, however, the two organisations, both of which were largely controlled from Moscow, created Zemgor as an agency to intervene in war supply, particularly in clothing. By 1916, L'vov controlled a budget of 2 billion roubles and a large workforce including labour brigades behind the front.

The emergence of Zemgor was followed by the creation in June 1915, in a further extension of the self-mobilisation process of business and industry, of the Tsentral'nyi Voenno-Promyshlennyi Komitet (TsVPK; Central War Industries Committee), under Guchkov, and other similar local Voenno-Promyshlennya Komitety (VPKs; War Industries Committees). The creation of the Moscow-dominated Association of Industry and Trade, the TsVPK and the regional VPKs, 78 of which were in existence by the end of July, drew a significant response from what might be termed the industrial bourgeoisie.

The significance of these public organisations and of the Progressive Bloc, which was closely linked to them, was the middle-class assertion of their role in the state. Indeed, the emerging wartime alliance of industry, Duma and Stavka posed an alternative to the Tsar in a state in which the aristocracy could not, since it was created and not hereditary. Indeed, the government preferred self-mobilisation by private initiative to risking an incorporation or legitimisation of the middle classes within government that might threaten its very existence. Consequently, the government was intensely suspicious of the VPKs and of Guchkov's attack on state bureaucracy and the Moscow-based challenge to the industrial monopoly of the metal industries centred on St Petersburg.[27]

Unfortunately, the duplication of effort between state and public organisations undermined the ability of both to maximise war production. Thus, while the VPKs had secured some 400 million roubles' worth of orders by March 1917, this represented only a small percentage (7.6 per cent by 1916) of the total orders placed with industry. As government suspicions of the VPKs grew, moreover, orders were further reduced, compelling the VPKs to turn to considerations of a possible post-war role in reconstruction.[28]

Under the direction of Guchkov and his deputy, A. I. Konovalov, leader of the Progressists, the VPKs became increasingly politicised as Miliukov lapsed into passivity in the expectation that only the recall of the Duma could solve Russia's problems. Thus, Guchkov famously addressed criticisms of the government to the army Chief of Staff, Alekseev, in August 1916 and subsequently attempted to draw other officers into some kind of action to force the Tsar to abdicate. In many respects, however, the most politically damaging aspect of the VPKs was their championing of labour representation within industry from July 1915 onwards. It proved so because the 58 resulting *rabochie gruppy* (workers' groups) failed to achieve any worthwhile gains for labour. This so radicalised the central workers' group in St Petersburg that, under Menshevik influence in November 1916, it demanded the immediate establishment of a provisional revolutionary government.

Both the Petrograd and Moscow central groups then called for a strike in January 1917 in commemoration of the 'Bloody Sunday' of the 1905 revolution. Most of the leadership was arrested in February 1917, but the so-called assistance groups established by the workers' groups in many factories appear to have continued to play a significant role in the increasing strike action and general unrest in Petrograd through February and March 1917.[29]

There was some attempt to stimulate patriotism in Russia, but, as already indicated, there was considerable official ambivalence towards the mobilisation of opinion. As elsewhere, popular graphic art forms such as cartoons and postcards and popular culture such as *estrade* (variety shows) were utilised, the Russian popular broadside or *lubok* equating in many ways to the French *images d'Epinal*. The same kinds of anti-German themes were apparent as in Britain and France. There was also the same kinds of anti-German riots, prohibition of German music, promotion of Slavic rather than German names, and stoning of dachshunds.

Cinema was the largest entertainment medium, with over 4,000 cinemas by 1916, but few specifically war-related films were produced and, in terms of reportage, there were only five film cameramen on the entire Eastern Front. Consequently, Russian cinema proved of little value in propaganda terms though the stop-motion film, *Lily of Belgium*, was a powerful contribution to Entente solidarity. As suggested by Russian cinematic fare, there was much emphasis on pure entertainment, with tango, gypsy music and imported American ragtime most popular in terms of sheet music sales, gramophone sales, restaurants and cabarets.

At the same time, the *filery* (detectives) and *sekretnye sotrudniki* (secret agents) of the Ministry of Internal Affairs' political police endeavoured to ensure no repetition of the 1905 revolution. In the event, however, the constant change of ministers and of the officials appointed by ministerial patronage under-mined the relationship between ministers and police, while manpower short-ages led to decreasing availability of quality political intelligence.

Some crime fell during the war, largely through the control of vodka and other liquors, but there were increases in prostitution among younger women and notable increases in juvenile crime, which had risen by 8.6 per cent by 1916. Among the offenders were the so-called *bezprizornye* (fatherless children) swelled by the 4 million refugees inside Russia. There was also the same criticism of excessive displays of consumption, of financial speculation and of draft dodging as experienced elsewhere.[30]

The increasing difficulties for the government were compounded by the slow disintegration of the army. While shortage of materiel has been advanced as the primary reason for Russian military disasters in the Great War, these have been exaggerated in the sense that the German and Austro-Hungarian forces on the Eastern Front were also frequently short of sup-plies. The Russian army also performed better than is sometimes suggested, capturing more German and Austro-Hungarian prisoners of war than the British and French combined and also accounting for a higher percentage of German combat deaths than the western Allies. Indeed, it won signific-ant victories against the Austro-Hungarian army in Galicia in 1915 and at least initially during the Brusilov offensive in June 1916.

It has been argued that the 'old army' was destroyed in 1915, that structural problems dramatically increased in 1916, and that only harsh discipline kept the army together. Certainly, problems increased and frater-nisation with German and Austro-Hungarian troops was perceived as grow-ing evidence of war-weariness. Most Russian soldiers were peasants, and they were affected by separation from home and land, and unsettled by events on the home front. They also appear to have had little interest in Russia's wider war aims although they would have fought willingly in defence of Russia itself. But, in many respects, the replication of peasant society in the army's ranks and the bonding of military service helped to preserve the army as a military instrument at least until early 1917, when the abdication of the Tsar removed the vital traditional cement underpinning discipline.[31]

The Russians did have a major military mobility problem, however, and, as previously indicated, one of manpower, with almost 6 million casualties by January 1917. Losses badly affected the officer corps. Many new officers, recruited from the middle classes and from students, were, to quote Allan Wildman, 'negatively disposed' towards the government through their previous involvement in politics or their awareness of progressive ideals. At the same time, the gulf between officers and men steadily widened as soldiers increasingly questioned poor treatment of wounded, censorship of mail and dwindling rations, a factor made more significant by the relatively generous provision of rations in 1914. Trained NCOs were also a decreasing asset.

By the autumn of 1916, therefore, there were a number of mutinies, the best documented of which, in the 223rd Odoevskii Regiment on the South-western Front, was caused primarily by battle fatigue and war-weariness rather than revolutionary agitation. Thus, while the mutinies illustrated the undermining of discipline at the front, politicisation of the army was mainly a feature of the rear, of garrisons and transport centres. As with the industrial workforce, most recruits tended to be trained in large centres such as Moscow, St Petersburg and Kiev, where they suffered the same privations as the civilian population and with few officers to control them.[32]

Sailors of the Baltic Fleet were to prove more radical than the army. The majority of the Russian seamen were of non-peasant background and literate. More significantly, owing to a combination of ice-bound ports and German naval domination of the Baltic, they spent long periods in bases such as Helsingfors in Finland, Revel in Estonia and Kronstadt close to St Petersburg, where they were frequently in contact with shipyard and other industrial workers. Moreover, many naval officers were of Baltic-German or Finnish origin and were thus distanced from their men by both class and nationality.

Discipline amid the enforced idleness of naval life was often harsh. In the case of the cruiser *Aurora*, for example, which was sent to undergo repair in St Petersburg in September 1916, a new commanding officer had attempted to tighten discipline at a time when the crew was working alongside workers in a Socialist Revolutionary stronghold. When the disturbances broke out in St Petersburg in March 1917, the crew was confined to the ship and some workers were detained in the ship's brig. The crew mutinied on 13 March, murdering the captain and his executive officer. There is little evidence that the majority of sailors belonged to any political organisation and revolt was almost certainly spontaneous. It spread to Kronstadt on the same day, to Revel on 15 March and to Helsingfors on 16 March. At least 76 naval officers were killed and over 300 arrested in the course of a few days.[33]

In St Petersburg itself, the chain of events leading to revolution had been set off on 8 March 1917 by a riot of women textile workers from the Vyborg district queuing for flour. Women comprised some 43.2 per cent of the Russian industrial labour force by 1917 and, as elsewhere, they experienced at first hand the problems of keeping their families fed. One calculation is that, by 1917, the average working woman in St Petersburg spent 40 hours a week in queues for food or other requirements. The women were quickly joined by militant metalworkers.

There were at least 180,000 troops available in the capital. The majority of these, however, were under training or recovering from wounds, with only perhaps 12,000 regarded as reliable. Troops were on the streets for three days without being called on to fire and were generally mingling with crowds. Therefore, when, on 11 March (26 February), the Tsar ordered the army to suppress the disturbances and to open fire, troops began to mutiny. Attempting to return to his capital from Stavka, to which he had returned only on 7 March, the Tsar's train was halted on 14 March.

The Tsar's brother, Grand Duke Michael, took the decision to abandon the Winter Palace on the night of 11/12 March at a time when the crowds had dispersed. Reinforcements, however, could not be sent owing to rail strikes. It was Alekseev who now took the initiative with his fellow generals in co-operation with the Duma, which the Tsar had once more dissolved in February but which had remained in unofficial session. Indeed, the liberal opposition had been assiduously cultivating the army since 1915, as suggested by Guchkov's contacts with Alekseev and others. A provisional government under Prince L'vov was nominated by the Duma's leaders acting as a provisional committee on 14 March. It forced the Tsar to abdicate on behalf of himself and his son in favour of Grand Duke Michael on 15 March (2 March). Michael then also renounced the throne on the following day. Alekseev became Commander-in-Chief, Guchkov War Minister, and Miliukov Foreign Minister. Alexander Kerensky, a lawyer and Trudovik deputy who now proclaimed himself a Socialist Revolutionary, also joined as Justice Minister, having been elected president of the self-styled 'soviet' within the Duma.[34]

At this point the army was still very much in existence with 6.5 million men under arms. The basic aspirations of workers and peasants alike as expressed in resolutions of various workers' and villagers' committees or soviets which began to spring up in March 1917 were largely economic rather than political: the two main demands were an eight hour day for workers and land redistribution for peasants. In many cases, the soviets, of which there were at least 77 by the end of March, acted to enforce their demands but there was no particular urge for an end to the war at this stage. Indeed, nationalist aspirations appeared to be a more serious threat to the state, particularly those emanating from the Baltic States and the Ukraine. In response, the provisional government recognised the principle of Polish independence and granted autonomy to Finland. Other reforms were also effected including freedom of the press and of association, the disestablishment of the Orthodox Church, the independence of the judiciary and the replacement of police with a militia.

The new government erred, however, in not pushing land redistribution, preferring to await the convening of a promised constituent assembly to authorise the erosion of property rights. The assembly was then delayed by the belief on the part of the Kadets that elections might result in a more radical assembly than was desirable. Similarly, influenced by the opposition of industrialists to price controls and increased taxes, the provisional government mismanaged the economy. It doubled the price of grain in September 1917, having failed to organise an efficient rationing system in May.

Adding to the difficulties of the provisional government, a division of authority soon emerged between, on the one hand, the government, which was backed by the generals, the bureaucrats, industrialists and the Duma, and on the other the soviets. In essence it was a contest between liberalism and socialism institutionalised by the duality in St Petersburg of the provisional government and the Menshevik-dominated Petrograd Soviet of Workers' and Soldiers' Deputies. A self-appointed creation of socialist intellectuals, the Petrograd Soviet was established on 10 March and soon became dominated by a Georgian Menshevik, Irakli Tsereteli. The Petrograd Soviet's power was a negative one, with the ability to veto and to paralyse the actions of the provisional government. This was quickly apparent in the Soviet's Army Order No. 1 issued from the Izvestiia printing works on 14 March. This authorised units of the Petrograd garrison to elect committees and representatives responsible to the Petrograd Soviet rather than to the Duma, and to enjoy civil rights such as not being maltreated by officers.

While intended to apply only to St Petersburg, the provisions of Army Order No. 1 rapidly spread to other fronts at a moment when abolition of the death penalty on 25 March further undermined discipline. Orders Nos 114 and 115, issued for the provisional government on 20 March, further muddied the waters. Troops began to sport red ribbons, and refused to salute or use military titles, although the new soldiers' committees and the various army and front congresses emerging from them generally favoured continuing the war. Commissars appointed by the Petrograd Soviet on 1 April, and subsequently subordinated to the provisional government, also assisted commanders in acting as intermediaries with their men amid deteriorating discipline. Desertion in the 31 months prior to the March revolution had run at a rate of 6,300 a month, but in the 5 months after March 1917 it ran at 34,000 a month.[35]

Seeking to reassure the Entente, Miliukov issued a new declaration of war aims on 9 April 1917. While rejecting territorial expansion and seeking a stable peace on the basis of self-determination, the government would continue to defend Russia and to meet its obligations to its allies. On making the declaration public on 1 May, however, Miliukov attached a note suggesting the general support of the Russian people for a decisive victory. As a result, there were widespread demonstrations and Miliukov and Guchkov were compelled to resign on 18 May. The government was restructured to include other socialists besides Kerensky, who now became War Minister.

Kerensky wanted to continue the war in the cause of what he called 'revolutionary defensism', preliminary talks with the Germans in March and April having suggested that the price being demanded for peace, namely the loss of Poland and the Baltic states, was too high. Kerensky appears to have succeeded in galvanising the soldiers' committees in support of the war but not the ordinary rank and file, who appear to have been disillusioned by the willingness of members of the Petrograd Soviet to join the government. Meanwhile, the Bolsheviks were working to regain the ground they had lost within the army, while both they and the Germans were encouraging fraternisation.

Like its army commanders, the government saw an offensive as a way of restoring internal discipline and preventing the army's disintegration, especially if units from the troublesome St Petersburg garrison could be sent to the front. Indeed, soldiers from the garrison joined workers in demonstrating against the offensive when it began on 1 July 1917 after a two-day preliminary bombardment. Directed by Brusilov, who had replaced Alekseev as Commander-in-Chief in June after Alekseev's opposition to further democratising the army, the offensive soon ground to a halt despite the use of specially trained shock battalions and companies. By the time the Germans counter-attacked, the Russians had already lost over 58,000 casualties on the South-western Front alone. As the offensive faltered, the Kadets withdrew from the coalition government over the issue of autonomy for the Ukraine and concessions being made on redistribution of land to peasants. L'vov also resigned, being replaced by Kerensky. Brusilov was removed by Kerensky and replaced by Lavr Kornilov.[36]

Under pressure from Kornilov, Kerensky agreed to reintroduce the death penalty on 25 July with military-revolutionary courts to restore discipline. In practice, however, little action was taken, the relative stability achieved being due more to the end of offensive operations.

In September, Kerensky agreed to the III Cavalry Corps's being sent to St Petersburg under A. M. Krymov to help suppress a rumoured Bolshevik rising. Krymov had been plotting the downfall of the government for some time and had offered his services to Kornilov. Kornilov seems to have understood that Kerensky would support a package of military reforms and a reconstruction of the government. It should be emphasised that Kornilov did not intend to restore the monarchy and believed he could save the government from the influence of the Petrograd Soviet. Kerensky, however, had become convinced that Kornilov was a threat to his own position and engineered the alleged plot in order to remove the general and enhance his own authority.

Accordingly, Kerensky accused Kornilov of an attempted coup and had him arrested on 14 September 1917. Krymov, whose cavalry was intercepted by pro-Soviet agitators en route to St Petersburg, committed suicide. It soon became apparent that hard-core support for Kornilov among officers was limited. Recalling Alekseev as Chief of Staff, Kerensky assumed the Supreme Command himself. With Kornilov's removal and the subsequent resignation of Alekseev, when Kerensky would not pursue the wider military reforms intended by Kornilov, desertion increased yet further. Conceivably, 900,000 men deserted between 1 January and 1 September 1917 in a constant process of self-demobilisation.

The provisional government's attempt to continue the war also resulted in increased Bolshevik influence within the Baltic Fleet. By greater effort than that of their rivals, the Bolsheviks won control of the key committees of the soviets, enabling them to carry resolutions according their own agenda. Their influence over the fleet was then consolidated through daily newspapers produced for the fleet by their activists.[37]

The Bolsheviks had been the only group advocating peace at any cost, one reason why the German General Staff had facilitated Lenin's return to Russia from Switzerland in April 1917 together with 31 other Bolsheviks. Most of the Bolshevik leadership had been in exile and the overthrow of the Tsar clearly took the party by surprise. Indeed, none of the revolutionary parties had played any significant role in the politicisation of the working class although the Socialist Revolutionaries were more active than is generally supposed.

Even Soviet historians later accepted that the Bolsheviks had secured control of only 27 out of 242 workers' soviets formed by the end of March 1917 and commanded the allegiance of only 40 of the 600 deputies on the Petrograd Soviet. As late as November, the party won only 25 per cent of the seats in the constituent assembly. By preaching 'all power to the soviets', however, the Bolsheviks were able to capitalise on the growing frustration with the provisional government for its inability to alleviate shortages and inflation, and also with the failure of the Mensheviks and Socialist Revolutionaries to capture the mood of the people.

Between March and November 1917, moreover, peasants had increasingly acted in their own interest, beginning to take over land and livestock from landowners. In urban areas, increasing inflation had forged a greater unity of interest between the more radical, skilled workers, who had taken the lead in forming soviets and factory militias, and newer migrants to industry such as women and youths. The resulting rise in militancy involved perhaps 2.4 million workers at one time or another between March and November. Wages and working hours, however, still featured more prominently than political demands.

More leftward-leaning Socialist Revolutionaries were the initial beneficiaries of the movement of peasants and workers to the political left and the demand for a government formed by the soviets. Subsequently, however, Bolshevik membership steadily increased from about 20,000 in April 1917 to 350,000 by November. The Bolshevik control of soviets had also increased in both St Petersburg and Moscow by August and September, as the Bolsheviks were transformed into a mass political movement somewhat removed from the original conception of an elitist intelligentsia. As Edward Acton has remarked, the Bolsheviks had successfully articulated the goals of the ordinary Russian but 'did not create either those goals or the mass radicalism that went with them'.[38]

By November 1917, the army was thoroughly demoralised and disorganised. Thus, although some 10,000 officers and officer cadets were available around St Petersburg on 6/7 November 1917 (24/25 October) few attempted to do anything to save Kerensky against the coup he feared likely to be mounted by the Bolsheviks. In fact, the Bolshevik Party's Central Committee had rejected an insurrection, compelling Lenin to appeal to party members to act to forestall anyone else attempting one. Indeed, the Petrograd Soviet's Military Revolutionary Committee (MRC), on which the Bolsheviks had a majority, launched the coup without formal party sanction.

Kerensky left St Petersburg to mobilise loyal troops and the Bolsheviks seized power virtually bloodlessly. Sailors from Kronstadt and the *Aurora*, now fully repaired, again played a key role, the cruiser lobbing a single blank salvo at the Winter Palace. The latter was abandoned by its defenders – mostly cadets and women of the Battalion of Death – with little loss of life. The other key element was the Red Guards, the predominantly young, single and skilled members of the workers' militias, which had emerged in Petrograd and other areas in February.

Following the repulse of a poorly organised counter-attack by Kerensky's forces on St Petersburg, Lenin called for an armistice on all fronts on 19 November. Subsequently, a Bolshevik delegation met the Germans at Brest Litovsk to begin negotiations on 2 December 1917. Lenin was quite ready to abandon one-third of the population of the Tsarist empire to obtain a peace which would enable him to consolidate control inside Russia. With the Germans continuing to advance, Lenin persuaded his colleagues to accept the terms on offer and the Treaty of Brest Litovsk was signed on 3 March 1918.[39]

Many of the subject nationalities were already fighting to rid themselves of Russian control by the time the Soviet Union was proclaimed on 31 January 1918. In the Ukraine, no less than 93 groups emerged to resist the Bolsheviks.

Estonia declared its independence in November 1918, to be followed by Latvia, Lithuania and Finland in December. The Bolsheviks also found themselves opposed by the first White Russian (Belorussian) force in the Don Cossack region, and the first Entente forces were committed to intervention against them in January 1918 with the arrival of 'Dunsterforce' in the Trans-caspian region. The agreement reached between Masaryk and the Bolsheviks to allow the Czech Legion to embark for Europe from Vladivostock also broke down. Ultimately, the Russian Civil War continued until 1921.[40] Estimates of the deaths in Russia between 1917 and 1921 as a result of the civil war and concomitant disease and starvation range between 2.8 million and 6 million, while the death deficit is put between 20 and 28 million.[41]

Brest Litovsk deprived the Bolsheviks of any immediate opportunity to spread revolution by war. Events in Russia between March and November, however, had an immediate political impact on all other belligerents in arousing fears that disaffection would spread. In both France and Macedonia, Russian troops proved troublesome. A disinclination to serve in the intervention forces in north Russia was a factor, albeit a minor one, in the British army's demobilisation disturbances in January 1919.[42] Socialists generally took heart from the events in St Petersburg and, as already indicated, the governments of the other belligerents invariably felt it necessary to renew their efforts to mobilise public opinion behind continuing the war. As suggested at the beginning of this chapter, it was the breakdown of the function and authority of the state which was most likely to create revolutionary conditions. In the light of the revolution in Russia, therefore, defeat in a war which had demanded so much sacrifice was increasingly to have catastrophic consequences.

Notes and references

1. Winter, *Experience of World War I*, pp.194–5; Horne, 'Remobilising for Total War', pp.195–211; Kocka, *Facing Total War*, pp.40–67.

2. Harvey, *Collision of Empires*, p.441.

3. Gordon Craig, 'The Political Leader as Strategist', in Paret, ed., *Makers of Modern Strategy*, pp.482–91; French, 'One-man Show', pp.77, 86–7; Hazlehurst, *Politicians at War*, pp.20, 103, 114–18, 128; Turner, *British Politics*, pp.1, 13–18, 61; Martin Pugh, 'Asquith, Bonar Law and the First Coalition' *HJ* 17 (1974), pp.813–36; George H. Cassar, *Asquith as War Leader* (London, 1994); David Sweet, 'The Domestic Scene: Parliament and People', in Liddle, ed., *Home Fires and Foreign Fields*, pp.9–19; A. J. P. Taylor, *Politics in Wartime* (London, 1964), pp.11–44.

4. Hazlehurst, *Politicians at War*, pp.232–69, 279–82; John Turner, 'British Politics and the Great War', in Turner, *Britain and First World War*, pp.117–38; idem, *British Politics*, p.51; David French, 'The Military Background to the Shell Crisis of May 1915', *JSS* 2 (1979), pp.192–205; Trevor Wilson, *The Downfall of the Liberal Party* (London, 1966), pp.53–5; R. P. Murphy, 'Walter Long, the Unionist Ministers and the Formation of Lloyd George's Coalition in December 1916', *HJ* 29 (1986), pp.735–45; Michael Fry, 'Political Change in Britain, August 1914 to December 1916: Lloyd George replaces Asquith', *HJ* 31 (1988), pp.609–27; Stephen Koss, 'The Destruction of Britain's Last Liberal Government', *JMH* 40 (1968), pp.257–77; Barry McGill, 'Asquith's Predicament, 1914–18', *JMH* 39 (1967), pp.283–303; Peter Fraser, 'British War Policy and the Crisis of Liberalism in May 1915', *JMH* 54 (1982), pp.1–26; idem, 'The British Shells Scandal of 1915', *CJH* 18 (1983), pp.69–86.

5. Turner, *British Politics*, pp.55–78, 86–103,109–11, 117–51; idem, 'The House of Commons and the Executive in the First World War', *Parliamentary History* 10 (1991), pp.297–316; Adams and Poirier, *Conscription Controversy*, pp.93–143; R. J. Q. Adams, 'Asquith's Choice: The May Coalition and the Coming of Conscription, 1915–16', *JBS* 25 (1986), pp.243–63; M. McEwen, 'The Struggle for Mastery in Britain: Lloyd George versus Asquith, December 1916', *JBS* 20 (1980), pp.131–56.

6. Turner, *British Politics*, pp.152–4, 165–70, 194–8, 204–9, 214–15, 239–42, 248–52, 294–305, 334–6, 387–9, 437–48; Chris Wrigley, '"In Excess of their Patriotism": The National Party and Threats of Subversion', in Chris Wrigley, ed., *War, Diplomacy and Politics: Essays in Honour of A. J. P. Taylor* (London, 1986), pp.93–119.

7. Godfrey, *Capitalism at War*, pp.52–62; Harvey, *Collision of Empires*, pp.452, 473–4; Robbins, *First World War*, pp.140–2.

8. Kitchen, *Silent Dictatorship*, pp.271–8; Kocka, *Facing Total War*, pp.128–33, 147–54; Bessel, 'Mobilisation and Demobilisation', pp.212–22; Herwig, *First World War*, pp.374–7; Chickering, *Imperial Germany*, pp.61–4, 80, 162–7.

9. Stone, *Eastern Front*, p.124; Gabor Vermes, 'Leap into the Dark: The Issue of Suffrage in Hungary during World War I', in Kann and Kiràly, eds, *Habsburg Empire*, pp.29–44; Tibor Zsuppán, 'The Hungarian Political Scene, 1908–18', in Cornwall, ed., *Last Years of Austria-Hungary*, pp.63–76; Lothar Höbelt, 'Parties and Parliament: Austrian Pre-war Domestic Politics', ibid., pp.41–61; Pastor, 'Home Front in Hungary', pp.131–4; Galántai, *Hungary*, pp.240–6.

10. Rauchensteiner, *Tod des Doppeladlers*, pp.371–90; Mamatey, 'Union of Czech Political Parties', pp.3–28; Cornwall, 'Experience of Yugoslav Agitation', pp.656–76; Zeman, *Break-up*, pp.129–30, 163–76.

11. Georges Haupt, *Socialism and the Great War: The Collapse of the Second International* (Oxford, 1972), pp.217–49; Becker, *Great War and French People*, pp.77–93, 170–2, 174–5; Susan Milner, 'August 1914: Nationalism, Internationalism and

the French Working Class', in Scriven and Wagstaff, eds, *War and Society in Twentieth Century France*, pp.15–33; Ferro, 'Cultural Life in France', pp.301–2; F. L. Carsten, *War against War: British and German Radical Movements in the First World War* (London, 1982), pp.11–34, 77–91; Tony Jowitt and Keith Laybourn, 'The Bradford Independent Labour Party and the First World War', in Keith Dockray and Keith Laybourn, eds, *The Representation and Reality of War: The British Experience* (Stroud, 1999), pp.152–69; idem, 'War and Socialism: The Experience of the Bradford Independent Labour Party, 1914–18', *Journal of Regional and Local Studies* 4 (1984), pp.57–72; I. G. C. Hutchison, 'The Impact of the First World War on Scottish Politics', in Macdonald and McFarland, eds, *Scotland and Great War*, pp.36–58; William Kenefick, 'War Resisters and Anti-conscription in Scotland: An ILP Perspective', ibid., pp.59–80.

12.   Geoff Eley, 'The SPD in War and Peace', in Fletcher, *Bernstein to Brandt*, pp.65–73; Kolko, *Century of War*, pp.118–19; A. J. Ryder, *The German Revolution of 1918: A Study of German Socialism in War and Revolt* (Cambridge, 1967), pp.1–139, 193–9; David Morgan, *The Socialist Left and the German Revolution: A History of the German Independent Social Democratic Party, 1917–22* (Ithaca, NY, 1975), pp.53–79; Walter Mühlhausen, 'Die Sozialdemokratie am Scheideweg: Burgfrieden, Parteikrise und Spaltung in Ersten Weltkrieg', in Michalka, ed., *Erste Weltkrieg*, pp.649–71; Elzbieta Ettinger, *Rosa Luxemburg: A Life* (London, 1987), pp.185–228; Mary Nolan, *Social Democracy and Society: Working Class Radicalism in Düsseldorf, 1890–1920* (Cambridge, 1981), pp.251–68; David Kirby, *War, Peace and Revolution: International Socialism at the Cross-roads* (New York, 1986), pp.42–8; Jelavich, 'German Culture', pp.46–7; Beller, 'Tragic Carnival', pp.148–54.

13.   Daniel, *War From Within*, pp.250–2; Englander, 'Military Intelligence and Defence of Realm', pp.24–32; Brock Millman, 'British Home Defence Planning and Civil Dissent, 1917–18', *WH* 5 (1998), pp.204–32; Keith Jeffery and Peter Hennessy, *States of Emergency* (London, 1983), pp.5–9; Wrigley, 'State and Challenge of Labour', pp.262–88.

14.   Schaffer, *America in Great War*, pp.13–15, 127–48; Kennedy, *Over Here*, pp.73–4, 85–6; Gruber, *Mars and Minerva*, pp.174–206; Wallace, *War and Image of Germany*, pp.125–40, 150–6, 159–60; Becker, *Great War and French People*, pp.152–4.

15.   Keith Robbins, *The Abolition of War: The Peace Movement in Britain, 1914–19* (Cardiff, 1976), pp.27–47, 61–9, 77–92, 120–1, 149–56; idem, 'British Experience of Conscientious Objection', pp.691–706; Gilbert, *First World War*, p.253; Marvin Schwartz, *The Union of Democratic Control in British Politics during the First World War* (Oxford, 1971), pp.11–84; C. Howard, 'MacDonald, Henderson and the Outbreak of War, 1914', *HJ* 20 (1977), pp.871–91; Jay Winter, 'Arthur Henderson, the Russian Revolution and the Reconstitution of the Labour Party', ibid., 15 (1972), pp.753–73; Cyril Pearce, 'A Community of Resistance: The Anti-war Movement in Huddersfield, 1914–18', in Dockray

and Laybourn, eds, *Representation and Reality*, pp.170–89; Wallace, *War and Image of Germany*, pp.90–9, 112–24; Horne, *Labour at War*, pp.302–49; idem, 'Remobilising for Total War', p.197; Carsten, *War against War*, pp.64–73; Martin Ceadel, *Pacifism in Britain, 1914–45: The Defining of a Faith* (Oxford, 1980), pp.31–56; Rae, *Conscience and Politics*, pp.68–133, 201–33; Kennedy, *Hound of Conscience*, pp.40–53, 124–32, 155–96, 240–51; Englander, 'Police and Public Order', pp.90–138.

16. G. Hayes McCoy, 'A Military History of the Easter Rising', in K. B. Nowlan, ed., *The Making of 1916* (Dublin, 1969), pp.255–304; Charles Townshend, 'The Suppression of the Easter Rising', *Bullán: An Irish Studies Journal* 1 (1994), pp.27–39; George Boyce, 'Ireland and the First World War', *History Ireland* 2 (1994), pp.48–53; Fitzpatrick, *Politics and Irish Life*, pp.90–7; Thomas Hennessey, *Dividing Ireland: World War I and Partition* (London, 1998), pp.125–78, 202–20, 228–33; J. B. O'Brien, *Dear Dirty Dublin: A City in Distress, 1899–1916* (Berkeley, CA, 1983), pp.258–74; M. Tierney, *Eoin MacNeill: Scholar and Man of Action, 1867–1945* (Oxford, 1980), pp.181–227; Brian P. Murphy, *Patrick Pearse and the Lost Republican Ideal* (Dublin, 1991), pp.41–63; W. K. Anderson, *James Connolly and the Irish Left* (Dublin, 1994), pp.72–5; Roger Sawyer, *Casement: The Flawed Hero* (London, 1984), pp.109–20; Jane Leonard, 'The Reaction of Irish Officers in the British Army to the Easter Rising of 1916', in Cecil and Liddle, eds, *Facing Armageddon*, pp.256–68; A. J. Ward, *Ireland and Anglo-American Relations, 1899–1921* (London, 1969), pp.101–25.

17. Flood, *France, 1914–18*, pp.107–17, 147–65; Becker, *French People and Great War*, pp.77–93, 195–204, 217–35, 239–45, 298–301; idem, 'That's the Death-knell of Our Boys', in Fridenson, ed., *French Home Front*, pp.17–36; idem, 'Opposition to the War in France: The Case of Clovis Andrieu', in Cecil and Liddle, eds, *Facing Armageddon*, pp.677–90; Horne, *Labour at War*, pp.122–70; Pierre Bouyoux, 'La Population de Toulouse et le Sentiment National pendant la Première Guerre Mondiale', in Becker and Audoin-Rouzeau, eds, *Les sociétés européennes*, pp.245–55; Pierre Renouvin, 'L'Opinion publique et la guerre en 1917', *Revue d'Histoire Moderne et Contemporaine* 15 (1968), pp.4–23; Catherine Slater, *Defeatists and their Enemies: Political Invective in France, 1914–18* (Oxford, 1981), pp.65–87.

18. Eley, 'SPD in War and Peace', pp.65–73; Carsten, *War against War*, pp.11–34, 77–91, 124–42; Chickering, *Imperial Germany*, pp.152–3; James Shand, ' "Doves among the Eagles": German Pacifists and their Government during World War I', *JCH* 10 (1975), pp.95–108.

19. Plaschka, 'Army and Internal Conflict', pp.338–53; Herwig, *First World War*, pp.361–8.

20. Harvey, *Collision of Empires*, p.435; H. Meynell, 'The Stockholm Conference of 1917', *International Review of Social History* 5 (1960), pp.1–25, 203–25; Kirby, *War, Peace and Revolution*, pp.83–92, 104–14, 152–70, 188–203, 230–46; Galántai, *Hungary*, pp.167–70; Ryder, *German Revolution*, pp.59–63, 103–5;

Ferro, *Great War*, pp.163–9, 193–9; Horne, *Labour at War*, pp.48, 302–49; Carsten, *War against War*, pp.35–63.

21. J. A. S. Grenville, *A World History of the Twentieth Century, 1900–45*, 2 vols (London, 1980), I, pp.218–19.

22. H. Seton Watson, *The Decline of Imperial Russia, 1855–1914*, 2nd edn (London, 1964), pp.261–310, 360–6; Jacob Walkin, *The Rise of Democracy in Pre-revolutionary Russia* (London, 1963), pp.179, 232–3; L. H. Haimson, 'The Problem of Social Stability in Urban Russia, 1905–17', *Slavic Review* 23/24 (1964/65), pp.619–42, 1–22; E. D. Vinogradoff, 'The Russian Peasantry and the Elections to the Fourth State Duma', in L. H. Haimson, ed., *The Politics of Rural Russia, 1905–14* (Bloomington, IN, 1979), pp.219–49; J. H. Bater, 'St Petersburg and Moscow on the Eve of Revolution', in D. H. Kaiser, ed., *The Workers' Revolution in Russia, 1917: The View from Below* (Cambridge, 1987), pp.20–58; Edward Acton, *Rethinking the Russian Revolution* (London, 1990), pp.52–82; Wildman, *End of Russian Imperial Army*, pp.47–58.

23. Stone, *Eastern Front*, pp.205, 285, 292–300; Rogger, *Russia in Age of Modernisation*, p.259; M. Perrins, 'The Politics of Russian Grain Procurement during the First World War', *Slavonic and East European Review* 61 (183), pp.388–401; Richard Pipes, *The Russian Revolution, 1899–1919* (London 1990), pp.272–4.

24. Stone, *Eastern Front*, pp.144–64, 196–7, 204–11, 284–5; idem, 'Organising an Economy for War: The Russian Shell Shortage, 1914–17', in Best and Wheatcroft, eds, *War, Economy and Military Mind*, pp.108–19; Ferguson, *Pity of War*, p.250; Jones, 'Imperial Russia's Forces', pp.262–72.

25. R. B. McKean, *The Russian Constitutional Monarchy, 1907–17* (London, 1977), pp.23–4, 33–4, 38; idem, *Between The Revolutions: Russia 1905–1917* (London, 1998), pp.23–6; idem, *St Petersburg between the Revolutions: Workers and Revolutionaries, June 1907 to February 1917* (New Haven, CN, 1990), pp.318–49; Sergei Kudryashov, 'The Russian Worker at War', in Cecil and Liddle, eds, *Facing Armageddon*, pp.545–8; Pipes, *Russian Revolution*, pp.234–8; Peter Gatrell and Mark Harrison, 'The Russian and Soviet Economies in Two World Wars: A Comparative View', *EcHR* 46 (1993), pp.425–52; Peter Gatrell, 'The First World War and War Communism', in R. W. Davies, M. Harrison and S. G. Wheatcroft, eds, *The Economic Transformation of the Soviet Union, 1913–45* (Cambridge, 1994), pp.216–37; D. Koenker and W. G. Rosenberg, 'Strikers in Revolution: Russia, 1917', in Haimson and Tilly, eds, *Strikes, Wars and Revolutions*, pp.167–96; Stone, *Eastern Front*, pp.286–91; Marwick, *War and Social Change*, p.35; Jones, 'Imperial Russia's Forces', pp.260–1; Ferro, *Great War*, p.178.

26. D. R. Jones, 'Nicholas II and the Supreme Command: An Investigation of Motives', *Shornik* 11 (1985), pp.47–83; Pipes, *Russian Revolution*, pp.246–50, 252–66; Orlando Figes, *A People's Tragedy: The Russian Revolution, 1891–1924* (London, 1996), p.278; Rogger, *Russia in Age of Modernisation*, pp.255–6; McKean, *Russian Constitutional Monarchy*, pp.36–7; R. Pearson, *The Russian Moderates and the Crisis of Tsarism, 1914–17* (London, 1977), pp.28–64.

27. Harvey, *Collision of Empires*, pp.296, 441; Lewis H. Siegelbaum, *The Politics of Industrial Mobilisation in Russia, 1914–17: A Study of the War-Industries Committee* (London, 1984), pp.40–84, 209–12; idem, 'Moscow Industrialists and the War Industries Committee during World War I', *Russian History* 5 (1978), pp.64–83; Thomas Fallows, 'Politics and the War Effort in Russia: The Union of Zemstvos and the Organisation of the Food Supply', *Slavic Review* 37 (1978), pp.70–90; W. Gleason, 'The All-Russian Union of Zemstvos and World War I', in T. Emmons and W. S. Vucinich, eds, *The Zemstvo in Russia* (Cambridge, MA, 1983), pp.365–82; Stone, *Eastern Front*, pp.198–211; Figes, *People's Tragedy*, pp.49–51, 271–2.

28. Siegelbaum, *Politics of Industrial Mobilisation*, pp.85–122, 156–8, 186–91; Stone, *Eastern Front*, pp.201–11.

29. Siegelbaum, *Politics of Industrial Mobilisation*, pp.159–82, 191–207.

30. Hubertus Jahn, *Patriotic Culture in Russia during World War I* (New York, 1995), pp.11–170; Denise J. Younghusband, 'A War Forgotten: The Great War in Russian and Soviet Cinema', in Paris, ed., *First World War and Popular Cinema*, pp.172–91; Richard Stites, 'Days and Nights in Wartime Russia: Cultural Life, 1914–17', in Roshwald and Stites, eds, *European Culture*, pp.8–31; Peter Kenez, 'Russian Patriotic Films', in Dibbets and Hogenkamp, eds, *Film and First World War*, pp.36–42; Fredric S. Zuckerman, 'The Political Police, War, and Society in Russia, 1914–17', in Coetzee and Shevin-Coetzee, eds, *Authority*, pp.29–56; Genadii Bordiugov, 'The First World War and Social Deviance in Russia', in Cecil and Liddle, eds, *Facing Armageddon*, pp.549–53.

31. Jay Luvaas, 'A Unique Army: The Common Experience', in Kann and Király, eds, *Habsburg Empire*, p.99; Stone, *Eastern Front*, pp.166–71; Wildman, *End of Russian Imperial Army*, pp.80–94; Bushnell, 'Peasants in Uniform', pp.567–70; Jones, 'Imperial Russia's Forces', pp.312–13; Davidian, 'Russian Soldier's Morale', pp.425–33; Vladimir Buldakov, 'The National Experience of War, 1914–17', in Cecil and Liddle, eds, *Facing Armageddon*, pp.539–44.

32. Wildman, *End of Russian Imperial Army*, pp.99–120; Stone, *Eastern Front*, pp.166–71, 212–18, 224–5; Jean Delmas, 'L'Armée Russe vue par les Officiers Français affectés en Russia, 1916–17', in Becker and Audoin-Rouzeau, eds, *Les sociétés européennes*, pp.375–83.

33. Norman E. Saul, *Sailors in Revolt: The Russian Baltic Fleet in 1917* (Lawrence, KS, 1978), pp.12–20, 27–36, 45–51, 64–80; Euan Mawdsley, *The Russian Revolution and the Baltic Fleet: War and Politics, February 1917–April 1918* (London, 1978), pp.3–21.

34. George Katkov, *Russia 1917: The February Revolution* (London, 1967), pp.173–7, 215–17, 247–84, 306–58; Figes, *People's Tragedy*, p.300; Jones, 'Imperial Russia's Forces', pp.281–5; Alexander Rabinowitch, *The Bolsheviks Come to Power: The Revolution of 1917 in Petrograd* (New York, 1976), pp.60–3, 125–71, 191–4, 210–18, 225–72, 311–14; Wildman, *End of Russian Imperial Army*,

pp.121–58; Tony Ashworth, 'Soldiers not Peasants: The Moral Basis of the February Revolution, 1917', *Sociology* 26 (1992), pp.455–70.

35. Wildman, *End of Russian Imperial Army*, pp.182–201, 246–90, 333–72; Ferro, *Great War*, pp.186–91, 223–34; idem, *The Russian Revolution of February 1917* (London, 1972), pp.115, 124–5, 134; Katkov, *Russia 1917*, pp.359–74; Donald J. Raleigh, 'Political Power in the Russian Revolution: A Case Study of Saratov', in Edith Rogovin Frankel, Jonathan Frankel and Baruch Knei-Paz, eds, *Revolution in Russia: Reassessments of 1917* (Cambridge, 1992), pp.34–53; Figes, *People's Tragedy*, pp.324–6; Rogger, *Russia in Age of Modernisation*, p.274; G. Gill, *Peasants and Government in the Russian Revolution* (London, 1979), pp.46–64, 75–89; Acton, *Rethinking*, pp.132–54.

36. Stone, *Eastern Front*, pp.300–1; Louise Heenan, *Russian Democracy's Fatal Blunder: The Summer Offensive of 1917* (New York, 1987), pp.11–21, 23–34, 38–46, 50–6, 109–24; A. K. Wildman, *The End of the Russian Imperial Army II: The Road to Soviet Power and Peace* (Princeton, NJ, 1987), pp.36–72, 89–119.

37. Katkov, *The Kornilov Affair: Kerensky and the Break-up of the Russian Army* (London, 1980), pp.47–64, 83–104; J. L. Munck, *The Kornilov Revolt: A Critical Examination of Sources Research* (Aarhus, 1987), pp.11–15, 44–9, 69–73, 81–8, 109–23, 138–42; William Rosenberg, *Liberals in the Russian Revolution: The Constitutional Democratic Party, 1917–21* (Princeton, NJ, 1974), pp.170–6, 205–12, 220–8; Rabinowitch, *Bolsheviks Come to Power*, pp.94–150; Wildman, *End of Russian Imperial Army*, II, pp.123–47, 153–83, 191–202, 230–34, 286–7; idem, 'Officers of the General Staff and the Kornilov Movement', in Frankel, Frankel and Knei-Paz, eds, *Revolution in Russia*, pp.76–102; Ziva Galili, 'Commercial–Industrial Circles in Revolution: The Failure of "Industrial Progressivism"', ibid., pp.188–216; Marc Ferro, 'The Russian Soldier in 1917: Patriotic, Undisciplined and Revolutionary', *Slavic Review* 30 (1971), pp.483–51; Saul, *Sailors in Revolt*, pp.91–6, 99–111, 119–22, 142–9; Mawdsley, *Russian Revolution and Baltic Fleet*, pp.51–66.

38. Michael Melancon, *The Socialist Revolutionaries and the Russian Anti-war Movement, 1914–17* (Columbus, OH, 1990), pp.167–278; Gill, *Peasants and Government*, pp.141–9, 157–69; Mary McAuley, *Bread and Justice: State and Society in Petrograd, 1917–22* (Oxford, 1991), pp.23–34; Ziva Galili y Garcia, *The Menshevik Leaders in the Russian Revolution: Social Realities and Political Strategies* (Princeton, NJ, 1989), pp.45–202, 294–337; S. A. Smith, *Red Petrograd: Revolution in the Factories, 1917–18* (Cambridge, 1983), pp.14–36, 48–53, 110–16, 160–7; idem, 'Petrograd in 1917: The View from below', in Kaiser, ed., *Workers' Revolution*, pp.59–79; Orlando Figes, *Peasant Russia, Civil War: The Volga Countryside in Revolution, 1917–21* (Oxford, 1989), pp.61–84; John Channon, 'The Peasantry in the Revolutions of 1917', in Frankel, Frankel and Knei-Paz, eds, *Revolution in Russia*, pp.105–30; Diane P. Koenker and William G. Rosenberg, 'Perceptions and Realities of Labour Protest, March to October 1917', ibid., pp.131–56; idem, *Strikes and Revolution in Russia, 1917* (Princeton, NJ, 1989), pp.61–95,

265–98; Rogger, *Russia in Age of Modernisation*, pp.272–91; Ian D. Thatcher, 'Trotskii, Lenin and the Bolsheviks, August 1914–February 1917', *Slavonic and East European Review* 72 (1994), pp.72–114; Acton, *Rethinking*, pp.118–22, 156–66, 182–209.

39. Wildman, *End of Russian Imperial Army*, II, pp.292–306; Rex A. Wade, *The Russian Search for Peace, February–October 1917* (Stanford, CA, 1969), pp.26–50; idem, *Red Guards and Workers' Militias in the Russian Revolution* (Stanford, CA, 1984), pp.80–114, 173–82; idem, 'The Red Guards: Spontaneity and the October Revolution', in Frankel, Frankel and Knei-Paz, eds, *Revolution in Russia*, pp.54–75; Robert Service, 'The Bolsheviks on Political Campaign in 1917: A Case Study of the War Question', ibid., pp.304–25; J. W. Wheeler-Bennett, *Brest Litovsk: The Forgotten Peace, March 1918* (London, 1963), pp.37–41; Saul, *Sailors in Revolt*, pp.169–74, 176–90; Figes, *People's Tragedy*, pp.482–500, 536–47; Mawdsley, *Russian Revolution and Baltic Fleet*, pp.51–66, 97–115.

40. See Euan Mawdsley, *The Russian Civil War* (London, 1987); Geoffrey Swain, *The Origins of the Russian Civil War* (London, 1996); Peter Kenez, *Civil War in South Russia*, 2 vols (Berkeley, CA, 1977); O. H. Radkey, *The Unknown Civil War in South Russia: A Study of the Green Movement in the Tambov Region, 1920–21* (Stanford, CA, 1976); Martha Olcott, 'The Basmachi or Freemen's revolt in Turkestan, 1918–24', *Soviet Studies* 33 (1981), pp.352–69; N. G. O. Pereira, *White Siberia: The Politics of Civil War* (Montreal, 1996); and Jonathan Smele, *Civil War in Siberia: The Anti-Bolshevik Government of Admiral Kolchak, 1918–20* (Cambridge, 1997).

41. Nicholas V. Riasanovsky, *History of Russia*, 2nd edn (New York, 1969), p.540; S. G. Wheatcroft and R. W. Davies, 'Population', in Davies, Harrison and Wheatcroft, eds, *Economic Transformation*, pp.62–4.

42. R. B. Spence, 'Lost to the Revolution: The Russian Expeditionary Force in Macedonia, 1916–18', *EEQ* 19 (1985), pp.417–37; Rothstein, *Soldiers' Strikes*, pp.37–9, 44, 46–7, 49, 58, 69, 86–9, 92–3.

Victors and Vanquished

It was as much a case of Germany losing the war as of the Entente winning it. The consequence, however, was not just a revolution in authority in the defeated states but also attempted social revolution in both Germany and Hungary. For a short while, between 1924 and 1931, the post-war settlement did make some of the world 'safe for democracy', but Versailles and its related treaties neither destroyed Germany nor conciliated it. Instead, Germany was left humiliated and resentful, but what most condemned the treaty arrangements was that the will to enforce them so rapidly disappeared in the light of the withdrawal of the United States into diplomatic isolation and the spectre of communism in Russia. Coupled with post-war economic problems, frustrated nationalism and general disillusionment, the settlements paved the way for Europe to become a battleground between political extremes. Of course, there are distinct differences between the causes of the two world wars, but it is hard to imagine the conflict that began in Europe in 1939 occurring without the legacy of the Great War.

Defeat and revolution

The strategic calculations of Hindenburg and Ludendorff after they took effective control of Germany in August 1916 were fundamentally flawed. In particular, the pursuit of war as an objective in its own right, not least through the adoption of unrestricted submarine warfare proved catastrophic. So, too, was the determination on ever wider expansion eastwards, which caused friction with both Austria-Hungary and Turkey. In theory, the resources of the east were to be directed towards victory in the west. Yet, continued expansion eastwards never resulted in sufficient troops being made available to secure such a victory on the Western Front although 48 divisions were sent west from Russia, Romania and Italy between November 1917 and March 1918, leaving 47 divisions in the east.

The five German spring offensives in the west, beginning on 21 March 1918 and concluding on 15 July, certainly achieved major territorial gains but no strategic breakthrough. Indeed, the German advance went furthest in those areas where the defence was weakest precisely because those areas had less strategic significance. Accordingly, local German successes did not fulfil any higher objective. As already indicated, German troops were soon exhausted by their exertions, often slowing their advance to loot British and French food supply depots. Influenza also took its toll of the German troops, though not the British or French, with at least 580,000 men being affected by July. There was increasing evidence, too, of a 'covert military strike' as men either went missing in the rear areas or declined to take any more risks at the front. As in most armies, the weakest link was in the rear areas, where movement of men to and from the front could not be as controlled as at the front. In the rear, tensions arising from supply problems and other difficulties, as Hew Strachan has put it, 'could simmer and seethe . . . without the direct pressure of the enemy to suppress them'.[1]

The Entente counter-attack from August 1918 onwards did not break the German army in the sense that, in November, it was still intact and still maintained a continuous front line. In theory, it could have continued the war into 1919. The Entente advance had slowed in the face of determined rearguard actions and with the difficulties experienced in supplying their armies across desolated battlefields. As late as 19 October 1918, therefore, Haig believed the Germans quite capable of retiring to their own frontiers and holding them. This does not detract from the achievement of the British army during the 'Hundred Days', capturing 188,700 prisoners and 2,840 guns in nine major actions between 8 August and 11 November. The 350,000 British casualties were a heavy price, but the German army had itself taken heavy casualties in the spring offensives in the process of extending the length of the German front from 390 to 510 kilometres. By November 1918, indeed, the Germans had sustained 1.7 million casualties since 21 March. Moreover, those losses had been among the best of Germany's remaining troops and those who had the highest morale. Ludendorff's hope of holding the line of the Meuse also began to look increasingly doubtful as the British Third and Fourth Armies forced the canalised River Sambre on 4 November. In effect, the German army had lost the belief that it could achieve victory.[2]

Ludendorff's power began to wane when the spring offensives manifestly failed to bring victory, many officers, including even Bauer, criticising the lack of strategic objectives. His nerve broken by the British offensive at Amiens on 8 August, Ludendorff tendered his resignation on 13 August only for the Kaiser to reject it. On 28 September 1918, with the news that Bulgaria had sought an armistice, Ludendorff had another nervous collapse and urged Hindenburg to seek an armistice.

The Entente had finally launched an offensive from Salonika under the direction of Franchet D'Esperey on 15 September. Bulgarian military morale collapsed with rebel units threatening to march on Sofia. King Ferdinand, still resentful that Bulgaria had not acquired the Dobrudja from the Treaty of Bucharest imposed on Romania in March, requested an armistice on 26 September 1918. Hostilities ended on 30 October 1918.

With the loss of Bulgaria, Germany was cut off from vital oil and corn supplies to the east. Allenby, meanwhile, had begun his offensive into Syria from Jaffa on 19 September, destroying two Turkish armies at Megiddo. Damascus fell on 1 October and Aleppo on 23 October. On the Mesopotamian front, too, Sir William Marshall advanced up the Tigris towards Mosul. The Turks opened negotiations on 26 October and concluded an armistice on Mudros on 30 October 1918, by which the Entente occupied the Dardanelles and Bosphorus. In Romania, prime minister Bratianu, who had been forced out of office in March, began new negotiations with the Entente in October. On 10 November 1918, Romania declared war on the Central Powers once more, linking with Entente forces advancing from Bulgaria, reoccupying Wallachia and sweeping across the Carpathians into Hungarian Transylvania.[3]

Accompanied by Hindenburg and the Foreign Secretary Admiral Paul von Hintze, Ludendorff informed the Kaiser of the need for an armistice on 29 September. While Hindenburg and Ludendorff wished to appeal for an eventual armistice, the Kaiser and Hintze assumed they wanted an immediate armistice. All were agreed, however, on the need for a new 'liberal' government to secure agreement with Woodrow Wilson, whose Fourteen Points seemed to suggest the chance of leniency. In effect, Ludendorff began laying the foundations of the post-war *dolchstoss* (stab in the back) myth by announcing to his staff on 1 October that 'those circles which we have above all to thank for having brought us to this point' could now 'eat the broth they have cooked for us'. Hertling was dismissed as Chancellor and Prince Max of Baden brought in on 3 October to handle the negotiations.

Max, who insisted on bringing the Social Democratic Party (SPD) into his government, had no illusions that the price of peace would be high. Max requested that Wilson arrange an armistice on 3 October 1918 on the basis of the Fourteen Points, to which Wilson responded by asking for clarification. Wilson's second note on 14 October was something of a shock for the German leadership in demanding absolute guarantees 'of the maintenance of the present military supremacy of the Armies of the United States and its Allies'. A third note on 23 October also made it clear that an armistice must make resumption of the war by Germany impossible and that peace terms must bring about the end of Prussian militarism. Ludendorff had now recovered his nerve and, with Hindenburg, proposed to renew the war, only to find that his position had been undermined. Thus, on 26 October 1918, on the insistence of Max, his resignation was accepted by the Kaiser. The latter pointedly complained that Ludendorff had first demanded an armistice and now, a month later, demanded its negotiation be broken off. The former head of the Supreme War Office, Groener, was brought back to Berlin to become First Quartermaster General in succession to Ludendorff on 29 October.[4]

Groener concluded that Germany could not continue the war once continuation had been called into question. Manpower shortages were becoming serious and there were increasing reports of collapsing military morale. The pressure to accept peace at any price also increased with the Turkish surrender and that of Austria-Hungary on 3 November 1918. Groener and his colleagues were determined to preserve the army itself, and on 8 November Groener told the Kaiser he must abdicate in the interests of the army and stability. The Social Democratic Party had also insisted that the Kaiser go or their two ministers, Philip Scheidemann and Otto Bauer, would resign.

The German Fleet had mutinied at Wilhelmshaven on 27/28 October, having refused to be sent out to fight one last great suicidal battle or *flottenvortoss* with the Royal Navy, a plan hatched by Vice-Admiral Adolf von Trotha, Chief of Staff to the High Seas Fleet, and Scheer in defiance of the government, which had suspended unrestricted submarine warfare on 20 October. Mutiny then spread to Kiel on 3 November and seamen's 'flying columns' seized Schleswig-Holstein, Lübeck, Cuxhaven, Bremen and Hamburg. Another seamen's column reached Berlin on 9 November. Max, however, despatched the SPD deputy, Gustav Noske, to Kiel. Noske conceded the far from revolutionary demands for amnesty, an end to censorship of mails and better treatment, and the seamen elected him chairman of the Sailors' Committee and governor of the city.[5]

The military leadership tried to persuade the Kaiser, with whom Wilson had refused to negotiate, to seek death at the front, but he refused. Max, therefore, announced the Kaiser's abdication before the Kaiser had actually given his consent and then resigned himself to make way for Ebert of the SPD. A republic was proclaimed on 9 November 1918 by Scheidemann, with Ebert forming a provisional government of six 'people's commissars' drawn from both SPD and USPD. On 10 November, Groener contacted Ebert and struck a deal which would be the basis of the Weimar Republic. The army would guarantee the state against revolution and, in turn, the state would uphold the authority of the army's officers, suppress 'Bolshevism', and take responsibility for peace negotiations. On 8 November an armistice commission headed by the Centrist Matthias Erzberger had met the Allied supreme commander, Foch, in a railway carriage at Compiègne. Instructed to secure the armistice at any price, Erzberger signed at 0510 hours on the morning of 11 November. The armistice then came into effect at 1100 hours on 11 November 1918 for a period of 36 days.[6]

Normally an armistice implied a cessation of hostilities only, and Ludendorff had clearly advocated it simply as a means of providing Germany with a breathing space. This armistice, however, was to become almost a peace treaty as the Entente incorporated provisions designed to ensure Germany's inability to resume hostilities. Receiving the initial German request to Wilson on 3 October, Entente political leaders drew up a list of eight conditions relating to German evacuation of occupied French and Belgian territory and retirement behind the Rhine, thus also vacating Alsace-Lorraine and the Rhineland. The Supreme War Council was then invited to formulate suitable terms on 8 October, a process not completed until 4 November largely through the desire of Foch and the British Admiralty to impose more severe conditions.

The terms agreed demanded the immediate German evacuation of occupied French and Belgian territory; evacuation of the left bank of the Rhine; three bridgeheads for Allied troops across the Rhine; the renunciation of the Treaty of Brest Litovsk; the withdrawal of German forces in the east; and the surrender of war *matériel*, including 5,000 railway engines, 15,000 rail cars, 5,000 artillery pieces, 25,000 machine guns and all submarines. Additionally, the surface elements of the High Seas Fleet were to be interned. German forces evacuated France by 18 November and Belgium by 26 November while the U-boat fleet sailed into Harwich on 20 November. Subsequently, the Germans scuttled the High Seas Fleet at Scapa Flow on 21 June 1919 rather than hand it over to the British under the terms of the Versailles treaty. An Allied occupation of the Rhineland began on 1 December 1918.

While the blockade of neutral and liberated states was rescinded by the Entente on 24 December 1918, it was applied to Germany until 12 July 1919 to create additional pressure so that the war could not be renewed. With famine conditions existing in much of Central Europe over the winter, Herbert Hoover became director of a relief operation in December 1918. In order to receive essential food supplies, however, the German government was obliged to surrender its merchant fleet and its gold reserves in March 1919.[7]

Defeat was certainly blamed on a *dolchstoss* promoted by the socialists and brought about primarily by the British economic blockade. As Hew Strachan has commented, any explanation of German defeat which excludes the effect of the blockade 'is as deficient as one which overemphasises it'. Yet, as previously suggested, the blockade was not effective until the United States' entry into the war in April 1917 finally enabled the Entente to enforce restrictions on neutrals without regard for diplomatic niceties. Progressively, therefore, the blockade had an impact on Germany, especially when coupled with the poor harvests of 1916 and 1917. Its real impact resulted, however, from the fact that, through massive wartime expansion, the German army no longer stood apart from society. Soldiers on leave or in transit between Western and Eastern Fronts could not be isolated from civilian privation. It was in the rear echelons of the army that collapse was most apparent, with the plundering of army food stocks and their redistribution to civilians by soldiers a particular sign of collapse. At home, there was also a breakdown of authority by 1918 with black marketeering increasing, near anarchy on the railways and the harvest being stolen in the the fields. In October 1918, front and home front interacted, though the collapse on the home front was a consequence of the decision to seek terms rather than a cause of it.[8]

The events in Germany in November 1918 were in effect a revolution from above rather than below, but there was then an attempt at revolution from below. The most radical elements, as epitomised by revolutionary shop stewards, the Berlin USPD, and the Spartacists, attempted to wrest control from Ebert amid a general strike in Berlin, which involved some 750,000 strikers. In Munich, Kurt Eisner of the USPD, who earned a living as a theatre critic, took advantage of a peace demonstration and proclaimed a Socialist Bavarian Republic on 8 November. Liebknecht, only recently released from prison, similarly declared a German Soviet Republic in Berlin on 9 November. Elsewhere, the USPD took the lead in forming workers' and soldiers' councils, which seized control of local administration. The USPD dominated in cities such as Leipzig and Halle or became the ruling minority in others such as Hamburg and Bremen.

There was not, however, the same revolutionary potential as in Russia. The political left was fragmented between SPD, USPD and Spartacists. Moreover, the largely constitutional SPD retained the loyalty of most workers, securing 40 per cent of the vote in the national elections for a new constituent assembly on 17 January 1919 compared with only 7.6 per cent for the USPD. There was also a much larger and more well developed middle class in Germany than in Russia. The forces of the political right remained strong and the peasantry had greater access to land. Despite the creation of the councils, the imperial bureaucracy remained virtually intact and it was noticeable that popular resentment was directed against officers rather than employers or capitalists. Unions and employers, of course, had reached broad agreement in November on recognition for unions.

Liebkneckt refused to co-operate with the SPD and USPD in government and tried to accelerate the revolutionary process through mass meetings and demonstrations. On 6 December 1918, troops acting on behalf of the government shot dead sixteen Spartacist demonstrators. On 23/24 December troops also shelled mutinous sailors in Berlin. The USPD promptly left Ebert's government although it did so largely because it was outmanoeuvred by the SPD. Against the advice of several of their leaders, the Spartacists attempted an uprising in Berlin on 6 January 1919 in response to the Prussian government's attempt to dismiss the left-wing police chief in Berlin.

The army had almost ceased to exist amid the ad hoc rapid demobilisation of some 6 million men. Demobilisation avoided some of the problems readily apparent in the reluctance of troops to fire on the sailors in Berlin in December, but it left the government without adequate forces. Accordingly, former soldiers – most often officers and NCOs – were formed into the paramilitary Freikorps (Free Corps), initially on the initiative of General Ludwig von Maercker and under the nominal direction of Noske, who had been appointed Defence Minister on the resignation of the USPD ministers. Younger middle-class conservatives boosted the strength of the Freikorps to over 400,000 men. Their suppression of the Spartacist rising was undertaken with much brutality, Liebkneckt and Rosa Luxemburg both being executed after being arrested and beaten on 15 January 1919.

Unrest continued with a general strike in Berlin in March, which led to the imposition of martial law, and equally unsuccessful attempted risings in Hamburg and some other cities. In Munich, Eisner was assassinated on 21 February 1919 by a nationalist. The Bavarian Revolutionary Central Committee, heir to Eisner's original Workers' and Soldiers' Council, declared martial law, as communists and others attempted to establish a Soviet Republic in Bavaria. One such republic was established on 7 April and, after an unsuccessful counter-coup by the provisional government, another proclaimed on 13 April. The Berlin government then acted to support the provisional government in Bavaria and the republic was overrun by government troops and Freikorps on 1 May 1919. At least 700 people were killed in Bavaria between January and June 1919.

The government's willingness to suppress left-wing disorder had given the new regime some limited legitimacy in the eyes of the centre and right but had not won it support. Moreover, the government had restored order at the price of dividing the socialist movement and driving its radicals to communism.[9]

Defeat brought similar tensions in Austria-Hungary, but it was in Hungary that revolution came closest to succeeding. Austria-Hungary had been hit by a wave of strikes in early 1918; as the unrest spread so disturbances began in the armed forces, some 4,000 seamen mutinying at Cattaro in February 1918. Primarily, it was a strike over poor conditions on board, but it collapsed rapidly and four men were executed. Problems continued, however, consuming a variety of national contingents within the army including Slovenes, Serbs, Czechs and Magyars. The process was sparked by reductions in the bread rations for troops in rear areas, the assumption being that those at the front required the food more. Undeniably political aspects began to emerge in army disturbances in May 1918, however, as Conrad planned a new offensive against Italy.

The High Command was particularly alarmed by the return of Austro-Hungarian prisoners of war from Russia after Brest Litovsk. There was no particular evidence that they had been undermined by communist propaganda, but it was certainly the case that few wished to return to front line units. In the event, Conrad's offensive, which opened on 15 June, was a disaster, leading not only to his dismissal but also to increasing desertion. At least 400,000 men deserted between June and September 1918. By October 1918, many appeared to be waiting for an Allied advance to which they could surrender as a British and Italian offensive on 24 October broke through at Vittorio Veneto. Indeed, some 500,000 Austro-Hungarian soldiers surrendered between 26 October and 3 November 1918, with only some 30,000 men becoming casualties in the same period.[10]

Emperor Karl appealed to Wilson for peace on the basis of the Fourteen Points, but Wilson replied only through Berlin. Karl then introduced a federal structure to Austria on 16 October, only for the German-speaking deputies from Austria to constitute a Provisional National Assembly on 21 October and proclaim an Austrian state. In Hungary, a National Council was established on 25 October under Count Mihály Károlyi, this being recognised as the government on 31 October 1918. That same day, Tisza was murdered by soldiers who blamed him for the war. A Czechoslovak Republic was proclaimed in Prague on 28 October and Austrian Galicia announced it would join a Polish state, though this was not formally proclaimed by the Polish nationalist, Pilsudski, until 11 November. On the following day, the Zagreb diet proclaimed the cessation of constitutional ties between the South Slav lands and Vienna. On 30 October, the port of Fiume declared its independence and its wish to be united with Italy.

Much of the Austro-Hungarian army was now affected by mutiny and on 28 October Austria-Hungary requested an armistice, though it was only signed at Villa Giusti near Padua on 3 November and did not come into effect until 4 November 1918. Emperor Karl abdicated political power on 11 November though not formally renouncing the throne.[11]

The events in Austria were not a social revolution but a revolution in power and authority. By contrast, subsequent events in Hungary assuredly were a social revolution, albeit one soon extinguished. The new Hungarian authorities initially declined to accept that the armistice applied to Hungary, but they signed one officially at Belgrade on 13 November 1918. On 16 November, Hungary was proclaimed as a republic in a bloodless process controlled largely by a middle-class alliance of social democrats and radicals. Károlyi, however, proved a disappointment to the poorer peasants in not pressing land redistribution. Still faced with the Entente blockade, the government also found itself incapable of curbing the soldiers' and workers' councils which had emerged at the end of the war.

A Hungarian Communist Party in exile had been established in March 1918 under Béla Kun, who had converted to communism while a prisoner of war in Russia. Its strength was such that, amid a series of damaging strikes and the demands by the Entente that Hungary surrender territory to Romania, the social democrats were compelled to accept a coalition with the communists in March 1919. The Revolutionary Governing Council of what was now the Hungarian Soviet Republic emerged on 23 March. The communists introduced wide-scale nationalisation of land but, rather than redistributing it, proposed state collectives. Courts were transformed into revolutionary tribunals, banks and industries were nationalised, education taken over by the state, universal suffrage introduced, and local administration assumed by offshoots of the workers' councils.

In April 1919, however, Czech, Yugoslav and Romanian forces intervened in Hungary to seize the territory they claimed. In July the Romanians broke the 'Hungarian Red Army' and Kun fled Budapest shortly before the Romanians occupied it on 3/4 August 1919. By November 1919 the Hungarian government had fallen under the control of Admiral Miklós Horthy, a former Commander-in-Chief of the old Imperial Navy. The communists were eradicated in a so-called White Terror and Horthy, who became regent in January 1920, continued to rule Hungary until 1944.[12]

The Paris peace conference and the peace settlements

Events in Hungary were one of many problems confronting the Entente powers as thoughts turned to a post-war settlement. There had been little expectation that the war would end quite as it did. In France, the first speculation that peace was near occurred only on 3 October 1918 and, when rumours of the possibility of an armistice began to circulate, many wanted to continue the war until the Germans had actually been driven from French soil. The actual armistice, however, was greeted with wild enthusiasm. The celebrations began four days earlier in the United States as a result of an American correspondent mistaking Erzberger's passage of the lines as the ceasefire. False rumours also reached Sydney on 8 November. In Britain, bells, sirens or maroons announced the armistice, while factories were closed and processions hastily organised. Australian, Canadian and British soldiers lit bonfires around Nelson's Column in Trafalgar Square, permanently scarring the monument. There were similar reactions throughout the Empire. The liberation of occupied Belgium, meanwhile, became a triumphal progress for King Albert, who moved quickly to appoint a coalition government and make good a previous concession of universal suffrage.[13]

There were to be six separate peace treaties, of which five were negotiated at Paris. The Treaty of Versailles was signed on 28 June 1919 to conclude the war with Germany, followed by the Treaty of St Germain concluded with Austria on 10 September 1919, and the Treaty of Neuilly with Bulgaria on 27 November 1919. Delayed by the Hungarian revolution, the Treaty of Trianon concluded the war with Hungary on 4 June 1920. The Treaty of Sèvres concluded the war with Turkey on 10 August 1920 and a further Treaty of Lausanne was then signed with Turkey on 24 July 1923.

Once the conference convened at Paris on 18 January 1919 with some 27 states represented – the defeated were not represented – the decision-making process was initially conducted by the so-called Council of Ten, comprising the heads of government and Foreign Ministers of Britain, France, Italy, Japan and the United States. In March 1919, as a means of resolving the many outstanding issues, decisions were made by the 'Council of Four', namely Lloyd George, Clemenceau, Wilson, and Orlando of Italy. After the end of the main negotiations in July1919, subsequent decisions were made between governments and various agencies of the Entente. The terms imposed on Turkey, negotiations for which were not completed at Paris, were then settled in London between February and April 1920 and finalised at San Remo in Italy in April, leading to the signing of the Sèvres treaty four months later.

As with the causes of the war, interpretations of the impact of the settlements have differed widely over the years. From the beginning, many commentators such as John Maynard Keynes condemned Versailles as unduly harsh, and A. J. P. Taylor was among those historians who believed it contributed significantly to the outbreak of the Second World War. More recently, other historians such as Alan Sharp have suggested that it was the best that could be achieved in the circumstances. Clearly, it proved an unhappy compromise between the French desire for a punitive settlement, the British desire for stability, and the American desire to create a better world based on principles of internationalism, democracy and self-determination.

In any case, the 'Big Four' could not of themselves enforce their collective will over some parts of Europe. The break-up of Austria-Hungary (and of Tsarist Russia) was established fact before the conference convened and the situation created thereby was irreversible. In most cases, achieving an economic and strategic frontier was simply incompatible with the geographical spread of nationalities on the ground, rendering self-determination all but impossible. The arrangements made for Turkey at Sèvres were soon rendered void.

It was also the case that, technically, none of the Central Powers had actually surrendered unconditionally, all having accepted military armistices. Moreover, in the case of Germany, Wilson had offered the Fourteen Points in reply to the German approach for terms prior to the armistice. Since Entente troops only occupied the Rhineland and they did not parade through Berlin as German troops had through Paris in 1871, it was never brought fully home to the German people that they had been defeated, hence the subsequent shock of the terms imposed. The Fourteen Points themselves were sufficiently vague to allow several interpretations, while the Entente had made widely contradictory wartime promises to Allies, which were frequently incompatible with the underlying principles of the Fourteen Points. Each Entente delegation at Paris also had to satisfy a public still imbued with the promises made them in return for their sacrifices.[14]

The three men whose views mattered most in shaping the settlement were Wilson, Lloyd George and Clemenceau. Wilson was in essence a 'progressive internationalist'. Translated into foreign policy terms as 'peace without victory', this implied a new world order established on the basis of arbitration, self-determination, collective security and disarmament through a League of Nations. Clearly, the United States had enormous financial muscle. The strength of Wilson's position, however, was deceptive.

The details of the League had not been discussed while the United States was at war, leaving the Republicans to impose their demand for German unconditional surrender upon the American public. Moreover, the mid-term elections in November 1918 had given the Republicans control of Congress. Wilson was not particularly influenced by domestic public opinion or interest groups, but he did have a developed sense of retributive justice which, in the short term, required appropriate punishment before Germany could be reintegrated into the new world order. Thus, the more the Germans resisted the idea of their 'war guilt', the more Wilson was convinced it was true. It was also the case that Wilson and his Paris team were inexperienced in diplomacy. Consequently, by humouring Wilson's overwhelming desire for the League, the Europeans wrested concessions on other Wilsonian principles.[15]

Britain had prepared carefully for the peace settlement. Despite his recent overwhelming electoral victory, however, Lloyd George was boxed in by election pledges to a public and press baying for retribution, and by a need to satisfy similar demands from his own back-benchers. A consummate politician, Lloyd George was a liberal realist on the needs of any peace settlement but this was tempered by British interests and his own parliamentary position. Nonetheless, Britain achieved most of its essential aims. Immediate British security requirements had been satisfied by the surrender of the High Seas Fleet but there was a need to compensate for the possible failure of the proposed League of Nations. Thus, the British stressed the necessity for a balance of power in Europe and were hostile to exaggerated Italian territorial claims and to French gains beyond Alsace-Lorraine. In eastern Europe, stability required a settlement largely based on ethnic lines. There was some support in the Foreign Office for recognition of Czechoslovakia, but wide divergences of opinion of the desirability of a greater Greece or a greater Poland. Generally, there was a determination to avoid any obligation requiring Britain to uphold the settlement in central or eastern Europe.

Beyond Europe, there was a need to juggle self-determination with imperial needs and to reconcile contradictory promises, not least those made to Arabs and Zionists. The British sought to cancel the Sykes–Picot Agreement so far as Syria was concerned, setting up Faisal as leader of an Arab state based on Damascus. Some wanted to involve the United States in Palestine as well as in Armenia and at Constantinople. There was less preparation on economic and legal questions and, in the event, political considerations led to deviation from prepared negotiating positions, notably on the issue of reparations.[16]

Clemenceau's overriding concern was France's future security in relation to Germany, although he also wished to reinvigorate France's position within Europe by territorial acquisitions and economic domination. Believing German democracy a smokescreen to modify Allied demands, Clemenceau wanted the wartime Entente continued as long as possible. Alsace-Lorraine would clearly be returned to France but Clemenceau wanted the 1814 frontier and not that of 1871. This would automatically include half the Saar, and the French sought not only the rest of the Saar but a foot on the Rhine.

Clemenceau was happy to give discreet encouragement to Rhenish separatism being advocated by the mayor of Cologne, Konrad Adenauer, and to support elements in Luxemburg seeking to overthrow its Grand Duke since it would seek closer ties with France. He wished to strongly establish the new states of eastern Europe, especially Poland, as an additional counterweight to Germany, while hoping that some kind of anti-Bolshevik and anti-German federation would emerge in Russia. Clemenceau also sought an Anglo-French alliance as an additional security guarantee. French imperial interests required the securing of Syria and Lebanon and, ideally, Palestine and Armenia.

Clemenceau's aims largely reflected French opinion. He was willing to be flexible, however, in how some of his aims might be achieved. Both the French political left and right attacked his negotiating positions and there was a far more prolonged debate on ratification of the settlement in France than elsewhere, but Clemenceau was in an unassailable political position. France did not get all it wanted, though its demands shaped much of the territorial settlement of Germany's frontiers. Economic gains were certainly achieved and there was a degree of flexibility in that the settlement made it possible to retain French forces in the Rhineland and the Saar in certain circumstances and to delay possible German entry into the League of Nations. The security guarantee that Clemenceau thought he had secured from Britain and the United States, however, collapsed with the American withdrawal into diplomatic isolation.[17]

In practice, the post-war settlements may be seen as addressing six principal issues: the acceptance by Germany of its responsibility for the war; the imposition of reparations; a territorial settlement, including the redistribution of the German colonies; a measure of arms control; the establishment of a League of Nations; and provision of safeguards against Bolshevism.

Article 231 of the Treaty of Versailles – there were 440 articles in all – ascribed responsibility for the war in what was largely a preface to Article 232 on reparations. It was intended, therefore, to imply a moral responsibility and a legal liability. Although carefully drafted, it was not assumed to be significant other than as a warrant for reparations. John Maynard Keynes remarked that it was 'only a matter of words, of virtuosity in draughtsmanship, which does no-one any harm'. Whatever the original intention, however, attribution of war guilt sowed an unfortunate legacy in Germany.

Having assumed a peace settlement broadly based on the Fourteen Points and that due regard would be paid to Germany's reformed democratic system, the German delegation was especially shocked by the draft treaty presented them. The problem was not just Article 231 but Articles 227–31, collectively known as the *Schmachparagraphen* (Articles of Shame). An attempt to extradite the Kaiser from the Netherlands failed and only a few 'war criminals' were ever brought to trial by the Weimar Supreme Court at Leipzig, receiving derisory sentences; the pursuit of Turkish war criminals was similarly fruitless. Many Germans, however, to use the phrase of the theologian, Ernst Troeltsch, had existed in a kind of 'dreamland' since the armistice and there was now a feeling that they had been intentionally deceived by Wilson. Indeed, the leader of the German delegation, the Foreign Minister Count Ulrich von Brockdorff-Rantzau, resigned and the rest of the Scheidemann government collapsed, a new administration being formed by Gustav Bauer on 21 June 1919. The treaty was signed seven days later by the new Foreign Minster, Hermann Müller, and Johannes Bell, the Minister of Colonies and Transport.

Despite the political turmoil in Berlin, the Germans still prepared a detailed counter-proposal to the draft terms. This proved a powerful statement of the German case, arguing for a peace based on the Fourteen Points and offering reparations in return for maintaining German territory largely intact. It fuelled a growing unease in Britain with terms based on the notion of Germany's sole guilt for the war, which would ultimately contribute to the concept of appeasement.[18]

While it may have been discredited subsequently, war guilt initially assuaged British and French public opinion favouring due retribution for the effects of war. Reparations with which war guilt was intimately connected also initially spoke to similar constituencies. It came down in most respects to how much Germany should pay and for how long, balanced against Germany's capacity to do so, and bearing in mind the technical problems of transferring German assets into cash without disrupting financial markets or international trade.

The original armistice terms had spoken only vaguely of 'compensation', which Wilson interpreted as being for 'unlawful' wartime action such as the invasion of neutral Belgium. He did not anticipate that it would include reimbursement of war expenditure, and the Fourteen Points had suggested that only Belgium and France could exact 'restoration' for civilian damages. Others, however, interpreted reparations rather more broadly, mindful of those the Germans had imposed upon Russia at Brest Litovsk and earlier on the French in the Frankfurt Treaty of 1871, and the price that would have been exacted had the Germans secured victory.

The Neuilly Treaty imposed £90 million worth of reparations on Bulgaria but, such was the disagreement over Germany, that Versailles did not specify any amount. Reparations were to be an annual payment for a period of 30 years of which 52 per cent was to go to France, 22 per cent to Britain, 10 per cent to Italy and 8 per cent to Belgium. A precise schedule for payment was to be set later, but an immediate payment of Dm20 billion could be met in kind. By May 1921, much of the German merchant fleet had been handed over as well as some 5,000 railway locomotives and 136,000 wagons, and 135,000 cattle. Whereas the Entente calculated that the goods handed over by May 1921 amounted to Dm2.6 billion and the production of the Saar was worth Dm2.5 billion, the Germans claimed they were worth Dm37 billion. The Reparations Commission then set the sum to be paid at Dm132 billion (US$33 billion or £6.6 billion) plus interest to be paid in 42 instalments.

Collecting the instalments became a long-running issue and it has often been argued that the only beneficiaries of reparations were the Nazis, since reparations undermined the German economy. Many historians such as Peter Krüger, Gerald Feldman and David Felix still argue that Germany could not have realistically paid reparations. A number of revisionists such as Steven Schuker, Sally Marks, Charles Maier and Marc Trachtenberg, however, argue that Germany could afford reparations although an economic crisis did result from the currency depreciation encouraged by the German government as evidence of their inability to pay.

At the time, however, the German claims were believed by those already disillusioned with the treaty settlement. Ultimately, the Lausanne conference in 1932 terminated reparations with a final payment, largely paid off by American loans. Germany had paid less than half the original sum set and only one-third of that was paid in cash.[19]

There was little Entente agreement on the economic aims of the settlement. Indeed, all that was achieved by an economic commission headed by Clémentel was a requirement for Germany to grant the Entente powers unilateral and most favoured nation rights for five years and for Austria, Hungary and Bulgaria to do so for three years. However, the new frontiers generally disrupted economic progress. The Bohemian industries in the new Czechoslovakia, for example, had enjoyed protected markets within the Austro-Hungarian Empire but now found it necessary to compete in the world market when immediate neighbours were themselves building up their own new national industries. Having existed largely by providing services in return for agricultural and industrial products from the rest of the Empire, the new Austria found itself almost economically unviable. Yugoslavia inherited five different railway systems with four different gauges.[20]

Turning to the wider aspects of the territorial settlement, Germany's frontiers were substantially redrawn. Alsace-Lorraine was returned to France but only on the basis of the 1815–70 frontier. Moreover, the British resisted a strategic frontier on the Rhine which would have breached the principle of self-determination, creating what Lloyd George referred to as a 'new Alsace-Lorraine'. Nor did France secure the Rhineland. Instead, the Rhineland was demilitarised and divided into three zones to be occupied by Allied contingents for five, ten and fifteen years, respectively.

Foch was especially opposed to surrendering the left bank of the Rhine, but Clemenceau accepted demilitarisation in return for an Anglo-American guarantee of intervention to support France in the event of future German aggression. Made public in May 1919, the British guarantee was amended in June 1919 to make it contingent upon the American guarantee, which Wilson was persuaded to offer in the apparent belief that it was only a temporary expedient. Thus, when the United States Senate did not ratify the treaty settlement, the British guarantee also lapsed.[21]

The British were equally determined to keep Luxemburg out of French hands and succeeded in securing a plebiscite, which voted for continued independence. Again largely owing to British pressure, the Saar was placed under League of Nations control although with its coal produce allocated to France. Belgium made small gains, achieving only what was regarded as the minimum strategic frontier line necessary for defence. Thus, Belgium's continued security rested upon British and French commitment to the treaty settlement as a whole.[22]

The settlement of Germany's eastern frontiers was even more contentious, with the determination of France and the United States to establish a strong Poland as an additional guarantor of French security. The new state, however, was created in blatant disregard of the principle of self-determination, with Posen (Poznań) and Hultschin passing to Poland and Memel earmarked for Lithuania. What remained of east Prussia was now separated from Germany by the Polish Corridor to the sea including the predominantly German city of Danzig (Gdansk), the only viable economic and geographic port available. Posen had been German since the eighteenth century.

Following the receipt of the German counter-proposals to the draft treaty, and at Lloyd George's insistence, plebiscites were arranged in Marienwerder, Allenstein and Upper Silesia as well as Schleswig, which was intended for Denmark. Plebiscites were also arranged for Austrian Sopron and Slovenia. As a result of the first plebiscites in February and March 1920, the northern part of Schleswig voted to join Denmark and a second zone to remain with Germany. In the east Prussian plebiscites in July 1920, both Marienwerder and Allenstein voted to remain German. This was also the case in Upper Silesia in March 1921 despite the fact that the majority population in both Allenstein and Upper Silesia spoke Polish. In the case of Upper Silesia, however, the frontier was settled in defiance of the plebiscite. Supported by France, who signed a treaty of alliance with the Poles in early 1921, Polish troops seized the territory. Danzig became a free city under League control, as did Memel, which was seized by Lithuania in 1923. One-fifth of the population of the new Poland were not Poles, the 9 million non-Polish citizens recorded in the disputed 1921 census including 4 million Ukrainians, 1 million White Russians, 1 million Germans and over 2 million Jews.

In all, Germany lost some 13.1 per cent of her former national territory and 10 per cent of her population. The new Germany's western frontiers were not formally fixed until the Treaty of Locarno in October 1925, by which the Weimar Republic accepted its frontiers with France and Belgium. Resentment in Germany at the terms imposed, however, was still considerable. Moreover, Germany did not accept its eastern frontiers and there remained the problem of ethnic German minorities inside newly created states such as the Sudetenland Germans now located in Czechoslovakia. St Germain likewise transposed Austrian Germans of the southern Tyrol into Italian citizens while Austria was prohibited from being united with Germany in the future for fear of creating an even larger German state than had existed in 1914.[23]

Under the related treaties, the new states of eastern Europe also gained at the expense of Austria-Hungary and Bulgaria. Bulgaria, which had anticipated that she might gain from the conference on the basis of self-determination, lost just 8 per cent of its territory, principally western Thrace, which went to Greece. The Greeks were only the second largest ethnic group in western Thrace but it was unthinkable to return it to the Turks, who had the majority. Southern Dobrudja represented something of a problem in that, while lost by Bulgaria to Romania in 1913, the Romanians had no ethnic claim to it. In the event, it was felt best to leave it in Romania. While not losing too much territory, however, Bulgaria was certainly weakened with respect to its neighbours.

In many respects, Hungary was the greatest loser from the treaties, being dispossessed of 60 per cent of its former population and two-thirds of its former territory. Indeed, 6.2 million Austrians and 7.6 million Hungarians bore disproportionate blame for the sins of the 52 million inhabitants of the Austro-Hungarian Empire. As Churchill later noted, of two soldiers who had served side by side during the war, one might now be considered 'a guilty wretch, lucky to escape with life the conqueror's vengeance' while the other 'appears to be one of the conquerors himself'.

Czechoslovakia, comprising Bohemia, Moravia from Austria, Slovakia and Ruthenia from Hungary and the Sudetenland from Germany, was duly recognised at Paris. So, too, was Yugoslavia, known until 1929 as the Kingdom of the Serbs, Croats and Slovenes, and incorporating Serbia, Montenegro and Slavic parts of the Austro-Hungarian Empire such as Croatia, Bosnia and Hercegovina and most of the Banat, which had been claimed in its entirety by Romania. Romania itself doubled in size and population, receiving the Bukovina from Austria-Hungary and Transylvania from Hungary, although forced to withdraw from Budapest by an ultimatum that the Entente would break off relations. Recognition was also accorded Finland, Estonia, Latvia and Lithuania.[24]

Ethnic minorities were thus created throughout central, eastern and southern Europe. New states containing frustrated national minorities were, in some respects, artificial unions that were collections of weaknesses rather than concentrations of strength that could be exploited by both external and internal revisionists. In all, an estimated 19 million people became minority citizens in nine new states with a combined population of 98 million. At the same time, many others became refugees, rather than accept their new rulers. At least 450,000 refugees moved into Bulgaria from Thrace, Macedonia, Yugoslavia and Dobrudja, contributing to pressures which led to the fall of the government in 1923.

Concerned especially by persecution of the Jews in the emergent Polish state, Wilson hoped to protect minorities through the League of Nations, seeking also some kind of general declaration of rights. Consequently, minorities had their rights guaranteed under various provisions of the peace treaties. The minorities could appeal to the secretary-general of the League of Nations for redress but only a member state could ensure a complaint was discussed in the League's council. German minorities, therefore, lacked any protection until Germany joined the League in 1926. Jews, who suffered persecution in Poland, Hungary and Romania, could find no state to champion them. Greater restrictions placed on immigration by the United States in 1924 also closed off another safety valve.[25]

While, as might be expected, it was the defeated states who most resented the peace settlement, one member of the 'Big Four', Italy, found its own ambitions frustrated. Italy did gain the southern Tyrol, Trentino, Trieste, the Istrian peninsula, parts of Dalmatia and islands in the Adriatic. The Italians, however, had anticipated much more despite the incompatibility of the promises made under the Treaty of London in 1915 and Wilson's Ninth Point, emphasising that Italian frontiers should be 'effected along clearly recognisable lines of nationality'. It had not been anticipated that a new Yugoslavia would contest Italian claims to Dalmatia and, especially, the port of Fiume. Nor had the Italians taken into account French ambitions in the Mediterranean. While nationalists like D'Annunzio demanded Dalmatia and Fiume, the Italian government objected to the inclusion of Croats and Slovenes in the Yugoslav delegation and declined to lift the wartime blockade of the Adriatic.

Dismayed by Italian irredentism, Wilson tried to appeal to the Italian people over the head of Orlando on the issue of Fiume. As a result, Orlando walked out of the conference on 24 April 1919, receiving a massive endorsement from the Italian parliament and its people. Absence, however, did not assist the Italian cause and, forced back to Paris by sheer necessity on 7 May, Orlando's government fell in June 1919. D'Annunzio further complicated matters by seizing Fiume with 8,000 'Legionaries' in September 1919 on the day the Italian garrison was supposed to hand over control to the British. At Rapallo in November 1920, however, the Italians and Yugoslavs reached agreement on autonomous status for Fiume and Italian troops drove out D'Annunzio in December 1920 after he declared war on the Italian government. Four years later, Mussolini incorporated Fiume into Italy. The Italians also evacuated Albania in July 1920, recognising its independence in the following month.[26]

Turkey, too, lost territory, Sèvres providing for the redistribution of Turkey's Middle Eastern possessions, independence for Armenia and autonomy for the Kurds. In terms of the Turkish presence in Europe, the chief beneficiary was Greece. Greece wanted the Dodecanese and northern Aegean islands, Macedonia, all of Thrace, northern Epirus (a part of Albania) and western Asia Minor. In deference to the need to secure British support, the Greeks did not raise the question of Cyprus. Equally, Britain made it clear that it was not the intention to reverse the verdict of the Balkan Wars with respect to Macedonia, which remained Bulgarian.

Britain, France and the United States, however, all supported Greek claims in some measure. The most controversial was that to western Asia Minor or Anatolia, which the British believed likely to overstretch Greek capabilities. In May 1919, however, with the Italians absent from Paris and unable to object, prime minister Venizelos was invited to occupy part of Anatolia, including Smyrna, in what proved one of the most momentous decisions of the whole peace process.

The terms were accepted under protest by Sultan Mohammed VI, but Mustapha Kemal, the general who had first distinguished himself in defence of the Dardanelles at Gallipoli, refused to accept them, having first raised a national revolt when the Greeks occupied Smyrna (Izmir). Subsequently, Kemal not only suppressed the attempted independence on the part of Armenia but also defeated the Greek attempts to annexe Thrace and Anatolia between June 1920 and August 1922. Kemal's victory brought the Turks into a new confrontation with the British occupation forces in the 'neutral zone' at Chanak near Constantinople. With the French and Italians having made terms with Kemal and unsupported by the dominions, apart from New Zealand and Newfoundland, Britain backed down from confrontation.

Lausanne therefore revised the original treaty terms to Turkey's advantage in terms of the restoration of Armenia, eastern Thrace, Smyrna and Anatolia, leading to a mass exchange of Greek and Turkish populations. Some 1.5 million Greeks left Anatolia and 400,000 Muslims left Greek territory. Lausanne, therefore, was the only negotiated peace treaty, the others all being imposed. The Straits were demilitarised but Turkish control was restored in 1936.[27]

Wilson had also intended that there should be 'free, open-minded, and absolutely impartial adjustment' of colonial claims based upon the interests of indigenous populations. Resenting Wilson's interference, neither the British, the dominions nor the French were willing to forgo their colonial claims and all favoured outright annexation of German and Turkish colonial possessions. Annexation, however, would have been politically embarrassing.

The solution which presented itself as a means of placating anti-imperial sentiment was the mandate. Under the mandate system, colonies would be administered on behalf of the League of Nations. Class A mandates would be those territories considered sufficiently advanced to need only temporary 'guidance' by colonial powers before proceeding to independence. Class B mandates would enjoy a degree of autonomy and Class C mandates would be the most 'backward' territories to be retained for the foreseeable future.

In terms of the Ottoman Empire, Britain received the mandates for Palestine (A), Transjordan (A) and Iraq (A) and a protectorate over Arabia. France received a mandate for Syria (A), including Lebanon. Wilson declined British and French pressure to accept a United States mandate for Armenia. Britain also received German East Africa (B), which it had hoped to annexe outright to achieve a closer East African union, while South Africa received German South-west Africa (C). France took most of Togo (B) and the Cameroons (B). Despite last ditch efforts by Hughes of Australia and Massey of New Zealand, who continued to demand outright annexation, former German possessions in the Pacific passed to Australia, New Zealand and Japan as C mandates. Belgium received Rwanda and Burundi (B) while the Portuguese received Kionga, a small coastal strip of German East Africa. Italy, still absent when colonial claims were discussed, got the Juba valley from German East Africa and a minor adjustment of the frontier between Libya and French Algeria.

In dividing the Ottoman possessions between Britain and France, wartime promises to Arab nationalists remained unfulfilled. A poisonous legacy was thereby left, which has continued to have an impact on Middle Eastern affairs. The full settlement of the Middle East was not finalised until a further inter-Allied conference at San Remo in April 1920, which simply ignored continuing Arab demands.

While the peace settlement resulted in both the British and French Empires reaching their greatest extent, the war had also unleashed indigenous nationalism. A policy of self-determination for the European subjects of Austria-Hungary was a clear signal to others. Britain in particular was to meet nationalist unrest in Ireland (1919–21), India (1919), Egypt (1919–23), Palestine (1920–21) and Iraq (1920) at a moment when financial pressures and the need for demobilisation severely stretched resources. By 1921, Britain had been forced to withdraw troops from Russia, the Caucasus, Transcaspia, Persia and Afghanistan, where it had briefly fought the Third Afghan War between May and August 1919 to deter the new amir, Amanulla, from encouraging Muslim nationalists in the North-west Frontier province of India. Nevertheless, Britain's only major loss was Ireland, partition leading to the establishment of the Irish Free State with dominion status in 1921.

As suggested by Chanak, the dominions were less willing to support imperial ventures, all declining to send troops to Iraq in 1920. Canada and South Africa also opposed renewal of the Anglo-Japanese alliance in 1921, which was favoured by Australia and New Zealand, owing to the fear that it might jeopardise Anglo-American relations.[28]

Japanese ambitions were of particular concern to Hughes of Australia, who fought hard but unsuccessfully at Paris for his concept of an 'Australian Monroe Doctrine' for the Pacific. China, however, was even more concerned, and rejected the settlement when Japan received Kiaochow and the Shantung peninsula. The Chinese had assumed that Wilson's support for them would sway the other powers, but their case was undermined by promises already made to the Japanese and wartime agreements between the Chinese and Japanese governments for the financing of railway construction in the peninsula. The outcome in Paris was met by widespread demonstrations in China in May 1919, compelling the government to refuse to sign the final treaty. Korean protests at continued Japanese occupation were ignored at Paris, while another frustrated nationalist, Nguyen Ai Quoc, later known as Ho Chi Minh, was refused access to Wilson to press for self-determination for French Indo-China.

In Japan itself, the end of what was regarded as a European war was met with general indifference, but the Paris conference was to prompt popular agitation. On the one hand, Japan was successful not only in securing German possessions and rights in China but also Germany's north Pacific colonies as mandates, although outright annexation would have been preferred. On the other hand, there was less satisfaction with the establishment of the League of Nations, which the Japanese anticipated might act against their future interests. In particular, however, in the face of American and, especially, Australian opposition, the Japanese failed to secure within the covenant a form of words outlawing racial discrimination and discriminatory policies. Subsequently, the lack of a precise period for Japanese control of Kiaochow was taken up by Britain and the United States after the conference closed and Japan gave up its lease in 1922.[29]

In terms of arms control, the peace settlement imposed particular restrictions on Germany but also attempted to apply wider limitations in central and eastern Europe. Entente politicians believed it essential to disarm Germany, especially as it was such a recent convert to democracy and appeared unlikely to remain so in view of its political instability. Few Entente soldiers agreed with the concept of far-reaching disarmament, British soldiers in particular believing in the need to keep Germany relatively strong, given the spectre of Bolshevism.

Foch suggested a 200,000-strong conscript force, but the British came up with the concept of a long-service regular army of 100,000 men as a surer safeguard against militarism. In addition, Germany's General Staff was dissolved, all frontier fortifications erased, and weapons such as tanks, gas, aircraft and submarines prohibited. Effective arms control relied not only upon German co-operation, but also on Anglo-French commitment to enforce the provisions. Subsequently, however, with little interest in the European settlement as a whole, British soldiers generally took a 'relaxed view' of the inspection system established in 1920. In any case, the Germans intended to evade the provisions and there was little subsequent Anglo-French agreement on how to respond to German evasions. Arms control was also applied to Austria, Bulgaria, Turkey and Hungary, a process complicated in the case of Hungary by the revolution and made redundant in the case of Turkey by Kemal's revolt against Sultan Mohammed. At Lloyd George's suggestion, there was also an attempt to limit the armed forces of eastern Europe, but Poland, Romania, Yugoslavia, Czechoslovakia and Greece all refused to consider restrictions in June 1919.[30]

The League of Nations, under whose covenant signatories abjured recourse to war, was not something in which many Europeans had much confidence. They yielded, however, to Wilson's wishes to incorporate his vision of the League's covenant into the first 26 articles of the Versailles treaty. Wilson hoped that the existence of the League would enable future adjustment of any faults in the treaties. He had to make some concessions to opposition in the United States Senate by stating that the application of the Monroe Doctrine lay beyond the League's jurisdiction and that it would not intervene in internal matters such as tariffs and immigration. It was not enough. The Republican-dominated Senate declined to ratify the treaty on 19 November 1919, or American participation, on the grounds that the League infringed national sovereignty by compelling the United States to defend other nations against aggression. The League's General Assembly was thus convened for the first time in November 1920 without the Americans, the Senate having again voted against the treaty on 19 March 1920.

The League was famously to fail over such issues as the Japanese invasion of Manchuria in 1931 and the Italian invasion of Abyssinia in 1935. At least initially, it was successful in implementing the provisions of the peace treaties and it did mediate in some early international disputes such as those over Vilna in 1920, Corfu in 1923 and Mosul in 1924. The League also assumed some international responsibilities such as the battle against global diseases. Clearly, however, it fell far short of Wilson's original vision.[31]

The Treaty of Versailles also made provision for the establishment of an International Labour Organisation in Geneva. It was intended to ensure just conditions for labour as a response to the socio-political threat from the Bolsheviks, who had given socialism credibility and provided a vehicle for socialist aspirations beyond its frontiers. Of course, Entente intervention forces were already committed against the Bolsheviks when the peace conference convened.

The Germans tended to overplay the Bolshevik threat in their response to the peace process, but the abrogation of Brest Litovsk had clearly left a power vacuum in those areas of eastern Europe ceded to Germany, which the negotiators at Paris sought to fill by recognising the independence of Poland, Finland and the Baltic states. With the Bolshevik reimposition of control over the Ukraine, White or Belorussia, Georgia, Azerbaijan and Russian Armenia, the creation of new buffer states in eastern Europe was seen as a significant check to communism spreading to the west. However, it was the Polish victory over the Bolsheviks outside Warsaw in August 1920 which effectively arrested the threat of Bolshevism, the subsequent Treaty of Riga in March 1921 settling the frontier on the so-called Curzon Line until 1939.[32]

Political values and the politics of the 'front generation'

Broadly defined, liberal democracy was victorious in 1918 and its principles were enshrined in the Paris settlement. The new states of central and eastern Europe all adopted written constitutions and universal suffrage, while Germany embraced social democracy rather than social revolution. Even Hungary, where revolution had also been turned back, had at least the appearance of democracy until the 1930s. With communism contained, the European world indeed appeared 'safe for democracy'. Indeed, it might be argued that the war made liberalism more resilient in the long term through forcing all governments to become more interventionist in the collective interests of the state.

In the short term, however, liberalism was to prove a victim of the war as the liberal democracies seemed incapable of dealing with either the economic consequences of the war or the threat posed to the status quo by extremists on both political left and political right. Indeed, fascism was as much a threat to liberalism and liberal democracy as communism. Conservatism triumphed politically in Britain in November 1918 and 1922; in France in November 1919 and 1924; and in the United States in November 1921. Similarly, the socialist vote split in Germany in 1919 and 1920. Although the Italian socialists became the largest party in the Chamber of Deputies in the November 1919 elections, its success was short-lived, fascism triumphing in 1922.

Yet, while conservatism underpinned the electoral success of the Lloyd George coalition in Britain, there was evidence of a continuing political change with the decline of the Liberals and the advance made by the Labour Party. Both trends were evident before the war. Labour could not have expected to increase the size of its representation in the election otherwise due, but for the war, in 1915, much beyond the 65 seats gained in the first election in 1910: its representation had fallen to 42 in the second 1910 election. As it happened, Labour won only 57 seats on 22.7 per cent of the votes polled in November 1918, but, in 1922, it was to win 142 seats on 29.5 per cent of the vote.

The advance of the Labour Party was therefore steady rather than dramatic and it did not benefit as much as has sometimes been suggested from the fact that the electorate was two and half times larger in 1918 than it had been in 1910. Indeed, the opposition of skilled unions to dilution had alienated many women voters during the war. Nonetheless, Labour's status was enhanced, the leadership finally being convinced that Labour could risk breaking the pre-war electoral pact with the Liberals.

Labour's strength lay in the unions for it was in essence a parliamentary pressure group intended to advance union interests rather than a political party as such and the increase in unionisation assisted the party. It has been argued that the increase of union domination of Labour through the effective removal of the pacifist elements of the Independent Labour Party during the war further arrested the influence of socialism within the party. The programme adopted in December 1917 and the new party constitution of February 1918 were both reformist and socialist in terms of such aims as nationalisation, welfare reform, a minimum wage and taxation of wealth by capital levy. Nonetheless, the commitment to socialism was distinctly tempered by the increase of union representation on the party's National Executive Committee.[33]

By breaking the pre-war electoral pact between the Liberals and Labour, the war also assisted the Unionists. The extension of the franchise in 1918 did not necessarily help them, but a redistribution of constituencies did. The middle class now generally preferred the Unionists to the Liberals, and the redistribution created many more suburban middle-class seats. Newly enfranchised women also favoured the Unionists. Protectionism was a more popular cause after the war while the Unionists had clearly the greater enthusiasm for securing Britain the fruits of victory. The removal of the Irish MPs also greatly helped the Unionists in the Commons itself.

Compared with 272 seats secured in 1910 on 46.3 per cent of the vote, the Unionists in 1918 secured 335 seats on only 32.6 per cent of the votes, with uncouponed Unionists securing another 48 seats. Thus, the extension of the franchise proved a significant factor in Unionist political hegemony between the world wars. If pre-war politics had been divided by religion, class and nationality, class was beginning to be more significant but the overriding impression of British politics is still one of stability.[34]

Deriving from the experience of increased state intervention in industrial relations, the concept of reformism within the trade union movement was as marked in France as in Britain. Yet, socialists were out of office in France by 1918 and the war all but destroyed the Radical Socialist Party, which had gained 13.3 per cent of the vote and 165 seats in 1914. The party participated in wartime coalitions but the experience tended to mute its radicalism while its weak local organisation was adversely affected by military mobilisation. Already discredited by pre-war scandal, its acknowledged leader, Caillaux, was arrested for allegedly plotting against a republican form of government in January 1918. Another leading figure, Louis Malvy, serving as Interior Minister, had been forced from office in August 1917 for his links to the pacifist journal *Bonnet Rouge*. He was brought to trial, Clemenceau exploiting the affair to discredit both the party and any possibility of a compromise peace.[35]

Many Italians saw a need for a wider post-war role on the part of the state, but visions differed depending upon political perspective. Thus, the middle class sought direct participation in political power; the urban working class, further advances; and the peasants, reform; while landowners and industrialists largely wanted the status quo. At the same time, the war had brought more social fragmentation with the notion of wartime *imboscoti* (shirkers) being accentuated by the north–south divide between urban workers and the southern peasants who had served in the army. Intellectual interventionists and peasant soldiers alike could share an antipathy towards both the traditional elite and the industrial working class.

With war accentuating existing divisions within Italian society, an Italian version of the 'stab in back' myth, deriving from the perceived 'mutilated victory', added its own scars. Caporetto had dealt a shattering blow to the prestige of the old order, as had the failure to secure at Paris those territories most Italians believed their due. Post-war governments seemed little improved, while those groups which had opposed the war remained tainted with defeatism and the spectre of Bolshevism. Fascism was well placed to seize on the mood of dissatisfaction. As an ideology, it was in many ways a celebration of the concept of total wartime mobilisation and, particularly, the idea that national unity could be regained by militarisation. War, therefore, provided the fascists with their most potent myths and symbols of blood sacrifice, a cult of heroism, community of trenches and symbolism of death. Mussolini and D'Annunzio drew the lesson from the war that parliamentary institutions could be ignored and that a population inured to violence would not resist a determined minority.[36]

Street politics also emerged in Germany and it has been suggested that the combination of increasing deprivation, national defeat and the prolonged absence of parents on military service or war work contributed significantly to the attraction of the young to the Nazi movement in the mid and late 1920s. Some care needs to be exercised, however, before assuming too readily that ex-servicemen of the 'front generation' were always at the forefront of the apparent increasing militarisation of European politics.

Governments had been as careful to maintain surveillance of veterans as of civilians; in most cases, however, ex-servicemen were a force for conservatism in one way or another. The demobilisation disturbances in Britain in January 1919 had a limited political element linked to the possibility of service in Russia, but the great majority were related solely to demands to go home or to familiar grievances over food, compulsory church parades, and working hours. Those involved in the demobilisation disturbances wanted not only to leave the army but also to sever all contact with it. Thus, most British ex-servicemen were indifferent to attempts by some veterans' organisations to forge a radical political movement.[37]

Ex-servicemen certainly had grievances. The National Association of Discharged Sailors and Soldiers (NADSS), formed in Blackburn in September 1916; the National Federation of Discharged and Demobilised Sailors and Soldiers (NFDDSS), formed in London in April 1917; and the Comrades of the Great War (CGW), formed in August 1917, were created as pressure groups in response to the government's ad hoc approach to such matters as pensions, rehabilitation and disabilities.

Both NADSS and NFDDSS were mildly radical, loosely sympathising with the Independent Labour and Liberal Parties, respectively. By contrast, CGW had been encouraged by Lord Derby as a conservative riposte after the NFDDSS put up a candidate against Derby's son in a by-election in Liverpool in June 1917. Twenty-nine candidates were put up by NADSS and NFDDSS in the 1918 election and one, Robert Barker from NADSS, was elected. Far more radical was the Soldiers, Sailors and Airmens' Union (SSAU). Formed in January 1919 with the support of the *Daily Herald* as an association of socialist servicemen, it was about 10,000 strong. There were also two splinter groups from NFDDSS, the National Union of Ex-servicemen (NUX), formed in May 1919 and the International Union of Ex-servicemen (IUX), formed in Glasgow the same month. Fragmentation of the movement resulted in bitter rivalries such as that which led to a serious riot at Luton in Bedfordshire during supposed 'peace celebrations' in July 1919, when the town hall was gutted by fire.

Much of the basis of veterans' grievance was removed by government concessions on pensions in August 1919, followed by preferential treatment at labour exchanges and official encouragement of assistance to ex-servicemen by voluntary agencies. By July 1921, NADSS, NFDDSS and CGW, too, had combined in a new British Legion under Haig's leadership. The Legion rejected political partisanship and, through the participation of ex-officers, replicated the army's hierarchy, albiet often to the annoyance of former rank and file members, who were also wary of the anti-socialist theme of the leadership.

If slow, the Legion's growth was steady with, by 1938, just over 409,000 members, many of whom were disabled. While there was some thought of being a political pressure group, the Legion soon became in effect a charitable organisation. The Legion's first Poppy Day in November 1921 began the annual process of raising funds for ex-servicemen after the success of a similar poppy appeal for American ex-servicemen by the American Legion. Indeed, poppies became the biggest annual charity appeal in inter-war Britain, gross receipts rising to over £578,000 by 1938.[38]

With the appearance of the British Legion, the other radical veterans' groups simply disbanded. Indeed, the closest comparison of any British ex-servicemen's organisations with those abroad are arguably the 7,000 members of the Black and Tans and the 1,418 members of the Auxiliary Division of the Royal Irish Constabulary (RIC), both recruited to fight in the Anglo-Irish War of 1919–21. In June 1922, too, ex-servicemen in Tonypandy, famously though innacurately known for the supposed order for troops to open fire on striking miners there in 1910, offered their services to the king to serve anywhere in the Empire following the Irish Republican Army's murder of Sir Henry Wilson. Some former activists in the veterans' movement became associates of Oswald Mosley's British Union of Fascists (BUF) in 1932. The BUF had some similarity of philosophy with the NUX and IUX, but Mosley did not seek to recruit veterans exclusively and relatively few were drawn to his movement.[39]

One specific measure taken for the relief of British ex-servicemen was in land settlement schemes, initially seen as a response to the task of rehabilitating disabled veterans. Provision was made for three experimental domestic colonies by the Small Holdings and Allotments Act of 1916. The war ended, however, before any wider scheme had been implemented and the scheme in Britain was killed off by financial retrenchment in 1921. Over the country as a whole, only some 24,000 candidates had been accepted by 1921, of whom only just over 9,000 had been allotted smallholdings. By 1923, the total had risen to about 19,000 while, in Scotland, some 6,000 allotments were provided for ex-servicemen.

In Ireland, it was believed that local authorities in the south, which had become dominated by nationalists, could not be trusted to house ex-servicemen, while state promotion of a scheme would give ex-servicemen a stake in the status quo. In the event, the scheme to provide smallholdings or cottages was affected by both post-war financial retrenchment and the creation of the Free State in 1921. After negotiation with the Free State and the establishment of the Irish Soldiers' and Sailors' Land Trust in 1922–23, the scheme was limited to 3,672 dwellings, of which 2,626 were in southern Ireland and 1,046 in the north. The target was only met in 1933 although the Trust survived until 1987. Unemployment was to prove higher among ex-servicemen in southern Ireland than in the rest of the United Kingdom owing to Sinn Féin's pressure on employers not to hire them, while cottages and smallholdings were vandalised. There were also many instances of intimidation and murder, at least 120 ex-servicemen being killed in the south between 1919 and 1924.[40]

With the failure of the domestic settlement scheme, imperialists such as Milner and Leo Amery, appointed as Colonial Secretary and Under-Secretary respectively in January 1919, promoted soldier settlement as an imperial policy. In April 1919 it was announced that free passage to the dominions would be granted for ex-servicemen and their dependants for a year from January 1920, the deadline subsequently extended to March 1923. In all, some 37,199 ex-servicemen accompanied by 48,828 dependants took up the free passage option, accounting for 12 per cent of British emigration to the Empire between 1919 and 1922. In fact, fears of dislocation after the war had prompted similar schemes within the dominions themselves.

With additional hopes of reducing rural depopulation, Canada began an assisted colonisation scheme in February 1917 and a Soldier Settlement Act was passed in May 1917. Ex-servicemen from Britain, however, were offered the chance for selective immigration to reinforce homogeneity after the problems experienced with aliens during the war. As a result, there was a revitalised effort under the Soldier Settlement Act of 1919. Under the British and Canadian schemes, almost 25,000 soldier settlers did try agriculture, of whom almost 11,000 or 43 per cent were still on the land in 1931. Moreover, even where the veterans failed, many of the farms were sold to other immigrants. Consequently, soldier settlement in Canada was by no means a total failure.

There was a similar attempt to increase British veteran migration to South Africa in order to restore British numbers after the failure of earlier attempts encouraged by the English-speaking Unionist Party. Afrikaners, however, opposed preference given to ex-servicemen at the expense of poor whites and the South African government was understandably wary of the scheme. Consequently, only 6,064 ex-servicemen and dependants, or 7 per cent of those taking up free passage from Britain, went to South Africa.

A New Zealand scheme was initiated as early as October 1915 under the Discharged Soldier Settlement Act, the government settling just over 9,000 Anzac veterans by 1919–20. The cost aroused much opposition since the state was buying cultivated land at inflated prices when large areas of Crown land remained undeveloped. Some New Zealanders opposed British veteran immigration unless carefully controlled, but only just over 13,000 ex-servicemen and dependants, or 15.5 per cent of the total, went to New Zealand on free passage. As elsewhere, depressed prices hit in the 1920s and government curtailed the acceptance of ex-servicemen unless they were already assured employment and accommodation. A small number of British veterans also settled in Kenya and Southern Rhodesia.[41]

In Australia there were also fears of visible veteran unemployment, especially during the war itself, when it was necessary to maintain voluntary recruitment. There was also concern at disturbances among returned servicemen, as in Melbourne in early 1916, and a desire to get soldiers out of the cities where they might join with organised labour. Queensland experienced disturbances by veterans in 1918 and 1919 and there were also riots during peace celebrations in Adelaide and Melbourne. The allocation of land to 37,000 former Anzacs was of some value in offsetting veteran discontent, even though about half failed to stay the course and returned to urban unemployment once depression hit in the 1930s. The 'Great Ocean Road' in Victoria from Torquay to Warrnambool, completed in 1932, was a public works project for unemployed ex-servicemen. Generally, despite fears that some arriving in Australia were unfit or unemployable, British veterans were welcomed, and the 37,000 ex-servicemen or dependants opting to take free passage to Australia were by far the largest proportion at 43.7 per cent of the total.

Generally, as in Britain, Australian ex-serviceman did not prove as radical as feared. In fact, veterans formed associations such as Legacy to care for war orphans, while there were also organisations for widows and even for bereaved fathers. The Limbless Soldiers' Association was more militant but, generally, radical veterans' organisations, such as the Returned Sailors' and Soldiers' Australian Democratic League (RSSADL) were marginalised through government promotion of the Returned Sailors' and Soldiers' Imperial League of Australia (RSSILA), later the Returned Services League (RSL), which had been formed in June 1916. Some veterans also became involved in right-wing quasi-military organisations like the Australian Protection League, King and Empire Alliance, and White Guard, all of which were seen as potential strike-breaking auxiliaries. Rather similarly, American veterans were relatively conservative, but were successful in obtaining the 'soldier's bonus' after the 1932 'bonus march and camp'.[42]

In France, the veterans or *anciens combattants* developed into a deeply pacifist movement. Disabled servicemen had formed their own association – the Union Nationale des Mutilés et Réformés (UNMR; National Union for the Disabled and Discharged) – in November 1917 with 125 delegates representing 125,000 men. Existing alongside the Union Fédérale (UF; Federal Union), which had been established by UNMR in February 1918, the Union Nationale des Combattants (UNC; National Union of Veterans) came into existence in November 1918. By 1932 the UF had 900,000 members and the UNC some 860,000 members. The national confederation of all such groups, set up with some difficulty in November 1927, claimed 3.4 million members in 1929. Naturally enough, the veterans campaigned vigorously for pension provision. While broadly patriotic, the veterans' groups became associated increasingly with pacifism and, although they did not have any particular political influence, their general dissatisfaction with the nature of the Third Republic prefigured the lack of commitment to the survival of the state in 1940.[43]

Pension deficiencies led to the establishment in Milan of the Association of Mothers and Widows of the Fallen in November 1917, which then campaigned alongside the Action Committee of the War Maimed, Disabled and Wounded. Italian veterans tended to remain outside the mainstream of politics immediately after the war, but this made their grievances ripe for exploitation. Thus, some 57 per cent of the rank and file membership of Mussolini's Fascist Party in 1921 were ex-servicemen. Many of them had served with the Arditi. The 'front generation', however, was not so prominent among the Nazis.[44]

The German government had opposed the emergence of any additional pressure group beyond its own National Committee for War Victims' Care of September 1915, but it was a curious hybrid of a voluntary organisation staffed by civil servants. Having thus set its face against agitation by war victims, the government did not look favourably on either the League of Blinded Soldiers (or Bund), formed in March 1916, or the Economic Association of Disabled Veterans (or Essen League) formed by Hans Adorf in April 1917. Consequently, Erich Kuttner's more radical National Association of Disabled Soldiers and Veterans (or Reichsbund) gathered pace from May 1917 onwards, numbering some 25,000 members by the spring of 1918, and holding a mass rally outside the War Ministry in Berlin in December 1918. With the Reichsbund alleged to be a tool of the Social Democratic Party, rival groups emerged in 1919, with the result that, by 1921, some seven groups existed with a combined membership of 1.4 million. The Reichsbund was still the largest with over 639,000.

The pressure exerted by the groups saw the passing of a National Pension Law in April 1920, but pension arrangements quickly became a victim of the economic collapse, with pension funds being totally exhausted by 1929. The veterans' groups split along political lines. Not surprisingly, the Nazis created a special party section in 1930 to woo the veteran vote, and most were merged into the Nazi party by 1932, becoming the nucleus of the National Socialist Reichsverband in April 1933.

Hitler was himself a product of the 'front generation', having won the Iron Cross, Second Class. Nevertheless, while often depicted as constituting 'institutionalised instability' within the Weimar Republic, the proportion of the 'front generation' who became involved in right-wing politics was small. Although between 70 and 80 per cent of the unemployed in Berlin in 1919–21 were ex-servicemen, German officers fared worst than ordinary soldiers in terms of post-war unemployment and it was they who were more active both in Weimar politics and in shaping the public memory of the war.[45]

Irrespective of the contribution of the 'front generation' to the militarisation of German or Italian politics, all points of reference in post-war Germany and Italy were fixed in relation to the war experience. While the results were less extreme in political terms elsewhere, much the same could be said of post-war Europe as a whole. The way in which the war had ended, and the way in which the peace had been established subsequently in the negotiations at Paris had together left a significant political legacy. Defeated states such as Germany, Austria and Hungary had particular reasons to feel aggrieved. The same, however, was true of some of the nominal victors such as Italy, Greece and China, and of many of those groups, such as the Arabs, who had allied themselves to the Entente in the expectation of achieving a significant measure of self-determination. Moreover, with the withdrawal of the United States into diplomatic isolation almost before the ink on the treaties was dry, policing of the settlement rested upon the increasingly uncertain commitment of Britain and France. That want of commitment in itself reflected, at least in part, the legacy of the war in terms of its psychological impact on policy-makers in London and Paris. In a real sense, however, as a usable past, the war experience had already become almost a mythic one.

Notes and references

1. Herwig, *First World War*, pp.410–11, 417–20, 424–5; Deist, 'Military Collapse', pp.186–207; Strachan, 'Morale of German Army', p.394. For the number of divisions transferred, see 'The Movement of German Divisions to the Western Front, Winter 1917–18', by, respectively, John Hussey, Tim Travers and Giordan Fong in *WH* 4 (1997), pp.213–20; 5 (1998), pp.367–70; and 7 (2000), pp.225–35.

2. J. P. Harris and Niall Barr, *Amiens to the Armistice: The BEF in the Hundred Days Campaign, 8 August to 11 November 1918* (London, 1998), pp.287–301; Deist, 'Military Collapse', pp.186–207; idem, 'Verdeckter Militärstreik im Kriegsjahr

1918?' in Wette, ed., *Krieg des kleinen Mannes*, pp.146–67; Kruse, 'Krieg und Klassenheer', pp.530–61; Bessel, *Germany after First World War*, pp.45–7; Ziemann, 'Fahnenflucht', pp.93–130; Strachan, 'Morale of German Army', pp.383–98; idem, *First World War*, pp.20–1.

3. Feldman, *Army, Industry, and Labor*, pp.144, 407; Sir Frederick Maurice, *The Armistices of 1918* (London, 1943), pp.14–26, 84–7; Richard Crampton, 'Deprivation, Desperation and Degradation: Bulgaria in Defeat', in Hugh Cecil and Peter Liddle, eds, *At The Eleventh Hour: Reflections, Hopes and Anxieties at the Closing of the Great War, 1918* (Barnsley, 1998), pp.255–65; Erik Zürcher, 'The Ottoman Empire and the Armistice of Mudros', ibid., pp.266–75.

4. Ernst Willi Hansen, 'The Military and the Military–Political Breakdown in Germany 1918 and France 1940', in Klaus-Jürgen Müller, ed., *The Military in Politics and Society in France and Germany in the Twentieth Century* (Oxford, 1995), pp.89–109; Ryder, *German Revolution*, pp.119–29.

5. Holger Herwig, *The German Naval Officer Corps: A Social and Political History, 1890–1918* (Oxford, 1973), pp.202–5; Wilhelm Deist, 'Die Unruhen in der Marine, 1917–18', in Deist, ed., *Militär, Staat und Gesellschaft*, pp.165–84; Richard Stumpf, 'Die Matrosenrevolte in Wilhelmshaven, 1918', in Wette, ed., *Krieg des kleinen Mannes*, pp.168–80; Daniel Horn, *Mutiny on the High Seas: The Imperial German Naval Mutinies of World War I*, 2nd edn (London, 1973), pp.94–137, 198–266; Ryder, *German Revolution*, pp.119–29, 140–9; Carsten, *War against War*, pp.112–23.

6. Herwig, *First World War*, pp.440–6; Ryder, *German Revolution*, pp.149–64.

7. Maurice, *Armistices*, pp.27–56, 93–100; Klaus Schwabe, *Woodrow Wilson, Revolutionary Germany, and Peacemaking, 1918–19: Missionary Diplomacy and the Politics of Power* (Chapel Hill, NC, 1985), pp.50–8, 81–117; Arthur Walworth, *America's Moment, 1918: American Diplomacy at the End of World War I* (New York, 1977), pp.32–73; Bullitt Lowry, *Armistice 1918* (Kent, OH, 1996), pp.7–76; idem, 'War Experience and Armistice Conditions: Generals and Politicians', in Cecil and Liddle, eds, *Facing Armageddon*, pp.103–18; idem, 'Pershing and the Armistice', *Journal of American History* 55 (1968), pp.281–91; idem, 'Negotiating and Signing the Armistices', in Cecil and Liddle, eds, *Eleventh Hour*, pp.17–30; Heinz Hagenlücke, 'Germany and the Armistice', ibid., pp.33–51; Nelson, *Land and Power*, pp.53–87; David French, ' "Had We Known How Bad Things Were in Germany, We Might Have Got Stiffer Terms": Great Britain and the German Armistice', in Manfred F. Boemeke, Gerald D. Feldman, and Elisabeth Glaser, eds, *The Treaty of Versailles: A Reassessment after 75 Years* (Cambridge, 1998), pp.69–86; Vincent, *Politics of Hunger*, pp.77–117.

8. Kocka, *Facing Total War*, pp.155–61; Strachan, *First World War*, pp.18–21.

9. Ryder, *German Revolution*, pp.142–9, 177–83, 188–92, 200–7, 212–17, 237–49; Carsten, *War against War*, pp.208–32; Morgan, *Socialist Left*, pp.118–82, 212–40; Nolan, *Social Democracy and Society*, pp.269–300; Ettinger, *Rosa Luxemburg*,

pp.229–46; Robert G. L. Waite, *Vanguard of Nazism: The Free Corps Movement in Post-war Germany, 1918–23* (Cambridge, MA, 1952), pp.17–167; N. H. Jones, *Hitler's Heralds* (London, 1987), pp.249–65; Mosse, *Fallen Soldiers*, pp.167–70; Bessel, 'Mobilisation and Demobilisation', pp.212–22; G. D. Feldman, 'Economic and Social Problems of the German Demobilisation, 1918–19', *JMH* 47 (1975), pp.1–47; Cole, 'Transition to Peace', pp.196–226; Dick Geary, 'Revolutionary Berlin, 1917–20', in Wrigley, ed., *Challenge of Labour*, pp.24–50; Martin Geyer, 'Munich in Turmoil: Social Protest and the Revolutionary Movement, 1918–19', ibid., pp.51–71; Wolfram Wette, 'Demobilisation in Germany, 1918–19: The Gradual Erosion of the Powers of the Soldiers' Councils', ibid., pp.176–95.

10. Herwig, *First World War*, pp.364–73, 433–6; Zeman, *Break-up*, pp.134–46; Plaschka, 'Army and Internal Conflict', pp.338–53; Gunther Rothenberg, 'The Collapse of the Central Powers in World War I: The Case of Austria-Hungary', in Titus, ed., *Home Front and War*, pp.57–66; Wawro, 'Morale in Austro-Hungarian Army', pp.399–412.

11. Zeman, *Break-up*, pp.217–45; Arthur May, *The Passing of the Habsburg Empire, 1914–18*, 2 vols (Philadelphia, NJ, 1966), II, pp.760–805; Herwig, *First World War*, pp.433–40; Lowry, *Armistice*, pp.101–16; Rauchensteiner, *Tod des Doppeladlers*, pp.533–53; Shafelt, *Secret Enemy*, pp.193–210; G. H. Cassar, *The Forgotten Front: The British Campaign in Italy, 1917–18* (London, 1998), pp.185–218; Maurice, *Armistices*, pp.87–90; Márton Farkas, 'The Military Collapse of the Austro-Hungarian Monarchy, October 24 to November 3, 1918', in Peter Pastor, ed., *Revolutions and Interventions in Hungary and its Neighbour States, 1918–19* (Boulder, CO, 1988), pp.11–23; Mark Cornwall, 'Austria-Hungary', in Cecil and Liddle, eds, *Eleventh Hour*, pp.285–300.

12. Arno Mayer, *Politics and Diplomacy of Peacemaking: Containment and Counter-revolution at Versailles, 1918–19* (New York, 1967), pp.521–603, 716–72, 827–52; Bogdan Krizman, 'The Belgrade Armistice of 13 November 1918', *Slavonic and East European Review* 48 (1970), pp.67–87; Mária Ormos, 'The Hungarian Soviet Republic and Intervention by the Entente', in B. K. Király, Peter Pastor and Ivan Sanders, eds, *Essays on World War I: Total War and Peacemaking, A Case Study on Trianon* (New York, 1982), pp.131–44; Gabor Vermes, 'Hungarian Politics and Society on the Eve of Revolution', in Pastor, ed., *Revolutions and Interventions*, pp.107–22; Helen Gabor, 'The Hungarian Revolution and Austrian Revolutions', ibid., pp.201–10; Ignác Romsics, 'The Social Basis of the Communist Revolution and the Counter-revolution in Hungary', ibid., pp.157–68; G. E. Torrey, 'The Romanian Intervention in Hungary', ibid., pp.301–20 [also in Torrey, *Romania*, pp.366–86]; F. L. Carsten, *Revolution in Central Europe, 1918–19* (Berkeley, CA, 1972), pp.239–47; Pastor, 'Home Front in Hungary', pp.131–4; Zsuzsa L. Nagy, 'Budapest and the Revolutions of 1918 and 1919', in Wrigley, ed., *Challenge of Labour*, pp.72–86; Ignác Romsics, 'The Hungarian Peasantry and the Revolutions of 1918–19', ibid., pp.196–214; András Siklós, *Revolution in Hungary and the Dissolution of the Multinational*

State, 1918 (Budapest, 1988), pp.38–64; Tibor Hájdu, *The Hungarian Soviet Republic* (Budapest, 1979), pp.11–22, 92–104, 153–69.

13. Becker, *Great War and French People*, pp.316–22; Kennedy, *Over Here*, pp.231–2; Peter Liddle, 'Britons on the Home Front', in Cecil and Liddle, eds, *Eleventh Hour*, pp.68–83; Allain Bernède, 'The French', ibid., pp.84–107; Mark Derez, 'Belgium: A Soldier's Tale', ibid., pp.108–41; Ashley Elkins, 'Australians at the End of the Great War', ibid., pp.157–80; Adrian Gregory, *The Silence of Memory: Armistice Day, 1919–46* (Oxford 1994), pp.64–7.

14. Steven A. Schuker, 'The End of Versailles', in Gordon Martel, ed., *The Origins of the Second World War Reconsidered: The A. J. P. Taylor Debate after Twenty-five Years* (Boston, 1986), pp.49–72; Gordon Martel, 'The Revisionist as Moralist: A. J. P. Taylor and the Lessons of History', ibid., pp.1–16; Klaus Hildebrand, *Das vergangene Reich: Deutsche Aussenpolitik von Bismarck bis Hitler, 1871–1945* (Stuttgart, 1995), pp.383–412; Alan Sharp, *The Versailles Settlement: Peacekeeping in Paris, 1919* (London, 1991), pp.19–41, 194–6; Antony Lentin, 'What Really Happened at Paris?', *Diplomacy and Statecraft* 1 (1990), pp.264–75; Marc Trachtenberg, 'Versailles after Sixty Years', *JCH* 17 (1982), pp.487–506; Michael Howard, 'The Legacy of the First World War', in Robert Boyce and Esmonde M. Robertson, eds, *Paths to War: New Essays on the Origins of the Second World War* (London, 1989), pp.33–54; Lloyd C. Gardner, 'The United States, the German Peril and a Revolutionary World: The Inconsistencies of World Order and National Self-determination', in Schröder, ed., *Confrontation and Co-operation*, pp.263–80; Arthur Walworth, *Wilson and His Peacemakers: American Diplomacy at the Paris Peace Conference, 1919* (New York, 1986), pp.23–39; Michael G. Fry, 'British Revisionism', in Boemeke, Feldman and Glaser, eds, *Treaty of Versailles*, pp.565–601.

15. Lloyd E. Ambrosius, *Woodrow Wilson and the American Diplomatic Tradition: The Treaty Fight in Perspective* (Cambridge, 1987), pp.1–14; idem, *Wilsonian Statecraft: Theory and Practice of Liberal Internationalism during World War I* (Wilmington, DE, 1991), pp.1–33; idem, 'The Orthodoxy of Revisionism: Woodrow Wilson and the New Left', *Diplomatic History* 1 (1977), pp.199–214; Schwabe, *Woodrow Wilson*, pp.393–402; Walworth, *Wilson and Peacemakers*, pp.1–5; N. Gordon Levitt, *Woodrow Wilson and World Politics: America's Response to War and Revolution* (New York, 1968), pp.123–82; Thomas J. Knock, *To End All Wars: Woodrow Wilson and the Quest for New World Order* (New York, 1992), pp.48–69, 111–15; idem, 'Wilsonian Concepts and International Realities at the End of the War', in Boemeke, Feldman and Glaser, eds, *Treaty of Versailles*, pp.111–29; William R. Keylor, 'Versailles and International Diplomacy', ibid., pp.469–505; Manfred F. Boemeke, 'Woodrow Wilson's Image of Germany, the War-guilt Question, and the Treaty of Versailles', ibid., pp.603–14.

16. Erik Goldstein, *Winning the Peace: British Diplomatic Strategy, Peace Planning, and the Paris Peace Conference, 1916–20* (Oxford, 1991), pp.9–89, 123–46, 150–86, 190–225; idem, 'The Foreign Office and Political Intelligence, 1918–20', *Review*

of International Studies 14 (1988), pp.275–88; idem, 'British Peace Aims and the Eastern Question: The P.I.D. and the Eastern Question, 1918', *Middle Eastern Studies* 23 (1987), pp.419–36; idem, 'Great Britain: The Home Front', in Boemeke, Feldman and Glaser, eds, *Treaty of Versailles*, pp.147–66; Antony Lentin, 'Several Types of Ambiguity: Lloyd George at the Paris Peace Conference', *Diplomacy and Statecraft* 6 (1995), pp.223–51; Michael Dockrill and J. D. Goold, *Peace Without Promise: Britain and the Peace Conference, 1919–23* (London, 1981), pp.17–30, 87–93, 143–50, 181–6; Michael Dockrill and Zara Steiner, 'The Foreign Office at the Paris Peace Conference in 1919', *IHR* 2 (1980), pp.56–86; Michael Dockrill, 'The Foreign Office Political Intelligence Department and Germany in 1918', in Dockrill and French, eds, *Strategy and Intelligence*, pp.160–83; idem, 'The British Empire and the Peace Conferences, 1919–23', *The Historian* 42 (1994), pp.3–8; Alan Sharp, 'Some Relevant Historians: The Political Intelligence Department of the Foreign Office, 1918–20', *Australian Journal of Politics and History* 34 (1989), pp.170–88.

17.   Mayer, *Policy and Diplomacy of Peacemaking*, pp.78–87; Stevenson, *French War Aims*, pp.89–137; idem, 'French War Aims and Peace Planning', in Boemeke, Feldman and Glaser, eds, *Treaty of Versailles*, pp.87–109; Georges Henri-Soutou, 'The French Peacemakers and their Home Front', ibid., pp.167–88; Charles L. Mee, *The End of Order: Versailles, 1919* (London, 1980), pp.54–6; Nelson, *Land and Power*, pp.111–19; Walter A. McDougall, 'Political Economy versus National Sovereignty: French Structures for German Economic Integration after Versailles', *JMH* 51 (1979), pp.4–23.

18.   Antony Lentin, *Lloyd George, Woodrow Wilson and the Guilt of Germany: An Essay in the Pre-history of Appeasement* (Leicester, 1984), pp.66–80, 84–104, 128–38; Klaus Schwabe, 'Germany's Peace Aims and the Domestic and International Constraints', in Boemeke, Feldman and Glaser, eds, *Treaty of Versailles*, pp.37–67; Fritz Klein, 'Between Compiègne and Versailles: The Germans on the Way from a Misunderstood Defeat to an Unwanted Peace', ibid., pp.203–20; Sally Marks, 'Smoke and Mirrors: In Smoke-filled Rooms and the Galerie des Glaces', ibid., pp.337–70; W. A. Coupe, 'German Cartoonists and the Peace of Versailles', *History Today* 32 (1982), pp.46–53; Peter Krüger, 'German Disappointment and Anti-western Resentment, 1918–19', in Schröder, ed., *Confrontation and Co-operation*, pp.323–35; J. F. Willis, *Prologue to Nuremberg: The Politics and Diplomacy of Punishing War Criminals of the First World War* (Westport, CN, 1982), pp.65–86, 98–112, 126–63; Dockrill and Goold, *Peace Without Promise*, pp.69–80.

19.   Sally Marks, 'The Myths of Reparations', *CEH* 11 (1978), pp.231–55; eadem, 'Smoke and Mirrors', pp.337–70; eadem, 'Reparations Reconsidered: A Reminder', *CEH* 2 (1969), pp.356–65; Sharp, *Versailles Settlement*, pp.77–101; Hardach, *First World War*, pp.246–8, 289–90; Kaiser, *Politics and War*, pp.354–62; Lentin, *Lloyd George, Wilson and Guilt*, pp.11–29, 48–53; Goldstein, *Winning Peace*, pp.237–40; Steven A. Schuker, *The End of French Predominance in Europe: The Financial Crisis of 1924 and the Adoption of the Dawes Plan* (Chapel Hill, NC,

1976), pp.3–56, 232–82, 359–73; idem, *American 'Reparations' to Germany, 1919–33: Implications for the Third-World Debt Crisis* (Princeton, NJ, 1988), pp.14–46, 106–8; idem, 'American "Reparations" to Germany, 1919–33', in G. D. Feldman, ed., *Die Nachwirkungen der Inflation auf die deutsche Geschichte, 1924–33* (Munich, 1985), pp.335–84; idem, 'Finance and Foreign Policy in the Era of the German Inflation: British, French and German Strategies for Economic Reconstruction after the First World War', in Otto Büsch and G. D. Feldman, eds, *Historische Prozesse der Deutschen Inflation, 1914–24: Ein Tagungsbericht* (Berlin, 1978), pp.343–62; idem, 'Origins of American Stabilisation Policy in Europe: The Financial Dimension, 1918–24', in Schröder, ed., *Confrontation and Cooperation*, pp.377–408; Peter Krüger, *Deutschland und die Reparationen 1918–19: Die Genesis de Reparationsproblems in Deutschland zwischen Waffenstillstand und Versailles Friedensschluss* (Stuttgart, 1973), pp.41–51; idem, 'Das Reparationsproblem der Weimarer Republik in fragwürdiger Sicht', *Vierteljahrshefte für Zeitgeschichte* 29 (1981), pp.21–47; idem, 'Die Reparationen und das Scheitern einer deutschen Verständigungspolitik auf der Pariser Friedenskonferenz im Jahre 1919', *Historische Zeitschrift* 221 (1975), pp.326–72; Maier, *Recasting Bourgeois Europe*, pp.249–53, 293–387; Niall Ferguson, 'The Balance of Payments Question: Versailles and After', in Boemeke, Feldman and Glaser, eds, *Treaty of Versailles*, pp.401–40; Bunselmayer, *Cost of War*, pp.35–51, 75–120, 126–44, 149–70; Carl-Ludwig Holtfrerich, *The German Inflation, 1914–23: Causes and Effects in International Perspective* (New York, 1986), pp.136–54; Marc Trachtenberg, *Reparation in World Politics: France and European Economic Diplomacy, 1916–23* (New York, 1980), pp.29–97, 193–223, 337–42; idem, 'Reparation at the Paris Peace Conference', *JMH* 51 (1979), pp.24–55; David Felix, 'Reparation Reconsidered with a Vengeance', *CEH* 4 (1971), pp.171–9; Bruce Kent, *The Spoils of War: The Politics, Economics and Diplomacy of Reparations, 1918–32* (Oxford, 1989), pp.17–140; Jon Jacobson, 'The Reparation Settlement of 1924', in G. D. Feldman, Carl-Ludwig Holtfrerich, Gerhard Ritter and P. C. Witt, eds, *Konsequenzen der Inflation* (Berlin, 1989), pp.79–108.

20. Hardach, *First World War*, pp.237–45; Soutou, *'L'Or et le sang'*, pp.478–568, 766–94, 836–43; Walworth, *Wilson and Peacemakers*, pp.511–27; Goldstein, *Winning Peace*, pp.192–204; Schuker, 'Origins of American Stabilisation', pp.377–408; Elisabeth Glaser-Schmidt, 'German and American Concepts to Restore a Liberal World Trading System after World War I', in Schröder, ed., *Cooperation and Confrontation*, pp.353–76; Trachtenberg, *Reparation in World Politics*, pp.1–27; Elisabeth Glaser, 'The Making of the Economic Peace', in Boemeke, Feldman and Glaser, eds, *Treaty of Versailles*, pp.371–99.

21. Antony Lentin, *The Versailles Peace Settlement: Peacemaking with Germany* (London, 1991), pp.7–8, 20; idem, 'The Treaty That Never Was: Lloyd George and the Abortive Anglo-French Alliance of 1919', in Judith Loades, ed., *The Life and Times of David Lloyd George* (Bangor, 1991), pp.115–28; Goldstein, *Winning Peace*, pp.233–7; Dockrill and Goold, *Peace Without Promise*, pp.34–9; J. C. King, *Foch versus Clemenceau: France and German Dismemberment, 1918–19* (Cambridge,

MA, 1960), pp.1–27, 61–4, 73–104; William Keylor, 'The Rise and Demise of the Franco-American Guarantee Pact, 1919–21', *Proceedings of the Annual Meeting of the Western Society for French History* 15 (1978), pp.367–77; Sally Marks, 'Ménage à trois: the negotiations for an Anglo-French-Belgian Alliance in 1922', *IHR* 4 (1982), pp.524–52; Walter A. McDougall, *France's Rhineland Diplomacy, 1914–24: The Last Bid for a Balance of Power in Europe* (Princeton, NJ, 1978), pp.17–32; Robert McCrum, 'French Rhineland Policy at the Paris Peace Conference, 1919', *HJ* 21 (1978), pp.623–48; Nelson, *Land and Power*, pp.198–281; Steven A. Schuker, 'The Rhineland Question: West European Security at the Paris Peace Conference of 1919', in Boemeke, Feldman and Glaser, eds, *Treaty of Versailles*, pp.275–312.

22. Sally Marks, *Innocent Abroad: Belgium at the Paris Peace Conference of 1919* (Chapel Hill, NC, 1981), pp.137–54, 170–254, 384–402; Dockrill and Goold, *Peace Without Promise*, pp.39–43; Nelson, *Land and Power*, pp.312–20; David Stevenson, 'Belgium, Luxembourg and the Defence of Western Europe, 1914–20', *IHR* 4 (1982), pp.504–23.

23. Lentin, *Versailles Peace Settlement*, pp.17–19; Sharp, *Versailles Settlement*, pp.118–24; Kai Lundgreen-Nielsen, *The Polish Problem at the Paris Peace Conference: A Study of the Policies of the Great Powers and the Poles, 1918–19* (Odense, 1979), pp.58–88, 357–414; idem, 'The Mayer Thesis Reconsidered: The Poles and the Paris Peace Conference, 1991', *IHR* 7 (1985), pp.68–102; Piotr S. Wandycz, 'The Polish Question', in Boemeke, Feldman and Glaser, eds, *Treaty of Versailles*, pp.313–35; idem, 'Dmowski's Policy at the Paris Peace Conference: Success or Failure?', in Paul Latawski, ed., *The Reconstruction of Poland, 1914–23* (London, 1992), pp.117–32; Anna M. Cienciala, 'The Battle of Danzig and the Polish Corridor at the Paris Peace Conference of 1919', ibid., pp.71–94; Dockrill and Goold, *Peace Without Promise*, pp.113–18; Goldstein, *Winning Peace*, pp.259–65; Nelson, *Land and Power*, pp.145–97, 321–62; E. Gregory Campbell, 'The Struggle for Upper Silesia, 1919–22', *JMH* 42 (1970), pp.361–85; Walworth, *Wilson and Peacemakers*, pp.255–76; 321–34.

24. Stephen D. Kertész, 'The Consequence of World War I: The Effects on East Central Europe', in Király, Pastor and Sanders, eds, *Essays on World War I*, pp.39–58; Káraly Vigh, 'The Causes and Consequences of Trianon: A Re-examination', ibid., pp.59–88; Winston S. Churchill, *The World Crisis: The Aftermath* (New York, 1929), pp.231–2; D. Kelly, 'Woodrow Wilson and the Creation of Czechoslovakia', *EEQ* 26 (1992), pp.185–207; Nelson, *Land and Power*, pp.282–311; Wandycz, *France and Eastern Allies*, pp.49–74; I. J. Lederer, *Yugoslavia at the Paris Peace Conference: A Study in Frontier-making* (New Haven, CN, 1963), pp.117–83, 218–45; S. D. Spector, *Romania at the Paris Peace Conference: A Study of the Diplomacy of Ioan Bratianu* (New York, 1962), pp.125–53, 167–90, 201–34, 251–77.

25. Crampton, 'Deprivation, Desperation and Degradation', pp.263–4; Kaiser, *Politics and War*, pp.367–70; Walworth, *Wilson and Peacemakers*, pp.468–84;

Alan Sharp, 'Britain and the Protection of Minorities at the Paris Peace Conference', in A. C. Hepburn, ed., *Minorities in History* (London, 1978), pp.170–80; Frank Koszorus, 'The Forgotten Legacy of the League of Nations Minority Protection System', in Király, Pastor and Sanders, eds, *Essays on World War I*, pp.547–72; Mark Levene, 'Nationalism and its Alternatives in the International Arena: The Jewish Question at Paris, 1919', *JCH* 28 (1993), pp.511–31; Carole Fink, 'The Minorities Question at the Paris Peace Conference: The Polish Minority Treaty, June 28, 1919', in Boemeke, Feldman and Glaser, eds, *Treaty of Versailles*, pp.249–74; Nelson, *Land and Power*, pp.282–311; Wandycz, *France and Eastern Allies*, pp.75–103.

26. Burgwyn, *Legend of Mutilated Victory*, pp.221–41, 269–83, 150–4, 303–9, 313–21; René Albrecht-Carrié, *Italy at the Paris Peace Conference*, 2nd edn (Hamden, CN, 1966), pp.114–52, 184–232; Goldstein, *Winning Peace*, pp.265–9; Lederer, *Yugoslavia*, pp.54–80; Sharp, *Versailles Settlement*, pp.139–41.

27. Douglas Dakin, *The Unification of Greece* (New York, 1972), pp.201–28; N. Petsalis-Diomidis, *Greece at the Paris Peace Conference, 1919* (Thessaloniki, 1978), pp.63–6, 200–27; Leontarritis, *Greece and First World War*, pp.367–95; Sharp, *Versailles Settlement*, pp.165–75; Goldstein, *Winning Peace*, pp.242–51; idem, 'Britain and Greater Greece', pp.339–56; P. C. Helmreich, *From Paris to Sèvres: The Partition of the Ottoman Empire at the Paris Peace Conference of 1919–20* (Columbus, OH, 1974), pp.83–106, 153–78, 230–41, 291–338; A. E. Montgomery, 'The Making of the Treaty of Sèvres of 10 August 1920', *HJ* 15 (1972), pp.775–87; Justin McCarthy, *Muslims and Minorities: The Population of Ottoman Anatolia and the End of the Empire* (New York, 1983), pp.117–44.

28. H. D. Hall, 'The British Commonwealth and the Founding of the League Mandate System', in Bourne and Watt, eds, *Studies in International History*, pp.345–68; Lowe, 'Australia in the World', pp.125–48; A. J. Crozier, 'The Establishment of the Mandates System, 1918–25: Some Problems Created by the Paris Peace Conference', *JCH* 14 (1979), pp.483–515; Dockrill and Goold, *Peace Without Promise*, pp.64–8, 150–79; Louis, *Great Britain and Germany's Lost Colonies*, pp.77–155; Sharp, *Versailles Settlement*, pp.178–84; Hughes, *Allenby and British Strategy*, pp.113–48; Jeffery, *British Army and Crisis of Empire*, pp.31–51, 75–95, 133–54; Charles Townshend, *Britain's Civil Wars* (London, 1986), pp.85–99, 134–9; Thomas Mockaitis, *British Counter-insurgency, 1919–60* (London, 1990), pp.63–99; Jide Osuntokun, 'Great Britain and the Final Partition of the Cameroons, 1916–22', *Afrika Zamani* 6/7 (1977), pp.53–71; Peter Yearwood, '"In a Casual Way with the Blue Pencil": British Policy and the Partition of Kamerun, 1914–19', *Canadian Journal of African Studies* 27 (1993), pp.218–44; idem, 'Britain and Repartition', pp.316–41; Brian Digre, *Imperialism's New Clothes: The Repartition of Tropical Africa, 1914–19* (New York and Berne, 1990), pp.157–72; Nish, *Alliance in Decline*, pp.263–76, 305–18, 368–82.

29. Walworth, *Wilson and Peacemakers*, pp.359–76; Gilbert, *First World War*, pp.509–10; Naoko Shimazu, 'Detached and Indifferent: the Japanese Response', in

Cecil and Liddle, eds, *Eleventh Hour*, pp.224–34; Paul Lauren, 'Human Rights in History: Diplomacy and Racial Equality at the Paris Peace Conference', *Diplomatic History* 2 (1978), pp.257–78.

30. Jaffe, *Decision to Disarm Germany*, pp.84–107, 120–64, 195–213; Philip Towle, *Enforced Disarmament: From the Napoleonic Campaigns to the Gulf War* (Oxford, 1997), pp.69–87, 94–110, 238–45; Dockrill and Goold, *Peace Without Promise*, pp.43–5; Goldstein, *Winning Peace*, pp.146–9.

31. Walworth, *Wilson and Peacemakers*, pp.106–24, 528–56; Sharp, *Versailles Settlement*, pp.42–64; Herbert F. Margulies, *The Mild Reservationists and the League of Nations Controversy in the Senate* (Columbia, MO, 1989), pp.137–260; Lentin, *Lloyd George, Wilson and Guilt*, pp.46–8; Hugh Cecil, 'Lord Robert Cecil and the League of Nations during the First World War', in Liddle, ed., *Homes Fires and Foreign Fields*, pp.69–82; Dockrill and Goold, *Peace Without Promise*, pp.56–63; George W. Egerton, *Britain and the Creation of the League of Nations: Strategy, Politics and International organisation, 1914–19* (Chapel Hill, NC, 1978), pp.24–43, 63–80, 110–69; idem, 'Ideology, Diplomacy and International Organisation: Wilsonism and the League of Nations in Anglo-American Relations', in B. J. C. McKercher, ed., *Anglo-American Relations in the 1920s: The Struggle for Supremacy* (London, 1991), pp.17–54; idem, 'Britain and the "Great Betrayal": Anglo-American Relations and the Struggle for United States Ratification of the Treaty of Versailles, 1919–20', *HJ* 21 (1978), pp.885–911; idem, 'The Lloyd George Government and the Creation of the League of Nations', *AHR* 72 (1974), pp.419–44; Peter Yearwood, '"On the Safe and Right Lines": The Lloyd George Government and the Origins of the League of Nations, 1916–18', *HJ* 32 (1989), pp.131–55; William Laird Kleine-Ahlbrandt, *The Burden of Victory: France, Britain and the Enforcement of the Versailles Peace, 1919–25* (Lanham, MD, 1995), pp.95–109, 115–29, 265–77; Antoine Fleury, 'The League of Nations: Towards a New Appreciation of its History', in Boemeke, Feldman and Glaser, eds, *Treaty of Versailles*, pp.507–22.

32. Lloyd C. Gardner, *Safe for Democracy: The Anglo-American Response to Revolution, 1913–23* (New York, 1984), pp.233–56; Kennedy, *Over Here*, pp.350–6; John M. Thompson, *Russia, Bolshevism, and the Versailles Peace* (Princeton, NJ, 1966), pp.62–130, 309–21, 325–46; Walworth, *Wilson and Peacemakers*, pp.125–39, 234–54; Dockrill and Goold, *Peace Without Promise*, pp.118–25; Fritz Klein, 'Krieg–Revolution–Frieden, 1914–20', *Zeitschrift für Geschichtswissenschaft* 28 (1980), pp.544–54.

33. Strachan, *First World War*, p.6; Wrigley, 'Impact of First World War on British Labour Movement', pp.151–9; idem, 'Labour and the Trade Unions', in K. D. Brown, ed., *The First Labour Party, 1906–14* (London, 1985), pp.129–57; M. Savage, *The Dynamics of Working Class Politics: The Labour Movement in Preston, 1880–1940* (Cambridge, 1987), pp.163–71; Horne, *Labour at War*, pp.218–301; Duncan Tanner, *Political Change and the Labour Party, 1900–18* (Cambridge, 1990), pp.317–37, 378–81; idem, 'The Parliamentary Electoral System,

the "Fourth" Reform Act and the Rise of Labour in England and Wales',
BIHR 56 (1983), pp.205–19; Cronin, *Politics of State Expansion*, pp.61–4, 426–
42; Turner, *British Politics*, pp.52–3, 317–32, 390–436; Ross McKibbin, *The
Evolution of the Labour Party, 1910–24* (Oxford, 1974), pp.43–7, 72–87, 178–82;
Jay Winter, 'Trade Unions and the Labour Party in Britain', in Wolfgang
Mommsen and H. G. Husung, eds, *The Development of Trade Unionism in Great
Britain and Germany, 1890–1914* (London, 1985), pp.359–70; Pugh, 'Domestic
Politics', in Constantine, Kirby and Rose, eds, *First World War in British His-
tory*, pp.9–28; idem, *Making of Modern British Politics*, pp.176–81, 193–9, 210–
16; H. C. G. Matthew, R. McKibbin and J. A. Kay, 'The Franchise Factor in
the Rise of the Labour Party', *EHR* 91 (1976), pp.723–52; E. David, 'The
Liberal Party Divided, 1916–18', *HJ* 13 (1970), pp.509–32.

34. J. O. Stubbs, 'The Impact of the Great War on the Conservative Party', in
     Gillian Peele and Chris Cook, eds, *The Politics of Reappraisal, 1918–39* (Lon-
     don, 1975), pp.14–38; Turner, *British Politics*, pp.18–37, 332–3, 434–6, 447;
     Pugh, *Electoral Reform*, pp.175, 183–4; Andrew Taylor, 'Conservative Elec-
     toral Strategy, Creating Political Stability and the Advent of Mass Democ-
     racy, 1914–18', in Dockray and Laybourn, eds, *Representation and Reality*,
     pp.126–51.

35. Horne, *Labour at War*, pp.95–6, 223–4, 350–94; idem, 'Comité d'Action',
     pp.241–79; Jean-Louis Robert, 'Co-operatives and the Labour Movement in
     Paris during the Great War', in Fridenson, ed., *French Home Front*, pp.280–
     316; Jean-Louis Robert, 'Mobilising Labour and Socialist Militants in Paris
     during the Great War', in Horne, ed., *State, Society and Mobilisation*, pp.73–88;
     Serge Berstein, 'The Radical Socialist Party during the First World War',
     ibid., pp.37–54.

36. Corner and Procacci, 'Italian Experience of Total War', pp.231–40; Paul
     Corner, 'La mémoire de la guerre et le fascisme italien', in Becker, Winter,
     Krumeich, Becker and Audoin-Rouzeau, eds, *Guerre et Cultures*, pp.329–35;
     Christopher Seton-Watson, *Italy from Liberalism to Fascism, 1870–1925* (Lon-
     don, 1967), pp.504–36, 570–629; Kolko, *Century of War*, pp.161–8; Sullivan,
     'Caporetto', pp.76–8; Adamson, 'Impact of World War I on Italian Political
     Culture', pp.308–29.

37. Jeffery, 'Post-war Army', pp.212–31; Rothstein, *Soldiers' Strikes*, pp.30–5, 91–
     9; S. R. Graubard, 'Military Demobilisation in Great Britain following the
     First World War', *JMH* 19 (1947), pp.297–311.

38. Englander and Osborne, 'Jack, Tommy and Henry Dubb', pp.593–621; David
     Englander, 'Troops and Trade Unions, 1919', *History Today* 37 (1987), pp.8–
     13; idem, 'Die Demobilmachung in Grossbritannien nach dem Ersten
     Weltkrieg', *Geschichte und Gesellschaft* 9 (1983), pp.195–210; idem, 'Military
     Intelligence and Defence of Realm', pp.24–32; idem, 'The National Union of
     Ex-Servicemen and the Labour Movement, 1918–20', *History* 76 (1991), pp.24–
     42; Stephen R. Ward, 'Intelligence Surveillance of British Ex-servicemen,

1918–20', *HJ* 16 (1973), pp.179–88; idem, 'Great Britain: Land Fit for Heroes Lost', in Stephen R. Ward, ed., *The War Generation: Veterans of the First World War* (Port Washington, NY, 1975), pp.10–37; idem, 'The British Veterans' Ticket of 1918', *JBS* 8 (1968), pp.155–69; Bourke, *Dismembering the Male*, pp.124–70; Leese, 'Problems Returning Home', pp.1055–67; Niall Barr, 'The British Legion after the Great War: Its Identity and Character', in Taithe and Thornton, eds, *War*, pp.213–33; Gregory, *Silence of Memory*, pp.51–61, 93–114; J. G. Dony, 'The 1919 Peace Riots in Luton', *Bedfordshire Historical Record Society* 57 (1978), pp.205–33; De Groot, *Haig*, pp.403–4; Niall Barr and Gary Sheffield, 'Douglas Haig, the Common Soldier and the British Legion', in Bond and Cave, eds, *Haig*, pp.223–39.

39. Winter, *Experience of World War*, p.213; F. S. Lyons, *Ireland since the Famine* (London, 1971), pp.414–15; Charles Townshend, *Britain's Campaign in Ireland, 1919–21: The Development of Political and Military Policies* (Oxford, 1975), pp.25, 45–6, 64, 75, 94, 102, 110–12, 209–12; Angela Gaffney, *Aftermath: Remembering the Great War in Wales* (Cardiff, 1998), pp.158–9.

40. Kent Fedorowich, *Unfit for Heroes: Reconstruction and Soldier Settlement in the Empire between the Wars* (Manchester, 1995), pp.25–37; Leah Leneman, *Fit for Heroes: Land Settlement in Scotland after World War I* (Aberdeen, 1989), pp.1–37; Carol A. Lockwood, 'From Soldier to Peasant? The Land Settlement Scheme in East Sussex, 1919–39', *Albion* 30 (1998), pp.439–62; Murray Fraser, *John Bull's Other Homes: State Housing and British Policy in Ireland, 1883–1922* (Liverpool, 1996), pp.240–71; Johnson, *Land Fit for Heroes*, pp.347–51; F. H. A. Aalen, 'Homes for Irish Heroes: Housing under the Irish Land (Provision for Sailors and Soldiers) Act, 1919 and the Irish Soldiers' and Sailors' Land Trust', *Town Planning Review* 59 (1988), pp.305–23; Jane Leonard, 'Facing "The Finger of Scorn": Veterans' Memories of Ireland after the Great War', in Martin Evans and Ken Lunn, eds, *War and Memory in the Twentieth Century* (Oxford, 1997), pp.59–72; eadem, ' "Getting Them at Last": The IRA and Ex-servicemen', in David Fitzpatrick, ed., *Revolution? Ireland, 1917–23* (Dublin, 1999), pp.118–29.

41. Fedorowich, *Unfit for Heroes*, pp.37–41, 46–65, 70–106, 115–39, 177–82, 191–8, 200–1; idem, 'The Assisted Emigration of British Ex-servicemen to the Dominions, 1914–22', in Stephen Constantine, ed., *Emigrants and Empire* (Manchester 1990), pp.45–71; J. A. Schultz, 'Finding Homes fit for Heroes: The Great War and Empire Settlement', *CJH* 18 (1983), pp.99–110; C. J. D. Duder, 'Beadoc: The British East Africa Disabled Officers' Colony and the White Frontier in Kenya', *Agricultural History Review* 40 (1992), pp.142–50; idem, ' "Men of the Officer Class": The Participants in the 1919 Soldier Settlement Scheme in Kenya', *African Affairs* 92 (1993), pp.69–87; J. M. Powell, 'Soldier Settlement in New Zealand, 1915–23', *Australian Geographical Studies* 9 (1971), pp.144–60; idem, 'The Debt of Honour: Soldier Settlement in the Dominions, 1915–40', *Journal of Australian Studies* 5 (1980), pp.64–87.

42. Beaumont, 'Anzac Legend', pp.149–80; Winter, 'Communities in Mourning', pp.325–55; Chris Coulthard-Clark, *Soldiers in Politics: The Impact of the Military*

on Australian Political Life and Institutions (St Leonard's, 1996), pp.149–54, 163–76; White, 'War and Australian Society', pp.401–2; Marilyn Lake, 'The Power of Anzac', in McKernan and Browne, eds, *Australia*, pp.194–222; eadem, *The Limits of Hope: Soldier Settlement in Victoria, 1915–38* (Melbourne, 1987), pp.11–25, 36; eadem, *A Divided Society* (Melbourne, 1975), pp.145–53, 172–5; Oliver, *War and Peace*, pp.133–63; J. Templeton, 'Set up to Fail? Soldier Settlers in Victoria', *Victorian Historical Journal* 59 (1988), pp.42–50; K. Fry, 'Soldier Settlement and the Australian Agrarian Myth after the First World War', *Labour History* 48 (1985), pp.29–43; Raymond Evans, '"Some Furious Outbursts of Riot": Returned Soldiers and Queensland's "Red Flag" Disturbances, 1918–19', *W&S* 3 (1985), pp.75–98; David Hood, 'Adelaide's First "Taste of Bolshevism": Returned Soldiers and the 1918 Peace Day Riots', *Historical Society of South Australia* 15 (1987), pp.42–53; Thomson, *Anzac Memories*, pp.118–28; Fedorowich, *Unfit for Heroes*, pp.144–90; idem, '"Society Pets and Morning Coated Farmers": Australian Soldier Settlement and the Participation of British Ex-servicemen, 1915–29', *W&S* 8 (1990), pp.38–56; Barry Smith, 'What if Australia had not participated in the Great War? An Essay on the Costs of War', in Craig Wilson and Janice Aldridge, eds, *The Great War: Gains and Losses – Anzac and Empire* (Canberra, 1995), pp.179–95; Joy Damousi, *The Labour of Loss: Mourning, Memory and Wartime Bereavement in Australia* (Cambridge, 1999), pp.46–102; Donald J. Lisio, 'The United States: Bread and Butter Politics', in Ward, ed., *War Generation*, pp.38–58.

43. Winter, 'Communities in Mourning', pp.342–4; Antoine Prost, *In the Wake of War: 'Les Anciens Combattants' and French Society, 1914–39* (Oxford, 1992), pp.30–41, 65–9, 83–93, 131–5, 137–47; Robert Soucy, 'France: Veterans' Politics between the Wars', in Ward, ed., *War Generation*, pp.59–103.

44. Lagorio, 'Italian Widows', pp.175–98; Michael A. Ledeen, 'Italy: War as a Style of Life', in Ward, ed., *War Generation*, pp.104–34; Sullivan, 'Caporetto', p.77.

45. Bessel, *Germany After the First World War*, pp.254–84; idem, 'The Great War in German Memory: The Soldiers of the First World War, Demobilisation and Weimar Political Culture', *German History* 6 (1988), pp.20–34; idem, 'Unemployment and Demobilisation in Germany after the First World War', in R. J. Evans and Dick Geary, eds, *The German Unemployed: Experiences and Consequences of Mass Unemployment from the Weimar Republic to the Third Reich* (London, 1987), pp.23–43; idem, 'The Front Generation and the Politics of Weimar Germany', in Mark Roseman, ed., *Generations in Conflict: Youth Revolt and Generation Formation in Germany, 1770–1968* (Cambridge, 1995), pp.121–36; Whalen, *Bitter Wounds*, pp.83–105, 117–29, 131–9, 167 79; James M. Diehl, 'Germany: Veterans' Politics under Three Flags', in Ward, ed., *War Generation*, pp.135–86; idem, 'Victors or Victims? Disabled Veterans in the Third Reich', *JMH* 59 (1987), pp.705–36; Cole, 'Transition to Peace', pp.196–226.

CHAPTER TWELVE

Wastelands?

The popular images of the Great War endure in part because of the way in which so many British schoolchildren are introduced to the war through a highly selective reading of a profoundly misleading literary legacy. In many respects, however, the collective memory of war was shaped from the beginning by the existing predilections of differing European cultures. It also evolved according to the events of the inter-war period. Such collective memory can be interpreted as a shared myth, often deriving from personal narratives, which both created and preserved the consensual interpretation of the war. Indeed, the most familiar 'war books' associated with the Great War are the memoirs distanced from events often by a decade or more. Such reflection on events represented a remembered war rather than a record of immediacy and created a myth of war experience that shaped the consensus of what the war had been like.

The myth of the war that arose in Britain was of a lost generation slaughtered in a futile war directed by the old, who had lied to the young. Thus, the survivors became disillusioned, embittered, and separated not only from the past but from their cultural inheritance. At the same time, in Germany, a different war myth was intended to displace the reality of war and defeat, a cult of the fallen soldier being consciously developed to strengthen the appeal of nationalism. Thus, the memory of war became a weapon against those German politicians perceived to have betrayed the nation by making peace in 1918.[1]

The means by which such myths of the war were transmitted were largely cultural and there is little doubt of the significance of the war for European cultural output. Over 2,000 poets had their work published in Britain during the war, with over 3,000 individual volumes of poetry published. A catalogue of the anthologies and volumes collected by Birmingham Public

Libraries already listed 1,200 different titles by 1921. Similarly, a French bibliography in 1927 listed 250 poetry volumes and a German bibliography of 1920 some 450 volumes of poetry. One calculation, indeed, is that 1.5 million poems were published in Germany in August 1914 alone. Novelists, playwrights, artists, composers, sculptors and architects equally contributed to the cultural legacy, over 800 such individuals being killed in the war.[2]

Yet, it should not be assumed that all of these victims of the war were equally talented, or that they were of one mind in their response to the war. Too often, indeed, it is accepted that poets, novelists and artists promoted a uniformly anti-war message. Moreover, it is also frequently asserted that, since traditional modes of linguistic and artistic representation proved inadequate to the task, the experience of modern mechanised war could only be expressed through 'modernist' forms. Increasingly, however, historians have pointed to the continuities in the usage of traditional cultural forms in shaping reactions to the war. As in other respects, however, this aspect of the myth of the war has proved highly resistant to historical revisionism. Indeed, there are still powerful factors at work, not least cinema, television and popular historiography, which perpetuate the considerable gap between myth and reality.

Memory and commemoration

Part of the difficulty with respect to the persistence of a mythic version of the war is that its memory was a 'usable past' from the beginning. Thus, in Germany, the 'cult of the fallen' assisted the resurrection of the ideal of the fatherland under Weimar. Even more German war memorials, which tended to have rather more aggressive statuary than normal in Britain and France, were erected under the Nazis after 1933. Langemarck had already proved a potent myth of fallen youth called forth to inspire a new Germany and, after 1918, in the words of George Mosse, 'the dead came truly alive'.[3]

Equally, the memory of the war dead served differing purposes in Britain. Bob Bushaway has argued that the symbolism of sacrifice was intended to inhibit serious criticism of post-war social and political structures. Thus, national commemoration elevated the war experience beyond critical analysis into a strange, almost mystical area in which war was neither celebrated nor condemned. Overall, indeed, the annual rituals of commemoration are 'the most obvious annual reaffirmation of British national identity'.

At a more local level, commemoration of the dead could serve differing purposes. In the case of one prominent Norwich Baptist killed in Palestine, for example, local Free Churches chose to commemorate Christian liberal

virtues such as faith, social service and voluntarism rather than more militaristic virtues. In the Lancashire town of Bury, the 'six VCs before breakfast'
won by 1st Battalion, The Lancashire Fusiliers, at Cape Helles, Gallipoli, in
April 1915, also became a potent myth. The Unionist candidate, Captain
Charles Ainsworth, who had served at Gallipoli, unseated the sitting Liberal
in 1918 and held the seat until he retired undefeated in 1935 in an area not
normally kind to Unionists. Church, grammar school OTC, old comrades
and local Territorials, albeit less successfully, all played a role in Gallipoli
Sunday, the nearest to 25 April, rivalling Armistice Day in significance. The
myth died with large-scale Commonwealth immigration into Bury after the
Second World War, the death of the last survivors and the disappearance of
the regiment, but Gallipoli Sunday survives with a modern emphasis on all
those fusiliers who have died in action.

Memorialising the dead, however, was not always used for overtly political purposes. It can be noted that, in Wales, the use of the Welsh language
was not an issue in commemoration. Indeed, Welsh memorials have frequent reference to England as an interchangeable symbol for Britain and its
Empire. It was simply not regarded as incompatible with Welsh identity.
Moreover, commemoration was one of the few links between employers
and employees on the south Wales coalfield not affected by industrial strife
in the inter-war years.[4]

It has also been argued that the myth of the war helped stifle dissent from
the point of view of Canada's political leadership while being consolatory
or explanatory. There was a search for a positive memory and the desire to
believe in a just war that had unified the nation. A broad consensus emerged
as to how the history of the war ought to be told. Much of the Canadian
response, indeed, was summed up by John McCrae's celebrated wartime
poem *In Flanders Fields*, with its call to honour the sacrifice of the dead and
to 'take up our quarrel with the foe'. In the process, the Canadian Expeditionary Force became the embodiment of the nation itself, the assimilationist
myth of the war defining Canadian citizenship in the 1920s and 1930s and
largely excluding immigrants, natives and French Canadians.[5]

In Australia and New Zealand, Anzac Day became a particularly important event given the difficulty for relatives in visiting distant graves. Anzac
Day had originated during the war partly as a recruiting device. Interest in
Anzac Day was waning in some areas when it was revived in the mid-1920s
as a 'popular patriotic pageant' by the RSSILA, which found it convenient
to draw attention to veterans' issues. All Australian states had adopted it by
1927 as an official public holiday despite opposition from Labor activists
and frequent debates as to whether public houses and places of gambling
or entertainment should be closed. There was another revival of interest
in Anzac Day in the 1980s, although it has also become simultaneously a

focus for opposition by feminists and Aborigines since it is still seen by some as divisive.[6]

Commemoration proved a particularly difficult concept for the Irish Free State, which preferred to forget that so many southern Irishmen had fought in the British army. Indeed, war losses were not deemed relevant to the new Ireland, and Irish culture was generally distanced from the war. A temporary cenotaph was erected at College Green in Dublin as an Irish National War Memorial in 1919, but, in 1924, the Free State government objected to a scheme to convert Merrion Square into a permanent war memorial park since it would be directly opposite the seat of government. A memorial arch in Phoenix Park was also vetoed in 1928 and, eventually, a memorial park designed by Sir Edwin Lutyens was created in 1929 at the distant Islandbridge. It was not formally opened, however, as intended in the spring of 1939 owing to the international situation. It remains incomplete though part of the original design was accomplished in 1994. In the words of Malcolm Smith, it was a 'telling tribute to the strength of the war memorial as a symbol of British identity' when the Provisonal IRA chose to bomb the memorial in Enniskillen on Remembrance Sunday in November 1987.[7]

While the emphasis thus far has been upon the political usage of commemoration, it should not be forgotten that it was also an attempt to give meaning to mass death and its emotional traumas. Greater meaning was given to sacrifice through the shrines of national worship erected in each state. It should be noted, however, that there was a contrast evident in both Britain and, especially, France between the wish to commemorate the dead at a national level and the desire of many families that soldiers' remains should be returned to their localities and not interred in war cemeteries at the front.[8]

Care of German war graves was vested in 1919 in the hands of the private association, Volksbund Deutsche Kriegsgräberfürsorge (German League for the Care of War Graves), although control of German cemeteries in France and Flanders did not pass into German hands until 1966, since it was the responsibility of every nation to care for the war dead on its own soil under provisions of the Versailles treaty. German war cemeteries tended to be stark, usually just a centralised monument such as a simple Iron Cross over a mass grave without individual headstones. Some, indeed, were so-called *Totenburgen* (fortresses of the dead), which remained the preference of the Nazis in the Second World War. Natural surroundings, however, were also important in linking with the ideal of landscape and, especially, the forest in German thought. Often, therefore, a *Heldenhain* (heroes' groves) of trees as a 'space within nature' took the place of headstones arranged around an oak or a boulder.

Some Germans identified commemoration with the lily-aster but, generally, the Volksbund contrasted the British penchant for poppies and cemetery flower beds with the 'tragic-heroic' spirit of German cemeteries. On the Italian front, the mountains themselves became symbolic of German identification with a pre-industrial spirit. Medieval symbols were frequently used on German memorials, commonly the Archangel Michael as representative of Germany slaying a dragon. The 'brutal edge' to the cult of the fallen in Germany was also characterised by use of classical semi-nude figures. Modernist symbols were rarely employed and those created by Ernst Barlach for some memorials were subsequently removed by the Nazis.[9]

While the British adoption of the poppy was a pastoral gesture in the association between death and renewal in nature, British war cemeteries also made a conscious link between the dead and Christian sacrifice. The 'silent cities' were an unprecedented imposition of the authority of the Empire and state over the rights of the citizens through the refusal to countenance repatriation of the dead. It made the collective cultural impact of the dead all the greater as did the uniformity of the cemeteries.

Non-repatriation originated with Fabian Ware, whose Red Cross mobile unit became the official war graves registration organisation in March 1915. Ware's organisation underwent several name changes before emerging as the Imperial War Graves Commission in May 1917. Conscious of the greater democratic mood of Britain at war, Ware forbade private exhumations in March 1915 and personalised monuments in May 1916. Increasingly convinced that all should be equal in death, Ware also directed in November 1917 that there should be no distinction between officers and men.

By 1930, some 891 British cemeteries had been completed on the Western Front with over 540,000 headstones. There was some pressure for separate memorials, which the Commission was unable to resist. Thus, one commemorated the Indian contribution, and this was followed by the construction of an Ulster Memorial Tower. The dominions similarly created their own national monuments on the Western Front. Large monuments also commemorated the missing, including the Menin Gate at Ypres, which was unveiled in July 1927, and that at Thiepval on the Somme, unveiled in August 1932. Initially, the British had favoured leaving the ruins of the Cloth Hall and cathedral in Ypres as a permanent memorial, a view not shared by the Belgians, who rebuilt both. At the Menin Gate, however, at the suggestion of the local chief of police, the Last Post was sounded at sundown between July and October 1928. It was revived in May 1929 and has been sounded continuously ever since except during German occupation in the Second World War. Similar cemeteries and memorials were constructed in Egypt, Gallipoli, Macedonia, Mesopotamia and east Africa.[10]

In Britain itself, there were memorials to the missing of the Royal Navy, Royal Air Force and the Merchant Navy, but there were also two national shrines, namely the Tomb of the Unknown Warrior in Westminster Abbey and the Cenotaph in Whitehall. The idea of the Cenotaph (Greek for empty tomb) originated in discussions as to a suitable saluting point in honour of the dead for the victory parade planned for Peace Day on 19 July 1919. Sir Alfred Mond, First Commissioner of Works, rejected Lord Curzon's idea of a catafalque similar to that intended for a parade in Paris as 'purely Catholic'. Mond therefore asked Lutyens to suggest a design. Lutyens had already designed a proposed replacement for a temporary war shrine in Hyde Park in August 1918 and now came up with a simple abstract form based on classical Greek designs, which he characterised as a cenotaph.

Originally just wood and plaster, the Cenotaph made a considerable impact at the victory parade. Almost immediately, there was considerable support for making it a permanent structure given the near universal belief that it represented a necessary and special point for commemoration, especially for those who could not afford to visit the resting places of their relatives abroad. Consequently, the Cenotaph was re-erected as a permanent shrine for Armistice Day in November 1920, some 400,000 people visiting it in just three days. The Cenotaph quickly became closely associated with the concept of the returning dead, being the subject of the 'psychic photography' of Mrs Emma Deane in 1922 and of a celebrated painting, Will Longstaff's *The Immortal Shrine*, in 1928: Longstaff did a similar 'spiritualist' painting of the Menin Gate in the same year.[11]

The Tomb of the Unknown Warrior also became a focus for pilgrimage in its own right. The concept originated at the suggestion of the Dean of Westminster in October 1920 as a result, in turn, of an idea put to him by the Reverend David Railton, MC. The French, however, had already mooted a similar idea in September 1919, when its emulation had been supported by the *Daily Express* and promoted by the Comrades of the Great War. On 9 November 1920, therefore, four bodies of unidentified soldiers were exhumed from the main British battlefields in France and Flanders and one selected. That chosen was transferred to England and interred in Westminster Abbey. Large crowds lined the route from Dover to London. At least 40,000 people passed through the Abbey on the first day and it is conceivable that 1.2 million visited the Abbey by the time the grave was closed on 18 November. A commemorative edition of the *Daily Mail* sold a record 1.9 million copies for a single issue.

A similar entombment took place beneath the Arc de Triomphe in Paris on the same day as the ceremony in London, the body chosen from eight unidentified soldiers taken from representative French battlefields. At the same time, the heart of Léon Gambetta, who had inspired the defence of France in 1871, was temporarily removed from the Panthéon to lie opposite the Unknown Warrior during the ceremony. An eternal flame was then lit under the Arc on 11 November 1923. Unknown Warriors were also interred in Washington, Brussels, Rome and Lisbon in 1921. In Germany, 20 Unknown Warriors were interred at Tannenberg in 1927 at a monument which actually commemorated Hindenburg's victory rather than the fallen. Another Unknown Warrior was interred at the eighteenth century guardhouse known as the Neue Wache in Berlin in 1931 and Munich followed suit. By 1930 there were also unknown soldiers entombed in Austria, Bulgaria, Czechoslovakia, Greece, Hungary, Poland, Romania and Yugoslavia. While Australia and New Zealand originally accepted the tomb in London to represent their own unknown soldiers, Australia brought home a body for its own Hall of Memory at the Australian War Memorial in Canberra as late as 11 November 1993. In time, however, there was a rather more unseemly aspect to the ritual exchange of each country's highest military decorations as honours for the others' unknown soldiers. Moreover, Mussolini was to make the tomb in Rome a site for fascist ceremony and Hitler began to refer to himself as the unknown soldier. Soviet Russia had no equivalent tomb until 1967 and that tomb commemorated the Second World War rather than the First.[12]

Such national shrines were the focus for activity with the concomitant concept of Armistice Day. In Britain, Armistice Day was observed by the Silence. This originated with the suggestion of a former High Commissioner in South Africa, Sir Percy Fitzpatrick, based on the model of the three minutes' silence customarily observed in South Africa during the war at noon each day. Fitzpatrick saw it as a symbol of integration and unity, embracing the bereaved and veterans, but also providing a lesson for children for the future. Endorsed by the War Cabinet, it was publicised as a personal request by King George V on 7 November for the first anniversary of the armistice in four days' time. Serving as both public and private commemoration, it was an immense success and was then made a central part of the unveiling of Cenotaph and the commitment of the body of the Unknown Warrior the following year.

Armistice Day became a common choice for the unveiling of town and parish memorials through the 1920s, although by no means exclusively so. Some of the early Armistice Days were also the focus for protest by unemployed ex-servicemen, as in Liverpool and Dundee in 1921. Interestingly, however, in the early 1920s, Armistice Day was also regarded as a day of festivity by some ex-servicemen's groups. The resulting public controversy led in 1925 to the cancellation of the former annual Victory Ball in the Albert Hall. Its replacement in 1926 was a performance of a requiem by John Foulds for war charities and, then, in 1927, the first Festival of Remembrance sponsored by the *Daily Express*. The first programme was broadcast by the BBC simultaneously to the Empire as a whole; the festival continues to this day.

The poppy was closely connected with Armistice Day and Remembrance. It was inspired in part by McCrae's poem, but also by the example of Moina Michael, who had persuaded American servicemen to adopt the poppy, artificial ones being manufactured for the benefit of children in devastated areas of France and Flanders. In August 1921, Madame Guerin, who organised the manufacture of the poppies in France, suggested to the British Legion that the same could be done in Britain, and the first Poppy Day was held on 11 November 1921. The Legion began making its own poppies rather than buying them from France in 1922. It added to the concept of commemoration the idea of an obligation to the living, as well as that of obligation to the dead, since the proceeds benefited disabled veterans.[13]

Armistice Day remained of great significance throughout the inter-war period. The annual crowd was usually over 20,000 and the ceremony was broadcast by the BBC from 1928 onwards, even being shown on the infant television service in 1937. It was partially observed during the Second World War, becoming Remembrance Sunday in 1946. Remembrance Sunday did not have the emotive power of Armistice Day, following a very different kind of war experience. However, the Silence was observed once again on 11 November itself in 1995, and more and more people have done so each year since.

Armistice Day became similarly fixed in France in November 1922, but as a national holiday. Veterans had led an outcry when the French government initially tried to fix it for the nearest Sunday. All Saints Day (1 November) had also become associated with commemoration and remembrance in France during the war itself. In Germany the Volksbund campaigned for a national memorial day close to Easter, but there was no agreement among the differing German Churches and states. Consequently, both 1 August and 11 November were used until the Nazis fixed a single Heroes' Memorial Day in 1934.[14]

While the national shrines provided a focus for commemoration at home, it was possible for some of the bereaved to visit the cemeteries and battlefields overseas. Indeed, there was to be an increasing number of sponsored pilgrimages to the battlefields after the war. A certain tension existed, however, between pilgrimage and tourism although, in many respects, secularism and religion met on battlefields such as the Ypres Salient and Verdun, which had taken on an almost sacred symbolism. Moreover, both tourism and pilgrimage generally increased in Europe after the war, pilgrimage to locations such as Lourdes and Walsingham also becoming more popular. Battlefield tourism was not unknown prior to the First World War, Waterloo being a particularly popular tourist venue throughout much of the nineteenth century. The most frequent visitors to the battlefields and cemeteries were the bereaved coming to terms with their loss, or ex-servicemen confronting their past. Indeed, the British Legion organised the largest pilgrimage of all in August 1928. A five-day visit by some 11,000 people culminated in a memorial service at the Menin Gate while others travelled independently so that an estimated 20,000 attended the service, which was also broadcast by the BBC.

Inspired by the American Legion pilgrimage to France in 1927, the British Legion's pilgrimage was also consciously promoted in 1928 as part of the 'conservative reconstruction' of the memory of war. Clearly, it did fill a need and, if individuals could not visit a cemetery personally, then organisations such as the St Barnabas Society, founded in Britain by the Reverend M. Millineaux in 1919, would place wreaths on graves for relatives. The Society also helped organise pilgrimages, as did the Salvation Army, the Ypres League and the Empire Service League, although this market was taken over by commercial companies such as Thomas Cook in the late 1920s. A slightly different aspect of pilgrimage was evinced by at least 76 British communities adopting around 100 villages and towns in France in the 1920s and 1930s in an early twinning process.

There was considerable tourist activity between 1919 and 1922 followed by a lull, and then a revival between 1927 and 1932, possibly as a result of the unveiling of the Menin Gate. Ypres proved popular but so, too, did Zeebrugge, which had a museum devoted to the British raid of April 1918, other naval events, and German atrocities, such as the execution of Charles Fryatt. Certain graves became attractions, such as those of John McCrae and the Irish constitutional nationalist MP William Redmond, as well as the relatively few sites where trenches were left untouched. Some felt that Ypres in particular had become too commercialised by the 1930s, with over 150 premises selling beer to tourists. Thomas Cook and other companies such as Pickfords did well from the battlefield trade and at least thirty guidebooks were published in English between 1919 and 1921 alone. The Michelin guides to battlefields published for motorists, of which 1.4 million had been sold by 1922, are still widely available. French and Belgian civilians, meanwhile, profited from selling objects made from shell cases and other wartime debris, such 'trench art' having been originally produced by the troops themselves during the war. Verdun became a similar magnet for French pilgrims and tourists and Tannenberg for Germans. The visitors' book at the Menin Gate recorded 60,000 visitors as late as 1937.[15]

More distant battlefields were difficult to reach and attracted less interest though some did go to Gallipoli and Palestine, the St Barnabas Society organising pilgrimages to the former in 1926 and to Jerusalem in 1927.

Both Gallipoli and Palestine were even more significant for Australians and New Zealanders. For the dominions, however, France and Flanders was equally a distant 'holy land' of pilgrimage. Distance added to the popularity of exhibitions of war relics in Canada and Australia, and Longstaff's painting, *The Menin Gate at Midnight*, was purchased for Australia and widely seen on a national tour in 1928 and 1929. A reunion of the Canadian Expeditionary Force in Toronto in 1934 attracted 100,000 ex-servicemen while 8,000 Canadians made the trip for the unveiling of Walter Allward's memorial on Vimy Ridge by King Edward VIII in July 1936. The first Australian pilgrimage, again in response to that of the American Legion to France, was in July and August 1929, about 100 people taking in Gallipoli, Palestine and the Western Front. About 400 veterans attended the unveiling of the Australian memorial at Villers Bretonneux in July 1938.

The American Legion pilgrimage to France in September 1927 embraced no less than 25,000 men and their families, crossing the Atlantic on fifteen liners. There was a mass parade down the Champs Elysées, which shocked many of the watching French by its near-carnival spirit, itself a reflection that the war had not been the same traumatic experience for the United States. Three years later, Congress authorised the expenditure of US$5 million to send mothers to visit their sons' graves, some 6,000 accepting the invitation and the first contingent of 234 going to France in May 1930.[16]

At the purely local level, commemoration was principally accomplished by the erection of war memorials, which complemented the official face of national remembrance, and were the more essential as a visible representation of grief and a reminder of the dead entombed in foreign fields.[17] In nearly all cases, British war memorials reflected traditional forms, guided by local choices and what Catherine Moriarty has characterised as the local 'market forces of materials and labour'. They were also expected to be of interest for the increasing number of leisure motorists in a curious link of technology, consumerism and memory in their density and visibility within the British urban landscape.

The memorial movement had in essence begun during the war itself with the compilation of local rolls of honour and, often, the erection of street shrines which tended to be promoted by more Catholic-minded Anglican clergy. Most post-war memorials were the work of local committees. Although meant to be representative, committees were often composed of local worthies, but they did usually consult the wider community, which was both paying for the memorial and wished to help shape its form. Such local committees were by no means consistent in the choices they made, commemoration being often a matter of local civic pride and, therefore, of intense debate. In Wales, for example, a Welsh National War Memorial was unveiled at Cathays Park in Cardiff in 1928 as a result of its promotion by the Cardiff-based *Western Mail*. Many of the authorities in north Wales, however, favoured a local rather than a 'Welsh' initiative and subscribed instead to the North Wales Heroes' Memorial, a commemorative archway to the university college in Bangor.

Sometimes, there was a choice made between a memorial and providing some form of community benefit such as a community hall or a hospital, as at Watford, or a hospital extension, as in Islington. Some villages in Cumberland even proposed installing electricity as a memorial. Other communities created rolls of honour. Some memorials, on the other hand, had no physical existence, being instead funds applied to a variety of individual or community purposes. Where a utilitarian monument was chosen, it could sometimes serve what Alan Borg has characterised as a passive purpose, such as a clocktower. Choices might also be influenced by local political or other rivalries, as in that between two leading local Unionist politicians in Stoke Newington, or between religious denominations as over a lych-gate memorial at Brompton in Yorkshire.

It has been argued by Alex King that the whole practice of commemoration was fundamentally political in terms of the involvement of local political institutions, the press and other organisations. Often, however, there was an underlying concern that, with a utilitarian monument, the dead would be forgotten. Communal acts of remembrance, therefore, tended to stress the need for remembrance, and community leaders often emphasised the value of sacrifice. Generally, however, memorials were cheaper than halls and hospital extensions and this factor should not be ruled out, one committee member at Barry in south Wales pointedly remarking, 'It seems strange that bricks and mortar should be so dear, and life so cheap.' Indeed, it needs to be recognised that commemoration was a profitable business for many. Charles Sargeant Jagger consciously set out to make his name as a sculptor with the Royal Artillery Memorial at Hyde Park Corner. Similarly, architects, who designed most of the memorials, often used architectural competitions, where these were organised, to increase their standing. At the other end of the scale, monumental masons competed in offering standard designs to local communities.

The most common method of raising money for the erection of memorials was by public subscription, sometimes by house to house collections, though occasionally individuals donated the bulk of the funds needed. Lotteries, which were illegal, were employed in some places such as Deptford and Stoke Newington. Most memorials were unveiled between 1920 and 1925 – one of the last appears to have been at Mumbles near Swansea in July 1939 – in remarkably similar ceremonies. These were invariably reported as displaying an un-English emotion, linking private grief and public remembrance though it was sometimes apparent that the bereaved were marginalised or alienated by the experience. Just as Armistice Day has been revived in Britain so, too, has the erection of war memorials, principally as a result of the activities of the Western Front Association, which has raised funds for several memorial projects in both Britain and France and Flanders since its foundation in 1980.[18]

A very few British communities were the 'thankful' or 'golden' villages, those which had lost none of their men in the war. A total of 36 such villages, which put up commemorative memorials of one kind or another, were listed in 1993 but the ongoing work of the National Inventory of War Memorials at the Imperial War Museum has revealed at least two more. Examples are Cayton near Scarborough, where all 43 men came back, and Meldon in Northumberland.[19]

French and Belgian monuments had less uniformity than those in Britain. In Belgium, three or four monuments were being unveiled every week between 1921 and 1924, but the only truly national memorial was an equestrian statue of King Albert erected near the sluices at Nieuwport, which had been opened in 1914 to flood the coastal area. The Flemish Tower in Diksmude reflected national divisions and, indeed, it was blown up in mysterious circumstances after the Second World War. Similarly, during the war, a Committee for the Yser Pilgrimages had made headstones available to soldiers for use by their comrades when the dead men's families were often in occupied Belgium. Few of these were retained by the families after the war and the Walloon-dominated government incensed Flemish groups by using the surplus for roadmaking.

In France, the debate over repatriation of bodies was even more intense than in Britain. No decision was made during the war and some bodies were clearly retrieved by the bereaved, leading to a prohibition on private exhumation and burials in November 1918. It did not work and, in September 1920, the government permitted the bereaved to reclaim bodies and transport them home at state expense. In all, by 1923, about 300,000 bodies or approximately 40 per cent were returned home though it was not always a smooth process, with parents' rights often triumphing over those of widows.

French war cemeteries and memorials also tended to the bizarre, such as the Trench of Bayonets at Verdun, supposedly where a French infantry company was buried alive by German bombardment, leaving their bayonets sticking above the earth. A memorial paid for by an American banker was created in 1920 some distance from the original supposed location. National ossuaries for the remains of the unidentified were also created at four representative sites that had become regarded as sacred battlefields, namely Douaumont for Verdun, Lorette in Artois, Dormans on the Marne, and Hartmanwillerkopf in Alsace. Douaumont contains the remains of 130,000 men.

There were also over 36,000 local memorials erected between 1916 and 1926, usually situated in cemeteries and many the work of the sculptor Maxime Réal del Sarte. As in Britain, commemoration was a business enterprise subject to local committee decisions and architectural competitions, though over 900 communes chose the factory-reproduced *Combattant victorieux* (victorious warrior).

Wider issues could be addressed by memorials. On Guadeloupe, for example, the drive to create war memorials was an affirmation of 'Frenchness' in that there was a fear that the island might be sold to the United States. In Alsace-Lorraine, the problem presented itself that some of the dead had fought, whether unwillingly or not, for the German army and not the French. The solution tended to be composite memorials combining themes of victory, sacrifice, memory and local identity. More often than not, they were destroyed by the Germans during the Second World War. Similarly, the railway carriage at Compiègne, in which the armistice had been signed, and which was set up as a memorial in November 1932, was taken off to Germany after being pressed into use once more by Hitler in June 1940. It was apparently destroyed at the end of the Second World War but was replaced by a replica.[20]

There were still other manifestations of commemoration to be found in museums. In November 1916, C. Reginald Grundy, editor of the art magazine *Connoisseur*, had suggested establishing local war museums in every major British centre to 'enable future generations to visualise the experiences, hopes, fears, disappointments and triumphs of the conflict'. The issue was raised in Parliament in February 1917, but appeared to receive little government support. Within a few weeks, however, the War Cabinet announced the creation of a National War Museum on 5 March 1917, partly because local museums were beginning to collect war material. The National War Museum, redesignated as the Imperial War Museum in January 1918, was to have the priority in collecting trophies. It opened at the Crystal Palace and received 2.5 million visitors in its first year, but it was poorly organised, with exhibits incongruously arranged among potted plants for many years and larger exhibits left without cover slowly decaying. A Scottish National War Museum was also established and some local museums created memorial galleries such as the Stockport Memorial Art Gallery and the war memorial court extension at Aberdeen. Individuals also sponsored memorial galleries.

Tanks and other war relics were also offloaded to local authorities by the War Office War Trophies Committee. In many ways, it was simply an extension of the 'tank banks' first used in March 1918 to sell additional war bonds. Indeed, at least 262 'presentation tanks' were awarded to those

British towns and villages in 1919 which had been successful in selling national war bonds or war savings certificates. Most went for scrap in the Second World War, including even the original 'Big Willie' prototype tank from Bovington Camp.[21]

Overseas, there were similar war collections. The Canadian War Records Office was established by Sir Max Aitken, later Lord Beaverbrook, in 1915, while the Australians created the Australian War Records Section in May 1917 – the genesis of the Australian War Memorial collection at Canberra – following suggestions by Charles Bean. By contrast, the beginnings of national documentary war collections in Paris, Stuttgart and Frankfurt were private initiatives like that at the University of Cambridge. There was even an anti-war collection begun in Berlin by Ernst Friedrich in 1924.[22]

In many ways, however, as Jay Winter has argued, alongside collective memory there was also what he terms fictive kinship. This was the kind of individual family memory of the war within which loss and bereavement of fathers, sons and husbands, or war wounds and injuries were initially accommodated. Individual memories could be served by medals, commemorative plaques – such as the 'dead man's penny' issued in Britain – or honour scrolls. Local war memorials were a kind of extension of such family accommodations, as were contacts of the bereaved with the dead's unit and comrades, amounting to an 'adoptive kinship'. Family memory was often also reflected in the recounting of war stories and has continued in the form of genealogical investigations, which have become increasingly popular in contemporary Britain.[23]

War and culture

It is apparent that most war memorials followed traditional forms and this very much bears upon the wider debate concerning the impact of the war upon culture. In the past, cultural historians have frequently posited a link between the Great War and modernism, the assumption being that the war marked a distinct break between older values and the 'modern', although there are subtle variations within the general theme that the war represented a clear discontinuity between past and future.

It is Paul Fussell's contention, for example, that the literature emerging from the war established a new pattern of ironical writing, which came to characterise twentieth-century literature as a whole and, especially, subsequent attempts to comprehend the nature of modern conflict. In Fussell's view, the scale of death, the collective trauma and the reduction of individuals to mere ciphers by machine-age modern war defied the expressive power of conventional literature and undermined traditional cultural sensibilities. Primarily, this meant the end of the cadences of 'Georgian' writing in poetry and prose and the 'high diction' of traditional elevated and euphemistic descriptions of war.[24]

Modris Eksteins argues, in some respects, that the war was a product of modernism rather than modernism a product of war. Cultural modernism was a backlash against the rationalisation and materialism of industrial modernity, leading to a cult of the irrational even before 1914 though the war then reinforced it by undermining order and morality. Eksteins also sees the war as something of a cultural clash between Britain, which is characterised as stable and traditional in terms of culture, and Germany, which became the standard bearer of the modern avant-garde and the driving force of the war. Generally, the desire to return to elemental primitivism led the artistic community to welcome the war as liberation and deliverance from past artistic constraints and conventions.[25]

Samuel Hynes argues that there was both continuity and change in terms of British culture as a result of the war, though there was a greater tendency towards the war opening a 'gap' in history, which separated one world of beliefs and values from another. The turning point in Hynes's estimation was 1916 in that artists and writers began to find a viable means of representing a war which had outrun not only traditional forms but, seemingly, modernism as well. The disgust for the horrors of war experienced among intellectuals resulted in a modernist 'counter-culture', which saw the war as the dividing line between innocence and disillusionment. War, therefore, put pre-war cultural innovations to new uses and gave modernism a new moral basis of protest against the war. A new kind of modernism emerged around 1917, which belonged neither to pre-war cultural trends nor to the war years, being associated with largely unknown writers such as James Joyce and T. S. Eliot, who had no direct war experience.[26]

One more variation on the theme is that of Robert Wohl, who identifies the emergence of a 'generational consciousness' by the early twentieth century and the attraction for it of the new cultural trends of the avant-garde. The war represented the opportunity for the regeneration of a dying culture, and though some discovered that they were but cogs in the war machine, others found the experience of war a revelation. Many, therefore, came back feeling that they were better men for the experience, but the war had invested the conflict of the younger and the older generation with new meaning. Many veterans felt the betrayal of their hopes, believing they lived in an 'abyss' between worlds, hence the attraction of political extremism in the post-war world.[27]

This cultural approach to the legacy of the war raises many problems. Most of Fussell's assumptions about the way in which the war was fought, for example, are quite wrong. He is contemptuous of the basic tools of the historian, and what Robin Prior and Trevor Wilson have rightly described as Fussell's 'Alice-in-Wonderland' account is riddled with errors of fact, date and geography. Above all, Fussell subscribes to the view that the generation of 1914 all responded to the war in exactly the same way.[28]

In reality, the war fitted both within the context of cultural existing movements as well as pushing them into newer directions, although often along the imaginative lines pioneered since 1890. Thus, the origins of modernism lie in the pre-war decades and the reaction against the romanticism of the nineteenth century. Imagist poetry by poets such as Ezra Pound, Richard Aldington and T. E. Hulme emerged around 1910. The first issue of Wyndham Lewis's Vorticist journal, *Blast*, was published in June 1914. Arnold Schoenberg's atonal works dated from before the war and, famously, Igor Stravinsky's ballet *The Rite of Spring*, composed for Sergei Diaghilev's company and its *primo uomo* Vaslav Nijinsky, provoked violence at its première in Paris in May 1913. Symbolism had appeared in literature, cubism and expressionism in French and German art, and futurism had been promoted by Filippo Tommasso Marinetti in Italy. Far from seeing themselves as traditionalists, 'Georgians' such as Edward Marsh, Rupert Brooke and Edward Thomas believed they, too, were in the forefront of the new movement in literature and a reaction against the rhetoric of older 'imperialist' poets.

Clearly, pre-war movements such as expressionism, futurism and cubism were primarily influential among the younger generation, who were most likely to be called up for wartime service and to be caught in the initial enthusiasm for war. Futurists, indeed, positively welcomed war from their belief that dynamism and change were to be welcomed as much in life as in art and sculpture. The war, therefore, may have propelled more artists and writers towards new forms of expression and increased the audience for modernism.[29]

At the same time, however, there was often a reaction against modernism as a perceived foreign influence. Moreover, as with the case of war memorials, the war did not mark a total break between one world and another in terms of literature and the arts. Indeed, Jay Winter has argued that the war did not witness the triumph of modernism. Far from representing a cultural discontinuity, the war saw the use of traditional forms in literature, art, music and sculpture and the persistence of the languages of earlier movements such as romanticism and classicism. With respect to commemoration, Winter argues that traditional approaches best suited the requirement of bereavement. Modernist statements in art or literature could express anger, but could not provide a means by which the bereaved could come to terms with loss.

Poetic forms arguably saw most apparent change but what has been characterised as high diction remained the most common linguistic approach to war for most of the English elite, as evinced in amateur poetry and the decidedly anti-modernist approach of the *Poetry Review*, which had been founded in 1912.[30]

Even those regarded as modernist poets embraced elements of the more traditional and pastoral. There is more than a hint of classical romanticism, for example, in some of Siegfried Sassoon's work. The same contrasting effects of war both reinforcing change but also looking backwards is equally true of the poetry of Charles Peguy in France or Rupert Brooke and Julian Grenfell in Britain. Equally, British propaganda agencies primarily mobilised traditional writers such as Thomas Hardy, J. M. Barrie, Henry Newbolt, John Buchan and Kipling to the war effort and not conscious futurists such as D. H. Lawrence, whose *The Rainbow* was officially proscribed in 1915. Well-known 'anti-war' books such as Henri Barbusse's *Under Fire* (1917) or Eric Maria Remarque's *All Quiet on the Western Front* (1929), retained the more traditional descriptive approach usually characterised as realistic rather than ironic. Indeed, much of the literature of the Great War was in essence traditional in being about the separation of the military from the civilian world and, above all, in being as much about bereavement as disillusion.

This was also true of the modernists of the 1920s such as Lawrence, Joyce, Pound and Eliot, who are sometimes regarded as undergoing a parallel literary transformation to the experience of those who actually fought in the war. Thus, Eliot's *The Wasteland* (1922) is often interpreted as a war poem, but it is not about the war itself, rather the post-war consciousness of its effect in creating a 'ruined' world. Indeed, these authors, to quote Arthur Marwick, display 'nothing remotely approaching a one-to-one relationship with the war'.[31]

There is a constant emphasis in cultural approaches to the war upon the literature of disillusionment, which did not actually appear until the period between 1928 and 1935. It needs to be appreciated, therefore, that only a small fraction of the extensive creative writing which emerged from the war actually fits the popular image of anti-war literature. Much of the sum of British war poetry was written by civilians, only one-fifth being the work of combatants, and one-quarter being by women. There is no clear chronological shift from pro- to anti-war poetry and no clear social transformation between older and newer poetic forms. If the war generated more poetry than earlier conflicts, this was largely because of greater literacy. Moreover, most 'anti-war' poetry is actually rather ambiguous, attacking neither the war nor the combat in which the protest poets were engaged. Rather, it was aimed against propaganda and those who manufactured it.[32]

The most popular poet in wartime Britain was John Oxenham whose *Hymn for the Men at the Front* sold 7 million copies. He was followed in terms of popularity by Reverend G. A. Studdert Kennedy ('Woodbine Willie') and Robert Service. By contrast, Wilfred Owen had only four poems published during the war and was unknown to the general public. The first edition of his collected verse appeared in December 1920 with Sassoon's name on the title page as author of the introduction. Only a few hundred copies of Owen's poems had been sold by the end of the 1920s, whereas Rupert Brooke's *1914 and Other Poems* went through twenty-three impressions by 1918 and had sold over 300,000 copies by 1930. Julian Grenfell's *Into Battle* was also extremely popular.

The outbreak of the war was met with considerable nationalistic and heroic poetry among all belligerents and the promotion of what Elizabeth Marsland characterises as 'mass heroism'. Anthologies tend to represent their times. Thus, contemporary wartime anthologies drew on the heroic poets, while it is the later anthologies that drew primarily on the anti-war poets and so reflected a presupposed view of the war. It can be argued that Sassoon and Owen were highly ambivalent about war. Indeed, it has been suggested by Adrian Caesar that Owen and Sassoon, 'for all their supposedly anti-war feeling, in fact express ideas and emotions which excite young and unwary readers, and covertly support war by providing positive consolations based on the idea that suffering is good'. Andrew Rutherford similarly has pointed out that, despite their anti-war poetry, Sassoon and others 'themselves remained committed to the activity which they condemned' as fighting soldiers. In other words, there is a distinct gulf between contemporary and current perceptions of the anti-war poets.[33]

As with poetry, so with novels. The most popular wartime novelists in Britain were Nat Gould and Victoria Cross (Victoria Cory), the former ignoring the war and continuing to produce stories based on hunting and horse racing, and the latter producing sentimental romances. Ernest Raymond's massively popular romantic war novel, *Tell England* (1922), a celebration of middle-class English youth based loosely on his Gallipoli experiences, was so popular that it was reprinted twenty times in two years. Much wartime fiction was patriotic, such as that by Ian Hay (John Hay Beith) and 'Sapper' (Cyril McNeile), both of whom saw active service. Hay's *The First Hundred Thousand* (1915) sold 115,000 copies in Britain and the Empire and a further 350,000 copies in the United States within a year. Its boyish humour not only caught the spirit of the New Armies, but has also been credited with helping to re-establish the sense of national identity in Scottish literature. Drama, too, broke little new ground during the war with most of the output patriotic. As L. J. Collins has remarked, if the theatre 'failed artistically, it was, however, rarely more popular or, given the limitations of the time, productively more popular'.

Post-war fiction about the war continued in the same vein. 'Middle brow' writers such as Robert Keable, A. S. M Hutchinson, Wilfrid Ewart, Gilbert Frankau and Richard Blaker did not hide the horrors of war but stressed traditional values such as comradeship, home and countryside. Their work was characterised by patriotism, vehemence against the enemy, and respect for military traditions, especially those of the regiment. With the exception of *All Quiet on the Western Front*, to quote Hugh Cecil, 'book for book, the British public, over a thirty year period . . . seem to have preferred the patriotic to the disenchanted type of war book'. There were those of a more sombre and questioning nature such as work by Oliver Onions, R. H. Mottram and Ford Maddox Ford. There was little specifically anti-war, however, until after the success of Remarque's book in 1929. Moreover, children's literature, often written by war veterans, continued to display a positive view of the war as justified sacrifice.[34]

Like anti-war poets, a number of the authors of books considered to be anti-war were ambiguous in their attitudes. C. E. Montague's early polemic, *Disenchantment* (1922), was inspired primarily by the harsh terms imposed on Germany at Versailles, which he regarded as an insult to the sacrifices made to achieve victory. Montague later wished that he had used a different title since he was invariably linked with the subsequent anti-war literature when his own text was far more balanced.[35]

The later anti-war literature, which followed the success of *All Quiet on the Western Front*, was equally ambiguous in its response to the war. A good example is the successful play *Journey's End* by R. C. Sheriff. Staged initially for two nights in London in December 1928, it went on to 593 consecutive performances, being staged in 25 languages by end of 1929 and selling over 175,000 copies. Sheriff always maintained that it was a play 'in which not a word was spoken against the war, in which no word of condemnation was uttered by any of its characters'. Sheriff apparently intended it as a means of perpetuating the memory of the fallen. As the *Daily Telegraph* commented at the time, it asked what the war was like, not what it meant. Most who saw the play, however, regarded it as an indictment of the war from its very realism, an effect heightened by its West End producer, Maurice Browne, a pacifist and conscientious objector who had spent the war in the United States, and the director, James Whale. Thus, the play has entered collective memory as a 'literary statement straddling an ambiguous line between con-demnation of war and representation of bygone values'.[36]

In addition to *Journey's End*, a number of other perceived anti-war books proved successful between 1928 and 1931, including Richard Aldington's autobiographical novel *Death of a Hero* (1929); Edmund Blunden's memoir *Undertones of War* (1928), which was reprinted three times in a month; Robert Graves's semi-fictional memoir *Goodbye to All That* (1929); Sassoon's 'not quite autobiographical' trilogy in three volumes, *The Memoirs of a Fox-hunting Man* (1928), *Memoirs of an Infantry Officer* (1930) and *Sherston's Progress* (1936); and V. M. Yeates's flying memoir *Winged Victory* (1934). It is often suggested that such works began appearing ten years after the war because such an interval was needed for reflection. Bruno Schultze, however, has argued that there was as much a political as a psychological influence, the collapse of the Geneva naval disarmament conference in 1927 representing a turning point when both political left and right in Britain reached a broad consensus in recognising the need to prevent future wars. In fact, Sassoon's trilogy and Graves's book, which was clearly influenced by the commercial success of Remarque, were not markedly anti-war and Graves himself did not regard his book, which much embellished and embroidered his experiences, as such.

If it is assumed that most creative writing portrayed the soldier as victim, the best writers recognised that the soldier also inflicted pain. Thus, Frederick Manning's autobiographical novel, *The Middle Parts of Fortune* (1929), published in a bowdlerised version as *Her Privates We* (1930) and which finally appeared in a fully unexpurgated verison under the original title in 1977, depicted the urge to wage war as originating within soldiers themselves. Manning was not as overtly anti-war as it is sometimes assumed. Indeed, he believed that ordinary soldiers had been in effect libelled by other 'war books'. That was a view with which the historians Douglas Jerrold and Cyril Falls, both with wartime service, could heartily agree. Jerrold's *The Lie About the War* (1930) and Falls's *War Books* (1930), attempted, therefore, to demonstrate that the spate of anti-war books had falsified the image of the war and contrived to make it appear that the war had no meaning.[37]

Alongside the anti-war memoirs there were plenty of those who had enjoyed their war and were prepared to acknowledge it. Such memoirs include those by Graham Greenwell and Charles Edmonds (Charles Carrington). Sidney Rogerson's *Twelve Days* (1933) specifically refuted the 'post-war propaganda, piling corpse on corpse, heaping terror on futility', while even Guy Chapman's *A Passionate Prodigality* (1933) reluctantly acknowledged the fascination of war. The self-educated Irish Catholic 'navvy' writer Patrick Macgill, who served in the London Irish Rifles, never wholly lost his positive view of traditional values such as comradeship, courage and self-sacrifice in a series of quasi-autobiographical wartime and post-war works.[38]

About one-quarter of the published British wartime poets were women, while many novels and memoirs were also the work of women writers. Perhaps best known among memoirs, Vera Brittain's *Testament of Youth* (1933) attempted to come to terms with the loss of her brother and his best friend. It fits well into the pattern of anti-war books and assisted in establishing

1 July 1916 as a symbol of tragedy, but Brittain was not as perceptive as sometimes assumed about either the men of whom she wrote or, indeed, her own experience.

As with male writers, however, there were women on both sides of the ideological divide on the war. Some female authors, such as Sheila Kaye-Smith, therefore, displayed a consciousness of the value of duty. Post-war best-selling authors like Rebecca West or Virginia Woolf, however, are primarily of interest for their reliance on what was becoming established as the popular myth of the war. Moreover, women writers were generally likely to transmit myths on the incommunicability of a battle experience they could not share in addition to a kind of 'white feather syndrome' in which they carried a sense of guilt for the lost generation they had urged to enlist.[39]

If women writers were distanced from the war in one way, American writers were distanced in another. The geographical distance from the front lines meant that the war had a different impact on Americans though the rhetoric of Entente propaganda had created the image of a crusade before the United States entered the war. The dominant theme of American war writing, however, was of an end to innocence, and few achieved any real sense of the experience of war until American veteran memoirs began to be published after 1918. To quote Stanley Cooperman, therefore, many early novelists, like Edith Wharton or Willa Cather, characterised the war experience 'as something of a cross between the Alamo and Bunker Hill'.

The American poet Alan Seeger, killed while serving with the French Foreign Legion in July 1916, was comparable to Rupert Brooke in his patriotic response to a war which he enjoyed. The wartime literature of patriotism was succeeded, however, by post-war novels by non-combatants such as F. Scott Fitzgerald and William Faulkner, which viewed the war as tragic waste. There was certainly a sense of alienation in John Dos Passos's *Three Soldiers* (1921). Ernest Hemingway also repudiated war in his novel set on the Italian front, *A Farewell to Arms* (1929), which it might be noted contains a wholly imaginary account of Caporetto since he himself only reached Italy in June 1918 and saw no major action.[40]

It is highly suggestive that much of the literature of disillusionment stemmed from the phenomenal success of Eric Maria Remarque's *Im Westen nichts Neues* (literally, Nothing New on the Western Front), translated by Arthur Wheen into English as *All Quiet on the Western Front* in 1929. Having first appeared in serialised form, the book sold 2.5 million copies in 25 languages within 18 months. Indeed, Remarque's book became the best known of all anti-war books, William Faulkner writing of its perception in the United States that, 'America has been conquered not by the German soldier that died in French and Flemish trenches, but by the German soldier that died in German books'. It inspired many others such as Graves to try their hand at the genre and Remarque himself followed it with two more novels, *The Road Back* (1931) and *Three Comrades* (1937).

Though ostensibly autobiographical, *All Quiet on the Western Front* is not an authentic record of war experience. Edmund Blunden, for example, questioned many of Remarque's details of military life, calling the book 'piddling, lying rubbish'. Indeed, conscripted in November 1916, Remarque (born Erich Paul Remarque) reached the front only in June 1917 and was seriously wounded by British shelling on 31 July 1917. He spent almost a year recovering and was passed fit for active duty just four days before the armistice. Remarque proclaimed in the preface to his book, a line repeated at the start of the subsequent film, that he wanted to tell 'of a generation of men, who, even though they may have escaped its shells, were destroyed by the war'. In fact, the book is really a reflection not on the war itself but on the memory of the war and the confused reaction of Remarque and the rest of the 'front generation' in the Weimar Republic to that memory ten years on.

Certainly, the book set the pattern of the anti-war genre in portraying the alienation of the front-line soldier from civilian society amid a brutal mechanistic warfare over which he could have no control. Remarque's equation of his suffering and the war struck a chord with the popular sense of Germany's suffering as a legacy of the war. Probably most read by veterans and youths, it suggested a universality of experience.[41]

In Germany, both political left and political right condemned the book. The left condemned it because Remarque did not indict the ruling elite or encourage a revolutionary consciousness, and the right because it ignored the ideal of heroic sacrifice in a national cause. There were certainly other German writers whose work took an anti-militarist perspective, such as Arnold Zweig, whose *Der Streit um den Sergeanten Grischa* (The Case of Sergeant Grischa) was published in 1927. Ludwig Renn's *Krieg* (War), published in 1929, was not as overtly political but still demonstrated a failure of purpose in the war. In many respects this kind of literature was aimed at nationalism and militarism as much as at the war, with an underlying condemnation of the values of the 'front generation'. This was deemed necessary for these values were being asserted by most post-war German authors, for whom they symbolised all that was wrong with Weimar. The most obvious manifestation was Ernst Jünger.[42]

Ernst Jünger was one of those veterans who had thoroughly enjoyed the war, winning two Iron Crosses and Germany's highest decoration, the *Pour le Mérite* (For Valour). Jünger's memoir *In Stahlgewittern* (Storm of Steel), which was privately published in 1920 and then commercially in 1922 and 1924, was a celebration of martial values. It was followed by *Das Wäldchen*

125 (Copse 125) in 1924, and *Feuer und Blut* (Fire and Blood) in 1925. Jünger also wrote an essay in 1922, *Der Kampf als imeren Erlebnis* (Battle as Inner Experience), which was later used by *Schutzstaffel* (SS) training schools.

Jünger was only moderately successful in Germany, selling about 39,000 copies of *Storm of Steel* by 1929 but very successful in Britain where the translated edition went through four reprints in 1924. Conceivably, it did better in Britain because Jünger was describing battle against the British and because memoirs by officers were more acceptable than in Germany, where the memory of war was much more politicised. In turn, *Copse 125*, like *Battle as Inner Experience*, was more a polemic than a memoir. Jünger, however, was not a Nazi and withdrew from public life in 1933.[43]

German modernist poets frequently supported the war at first, a number such as Hans Leybold and August Stramm, being killed. Others, however, became disillusioned though the German poetic tradition tended towards an idealism, abstraction and remoteness from reality which made it difficult to get to grips with the experience of war. Nonetheless, the best, like Georg Trakl and Anton Schnak, are comparable to Wilfred Owen.[44]

French literary response to the war was surprisingly muted considering that it was being fought on French soil. Marcel Proust continued to work on *À la recherche du temps perdu* (Remembrance of Things Past) while Guillaume Apollinaire's *Calligrammes* was published in a small edition in April 1918, which had little impact at the time. The other most notable wartime productions were Paul Valéry's *Civilisations* and Henri Barbusse's *Le feu, journal d'une escouade* (Under Fire: The Story of a Squad). Many French poets under the influence of symbolism and surrealism, like Louis Aragon, did not respond to the war in the direct terms of their British counterparts. French women writers had little to say on the war.

Those French writers who did confront the war displayed a variety of responses. Pierre Drieu La Rochelle, whose *Interrogation* (1917) celebrated the virtues of war, turned to fascism, while Barbusse turned to communism. There was also a 'literature of the absurd', as evinced in 1932 by *Voyage au bout de la nuit* (Journey to the End of Night) written by Céline (Louis-Ferdinand Destouches), who had been invalided out of the army in 1915. There were novels from pro-war writers such as René Benjamin, whose *Gaspard* (1915) won the Prix Goncourt that year. Some novelists who fought in the war published realistic novels without having any particular political viewpoint, such as Georges Duhamel and Roland Dorgelès, whose best known novel, *Les croix de bois* (Wooden Crosses), appeared in April 1919.

If Dorgelès wrote to memorialise the dead, Barbusse wrote to mobilise the living as an internationalist rather than a pacifist. A journalist who had published symbolist poetry and novels before the war, Barbusse won the *Croix de guerre* for bringing in wounded from No Man's Land in 1915.

According to his own account, this 'Jeremiad of the Trenches' had enlisted at the age of 41 to fight imperialism and German militarism, cultivating a notion of a 'socialist just warrior'. Apocalyptic in tone, the book was published in instalments in *L'Oeuvre* from August 1916 onwards, appearing in book form in December 1916. Its uncompromising realism was denounced by some as German propaganda, but it not only passed the censors but also won the Prix Goncourt for 1916. Unusually for anti-war literature at the time, it sold 200,000 copies by July 1918, but it seems that the bulk of the book was accepted as a realistic depiction of war and the last chapter, which denounced war, was dismissed as 'literature'. The success of *Under Fire*, however, did not result in the disappearance of patriotic material and there was something of a revival in the publication of French heroic literature at the end of the war.[45]

Like some of the German expressionists, the Italian futurists welcomed the challenge of war. Gabriele D'Annunzio, for example, who temporarily lost his sight as a result of an air crash in January 1916, had his daughter transcribe his celebration of death, *Notturno*. It was eventually published in 1921. Marinetti's *L'alcova d'acciaio* (The Steel Alcove), which also appeared in 1921, similarly lauded the destructive potential of the autonomous world of the machine. Not all Italian intellectuals, however, fully supported the war. Benedetto Croce, who had voted for war as a deputy in the Chamber in 1915, became a neutralist and withdrew to work on his history books. Adolfo Omodeo's *Momenti della vita di guerra* (Moments of a Wartime Life), originally published in instalments between 1929 and 1933, was intended both as a memorial to his fallen comrades and as an attempt to rescue his generation from fascist distortions. Thus, he contended that the best of Italy's war generation had been motivated by a sense of duty and the dream of a Europe of free peoples, and not by hate, glory or enjoyment of war.[46]

In Austria-Hungary, two notable anti-war, and anti-German, plays were Stefan Zweig's thinly veiled biblical allegory *Jeremias*, and Karl Kraus's *Die letzen Tage der Menschheit* (The Last Days of Mankind). Written between 1915 and 1917, the latter was completed in 1919 though not published until 1922. While Zweig's play had elements of Zionism, Kraus's work was anti-semitic, the play being both anti-capitalist and, in some respects, anti-modernist. The underlying message, however, was certainly pacifist. Elsewhere in the Empire, Jaroslav Hasek's *The Good Soldier Svejk* (1921) was the recreation of a pre-war character in Hasek's writing to reflect the ambiguities of Czech existence during the war.[47]

Turning from literature and poetry to other artistic forms, just as modernist literary trends were viewed as foreign, so modern art came under attack, an exhibition of the London Group of Futurists in March 1915 being pointedly denounced by *The Times* as 'Junkerism in art'. As with literature, too, more traditional art forms continued to be produced along-side modernist attempts to capture the essence of the war.

In Britain, traditional neoclassical battle art was still produced by artists such as Richard Caton Woodville, Fortunio Matania, William Barnes Wollen, James Prinsep Beadle and Lady Butler well into the post-war period. Indeed, traditional art had a much greater visibility to the public than modernist work. Work exhibited at the Royal Academy summer exhibitions got a wider audience, but this also tended to be more traditional. Eric Kennington's painting on glass, *The Kensingtons at Laventie*, was widely exhibited to raise money for the Star and Garter Fund, but Kennington's work was not avant-garde but a 'fusion of archaic styles' reminiscent especially of the pre-Raphaelites. By contrast, traditional and heroic themes were widely disseminated as illustrations in popular periodicals and part-works such as *The Illustrated London News*, *The War Budget* and *The War Illustrated*.[48]

In terms of official art, Wellington House formed a pictorial section in April 1916, which then published *War Pictorial* as a means of making use of the photographs being taken. Masterman believed that there was a strong case for supplementing the photographers, whose activities were limited by censorship and circumstances. Encouraged by figures within the art world, he moved towards sponsoring official war artists, the first of whom was Muirhead Bone, a Scottish landscape artist, in July 1916. Beaverbrook had also begun to sign up artists for his Canadian War Records Office. After Wellington House became part of Beaverbrook's Ministry of Information, a British War Memorials Committee within it continued to sponsor art with the ultimate intention of displaying it in Halls of Remembrance in Britain and Canada. Indeed, a number of large paintings were commissioned for the London Hall of Remembrance including John Singer Sargent's *Gassed* and Paul Nash's *The Menin Road*. In the event, the halls never materialised. In addition, there were already many artists serving in the army working for themselves on regimental Christmas cards or for the illustrated London journals. Some notable art had also been produced for propaganda purposes by artists like David Allen and, especially, Frank Brangwyn, working on recruiting and other posters.

Many of the official war artists had been influenced by modernist artistic movements such as cubism and futurism before the war. C. R. W. Nevinson, for example, had co-written a pamphlet on futuristic art with Marinetti, and his *La Mitrailleuse* fused cubism and futurism. Paul Nash and Percy Wyndham Lewis, a vorticist, did not continue their more experimental pre-war work, however, as they seemed to feel it unnecessary when the reality of the Western Front appeared to meet modernist concepts more than half-way. A kind of 'anti-landscape' was created, Nash in particular using titles to convey the irony in depicting the death of landscape and the violation of nature. Only Nevinson's *The Paths of Glory*, depicting dead British soldiers caught on barbed wire, ran into censorship difficulties, though Sir William Orpen had to revise his satire on the signing of the Versailles treaty, *To the Unknown British Soldier in France*, before the Imperial War Museum would accept it.

Once the war was over, modernists like Nash, Nevinson and Lewis turned away from the subject, vorticists in particular now associating war with destruction rather than progress. Accordingly, unlike the case in literature, there was was little retrospective war art in Britain. An exception was Stanley Spencer, who had served as hospital orderly in Macedonia. His series of frescoes at Cookham and, especially those executed at Burghclere in Berkshire between 1928 and 1932, were unique in Britain in reflecting the apocalyptic vision of some German artists.[49]

As in Britain, traditional French art forms such as *images d'Epinal* tended to push newer forms such as cubism to the sidelines, especially as foreign-born artists residing in France like Pablo Picasso were somewhat suspect. Many of the French avant-garde were in uniform during war, and maintaining the spirit of cubism was largely left to journals like Jean Cocteau's *Le Mot*. Much appeared that was traditional and there was even a reversion to classical themes in war art. Moreover, it should be noted that Cocteau resisted what he regarded as German influences in modernism and that his work also looked backwards to pre-war styles. Thus, with Picasso and Juan Gris, Cocteau chose to abandon techniques that did not appear sufficiently French. Their collaboration on the Diaghilev Company's ballet *Parade* in September 1917, therefore, used French folk art, circus and music hall traditions, but with the dancers wearing cubist masks designed by Picasso. Thus it looked backwards and forwards in time and form simultaneously.

Ironically, cubist designs were used by camouflage artists at the front such as Luc-Albert Moreau and André Dunoyer de Seganzac in what has been characterised as non-representational art. Begun in February 1915, the camouflage section had over 3,000 workers by 1917. Similar techniques were used by 'dazzle' artists such as Edward Wadsworth on Royal Navy ships. The *camoufleurs*, however, represented only a minority of mobilised artists. In many ways, however, the work of French artists showed little war influence in the longer term.[50]

In Germany, there was less emphasis upon official war art but, in many respects, German artists were to be more deeply affected by the experience of war. Like the Italian futurists, German artists like Otto Dix and Max Beckmann initially welcomed the war as a means of burying pre-war culture and as a new opening for creativity. The most radical response was that of the Dadaists like Hans Arp, Hugo Ball, Richard Huelsenbeck, all of whom had taken refuge in Switzerland, and the Herzfelde brothers. Dadaism emerged as a means of portraying the realism of war, which they believed the expressionists were too traditional to accomplish. In fact, much of their work depicted the home front rather than the war itself.

Most war art, however, was expressionist, though some artists like Paul Klee and Franz Marc, who was killed in March 1916, found it limiting and turned to the abstract. Beckmann, who was discharged from the army after a nervous breakdown in 1915, exhibited a profound change in style. Prior to the war, he had opposed both cubism and futurism but was converted to extreme expressionism.

Dix and Georg Grosz found even the abstract limiting, Dix converting from futurism, which tended to glorify war, to allegorical and biblical anti-war apocalypticism and expressionism during his wartime service. Apocalyptic images had featured before the war, but war shifted its emphasis from the urban to the rural setting of the Western Front. Dix saw service as an artilleryman and machine gunner on both Western and Eastern Fronts, while Grosz suffered a nervous breakdown in 1917 without experiencing battle. Their art was brutalist in tone during the war and revolutionary in message after it, although their attitude to the war was ambivalent at times.

Both Grosz and the Herzfelde brothers undertook propagandist cartoon projects for Ufa during the war. Grosz, however, was increasingly drawn into the class struggle, notably satirising the suppression of the Spartacists. His paintings were exhibited in Friedrich's anti-war museum in 1924. Dix also grew increasingly hostile to war, as evinced in his fifty etchings entitled collectively as *Der Krieg* in 1924; his triptych, also entitled *Der Krieg*, in 1932; and his 1936 painting *Flanders*, based on an episode recounted in Barbusse's *Under Fire*.[51]

Austro-Hungarian artists also became disillusioned as the war progressed. Albin Egger-Leinz, whose *Helden 1915* (Heroes, 1915), of soldiers marching heroically into battle, could be contrasted with his 1916 painting, *Der Namenlosen 1914* (To the Nameless Ones, 1914), in which troops now advanced bowed down and crouching. On the other hand, Gustav Klimt's art was unchanged and untouched by the war.[52]

The same contrast in response to the war between traditional and modernist styles was also apparent in music, and war had the same contradictory influences. Modernism was represented in pre-war music by use of what might be regarded as disharmony and cacophony, and a deliberate negation of metre. Schoenberg and Stravinsky had been roundly condemned for their musical excesses before 1914. The jazz music introduced to the French by American servicemen was equally as shocking to Parisian audiences as cubist art, but by no means outside the progressive pre-war trend.

It has been suggested that the war gave a new validity to the discordant effect of Stravinsky's music, but Schoenberg produced virtually no music at all during the war or in its immediate aftermath beyond *Jacob's Ladder*, which was never completed. Indeed, Schoenberg discovered his serial twelve-note technique only in 1921. Carl Nielsen's Fourth Symphony, known as *The Inextinguishable* and composed between 1915 and 1916, has been taken as representative of the influence of war. Nielsen, however, had begun work on it before 1914 and was isolated from actual impact of the war in neutral Denmark.

Similarly, the work of Ravel, who briefly served in the French artillery before being discharged as unfit, shows no obvious change in style before, during and after the war. His *Le Tombeau de Couperin*, a piece theoretically composed in memory of the eighteenth-century French composer François Couperin, had each of its six movements dedicated to a different friend killed in the war. Yet most of it had been written in July 1914. Ravel's piano concerto for the left hand, composed in 1929 and 1930 for Paul Wittgenstein, who had lost his right arm during the war, might appear more directly related to the war. Again, however, it can be argued that it was more suggestive of Ravel's long-term obsession with death. Sergei Prokofiev and Sergei Rachmaninov also appear to have been little influenced by the war.

British music continued in traditional vein. George Butterworth was killed on the Somme in August 1916 and Ralph Vaughan Williams wrote little during the war, but Gustav Holst, who had been rejected for military service, completed *The Planets*. Sir Hubert Parry also wrote the stirring musical setting of William Blake's *Jerusalem*. Edward Elgar's *The Spirit of England*, first performed in its entirety in November 1917, was also traditional, setting to music three poems by Laurence Binyon including the famous *For the Fallen*. If anything, however, the war stifled Elgar's creativity. Again, there was little long-term impact on British music, although Arthur Bliss's *Morning Heroes* (1930) and his score for the film *Things To Come* (1935) arguably did show the influence of the war. For Holst and Vaughan Williams, indeed, it was 'progressive to be regressive'.[53]

Architecture displayed some new influences in post-war reconstruction, particularly in the imaginative use of glass, while the Swiss architect Le Corbusier began an important and influential series of articles in October 1922. British architects, however, appear to have been little influenced by the war and those young enough to have served, such as Oliver Hill and Clough Williams-Ellis, turned back to a neo-Georgian past for their inspiration. The work of architects such as Lutyens and Sir Reginald Blomfield on war memorials, while often innovative, still went against the abstract and constructivist trends of mainstream modern artistic style: it would have been deemed inappropriate to incorporate the abstract or experimental in monumental architecture. Indeed, non-conventional monuments were rarely considered successful, with the notable exception of C. Bruce Dellit's Anzac Memorial in Sydney, executed in Art Deco style and centred around Rayner Hoff's sculpture of a naked corpse supported by mourning women. The prevailing results of the memorial movement have often been dismissed for the very reason that the memorials were traditionalist rather than experimental, but Lutyens in particular produced what some regard as incomparably the most impressive memorials of the twentieth century.

The architectural impact of the war was more pronounced on the continent, especially in the work of German expressionist architects such as Fritz Höger, Hans Poelzig and Erich Mendelsohn. Of the four major post-war architects, Ludwig Mies van der Rohe, Le Corbusier, Frank Lloyd Wright and Walter Gropius, only Gropius had fought in war, but he did claim that his work was affected by his experience and his sense of needing an intellectual change of front.

As in the case of monumental architecture, it has also been argued that the war set back stylistic advance in sculpture. Again, too experimental an approach was not appropriate for the main outlet for British sculptors, which was in the form of sculptured figures for war memorials. Certainly, stylised and moderately futuristic figures produced by Eric Kennington for the 24th Division memorial in Battersea were much criticised, as was Sir George Frampton's 'severe' statue of Edith Cavell in St Martin's Place, London. Moreover, Jacob Epstein, who had outraged sensibilities with the figures on the British Medical Association building in London in 1908, was pointedly not considered as an official war artist. Yet, the work of other younger sculptors associated with the 'new sculpture movement' of the 1890s, like Jagger, Gilbert Ledward and Eric Gill, was deemed quite acceptable possibly because Kennington, Jagger and Philip Lindsay Clark were largely inspired by traditional representations of masculinity and influenced by an appreciation of Rudyard Kipling's vision of the ordinary 'Tommy'. Indeed, Ledward and Jagger were chosen as the two sculptors for the narrative friezes which would have appeared alongside art in the proposed Hall of Remembrance. While often in the style of Victorian public sculpture, therefore, war memorial sculpture was often imaginative. Outstanding examples were Goscombe John's three-dimensional sculptural monument at Port Sunlight in Cheshire, and Eric Gill's relief panels at the University of Leeds and at Trumpington near Cambridge. Jagger's figures for Lionel Pearson's Royal Artillery Memorial have been characterised as 'one of the outstanding examples of twentieth century British art'.[54]

Photographs could also be transformed into an art form, professionals appointed as official war photographers in particular having opportunities denied the amateur, and even the press photographer. In the case of Britain and the dominions, over 40,000 official photographs were taken, well over half on the Western Front. In Palestine, the American journalist Lowell Thomas was instrumental in creating the post-war image of Lawrence of Arabia through combining his reportage with the wartime photography of Harry Chase. On the home front, Horace Nicholls, appointed official photographer of Great Britain in July 1917, produced a memorable series of scenes in munitions and ordnance factories. The Germans had at least fifty photographers at the front, and the French about thirty-five. The US Army Signal Corps performed the same task for the American Expeditionary Force.

Later war photographers of the Spanish Civil War and the Second World War had smaller, more compact cameras, and pushed back much further the parameters of what was acceptable. The photographers of the Great War, however, began the process and helped to transform photography into a mass medium. Photographic exhibitions were arranged in Britain by Beaverbrook and, in October 1918, the Ministry of Information opened a shop to sell official photographs. Sales were also licensed through postcards issued by the *Daily Mail* and stereoscopic prints produced by various firms.[55]

War and the silver screen

If photographs were increasingly a visual medium of immense importance, then this was even more true of cinema, which was both a product and a creator of popular culture. Indeed, in reaching a mass audience, cinema was arguably far more influential than literature in shaping the popular memory of the war. No film of the silent era could reproduce the noise and smell of war but, in the 1920s, film-makers began to try to convey more of the reality. In the process, they merely compounded the effect already produced by wartime documentaries such as *The Battle of the Somme* by perpetuating a series of visual clichés which, as Pierre Sorlin has suggested, in themselves ceated a false reality. Certainly, the same images have recurred so often in the cinematic portrayal of the Great War that audiences have become accustomed through constant repetition to the mythic image of the war.[56]

In many respects, however, this was not the intention of film-makers immediately after the war. In Britain, there was a series of films made between 1919 and 1927 almost as documentaries, or 'reconstructions' as they were billed at the time, by Harry Bruce Woolfe's company, British Instructional Films, in co-operation with the War Office and the Admiralty. Mostly, these films, which included versions of Mons, the Somme, Jutland and the Zeebrugge Raid, concentrated on the exploits of winners of the Victoria Cross. Clearly, these were not intended to be critical of the conduct

of the war, nor to depict the war as a grisly horror. Similar positive reconstructions were made by others such as Maurice Elvey and Arthur Maude.
An heroic view of the war experience also emerged from German quasi-
documentaries during the Weimar years and included *Der Weltkrieg* (1927),
Douaumont (1931) and *Tannenberg* (1932). Nazi cinema, of course, took a
decidedly positive view of wartime sacrifice.

Hollywood took a rather similar view and its films on the war oscillated
between the realistic and the epic. This again helped mythologise the conflict
by recreating it in a more palatable form through the unfolding of themes
such as love, loyalty, death and resurrection. As Jay Winter has commented,
this sanitation of the war and removal of its harsher features enabled 'both
those who went through it and those who were born long after 1918 to create
in their mind a different war, a filmic war which could be remembered in
an heroic or romantic haze'. This remained the case into the era of sound.[57]

In a very real way, there was a clear mythic theme in such films as Rex
Ingram's version of Vincente Blasco Ibáñez's novel *The Four Horsemen of the
Apocalypse* (1921), starring Rudolf Valentino. The classic *J'Accuse*, made by
the French director Abel Gance with the assistance of a disabled Foreign
Legion veteran, Blaise Cendrars, during the war, but released only in 1919,
was similarly mythic. The dead rise from their graves to see if their sacrifice
has been in vain, compelling the civilians whom they visit to become wor-
thy of the dead. Ironically, many of the extras were soldiers home on leave
who were later killed. The same use of the image of the returned dead was
used at the end of Raymond Bernard's 1932 film version of Dorgelès's
novel *Les croix de bois* and, indeed, in the last scene of the film version of *All
Quiet on the Western Front*.[58]

Camaraderie was celebrated in such films as Howard Hawks's *The Road
to Glory* (1936), centring on a group of French soldiers ordered to hold their
posts to the last man. In fact, it was a remake of *Les croix de bois*, even
including footage from the French original. The theme was perhaps best
presented, however, in Jean Renoir's *La Grande Illusion* (1937), in which a
group of French airmen shot down over the German lines and held in a
fortress prison represent a cross-section of French society. Partly based on
De Gaulle's attempted escape from Rosenberg castle near Bayreuth after
his capture in March 1916, the film showed camaraderie stronger than the
class affinity enjoyed by the aristocratic French officer de Boeldieu and the
German camp commandant von Rauffenstein. Renoir, who had served
with the French airforce during the war, was associated with the Popular
Front. His film, therefore, emphasised class difference as more significant
than national enmity. It was banned in Italy, Belgium and Japan as well as
in France during the Second World War. Wartime romance also remained
a favoured Hollywood theme as in *The White Sister* (1923), with Lillian Gish

and Ronald Colman, and *Dark Angel* (1935), with Herbert Marshall and Merle Oberon. Both Colman and Marshall had served in the war and both had been wounded, Marshall losing a leg.[59]

If romantic themes humanised the war, so did comedy. Charlie Chaplin was by far the most popular film entertainer of the war years and one of his greatest successes was *Shoulder Arms* (1918), in which he dreamed of capturing the Kaiser. The film was carefully constructed in such a way as not to offend and it was especially popular with military audiences. Laurel and Hardy made the similar *Pack Up Your Troubles* in 1932, and the Marx Brothers produced the war satire *Duck Soup* in 1937.[60]

Jay Winter has also argued that the image of war was softened by those film-makers who became almost obsessed with the visual beauty of conflict. This was most often characterised by the use of the silhouettes of soldiers on battlefields. Some intended to show the ugly side of combat, like the German director Georg Pabst in *Westfront 1918* (1930). Overshadowed at the time by *All Quiet on the Western Front*, Pabst's powerful battle scenes produced an ambiguous effect on the audience through their artistry and the use of sky and landscape. The same was true of the dramatic depiction of the air war, as in the two early Hollywood epics, *Wings* (1927) and Howard Hughes's *Hell's Angels* (1930).

Other films were more sombre, such as the stoical acceptance of duty portrayed in the 'Hollywood British' co-production of *Journey's End* (1930). Directed like the original play by James Whale, the cinematic version of *Journey's End* created an ambiguous image of tension and hardship modified by heroism. In many respects, the British film production by Anthony Asquith of *Tell England* (1931), based on Raymond's novel, was very similar. Indeed, the film ended with the Thermopylae-like epitaph on a character's headstone: 'Tell England, ye who pass this monument, We died for her, and here we rest content.'[61]

Grittier still were the Hollywood productions *What Price Glory* (1926, directed by Raoul Walsh) and *The Big Parade* (1925, directed by King Vidor), which were both influenced by contributions from the author, Laurence Stallings, who had lost a leg as a wartime Marine. *The Big Parade* was the first feature film to try to portray the trenches realistically and Vidor, who had some military experience, viewed US Signal Corps footage for authenticity. He was rewarded with commercial success: *The Big Parade* cost US$382,000 and made US$3.4 million.[62]

With one exception, however, as Jay Winter had remarked, political and pacifist statements about the war were 'not central to the cinematic recapitulation of the war' between 1919 and 1939. That one exception was the 1930 version *All Quiet on the Western Front*, which has been seen by an estimated 100 million people since it was made.

459

The film was directed by Lewis Milestone, a veteran of the US Army Signal Corps's photographic section though he never served outside the United States. Confined to seeing photographic images of the war, Milestone later remarked significantly that, 'I knew precisely what it was supposed to look like'. *All Quiet on the Western Front* starred the then unknown Lew Ayres, a later pacifist and conscientious objector during the Second World War. It was produced by Carl Laemmle's Universal at a time when it was thought the public had tired of the war. A pacifist, Laemmle had quickly noted the sales phenomenon and rushed to Germany to acquire the film rights in August 1929.

Milestone used the still new techniques of sound to heighten the impact and the images became a powerful indictment of the war, as in the hero's death from a sniper's bullet as he reached for a butterfly, a scene not in the book and added after the initial previews but before the première on 29 April 1930. Indeed, *All Quiet on the Western Front* built upon the already accepted visual myth of the Great War and offered ready-made images constantly recycled ever since.

The film was a great commercial success, quickly recouping its US$1.4 million cost and winning two Oscars, but it also attracted hostility. It fell foul of right-wing groups even in the United States and, somewhat surprisingly, the first country to ban it was New Zealand on the grounds that it was not an entertainment, though cuts satisfied the censors. In Germany, the second largest market in Europe, a number of cuts were made to scenes which were thought to detract from the image of Germany and its army, to enable it to be shown in Berlin on 5 December 1930. Led by Goebbels, Nazis rioted to prevent it being shown and it was withdrawn from general exhibition on 11 December. The Social Democrats agitated for a modification, which allowed private exhibition, and a new shorter revised version was allowed in September 1931 for public exhibition. It was then entirely banned in January 1933 and shown again only in 1952. It was also banned in Italy and not shown there until 1956.[63]

German diplomats had tried to correct Hollywood's view of Germany in films like *Four Horsemen of the Apocalypse*, but they had little leverage in the 1920s though Herbert Wilcox's *Dawn* (1928) was banned in the interests of Anglo-German relations. It was later remade as *Nurse Edith Cavell* (1939). The Nazis were more successful in terms of Hollywood through controlling distribution rights in Germany. Thus, Universal modified its 1937 version of Remarque's subsequent book, *The Road Back*, though Metro-Goldwyn-Meyer declined to stop a film production of Remarque's third book, *Three Comrades* in 1938.[64]

While *All Quiet on the Western Front* was unusual among the films produced prior to the Second World War, its message was common to those films dealing with the Great War after 1945. Thus, the familiar images were recalled in Stanley Kubrick's *Paths of Glory* (1957). Based on a 1935 novel by a Canadian veteran, Humphrey Cobb, it dealt with a failed French attack and the arrest, trial and execution of three of the troops in order to cover up the incompetence of the High Command, who had ordered a frontal assault on an impregnable position. It was effectively suppressed in France until 1975, though not actually banned, seemingly owing to French involvement in Algeria at the time of release. The British film by the Hollywood-blacklisted Joseph Losey, *King and Country* (1964), with Tom Courtney, had a similar theme.[65]

A related but distinct sub-genre in recent years has been the treatment of Australians by the British High Command. This particular aspect of the Anzac myth has been displayed both in a film about the South African War, *Breaker Morant* (1979), but also in Peter Weir's *Gallipoli* (1981) and *The Light Horsemen* (1987), set in Palestine. These major commercial successes were partly fuelled by a revival in Australian cultural nationalism, promoted by successive governments in the 1970s and 1980s. In the process, the myths have been perpetuated and have had a major influence on the popular memory of a younger generation. Thus, in *Gallipoli* the attack on the Nek, which forms the film's climax, is ordered by a British officer. In reality, it was an Australian who ordered the attack.[66]

Military incompetence was also a theme of the film version of Joan Littlewood's 1963 Theatre Workshop play *Oh! What a Lovely War*, made by Richard Attenborough in 1969. Much of the play's script was written by Raymond Fletcher, later Labour MP for Ilkeston, of whom it is said that his 'fixity of purpose' supplied the production with 'its precepts and its strong socialist undertow'. Fletcher also conceived what he called a 'message for the sixties', being much influenced by the apocalyptic vision of nuclear war in the light of the Cuban Missile Crisis. Thus, what was billed as musical entertainment was meant to be a cautionary tale for the audience. The film version, in some ways, was more anti-authority and anti-establishment than anti-war but the message was still one of the futility of the conflict. The theme of futility has continued, as in a 1976 remake of *Journey's End*, now transferred from the Western Front to the air war as *Aces High*. *Regeneration* (1997), based on Pat Barker's novel about Siegfried Sassoon and Wilfred Owen meeting at Craiglockhart military hospital in the summer of 1917, reinforced all the clichés.

Television has had the same effect. Mention was made in the first chapter of the impact on the audience of the visual images of the BBC's *Great War* series in 1964, despite the revisionist narration scripted by the likes of John Terraine and Corelli Barnett. Television documentaries and dramas have continued to peddle the now familiar version of the war, arguably the most notorious being the travesties perpetuated by the BBC's *The Monocled Mutineer* in 1986. The unrelenting gloom of the 1996 BBC documentary series *1914–18* was such that it was characterised by Corelli Barnett as 'Oh! What a Whinging War'. As Gary Sheffield has noted, *Blackadder Goes Forth*, first broadcast in 1989, was so successful because the characters and situations needed no explanation, so familiar was the audience with the received version of the war. In 1999 the final moments of the series, where the characters become freeze-framed as they go over the top, was first among the ten clips voted, with no apparent irony, 'the nation's all-time favourite' moment from a television comedy. Perhaps significantly, another favourite was a typically comic moment from the entirely affectionate series built on the popular memory of the Home Guard in the Second World War, *Dad's Army*.[67]

War and history

A comparison of *Blackadder Goes Forth* and *Dad's Army* is a reminder of A. J. P. Taylor's observation that, by comparison with the Great War, the Second World War has been regarded as a 'good war'. Taylor's popular illustrated account, *The First World War* (1963), which had sold at least 250,000 copies by 1989, reinforced the point with its caustic captions. Indeed, while film-makers, television producers and English teachers have much to answer for in the perpetuation of the image of the Great War as one in which a generation of 'lions' were needlessly sacrificed by the 'donkeys', it is as well to acknowledge the responsibility of some historians in the process.[68]

Moreover, futility was already a theme by the 1930s. The idea that Britain had suffered a lost generation was expressed by Stanley Baldwin in 1935 as the country 'living under the shadow' of the war. That image of a lost generation arose from the smallness of the elite and its prominent losses such as Asquith's son Raymond, two of Bonar Law's sons, Arthur Henderson's eldest son and Neville Chamberlain's two cousins. It enabled many to eulogise a lost English Arcadia, which had never actually existed beyond their imagination. Thereafter, the 'lost generation' was frequently intoned to explain subsequent British decline. Thus, in 1986, Sir Ian MacGregor, the industrialist brought in to salvage British Steel, remarked that, 'even today we have not fully replaced the dynamism and leadership qualities of the generation we threw away in the First World War'. The reality, as Corelli Barnett has written, was that the war crippled Britain psychologically but in no other way.

When the chairman of the American Joint Chiefs of Staff, George C. Marshall, visited London to urge the early opening of a Second Front during the Second World War, he was told by Churchill's adviser, Lord Cherwell, 'It's no use, you are arguing against the casualties on the Somme.' Such was the received image that the assumption among many Second World War servicemen was that they would experience the same conditions as their fathers. In fact, as Gary Sheffield has suggested, the experience of attritional warfare in Italy in 1943–44 or Normandy in 1944, or conditions at Kohima in Burma (1944) were probably far worse than anything experienced in the Great War. Yet, most Second World War servicemen convinced themselves that their war was not as bad as the previous one. They had acccepted a mythologised version of the Great War and then mythologised their own experience in relation to it.[69]

The version of the war already accepted by the 1930s was not simply a result of anti-war books and poetry or the visual images. A third factor was the actual historiography of the war. Initially, histories had served the nation's cause, be they popular illustrated accounts such as J. A. Hammerton's *The War Illustrated* and Hammerton and H. W. Wilson's *The Great War*, or attempts at general histories such as Conan Doyle's *The British Campaign in France and Flanders* in six volumes (1916–20). Beginning with the 'battle of the memoirs' in the 1920s, however, a more critical view of the conduct of the war soon emerged in Britain. It found a parallel elsewhere, as in the post-mortems in Germany on the failures of the Schlieffen Plan, Verdun and the 1918 offensives rehearsed in memoirs by Ludendorff and Falkenhayn.

In the absence of any access to unpublished official documents in Britain until the 1960s, memoirs held the field. Some proved very influential, such as Beaverbrook's two-volume *Politicians and the War* (1928 and 1932) and, especially, the magisterial volumes of Churchill's *The World Crisis* (1923–29) and Lloyd George's *War Memoirs* (1933–36). Some of the distortions produced by these accounts with regard to the traditional Westerners versus Easterners interpretation of British strategy have been mentioned already. Such memoirs were successful commercially in the eagerness of the British public to know the truth of the war. Churchill's first volume was reprinted twice within a month of publication in April 1923. Lloyd George sold 54,237 copies of his six volumes in Britain alone by February 1937 and 246,429 copies of the two-volume abridged version (1938) by 1944.

The resulting financial gains were important to some: Asquith, Lloyd George and Churchill all needed cash at the time they began to write. It was also a matter, however, of putting one's own case. Indeed, Churchill summed up the balance nicely in December 1921, writing to his wife that his memoirs represented 'a great chance to put my whole case in an agreeable form to an attentive audience. And the pelf will make us v[er]y comfortable'.

In particular, Lloyd George's *War Memoirs* did immense damage to the reputation of British generalship. The index alone is a sufficient example, its entries on 'military mind' including 'narrowness of', 'stubbornness of', 'does not seem to understand arithmetic', 'regards thinking as form of mutiny', and so on.[70] Influential critiques of British generalship, however, were also advanced by J. F. C. Fuller and Basil Liddell Hart. The latter was initially sympathetic to British generals in *Reputations* (1928), but, partly influenced by the publication of the diaries of Sir Henry Wilson, changed his view. *The Real War* (1930), which remains in print as Liddell Hart's *History of the First World War*, was a sustained strategic critique. Partial and selective, Liddell Hart had a great influence over later historians, who were given free access to his large personal archive. C. R. M. F. Cruttwell's *A History of the Great War* (1934) was far more objective and balanced, but it was overshadowed by Liddell Hart's book, as was that of Cyril Falls, whose *The First World War* only appeared in 1960.[71]

Official histories had little corrective impact in Britain since much remained deliberately hidden. In any case, the official history had a long gestation period between 1922 and 1948, and criticism tended only to appear in the voluminous appendices. Captain G. C. Wynne, one of the assistants of the official historian, Brigadier Sir James Edmonds, had his name removed from the title page of the volume on Passchendaele – the last to be published in 1948 – because Edmonds had twisted the truth. Certainly, Edmonds suppressed evidence on occasions and, for example, massaged the German casualty figures for the Somme to make it appear that they had lost as many as the British.

Somewhat similarly, C. E. W. Bean's volumes in the Australian official history reinforced the Anzac legend, while the Canadian official history also reflected the broad consensus on how the war's history should be recorded. But then 'official history' was not the same as history. Indeed, all the major belligerents launched their own series of selected documents in the inter-war years to support their version of the war's outbreak.[72]

Little of what was said in the revival of interest in the war in the 1960s differed from that already said in the 1920s and 1930s. Prior to the 1960s and 1970s, however, it was most often Passchendaele that was identified as the most suitable illustration of military futility. Classic monuments to the 'angry young men' school of the late 1950s, Leon Wolff's *In Flanders Fields* (1959) and Alan Clark's *The Donkeys* (1961) dealt with Passchendaele and 1915: both are still in print. It was the output based on oral testimony by popular authors like Martin Middlebrook and Lyn MacDonald in the 1970s and early 1980s which then newly established the Somme and the experience of the Pals battalions in particular in the public consciousness. Rarely have the burgeoning accounts of the Pals looked beyond 1 July 1916. Moreover, oral history involves distinct dangers. Indeed, Alistair Thomson's investigation of the Anzac legend shows how Anzac veterans themselves articulated the legend through selection, simplification and generalisation, absorbing the myth so that their memories 'had become entangled with the legend of their lives'.[73]

The myth of the Great War is still routinely invoked in the British national press. By contrast, academe's image of the war has been transformed in the past fifteen years or so and a broad historical consensus has emerged, taking the war out of myth and returning it to history. Historians have probably almost arrived at that point looked forward to by Brian Bond when the war would be studied 'simply as history without polemic intent or apologies'.[74] Unfortunately, among the public back in 'Blighty' it is seemingly for ever 1 July 1916.

Notes and references

1. Gregory, *Silence of Memory*, pp.2–6; Samuel Hynes, *A War Imagined: The First World War and English Culture* (London, 1990), pp.ix–xi, 469; idem, 'Personal Narratives and Commemoration', in Winter and Sivan, eds, *War and Remembrance*, pp.207–8, 211–12, 219–20; Mosse, *Fallen Soldiers*, pp.3–11; idem, 'Two World Wars and the Myth of War Experience', *JCH* 21 (1986), pp.491–513.

2. Catherine Reilly, *English Poetry of the First World War: A Bibliography* (London, 1978), p.xix; Elizabeth A. Marsland, *The Nation's Cause: French, English and German Poetry of the First World War* (London, 1991), p.2; Tim Cross, ed., *The Lost Voices of World War I* (London, 1988), pp.387–406.

3. Mosse, *Fallen Soldiers*, pp.70–4, 79–80; idem, 'National Cemeteries and National Revival: The Cult of the Fallen Soldier in Germany', *JCH* 14 (1979), pp.1–20; idem, 'Souvenir de la guerre et place du monumentalisme dans l'identité culturelle du national-socialisme', in Becker, Winter, Krumeich, Becker and Audoin-Rouzeau, eds, *Guerre et Cultures*, pp.278–86; Bernd Ulrich, '"Als wenn nichts geschehen wäre": Anmerkungen zur Behandlung der Kriegsopfer während des Ersten Weltkrieges', in Hirschfeld and Krumeich, eds, *Keiner fühlt sich hier als mensch*, pp.115–29; Reinhart Koselleck, 'Kriegerdenkmale als Identitätsstiftungen der Überlebenden', in O. Marquard and K. Stierle, eds, *Identität* (Munich, 1979), pp.237–76; idem, Der Einfluss der beiden Weltkriege auf das soziale Bewusstsein', in Wette, *Krieg des kleinen Mannes*, pp.324–43.

4. Bob Bushaway, 'Name Upon Name: The Great War and Remembrance', in Roy Porter, ed., *Myths of the English* (Cambridge, 1992), pp.136–67; Thomas W. Laqueur, 'Memory and Naming in the Great War', in J. R. Gillis, ed., *Commemorations: The Politics of National Identity* (Princeton, NJ, 1994), pp.150–67; Alex King, *Memorials of the Great War in Britain: The Symbolism and Politics of*

Remembrance (Oxford, 1998), pp.205–12; Michael Heffernan, 'For Ever England: The Western Front and the Politics of Remembrance in Britain', *Ecumene* 2 (1995), pp.293–323; Barry M. Doyle, 'Religion, Politics and Remembrance: A Free Church Community and its Great War Dead', in Evans and Lunn, eds, *War and Memory*, pp.223–38; Geoffrey Moorhouse, *Hell's Foundations: A Town, Its Myths and Gallipoli*, 2nd edn (London, 1993), pp.118–22, 141–59, 182–200, 211–12, 225–32; Gaffney, *Aftermath*, pp.96–115, 133–69.

5. Jonathan F. Vance, *Death So Noble: Memory, Meaning and the First World War* (Vancouver, 1997), pp.12–34, 102–8, 111–62, 198–260, 266–7; Alan Young, ' "We Throw the Torch": Canadian Memorials of the Great War and the Mythology of Heroic Sacrifice', *Journal of Canadian Studies* 24 (1989/90), pp.5–28.

6. Beaumont, 'Anzac Legend', pp.149–80; Ken Inglis, 'Le 25 avril en Australie et en Nouvelle-Zélande', in Becker, Winter, Krumeich, Becker and Audoin-Rouzeau, eds, *Guerre et Cultures*, pp.397–410; idem, 'Memorials of the Great War', *Australian Cultural History* 6 (1987) pp.5–17; Ken Inglis and Jock Philips, 'War Memorials in Australia and New Zealand: A Comparative Survey', *Australian Historical Studies* 24 (1991), pp.179–91; Richard Ely, 'The First Anzac Day: Invented or Discovered?', *Journal of Australian Studies* 17 (1985), pp.41–58; Mary Wilson, 'The Making of Melbourne's Anzac Day', *Australian Journal of Politics and History* 20 (1974), pp.197–209; Maureen Sharpe, 'Anzac Day in New Zealand, 1916–39', *New Zealand Journal of History* 15 (1981), pp.97–114; Thomson, *Anzac Memories*, pp.128–42, 193, 197–204; J. F. Williams, *Anzacs, the Media and the Great War* (Sydney, 1999), pp.98–110; Adrian Howe, 'Anzac Mythology and the Feminist Challenge', in Joy Damousi and Marilyn Lake, eds, *Gender and War: Australians at War in the Twentieth Century* (Cambridge, 1995), pp.302–10.

7. Smith, 'War and Culture', p.172; Keith Jeffery, 'The Great War in Modern Irish Memory', in Fraser and Jeffery, eds, *Men, Women and War*, pp.136–57; idem, 'Irish Culture and the Great War', *Bullán: An Irish Studies Journal* 1 (1994), pp.87–96; idem, 'Irish Prose Writers of the First World War', in Kathleen Devine, ed., *Modern Irish Writers and the Wars* (Gerrards Cross, 1999), pp.1–17; Jane Leonard, 'The Twinge of Memory: Armistice Day and Remembrance Sunday in Dublin since 1919', in Richard English and Graham Walker, eds, *Unionism in Modern Ireland: New Perspectives on Politics and Culture* (London, 1996), pp.99–114; eadem, 'Lest we Forget', in David Fitzpatrick, ed., *Ireland and the First World War*, 2nd edn (Mullingar, 1988), pp.59–67.

8. David Cannadine, 'War and Death, Grief and Mourning in Modern Britain', in J. Whaley, ed., *Mirrors of Mentality: Studies in the Social History of Death* (London, 1981), pp.187–242.

9. G. L. Mosse, 'War and the Appropriation of Nature', in Berghahn and Kitchen, eds, *Germany in Age of Total War*, pp.102–22; idem, *Fallen Soldiers*, pp.82, 84–91, 100–6, 111–12, 114–19.

10. Smith, 'War and British Culture', p.171; Philip Longworth, *The Unending Vigil* (London, 1967), pp.1–55; Heffernan, 'For Ever England', pp.293–323; Winter, *Sites of Memory*, pp.105–8; Derez, 'Belgian Salient for Reconstruction', pp.448–54; *War Graves of the Empire*, pp.47–70.

11. David W. Lloyd, *Battlefield Tourism: Pilgrimage and the Commemoration of the Great War in Britain, Australia and Canada, 1919–39* (Oxford, 1998), pp.49–63; Wilkinson, *Church of England and First World War*, pp.294–310; Eric Homberger, 'The Story of the Cenotaph', *Times Literary Supplement* 12 November 1976, pp.1429–30; Penelope Curtis, 'The Whitehall Cenotaph: An Accidental Monument', *IWMR* 9 (1994), pp.31–41; Allan Greenberg, 'Lutyens' Cenotaph', *Journal of the Society of Architectural Historians* 48 (1989), pp.5–23; James Brazier, 'War Shrines', *Bulletin of Western Front Association* 54 (1999), pp.38–9; Winter and Baggett, *1914–18*, p.385; King, *Memorials*, pp.55–6, 141–7; Winter, *Sites of Memory*, pp.60–1, 73–6, 102–5.

12. Mosse, *Fallen Soldiers*, pp.94–8; Lloyd, *Battlefield Tourism*, pp.63–75, 83–7; Ken Inglis, 'Entombing Unknown Soldiers: From London and Paris to Baghdad', *History and Memory* 5 (1993), pp.7–31 [also in Lack, ed., *Anzac Remembered*, pp.194–215]; Volker Ackermann, 'La vision allemande du soldat inconnu: débats politiques, réflexion philosophique et artistique', in Becker, Winter, Krumeich, Becker and Audoin-Rouzeau, eds, *Guerre et Cultures*, pp.385–96; Becker, *War and Faith*, pp.170–6; Michael Gavaghan, *The Story of the Unknown Warrior, 11 November 1920* (Cambridge, 1995), pp.7–13, 17–23, 74; Gregory, *Silence of Memory*, pp.24–6; Marilene Patten Henry, *Monumental Accusations: The Monuments aux Morts as Expressions of Popular Resentment* (New York, 1996), pp.104–15.

13. Gregory, *Silence of Memory*, pp.8–24, 28–34, 56–60, 65–84, 99–104; Matthew Richardson, 'A Changing Meaning for Armistice Day', in Cecil and Liddle, eds, *At Eleventh Hour*, pp.347–64; Graham Wootton, *The Official History of the British Legion* (London, 1956), pp.38–41; Hynes, *War Imagined*, pp.275–6.

14. Gregory, *Silence of Memory*, pp.118–42, 149–76, 215–22; Becker, *War and Faith*, pp.119–20; Mosse, *Fallen Soldiers*, pp.94–8.

15. A. V. Seaton, 'War and Thanatourism', *Annals of Tourism Research* 26 (1998), pp.1–29; Lloyd, *Battlefield Tourism*, pp.19–48, 101–30, 134–79; Longworth, *Unending Vigil*, p.105; Winter, 'Communities in Mourning', pp.348–50; Tony Walter, 'War Grave Pilgrimage', in I. Reader and T. Walter, eds, *Pilgrimage in Popular Culture* (London, 1993), pp.63–91; Terence Denman, ' "A Voice from the Lonely Grave": The Death in Action of Major William Redmond MP', *Irish Sword* 18 (1992), pp.286–96; idem, *A Lonely Grave: The Life and Death of William Redmond* (Dublin, 1995), pp.117–36; Mosse, *Fallen Soldiers*, pp.152–5; Susanne Brandt, 'Le voyage aux champs de bataille', in Becker, Winter, Krumeich, Becker and Audoin-Rouzeau, eds, *Guerre et Cultures*, pp.411–16; Modris Eksteins, 'Michelin, Pickfords et la Grande Guerre: le tourisme sur le

front occidental, 1919–91', ibid., pp.417–28; *Bulletin of Western Front Association* 44/45 (1996), pp.23, 28; G. Stinglhamber, *Guide to the Zeebrugge War Museum*, 4th edn (Bruges, 1928), pp.1–31; Nicholas Saunders, 'Memories of Metal: Trench Art, a Lost Resource of the Great War', *Stand To* 58, 2000, pp.14–17.

16. Lloyd, *Battlefield Tourism*, pp.95–100, 107–8, 181–215; Vance, *Death So Noble*, pp.64–71; D. Thomson, 'National Sorrow, National Pride: Commemoration of the Great War in Canada, 1918–45' *Journal of Canadian Studies* 30 (1995/96), pp.5–27; J. Pierce, 'Constructing Memory: The Vimy Memorial', *Canadian Military History* 1 (1992), pp.5–14; Kennedy, *Over Here*, pp.363–9; G. K. Piehler, 'The War Dead and the Gold Star: American Commemoration of the First World War', in Gillis, ed., *Commemorations*, pp.168–85.

17. For general surveys of war memorials, see Derek Boorman, *At the Going Down of the Sun: British First World War Memorials* (York, 1988); Ken Inglis, *Sacred Place: War Memorials in the Australian Landscape* (Melbourne, 1998); C. Maclean and J. Phillips, *The Sorrow and the Pride: New Zealand War Memorials* (Wellington, 1990); R. Shipley, *To Mark Our Place: A History of Canadian War Memorials* (Toronto, 1987); James M. Mayo, *War Memorials as Political Landscape: The American Experience and Beyond* (New York, 1984); and Patricia Dogliani, 'Les monuments aux morts de la Grande Guerre en Italie', *GMCC* 167 (1992), pp.87–94.

18. B. Huppauf, 'War and Death: The Experience of the First World War', in M. Crouch and B. Huppauf, eds, *Essays in Mortality* (Sydney 1985), pp.65–87; King, *Memorials*, pp.5, 23, 26–36, 44–61, 66–82, 86–103, 106–25, 129–41, 146–50, 158–68, 173–91, 234–6; Jon Davies, 'War Memorials', in David Clark, ed., *The Sociology of Death* (Oxford, 1993), pp.112–28; Alan Borg, *War Memorials: From Antiquity to the Present* (London, 1991), pp.86–143; Christine Moriarty, 'Christian Iconography and First World War Memorials', *IWMR* 6 (1991), pp.63–75; eadem, 'Private Grief and Public Remembrance: British First World War Memorials', in Evans and Lunn, eds, *War and Memory*, pp.125–42; eadem, 'The Absent Dead and Figurative First World War Memorials', *Transactions of the Ancient Monuments Society* 39 (1995), pp.7–40; Gaffney, *Aftermath*, pp.25–95; N. Mansfield, 'Class Conflict and Village War Memorials, 1914–24', *Rural History* 6 (1995), pp.67–87; Ken Inglis, 'War Memorials: Ten Questions for Historians', *GMCC* 167 (1992), pp.5–22; idem, 'World War I Memorials in Australia', ibid., pp.51–8; idem, 'The Homecoming: The War Memorial Movement in Cambridge, England', *JCH* 27 (1992), pp.583–606; Alice Goodman, *The Street Memorials of St Albans Abbey Parish* (St Albans, 1987), pp.22–7, 36–52; J. Bartlett and K. M. Ellis, 'Remembering the Dead in Northop: First World War Memorials in a Welsh Parish', *JCH* 34 (1999), pp.231–42.

19. *This England* (Spring 1993), pp.11, 13; *Gunfire* 13 (1990), p.52; Janet Brown, 'Recording War Memorials in Northumberland', *The Local Historian* 26 (1996), pp.209–22.

20. Derez, 'Belgian Salient for Reconstruction', pp.454–6; Winter, *Sites of Memory*, pp.22–8, 86–96, 99–102; Becker, *War and Faith*, pp.118–19, 123–39, 146–58; idem, *Les Monuments aux morts: mémoire de la Grande Guerre* (Paris, 1989), pp.26, 75–6, 81, 112; idem, 'From Death to Memory: The National Ossuaries in France after the Great War', *History and Memory* 5 (1993), pp.32–49; Antoine Prost, 'Mémoires locales et mémoires nationales: les monuments de 1914–18 en France', *GMCC* 167 (1992), pp.41–50; idem, 'Les monuments aux morts. Culte républicain? Culte civique? Culte patriotique?, in Pierre Nora, ed., *Les Lieux de mémoire: La République* (Paris 1984), pp.195–225; Henry, *Monumental Accusations*, pp.8, 99; William Kidd, 'Memory, Memorials and Commemoration of War: Memorials in Lorraine, 1908–88', in Evans and Lunn, eds, *War and Memory*, pp.143–59; idem, 'Identity and Iconography: French War Memorials, 1914–18 and 1939–45', in R. Chapman and N. Hewitt, eds, *Popular Culture and Mass Communication in Twentieth Century France* (Lampeter, 1992), pp.220–40; E. T. Jennings, 'Monuments to Frenchmen? The Memory of the Great War and the Politics of Guadeloupe's Identity, 1914–45', *French Historical Studies* 21 (1998), pp.561–92.

21. Kavanagh, *Museums and First World War*, pp.105–16, 121–3, 126–51, 155–7; idem, 'Museum as Memorial: The Origins of the Imperial War Museum', *JCH* 23 (1988), pp.77–97; Trudi Tate, *Modernism, History and the First World War* (Manchester 1998), pp.127–34; James Brazier, 'Presentation Tanks', *Gunfire* 39 (1996), pp.48–52.

22. Michael Mckernan, *Here is There Spirit: A History of the Australian War Memorial, 1917–90* (St Lucia, 1991), pp.37,40; Ken Inglis, 'A Sacred Place: The Making of the Australian War Memorial', *W&S* 3 (1985), pp.99–127; Winter, *Sites of Memory*, pp.80–2.

23. Winter, 'Kinship and Remembrance', pp.40–7, 54–9; idem, 'Communities in Mourning', pp.325–55; *Sites of Memory*, pp.29–53, 108–13; Philip Dutton, ' "The Dead Man's Penny": A History of the Next of Kin Memorial Plaque', *IWMR* 3 (1988), pp.60–8; Regina Schulte, 'Käthe Kollwitz's Sacrifice', *HWJ* 41 (1996), pp.193–221.

24. Fussell, *Great War and Modern Memory*, pp.21–2, 51–69, 310–35; John Cruickshank, *Variations on Catastrophe: Some French Responses to the Great War* (Oxford, 1982), pp.27–41.

25. Modris Eksteins, *Rites of Spring: The Great War and the Birth of the Modern Age*, 2nd edn (London, 1990), pp.15–19, 122–8, 183–90, 216–17; idem, 'The Cultural Impact of the Great War', in Dibbets and Hogenkamp, eds, *Film and First World War*, pp.201–12.

26. Hynes, *War Imagined*, pp.ix–xi, 99–108, 166–7, 235–7.

27. Wohl, *Generation of 1914*, pp.203–37.

28. Fussell, *Great War and Modern Memory*, pp.203–20, 231–309; Robin Prior and Trevor Wilson, 'Paul Fussell at War', *WH* 1 (1994), pp.63–80; Martin Stephen,

The Price of Pity: Poetry, History and Myth in the Great War (London, 1996), pp.230–6; Daniel Pick, *War Machine: The Rationalisation of Slaughter in the Modern Age* (New Haven, CN, 1993), pp.189–204.

29. G. D. Josipovici, 'The Birth of the Modern, 1885–1914', in John Cruickshank, ed., *French Literature and its Background* (Oxford, 1970), VI, pp.1–20; Mosse, *Fallen Soldiers*, pp.53–69; Arthur Marwick, 'War and the Arts – Is There a Connection? The Case of the Two World Wars', *WH* 2 (1995), pp.65–86; Eksteins, *Rites of Spring*, pp.32–40; Stephen, *Price of Pity*, pp.25–41; Hynes, *War Imagined*, pp.7–10; Ferguson, *Arts in Britain*, pp.1–14; Stromberg, *Redemption by War*, pp.24–30.

30. Winter, *Sites of Memory*, pp.2–11, 113–16, 204–22, 225–9; Ted Bogacz, ' "A Tyranny of Words": Language, Poetry, and Anti-modernism in England in the First World War', *JMH* 58 (1986), pp.643–68; Ferguson, *Arts in Britain*, pp.43–4, 53–6, 115; Wohl, *Generation of 1914*, pp.92–5.

31. Marwick, *War and Social Change*, pp.85–6; idem, *Deluge*, pp.157, 237–44; Smith, 'War and British Culture', pp.169, 176, 180; Winter, *Sites of Memory*, pp.191–6; idem, 'Popular Culture in Wartime Britain', pp.344–7; idem, 'Les poètes combattants de la grande guerre: une nouvelle forme du sacré', in Becker, Winter, Krumeich, Becker and Audoin-Rouzeau, eds, *Guerre et Cultures*, pp.28–35; Hynes, *War Imagined*, pp.135–44, 342–4; Bernard Bergonzi, *Heroes' Twilight: A Study of the Literature of the Great War*, 2nd edn (London, 1980), pp.32–51; Frank Field, *British and French Writers of the First World War: Comparative Studies in Cultural History* (Cambridge, 1991), pp.211–28; Tate, *Modernism, History and First World War*, pp.102–9.

32. Marsland, *Nation's Cause*, pp.14–22, 107–8. Wide-ranging anthologies are: Dominic Hibberd and John Onions, eds, *Poetry of the Great War: An Anthology* (Basingstoke, 1986); and David Roberts, *Minds at War: The Poetry and Experience of the First World War*, 2nd edn (London, 1998).

33. Bourne, *Britain and Great War*, pp.225–7; Alan Wilkinson, 'Is Poetry a Part of History?', *Modern History Review* April 1996, pp.22–3; Stephen, *Price of Pity*, pp.138–48, 188–93, 220–7; Brian Bond, 'British "Anti-War" Writers and their Critics', in Cecil and Liddle, eds, *Facing Armageddon*, pp.817–30; Ferguson, *Arts in Britain*, pp.17–20, 52; Adrian Caesar, *Taking It Like a Man: Suffering, Sexuality and the War Poets – Brooke, Sassoon, Owen, Graves* (Manchester, 1993), pp.66–99, 141–68, 229; Andrew Rutherford, *The Literature of War: Studies and Heroic Virtue*, 2nd edn (Basingstoke, 1989), p.80; Field, *British and French Writers*, pp.105–22, 153–76, 229–44; Wohl, *Generation of 1914*, pp.85–92; A. E. Lane, *An Adequate Response: The War Poetry of Wilfred Owen and Siegfried Sassoon* (Detroit, MH, 1972), pp.87–166; Bergonzi, *Heroes' Twilight*, pp.109–21, 171–97.

34. Hugh Cecil, *The Flower of Battle: British Fiction Writers of the First World War* (London, 1995), pp.1–8, 42–73, 91–116, 119–212, 307–37, 338–41; idem, 'The Literary Legacy of the War: The Post-war British War Novel – A Select Bibliography', in Liddle, ed., *Home Fires and Foreign Fields*, pp.205–30; idem,

'British War Novelists', in Cecil and Liddle, eds, *Facing Armageddon*, pp.801–16; Gordon Urquhart, 'Confrontation and Withdrawal: Loos, Readership and *The First Hundred Thousand*', in Macdonald and McFarland, eds, *Scotland and Great War*, pp.125–44; Collins, *Theatre at War*, pp.177–211, 216–17, John Onions, *English Fiction and Drama of the Great War, 1918–39* (Basingstoke, 1990), pp.30–5, 49–64, 99–109, 116–34; Thomas Vincent, 'Canadian Poetry of the Great War and the Effect of the Search for Nationhood', in Franz Karl Stanzel and Martin Löschnigg, eds, *Intimate Enemies: English and German Literary Reactions to the Great War, 1914–18*, 2nd edn (Heidelberg, 1994), pp.165–80; Rosa Maria Bracco, *Merchants of Hope: British Middlebrow Writers and the First World War, 1919–39* (Providence, RI, 1993), pp.22–6, 65–76, 124–41, 198; W. Mellers and R. Hildyard, 'The Edwardian Age and the Inter-war Years', in Boris Ford, ed., *Cambridge Cultural History of Britain: Early Twentieth Century Britain* (Cambridge, 1992), pp.22–7; Jacques Berthoud, 'Literature and Drama', ibid., pp.47–99; Michael Paris, 'A Different View of the Trenches: Juvenile Fiction and Popular Perceptions of the First World War, 1914–39', *War Studies Journal* 3 (1997), pp.32–46.

35. Keith Grieves, 'C. E. Montague and the Making of *Disenchantment*, 1914–21', *WH* 4 (1997), pp.35–59; Hynes, *War Imagined*, pp.283–91, 307–10.

36. Bracco, *Merchants of Hope*, pp.145–88.

37. Bruno Schultze, 'Fiction and Truth: The Politics of the War Novel', in Stanzel and Löschnigg, eds, *Intimate Enemies*, pp.297–311; Tate, *Modernism, History and First World War*, pp.75–7; Wohl, *Generation of 1914*, pp.105–8; Bergonzi, *Heroes' Twilight*, pp.146–70, 198–212; Onions, *English Fiction and Drama*, pp.64–76, 135–63; Hynes, 'Personal Narratives', pp.213–19; idem, *War Imagined*, pp.425–43, 449–55; Cecil, 'British War Novelists', pp.801–30; idem, 'Literary Legacy', pp.205–30.

38. Bond, 'British "Anti-war" Writers', pp.817–30; David Taylor, '"A Little Man in a Great War": Patrick Macgill and the London Irish Rifles', in Taithe and Thornton, eds, *War*, pp.235–49; idem, '"The Minstrel Boy to the War Has Gone": Rifleman 3008, Patrick Macgill and A Soldier's Experience of the First World War', in Dockray and Laybourn, eds, *Representation and Reality of War*, pp.190–202; Jeffery, 'Irish Prose Writers', pp.1–17.

39. Claire M. Tylee, *The Great War and Women's Consciousness: Images of Militarism and Womanhood in Women's Writings, 1914–64* (London, 1990), pp.33–9, 47–53, 108–13, 121–9, 150–67, 209–23, 256; Jo Newberry Vellacott, 'Feminist Consciousness and the First World War', *HWJ* 23 (1987), pp.81–101; Nicola Beauman, '"It is not the place of women to talk of mud": Some Responses by British Women Novelists to World War I', in Dorothy Goldman, ed., *Women and World War I: The Written Response* (London, 1993), pp.128–49; Jane Gledhill, 'Impersonality and Amnesia: A Response to World War I in the Writings of H. D. and Rebecca West', ibid., pp.169–87. See also the anthologies compiled by Catherine Reilly, *Scars Upon My Heart: Women's Poetry and Verse of the*

First World War (London, 1981), and Margaret Higonnet, *Lines of Fire: Women Writers of World War One* (New York, 1999), as well as the wide-ranging bibliography by Sharon Ouditt, *Women Writers of the First World War: An Annotated Bibliography* (London, 1999).

40. Stanley Cooperman, *World War I and the American Novel*, 2nd edn (Baltimore, MD, 1970), pp.44–56, 69–77, 175–81; Dorothy Goldman, ' "Eagles of the West"? American Women Writers and World War I', in Goldman, ed., *Women and World War I*, pp.188–208; Patrick Quinn, 'The Experience of War in American Patriotic Literature', in Cecil and Liddle, eds, *Facing Armageddon*, pp.752–66.

41. Faulkner quoted in *New Republic* 20 May 1931, pp.23–4; Eksteins, *Rites of Spring*, pp.368–98; idem, '*All Quiet on the Western Front* and the Fate of a War', *JCH* 15 (1980), pp.345–66; Bessel, *Germany After First World War*, pp.266–8; Cecil, 'British War Novelists', pp.813–14; Andrew Kelly, *Filming All Quiet on the Western Front* (London, 1998), pp.39–56; Martin P. A. Travers, *German Novels on the First World War and their Ideological Implications, 1918–33* (Stuttgart, 1982), pp.84–105.

42. Travers, *German Novels*, pp.17–31, 44–82, 149–67, 180–92, 195; Jelavich, 'German Culture', pp.47–53; Gerd Krumeich, 'La Place de la Guerre de 1914–18 dans l'Histoire Culturelle de l'Allemagne', in Becker, Winter, Krumeich, Becker and Audoin-Rouzeau, eds, *Guerre et Cultures*, pp.36–45; Helmut Fries, 'Deutsche Schriftsteller im Ersten Weltkrieg', ibid., pp.825–48.

43. Hans-Harald Müller, ' "Herr Jünger thinks war a lovely business": On the Reception of Ernst Jünger's *Im Stahlgewittern* in Germany and Britain before 1933', in Stanzel and Löschnigg, eds, *Intimate Enemies*, pp.327–42; Roger Woods, *Ernst Jünger and the Nature of Political Commitment* (Stuttgart, 1982), pp.99–136, 199–231; Thomas Nevin, *Ernst Jünger and Germany: Into the Abyss, 1914–45* (London, 1997), pp.39–74, 141–71; 'Ernst Jünger: German Stormtrooper Chronicler', in Cecil and Liddle, eds, *Facing Armageddon*, pp.269–77; Thomas Rohkrämer, 'Die Verzauberung der Schlange: Krieg, Technik und Zivilisationskritik beim frühen Ernst Jünger', in Michalka, ed., *Erste Weltkrieg*, pp.849–74.

44. W. Patrick Bridgwater, *The German Poets of the First World War* (London, 1985), pp.15, 19–152; idem, 'German Poetry and the First World War', *ESR* 1 (1971), pp.147–86; Agnès Cardinal, 'Women on the Other Side', in Goldman, ed., *Women and World War I*, pp.31–50; Hans-Otto Binder, 'Zum Opfern bereit: Kriegsliteratur von Frauen', in Hirschfeld, Krumeich, Langewiesche and Ullman, eds, *Kriegserfahrungen*, pp.107–28; Winter, *Sites of Memory*, p.199; Martin Jay, 'Against Consolation: Walter Benjamin and the Refusal to Mourn', in Winter and Sivan, eds, *War and Remembrance*, pp.221–39.

45. Ferro, 'Cultural Life in France', pp.304–5; Becker, *Great War and French People*, pp.161–77; Leonard V. Smith, 'Masculinity, Memory and the French World

War I Novel: Henri Barbusse and Roland Dorgelès', in Coetzee and Shevin-Coetzee, eds, *Authority*, pp.251–74; Frank Field, *Three French Writers and the Great War: Studies in the Rise of Communism and Fascism* (Cambridge, 1975), pp.21–138; idem, 'The French War Novel: The Case of Louis-Ferdinand Céline', in Cecil and Liddle, eds, *Facing Armageddon*, pp.831–40; idem, *Variations on Catastrophe*, pp.75–113; Winter, *Sites of Memory*, pp.178–86; Wohl, *Generation of 1914*, pp.5–41; Agnès Cardinal, 'Women and the Language of War in France', in Goldman, ed., *Women and World War I*, pp.150–68.

46. Adamson, 'Impact of World War I on Italian Political Culture', pp.319–22; David Roberts, 'Croce and Beyond: Italian Intellectuals and the First World War', *IHR* 3 (1981), pp.201–35; Thayer, *Italy and Great War*, pp.371–90; Ulrich Schulz-Buschhaus, 'Exaltation des Krieges und Zerstörung der Syntax bei F. T. Marinetti', in Stanzel and Löschnigg, eds, *Intimate Enemies*, pp.257–74.

47. Kann, 'Trends in Austrian-German Literature', pp.159–83; Winter, *Sites of Memory*, pp.186–91; Frank Field, 'Karl Kraus, Bernard Shaw and Romain Rolland as Opponents of the First World War', in P. Scheichl and Edward Timms, eds, *Karl Kraus in neuer Sicht* (Munich, 1986), pp.158–73; Nolte, 'Ambivalent Patriots', pp.165–7; Beller, 'Tragic Carnival', pp.148–54; Edward Timms, *Karl Kraus: Apocalyptic Satirist: Culture and Catastrophe in Habsburg Vienna* (New Haven, CN, 1986), pp.267–376; Wachtel, 'Culture in South Slavic Lands', pp.206–7.

48. Peter Harrington, *British Artists and War: The Face of Battle in Paintings and Prints, 1700–1914* (London 1993), pp.301–10; idem, 'Early Paintings of the Great War', *IWMR* 7 (1992), pp.46–54; Angela Wright, 'The Kensingtons at Laventie: A Twentieth Century Icon', *IWMR* 1 (1986), pp.14–18; Stuart Sillars, *Art and Survival in First World War Britain* (New York, 1987), pp.39–47, 72–3, 90–115, 157–8.

49. Smith, 'War and British Culture', pp.173–5; M. Harries and S. Harries, *The War Artists: British Official War Art of the Twentieth Century* (London, 1983), p.7; Maria Tippett, *Art at the Service of War: Canada, Art and the Great War* (Toronto, 1984), pp.17–35; Keith Jeffery, 'Irish Artists and the First World War', *History Ireland* 1 (1993), pp.42–5; Paul Gough, '"An Epic of Mud": Artistic Interpretations of Third Ypres', in Liddle, ed., *Passchendaele in Perspective*, pp.409–21; idem, 'The Experience of British Artists in the Great War', in Cecil and Liddle, eds, *Facing Armageddon*, pp.841–53; Charles Doherty, 'The War Art of C. R. W. Nevinson', *IWMR* 8 (1993), pp.48–62; Jay Winter, 'Painting Armageddon: Some Aspects of the Apocalyptic Imagination in Art from Anticipation to Allegory', ibid., pp.854–78; idem, *Sites of Memory*, pp.167–71; Hynes, *War Imagined*, pp.159–66, 194–202, 294–8, 459–63; Richard Cork, 'The Visual Arts', in Ford, ed., *Early Twentieth Century Britain*, pp.157–95.

50. Kenneth E. Silver, *Esprit de Corps: The Art of the Parisian Avant-garde and the First World War, 1914–25* (Princeton, NJ, 1989), pp.28–73, 115–30; Richard Cork,

A Bitter Truth: Avant-garde Art and the Great War (New Haven, CN, 1994), pp.230–2; Ferro, 'Cultural Life in France', p.298; Danièlle Dellouche, 'Cubisme et camouflage', in Becker, Winter, Krumeich, Becker and Audoin-Rouzeau, eds, *Guerre et cultures*, pp.239–52; Elizabeth Louise Kahn, *The Neglected Majority, 'Les Camoufleurs', Art History and World War I* (Lanham, MD, 1984), pp.11–45, 49–139; Marwick, 'Wars and Arts', pp.75–6.

51. Mommsen, 'German Artists, Writers and Intellectuals', pp.21–38; Jost Dülffer, 'Kriegserwartung und Kriegsbild in Deutschland vor 1914', in Michalka, ed., *Erste Weltkrieg*, pp.778–98; Winter, *Sites of Memory*, pp.145–67; idem, 'Painting Armageddon', pp.854–78; Klaus Vondung, 'Apokalyptische Deutungen des Ersten Weltkriegs in Deutschland', in Stanzel and Löschnigg, eds, *Intimate Enemies*, pp.59–69; Patrick Bridgwater, 'The German Painters of the First World War', ibid., pp.517–40; Marwick, 'War and Arts', pp.76–9; B. C. Buenger, 'Max Beckmann in the First World War', in R. Rumold and O. K. Werckmeister, eds, *The Ideological Crisis of Expressionism: The Literary and Artistic German War Colony in Belgium, 1914–18* (Columbia, SC, 1990), pp.237–75; C. W. Haxthausen, 'Beckmann and the First World War', in C. Schulz-Hoffmann and J. C. Weiss, eds, *Max Beckmann Retrospective* (Munich, 1985), pp.69–80; Susanne Brandt, 'Bilder von der Zerstörung an der Westfront und die doppelte Verdrängung der Niederlage', in Hirschfeld, Krumeich, Langewiesche and Ullman, eds, *Kriegserfahrungen*, pp.439–54; Jelavich, 'German Culture', pp.53–6; Matthias Eberle, *World War I and the Weimar Artists: Dix, Grosz, Beckmann, Schlemmer* (New Haven, CN, 1985), pp.22–105.

52. Beller, 'Tragic Carnival', pp.141, 146.

53. Marwick, *War and Social Change*, pp.83–6; idem, *Deluge*, pp.154–5; idem, 'War and Culture', in Arthur Marwick, Bernard Waites, Clive Emsley and John Golby, eds, *War and Change in Twentieth Century Europe* (Buckingham, 1990), pp.140–2; idem, 'War and the Arts', pp.65–86; Hynes, *War Imagined*, pp.36–9; Beller, 'Tragic Carnival', pp.147–8; Ferguson, *Arts in Britain*, pp.23–4, 56–62, 100–2; Stites, 'Days and Nights in Wartime Russia', pp.13–15; Michael Kennedy, 'Music', in Ford, ed., *Early Twentieth Century Britain*, pp.117–54; Mellers and Hildyard, 'Edwardian Age', ibid., pp.10, 26.

54. Allyson Booth, *Postcards from the Trenches: Negotiating the Space between Modernism and the First World War* (New York, 1996), pp.125–44, 153–6; Jonathon Black, 'War without the Gloss: Conscientious Masculinity and the Image of the British Soldier in Great War Memorial Sculpture, 1919–30', paper presented at Anglo-American Conference of Historians, London, July 2000; Borg, *War Memorials*, pp.69–85, 114–16, 121–2, 134–5; Ken Inglis, 'Men, Women, and War Memorials: Anzac Australia' and 'Monuments in the Modern City: The War Memorials of Melbourne and Sydney', in Lack, ed., *Anzac Remembered*, pp.97–119, 171–93; Nicholas Penny, 'English Sculpture and the First World War', *Oxford Art Journal* 4 (1981), pp.36–42; John Summerson, 'Architecture', in Ford, ed., *Early Twentieth Century Britain*, pp.21–53.

55. Jane Carmichael, *First World War Photographers* (London, 1989), pp.36–7, 48–75, 81–2, 131, 142, 145, 148–9, 151–4; Kevin Brownlow, *The War, the West and the Wilderness* (London, 1979), pp.119–30; Bernd Hüppauf, 'Kriegsfotografie', in Michalka, ed., *Erste Weltkrieg*, pp.875–910; Laurent Veray, 'Montrer la guerre: la photographie et le cinématographe', in Becker, Winter, Krumeich, Becker and Audoin-Rouzeau, eds, *Guerre et Cultures*, pp.229–38.

56. Pierre Sorlin, 'War and Cinema: Interpreting the Relationship', *HJFRT* 14 (1994), pp.357–66; idem, 'Cinema and the Memory of the Great War', in Paris, ed., *First World War and Popular Cinema*, pp.5–26.

57. Hynes, *War Imagined*, pp.443–7; Michael Paris, 'Enduring Heroes: British Feature Films and the First World War, 1919–97', in Paris, ed., *First World War and Popular Cinema*, pp.51–73; Rother, 'Experience of First World War and German Film', ibid., pp.217–46; Winter, *Experience of World War I*, p.245.

58. Winter, *Sites of Memory*, pp.15–22, 133–42; idem, *Experience of World War I*, pp.240; Kelly, *Cinema and Great War*, pp.102–5.

59. Winter, *Experience of World War I*, pp.242–3, 246; Kelly, *Cinema and Great War*, pp.106–26.

60. Winter, *Experience of World War I*, p.245; Michael T. Isenberg, *War on Film: The American Cinema and World War I, 1914–41* (London and Toronto, 1981), pp.204–14; Brownlow, *War, West and Wilderness*, pp.38–43.

61. Winter, *Experience of World War I*, pp.241–2; Kelly, *Cinema and Great War*, pp.63–77, 87–96; Brownlow, *War, West and Wilderness*, pp.205–11; Rother, 'Experience of First World War and German Film', pp.217–46.

62. Isenberg, *War on Film*, pp.118–26; idem, 'The Great War Viewed from the Twenties: *The Big Parade* (1925)', in John E. O'Connor and Martin A. Jackson, eds, *American History / American Film: Interpreting the Hollywood Image* (New York, 1979), pp.17–38; Brownlow, *War, West and Wilderness*, pp.184–98; Kelly, *Cinema and the Great War*, pp.29–42.

63. Winter, *Experience of World War I*, p.245; Modris Eksteins, 'War, Memory and Politics: The Fate of the Film, *All Quiet on the Western Front*', *CEH* 13 (1980), pp.60–82; idem, 'Cultural Impact of Great War', pp.201–12; John Whiteclay Chambers, '*All Quiet on the Western Front* (1930): The Anti-war Film and the Image of the First World War', *HJFRT* 14 (1994), pp.377–412; Kelly, *Filming All Quiet*, pp.57–81, 83–132, 150–65; idem, '*All Quiet on the Western Front*: "Brutal Cutting, Stupid Censors and Bigoted Politicos", 1930–84', *HJFRT* 9 (1989), pp.135–50; idme, *Cinema and Great War*, pp.43–57; Isenberg, *War on Film*, pp.132–41; Brownlow, *War, West and Wilderness*, pp.214–19; J. Simmons, 'Film and International Politics: The Banning of *All Quiet on the Western Front* in Germany and Austria, 1930–31', *Historian* 52 (1989), pp.40–60.

64. Thomas J. Saunders, 'German Diplomacy and the War Film in the 1920s', in Dibbets and Hogenkamp, eds, *Film and First World War*, pp.213–22; Daniel J.

Leab, 'Viewing the War with the Brothers Warner', ibid., pp.223–36; Kelly, *Cinema and Great War*, pp.63–4, 141–46, 148–61; idem, *Filming All Quiet*, pp.133–50; J. C. Robertson, *'Dawn* (1928): Edith Cavell and Anglo-German Relations', *HJFRT* 4 (1984), pp.15–28.

65. Andrew Kelly, 'The Brutality of Military Incompetence: *"Paths of Glory"'*, *HJFRT* 13 (1993), pp.215–27; idem, *Cinema and Great War*, pp.162–80.

66. Thomson, Anzac Memories, pp.192–3, 196–7; Peter Burness, *The Nek: The Tragic Charge of the Light Horse at Gallipoli* (Kenthurst, 1996), pp.110–23, 151–7.

67. Danchev, 'Bunking and Debunking', pp.263–88; Derek Paget, 'Remembrance Play: *Oh! What a Lovely War* and History', in Tony Howard and John Stokes, eds, *Acts of War: The Representation of Military Conflict on the British Stage and Television since 1945* (Aldershot, 1996), pp.82–97; Corelli Barnett, 'Oh! What a Whinging War', *The Spectator* 18 January 1997; Putkowski, 'Toplis, Etaples and the "Monocled Mutineer"', pp.6–11; Gary Sheffield, 'Oh! What Futile War: Representations of the Western Front in Modern British Media and Popular Culture', in Ian Stewart and Susan Carruthers, eds, *War, Culture and the Media* (Trowbridge, 1996), pp.54–74.

68. A. J. P. Taylor, *The Second World War* (London, 1976), p.234; Beckett, 'Military Historian and Popular Image', pp.11–14; Bond, 'Victory Worse than Defeat', pp.1–16; Danchev, 'Bunking and Debunking', pp.263–88.

69. MacGregor quoted in *Sunday Times* 31 August. 1986; F. C. Pogue, *George C. Marshall: Ordeal and Hope* (London, 1968), p.317; Corelli Barnett, *The Collapse of British Power*, 2nd edn (Gloucester, 1984), pp.424–38; idem, 'Of Horrors and Scapegoats: Ending World War I Legends', *Encounter* 50 (1978), pp.66–74; idem, 'A Military Historian's View of the Great War', *Essays by Divers Hands, Being the Transactions of the Royal Society of Literature* 36 (1970), pp.1–18; John Terraine, *The Smoke and the Fire: Myths and Anti-myths of War, 1861–1945* (London, 1980), pp.35–47, 104; Gary Sheffield, 'The Shadow of the Somme: The Influence of the First World War on British Soldiers' Perceptions and Behaviour in the Second World War', in Addison and Calder, eds, *Time to Kill*, pp.29–39.

70. Keith Grieves, 'Early Historical Responses to the Great War: Fortescue, Conan Doyle and Buchan', in Bond, ed., *First World War and British Military History*, pp.15–39; Richard Holmes, 'Sir John French and Lord Kitchener', ibid., pp.113–39; Keith Simpson, 'The Reputation of Sir Douglas Haig', ibid., pp.141–62; Ian F. W. Beckett, ed., *The Judgement of History: Sir Horace Smith-Dorrien, Lord French and 1914* (London, 1993), pp.vii–xxvi; idem, 'Frocks and Brasshats', pp.89–112; George Egerton, 'The Lloyd George War Memoirs: A Study in the Politics of Memory', *JMH* 60 (1988), pp.55–94; David French, 'Sir Douglas Haig's Reputation, 1918–28: A Note', *HJ* 28 (1985), pp.953–60; J. O. Stubbs, 'Beaverbrook as Historian: *Politicians and the War* Reconsidered', *Albion* 14 (1982), pp.235–53; Peter Fraser, 'Lord Beaverbrook's Fabrications in *Politicians*

and the War, 1914–16', *HJ* 25 (1982), pp.147–66; idem, 'Cabinet Secrecy and War Memoirs', *History* 70 (1985), pp.397–409; T. M. McEwen, 'Lord Beaverbrook: Historian Extraordinary', *Dalhousie Review* 59 (1979), pp.129–43.

71. Hew Strachan, '"The Real War": Liddell Hart, Cruttwell, and Falls', in Bond, ed., *First World War and British Military History*, pp.41–67; Brian Holden Reid, 'T. E. Lawrence and his Biographers', ibid., pp.227–59; idem, 'T. E. Lawrence and Liddell Hart', *History* 70 (1985), pp.218–31 [also in Brian Holden Reid, *Studies in British Military Thought: Debates with Fuller and Liddell Hart* (Lincoln, NB, 1998), pp.150–67]; Bond, 'Victory Worse than Defeat', pp.8–9.

72. David French, 'Sir James Edmonds and *The Official History: France and Belgium*', in Bond, ed., *First World War and British Military History*, pp.69–86; idem, '"Official but not History?" Sir James Edmonds and the Official History of the Great War', *JRUSI* 131 (1986), pp.58–63; M. J. Williams, 'The Treatment of the German Losses on the Somme in the British Official History', *JRUSI* 111 (1966), pp.69–74; idem, 'Thirty Per Cent: A Study in Casualty Statistics', *JRUSI* 109 (1964), pp.51–5; Travers, *Killing Ground*, pp.203–49; idem, 'Allies in Conflict', pp.301–25; Jay Luvaas, 'The First British Official Historians', in Robin Higham, ed., *Official Histories* (Manhattan, KS 1970), pp.485–505; Thomson, *Anzac Memories*, pp.142–56; K. A. Hamilton, 'The Pursuit of Enlightened Patriotism: The British Foreign Office and Historical Researchers during the Great War and its Aftermath', *BIHR* 61 (1988), pp.316–44; Vance, *Death So Noble*, pp.163–97.

73. Brian Bond, 'The Somme in British History', unpublished paper, May 1992; Peter Simkins, 'Everyman at War: Recent Interpretations of the Front Experience', in Bond, ed., *First World War and British Military History*, pp.289–313; Paul Thompson, *The Voice of the Past*, 2nd edn (Oxford, 1988), pp.101–49; Thomson, *Anzac Memories*, pp.7–11, 183–7, 225–39; idem, 'Anzac Memories: Putting Popular Memory Theory into Practice in Australia', *Oral History* 18 (1990), pp.25–31. For a defence of oral history, see Peter Liddle and Matthew Richardson, 'Voices from the Past: An Evaluation of Oral History as a Source for Research into the Western Front Experience of the British Soldier, 1914–18', *JCH* 31 (1996), pp.651–74.

74. Sheffield, 'Oh! What Futile War', pp.54–74; Brian Bond, 'Introduction', in Bond, ed., *First World War and British Military History*, p.12; Ian Beckett, 'Revisiting the Old Front Line', *Stand To* 43 (1995), pp.10–14.

EPILOGUE

Geoffrey Blainey has suggested that it is hard to find a war that could be termed either accidental or unintentional.[1] Certainly, the outbreak of the Great War was neither. The assassination of Franz Ferdinand offered the Austro-Hungarian leadership the opportunity it sought to crush Serbia. In turn, that localised conflict gave the German leadership the opportunity to realise its own manifold ambitions. Faced with the prospect of German hegemony, politicians in London, Paris or St Petersburg would have found it difficult to have chosen different courses in reaction to the decisions taken in Vienna and Berlin. The consequences of that reaction to German aggression were momentous and, for millions, ultimately fatal. The cost was enormous, but the fact that the eventual victory parades were in London and Paris, and not in Berlin, meant that the sacrifice was far from futile.

Most Europeans believed that the war would be short and that they would win without serious loss or inconvenience. From the beginning, however, the involvement of European colonial empires brought an escalation of the conflict beyond Europe. A combination of belligerent war aims and self-interest among other powers ensured that a global conflict ensued. Moreover, the impact of industrialisation had transformed the nature of warfare. The initial campaigns in 1914 went much as soldiers had expected, but as the strength of the defensive became apparent, so a military deadlock occurred. Too many leading soldiers took too long to glimpse the nature of the military problems confronting them. In many respects, however, this was still a transitional military conflict, in which the new military technologies were as yet imperfect for the task of providing a ready solution to deadlock.

Deadlock encouraged states to draw upon all their national resources in order to out-produce their opponents. To ensure the full mobilisation of resources, it was necessary for governments to intervene massively in their domestic economies. The growth of government was marked and permanent, although many wartime controls were subsequently divested. The short-term impact of the war upon society and, indeed, culture was inescapable, though, in the longer term, there were more continuities than discontinuities between pre-war and post-war societies. Indeed, even military service on the part of the citizen soldiers who fought the war may not have had the lasting impact usually assumed from a highly selective reliance upon the evidence of an unrepresentative group of literary intellectuals. To portray the soldiers of the Great War as nothing more than passive victims does the ideals for which they fought and the men themselves a profound disservice.

The greater changes were to occur in those states that failed the challenges of war and were defeated. Where the authority of the state was undermined by defeat, revolutionary conditions could arise, and all belligerents were compelled to attempt the management of national morale. Ever-expanding war aims to justify the sacrifices being made were an essential and dangerous component of such political strategies, since failure only increased pressures on governments to deliver. In such circumstances, the legacy of war was that post-war politics was fixed in relation to the war experience. Thus, the memory of the war quickly became a usable past for both victors and vanquished. In some respects, indeed, the mythic version of the war has endured longer among the former than the latter.

Not unexpectedly, the war's most significant consequences were political. The defeat of the Central Powers and the collapse of Tsarist Russia clearly resulted in the redrawing of the map of Europe, the Middle East and Africa. In the process, the long-term global balance of power was changed. The United States emerged as a significant military and economic power, and the opportunity for power granted the Bolsheviks established communism as a potent ideology. Indeed, irrespective of whether the two world wars of the twentieth century are regarded as a single period of conflict divided by a twenty-one year truce, it can be argued that the world created by the Great War endured until the collapse of communism in Europe in 1989.[2]

Notes and references

1. Geoffrey Blainey, *The Causes of War* (Melbourne, 1988), p.141.

2. Michael Howard, 'The Springtime of Nations', *Foreign Affairs* 69 (1990), pp.17–32.

SELECT BIBLIOGRAPHY

Note: Unless otherwise stated, the place of publication is London. Since full sources are given in the footnotes, this highly selective bibliography is confined to those general volumes most useful and accessible to English readers.

There is no wholly adequate single volume history of the war available for undergraduate use. Martin Gilbert, *The First World War* (1995) is relentlessly anecdotal. John Keegan, *The First World War* (1998), despite its elegant style, is a somewhat old-fashioned military narrative, while Spencer Tucker, *The Great War, 1914–18* (1998) is even more so. Of those histories which attempt an analytical rather than a chronological approach, Marc Ferro, *The Great War, 1914–18* (1973) is too idiosyncratic, and the otherwise excellent Keith Robbins, *The First World War*, 2nd edn (Oxford, 1993) is simply too short. In many respects, the best analytical treatments available are the heavily illustrated Jay Winter, *The Experience of World War I* (1988) and Hew Strachan, ed., *The Oxford Illustrated History of the First World War* (Oxford, 1998).

A wide-ranging collection of essays appears in Hugh Cecil and Peter Liddle, eds, *Facing Armageddon: The First World War Experienced* (1996). Gerd Hardach, *The First World War, 1914–18* (1973) covers mostly economic matters, and John Stevenson, *The First World War and International Politics* (Oxford 1988), diplomacy.

Britain has fared well in terms of general histories. Trevor Wilson, *The Myriad Faces of War* (Cambridge, 1986) is a dense and detailed analytical narrative. John Bourne, *Britain and the Great War, 1914–18* (1989) is good on military and political aspects. Social issues are well covered by Jay Winter, *The Great War and the British People* (1985) and the conservatively minded Gerard De Groot, *Blighty: British Society in the Era of the Great War* (1996), which contrasts with the older interpretation of Arthur Marwick, *The Deluge: British Society and the First World War*, 2nd edn (1991). A variety of aspects are covered in the essays in Peter Liddle, ed., *Home Fires and Foreign Fields: British Social and Military Experience in the First World War* (1985) and John Turner, ed., *Britain and the First World War* (1988). Those essays in Stephen Constantine, Maurice Kirby and Mary Rose, eds, *The First World War in*

480

British History (1995) provide a comprehensive summary of recent research. Niall Ferguson, *The Pity of War* (London, 1998) is primarily about Britain but, while good on economics, its military judgements are questionable. A welcome regional perspective can be found in Catriona Macdonald and E. W. McFarland, eds, *Scotland and the Great War* (East Linton, 1999).

Germany and Austria-Hungary are now well served by Holger Herwig, *The First World War: Germany and Austria-Hungary 1914–18* (1997), though it is at times an uneasy mix of narrative and analysis. In some respects Roger Chickering, *Imperial Germany and the Great War* (Cambridge, 1998) is to be preferred, although Herwig gives more detail. Older interpretations of the Austro-Hungarian experience include Arthur May, *The Passing of the Habsburg Empire, 1914–18*, 2 vols (Philadelphia, PA, 1966), and Z. A. B. Zeman, *The Break-up of the Habsburg Empire, 1914–18: A Study in National and Social Revolution* (Oxford, 1961). There are some useful essays in Robert Kann, B. Király and Paula Fichtner, eds, *The Habsburg Empire in World War I: Essays on the Intellectual, Military, Political and Economic Aspects of the Habsburg War Effort* (Ithaca, NY, 1977).

Eastern Europe is covered generally by B. Király and N. F. Dreisziger, eds, *East Central European Society in World War I* (New York, 1985); while Glenn Torrey, *Romania and World War I* (Iasi, 1998) collects together a number of his essays from various journals and volumes. Two large-scale accounts of Russia in war and revolution are Richard Pipes, *The Russian Revolution, 1899–1919* (1990), and Orlando Figes, *A People's Tragedy: The Russian Revolution, 1891–1924* (1996). Current interpretations are reviewed in Edward Acton, *Rethinking the Russian Revolution* (1990) and Edith Frankel, Jonathan Frankel and Baruch Knei-Paz, eds, *Revolution in Russia: Reassessments of 1917* (Cambridge, 1992).

There is no overall treatment of the French experience available in English, but social aspects are well covered in Jean-Jacques Becker, *The Great War and the French People* (Leamington Spa, 1985) and the essays in Patrick Fridenson, ed., *The French Home Front, 1914–18* (Providence, RI, 1992).

The United States experience is covered from a largely social perspective in David Kennedy, *Over Here: The First World War and American Society* (New York, 1980); Ronald Schaffer, *America in the Great War: The Rise of the War Welfare State* (New York, 1991) and Neill Wynn, *From Progressivism to Prosperity: World War I and American Society* (New York, 1986).

Still wider perspectives are provided by Desmond Morton and J. L. Granatstein, *Marching to Armageddon: Canadians and the Great War, 1914–19* (Toronto, 1989), Joan Beaumont, ed., *Australia's War, 1914–18* (St Leonards, 1995); Melvin Page, ed., *Africa and the First World War* (1987) and Bill Albert, *South America and the First World War: The Impact of the War on Brazil, Argentina, Peru and Chile* (Cambridge, 1988).

On the causes of the war, the best summaries of recent historiography are to be found in Volker Berghahn, *Germany and the Approach of War in 1914* (1973), John Keiger, *France and the Origins of the First World War* (1983), D. C. B. Lieven, *Russia and the Origins of the First World War* (1983), Samuel Williamson, *Austria-Hungary and the Origins of the First World War* (1991), Richard Bosworth, *Italy and the Approach of the First World War* (1983) and Zara Steiner, *Britain and the Origins of the First World War* (1977). The focus is on individual state decisions in R. J. W. Evans and Hartmut Pogge von Strandmann, eds, *The Coming of the First World War*, 2nd edn (Oxford, 1990) and Keith Wilson, ed., *Decisions for War 1914* (1995). More general treatments are to be found in James Joll, *The Origins of the First World War* (1984); and H. W. Koch, ed., *The Origins of the First World War*, 2nd edn (1984).

Military planning is covered in Paul Kennedy, ed., *The War Plans of the Great Powers, 1880–1914* (1979). The conduct of the war generally is the subject of the essays on each major belligerent in Allan Millett and Williamson Murray, eds, *Military Effectiveness: The First World War* (Boston, MA, 1988). Some of the current debates on the operational effectiveness of the British army in particular are covered in the essays in Paddy Griffith, ed., *British Fighting Methods in the Great War* (1996) and Brian Bond, ed., *Look to Your Front: Studies in the First World War* (Staplehurst, 1999). For the eastern theatre, Norman Stone, *The Eastern Front, 1914–17* (1975) is indispensable. A general survey of strategy and war aims is to be found in the essays in Barry Hunt and Adrian Preston, eds, *War Aims and Strategic Policy in the Great War* (1977). Similarly, the essays in Ian Beckett and Keith Simpson, eds, *A Nation in Arms: A Social Study of the British Army in the First World War* (Manchester, 1985) provide an introduction to social aspects of the British military presence on the Western Front.

For the war at sea, see Arthur Marder, *From the Dreadnought to Scapa Flow: The Royal Navy in the Fisher Era, 1904–1919*, 5 vols (Oxford, 1961–70) and Paul Halpern, *A Naval History of World War I* (Annapolis, MD, 1994). A good general account of the air war is John Morrow, *The Great War in the Air: Military Aviation from 1909 to 1921* (Washington DC, 1993).

On the impact of the war upon government see the essays in Kathleen Burk, ed., *War and the State: The Transformation of British Government, 1914–18* (1982), while mobilisation generally is treated in John Horne, ed., *State, Society and Mobilisation in Europe during the First World War* (Cambridge, 1997). European social responses as a whole are covered by the essays in Jay Winter and Richard Wall, eds, *The Upheaval of War: Family, Work and Welfare in Europe, 1914–18* (Cambridge, 1988); while a similar comparative perspective is offered by those in Jay Winter and Jean-Louis Robert, eds, *Capital Cities: London, Paris, Berlin, 1914–18* (Cambridge, 1997). Labour relations are covered in L. Haimson and G. Sapelli, eds, *Strikes, Social Conflicts and the First World War: An International Perspective* (Milan, 1991).

An excellent survey of European cultural responses to the war is found in the essays in Aviel Roshwald and Richard Stites, eds, *European Culture in the Great War: The Arts, Entertainment and Propaganda, 1914–18* (Cambridge, 1999). Aspects of the literary legacy are covered in Franz Karl Stanzel and Martin Löschnigg, eds, *Intimate Enemies: English and German Literary Reactions to the Great War, 1914–18* (Heidelberg, 1992). There are some useful essays in Karel Dibbets and Bert Hogenkamp, eds, *Film and the First World War* (Amsterdam, 1994) and Michael Paris, ed., *The First World War and Popular Cinema, 1914 to the Present* (Edinburgh, 1999), while Richard Cork, *A Bitter Truth: Avant Garde Art and the Great War* (New Haven, CN, 1994) is splendidly illustrated. George Mosse, *Fallen Soldiers: Shaping the Memory of the World Wars* (New York, 1990) and Jay Winter, *Sites of Memory, Sites of Morning: The Great War in European Cultural History* (Cambridge, 1995) offer overviews of the post-war memory of the war. An introduction to veterans' issues can be found in the essays in Stephen Ward, ed., *The War Generation: Veterans of the First World War* (Port Washington, NY, 1975).

Reactions to the end of the war are examined in Hugh Cecil and Peter Liddle, eds, *At the Eleventh Hour: Reflections, Hopes and Anxieties at the Closing of the Great War, 1918* (Barnsley, 1998). The peace settlement is covered generally by Alan Sharp, *The Versailles Settlement: Peacekeeping in Paris, 1919* (1991) and by the essays in the weighty Manfred Boemeke, Gerald Feldman, and Elisabeth Glaser, eds, *The Treaty of Versailles: A Reassessment after 75 Years* (Cambridge, 1998). Aspects of the historiography of the war since 1919 are examined in Brian Bond, ed., *The First World War and British Military History* (Oxford, 1991).

MAPS

Map 1 Europe in 1914

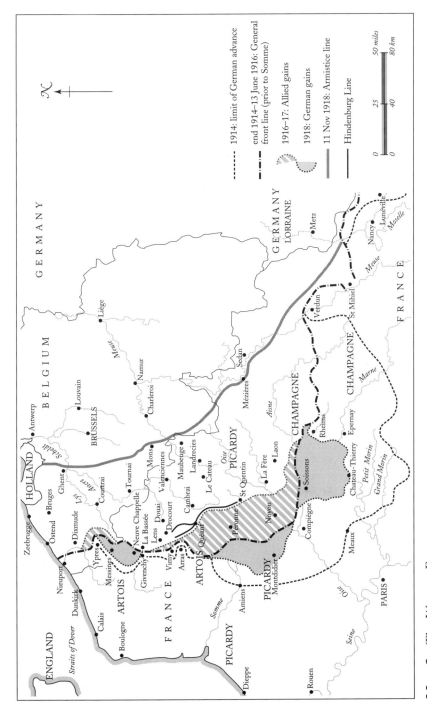

Map 2 The Western Front

Map 3 The Russian Front

Map 4   The Balkans

Legend:
- Dodecanese: won by Italy, 1912
- Won by Romania from Bulgaria, 1913
- Won by Bulgaria from Turkey, 1913
- Won by Serbia, 1913
- Won by Greece, 1913

RUSSIA

AUSTRIA-HUNGARY

ROMANIA

Bucharest

Belgrade

SERBIA

Sarajevo

MONTE-
NEGRO

BULGARIA

Sofia

ALBANIA

MACEDONIA

Salonika

Constantinople

TURKEY

GREECE

Smyrna

Athens

0   100   200 miles

0   100   200 km

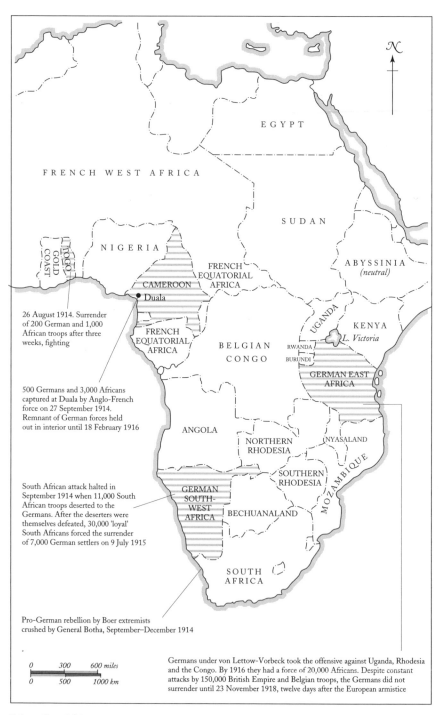

26 August 1914. Surrender
of 200 German and 1,000
African troops after three
weeks, fighting

500 Germans and 3,000 Africans
captured at Duala by Anglo-French
force on 27 September 1914.
Remnant of German forces held
out in interior until 18 February 1916

South African attack halted in
September 1914 when 11,000 South
African troops deserted to the
Germans. After the deserters were
themselves defeated, 30,000 'loyal'
South Africans forced the surrender
of 7,000 German settlers on 9 July 1915

Pro-German rebellion by Boer extremists
crushed by General Botha, September–December 1914

| 0 | 300 | 600 miles |
| 0 | 500 | 1000 km |

Germans under von Lettow-Vorbeck took the offensive against Uganda, Rhodesia
and the Congo. By 1916 they had a force of 20,000 Africans. Despite constant
attacks by 150,000 British Empire and Belgian troops, the Germans did not
surrender until 23 November 1918, twelve days after the European armistice

Map 5   Africa

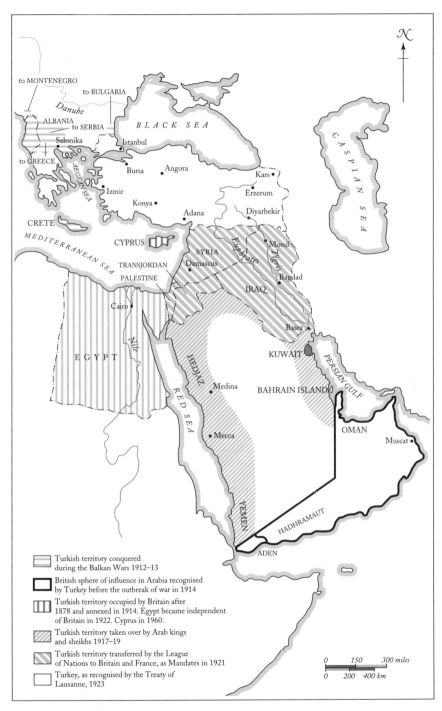

Map 6 The Middle East

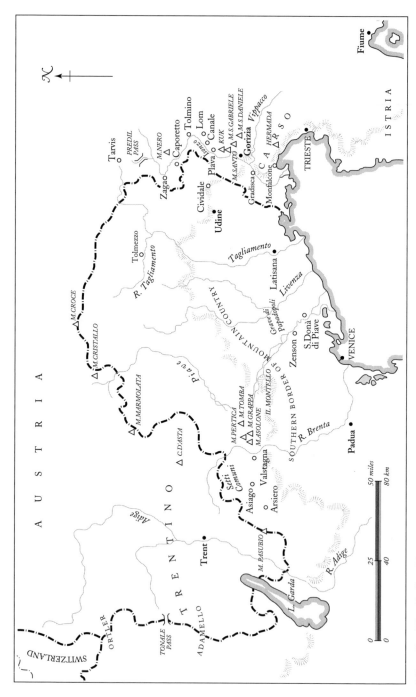

Map 7 The Italian Front

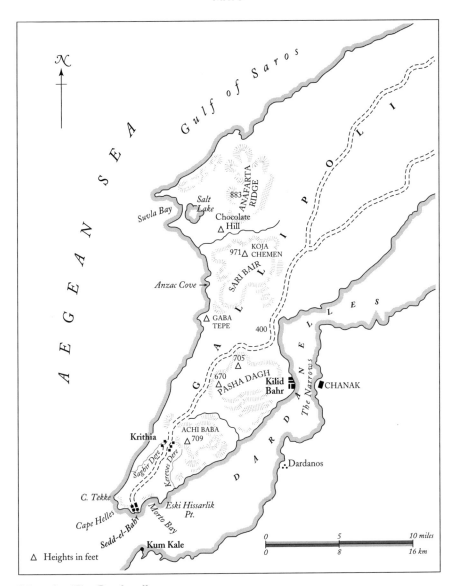

Map 8 The Dardanelles

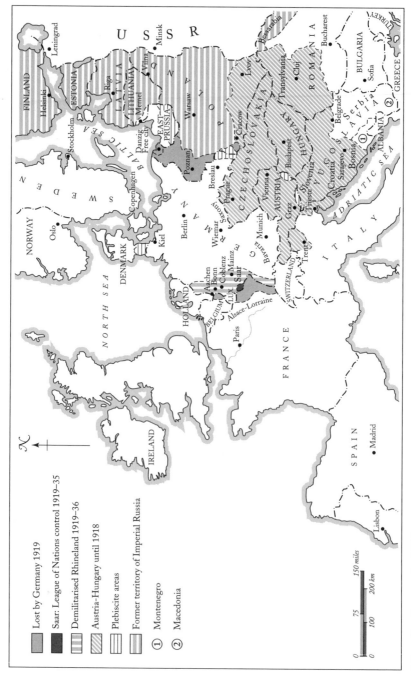

Map 9 Europe in 1919

Legend:

- Lost by Germany 1919
- Saar: League of Nations control 1919–35
- Demilitarised Rhineland 1919–36
- Austria-Hungary until 1918
- Plebiscite areas
- Former territory of Imperial Russia
- ① Montenegro
- ② Macedonia

Scale:
0   75   150 miles
0   100   200 km

INDEX